D1544789

Christ and the Catholic Priesthood

Christ and the Catholic Priesthood

Ecclesial Hierarchy and the Pattern of the Trinity

Matthew Levering

HillenbrandBooks

Chicago / Mundelein, Illinois

CHRIST AND THE CATHOLIC PRIESTHOOD: ECCLESIAL HIERARCHY AND THE PATTERN OF THE TRINITY © 2010 Archdiocese of Chicago: Liturgy Training Publications, 3949 South Racine Avenue, Chicago IL 60609; 1-800-933-1800, fax 1-800-933-7094, e-mail orders@ltp.org. All rights reserved. See our Web site at www.LTP.org.

Hillenbrand Books is an imprint of Liturgy Training Publications (LTP) and the Liturgical Institute at the University of Saint Mary of the Lake (USML). The imprint is focused on contemporary and classical theological thought concerning the liturgy of the Catholic Church. Available at bookstores everywhere, through LTP by calling 1-800-933-1800, or visiting www.LTP.org. Further information about the **Hillenbrand Books** publishing program is available from the University of Saint Mary of the Lake/ Mundelein Seminary, 1000 East Maple Avenue, Mundelein, IL 60060 (847-837-4542), on the Web at www.usml.edu/liturgicalinstitute, or e-mail litinst@usml.edu.

On the cover: Holy Trinity Church (formerly Saints Peter and Paul), Cincinnati, Ohio. Edward Schulte, architect. Photo © Denis R. McNamara.

Printed in Mexico.

Library of Congress Control Number: 2009939811

978-1-59525-029-2

HCCP

Contents

Acknowledgments

This book was written thanks to Professor David Solomon, who invited
me to be the Myser Fellow at his Center for Ethics and Culture at
the University of Notre Dame for the academic year 2006–2007.
Thanks also to Michael Dauphinais, Dean of Faculty at Ave Maria
University, and to Father Matthew Lamb, Chair of the Department
of Theology at Ave Maria, for granting me the year's leave and for
their friendship.

At three conferences, I presented material that became part of
the book. Thanks again to David Solomon for accepting my paper for
the fall 2006 Center for Ethics and Culture conference on "Modernity:
Yearning for the Infinite." John Boyle kindly invited me to speak at
the session that he hosts at the International Congress for Medieval
Studies at Kalamazoo. I also presented part of the work at the Aquinas
Center for Theological Renewal's "Sacraments in Aquinas" conference.
During these presentations, I received helpful suggestions for improve-
ment from Peter Casarella; Lawrence Dewan, OP; David Fagerberg;
Paul Griffiths; Reinhard Hütter; and Joseph Koterski, SJ. Thanks as
well to Joseph Torchia, OP, and Gregory LaNave of *The Thomist*, who
accepted for publication a study that forms part of chapter 2. I have
also incorporated, at various places in the book, portions of an essay
that was published in a Festschrift honoring Matthew Lamb.

Lunch conversations at Notre Dame with David Fagerberg,
who shared his knowledge of contemporary Orthodox theology,
stimulated and enhanced my research. Raymond Hain, a doctoral
student at Notre Dame in philosophy, did a great job in helping me
obtain books and articles. His friendship and that of Drew Rosato,
Tom and Susan Scheck, Patrick and Jenny Clark, Regina and
Tremayne Cates, Jim Lee, and Austin Murphy, OSB, helped my family
and me greatly during the year. Thanks also to St. Matthew's
Cathedral, its school, and its pastor Father Michael Heintz. Kevin
Thornton's support for the manuscript at Hillenbrand Books made
the writing much easier. Thanks also to Louise Mitchell for preparing
the bibliography and for assisting with the index.

Four scholars read the entire manuscript while it was under construction in 2007: Bernhard Blankenhorn, OP; Andrew Hofer, OP; Guy Mansini, OSB; and Jörgen Vijgen. Their generosity with their time and erudition made this manuscript far better than it otherwise would have been. I cannot emphasize enough how grateful I am for their intellectual companionship.

A move from Florida to South Bend for a year is not something that most families with five young children would willingly undertake. My wife Joy undertook it with her characteristic grace and generosity of spirit. I thank God for giving me such a wife and family and for drawing close to us in Christ Jesus and his Holy Spirit.

This book is dedicated to my maternal grandmother, Irene B. Webb, whose generosity and love bestowed upon me and my family innumerable blessings. She passed into eternal life on May 28, 2007. We miss you, Grandmother. May you share in the life of God through Christ Jesus!

Introduction

Ecclesial Hierarchy

Just as God is not an external Master but rather is supreme Love, so also, says the Orthodox theologian Paul Evdokimov, the bishop is not "an executive, a patron, a power who constrains," but an image of God's gifting.[1] In the light of faith, the truth that "the bishop is responsible for correct teaching and the pastoral direction of the community" appears as a role of service, of mediation of the gifts of Love.[2] Does Evdokimov's depiction, however, fit the actual reality of the Church? In the hierarchical Church, made up of fallen human beings, the bishop has an authoritative role that will inevitably make him sometimes be "a power who constrains." Can such an unequal power structure truly express the mutually self-giving love that Christians are called to manifest?[3] When organized in a hierarchical fashion, can the Church be transparent to the self-emptying love of the crucified one? In a nutshell, does hierarchy by its very nature hinder the mutual self-subordination that configures believers to the image of the Father?[4]

---

1. Paul Evdokimov, "Freedom and Authority," in *In the World, of the Church: A Paul Evdokimov Reader*, ed. and trans. Michael Plekon and Alexis Vinogradov (Crestwood, NY: St. Vladimir's Seminary Press, 2001), 217–30, at 230.

2. Ibid., 229.

3. In asking this question, I take inspiration from *In One Body through the Cross: The Princeton Proposal for Christian Unity*, ed. Carl E. Braaten and Robert W. Jenson (Grand Rapids, MI: Eerdmans, 2003). The Princeton Proposal, signed by 16 leading theologians, calls for "sustained attention to the structures and forms of communion, and to their foundation in a common faith and discipleship" (18); cf. the essays of these theologians in *The Ecumenical Future*, ed. Carl E. Braaten and Robert W. Jenson (Grand Rapids, MI: Eerdmans, 2004). See also some of the issues raised by Avery Dulles, sj, Eugene L. Brand, Ephraim Radner, Geoffrey Wainwright, Gabriel Fackre, and Timothy George in a Symposium on the Congregation for the Doctrine of the Faith's *Dominus Iesus* (August 6, 2000) in *Pro Ecclesia* 10 (2001): 5–16.

4. For the view that "hierarchy" is a negative imposition of Hellenistic culture upon Christianity, see Ghislain Lafont, osb, *Imagining the Catholic Church: Structured Communion in the Spirit*, trans. John J. Burkhard, ofm conv. (French 1995; Collegeville, MN: Liturgical Press, 2000), 13f. Lafont notes with some urgency, "The Catholic Church chose to be

Certain passages from the Gospels make such concerns even more pressing. In reply to the disciples' question "Who is the greatest in the kingdom of heaven?" Jesus brings forward a little child and says to the disciples that "unless you turn and become like children, you will never enter the kingdom of heaven. Whoever humbles himself like this child, he is the greatest in the kingdom of heaven" (Matthew 18:3–4). Does not the very possession of hierarchical authority, the possession by some Christians of a permanently elevated status vis-à-vis other Christians, militate strongly against the ability of the one in authority to "humble himself like this child"? Likewise, when the two sons of Zebedee strive to obtain a particular position of eminence among the disciples, Jesus tells the disciples,

> You know that the rulers of the Gentiles lord it over them, and their great men exercise authority over them. It shall not be so among you, but whoever would be great among you must be your servant, and whoever would be first among you must be your slave; even as the Son of man came not to be served but to serve, and to give his life as a ransom for many. (Matthew 20:25–28)[5]

Do not the bishops and the pope—or even all ordained priests[6]—possess offices that make them seem much more like "the rulers of the

---

'antimodern' rather than 'modern, but in a different sense.' This failure has cost the Church dearly, but it has also been disastrous for civilization. Instead of offering each other possibilities of correcting one-sided positions and of mutually corroborating each other in the search for a just way for humanity to survive in a world increasingly abandoned by hierarchical thought, the Church and the world grew farther apart, each perilously weakened by the divorce" (32). Seeking to move beyond "powers" (corresponding to the choice between "hierarchical" and "democratic") to "charisms," Lafont calls for the election of bishops by the congregations, to be confirmed by the presiding bishop: see Lafont, *Imagining the Catholic Church*, 174–75. For diagnosis of the broader currents behind this kind of approach, see Hans Urs von Balthasar, *The Office of Peter and the Structure of the Church*, trans. Andrée Emery (German 1974; San Francisco: Ignatius Press, 1986), 60–127. For criticism of late-medieval and modern "hierarchology," whose emphasis on power is mirrored in much anti-hierarchical Catholic ecclesiology today, see Louis Bouyer, *The Church of God: Body of Christ and Temple of the Spirit*, trans. Charles Underhill Quinn (French 1970; Chicago: Franciscan Herald Press, 1982), 29–46; Yves Congar, OP, "De la communion des églises à une ecclésiologie de l'Église universelle," in *L'Épiscopat et l'Église universelle*, eds. Y. Congar et B. Dupuy (Paris: Cerf, 1962), 227–60; idem, *L'Église de saint Augustin à l'époque moderne* (Paris: Cerf, 1970).

5. For further discussion of this biblical text and other similar ones, see Yves Congar, "The Hierarchy as Service: Scriptural Sources and Historical Development," in idem, *Power and Poverty in the Church*, trans. Jennifer Nicholson (Baltimore: Helicon, 1964), 17–100, at 24.

6. This seems to me to be the difficulty with positions such as that of Dumitru Stăniloae, who affirms the "ontological equality" of bishops ("synodality") and holds, as Dănuţ Mănăstireanu puts it, that the papacy instantiates an "*ad principatum* principle" while synodality follows "the

Gentiles" than like "slaves"? Given that the disciples/apostles possessed authority in the early Church, how could their authority have been conceived along hierarchical lines, given that Jesus wished them to humble themselves like children and servants? How can mutual self-subordination truly express itself within hierarchical relationships, in which power is not equal? Could the incarnate Son of God, who instructs his disciples to "love one another as I have loved you" (John 15:12), have willed for his disciples to be united in "fellowship (*koinōnia*)" (1 Corinthians 1:9)[7] in a hierarchical manner?

This question, of course, evokes controversies and crises, both past and present, regarding the Church's hierarchy and her exercise of authority.[8] Before one can resolve the questions of who should possess authority in Christian communities and how this authority should be exercised, one must ask whether there should be a hierarchical

---

ad servitutem principle" (Mănăstireanu, "Dumitru Stăniloae's Theology of Ministry," in *Dumitru Stăniloae: Tradition and Modernity in Theology*, ed. Lucian Turcescu [Oxford: Center for Romanian Studies, 2002], 126–44, at 138). As advocates of episcopal elections and lay presiders have recognized, if papal authority is guilty of imposing an *ad principatum* rather than *ad servitutem* model, thereby distorting the Gospel, why not the same for episcopal authority in the diocese or priestly authority in the parish?

7. See Avery Dulles, SJ, "The Church as Communion," in *New Perspectives on Historical Theology: Essays in Memory of John Meyendorff*, ed. Bradley Nassif (Grand Rapids, MI: Eerdmans, 1996), 125–39, at 128. For further biblical exploration of the meaning of *communion* see Joseph Ratzinger, "Communion: Eucharist—Fellowship—Mission," in his *Pilgrim Fellowship of Faith: The Church as Communion*, ed. Stephan Otto Horn and Vinzenz Pfnür, trans. Henry Taylor (German 2002; San Francisco: Ignatius Press, 2005), 60–89.

8. Such crises produce a profusion of journalistic pieces: see for example Stephen J. Pope, "Accountability and Sexual Abuse in the United States: Lessons for the Universal Church," *Irish Theological Quarterly* 69 (2004): 73–88. Even from a more strictly theological perspective, ecclesial hierarchy is a controversial topic. Cf. John Milbank's concerns about Henri de Lubac, SJ, and Hans Urs von Balthasar: "Is there not some contradiction here between his [de Lubac's] and von Balthasar's formal capitulation to papal authority on the one hand, and their ecclesiology on the other, which stressed the primacy of the sacramental influence of the bishops as eucharistic mediators? What of de Lubac's acknowledgment that papal power in the Middle Ages was falsely and permanently directed into an overly judicial and non-spiritual direction?" (Milbank, *The Suspended Middle: Henri de Lubac and the Debate Concerning the Supernatural* [Grand Rapids, MI: Eerdmans, 2005], 104). The question is what "judicial" role comports with the bishops' role as "eucharistic mediators." Likewise Milbank criticizes de Lubac's and von Balthasar's theological defense of the male priesthood, grounded in their "dualist models of the Church, distinguishing between a lay, receptive, mystical, cultural 'Marian' aspect and a more legal, regulative, intellectual, abstract 'Petrine' aspect" (105). De Lubac and von Balthasar were seeking to understand what role human male and female bodiliness has in the sacramental symbolism of the Church, and they were doing so within the framework of received authoritative *sacra doctrina*: see, e.g., von Balthasar, "Thoughts on the Priesthood of Women," trans. Adrian Walker, *Communio* 23 (1996): 701–9; cf. Sara Butler, MSBT, *The Catholic Priesthood and Women* (Chicago: Hillenbrand, 2007).

priesthood in the Church at all. As Yves Congar says, one must ask whether ecclesial hierarchy is "of the Lord and in the Lord."[9] Ecclesial hierarchy must be shown to belong to the Trinitarian and Christological pattern of the communication of the divine life, a pattern that cannot be separated from the election of Israel and the covenantal structures of gifting, receptivity, and mediation that have shaped the people of God from the beginning.[10] Does ecclesial hierarchy flow from Christ's Spirit-filled fulfillment of Israel's Torah and Temple by his Paschal Mystery ("of the Lord")?[11] Does hierarchy in the Church, as manifested

---

9. Congar, "The Hierarchy as Service," 99. See also Henri de Lubac, sj, *The Splendor of the Church*, trans. Michael Mason (French 1953; San Francisco: Ignatius Press, 1986), 266–67, 300–1; idem, *The Motherhood of the Church*, trans. Sister Sergia Englund, ocd. (French 1971; San Francisco: Ignatius Press, 1982), 228; Avery Dulles, sj, *The Catholicity of the Church* (Oxford: Oxford University Press, 1985), 106–26. See also the approach of the Anglican theologian John Webster, "The Self-Organizing Power of the Gospel of Christ: Episcopacy and Community Formation," in his *Word and Church: Essays in Christian Dogmatics* (New York: T. & T. Clark, 2001), 191–210. Quoting Rowan Williams, Webster states, "Episcopal ministry 'is that ministry whose special province is both to gather the believing community around the centre which it proclaims, the preaching of the resurrection, and *in* that gathering, to make sure that this community is critically aware of itself'. The gospel requires this simply because Jesus Christ elects to manifest himself to the world not without a visible human, historical society with a specific calling" (203).

10. The very presence of a hierarchical priesthood witnesses against Scott Bader-Saye's view that "early Christian theology spiritualized and individualized election, detaching it from corporate, bodily existence and reformulating it on the basis of spirit and belief. That is to say, election fell prey to a gnostic redescription. No longer a communal claim about the formation of a people in this world, election became information about individual salvation in the next world. Instead of being forever linked to the people of Israel, Christian election was correlated with a dualistic rejection of Israel qua Israel. Election was reduced to a belief about the destiny of the individual soul rather than a calling to participate in a particular communal vocation. This meant that the Christian doctrine of election, unlike the Jewish teaching, was not considered materially determinative for the community's earthly life and practice" (Bader-Saye, *Church and Israel after Christendom: The Politics of Election* [Boulder, CO: Westview Press, 1999], 55).

11. Cf. Terence L. Nichols, "Participatory Hierarchy," in *Common Calling: The Laity and the Governance of the Catholic Church*, ed. Stephen J. Pope (Washington, DC: Georgetown University Press, 2004), 111–26. Nichols focuses on "the displacement of participatory hierarchy by command hierarchy" (115). The deleterious effects of this displacement, he argues, can be seen in recent times in Vatican I's affirmation of papal infallibility and Pope Paul VI's promulgation of *Humanae Vitae* against the judgment of the majority of the papal commission. Nichols does not advocate full democratization of Church structures; he fears that "disunity and fragmentation" follow upon this path (112). Instead, he argues that what is needed is a model of authoritative hierarchy where those in authority aim "to lead those in their charge into a sharing of the goods that the leaders themselves possess" (113). The key question, then, is what "goods" the leaders "possess" and how the "sharing of the goods" takes place. Nichols's account of these goods, and their sharing, focuses on the model of teaching. As examples of "participatory hierarchy," he gives the "wise teacher," the "parent-child relationship," and the "religious master-disciple relationship." Teaching is the means by which the "goods" are shared. Furthermore, the teachers "possess" these goods because they, the teachers, are good.

especially in the celebration of the Eucharist, serve to draw us into the Trinitarian communion ("in the Lord")?

The Structure of the Book

In exploring these questions, I will not "be preoccupied with questions of order and the basis of order . . . to the neglect of more fundamental questions about the nature of the church."[12] As Charles Journet remarks, "It would be a fatal thing" to "believe in the existence of two distinct theological treatises, one, on the Church, dealing with the hierarchical organization, the other, on the Mystical Body, with the inner life of the members of Christ."[13] The book's five chapters

---

He recognizes that a "pure form of participatory hierarchy" is not possible in an institutional setting, where some elements of "command hierarchy" will inevitably intrude. For Nichols, Jesus practiced solely participatory hierarchy, the "hierarchy" of a good teacher, if he practiced any kind of hierarchy at all. Thus a "command hierarchy" makes the Church "a countersign, a stumbling block to the faithful, a sign not of participation but of domination, authoritarianism, and oppression" (115). Yet, Nichols's purely educative "participatory hierarchy" seems to fall into the same soteriological hollowness found in the "command hierarchy" that he criticizes. In Nichols's vision of "participatory hierarchy," Jesus appears as the great teacher, and the goods that the hierarchy mediates are teachings—the (practical) truth of which can be tested solely by the experience of the Church's moral virtue. See also Terence L. Nichols, *That All Might Be One: Hierarchy and Participation in the Church* (Collegeville, MN: Liturgical Press, 1997).

12. J. Augustine Di Noia, OP, "The Church in the Gospel: Catholics and Evangelicals in Conversation," *Pro Ecclesia* 13 (2004): 58–69, at 61. The full passage from Di Noia reads: "It is true that Catholic ecclesiology, particularly in response to Reformation critiques of the late medieval church, came to be preoccupied with questions of order and the basis of order in the New Testament, sometimes to the neglect of more fundamental questions about the nature of the church. It was not always so in churchly theology. Patristic and scholastic theologians sought to articulate the nature of the fundamental unity of the church, chiefly in terms of the grace of communion with the Father through Christ and in the Holy Spirit. While surely not independent of the visible Catholic institutions that embodied this communion and safeguarded its temporal unity, this account of the ecclesial dimensions of the 'theological life' of the baptized was nonetheless seen as the basis of the sacramental, doctrinal and governmental structures of the church. The central themes of this classical ecclesiology continue to be actively recovered in present-day Catholic ecclesiology and in large measure provided the impetus for the renewal of the doctrine, practice and theology of the church at the Second Vatican Council and its aftermath" (61–62). For an overview of Catholic ecclesiology since 1940, see Avery Dulles, SJ, "A Half Century of Ecclesiology," *Theological Studies* 50 (1989): 419–42. For the development of ecclesiology see also Georges Florovsky, "On the History of Ecclesiology," in *Collected Works of Georges Florovsky*, vol. 14, *Ecumenism II: A Historical Approach*, ed. Richard S. Haugh (Vaduz: Büchervertriebsanstalt, 1989), 9–17.

13. Charles Journet, *The Church of the Word Incarnate: An Essay in Speculative Theology*, vol. 1, *The Apostolic Hierarchy*, trans. A. H. C. Downes (London: Sheed & Ward, 1955), xxvi. Journet observes that unfortunately, "Works on the Church undertaken since St. Thomas's time have been chiefly directed—even the *Summa de Ecclesia* of Turrecremata is not altogether an exception—to defending the Church's authority, called in question since the end of the medieval

therefore approach the topic of hierarchical priesthood in the Church through Trinitarian and soteriological reflection, unified by dialogic engagement with the biblical, patristic, and metaphysical resources of Saint Thomas Aquinas's theology.

The first chapter takes its starting point from the nature of the Church as a graced participation in the divine communion of persons: as Karol Wojtyła puts it in his *Sources of Renewal: The Implementation of the Second Vatican Council,* "The Church as People of God, by reason of its most basic premises and its communal nature, is oriented towards the resemblance there ought to be between 'the union of the sons of God in truth and love' [*Gaudium et Spes* §24] and the essentially divine unity of the divine persons, in *communione Sanctissimae Trinitatis.*"[14] Since the Persons of the Trinity are supremely co-equal, it would seem that the structure of the community of believers should mirror this perfect equality. Indeed, the ecclesiologies of Joseph Ratzinger (now Pope Benedict XVI) and John D. Zizioulas (now Metropolitan John of Pergamon) aim to show how hierarchical priesthood belongs to the Church's mode of participating in the Trinitarian communion. Miroslav Volf, however, has argued in detail that their perspectives remain monistic. As a contribution to this discussion, I explore the theme through the perspective of Thomas Aquinas. Regarding Aquinas's perspective Jean-Pierre Torrell remarks, "Viewed, as it is, in the movement of the 'exit' from the Trinity and the 'return' toward it, at the initiative of the Father and thanks to the conjoint work of the Son and Holy Spirit, Christian life according to Saint Thomas is a resolutely

---

period either by the civil power or by various forms of heresy. The result is that even to-day the questions discussed in treatises on the Church mainly concern either the hierarchy, that is to say the power of order and the power of jurisdiction, or the marks by which the true Church is to be recognized. . . . This concentration upon apologetic has tended to exclude from treatises *de Ecclesia* all deeper study of the intimate constitution and essential mystery of the Church. It is precisely these, however, that most interest us to-day" (xxv-xxvi). Ironically, Journet's four-volume ecclesiology, in which each volume treats one of the four "notes" of the Church in light of one of the four causes (material, efficient, formal, final—a method that Journet takes over from Reginald Garrigou-Lagrange), is often criticized today precisely as overly juridical. John P. Galvin, for instance, sums up Journet's approach as "characterized by strong emphasis on jurisdiction and by an inclination to analyze realities in terms of their causes," although Galvin does not therefore reject Journet's work (Galvin, "Papal Primacy in Contemporary Roman Catholic Theology," *Theological Studies* 47 [1986]: 653–67, at 654; cf. 666).

14. Karol Wojtyła, *Sources of Renewal: The Implementation of the Second Vatican Council,* trans. P. S. Falla (San Francisco: Harper & Row, 1980), 138; cited in Michael Waldstein, introduction to John Paul II, *Man and Woman He Created Them: A Theology of the Body,* trans. Michael Waldstein (Boston: Pauline Books & Media, 2006), 1–128, at 90.

theological, trinitarian reality."[15] Aquinas's theology may thus be expected to assist in understanding why the Church, in accordance with its particular mode of sharing in and imaging the Trinitarian communion, has a hierarchical structure.

The second chapter considers whether Christ's action on the cross was a "priestly" action. How did Jesus conceive of his death, and how did he intend his followers to share in his death? This question lies at the heart of debates about Christian priesthood, because if Christ did not understand his death or our participation in it cultically, then there would be no basis for a sacramental-hierarchical priesthood within the community of his followers. In order to gain insight into this topic, I examine in some detail recent historical-critical analyses by N. T. Wright, Steven Bryan, Scot McKnight, and Brant Pitre. On this basis, I identify four ways in which Jesus appears to have inter-preted his approaching death—eschatological, sacrificial/eucharistic, sanctifying, and unitive. These interpretive lenses, which provide a nuanced portrait of Jesus in his historical context, suggest that he deliberately undertook a priestly action. While this conclusion helps explain the presence among his followers of a hierarchical priesthood through which his followers share in his Paschal action, one may still wonder why Jesus' bloody self-sacrifice would be way of bringing God's salvific work in Israel to completion. Given this concern, I engage the four interpretive lenses in dialogue with Aquinas's theology of Christ's priesthood. Here I ask what it means theologically to identify Jesus Christ as a "priest."

The third chapter investigates leadership in the first Christian communities. I begin by examining the recent historical work of

---

15. Jean-Pierre Torrell, OP, *Saint Thomas Aquinas*, vol. 2: *Spiritual Master*, trans. Robert Royal (French 1996; Washington, DC: The Catholic University of America Press, 2003), 371. According to Torrell, Aquinas's theology of the Church "is very specifically a theology of the Body of Christ," in which the Body is constituted by the Head's gift of the Holy Spirit (188–89). Torrell notes that for Aquinas "the role of the Holy Spirit is precisely to establish the 'continuity' between Christ the Head and the faithful members, for he has the property of remaining numerically *one and the same* in the Head and in the members" (189). See also Torrell's discussion of the Holy Spirit as the "soul of the Church" (190f.). Torrell here has high praise for Charles Journet's treatment of this topic in *L'Église du Verbe Incarné*, vol. 2 (Paris: Desclée de Brouwer, 1951), 510–80; cf. Journet, "La sainteté de l'Église. Le livre de Jacques Maritain," *Nova et Vetera* 46 (1971): 1–33, on Jacques Maritain's *De l'Église du Christ* (Paris: Desclée de Brouwer, 1970). Torrell points out that Congar agrees with Journet: see Yves Congar, "La personne de l'Église," *Revue Thomiste* 71 (1971): 613–40. See also Emile Mersch, SJ, *The Theology of the Mystical Body*, trans. Cyril Vollert, SJ (St. Louis: Herder, 1951).

James Burtchaell and Francis Sullivan, who expose the central problem: did early Christian leadership derive from anything more than the organizational exigencies of teaching and service? In light of this problem, I turn to Saint Paul's first letter to the Corinthians and the Gospel of Matthew. I argue that Paul recognizes in his mandate a special power to communicate Christ's saving power, which enables Paul rightly to claim hierarchical authority in the community of believers.[16] Likewise, the Gospel of Matthew presents the disciples/apostles as possessing a distinctive participation in the sanctifying power of Christ's Pasch. Not merely teaching and service, but a distinctive sacred "power" undergirds their leadership role. On the basis of this biblical exegesis, I inquire into what this distinctive sacred "power" means for Christian theology of the hierarchical priesthood. Here I examine the eucharistic and metaphysical accounts of hierarchical priesthood offered by John Zizioulas and Thomas Aquinas.

The fourth chapter raises the topic of the papacy. It does so through the lens of contemporary Orthodox theology, specifically the influential work of Nicholas Afanasiev and the recent response by Olivier Clément to John Paul II's encyclical *Ut Unum Sint*.[17] Afanasiev

---

16. Philip Turner, drawing upon the work of Yves Simon and Hannah Arendt, remarks regarding the related meanings of "power" and "authority": "Within the classical tradition, authority in its political sense is understood as a form of social control, or better a means to order the common life of a society, that lies between power (i.e. domination or manipulation) on the one hand and the non-executive authority of simple persuasion by example, rhetoric or competence on the other. To have authority is different from being a dictator who relies on force, and it is different from being a leader who relies simply on the ability to *persuade* others by charisma or eloquence to follow. . . . In short, authority is a way of investing power with moral and religious accountability. It is a way of ordering power within a community in such a way that the power of the community itself is augmented and directed to purposes acceptable to the community as a whole" (Turner, "Episcopal Authority within a Communion of Churches," in Ephraim Radner and Philip Turner, *The Fate of Communion: The Agony of Anglicanism and the Future of the Global Church* [Grand Rapids, MI: Eerdmans, 2006], 135–62, at 138, 140). Thus "authority" orders "power" to the common good of the community, and allows one to distinguish between disordered uses of power and ordered ones. Power in the Church has an additional meaning: sacramental "power," an ontological participation in Christ. This sacramental (and hierarchical) meaning of power is normative for what constitutes an ordered exercise of "power" ("authority") in the Church.

17. The impact of these thinkers, especially Afanasiev and Zizioulas, upon Catholic theology is shown by Ernest Skublics, "Communion Ecclesiology: A Vision of the Church Reshaping Theology and Seminary Formation," *Pro Ecclesia* 7 (1998): 288–306. Writing as Academic Dean of Mount Angel Seminary, a Catholic seminary in St. Benedict, Oregon, Skublics shows how the revision of the curriculum in the mid 1990s at Mount Angel Seminary drew upon the work of Afanasiev and Zizioulas. Skublics argues that their vision will be constitutive for the future Church: "There is a dichotomy to be observed at present between the eucharistic

and Clément relegate the traditional controversies—regarding the
biblical role of Peter, apostolic succession, and the historical development
of the role of the Bishop of Rome—to a secondary position, and
instead focus on whether Catholic ecclesiology has understood the role
of the Bishop of Rome primarily in terms of juridical power, rather
than primarily in light of the Eucharist as constitutive of the Church's
(and the world's) unity in love. After presenting the perspectives and
concerns of Afanasiev and Clément, I probe what contribution Aquinas
has to make to contemporary theology of the papacy. His understanding of the papacy depends not upon juridical arguments but upon his
theology of believers' participation in Christ's Paschal Mystery through
the Eucharist, a participation that requires the virtues of faith and
charity.[18] The role of the papacy is to foster the fullness of the
Church's eucharistic receptivity and gifting.

The first four chapters address four significant theological
barriers to positive contemporary theological evaluation of ecclesial
hierarchy—namely, the equality of the divine Persons, the nature of
Christ's death and our participation in it, the nature of leadership in
the early Church, and the contested authority of the pope. The last
chapter treats a theme that underlies all these earlier chapters: sacramental mediation. From a variety of perspectives, the leading figures
of the Reformation and the Enlightenment subjected the Catholic
understanding of ecclesial hierarchy and sacramental mediation to a

---

ecclesiology shared by Roman Catholic, Orthodox, Anglican and Lutheran Christians and
theologians, expressed and affirmed by the highest offices of these churches, on the one hand,
and a continued denominational institutional identity, on the other hand, which is impressed
upon the next generation of clergy as highest priority, in fact militating against the new and
eschatological vision of the church, which should be seen as normative. The priestly minister
must be an agent of this coming church, *the true church*, for which he has been ordained" (305).
See also the eucharistic ecclesiology of Donald J. Keefe, "Authority in the Church: An Essay
in the Theology of History," *Communio* 7 (1980): 343–63, which follows the historical thesis
of Henri de Lubac's *Corpus Mysticum*; for certain criticisms of this thesis, see Martin Morard,
"Les expressions 'corpus mysticum' et 'persona mystica' dans l'oeuvre de saint Thomas
d'Aquin. Références et analyse," *Revue Thomiste* 95 (1995): 653–64; and Ephraim Radner, *The
End of the Church: A Pneumatology of Christian Division in the West* (Grand Rapids, MI:
Eerdmans, 1998), 228–30.

18. See also, for the theology of creation that undergirds the theology of redemption East
and West, Charles Miller, *The Gift of the World: An Introduction to the Theology of Dumitru
Stăniloae* (Edinburgh: T. & T. Clark, 2000); Kenneth L. Schmitz, *The Gift: Creation*, The
Aquinas Lecture, 1982 (Marquette: Marquette University Press, 1982), with its helpful
contrast of Aquinas and Hegel.

withering critique.[19] This critique, in a contemporary form, has been well expressed by Miroslav Volf. To contextualize theologically the challenges raised by Volf, I return to an eighteenth-century debate between the Jewish philosopher Moses Mendelssohn and the Christian thinker Johann Georg Hamann, the former holding that Judaism and Christianity solely mediate philosophical instruction and devotional piety, the latter that both Jewish and Christian mediation involves the power of divine realities. In light of this debate, I take up the classic Jewish response to the issues raised by Mendelssohn, namely Franz Rosenzweig's *The Star of Redemption*, which emphasizes the primacy of liturgical mediation. I then examine Pseudo-Dionysius's similar emphasis in his *The Ecclesiastical Hierarchy*, which explores the connection between liturgical mediation and a hierarchical priesthood. Returning on this basis to the concerns raised by Volf, I argue that many of his concerns find resolution in Aquinas's Dionysian theology of the priesthood.

GIFTING AND RECEPTIVITY

Throughout the book, I propose that the Father, Son, and Holy Spirit willed a hierarchical Church, notwithstanding the inevitable sinfulness of the members of the hierarchical priesthood, because of the theo-centric pattern of gifting and receptivity that hierarchy fosters in the

---

19. For recent ecumenical reflection on the Church, see, e.g., George Lindbeck, "The Church," in *Keeping the Faith: Essays to Mark the Centenary of Lux Mundi*, ed. Geoffrey Wainwright (Allison Park, PA: Pickwick Publications, 1998), 179–208; G. R. Evans, *The Church and the Churches: Toward an Ecumenical Ecclesiology* (Cambridge: Cambridge University Press, 1994); James J. Buckley, "The Wounded Body: The Spirit's Ecumenical Work on Divisions among Christians," in *Knowing the Triune God: The Work of the Spirit in the Practices of the Church*, ed. James J. Buckley and David S. Yeago (Grand Rapids, MI: Eerdmans, 2001), 205–230. See also Joseph Ratzinger, "Luther and the Unity of the Churches" and his "Postscript" to this piece, in his *Church, Ecumenism and Politics: New Essays in Ecclesiology*, trans. Robert Nowell (German 1987; New York: Crossroad, 1988), 99–134. In the "Postscript," Ratzinger responds particularly to Heinrich Fries and Karl Rahner's proposal for Lutheran–Catholic reunion: Fries and Rahner, *Einigung der Kirchen—reale Möglichkeit* (Freiburg: 1983). Ratzinger observes that "as far as things stand with Rahner the possibility of unity rests on nobody knowing any longer exactly whether he or she has correctly understood the Church's teaching (based on the Bible), whether he or she has rightly grasped the other's theology" (131). *Pace* Rahner, "A formal unity without any clear content is fundamentally no unity at all, and a mere linking together of institutions is no value in itself. Unity conceived of in this way is based on common scepticism, not on common knowledge" (131). For a Lutheran response to "Luther and the Unity of the Churches," see David S. Yeago, " 'A Christian, Holy People': Martin Luther on Salvation and the Church," *Modern Theology* 13 (1997): 101–20.

Church. This pattern of gifting and receptivity characterizes the Church as our "mother": "But the Jerusalem above is free, and she is our mother" (Galatians 4:26).[20] I owe this emphasis upon the pattern of gifting/receptivity not only to Aquinas, but also and especially to the writings of Joseph Ratzinger and Hans Urs von Balthasar. One finds in Joseph Ratzinger's work a consistent depiction of ecclesial hierarchy—whose foibles and failures he knows well—as fostering receptivity to God's gifting.[21] Discussing Paul's understanding of his

20. Roch Kereszty, OCIST, points out that "one of the most fundamental biblical and patristic images of the Church, woman as Virginal Bride and Mother, has nearly vanished from today's ecclesial consciousness" (Kereszty, " 'Bride' and 'Mother' in the *Super Cantica* of St. Bernard: An Ecclesiology for Our Time?" *Communio* 20 [1993]: 415–36, at 415). He proposes that "a re-discovery of the Church as Bride and Mother could lead to new insights uniquely suited to answer a threefold question that today concerns not only professional theologians but the Christian public at large: 1) Why does one need a Church instead of or in addition to a direct personal relationship to Christ? 2) What is the role of the ministerial priest, and how could one work out an effective priestly spirituality? 3) What is the theological relevance of the 'Feminine'?" (416). When hierarchy in the Church is seen solely in terms of sociological power, the maternal imagery for the Church, rooted in gifting and receptivity, is lost. See also Hans Urs von Balthasar, *Unless You Become Like This Child*, trans. Erasmo Leiva-Merikakis (German 1988; San Francisco: Ignatius Press, 1991).

21. On Ratzinger see Aidan Nichols, OP, *The Theology of Joseph Ratzinger* (Edinburgh: T. & T. Clark, 1988), as well as Avery Dulles, SJ, *The Priestly Office: A Theological Reflection* (Mahwah, NJ: Paulist Press, 1997), 21–22, where Dulles briefly traces the development of Ratzinger's theology of the priesthood from Ratzinger's early criticisms of cultic language (in his *The Meaning of Christian Brotherhood* [German 1960; San Francisco: Ignatius Press, 1993], 61–62 and his *Theological Highlights of Vatican II* [New York: Paulist Press, 1966], 175–78) to his later emphasis on the Church's dialogic structure and the priest as representing Christ. Christopher Ruddy praises Ratzinger's ecclesiology as "not a repressive 'hierarchology,' but thoroughly sacramental, centered above all on the eucharistic celebration. Its dominant tone is mystical, even romantic, in its emphases upon the communal, the interior and intuitive, the familial. Most fundamental, perhaps, is his sense of divine gift: the church and its liturgy are to be received by men and women in wonder, rather than actively made or constructed" (Ruddy, *The Local Church: Tillard and the Future of Catholic Ecclesiology* [New York: Crossroad, 2006], 100). This last aspect stands at the center of Ratzinger's theology of ecclesial hierarchy. Disagreeing with Ratzinger's prioritizing of the "universal" Church, Ruddy argues for the simultaneity of the local and universal Church (106–7). Ruddy does not adequately engage Ratzinger's insistence upon the primacy of receptivity in ecclesiology, which grounds his sense of the "priority" of the "universal" Church. See especially Ratzinger, *Called to Communion: Understanding the Church Today*, trans. Adrian Walker (German 1991; San Francisco: Ignatius Press, 1996), chapter 3: "The Universal Church and the Particular Church: The Task of the Bishop," 75–103; idem, *Principles of Catholic Theology: Building Stones for a Fundamental Theology*, trans. Sister Mary Frances McCarthy, SND. (German 1982; San Francisco: Ignatius Press, 1987), 292–93; idem, *Church, Ecumenism and Politics,* , chapter 1; idem, "The Local Church and the Universal Church: A Response to Walter Kasper," *America* 185 (November 19, 2001): 7–11. For a survey of Ratzinger's debate with Walter Kasper on the universal and particular Church, favoring Kasper's position, see Kilian McDonnell, "The Ratzinger/Kasper Debate: The Universal Church and Local Churches," *Theological Studies* 63 (2002): 227–50 (McDonnell evaluates the debate on 246–50); cf. McDonnell's appreciative "Walter Kasper

apostolic mandate, Ratzinger focuses on how Paul's "ministry of reconciliation" (2 Corinthians 5:18–20) communicates to others the reconciliation accomplished by Jesus Christ. For Ratzinger, such apostolic power serves to carry "forward that dialogical structure that pertains to the essence of revelation,"[22] by inscribing a structure of receptivity within which the divine gifting operates. Arguing that this "dialogical structure" of gifting/receptivity belongs intrinsically to the Church, Ratzinger cites Paul's farewell exhortation to the "elders" of the Ephesian Church as recorded in Acts 20:28. Their task, like Paul's, is to communicate the divine gifting so that the universal priesthood of Christ—the "communion of saints"—may be nourished.[23] As Ratzinger explains elsewhere, hierarchy "means not holy domination

---

on the Theology and the Praxis of the Bishop's Office," *Theological Studies* 63 (2002): 711–29. Guy Mansini, OSB, points out the significance of the distinction between "local" and "particular" with regard to the Church of Pentecost: "Evidently, this Church is a local Church, since it is in Jerusalem. But it is not a particular Church; it is rather the whole Church, all the Church there is, the universal Church" (Mansini, "On the Relation of Particular to Universal Church," *Irish Theological Quarterly* 69 [2004]: 177–87, at 181). See also Benoît-Dominique de La Soujeole, OP, *Introduction au mystère de l'Église* (Paris: Parole et Silence, 2006), 579–91; de Lubac, *The Motherhood of the Church*, 207–8.

22. Ratzinger, "On the Essence of the Priesthood," in his *Called to Communion*, 105–31, at 120; cf. Ratzinger, "The Papal Primacy and the Unity of the People of God," in his *Church, Ecumenism and Politics*, 29–45; Ratzinger, "The Ministry and Life of Priests," in his *Pilgrim Fellowship of Faith*, 153–75. See also my "A Note on Joseph Ratzinger and Contemporary Theology of the Priesthood," *Nova et Vetera* 5 (2007): 271–83, from which this paragraph is adapted. Geoffrey Preston, OP, likewise emphasizes the significance of "the dialogue of the [eucharistic] assembly with a president who is given to it from without and so represents the Christ who was sent to that assembly by the Father. That is, the president is Christ's ambassador, whom the assembly receives rather than gives to itself. The president is the 'vicar of Christ,' the representative of the sacrificing, sanctifying, preaching Christ" (Preston, *Faces of the Church: Meditations on a Mystery and Its Images*, ed. Aidan Nichols, OP [Grand Rapids, MI: Eerdmans, 1997], 159).

23. Ratzinger presents this point by quoting Jean Colson's words about the Old Testament priesthood, " 'It is the chief function of the *kohanim* (ιερεις) to keep the people aware of its priestly character and to work so that it might live in accordance with it, so that it might glorify God with its entire existence' " (127, quoted from J. Colson, *Ministre de Jésus-Christ ou le Sacerdoce de l'Évangile* [Paris: 1966], 185). Ratzinger comments on this quotation: "This statement is unmistakably close to the already-cited formula in which Paul speaks of his mission as *leitourgos* of Jesus Christ; the only difference is that the dynamic, missionary character of this expression now comes much more clearly to light as a consequence of the bursting open of the boundaries of Israel by the Cross of Christ. The ultimate end of all New Testament liturgy and of all priestly ministry is to make the world as a whole a temple and a sacrificial offering for God" (127). See also the perspective taken by the Bilateral Working Group of the German National Bishops' Conference and the Church Leadership of the United Evangelical Lutheran Church of Germany, *Communio Sanctorum: The Church as the Communion of Saints*, trans. Mark W. Jeske, Michael Root, and Daniel R. Smith (Collegeville, MN: Liturgical Press, 2004).

but holy origin. Hierarchical service and ministry is thus guarding an origin that is holy, and not making arbitrary dispositions and decisions."[24] Hierarchy's purpose is to recall all believers to "fundamental goods" that are "not something that we ourselves have discovered," but instead are received from God.[25]

For his part, Hans Urs von Balthasar observes that "the chief stumbling block against which non–Catholics come up in the Church is authority, the impersonal institution."[26] As he describes the problem: "But what, we might well ask, can the most personal of all relationships and experiences, those of vocation and discipleship, have to do with an authority that can still function substantially despite personal sinfulness? Surely the whole logic of the Gospel teaching must make us regard it as a mere means of preserving social order within the Christian community?"[27] In response, he emphasizes the disciples' call to follow the Lord. Distinguishing between Christian

---

24. Joseph Ratzinger, "Postscript" to "Luther and the Unity of the Churches," in his *Church, Ecumenism and Politics*, 128.

25. Ibid., 129. Ratzinger's emphasis on sacramental receptivity merits more attention in William J. Abraham's otherwise insightful summary of Ratzinger's theology in Abraham, *The Logic of Renewal* (Grand Rapids, MI: Eerdmans, 2003), 54–69, 167. Despite Ratzinger's best efforts, Abraham argues, he cannot avoid "the quick impasse that emerges when we appeal to the historical Jesus and the historical church" (68). How to know what Jesus wills for his Church? Abraham states, "The appeal to Petrine primacy and papal infallibility does not solve the problem. . . . The bishop of Rome, once a revered and crucial bishop in the church as a whole, has been turned into an epistemic mechanism for securing the right interpretation of the gospel" (ibid.). For Ratzinger, however, the pope serves not as an "epistemic mechanism" but as an instrument of the Church's gifting/receptivity.

26. Hans Urs von Balthasar, "Office in the Church," trans. A. V. Littledale with Alexander Dru, in *Explorations in Theology*, vol. 2, *Spouse of the Word* (San Francisco: Ignatius Press, 1991), 81–141, at 81. On von Balthasar's ecclesiology see especially Larry S. Chapp, "Who Is the Church? The Personalistic Categories of Balthasar's Ecclesiology," *Communio* 23 (1996): 322–38; cf. Stephan Ackermann, "The Church as Person in the Theology of Hans Urs von Balthasar," trans. Emily Rielley, *Communio* 29 (2002): 238–49.

27. Von Balthasar, "Office in the Church," 81. For further insight into these questions, see also von Balthasar's identification of "Marian," "Johannine," and "Petrine" dimensions of the Church, in idem, *The Office of Peter and the Structure of the Church*); idem, *Theo-Drama: Theological Dramatic Theory*, vol. 3, *Dramatis Personae: Persons in Christ*, trans. Graham Harrison (German 1978; San Francisco: Ignatius Press, 1992), 353–60. Somewhat similarly, Avery Dulles, sj, proposes "to distinguish among the various classes of disciple of whom we read in the Gospels, including Peter as prototype of the apostle-disciple and Mary as prototype of the believer-disciple." See Dulles, *A Church to Believe In: Discipleship and the Dynamics of Freedom* (1982; New York: Crossroad, 1987), 9; as well as idem, "A New Orthodox View of the Papacy," *Pro Ecclesia* 12 (2003): 345–58, at 348. See also on von Balthasar's typology, Antonio Sicari, "Mary, Peter and John: Figures of the Church," trans. Michael Waldstein, *Communio* 19 (1992): 189–207.

discipleship and discipleship in world religions and philosophies, he argues that " 'imitation' in the Christian sense is no other than the disciples' following as conceived and ordained by Christ himself, whose 'leaving all things' and 'going with' him were changed from a material to a spiritual act and carried out in all seriousness."[28] This spiritual act comprises four elements: faith's act of "surrender," Christ's cruciform revelation of himself, Christian self-renunciation, and "the investiture with the form of Christ."[29] In this fourfold way, von Balthasar says, the divine gifting occurs within "the open heart of God, which receives all the humbled in its own humiliation that they may find rest and can only do so by giving them to share this yoke of humiliation."[30] In other words, by renouncing any effort to give ourselves "form," we open ourselves most fully to receive and be configured to Christ's kenotic form, which is the form of divine gifting.[31] Hierarchical authority in the Church serves the personal *kenosis*—active love—of the universal priesthood of all believers, who receive Christ's form so as to share it with others.[32]

As von Balthasar puts it elsewhere, "It is Church office that wrests the individual's own criteria from him and hands them over to the Lord of the Church, guaranteeing that the Church's experience of love shall transcend itself in the direction of the love of Christ (as Head of the Church) and shall overcome all subjectivisms and attain the objectivity of that love that 'believes all things, hopes all things, endures all things' (1 Cor 13:7)."[33] In acknowledgment of the gifting that constitutes us, we learn to *receive*—rather than grasp on our own terms—the divine goodness.[34] Such receptivity, so opposed to our

---

28. Von Balthasar, "Office in the Church," 96–97.

29. Ibid., 108.

30. Ibid., 101.

31. For discussion see Chapp, "Who Is the Church? The Personalistic Categories of Balthasar's Ecclesiology." Chapp speaks of "the singular theological 'subjectivity' that permeates, unites and elevates the Church's 'form' into a christological form" (338). See also David L. Schindler, "Towards a Eucharistic Evangelization," *Communio* 19 (1992): 549–75.

32. See von Balthasar, "Office in the Church," 139. See also, for the active and engaged character of kenotic love, von Balthasar, *Truth Is Symphonic: Aspects of Christian Pluralism*, trans. Graham Harrison (German 1972; San Francisco: Ignatius Press, 1987), 104–7.

33. Von Balthasar, *Truth Is Symphonic*, 102.

34. See also Hans Urs von Balthasar, "Theology and Holiness," trans. Peter Verhalen, ocist, *Communio* 14 (1987): 341–50. Jean-Luc Marion likewise has the pattern of gifting and receptivity in view when he suggests that "just as a priest who breaks his communion with the

pride, requires concrete practice. God makes this possible by mediating his gifting (in Christ and by the Spirit) through other sinful human beings, priests. The kenosis required by the mediation of the incarnate Word in and through hierarchical ecclesial structures assists Christians in attaining the self-giving reality of Love.

Hierarchy and the Church's Common Good

Yet, are not such claims about the ecclesial structure of gifting/ receptivity insufficiently attentive to the problems caused by unequal power structures? It might seem that theologians such as Ratzinger and von Balthasar do not sufficiently consider the possibility that kenotic receptivity toward the hierarchical priesthood produces a structure of oppression, by leaving largely unchecked the power of the hierarchical priesthood and by placing the non-ordained members of the Church in an overly passive role.[35] While I discuss such concerns

bishop can no longer enter into ecclesiastical communion, so a teacher who speaks without, even against, the Symbol of the apostles, without, even against, his bishop, absolutely can no longer carry on his discourse in an authentically *theo*logical site." See Marion, *God Without Being: Hors-Texte*, trans. Thomas A. Carlson (Chicago: The University of Chicago Press, 1991), 153. Marion observes that "to detach oneself from the bishop does not offer to 'theological science' an 'object' that is finally neutral, but does away with the eucharistic site of the hermeneutic. . . . The more the teacher inscribes himself in the eucharistic rite opened by the bishop, the more he can become a *theo*logian" (*God Without Being*, 153–54). In a similar manner Marion criticizes the view that human beings constitute their own faith, in his " 'They Recognized Him; and He Became Invisible to Them,' " *Modern Theology* 18 (2002): 145–52. See also Reinhard Hütter's criticism that "in both the 'Kantian church' of moral motivation and the 'Schleiermachian church' of religious communication, the moral and/or religious subject antecedes the church. The fixed point is the subject to whom the 'church' stands in a functional relationship of service—be it of a moral or a religious kind" (Hütter, "The Church: The Knowledge of the Triune God: Practices, Doctrine, Theology," in *Knowing the Triune God: The Work of the Spirit in the Practices of the Church*, ed. James J. Buckley and David S. Yeago [Grand Rapids, MI: Eerdmans, 2001], 23–47, at 25). Drawing upon the research of Henri de Lubac, and Michel de Certeau, John Milbank argues that Marion's account applies to the Church only up to the Tridentine period, after which a non-eucharistic account of the bishop, present since the late-medieval period, became dominant. For Milbank, "Theology is answerable to the Bishop as the occupant of the *cathedra* and as President at the Eucharist. But this means that the theologian is primarily answerable, not so much to a Church hierarchy in its synchronic spatiality—this is all too modern—but rather to a hierarchical, educative *manuductio* of the faith down the ages" (Milbank, "Ecclesiology: The Last of the Last," in idem, *Being Reconciled: Ontology and Pardon* [London: Routledge, 2003], 105–37, at 126). I wonder, however, whether this separation between "synchronic spatiality" and the *manuductio* "down the ages" works.

35. For example, in an essay originally published in 1980, Avery Dulles, sj, advances concerns along these lines regarding von Balthasar's approach: "He tends to be rather

in the chapters that follow, and particularly in the Conclusion, Yves Simon's analysis of authority and the common good suggests a preliminary answer. Simon argues, "The common good is central to every theory of authority. It is only in relation to it that authority exercises essential functions, i.e., functions whose necessity does not result from any evil or deficiency, but from the nature and the excellence of things human and social."[36] This is so because human beings have what Simon terms "other-centered needs," so that human beings "would rather stand physical destitution than be denied opportunity for disinterested love and sacrifice."[37] Human community is a common good precisely as fostering (in the midst of human selfishness brought about by sin) these "other-centered needs" in and through "united action," which requires the exercise of authority within the community.[38]

---

defensive against democratization and sociological analysis, and one-sided in his emphasis on receptivity, obedience, and submission. He fails to insist that initiative, personal responsibility, candor, and creativity are inseparable from true discipleship" (Dulles, "Institution and Charism in the Church," in *A Church to Believe In*, 28). At the same time, however, Dulles gives von Balthasar high praise for having "developed a profound theology of ecclesiastical office, in which the charismatic and the institutional are richly interwoven" (28). Von Balthasar's understanding of *kenotic* existence is more active and creative than Dulles here allows; cf. Dulles's own later work.

36. Yves Simon, *A General Theory of Authority* (Notre Dame, IN: University of Notre Dame Press, 1962), 157. For further reflection on authority indebted to Simon, and especially to his *The Philosophy of Democratic Government*, see Philip Turner, "Episcopal Authority within a Communion of Churches," 150 and elsewhere; Michael J. Buckley, sj, *Papal Primacy and the Episcopate: Towards a Relational Understanding* (New York: Crossroad, 1998), 64–65. Buckley draws upon Simon's distinction between "substitutional" and "essential" (which Buckley terms "habitual") functions of authority. In Buckley's view, the popes, since the early Middle Ages if not before, have taken on too many "substitutional" functions. Buckley suggests that papal jurisdiction has weakened the local churches in the second millennium, but one wonders whether in fact the local churches have been as weak as he suggests, and furthermore whether their spiritual strength ("communion") has been weakened or in fact augmented by papal jurisdiction. See also Matthew L. Lamb, "Modern Liberalism, Authority and Authoritarianism: Political Theology against Deceptive Modern Categories," in *Missing God? Cultural Amnesia and Political Theology*, ed. John K. Downey, Jürgen Manemann, and Steven T. Ostovich (Berlin: LIT Verlag, 2006), 104–24, especially Lamb's critique of Max Weber's account of authority in terms of command/control.

37. Simon, *A General Theory of Authority*, 26.

38. Ibid., 29, 33. Simon goes on to note, "The existence of a plurality of genuine means in the pursuit of the common good excludes unanimity as a *sufficient* method of steadily procuring unity of action. . . . *The power in charge of unifying common action through rules binding for all is what everyone calls authority*" (47–48). To this point he adds, "*The most essential function of authority is the issuance and carrying out of rules expressing the requirements of the common good considered materially*" (57).

If authority is requisite for communities marked by self-sacrificial love, what kind of authority befits the Church as the locus of redemption from sin? In other words, what kind of authority enables the Church to pursue her particular common good, communion with the triune God, through united action in faith and charity?[39] First and foremost, the Church requires authority that is rooted sacramentally, so as to be able to communicate a common good that can only be given from above. Second, in order to foster united action flowing from shared wisdom, authority in the Church extends to teaching and governance.[40] The sacramental nature of authority in the Church

---

39. For further discussion see Kenneth L. Schmitz's excellent "The Authority of Institutions: Meddling or Middling?" *Communio* 12 (1985): 5–24. Cf. on faith and action Francis Martin, "The Integrity of Christian Moral Activity: The First Letter of John and *Veritatis Splendor*," *Communio* 21 (1994): 265–85.

40. Not sufficiently recognizing their connection with sanctifying, Bernard Hoose too strongly divides authority to teach and authority to govern in the Church: see Hoose, "Authority in the Church," *Theological Studies* 63 (2002): 107–22. Fearing that God's word has been treated as "the privileged possession of a privileged few members of the Church" (108), he has particularly in view the moral teachings of the Church, such as *Humanae Vitae*, which often seem to have "only a remote connection to revelation" (114); cf. Hoose's *Received Wisdom? Reviewing the Role of Tradition in Christian Ethics* (New York: Geoffrey Chapman, 1994). This reduction of ecclesial hierarchy to "a privileged few members of the Church" leaves out the sacramental dimension, and thereby leaves out as well the principle that delimits authority in the Church (as a sacramental organism in which not solely priests, but all believers, have a sacramental vocation toward the "end" of union with Christ). The result does not curtail disordered governance, but rather restricts teaching to a conceptual realm to which governance is extrinsic. For his part, Nicholas Lash calls for a retrieval of the full dimensions of the threefold office (priest, prophet, king), on the view that deeper appreciation of the prophetic office broadens the notion of "authority" in the Church. Lash warns, " 'Authority,' especially in a Christian context, is a far wider term than 'governance.' And yet, to an alarming extent, it is in terms of governance that authority in the Catholic Church is understood and exercised— even, perhaps especially, what we call 'teaching authority' or magisterium. . . . 'Teaching,' in Christianity, is not a form of governance. On the contrary, governance is an aspect of teaching—set, from start to finish, at the service of our common apprenticeship in holiness and understanding" (Lash, "Authors, Authority and Authorization," in *Authority in the Roman Catholic Church: Theory and Practice*, ed. Bernard Hoose [Aldershot: Ashgate, 2002], 59–71, at 68). It seems a stretch to argue that recent magisterial teaching has possessed a juridical rather than educative tenor, but even so, why subsume governance under teaching so as to produce (de facto) a twofold rather than threefold office? Certainly governance belongs to Christian pedagogy in the broad sense, but blurring the distinction between teaching and governance causes difficulties in accounting for Christian obedience and distinguishing the bishop's role from the theologian's. In a largely similar vein see such diverse recent studies as *Governance and Authority in the Roman Catholic Church: Beginning a Conversation*, ed. Noel Timms and Kenneth Wilson (London: SPCK, 2000); David Stagaman, *Authority in the Church* (Collegeville, MN: Liturgical Press, 1999); Linda Hogan, *Confronting the Truth: Conscience in the Catholic Tradition* (New York: Paulist, 2000); John P. Boyle, *Church Teaching Authority: Historical and Theological Studies* (Notre Dame, IN: University of Notre Dame Press, 1995); Bernard

means that no exercise of ecclesial authority can isolate itself from the kenotic pattern of true "power." The inscription of receptivity and gifting within the very meaning of hierarchical "power" in the Church marks ecclesial power with *dispossession*. As Congar says of hierarchy in the Church:

> The Church's powers come to it from Christ as those of Christ come to him from God. Consequently, through the whole range of its activities, there is always observed what might be called the law of hierarchical procession. Everything therein comes from above, from the bosom of the Father, through Christ and apostles. The whole external order, therefore, of its constitution and life is an application, as well as a sensible represen-tation, of the law according to which all it has comes from above. That is the inner meaning of the whole ordering of the consecrations, the sacraments, the liturgy, teaching and even of jurisdiction, where it is always a matter of communication from above to beneath, hierarchically. Those who speak disparagingly of human intermediaries and sacerdotalism may, indeed, show their keen sense of certain evangelical values, such as liberty and the interior spirit; but often enough they show a failure to grasp how, in the Church, all comes from above and how the Church itself is the great and universal sacrament of the sole mediation of Christ."[41]

Sesboüé, SJ, *Le Magistère à l'épreuve. Autorité, vérité et liberté dans l'Église* (Paris: Desclée, 2001).

41. Yves Congar, "The Church and Its Unity," in his *The Mystery of the Church*, trans. A. V. Littledale (French 1956; Baltimore: Helicon Press, 1960), 58–96, at 90; see also his "The Eucharist and the Church of the New Alliance," in his *The Revelation of God*, trans. A. Manson and L. C. Sheppard (French 1962; New York: Herder and Herder, 1968), 168–88, at 187. Reinhard Hütter, from a Lutheran perspective, likewise articulates the necessity of a concrete ecclesial receptivity (which he terms "pathos"): see his *Suffering Divine Things: Theology as Church Practice*, trans. Doug Stott (German 1997; Grand Rapids, MI: Eerdmans, 2000). On the Church as a "sacrament," see Congar's "The Idea of the Church in St. Thomas Aquinas," in idem, *The Mystery of the Church*, 115; Henri de Lubac, SJ, *The Splendor of the Church*, trans. Michael Mason (French 1953; San Francisco: Ignatius Press, 1986), chapter 6; Timothy George, "The Sacramentality of the Church: An Evangelical Baptist Perspective," *Pro Ecclesia* 12 (2003): 309–23. Congar concludes that for Aquinas "the Church-as-Institution is the sacrament of the Cross, the sacrament of the unique mediatorship of Christ Crucified. Again she is the sacrament, the effective sign and giver of the gift of new life and of union of men in Christ their Saviour. This mystery St. Thomas studies in detail in the *Tertia Pars, De ipso Salvatore, de Sacramentis ejus quibus salutem consequimur* (prol.). We can now understand the literalness, the realism, and depth of this doctrine, itself part of the common tradition of Catholic theology since Augustine. The unity of the Mystical Body is the reality attained by that sacrament which is the source, the end, the beginning and the consummation, of all the others, that by which and for which the Church is made—the Church the mystery of faith, of which we are speaking, as well as the material building—namely the Eucharist. In numerous texts St. Thomas asserts that the *Res hujus Sacramenti*, that is, the thing attained by the effective symbolism of the sacrament, is the *Unitas corporis mystici*" (Congar, "The Idea of the

The Church, on this theocentric view, is "hierarchical" because the Church receives everything from above, from the Father, Son, and Holy Spirit and embodies, by "application" and "sensible representation," these cruciform gifts in the world.

In exercising its proper authority for the common good, therefore, the hierarchy of the Church does not rely upon merely human resources. Authority in the Church—ordered power—depends upon Christ and his Spirit. Aquinas notes that "the ministers of the Church do not by their own power cleanse from sin those who approach the sacraments, nor do they confer grace on them: it is Christ Who does this by His own power while He employs them as instruments. Consequently those who approach the sacraments receive an effect whereby they are enlikened not to the ministers but to Christ."[42] It follows that even if priests fail in holiness, Christ can mediate the supernatural common good through the hierarchical priesthood: "a man can be Christ's minister even though he be not one of the just. And this belongs to Christ's excellence, Whom, as the true God, things both good and evil serve, since they are ordained by His providence for His glory."[43]

Yet, can unrepentant sinners truly exercise authority in Christ's Church? Recall Catherine of Siena's description of sinful priests and bishops as messengers empowered by being sent: "You know well enough that if someone filthy or poorly dressed were to offer you a great treasure that would give you life, you would not disdain the bearer for love of the treasure and the lord who had sent it, even

---

Church in St. Thomas Aquinas," 115). See also Jean-Pierre Torrell, OP, "Yves Congar et l'ecclésiologie de saint Thomas d'Aquin," *Revue des sciences philosophiques et théologiques* 82 (1998): 201–42.

42. III, q. 64, a. 5, ad 1; cf. III, q. 82, a. 5. For an ecclesiology attuned to questions of causality, see Christian Gouyard, *L'Église instrument du Salut* (Paris: Pierre Téqui, 2005). A classic approach from this direction is Charles Journet, *L'Église du Verbe Incarné*, 4 vols. (Saint-Maurice: Saint-Augustin, 1999–2000).

43. III, q. 82, a. 5. As the Protestant biblical theologian Timothy Laniak remarks, "The God of Scripture passionately seeks humans to enlist in his mission, risking it regularly in their hands. This predilection is rooted in an ideal whereby human rule is a derivative extension of divine rule. Our theology of leadership is informed by this breathtaking choice of God to grant royal prerogatives to his creatures. . . . Already the temptation to hubris is present throughout the accounts of biblical leaders, beginning with the first couple. In order to qualify this tendency, leaders are constantly reminded of their contingent status. Every shepherd leader is first and always a sheep who relates to God as 'my Shepherd' " (Laniak, *Shepherds after My Own Heart: Pastoral Traditions and Leadership in the Bible* [Downers Grove, IL: InterVarsity Press, 2006], 248).

though the bearer was ragged and filthy. . . . For love of the lord you would do what you could to persuade him to get rid of his filth and put on better clothes."[44] When members of the hierarchical priesthood abuse their received power by failing to act for the Church's common good, Catherine says, we must pray for these members and "hold them out to me [God] with tears and great desire, so that I in my goodness may clothe them with the garment of charity."[45] Recognizing herself as a sinner, however, Catherine desires, with tears of repentance, to be clothed with the same garment herself. Thus the divine gifting comes to us through the hands of dispossessed sinners because all human beings are dispossessed sinners. Intrinsic to our cruciform receptivity to the divine gifting in Christ's Mystical Body is our prayer that the Holy Spirit convert us.[46]

FAITH'S FREEDOM

It will be clear that I neither assume "a provisionality to present ecclesial actuality that allows us to infer a continuing creation and re-creation of the Church's being" nor hold that the Church is marked by an

---

44. Catherine of Siena, *The Dialogue*, trans. Suzanne Noffke, OP. (New York: Paulist Press, 1980), 230. In this view the Church remains intact despite its occasionally "ragged and filthy" appearance. For a vision of the Church as having abandoned the Lord (and living therefore only in and through the mercy of Christ's cross), see Radner, *The End of the Church*, as well as Bruce D. Marshall's appreciative review essay of this book: "Review Essay: The Divided Church and Its Theology," *Modern Theology* 16 (2000): 377–96. To my mind, Catherine of Siena provides a better solution than Radner's. See also Bruno Forte, "The Church Confronts the Faults of the Past," *Communio* 27 (2000): 676–87.

45. Catherine of Siena, *The Dialogue*, 230.

46. Thus, discussing the Mystical Body, Yves Congar remarks that "all the initiative belongs to him [Christ]. It is not so much we who appropriate his holiness or mimic him in his life of sonship; it is rather he who, having come for our sakes, continues in mankind the act of love and praise of the Father which he performed first on this earth as both God and one of us, in the name of us all; it is he who, 'having become man that we might become God,' works not only his own Incarnation, but our divinization. It is, in truth, a divine life he gives us to lead in the body through his grace; the power of the Holy Spirit is not confined to the generation of Christ in Mary's womb, but also is what generates Christians in the womb of the Church" (Congar, "The Mystical Body of Christ," in his *The Mystery of the Church*, 118–37, at 119). For further discussion of the Church as the Mystical Body, see Congar, "*Lumen Gentium*, 7: L'Église, Corps mystique du Christ, vu au terme de huit siècles d'histoire de la théologie du Corps mystique," in *Au service de la Parole de Dieu. Mélanges offerts à Mgr. A.-M. Charue* (Gembloux: Duculot, 1969), 179–202; de Lubac, *The Splendor of the Church*, 119–33.

"under-determinedness which is its freedom to become itself."[47] Indeed, were the Church's very "being" underdetermined in this way, such a situation would be the opposite of true Christian freedom, which is found in Christ's full gift of himself to believers in the Holy Spirit, through the teachings and sacraments of his Body. As Alexander Schmemann points out, "there is no freedom *in* the Church, but the Church herself *is* freedom, and only the Church is freedom"[48]—and this because the Church is the locus of the salvific operation of Christ and the Holy Spirit. The Church's freedom is precisely her capacity afforded by the grace of the Holy Spirit to act according to her supernatural nature as Christ's mystical Body, and to attain to her fulfillment (communion with the Trinity).[49] Saint Paul teaches, "God

---

47. Sue Patterson, *Realist Christian Theology in a Postmodern Age* (Cambridge: Cambridge University Press, 1999), 141. This notion of "freedom" has been challenged by Servais Pinckaers, OP, *The Sources of Christian Ethics*, 3rd ed. translated by Sister Mary Thomas Noble, OP (Washington, DC: The Catholic University of America Press, 1995); see also in this vein Avery Dulles, SJ, *A Church to Believe In*, chapter 5: "The Meaning of Freedom in the Church," 66–79; Joseph Ratzinger, "Freedom and Liberation: The Anthropological Vision of the Instruction 'Libertatis Conscientia,'" trans. Stephen Wentworth Arndt, *Communio* 14 (1987): 55–72. David L. Schindler characterizes "creaturely freedom and autonomy" as "properly spousal—or, more exactly, bridal—and hence *receptive and responsive* in nature. To be sure, the invitation to spousal intimacy which God extends already at creation presupposes man as a free determining subject. But this *invitation* to spousal intimacy has always-already (in the one real order of history) been inscribed within man, and thus functions as an anterior condition for man's reality as a free determining subject. Man does not possess a freedom which is first neutral, which then either contracts or does not contract a relation with the God is first (simply) outside of man" (Schindler, "Christology and the *Imago Dei*: Interpreting *Gaudium et Spes*," *Communio* 23 [1996]: 156–84, at 162). As an Anglican priest, Patterson is concerned about the Church's "capacity to create false and distorted worlds that are diminishing and destructive of the relationality on which personhood depends, as the historical record shows" (Patterson, 141).

48. Alexander Schmemann, *Church, World, Mission: Reflections on Orthodoxy in the West* (Crestwood, NY: St. Vladimir's Seminary Press, 1979), 184. Following A. S. Khomiakov, Schmemann goes on to blame the West—Roman Catholicism—for the "freedom-authority" dichotomy in the Church. Schmemann notes, "For Khomiakov the initial tragedy of the West, transcending its internal schism, or rather provoking it, was the identification of the Church with something alien to her nature—an external and objective authority. It made inevitable a revolt against this authority, but the revolt remains necessarily within the framework of that which it negates—and resulted therefore in a simple replacement of one external authority with another" (183). Authority must be seen as intrinsic, not extrinsic, to the mystical Body, filled with the Holy Spirit.

49. I owe this formulation to Bernhard Blankenhorn, OP. As Schmemann states, "All this means that in the Church freedom is manifested as obedience of all to all in Christ, for Christ is the one who, by the Holy Spirit, lives in all in communion with God. No one is above and no one is beneath. The one who teaches has no 'authority,' but a gift of the Holy Spirit. And the one who receives the teaching receives it only if he has the gift of the Holy Spirit, which reveals to him the teaching not as 'authority' but as Truth. And the prayer of the Church is not

is faithful, by whom you were called into the fellowship of his Son, Jesus Christ our Lord" (1 Corinthians 1:9).

Since the Holy Spirit establishes the Church's fellowship in Christ, one can agree with Henri de Lubac that the Church "stands wide open to us, but its depths defy our sounding; it is intelligible, to be sure, but not 'comprehensible.' "[50] That the Father, Son, and Holy Spirit have chosen to reverse our fallenness *from within* sinful humanity possesses inexhaustible depths. Through study of ecclesial hierarchy, may we enter ever more deeply into Saint Paul's exhortation to the Philippians:

> So if there is any encouragement in Christ, any incentive of love, any participation in the Spirit, any affection and sympathy, complete my joy by being of the same mind, having the same love, being in full accord and of one mind. Do nothing from selfishness or conceit, but in humility count others better than yourselves. Let each of you look not only to his own interests, but also to the interests of others. Have this mind among yourselves, which was in Christ Jesus, who, though he was in the form of God, did not count equality with God a thing to be grasped, but emptied himself, taking the form of a servant, being born in the likeness of men. And being found in human form he humbled himself and became obedient unto death, even death on a cross. Therefore God has highly exalted him and bestowed on him the name which is above every name, that at the name of Jesus every knee should bow, in heaven and on earth and under the earth, and every tongue confess that Jesus Christ is Lord, to the glory of God the Father. Therefore, my beloved, as you have always obeyed, so now, not only as in my presence but much more in my absence, work out your own salvation with fear and trembling; for God is at work in you, both to will and to work for his good pleasure. (Phil 2:1–12)

---

for 'sanctions' and 'guarantees,' but for the Spirit Himself—that He may come and abide in us, transforming us into that living unity in which the obedience of all to all is unceasingly revealing itself as the only freedom" (190). Thus "the mystery of the Church as freedom is hidden in the mystery of God as the Blessed Trinity—in the grace of our Lord Jesus Christ, the love of God the Father, in the communion of the Holy Spirit. And this mystery begins to be revealed and communicated to us when the same man [Paul] says of himself '*doulos Iesou Christou*'—'The slave of Jesus Christ'—and then, to each one and to all of us, 'Stand fast in the freedom in which Christ has set us free' (Gal. 5:1)" (190–91). All "authority" in the Church is sacramental and therefore Christological and pneumatological. For a positive understanding of authority, see my discussion of Yves Simon above.

50. De Lubac, *The Splendor of the Church*, 28, quoting Andrew of St. Victor.

Chapter 1

Hierarchical Priesthood and Trinitarian Communion

Unitatis Redintegratio, the Second Vatican Council's Decree on Ecumenism, teaches that the unity of the Church "finds its supreme exemplar and source in the unity of the Persons of the Trinity: the unity of the one God, the Father and the Son in the Holy Spirit."[1] The principle that ecclesial communion should manifest the Trinitarian communion is well attested in the New Testament. Jesus promises his disciples that their communion in truth will be a communion in the Father, Son, and Holy Spirit: "When the Spirit of truth comes, he will guide you into all the truth. . . . He will glorify me, for he will take what is mine and declare it to you. All that the Father has is mine" (John 16:13–15). The disciples' communion in the truth, which constitutes their unity, is a sharing in the Father, Son, and Holy Spirit. Similarly, Jesus prays for a graced unity of the disciples rooted in the unity of the Trinity: "The glory which thou [the Father] hast given me I have given to them, that they may be one even as we are one, I in them and thou in me, that they may become perfectly one, so that the world may know that thou hast sent me and hast loved them even as

---

1. *Unitatis Redintegratio*, 2, in *Decrees of the Ecumenical Councils*, vol. 2, *Trent to Vatican II*, ed. Norman P. Tanner, sj (Washington, DC: Georgetown University Press, 1990), p. 909. On the Church as an "icon of the Trinity" see Walter Kasper, "The Church as Sacrament of Unity," trans. Charles R. Hohenstein, *Communio* 14 (1987): 4–11. With respect to the place of hierarchy in a Trinitarian ecclesiology, Kasper states that "trinitarian *communio*-unity is to be considered hierarchical, in the sense of the theology of the Eastern churches, despite all that must be said about the equality of the Persons in essence, dignity and the worship owed to each" (11). Without positing that the divine Persons require "their own special domains" in the sense implied by this term, one can appreciate Kasper's elucidation of the Trinity as having an "inner order" that does not derogate from co-equality. The question is what goods belong intrinsically to Christian equality. This question has to be answered first from the perspective of charity, rather than first from the perspective of temporal power.

thou hast loved me" (John 17:22–23). Their unity, the unity of the Church, manifests not just the unity of God, but the unity of Father and Son (in the Spirit), the unity of the Trinity.[2] Likewise, just as the Church is built up by sharing in the Paschal Mystery of the Son in the Spirit, so the Church's prayer embodies the Trinitarian unity that God wills to give the Church (see Romans 8:14–17).

However, can hierarchical ecclesial structure, as *Unitatis Redintegratio* affirms, truly invite communion in the Trinitarian life?[3] In other words, does the presence of hierarchy within Christian ecclesial communion in fact obscure rather than make manifest the Trinitarian communion of co-equal Persons? It would seem that hierarchy's emphasis on promoting visible unity more clearly manifests divine unity than it does Trinitarian communion. If Christians are not in an absolute sense a community of equals, how can they truly proclaim and witness to a divine community of equals?

On these grounds, Miroslav Volf has recently challenged Catholic and Orthodox "communion ecclesiologies," as represented respectively by the work of Joseph Ratzinger and John D. Zizioulas.[4]

---

2. Cf. the remark of George Sabra in his *Thomas Aquinas' Vision of the Church: Fundamentals of an Ecumenical Ecclesiology* (Mainz: Matthias-Grünewald-Verlag, 1987), 70: "If one were to study all of Thomas' ecclesiological statements in all of his writings with the intention of discovering which mark of the Church occupied him most, the result would be quite clear: unity." Cited in Frederick Christian Bauerschmidt, " 'That the Faithful Become the Temple of God': The Church Militant in Aquinas's *Commentary on John*," in *Reading John with St. Thomas Aquinas*, ed. Michael Dauphinais and Matthew Levering (Washington, DC: The Catholic University of America Press, 2005), 293–311, at 301, fn. 22.

3. In asking this question, I wish to avoid any sense that the Church *is* the hierarchy. Richard F. Costigan, SJ, argues that both the Gallican and the "papalist" or Ultramontane sides in the controversies over papal authority (from the seventeenth through the nineteenth centuries) understand the term "*Ecclesia*" to refer to the hierarchy rather than to the whole people of God. See Costigan, *The Consensus of the Church and Papal Infallibility: A Study in the Background of Vatican I* (Washington, DC: The Catholic University of America Press, 2005), 32; cf. Yves Congar, "L'ecclésiologie de la Révolution française au Concile du Vatican, sous la signe de l'affirmation de l'autorité," in *L'ecclésiologie au XIXe siècle*, ed. Maurice Nédoncelle et al. (Paris: Cerf, 1960), 77–114; Francis A. Sullivan, SJ, *Magisterium: Teaching Authority in the Catholic Church* (New York: Paulist Press, 1983), 90ff.

4. Miroslav Volf, *After Our Likeness: The Church as the Image of the Trinity*, trans. Doug Stott (Grand Rapids, MI: Eerdmans, 1998), 25. He argues that "the *this-worldly character* of God's self-revelation makes it possible to convert Trinitarian ideas into ecclesiological ideas" (199). In so doing, it should be noted, he retains a solid grasp upon the analogous character of Trinitarian discourse: "The trinitarian models . . . are not simply projections of ideal social models. Insofar as trinitarian models do in fact speak about the triune God who is to be distinguished from human beings, models of the triune God and of the church must also be distinguished. 'Person' and 'communion' in ecclesiology cannot be identical with 'person' and

I first examine in detail Volf's arguments against Ratzinger and Zizioulas. Since Volf's arguments have to do not merely with twentieth-century theology, but with the Church's entire ecclesiological tradition, I engage Volf's arguments critically by means of Thomas Aquinas's theology of the Church, rooted in theology of the triune God and based concretely on participation in Christ's Paschal Mystery by faith and the sacraments.[5] I hope thereby to show how ecclesial hierarchy belongs to the Church's imaging of the Trinity.

VOLF ON RATZINGER AND ZIZIOULAS

Critique of Ratzinger

Volf's criticism of Ratzinger's ecclesiology is advanced through Trinitarian theology.[6] Ratzinger, Volf notes, largely agrees with Heribert Mühlen that, in Ratzinger's words, " 'The church's action and behaviour must correspond to the "we" of God by following the pattern of

---

'communion' in the doctrine of the Trinity; they can only be understood as *analogous* to them" (199). For discussion of Volf's work—including his later essays " 'The Trinity Is Our Social Program': The Doctrine of the Trinity and the Shape of Social Engagement," *Modern Theology* 14 (1998): 403–23; and idem, "Trinity, Unity, Primacy: On the Trinitarian Nature of Ecclesial Unity and Its Implications for the Question of Primacy," in *Petrine Ministry and the Unity of the Church*, ed. James F. Puglisi (Collegeville, MN: Liturgical Press, 1999), 171–84—see Dennis M. Doyle, *Communion Ecclesiology: Vision and Versions* (Maryknoll, NY: Orbis Books, 2000), 161–67. John J. Burkhard, OFM CONV, discusses Volf's critiques of Joseph Ratzinger's and John Zizioulas's ecclesiology in Burkhard, *Apostolicity Then and Now: An Ecumenical Church in a Postmodern World* (Collegeville, MN: Liturgical Press, 2004), 84–88.

5. Cf. Sabra, *Thomas Aquinas' Vision of the Church*, 77–106, 144–51. For further discussion of the relationship between faith and sacraments, see also Anscar Vonier, OSB, *A Key to the Doctrine of the Eucharist* (1925; Bethesda, MD: Zaccheus Press, 2003), 1–6.

6. It is worth noting that Zizioulas agrees with the basic thrust of Volf's critique of Ratzinger's ecclesiology. With Ratzinger (and Volf) in mind, Zizioulas writes, "There is an ecclesiology in which hierarchical structures are regarded as central and necessary, but they are so on the basis of a Trinitarian model in which otherness is secondary to unity and is understood as existing only in order to serve unity. A substantialist Trinitarian theology is, in this case, transferred into ecclesiology. This priority of the 'one' over the 'many', or of substance over personhood, turns hierarchy into a means not of producing and securing otherness, as is the case in the Cappadocian understanding of divine causality, but of enforcing unity" (Zizioulas, "The Father as Cause," in his *Communion and Otherness*, ed. Paul McPartlan [New York: T. & T. Clark, 2006], 113–54, at 145–46). Zizioulas also notes that Colin Gunton, for many years Zizioulas's colleague at King's College, London, advances similar criticisms of Catholic Trinitarian theology and ecclesiology: see Gunton's *The Promise of Trinitarian Theology* (Edinburgh: T&T Clark, 1991).

this [Trinitarian] relationship.' "[7] How then does Ratzinger conceive of this "pattern"? He begins with the medieval dictum, found in Aquinas and elsewhere, that *"persona est relatio."*[8] Volf interprets this claim to mean that a divine Person is nothing but *"pure* relationality."[9] The Persons in the Trinity are the same as the Trinitarian actions (e.g., the Father *is* begetting), and so the distinct Persons have no non-relational identity. Christ manifests the Person of the Son because Christ, too, has no non-relational identity: Christ has nothing of his own, but is simply what he receives from the Father. All human beings find the model of human perfection in Christ. Like Christ, we are called to lose ourselves so as to gain ourselves; we are called to become pure receptivity and relationality vis-à-vis the triune God. Like Christ, we cannot have a "'fenced-off private ground'" where we stake out an area of autonomy from the triune God.[10]

What problem does Volf identify in this approach? Put simply, "Pure relations can neither speak nor hear."[11] Ratzinger, in Volf's view, empties out any possibility for a real Trinitarian communion of Persons, because the Persons are ciphers. As Volf notes, following

---

7. Cited by Volf, *After Our Likeness*, 67; see Joseph Ratzinger, *Church, Ecumenism, and Politics: New Essays in Ecclesiology* (German 1987; New York: Crossroad, 1988), 31. As Volf points out, the effort to ground ecclesiology in Trinitarian theology is characteristic of Catholic and Orthodox theology, although he also suggests that it has not been successful (Volf, *After Our Likeness*, 4). For discussion of Saint Paul's Trinitarian ecclesiology see Hans Urs von Balthasar, *Paul Struggles with His Congregation: The Pastoral Message of the Letters to the Corinthians* (German 1988; San Francisco: Ignatius Press, 1992), 18–19.

8. Volf, *After Our Likeness*, 67. Cf. Ratzinger's "The New Covenant: A Theology of Covenant in the New Testament," trans. Maria Shrady, *Communio* 22 (1995): 635–51. Ratzinger remarks, "Within the Aristotelian chart of categories, relation is listed under accidents, which refer to substance and are dependent on it. Hence, one cannot speak of accidents in God. Because of the Christian doctrine of the Trinity, relation steps out of the substance-accidents schema. God himself is now described as a structure of trinitarian relationship, as *relatio subsistens.* When it is said of man that he is the image of God, it indicates that he is the being designed for being-in-relation, that he seeks throughout all his relationships the one relationship which is the ground of his being" (651).

9. Volf, *After Our Likeness*, 67. Aquinas affirms that the Persons are subsistent relations, not "pure" relations (of which there are four in God). Without analyzing Ratzinger's position, which as Volf admits is not systematically developed, it is clear that Volf is describing something that Aquinas, representative in this regard of the Latin tradition of Trinitarian theology, would reject. For further discussion see Gilles Emery, OP, *Trinity in Aquinas*, trans. Matthew Levering, et al. (Ypsilanti, MI: Sapientia Press, 2003), especially ch. 5, "Essentialism or Personalism in the Treatise on God in St. Thomas Aquinas?"

10. Volf, *After Our Likeness*, 68, quoting Ratzinger, *Introduction to Christianity* (London: Burns & Oates, 1969), 134.

11. Ibid., 69.

Wolfhart Pannenberg, "Admittedly, this is not only Ratzinger's problem, but that of the tradition that identifies persons with relations. This tradition has never succeeded in demonstrating persuasively how these relations can become concentrated in persons."[12] Once the Persons are seen as ciphers, the divine unity or substance becomes dominant. Since there are no Persons prior to or distinct from the relations, Volf explains, "their unity cannot come about by way of their specific personal selfhood."[13] They do not constitute a unity through their personal engagement; rather, their unity is something that underlies their Personhood. Volf states, "From this perspective, it is consistent when Ratzinger locates the unity of the triune God not at the level of persons, but rather together with the whole tradition of Western Trinitarian thought at the level of substance. The result, however, is that the one substance gains the upper hand over the three relations."[14] Volf grants that Ratzinger seeks to avoid this outcome by arguing for the "equiprimacy" of unity and Trinity, but for Volf the question remains as to how this "equiprimacy" can be maintained without a stronger account of "Person." As Volf says, "if *no* person possesses anything of its own (and according to Ratzinger, the Father apparently constitutes no exception), then they can hardly be distinguished from one another and from the divine substance sustaining them."[15]

Lacking ability to distinguish the Persons as distinct agents, one necessarily arrives at a twofold conclusion. First, the divine Persons do not form a structured pattern; such would be possible only if the divine Persons stood in some sense "on their own," rather than being pure relationality.[16] All talk of *perichoresis* aside, the only divine pattern that emerges from pure relationality is the underlying pattern of the one. Second, the divine substance, whether explicitly or implicitly,

---

12. Ibid., 71, fn. 224.

13. Ibid., 70.

14. Ibid.

15. Ibid., 71.

16. Volf comments, "Although Ratzinger criticizes Augustine's doctrine of the Trinity insofar as in it 'the persons of God are enclosed completely in God's interior, and that externally God becomes a pure I,' nonetheless, if all persons are total relationality with regard to one another, then the agent in the deity can only be the one substance, both externally and internally" (71; the citation is from Ratzinger, *Dogma and Preaching* [Chicago: Franciscan Herald, 1984], 223).

takes on the role of the agent of every divine work. In short, a thorough-going monism arises.

Volf observes that in the past such monism stemmed from the Person of the Father, who possessed a monarchical role that, in Volf's view, "functioned as a model for hierarchical relations in the church."[17] Ratzinger, however, ascribes pure relationality to the Father; the Father no more stands on his own than any other divine Persons. Despite his relational intention, however, Ratzinger (according to Volf) falls into a monism that privileges the divine substance: "The one, externally acting divine substance corresponds to the one church that, together with Christ, constitutes one subject and in that way becomes capable of action. A *monistic structure* for the Church emerges from this. The one Christ acting as subject in the church is represented by the one visible head of the church, and by the bishop as head of the local church."[18] The Church iconically manifests the divine unity, not the divine Trinity.

In Ratzinger's defense, one might ask whether the Church's hierarchical structure, understood as a pattern of receptivity or self-emptying, manifests the Trinity iconically. Volf accepts that Ratzinger's insistence upon the receptivity or selflessness of the bishops aims to manifest the Trinity.[19] But Volf points out that this selflessness depends upon unusual personal virtue that, in reality, cannot be expected to be present among all, or even many, of the bishops. He remarks that for Ratzinger, "Because these relations are conceived as pure, one ideally has a linear series of selfless hierarchs. Just as the Son is pure relation with regard to the Father, so also are the Pope and bishops to possess pure 'power as vicars.' Pure Trinitarian relationality seems to

---

17. Volf, *After our Likeness*, 71.

18. Ibid., 71–72.

19. For Ratzinger's own explanation of his position, see, e.g., his "The Papal Primacy and the Unity of the People of God," in his *Church, Ecumenism and Politics: New Essays in Ecclesiology*, trans. Robert Nowell (German 1987; New York: Crossroad, 1988), 29–45. In this essay, too, Ratzinger expresses his doubts about a Trinitarian ecclesiology that would weaken "primacy" (32). Here he engages with the ecclesiology of Vladimir Soloviev, which receives a detailed appreciation in Aidan Nichols, OP, "Solovyov and the Papacy: A Catholic Evaluation," *Communio* 24 (1997): 143–59, an essay delivered at a conference whose contributions are summarized by Gregory Glazov, "Vladimir Solovyov and the Idea of the Papacy," *Communio* 24 (1997): 128–42; cf. Georges Florovsky's highly critical discussion of Soloviev in Florovsky, *Ways of Russian Theology, Part Two*, trans. Robert L. Nichols, vol. 6 of Florovsky's *Collected Works*, ed. Richard S. Haugh (Vaduz: Büchervertriebsanstalt, 1987), 243–51.

relativize the power of the hierarchs"[20]—but in fact does not because the hierarchs are far from divine. Moreover, when one understands Christologically the human person along the model of the divine Person (pure relationality), one can never mount a critique of the exercise of power of the hierarchal bishops and priests. No human persons in the Church stand "on their own," and so no one in the Church has rights that flow from the integrity of standing "on one's own." It follows that the power of the Church's hierarchy is limited only by the virtue of the Church's hierarchy, a slim reed indeed.[21]

Volf draws a connection here between the pure relationality of the divine Persons and Ratzinger's approach to the Church as "one subject" with Christ. Ratzinger's "eucharistic ecclesiology," Volf points out, depends on "the assumption that the church is one subject with Christ,"[22] that is, that the "notion of the body of Christ" is "non-metaphorical."[23] Volf argues that this "one-subject" view deprives the

---

20. Volf, *After Our Likeness*, 72. As Serge-Thomas Bonino has shown, Aquinas's position is similar to Ratzinger's. Quoting John 17:8, where Jesus says, "I have given them the words which thou [the Father] gavest me," Bonino comments: "Saint Thomas makes explicit this double subordinate communication, which follows a structure frequently found in the Gospel of John, in which the relation Father/Son is extended and reflected in the relation Son/disciples. In a first moment, the Father communicates his *doctrina* to the Son, either in the eternal instant of generation or at the conception of his human nature. This is the first gift. . . . As the first beneficiaries of the teaching of Christ, and the ones who must communicate it to all men, the apostles are by rights the solid and permanent foundations of the *congregatio fidelium*, of the Church gathered together by the apostolic faith—'the Church, which was built on [Peter's] confession of faith' (*Ioan.* 1, lect. 15, n. 306)—and of which the *doctrina apostolorum* is one of the great riches (cf. *Ioan.* 2, lect. 2, n. 383)." See Serge-Thomas Bonino, OP, "The Role of the Apostles in the Communication of Revelation According to the *Lectura super Ioannem* of St. Thomas Aquinas," trans. Teresa Bede and Matthew Levering, in Dauphinais and Levering, *Reading John with St. Thomas Aquinas*, 318–46, at 321–22.

21. See Volf, *After Our Likeness*, 72.

22. Ibid., 46–47. Also in debate with eucharistic ecclesiology, although otherwise from a perspective quite different from Volf's, John Webster remarks that "the notion of the *totus Christus*—of Christ's completeness as inclusive of the church as his body—will be impermissible if it elides the distinction between Christ and the objects of his mercy" (Webster, "On Evangelical Ecclesiology," in his *Confessing God: Essays in Christian Dogmatics II* [New York: T. & T. Clark, 2005], 153–93, at 174). Insofar as Webster intends to invoke the distinction between the Head and the members, his point is incontestable. What seems lacking, however, is an understanding of the grace of headship able to articulate the continuity of the Holy Spirit's presence in Christ and in Christ's members.

23. Volf, *After Our Likeness*, 47. See contemporary biblical scholarship on this topic: e.g., Paul S. Minear, *Images of the Church in the New Testament* (Philadelphia: Westminster Press, 1960), ch. 6; Rudolf Schnackenburg, *The Church in the New Testament*, trans. W. J. O'Hara (New York: Seabury Press, 1965); 165–76; Daniel J. Harrington, SJ, *The Church According to the New Testament: What the Wisdom and Witness of Early Christianity Teach Us Today* (Chicago:

Church, both as the local congregation and as the "universal church," of its own integrity, its dimension of standing on its own. This deprivation is particularly noticeable at the congregational level: "If . . . one thinks of the one visible universal church as a subject, as does Ratzinger, and if this universal church is conceived in a primary sense as the body of Christ, then the local churches become organically connected *parts* of the universal church."[24] As mere parts, these local churches would not truly embody the Church. While particularly

---

Sheed & Ward, 2001), 64–66. Discussing Paul's image of the body of Christ, Harrington states that "Paul's distinctive contribution lies in his insistence that Christ makes the body, that it is Christ's initiative that transforms all these disparate persons into the Body of Christ, and that Christ enables them to work effectively together" (Harrington, *The Church According to the New Testament: What the Wisdom and Witness of Early Christianity Teach Us Today* [Chicago: Sheed & Ward, 2001], 67–68). For Harrington the image is thus not strictly metaphorical because Christ brings together the Body. Schnackenburg argues that for Paul in 1 and 2 Corinthians, "the Body of Christ is more than a metaphor. The term directly expresses something about the relationship of Church to Christ, its profound union with him through the Spirit, indeed unity with him in the Spirit, the constituting of this unity by baptism and its renewal by the eucharist, and about the intrinsic union of the members among themselves, with the obligation of making this unity visible and fruitful" (Schnackenburg, *The Church in the New Testament*, 170). Ephesians and Colossians, Schnackenburg suggests, develop the "Body of Christ" much further. Writing from a Protestant perspective, Minear notes that "any appraisal of the meanings of this image will be highly controversial" (Minear, 173). Observing that it has various meanings at various points in the Pauline corpus, Minear finds that in Romans "the term 'body' enabled him [Paul] to convey, almost in shorthand fashion: (1) the universal solidarity of all persons in one man, whether the old or the new, (2) the particular selfhood of each person with his separate decisions, (3) the diverse acts by which a person was transferred from one humanity to another, and (4) the overarching promise and hope of a single consummation for the whole creation" (177). While Minear generally holds that "it would distort Paul's thought . . . to make *church* and *body* interchangeable or identical terms" (185; cf. 248–49), he grants that "the community's participation in the Lord's body is seen to be intrinsic to its life. Its unity stems from the oneness of the loaf and cup. Its interdependence stems from its dependence on the Lord's death" (185). Minear concludes with a comment on Ephesians 3:19: "only the power of the Spirit of the Christ to knit a community together in love can enable men to know the knowledge-surpassing dimensions of the fullness of God" (220). See also Louis Bouyer, *The Spirituality of the New Testament and the Fathers*, trans. Mary P. Ryan (French 1960; London: Burns & Oates, 1963), 71–73.

24. Volf, *After Our Likeness*, 47. Cf. Douglas Farrow's presentation of Irenaeus's "eucharistic ecclesiology," in Farrow, *Ascension and Ecclesia: On the Significance of the Doctrine of the Ascension for Ecclesiology and Christian Cosmology* (Grand Rapids, MI: Eerdmans, 1999), 66–73. Irenaeus holds, says Farrow, that the Eucharist "imparts to us a share in the priestly humanity of our Lord, and interprets to us our ecclesial vocation" (69). While not adverse to the notion of "ecclesial man, corporate man" (68), Farrow agrees in significant part with Volf's critique of hierarchy: "Irenaeus shows no inclination to try on the oversized armour of institutionalism which others were beginning to forge at the expense of the *indicium libertatis*; why he does not turn to clericalism to guarantee the integrity of the church in the way that Ignatius does, for example" (71–72). By contrast, for the basic complementarity of Ignatius and Irenaeus, see Zizioulas, *Being as Communion*, 78–82 (cited by Farrow); Zizioulas, *Eucharist, Bishop, Church: The Unity of the Church in the Divine Eucharist and the Bishop During the First Three Centuries*,

clear at the level of the local Church, however, the deprivation in Volf's view also marks the Church as a whole. If the Church is "one subject" with Christ, would this not cancel out the Church's distinctive subjectivity on her own—resulting both in presumption (conflating the Church with Christ) and in denigration (of the Church's own identity as a human community)? Furthermore, the individual members of the Church entirely lose their distinctive subjectivities. In this regard Volf asks what "a collective subject" might mean: How can individual subjectivities be so thoroughly blended into a collective?[25] On all these grounds, the idea that the Church is "one subject" with Christ ends up, Volf suggests, increasing the monistic power of the pope and, to a lesser degree, the bishop.

Critique of Zizioulas

Volf offers a similarly detailed critique of Zizioulas's ecclesiology.[26] He grants that Zizioulas's emphasis upon the Father's "monarchy" enables

---

2nd ed., trans. Elizabeth Theokritoff (1965; Brookline, MA: Holy Cross Orthodox Press, 2001), Part II, ch. 2.

25. Volf, *After Our Likeness*, 38. On the mystical Body see Yves Congar, "The Church and Its Unity," in his *The Mystery of the Church*, trans. A. V. Littledale (French 1956; Baltimore: Helicon Press, 1960), 58–96. The proclamation of the kingdom in Daniel 7, Congar suggests, presents "one of the features which will be dominant, even decisive, in the Christian idea of the Kingdom and of the Church—the real identity of an individual and a collectivity, all being in a single one, all belonging to a single one, and yet all being realized in a collectivity, all belonging to a people" (60). Congar adds in this regard that "St. Paul's idea of the mystical Body as the idea of a certain relationship between an individual and a group has a Jewish background, and rests on the extremely vivid awareness, in the Old Testament, of the solidarity of the members of Israel with God" (60). Congar goes on to describe the marks of the Church: "The Church is one because Christ is one of whom it is the body; it is holy because the being Christ gives it is something holy, something heavenly, 'pneumatic'; it is Catholic, because its head has the power to communicate it a life and a force capable of reuniting through its means, in him, all things, those in heaven and those on earth" (68). In the letters of Saint Paul, Congar notes, the phrase "in Christ Jesus" and its variations occurs 144 times. See also Joseph Ratzinger, *Called to Communion: Understanding the Church Today*, trans. Adrian Walker (German 1991: San Francisco: Ignatius Press, 1995), 35–40. Ratzinger notes the "Semitic conception of the 'corporate personality' . . . expressed, for example, in the idea that we are all Adam" (35) and "the idea of nuptiality, or—to express it in profane terms—the biblical philosophy of love," where the two become one flesh (37).

26. For further discussion of Zizioulas's ecclesiology, see also Paul McPartlan, *The Eucharist Makes the Church: Henri de Lubac and John Zizioulas in Dialogue* (Edinburgh: T. & T. Clark, 1993). In his recent *Communion and Otherness*, Zizioulas responds to Volf's *After Our Likeness*: "There is a kind of ecclesiology in which all hierarchical notions are suspected as threatening communion as well as otherness. The most typical and representative expression of this non-hierarchical (if not anti-hierarchical) ecclesiology is to be found in

Zizioulas at least to avoid the primacy of the one substance that, as both Volf and Zizioulas think, plagues Ratzinger's Trinitarian theology. For Zizioulas, the Father (Person) is the source of divine being (substance); the Persons do not depend upon a substratum of divine substance, but rather the divine substance has its origin in the Person of the Father. As Volf summarizes Zizioulas's position on the Trinitarian communion of Persons, "The communion is always *constituted and internally structured by an asymmetrical-reciprocal relationship between the one and the many*."[27] The reciprocity consists in the equality and interdependence of the divine Persons; the asymmetry in the monarchy of the Father as the "cause" of the Son and the Holy Spirit.[28]

Yet, Volf points out that Zizioulas continues to assume that numerical oneness (the one Father as the source of the one substance) is necessary for grounding the unity of the Trinity. As Volf remarks in this regard, "This arouses the suspicion that he [Zizioulas] is not actually grounding the necessity of the one for the unity of the church by way of the Trinity, but rather quite the reverse is projecting the hierarchical grounding of unity into the doctrine of the Trinity from

---

Congregationalist and Free Church Protestantism. In the rest of Protestantism, hierarchical structures are centered mainly on ministries of Word and Sacrament, which, however, are conceived in terms of function rather than ontology, having little to do with the establishment and experience of *personal relations of an ontological kind* between the minister and the rest of the Church. Such an ecclesiology naturally and understandably reacts against the Cappadocian teaching of the Father as 'cause,' fearing that such a Trinitarian theology might have undesirable consequences for ecclesiology" (Zizioulas, "The Father as Cause," in idem, *Communion and Otherness*, 145). Zizioulas goes on to point out, "Even in the most 'congregationalist' type of Church, there are those who give (e.g., by preaching the word or performing the sacrament) and those who receive (by listening to the word, being baptized, etc.). The fact that such ministers are not permanent simply means that between the 'giver' and the 'receiver' there is no permanent (ontological) relationship, but only a functional one. However, the relationship is there, and it is an asymmetrical one, even if only for as long as the function lasts. Now, one may argue that calling this relationship hierarchical is an abuse of terminology, but terms mean what the source from which they derive dictates, and if our source is the revelation of God as Trinity, as the Fathers interpreted it for us, the essential aspect of divine hierarchy is precisely this relationship of 'giver' and 'receiver,' provided that it generates otherness and respects particularity as 'whole of the whole.' The issue, therefore, is not whether there is hierarchy in the Church, but what kind of hierarchy it is that does justice to the Trinitarian model" (146).

27. Volf, *After Our Likeness*, 38.

28. For an appreciative, occasionally critical reading of Zizioulas's Trinitarian theology in dialogue with that of Vladimir Lossky, see Aristotle Papanikolaou, *Being with God: Trinity, Apophaticism, and Divine-Human Communion* (Notre Dame, IN: University of Notre Dame Press, 2006). For a critique of Zizioulas's Trinitarian theology see my *Scripture and Metaphysics: Aquinas and the Renewal of Trinitarian Theology* (Oxford: Blackwell, 2004), ch. 7.

the perspective of a particular ecclesiology."[29] In other words, presuming a hierarchical Church whose unity flows from the Eucharist celebrated by the bishop, Zizioulas envisions Trinitarian unity in the same manner, with the Father in the role of the bishop. Correspondingly, Volf points out, Zizioulas has difficulty grounding "Person" in "communion." It seems on the contrary that for Zizioulas the divine Person of the Father precedes "communion." As Volf puts it, "The Father is not constituted relationally; rather, his fatherhood is necessarily expressed and confirmed relationally. This seems for me to be the implication of Zizioulas's assertion that the being of the *Father* is 'a result of the "willing one"—the Father Himself.' "[30]

Turning to ecclesiology proper, Volf finds the same strengths and problems. On the one hand, much more than Ratzinger, Zizioulas is able to account for the full ecclesiality of the local Church, a crucial aspect from Volf's Free-Church perspective. For Zizioulas, "the local church stands at the center of ecclesiology. It is identical with the church, indeed, *is* the *whole* church, because it is identical with the Eucharist, at which the whole Christ is present."[31] The members of the local Church are not fully swallowed up by a "collective subject." Their assent, registered by acclamation, is necessary for an episcopal ordination validly to occur—even though for Zizioulas the members of the local Church do not and need not participate in the *choice* of the bishop.[32] The bishop, too, does not receive his authoritative status

---

29. Volf, *After Our Likeness*, 79.

30. Ibid., 79–80, citing Zizioulas, "On Being a Person: Towards an Ontology of Personhood," in *Persons, Divine and Human*, ed. C. Schwöbel and C. Gunton (Edinburgh: T. & T. Clark, 1991), 33–46, at 42. For a critique of Zizioulas on personhood, see Lucien Turcescu, " 'Person' versus 'Individual,' and Other Modern Misreadings of Gregory of Nyssa," in *Re-Thinking Gregory of Nyssa*, ed. Sarah Coakley (Oxford: Blackwell, 2003), 97–110.

31. Volf, *After Our Likeness*, 123. Earlier Volf remarks that for Zizioulas "relationships between local churches are fundamentally symmetrical, with no superiority or subordination; every local church is 'capable of passing final judgment of everything.' Such an understanding of unity and ecclesiality seems to tend toward a confederation of local churches, even if the communities existing outside this 'confederation' would not be considered churches. Zizioulas, however, offsets this tendency through the 'one-many' dialectic between the local churches and their bishops, and does so not only at the level of the patriarchate, but also (cautiously) at that of the universal church. This dialectic takes its orientation from trinitarian hierarchical relationships and corresponds to the dialectic between the one (bishop) and the many (priests, laity) within the local church" (107).

32. See ibid., 121. Volf explains critically, "If such congregational participation in the choice of bishop were indeed a presupposition of ordination, then according to Zizioulas the bestowal of charisma would be dependent on the decision of the people made *outside* the eucharistic

"through the relationships with other bishops," but rather owes it to "the *concrete eucharistic community*" in and through which God acts to consecrate the bishop.[33] Similarly, for Zizioulas, "At the trinitarian level, the one person constitutes the communion; at the ecclesiological level, persons are constituted by the communion."[34] It would seem that this understanding might work to uphold the irreducible significance of persons.

On the other hand, despite its promising aspects, Volf finds that Zizioulas's approach fails to preserve a balance between the one and the many, person and communion. Most importantly, Zizioulas's understanding of the bishop as the guarantee of the unity of the Church has the same weaknesses as does Zizioulas's monarchical understanding of the Father as the cause of the divine "substance" and of the Son and Holy Spirit. Rather than having unity arise from a full communion of equal persons, unity flows monarchically to the communion of persons. For example, Zizioulas's account of ecclesial ordo limits the particularity of persons by making eucharistic communion into the interaction of diverse modes of ordo.[35] Thus Zizioulas's account of the ordo of the laity magnifies the bishop's monarchical status: "The bishop occupies a position even more superior to that of the individual layperson than to that of the entire *ordo* of the laity; while the *ordo* of the laity is ecclesiologically indispensable, the individual person by contrast seems almost insignificant."[36] Although the two modes of ordo—laity and bishop—are united in the eucharistic synaxis, it is less a communion of persons than a "strictly *bipolar event*."[37] Even if the bishop "represents" the laity, only the bishop is fully the "*alter* Christ."[38]

---

gathering. God's charismatic activity, however, cannot [for Zizioulas] be bound to any worldly, that is, noneschatological, causal nexus. The charismatic character of the office can be secured only by the immediacy of God's actions within the eucharistic gathering as a pneumatic eschatological event. Zizioulas does anticipate, however, that the choice of bishop by the synod takes place under the chairmanship of the first. A synod, however, is not a eucharistic event. To remain consistent, Zizioulas would have to argue against election by the synod as a condition for ordination. In any case, his ecclesiological assumptions do not explain why the extraeucharistic decision of the bishops should be acceptable while that of the entire congregation is not" (121–22).

33. Ibid., 119.

34. Ibid., 106.

35. See ibid., 116.

36. Ibid.

37. Ibid.

38. Ibid., 114.

Volf states, "The devaluation of the laity, judged from my perspective, corresponds to the soteriological and ecclesiological enhancement of the bishop; whoever assumes 'the place of God' must simply be followed."[39]

In his understanding of human "personhood," furthermore, Zizioulas claims more than the analogous character of Trinitarian discourse allows: human "persons are not identical with their tasks but persons who are already distinct are assigned different tasks,"[40] To understand this point requires some background in Zizioulas's view of human personhood. For Zizioulas, just as substance cannot have priority over Persons (rooted in the Father), so substance cannot have priority over human personhood. "Substance" for human beings, according to Zizioulas, is their biological-psychological individuality by which each human being is distinguished and separated from others.[41] By contrast, "person" rises above such limitations (including spatial-temporal ones) and possesses " 'absolute ontological freedom.' "[42] Human "personhood" thus can only be found in eschatological communion with the triune God, whose paradigmatic instance is the Incarnation. Jesus Christ is never a fragmented individual; rather, his Personhood is that of the divine Son, and Christ bears all human beings within himself as the new Adam and Head of the Church.[43] Christ, "through the eschatological Spirit of communion in which Christ's entire existence transpires,"[44] is the first instance of the true "personalization" or de-individualization of human beings. The task for other human beings is to come to share in Christ's personhood.

How, then, do human beings become transcendent, radically free "persons" in Christ? How can a mere human being become "a person who exists in the mode of being of God," that is, the Son's relationship to the Father?[45] As Volf states, Zizioulas holds that "the concrete locus of deindividualization and personalization is the church.

---

39. Ibid., 114.

40. Ibid., 115.

41. Thus, as Volf says, "Creation and Fall coalesce into a single entity in Zizioulas's thinking" (ibid., 81).

42. Ibid., 83.

43. See ibid., 84–85.

44. Ibid., 85.

45. Ibid., 86.

The church can be so, however, only because it is the pneumatologically constituted body of Christ."[46] Already Christ, in his Spirit-filled divine humanity, contains the Church in himself. Human beings become "persons," members of the Church, by being ontologically changed. It is first of all "in baptism that the personal structure of the Trinity is made into the structure of the human hypostasis";[47] Baptism in the Spirit gives human beings eschatological personhood in the new Adam (and thus in the Church). This ontological change inserts the human being into the "truth" of being, which is not a cognitive relation but "an event of love between persons."[48] This personhood is completed in the Eucharist, understood as a liturgical act rather than as an object. By consuming Christ sacramentally, his members become what they are, one body with him. Volf summarizes, "Just as through baptism human beings are constituted into persons anhypostatically in Christ, so also does the church exist in the Eucharist anhypostatically and acquire its entire identity from the identity of Christ."[49]

Given this understanding of humans sharing in Christ's divine Personhood in and through the eucharistic synaxis, Zizioulas affirms that hierarchy in the Church " 'emerges freely from the communion of love.'"[50] Volf grants that this view of hierarchy "may well be persuasive with regard to the Trinity (presupposing his [Zizioulas's] problematic understanding of trinitarian relationships), since God *is* love," and love would thus come forth from the Father's monarchy.[51] Regarding

---

46. Ibid., 83.

47. Ibid., 88.

48. Ibid., 93. Thus "being in truth means being in communion" (ibid.). This grounds a sacramental understanding of "truth": "one's disposition toward God's word as truth is not to be one of cognitive understanding or of belief; rather, one should *experience God's word* communally 'as the sacramental intimation of God's life' " (ibid.). Volf observes that for Zizioulas, "This noncognitive interiority of the word in relation to the church can only be secured sacramentally. Deindividualization demands direct or immediate relationships, and there in their turn demand the replacement of language by sacrament. This is why the Eucharist is *the* place where truth occurs. As a communal event *par excellence*, the Eucharist incarnates and actualizes our communion with the life and communion of the Trinity itself" (94). Volf criticizes Zizioulas's position for leaving out the cognitive act of faith. He quotes Zizioulas as saying that "dogmas 'carry no *relationship with truth in themselves*, but only in their being doxological acclamations of the worshiping community' " (95–96, his emphasis, citing Zizioulas, *Being as Communion* [Crestwood, NY: St. Vladimir's Seminary Press, 1985], 116f.).

49. Ibid., 100.

50. Ibid., 112.

51. Ibid., 112.

the Church, however, Volf finds that the assymetrical communion that Zizioulas proposes will not work, despite Zizioulas's efforts to relativize this asymmetry in the eucharistic event.

In sum, for Volf, Zizioulas's approach fails to live up to its promise of going beyond Ratzinger's monism. Personhood comes to depend not on intersubjectivity, but on being non-cognitively inserted into the eucharistic synaxis.[52] The monarchical structure of Zizioulas's Trinitarian and ecclesiological thought results not in the attainment of an equiprimacy of "person" and "communion," but rather in a situation where the bishop alone stands out as fully a Christological person. As in the Trinity, the Father's monarchy undermines the fully perichoretic communion of equals, so in the Church regarding the office of bishop.[53]

---

52. Ibid., 105. Volf's theology of the Eucharist has developed since the publication of *After Our Likeness*, perhaps in part due to his becoming an Episcopalian: for brief discussion of his movement from Pentecostalism to the Episcopalian Church, see his interview with Rupert Shortt in Shortt's *God's Advocates: Christian Thinkers in Conversation* (Grand Rapids, MI: Eerdmans, 2005), ch. 12, at 228. Volf's critique of Ratzinger's and Zizioulas's ecclesiology has not changed (see Shortt, 217–18). In his most recent book, *The End of Memory: Remembering Rightly in a Violent World* (Grand Rapids, MI: Eerdmans, 2006), Volf states with regard to the Eucharist: "Central to the rite is the solidarity of God with each human being and the reconciliation of each human being to God. Inseparable, however, from reconciliation to God is reconciliation to fellow human beings. As Alexander Schmemann puts it in *The Eucharist*, in this holy ritual, 'we *create the memory of each other*, we identify each other as living *in* Christ and being united with each other in him' " (*The End of Memory*, 119). He goes on to write with regard to his memory of someone who persecuted him in communist Yugoslavia: "Imagine what would happen if during Holy Communion I participated in the communal celebration of the Lamb of God, now seated at the right hand of the Holy One, who both suffered with all those who suffer and removed the guilt of their transgressors! Imagine what would happen if I celebrated the presence of *this* Christ in the life of the community and in my own life! In such a liturgical setting, both Captain G. and I would participate in the worship (I directly and he in my imagination) precisely in our capacities as the wronged and the wrongdoer. Equally importantly, the whole community would be celebrating my transformed memory of his wrongdoing—a memory that allows me to name the Captain's offenses as wrongdoing but that does not elicit in me only condemnation and disgust; a memory through which I, in receiving Christ in the sacrament of his body and blood, also receive myself as a new creature, made in the image of the God who loves the ungodly, with an identity that transcends anything anyone could ever do to me; a memory that frees me from the hold of my suffered wrong and motivates me to extend a reconciling hand to the Captain, whom Christ has already embraced with open arms on the cross; a memory that I ponder in the hope of the final reconciliation" (127–28).

53. Cf. the equality envisioned by John Milbank on the basis of his reading of Nicholas of Cusa in Milbank's "Ecclesiology: The Last of the Last," in idem, *Being Reconciled: Ontology and Pardon* (London: Routledge, 2003), 128–29. Although Milbank's equality differs somewhat from Volf's, nonetheless for both what Milbank calls the *"event of concordantia"* seems principally to be "on a level" rather than principally displaying the hierarchical and eucharistic pattern of gifting/receptivity. For further insight into Milbank's theology of gift, see the texts discussed by J. Todd Billings, "John Milbank's Theology of the 'Gift' and Calvin's Theology of Grace:

Every institution, Volf argues, must be evaluated on the basis of two factors, namely "the pattern of power distribution and the manner of its cohesion."[54] In his view, the Roman Catholic and Eastern Orthodox Churches do not fare well when evaluated in this manner. He remarks, "With regard to the distribution of power, one can distinguish between symmetrical-polycentric and asymmetrical-monocentric models; with regard to cohesion, one can distinguish between coerced and freely affirmed integration."[55] Both Ratzinger's "monocentric" understanding of Trinitarian and ecclesial relations and Zizioulas's "asymmetrical" (hierarchical) understanding result, due to imperfect hierarchs, in "partially coerced subordination of the many to the dominant one."[56] This conclusion leads Volf to argue that ecclesial hierarchy cannot be squared with the inner-Trinitarian communion of equals. In Volf's view, both ecclesial unity and Trinitarian unity must arise from the communion of strictly co-equal persons.[57]

As I have already suggested, I think that Volf's criticisms of Ratzinger and Zizioulas, as criticisms of the hierarchical structure that has characterized the Church since its first centuries, are best engaged by embedding the discussion more deeply in the Christian theological heritage.[58] On this basis, I will examine three pillars of Thomas

---

A Critical Comparison," *Modern Theology* 21 (2005): 87–105. See also the discussion of Milbank, Maximus the Confessor, and Kathryn Tanner in David Albertson, "On 'the Gift' in Tanner's Theology: A Patristic Parable," *Modern Theology* 21 (2005): 107–18.

54. Volf, *After Our Likeness*, 236.

55. Ibid.

56. Ibid.

57. For Volf's constructive position see *After Our Likeness*, Part II, 127–282. For Volf, following Jürgen Moltmann, it is crucial for ecclesiology that the divine Persons not "dissolve into relations; the Father becomes fatherhood; the Son, sonship; and the Spirit, procession. Understood in this way, these persons are not only superfluous but also incapable of action. Pure relations—the 'act of begetting,' the activity of being begotten, and that of procession—can no more act in salvation history than they can be petitioned in prayer or praised in worship. To do justice to the salvation history from which knowledge of the Trinity is actually acquired, one must conceive the trinitarian persons *as subjects*. God's external works are not to be attributed to the one undifferentiated divine essence, but rather proceed from the divine persons" (*After Our Likeness*, 205). Volf, however, has misunderstood the Trinitarian theology that he is criticizing: for a better account see Gilles Emery, OP, "The Personal Mode of Trinitarian Action in St. Thomas Aquinas," trans. Matthew Levering, in his *Trinity, Church, and the Human Person: Thomistic Essays* (Naples, FL: Sapientia Press, 2007), 115–53; Thomas G. Weinandy, OFM CAP, *Does God Suffer?* (Notre Dame, IN: University of Notre Dame Press, 2000).

58. Avery Dulles, SJ, examines Volf's *After Our Likeness*, as well as other contemporary ecclesiological approaches, in "The Trinity and Christian Unity," in *God the Holy Trinity: Reflections on Christian Faith and Practice*, ed. Timothy George (Grand Rapids, MI: Baker

Aquinas's theology of the Church: the divine unity and Trinity, the virtue of faith, and sacramental mediation. I first suggest that Aquinas's contrast between numerical multitude and formal multitude, only the latter of which applies to God, helps to avoid the confrontation of one and three in the doctrine of the triune God. Once this seeming confrontation has been overcome, Aquinas's Trinitarian theology—in which the Son receives all from the Father, and the Spirit is the Gift of the Father and the Son—can be seen to constitute the pattern, through the missions in history of the Son and Spirit, for the gifting and receptivity that unite the Church in communion through faith and the sacraments of faith.

AQUINAS ON CHURCH STRUCTURE AND THE TRIUNE GOD

Unity and Trinity in God

It is necessary first to show that divine unity does not conflict with divine Trinity, a point that has evident ecclesiological implications. In Deuteronomy 6:4, Moses exhorts the people of Israel: "Hear, O Israel: The Lord our God is one Lord." Aquinas quotes this scriptural passage in affirming, in the *Summa Theologiae*, that God is one.[59] While what it means to say that God is one might seem evident, the danger consists in suggesting that God is "one" being, as though he were one being among other beings, or as though he possessed a numerical oneness that delimits his infinite "to be." This danger makes manifest the need to begin by emphasizing that when we speak of God as "one" and "three," these terms, like all language about God, apply to God analogously rather than univocally.

Academic, 2006), 69–82. Like Volf, Dulles recognizes that any solid ecclesiology must be rooted in the two divine processions, those of the Son and the Holy Spirit, which are continued in their respective missions" (82; cf. Vatican Council II, *Unitatis Redintegratio*, 2). For Aquinas, Dulles points out, the Petrine office (as the Vicar of Christ) belongs to the Church's participation in the Son's (receptive) relationship to the Father, and the concord or collegiality of the bishops reflects the procession of the Holy Spirit as Love from the Father and Son; in this regard Dulles cites Aquinas's *Contra errores graecorum*, ch. 32. On this text from the *Contra errors graecorum*, see also Congar, "The Holy Spirit and the Apostolic Body, Continuators of the Work of Christ," in idem, *The Mystery of the Church*, 153.

    59. Thomas Aquinas, *Summa Theologiae* (ST) I, q. 11, a. 3, *sed contra*.

Aquinas's discussion of divine unity follows his treatment of God's simplicity and perfection. To say that God is "simple" means that God has no composition. Not only does God have no parts, God also has no accidental characteristics that differ from God. Everything that he is, is none other than God. Since God is simple, he is unrestricted Actuality.[60] This means that unlike numerical oneness, where a thing's unity sets it off from other things, God's oneness does not delimit his being by separating what is integral to God from what belongs to others. Instead, God's oneness signals an absolute fullness, an infinite range of being, which allows for no division. There are no parts in God that could be divided in order to make multiple gods; there are no potentialities in God that express an inner division. To say that "God is one" does not mean that we thereby separate God off from the many, but rather means that in God no separation, division, or delimitation is possible.[61] To say that God is "one," therefore, does not attach numerical oneness to God (to which three Persons would then seem antithetical), but rather expresses a privation or negation, just as when we say that God is "incorporeal" or "infinite."[62] God is one in the sense of "*not* many."[63] The term *undivided* gives insight into

60. One can appeal to Hans Urs von Balthasar here: "one can only frame a constructive philosophy of being in the categories of actuality, and natures cannot be understood otherwise than as sources of acts (*natura est principium actum*), form only explained in relation to its finality (though this is not to be taken in the narrow, technical sense of the Enlightenment), and to the being of the thing itself (*esse sequitur formam*)." Hans Urs von Balthasar, "Office in the Church," trans. A. V. Littledale with Alexander Dru, in *Explorations in Theology*, vol. 2; *Spouse of the Word* (German 1961; San Francisco: Ignatius Press, 1991), 137.

61. Aquinas explains, "*One* which is the principle of number is not predicated of God, but only of material things. For *one* the principle of number belongs to the *genus* of mathematics, which are material in being, and abstracted from matter only in idea. But *one* which is convertible with being is a metaphysical entity, and does not depend on matter, in its being" (ST I, q. 11, a. 3, ad 2). In this latter sense, God is "supremely" one, infinitely more so than any created unities, because his perfectly simple being means that "He is being itself, subsistent, absolutely undetermined" and "supremely undivided inasmuch as He is divided neither actually, nor potentially, by any mode of division" (ST I, q. 11, a. 4).

62. Aquinas states that "although in God there is no privation, still, according to the mode of our apprehension, he is known to us by way only of privation and remotion" (ST I, q. 11, a. 3, ad 2).

63. Drawing upon Aristotle's *Metaphysics*, Aquinas explains that "the *one* which is the principle of number, is opposed to *multitude* which is number, as the measure is to the thing measured. For *one* implies the idea of a primary measure; and number is *multitude* measured by *one*. . . . But the *one* which is convertible with *being* is opposed to *multitude* by way of privation; as the undivided is to the thing divided" (ST I, q. 11, a. 2). Taken metaphysically, "one" is not "an addition to *being*, in the sense of limiting it" (ST I, q. 11, a. 1, *sed contra*). Even while oneness (as "undivided," not as the principle of number and measure) is strictly "convertible

God's oneness, but even this term takes its starting point from the notion of divisibility, which is antithetical to God's oneness.

On the basis of this metaphysical understanding of oneness as undivision, Aquinas approvingly quotes Bernard of Clairvaux: " 'Among all things called one, the unity of the Divine Trinity holds the first place.' "[64] Far from implying a monism, it is precisely the unity of the *Trinity* that is infinitely the greatest. Since this may seem a surprising claim, let us investigate it further. Aquinas argues that just as one has to distinguish between numerical and metaphysical unity, so also, in discussing God the Trinity, one must distinguish between a numerical and a formal multitude.

What does it mean to say that the Trinity is a "formal" multitude but not a numerical multitude? How can there be real threeness, if it is not "numerical"? In a numerical triad, procession from the Father would envision a linear progression forming a composite whole, with the Father as number one and the Son and Spirit as numbers two and three. These three together would compose the Trinity, as numerical parts of the triad. In contrast, a formal triad does not have to do with quantity, which belongs to material things. Aquinas explains that formal division "is effected by opposite or diverse forms; and this kind of division results in a multitude which does not belong to a genus, but is transcendental in the sense in which being is divided by one and by many."[65] The "multitude" that is the Trinity is not a numerical multitude—for this would be to insert quantity into the Trinity—but rather is a formal multitude, which indicates that the many (the divine Persons) are "each undivided in itself."[66] The divine Persons are thus not three parts: the three are one, and yet each is distinct from the others, and the distinctions produce a "formal multitude."

---

with *being*," oneness "adds an idea to *being*" (ST I, q. 11, a. 1, ad 1 and 3). This "idea" is "the negation of division: for *one* means undivided *being*" (ST I, q. 11, a. 1). He adds, "This is the very reason why *one* is the same as *being*."

64. ST I, q. 11, a. 4, *sed contra*, citing Bernard, *De Consid.* v.

65. ST I, q. 30, a. 3. Formal multitude thus belongs to the angels as well.

66. Ibid. Aquinas observes that "numeral terms predicated of God are not derived from number, a species of quantity, for in that sense they could bear only a metaphorical sense in God, like other corporeal properties, such as length, breadth, and the like" (ibid.).

In order to shed further light on what is meant by "formal multitude," Aquinas (following Augustine)[67] turns to the analogy of the soul and its formalities of knowing and loving. The "soul knowing" is formally distinct from the soul, and yet it is fully the soul.[68] The "soul loving" what it knows is formally distinct from both the soul and the "soul knowing," and yet it too is fully the soul.[69] The distinctions involved, Aquinas recognizes, are relations, specifically relations of origin.[70] They do not instantiate a numerical multitude: there are not three souls. But as distinct relations they do instantiate a formal multitude. Each comprises an undivided whole that is distinct formally from the other two. Using this analogy, Aquinas can thus describe the Trinity as "the number of persons related to each other," without giving number a quantitative, material meaning.[71] Consider also that

---

67. For further discussion of this influence, see the essays by Gilles Emery, OP, Harm Goris, Bruce Marshall, and John O'Callaghan in *Aquinas the Augustinian*, ed. Michael Dauphinais, Barry David, and Matthew Levering (Washington, DC: The Catholic University of America Press, 2007).

68. Aquinas explains, "The act of human understanding in ourselves is not the substance itself of the intellect; hence the word which proceeds within us by intelligible operation is not of the same nature as the source whence it proceeds; so the idea of generation cannot be properly and fully applied to it. But the divine act of intelligence is the very substance itself of the one who understands (Q. 14, A. 4). The Word proceeding therefore proceeds as subsisting in the same nature; and so is properly called begotten, and Son" (ST I, q. 27, a. 2).

69. Divine knowing embraces all reality; divine loving inclines toward all reality. Aquinas therefore holds that "there is no need to go on to infinitude in the divine processions; for the procession which is accomplished within the agent in an intellectual nature terminates in the procession of the will" (ST I, q. 27, a. 3, ad 1). He further differentiates between the two processions: "The procession of love in God ought not to be called generation. In evidence whereof we must consider that the intellect and the will differ in this respect, that the intellect is made actual by the object understood residing according to its own likeness in the intellect; whereas the will is made actual, not by any similitude of the object willed within it, but by its having a certain inclination to the thing willed. Thus the procession of the intellect is by way of similitude, and is called generation, because every generator begets its own like; whereas the procession of the will is not by way of similitude, but is rather by way of impulse and movement toward an object. So what proceeds in God by way of love, does not proceed as begotten, or as son, but proceeds rather as spirit; which name expresses a certain vital movement and impulse" (ST I, q. 27, a. 4).

70. For discussion of the four real relations—paternity and filiation, spiration and procession—which comprise three distinct or subsisting relations in God (Persons) because "spiration" is encompassed in paternity and filiation, see ST I, qq. 28–29; cf. on spiration, ST I, q. 36, aa. 2–4.

71. ST I, q. 31, a. 1, ad 1. As Gilles Emery has shown, Aquinas's account of the revealed processions aims at arriving at an understanding of the Person as subsisting relation. The Persons are not "mere" relations devoid of any act and agency; rather, as subsisting relations, they are fully God, pure Act. This formulation might seem to suggest that Aquinas conceives of each divine Person as the one God manifesting himself in a distinct relational fashion. But

the formal distinction is brought about by distinct relations of origin, and that a relation always has two aspects: the relation as it exists in the related term, and the relation as the dynamism toward that to which it is related. The divine relation in God expresses supreme unity, whereas the divine relation toward its opposite (e.g., Father-Son) constitutes a formal multitude.[72]

Without claiming to have bridged the differences between Volf's Moltmannian Trinitarian theology and Aquinas's, therefore, I would argue on three grounds that Aquinas's Trinitarian theology exhibits the compatibility of a strong affirmation of divine unity with a thorough rejection of a monist understanding of God—and thus, by extension, the compatibility of a strong account of ecclesial unity with an equally strong affirmation of ecclesial communion.

First, Aquinas conceives of the divine Persons in terms of subsisting relations. This enables him both to affirm the Father's "monarchy" as the source of the Trinity[73] and to avoid presenting the Trinity in an overly linear fashion (in contrast to Zizioulas). For Aquinas the three Persons, distinguished by their proper acts, are equally at the center of the theology of God.

Second, as subsisting relations, the Persons are not purely relation with no distinctive subsistence or agency (as opposed to Volf's account of Ratzinger's alleged "pure relation"). As Gilles Emery puts it, Aquinas "maintains a *relational mode of acting* of each person, a proper and distinct mode that consists in the personal intra-Trinitarian relationship qualifying intrinsically the act of the Father, Son, and Holy Spirit."[74] It follows that as "the source in the Trinity, the Father is the 'ultimate term' to which the Holy Spirit and the Son lead human

---

on the contrary, Aquinas does not think through subsisting relation on the basis of divine unity, but instead thinks through divine unity on the basis of subsisting relation. See Gilles Emery, OP, *Trinity in Aquinas*, especially ch. 5, "Essentialism or Personalism in the Treatise on God in St. Thomas Aquinas?" 165–208 and ch. 1, "The Threeness and Oneness of God in Twelfth- to Fourteenth-Century Scholasticism," 1–32. See also my *Scripture and Metaphysics: Aquinas and the Renewal of Trinitarian Theology*; and a related essay, idem, "Friendship and Trinitarian Theology: Response to Karen Kilby," *International Journal of Systematic Theology* 9 (2007): 39–54.

72. See Emery's "Essentialism or Personalism in the Treatise on God in St. Thomas Aquinas?"

73. Aquinas quotes Augustine with regard to the Father's "monarchy": "Augustine says (*De Trin* iv. 20), *The Father is the Principle of the whole Deity*" (ST I, q. 33, a. 1, *sed contra*). Aquinas emphasizes that principle "does not signify priority, but origin" (ST I, q. 33, a. 1, ad 3). See also on the Persons' equality, ST I, q. 42, aa. 1–4.

74. Emery, "The Personal Mode of Trinitarian Action in St. Thomas Aquinas," 152–53.

beings. Creation and salvation are accomplished in the rhythm of the Trinitarian relations."[75] Perhaps misled by Ratzinger's emphasis on the pure relationality (mission) of human persons in Christ, Volf misconstrues Augustinian Trinitarian theology to the point of claiming that the divine Persons "are not only superfluous but also incapable of action" and "can no more act in salvation history than they can be petitioned in prayer or praised in worship."[76]

Third, Aquinas conceives of neither the divine Persons nor the divine unity in the numerical, quantitative terms. Rather, undividedness provides the key for both the formal multitude of the Persons and their unity, and so one avoids thinking of God through a numerical opposition between one and three. Volf's account of numerical opposition requires him to reject any strong affirmation of the unity of the "body of Christ" as antithetical to the diversity of its members. On the grounds that "within interpersonal relations there is nothing that might correspond to the numerically identical divine nature," Volf concludes, "For both trinitarian and ecclesiological reasons, the one numerically identical divine nature can play no role in the analogy between the Trinity and the church."[77] Fortunately, such a disastrous opposition between divine unity and Trinity is unnecessary.

Thus when Aquinas agrees with Saint Bernard of Clairvaux that "among all things called one, the unity of the Divine Trinity holds the first place,"[78] Aquinas does not have in view a tension between the requirements of the many and the requirements of the one. For Volf, only the "notion of perichoresis" can overcome "the alternatives *unio personae—unitas substantiae.*"[79] Defining the divine Persons as "perichoretic subjects," Volf accepts Wolfhart Pannenberg's view that the Father, Son, and Holy Spirit are " 'living realizations of separate centers of action,' "[80] in Volf's words "(interdependent and

---

75. Ibid., 153.

76. Volf, *After Our Likeness*, 205.

77. Ibid., 204.

78. ST I, q. 11, a. 4, *sed contra.*

79. Volf, *After Our Likeness*, 210.

80. Ibid., 215. For critical engagement with Pannenberg's and Moltmann's Trinitarian theology, see Anselm K. Min, *Paths to the Triune God: An Encounter between Aquinas and Recent Theologies* (Notre Dame, IN: University of Notre Dame Press, 2005). See also Anne Hunt, "The Trinity and the Church: Explorations in Ecclesiology from a Trinitarian Perspective," *Irish Theological Quarterly* 70 (2005): 215–35. While appreciative of Volf's work,

mutually internal) autonomous centers of action."[81] A deeper understanding of *perichoresis* sees that the "alternatives" are not in tension. Rather, each Person is the one substance (relation "in"), and so *perichoresis* occurs at the level of unity of substance. Similarly, each Person belongs within the definition of the other Persons, and so the indwelling appears also from the perspective of relation "to," based upon distinctive personal agency.[82] The proper agency of the divine Persons does not require them to be "autonomous"—which would be tritheistic no matter how tight the unity achieved by perichoretic mutuality—but simply requires that they be distinct.

Trinitarian Gifting and Receptivity

Does Aquinas's account of the Trinity, however, manifest the pattern of gifting and receptivity that marks ecclesial communion? In the Trinity, the Father is the "principle." As Aquinas explains, this does not mean "a distance of perfection or of power" or of "priority."[83] Rather, it means solely "a certain order to each other," an order of non-temporal origin.[84] The Father's role as "principle" is therefore a gifting that is already bound to the "receptivity" of filiation—although Aquinas employs the cognate *accipere* ("to receive") in order to rule out the notion that the Son is an already-constituted subject who receives the Father's gifting.[85] The Son exhibits the bond of gifting and receptivity

---

Hunt emphasizes that "our understanding of the mystery of the Trinity does not and in fact cannot serve to legitimate particular social or ecclesial structures. When we seek to express the incomprehensible mystery of God, we speak by way of analogy, moving from truths known naturally to an understanding of the divine mysteries. Throughout the process, an ever greater dissimilarity prevails" (234).

81. Volf, *After Our Likeness*, 220. Cf. Volf's critique of the office of the papacy in his "Trinity, Unity, Primacy: On the Trinitarian Nature of Ecclesial Unity and Its Implications for the Question of Primacy," in Puglisi, *Petrine Ministry and the Unity of the Church*, 171–84.

82. For discussion see ST I, q. 42, a. 5.

83. ST I, q. 33, a. 1, ad 1.

84. Ibid. This order does not mean that the divine Persons themselves constitute a hierarchy: see ST I, q. 108, a. 1.

85. Thus Aquinas states, "Not everything derived from another has existence in another subject; otherwise we could not say that the whole substance of created being comes from God, since there is no subject that could receive the whole substance. So, then, what is generated in God receives its existence from the generator, not as though that existence were received into matter of into a subject (which would conflict with the divine self-subsistence); but when we speak of His existence as received, we mean that He Who proceeds receives divine existence from another; not, however, as if He were other from the divine nature. For in

(in the sense distinguished by *accipere*) both because the name "Word" involves relation to the Father and to creatures, and because the Father and the Son spirate the Spirit who is Gift and Love.[86]

Reflecting on the Spirit's name of "Love," Aquinas observes, "For the name spirit in things corporeal seems to signify impulse and motion; for we call the breath and the wind by the term spirit. Now it is a property of love to move and impel the will of the lover towards the object loved."[87] The Holy Spirit is "Love proceeding" from the spiration of the Father and Son.[88] With respect to the Spirit as "Gift," Aquinas observes that "it is manifest that love has the nature of a first gift, through which all free gifts are given."[89] He adds that by grace rational creatures can receive the gift of sharing the Trinitarian life: "The rational creature does sometimes attain thereto; as when it is made partaker of the divine Word and of the Love proceeding, so as freely to know God truly and to love God rightly. Hence the rational creature alone can possess the divine person," although "this must be given it from above."[90]

Both the Son and the Holy Spirit proceed from the Father so as to receive the Father's likeness (although only the Son is properly named "Image") and so as to be "given" (although only the Holy Spirit is properly named "Gift"). The Son receives everything from the

---

the perfection itself of the divine existence are contained both the Word intelligibly proceeding and the principle of the Word, with whatever belongs to His perfection (I, q. 4, a. 2)" (ST I, q. 27, a. 2). The key portion of this passage in Latin reads, "Non omne acceptum est receptum in aliquo subiecto. . . . Sic igitur id quod est genitum in divinis, accipit esse a generante, non tamquam illud esse sit receptum in aliqua material vel subiecto (quod repugnant subsistentiae divini esse); sed secundum hoc dicitur esse acceptum, inquantum procedens ab alio habet esse divinum, no quasi aliud ab esse divino existens."

86. ST I, q. 34, a. 3, *sed contra*, quoting Augustine's QQ. lxxxiii, qu. 63.

87. ST I, q. 36, a. 1.

88. ST I, q. 37, a. 1.

89. ST I, q. 38, a. 2.

90. ST I, q. 38, a. 1. Herwi Rikhof, Bruce Marshall, and others have responded to the view that the Latin West downplays the Holy Spirit. See Rikhof, "Thomas on the Church: Reflections on a Sermon," in *Aquinas on Doctrine: A Critical Introduction*, ed. Thomas G. Weinandy, OFM CAP, Daniel A. Keating, and John P. Yocum (New York: T. & T. Clark, 2004), 199–223, at 212–14; Bruce Marshall, "What Does the Spirit Have to Do?" in Dauphinais and Levering, *Reading John with St. Thomas Aquinas*, 62–77. See also Daniel Keating's essay in Weinandy, Keating, and Yocum, *Aquinas on Doctrine*, "Justification, Sanctification and Divinization in Thomas Aquinas," 139–58. For examples of the critique of the Latin West, see Vladimir Lossky, *In the Image and Likeness of God* (London: Mowbray, 1975), 103; Robert W. Jenson, *Systematic Theology*, vol. 1, *The Triune God* (Oxford: Oxford University Press, 1997), 153.

Father; the Spirit receives everything from the Father and Son. Aquinas observes, "For that the Son is given is from the Father's love."[91] Because without the Son there would be no Father, in this sense the Father too "receives" or is his Personhood from within his gifting.

The Trinitarian life, then, is characterized both by a supreme undivided unity and by a communion of gifting/receptivity. Does this same pattern intrinsically characterize the relationship of the "one" and the "many" in the Church? As we will see, the answer is yes. Faith and the sacraments of faith establish believers' participation in the Trinitarian communion of gifting/receptivity.[92]

Ecclesial Faith: The Pattern of Gifting/Receptivity

For Aquinas, faith is an intellectual assent to God revealing, and as such, faith relates each believer directly to the triune God as its "formal object."[93] In this sense, faith is the intellectual assent to God on account of God's authority, thereby requiring the will's movement.[94]

---

91. ST I, q. 38, a. 2, ad 1.

92. On faith and the sacraments of faith, see also Yves Congar, "The Church and Its Unity," 58–96, especially 71ff.; idem, "The Idea of the Church in St. Thomas Aquinas," in idem, *The Mystery of the Church*, 97–117, at 114; idem, "The Mystical Body of Christ," in *The Mystery of the Church*, 118–37. For Congar's relationship to the theology of Aquinas (and much else) cf. Fergus Kerr, OP, "Yves Congar and Thomism," in *Yves Congar: Theologian of the Church*, ed. Gabriel Flynn (Louvain: Peeters, 2005), 67–97, which draws upon Congar's "St. Thomas Aquinas and the Spirit of Ecumenism," *New Blackfriars* 55 (1974): 196–209. As Kerr remarks, Congar sympathetically cites Karl Barth's comment in *Church Dogmatics* I/2, 614: "An attentive reading of the works of the *Doctor Angelicus* permits one to verify in him certain lines of force which, even if they do not lead directly to the Reformation, do not tend, any the more, towards Jesuitical Romanism. Thus when one knows how to use intelligently this immense compendium of the previous tradition which constitutes the *Summa*, one remarks that its author is, on many issues, an evangelical theologian useful to know" (see Kerr, "Yves Congar and Thomism," 94–95). Kerr emphasizes the importance of reading Aquinas's theology "as the 'compendium' of all previous tradition" (95).

93. On "formal" and "material" object, see ST II-II, q. 1, a. 1; cf. Henry Donneaud, OP, "Objet formel et objet matériel de la foi: Genèse d'un instrument philosophique chez s. Thomas et quelques autres," *Revue Thomiste* 100 (2000): 5–44. For discussion of the various elements of Thomistic theology of faith, see Romanus Cessario, OP, *Christian Faith and the Theological Life* (Washington, DC: The Catholic University of America Press, 1996).

94. On this point see ST II-II, q. 2, aa. 1–2; cf. q. 2, a. 9, on the meritorious character of the act of faith when formed by charity. On the intellect and will in faith, see further q. 4, aa. 2–3, which explain that faith is a virtue of the intellect and that charity is the "form" of faith. See also the brief but insightful presentation by Thomas G. Weinandy, OFM CAP, "The Supremacy of Christ: Aquinas' *Commentary on Hebrews*," in *Aquinas on Scripture: An Introduction to His Biblical Commentaries*, ed. Thomas G. Weinandy, OFM CAP, Daniel A. Keating, and John P. Yocum (New York: T. & T. Clark, 2005), 223–44, at 241–43.

By judging certain things to be true propositionally (faith's "material object"), human beings make the assent to God revealing. Aquinas observes that "we can only get a glimpse of Divine truth by way of analysis, since things which in God are one, are manifold in our intellect."[95] The truth-claims through which we assent to God revealing, and thereby come to share his life, are those about "the Trinity of Persons in Almighty God, the mystery of Christ's Incarnation, and the like."[96] As Aquinas suggests, the history of salvation thereby belongs within the act of faith: "Things concerning Christ's human nature, and the sacraments of the Church, or any creatures whatever, come under faith, in so far as by them we are directed to God, and in as much as we assent to them on account of the Divine Truth."[97] The history of salvation includes the Church as its matrix: in this regard the act of faith depends upon the communion of the Church.[98] Guided by the Holy Spirit, the Church presents by means of credal affirmations the teachings that belong to the "material object" of faith. Here Aquinas appeals to ecclesial authority: "The universal Church cannot err, since she is governed by the Holy Ghost, Who is the Spirit of truth: for

---

95. ST II-II, q. 1, a. 6, *sed contra*.

96. ST II-II, q. 1, a. 6, ad 1. Regarding the faith of people who never heard the Gospel, Aquinas observes that "all the articles [of faith] are contained implicitly in certain primary matters of faith, such as God's existence, and His providence over the salvation of man, according to Heb. xi: 'He that cometh to God, must believe that He is, and is a rewarder to them that seek Him.' For the existence of God includes all that we believe to exist in God eternally, and in these our happiness consists; while belief in His providence includes all those things which God dispenses in time, for man's salvation, and which are the way to that happiness: and in this way, again, some of those articles which follow from these are contained in others: thus faith in the Redemption of mankind includes belief in the Incarnation of Christ, His Passion and so forth" (ST II-II, q. 1, a. 7).

97. ST II-II, q. 1, a. 1, ad 1. Cf. Jean-Pierre Torrell, OP, "Saint Thomas et l'histoire. État de la question et pistes de recherches," *Revue Thomiste* 105 (2005): 355–409.

98. As Thomas Weinandy puts it, "while the act of faith is an act of an individual person, it is equally an ecclesial act, for the person, through faith, becomes a member of the body of Christ, the Church. Thus, in union with the whole earthly Church, individual believers come to perceive and are in communion with the heavenly realities they hope for. This again finds its completion in heaven. 'In heavenly glory there are two things which will particularly gladden the just, namely the enjoyment of the godhead and companionship with the saints. For no good is joyfully possessed without companions.' As the Trinity of persons are only able to enjoy their godhead in communion with one another so the blessed in heaven are only able to enjoy that Trinitarian communion in communion with one another. True happiness, for Aquinas, always consists in the joy, founded upon truth and goodness, shared in communion with others, whether those others be the communion of the divine persons or the communion of the saints" (Weinandy, "The Supremacy of Christ," 243, citing Aquinas's *In Heb.* 12.18-24 [706]). See also Avery Dulles, SJ, "The Ecclesial Dimension of Faith," *Communio* 22 (1995): 418–32.

such was Our Lord's promise to His disciples (Jo. xvi. 13): *When He, the Spirit of truth, is come, He will teach you all truth.* Now the symbol is published by the authority of the universal Church. Therefore it contains nothing defective."[99]

Judging by this brief synopsis of Aquinas's theology of faith, he seems to move in two quite different directions: faith as the individual believer's intellectual assent (moved by the graced will) to God revealing, and faith as mediated to the community of believers by the hierarchical Church's infallible authority as sustained by the Holy Spirit.[100] Although Aquinas gives full recognition to faith as a free personal assent to God, the personal and direct character of this assent would appear threatened by a hierarchical Church. This apparent tension seems strengthened by Aquinas's affirmation that an ecclesially authorized creed is needed because individual reading of scripture is not adequate to the assent of faith. He states, "The truth of faith is contained in Holy Scripture, diffusely, under various modes of expression, and sometimes obscurely, so that, in order to gather the truth of faith from Holy Scripture, one needs long study and practice, which are unattainable by all those who require to know the truth of faith, many of whom have no time for study."[101] Rather than depend-

---

99. ST II-II, q. 1, a. 9, *sed contra*. Note that this argument is both pneumatological and Christological. The passage from John 16 continues, "for he [the Spirit] will not speak on his own authority, but whatever he hears he will speak, and he will declare to you the things that are come. He will glorify me, for he will take what is mine and declare it to you. All that the Father has is mine; therefore I said that he will take what is mine and declare it to you" (John 16:13–15). Cf. Karl Barth's emphasis that ecclesial unity is Christological: "The quest for the unity of the Church must in fact be identical with the quest for Jesus Christ as the concrete Head and Lord of the Church. The blessing of unity cannot be separated from Him who blesses, for in Him it has its source and reality, through His Word and Spirit it is revealed to us, and only in faith in Him can it become a reality among us. I repeat: Jesus Christ as the one Mediator between God and man is the oneness of the Church, is that unity within which there may be a multiplicity of communities, of gifts, of persons within one Church, while through it a multiplicity of churches are excluded" (Barth, *The Church and the Churches* [German 1936; Grand Rapids, MI: Eerdmans, 2005], 13–14).

100. Discussing Aquinas's sermon-commentary on the Apostles' Creed, Herwi Rikhof underscores the connection that Aquinas makes between the Holy Spirit and the Church. Aquinas questions "the validity of the formula 'believe *in* the Church.' As Pope Leo had observed already, this is not a reliable formula. It is better to use simply *ecclesiam*. In the commentary on the Creed, Thomas follows his own advice and uses the formula: *credere sanctam Ecclesiam Catholicam.* . . . If one wants to keep the 'in,' Thomas argues, then one has to understand the phrase 'I believe in the Church' as 'I believe in the Holy Spirit sanctifying the Church' " (Rikhof, "Thomas on the Church," 202).

101. ST II-II, q. 1, a. 9, ad 1.

ing upon individual reading of scripture, the truth of faith requires to be set forth "in the person, as it were, of the whole Church, which is united together by faith."[102] Within this unified "person," councils of bishops and the pope draw up and confirm the credal summary.[103]

The Pope, the Bishop of Rome, is responsible for convening a council and confirming its teachings, and also possesses the authority to combat heresy by issuing a new credal statement of the Church's faith. It belongs to the authority of the pope "to decide matters of faith finally, so that they may be held by all with unshakable faith."[104]

---

102. Ibid., ad 3. For the importance of ecclesial unity in the New Testament, see Rudolph Schnackenburg, *The Church in the New Testament*, trans. W. J. O'Hara (New York: Seabury Press, 1965), 128–32. Schnackenburg observes, "Ultimately what binds the Christians together is the common confession of their Lord and Messias, expressed in the formula which was already known from the Old Testament (and its Greek Septuagint translation), but which was now transferred to Jesus Christ: 'those who call on the name of the Lord' or its equivalents (1 Cor 1:2; Rom 10:13; Acts 9:14, 21; 22:16). The sign and seal of this, however, is baptism 'in the name of the Lord Jesus' at which this 'good name' was also invoked upon the baptized person (cf. James 2:7)" (130).

103. When early councils anathematized any change of the Creed, Aquinas remarks, the anathemas were "intended for private individuals, who have no business to decide matters of faith" (ST II-II, q. 1, a. 10, ad 2). He adds, "For every council has taken into account that a subsequent council would expound matters more fully than the preceding council, if this became necessary through some heresy arising" (ibid.).

104. ST II-II, q. 1, a. 10. Ulrich Horst asks why, in the body of the article (as opposed to the *sed contra*), Aquinas does "not take the role of councils into consideration" (Horst, "Thomas Aquinas on Papal Teaching Authority," ch. 1 of his *The Dominicans and the Pope: Papal Teaching Authority in the Medieval and Early Modern Thomist Tradition*, trans. James D. Mixson [Notre Dame, IN: University of Notre Dame Press, 2006], 5–21, at 18). Drawing upon *De potentia* q. 10, a. 4, ad 13, Horst answers that the development of the explicit doctrine of the *filioque*, combined with the role given the Bishop of Rome in the Acts of the Council of Chalcedon, suggested to Aquinas that "just as a later synod has the authority to interpret an earlier one, so the Roman pontiff also has the power to make such an interpretation, since he alone can call a council and confirm its decrees" (Horst, "Thomas Aquinas on Papal Teaching Authority," 19). For Aquinas in the *De potentia*, Horst says, "It was without doubt that the pope had the rights and powers in question, such that councils are not absolutely necessary" (19) when war or similar events prevent the gathering of a council. In *Summa Theologiae* II-II, q. 1, a. 10, Aquinas does not limit the pope's powers to such unusual occasions. As Horst notes, Aquinas takes the requirement of "unshakable faith" in the pope's decision from the Acts of the Council of Chalcedon, and the requirement that the "more important and more difficult questions that arise in the Church" be brought to the pope comes from Gratian's *Decretum*. In his interpretation of Luke 22:32, furthermore, Aquinas does not hold that Christ "prayed for Peter *in figura ecclesiae*" (20) or mention that the pope could fall into heresy. While Aquinas never applies the term *infallibilis* to the pope and never says that the pope cannot err, it remains the case that the *Summa Theologiae* prepares for Vatican I's definition of papal infallibility. See also Yves Congar, "Saint Thomas Aquinas and the Infallibility of the Papal Magisterium (*Summa Theol.*, II-II, q. 1, a. 10)," *The Thomist* 38 (1974): 81–105; Francis Sullivan, sj, *Magisterium: Teaching Authority in the Catholic Church* (New York: Paulist Press, 1983), 90–91. For the argument that Aquinas's comments in the *Summa Theologiae* apply simply to the pope as the head of a council, see Klaus

Private individuals may not decide for themselves what to hold in faith, but the pope may decide for them. Aquinas grounds this position in the person/office of Peter, chosen by Christ Jesus: "Hence our Lord said to Peter whom he made Sovereign Pontiff (Luke xxii. 32): *I have prayed for thee*, Peter, *that thy faith fail not, and thou, being once converted, confirm thy brethren.*"[105]

Why should one human being have such authority in determining the content to be held in faith by all others in the communion of the Church? Jesus, by his prayer in the Holy Spirit, wills in this way to preserve the Church's receptive unity in faith, by which believers share in the Trinitarian gifting. Aquinas affirms that "there should be but one faith of the whole Church, according to 1 Cor. i. 10: *That you all speak the same thing, and that there be no schisms among you*: and this could not be secured unless any question of faith that may arise be decided by him who presides over the whole Church, so that the whole Church may hold firmly to his decision."[106] Otherwise, when differences in the interpretation of revelation arise not only among individuals but also between local congregations, how could these differences not destroy faith's receptive unity?

Yet, has the "one" thus come to dominate the "many," so that rather than a communion of equals the Church becomes divided hierarchically into dominant shepherds and obedient sheep, with the latter being merely passive recipients of the hierarchy's decisions? If receptive unity in faith requires not merely scriptural revelation but also an ecclesial hierarchy, then could it be that the Church witnesses to the triune God's unity but not to the Trinitarian communion of co-equal Persons? In answer, the Church's unity—as the image of the Trinity—is not simply the aggregation of rights-bearing persons. Rather, ecclesial unity goes deeper: it is the eucharistic unity of the mystical Body, in which persons come to indwell each other in Christ

---

Schatz, sj, *Papal Primacy: From Its Origins to the Present*, trans. John A. Otto and Linda M. Maloney (German 1990; Collegeville, MN: Liturgical Press, 1996), 119. Brian Tierney blames the medieval Franciscan theologian Peter Olivi for the doctrine: Tierney, *Origins of Papal Infallibility 1150–1350: A Study of the Concepts of Infallibility, Sovereignty and Tradition in the Middle Ages* (Leiden: E. J. Brill, 1972).

105. ST II-II, q. 1, a. 10.

106. Ibid.

through the grace of the Holy Spirit, a unity-in-communion that transcends the opposition of the one and the many.[107]

As already intimated, ecclesial unity thus emerges from within human sharing in the Trinitarian and Christological pattern of gifting/receptivity. When the Father gives the gift of his Word and human beings receive the gift in the Holy Spirit through faith and the sacraments of faith, this divine gifting is sacramentally mediated by fellow human beings in the Church. The believer's adoptive sonship is experienced as active reception of a gift within the matrix of a sacramental communion shaped by gifting/receptivity. Precisely by configuring the believer to the analogous gifting and receptivity constitutive of the Persons of the Father, Son, and Holy Spirit, hierarchy belongs to the salvific accomplishment of the unity that befits the Church.[108]

---

107. Volf's univocal understanding of unity requires him, as we have seen, to reject a strong Pauline sense of the mystical Body. Benedict Ashley, OP, differentiates Aquinas's understanding of the one and the many from that of Plotinus: "the world order of Aquinas is not primarily a hierarchy or linear cascade from the One to Non-Being, but rather it is a *community of complementary entities with God* as the *coincidentia oppositorum* or *concors discordantium* at the center. Around this center a spiral unfolds in which a hierarchical order as regards generic perfections is combined with a radial order as regards specific perfections" (Ashley, "Hierarchy in Ecclesiology," in idem, *The Ashley Reader: Redeeming Reason* [Naples, FL: Sapientia Press, 2006], 171–83, at 175). Ashley goes on to observe that Aquinas conceives "of the world order as a *community*. He understands this community as a plurality of beings that has a certain hierarchical inequality, yet in which every being makes a unique and irreplaceable contribution to the whole. Furthermore, this community, insofar as it is made of *persons*, is an advancing communication of life and experience in which inequality is overcome by mutual sharing, culminating in the graceful invitation of all created persons to enter the Triune Community in which there is perfect coequality of power, awareness, and love" (182).

108. William J. Abraham's account of papal infallibility seems to miss this soteriological context, despite his own salutary insistence upon the necessity of such a context. Abraham remarks that "papal infallibility is part and parcel of the effort to keep alive a doctrine of the infallibility of the Bible within the Western tradition. We can readily see why this is the case. The doctrine of scripture alone, conceived along the lines of a criterion of truth, cannot survive without some way of resolving the perennial problem of the proper interpretation of scripture. . . . One simple and attractive way to do this is to designate one person to carry the necessary burden by conceiving of him in the appropriate circumstances as an epistemic mechanism to do the required job. This is exactly the role assigned to the bishop of Rome in Vatican I. Thus papal infallibility is intimately linked to the thoroughly Western and thoroughly Protestant doctrine of Scripture alone. It is in fact a radical way of salvaging the doctrine. The Pope is the grandest of Protestants. He is a creation of modern Protestantism and a solution to the epistemological problems it has generated" (Abraham, *The Logic of Renewal* [Grand Rapids, MI: Eerdmans, 2003], 168). This historical claim does not do justice to the pattern of gifting/receptivity in Aquinas's ecclesiology. Abraham subjects Aquinas's understanding of theology to a withering critique in his *Canon as Criterion: From the Fathers to Feminism* (Oxford: Oxford University Press, 2002), viii–xi and 86–110; for a response, indicating that Abraham's reading of Aquinas suffers from the epistemological focus that it

For Aquinas, as Serge-Thomas Bonino observes, "the relation Father/ Son is extended and reflected in the relation Son/disciples."[109] Due to the pattern of gifting/receptivity, the (hierarchical) ecclesial communion of believers makes manifest the (ordered) communion of Trinitarian Persons, at the same time as it makes manifest the unity of the Trinity.

Sacramental Mediation: The Pattern of Gifting/Receptivity

Even if the hierarchical priesthood assists in configuring others to the Trinitarian pattern of gifting and receptivity, however, does not hierarchy mean that some Christians give more and others receive more? If this is so, how can a hierarchical Church be a true image of either the divine unity or the communion of the divine Trinity? These questions require deeper investigation of the unity and communion formed by sacramental mediation in the Church.

Aquinas affirms that human beings receive the salvific power of Christ's Passion by faith and charity, which produce the forgiveness of sins.[110] In conjunction with this spiritual mode of union with

---

condemns, see my "St. Thomas Aquinas and William Abraham," *New Blackfriars* 88 (2007): 46–55.

109. Bonino, "The Role of the Apostles in the Communication of Revelation," 321. See for further discussion Armando Bandera, OP, *Configuración teologal-eucarística de la Iglesia según santo Tomás de Aquino* (Toledo: Servicio de Publicaciones del Instituto Teológico San Ildefonso, 1988); Luc-Thomas Somme, OP, *Fils adoptifs de Dieu par Jésus Christ: La filiation divine par adoption dans la théologie de saint Thomas d'Aquin* (Paris: Vrin, 1997); as well as the dissertation of A. Cirillo, *Cristo Rivelatore del Padre nel Vangelo di S. Giovanni secondo il Commento di San Tommaso d'Aquino* (Rome: Angelicum, 1998); and D. Bourgeois, " 'Inchoatio vitae aeternae': La dimension eschatologique de la virtue théologique de foi chez S. Thomas d'Aquin," *Sapientia* 17 (1974): 276–86.

110. Aquinas states, "Christ dwells in us *by faith* (Eph. iii. 17). Now the power of blotting out sin belongs in a special way to His Passion. And therefore men are delivered from sin especially by faith in His Passion, according to Rom. iii. 25: 'Whom God hath proposed to be a propitiation through faith in His Blood' " (ST III, q. 62, a. 5, ad 2). Because of his theology of faith, Aquinas can affirm that Christ's mystical Body includes people from every time and place, including people who lived before Christ: see ST I-II, q. 106, a. 3, ad 2; I-II, q. 102, a. 5, ad 4; I-II, q. 107, a. 1, ad 2; III, q. 8, a. 3; III, q. 45, a. 3; III, q. 49, a. 5, ad 1; III, q. 62, a. 6. Serge-Thomas Bonino comments that for Aquinas "the difference between the time that preceded Easter and the time that followed it consists in the difference between the limited character and the fuller—superabundant—character of the gift of the Spirit to the apostles. After the resurrection, the Spirit is no longer given, as it were, in passing, but he establishes between himself and the apostles in whom he dwells a true *familiaritas*" (Bonino, "The Role of the Apostles in the Communication of Revelation," 332). This *familiaritas* comes about at Pentecost: "It is, therefore, only on the day of Pentecost that the apostles attained through the Spirit the fullness and perfection of the knowledge of faith" (335). For further discussion see

Christ's Passion, however, he affirms a sacramental mode of union.[111] "Divine wisdom provides for each thing according to its mode,"[112] and the human "mode" is hylomorphic, body-soul. Given the kind of creatures that human beings are, Aquinas (following Augustine) holds that without sensible sacraments, communities of faith cannot sustain the unity of their communion.[113] Not only do human beings learn intelligible truths through sensible things, but also, given the exigencies of human life, "man is prone to direct his activity chiefly towards material things."[114] Bodily actions or practices are inseparable from human knowing within communities. Therefore, Aquinas points out, "bodily exercise was offered to him [man] in the sacraments, by which he might be trained to avoid superstitious practices" along with "all manner of harmful action."[115] The Fall only makes clearer the need for a sacramental, and not only intellectual, union with the power of Christ's Passion. By subjecting human beings to love of visible creatures above love of the invisible God, the Fall establishes the need for a sacramental remedy: "for if man were offered spiritual things without a veil, his mind being taken up with the material world would be unable to apply itself to them."[116]

The fact that after his Resurrection Christ ascends to the Father shows that Christ wills to be present in a mediated fashion among human beings. Aquinas proposes three ways, taken from scripture, that Christ's Ascension to heaven causes our salvation: Christ ascends to "prepare a place" (John 14:2) for us and lead to heaven the holy souls who died before his Passion; he ascends to "make intercession" (Hebrews 7:25) for us to the Father through his exalted human nature;

---

my *Christ's Fulfillment of Torah and Temple: Salvation According to Thomas Aquinas* (Notre Dame, IN: University of Notre Dame Press, 2002), 111–12.

111. Aquinas states, "the power of Christ's Passion is united to us by faith and the sacraments, but in different ways, because the link that comes from faith is produced by an act of the soul; whereas the link that comes from the sacraments is produced by making use of exterior things." ST III, q. 62, a. 6.

112. ST III, q. 60, a. 4.

113. Augustine writes in *Contra Faust.* xix (quoted in ST III, q. 61, a. 1, *sed contra*): "It is impossible to keep men together in one religious denomination, whether true or false, except they be united by means of visible signs or sacraments."

114. ST III, q. 61, a. 1.

115. Ibid.

116. Ibid. On the sacraments as signs, see Vonier, *A Key to the Doctrine of the Eucharist*, 7–22.

and, in accord with Ephesians 4:8–10, he ascends to "send down gifts upon men."[117]

These gifts have a twofold purpose: healing from sin and uniting the person to the communion of the divine worship. With regard to the latter, Aquinas develops his theology of sacramental "character": "Since, therefore, by the sacraments men are deputed to a spiritual service pertaining to the worship of God, it follows that by their means the faithful receive a certain spiritual character."[118] The "character" denotes a spiritual power that enables believers to receive divine gifting and to mediate divine gifting.[119] Believers are configured to Christ's priesthood, and thereby fitted by the Holy Spirit for the worship of the Father in Christ the Son, through "the sacramental characters, which are nothing else than certain participations of Christ's Priesthood, flowing from Christ Himself."[120] Whether or not they

---

117. ST III, q. 57, a. 6. S. Bonino notes that for Aquinas "the apostles continue Christ's mission of teaching. They prolong and imitate it. They do so not as delegates of an absent one but in virtue of their union of love with Jesus who acts even now, that is, in virtue of their mystical configuration to Christ. Fully taking up the Pauline theme of the mystical body, St. Thomas shows how the mission of the members is not other than the mission of the Son. Christ 'speaks in and through the apostles' (*Ioan.* 16, lect. 3, n. 2093)" (Bonino, "The Role of the Apostles in the Communication of Revelation," 343). See also Douglas Farrow, *Ascension and Ecclesia: On the Significance of the Doctrine of the Ascension for Ecclesiology and Christian Cosmology* (Grand Rapids, MI: Eerdmans, 1999).

118. ST III, q. 63, a. 1. As a participation in Christ's priesthood, the spiritual power depends entirely upon the activity of Christ as the heavenly high priest.

119. ST III, q. 63, a. 2. Aquinas states, "Now the worship of God consists either in receiving Divine gifts, or in bestowing them on others. And for both these purposes some power is needed; for to bestow something on others, active power is necessary; and in order to receive, we need a passive power."

120. ST III, q. 63, a. 3. Indebted to Augustine, Aquinas notes that the sacramental "character," properly speaking, is a configuration to Christ (and thereby a re-creation in the Trinity): "the eternal Character is Christ Himself, according to Heb. i. 3: *Who being the brightness of His glory and the figure*, or character, *of His substance*" (ST III, q. 63, a. 3, *sed contra*). See Pierre-Marie Gy, OP, "Évolution de saint Thomas sur la théologie de l'ordre," *Revue Thomiste* 99 (1999): 187, where he notes that Aquinas's reading of Hebrews led him to "recenter the theology of the character on participation in the priesthood of Christ." See also Jean Galot, SJ, *La nature du caractère sacramentel. Étude de théologie médiévale* (Paris: Desclée, 1956), 187–90; Colman O'Neill, OP, "The Instrumentality of the Sacramental Character," *Irish Theological Quarterly* 25 (1958): 262–68; Yves Congar, *Lay People in the Church*, rev. ed., trans. Donald Attwater (London: Geoffrey Chapman, 1965), 140–45; John P. Yocum, "Sacraments in Aquinas," in Weinandy, Keating, and Yocum, *Aquinas on Doctrine*, 159–81, at 172–73. Yocum points to the significance that 2 Corinthians 1:21–22 has for Aquinas's theology of sacramental character: "But it is God who establishes us with you in Christ, and has commissioned us; he has put his seal upon us and given us his Spirit in our hearts as a guarantee." For the development of the theology of sacramental character at Vatican II with respect to the hierarchical priesthood, see Guy Mansini, OSB, "Episcopal *Munera* and the

belong to the hierarchical priesthood, all Christians possess a receptive-relational configuration to Christ by means of the sacramental characters.

The universal priesthood is sustained by two characters. First, all believers receive the sacrament of Baptism, which inscribes a character or configuration to Christ's priesthood that enables all to receive the gifts bestowed by Christ and the Holy Spirit in divine worship. Second, the sacrament of Confirmation bestows a further character that nourishes and strengthens the ability to live out these gifts during the trials of life. Related to these two characters of the universal priesthood is the sacrament of Holy Orders, which gives a further character that enables the hierarchical priesthood "to confer sacraments on others."[121] These diverse sacramental participations in Christ's priesthood are ordered to one end: Eucharistic consummation in the divine worship, the pattern of gifting and receiving whereby believers come to share in Christ's communion with the Father in the unity of the Holy Spirit. Divine worship's priestly pattern of gifting and receiving provides the pattern for all other aspects of Christian life.

CONCLUSION

Paul says of the apostles and those who share in their authority: "This is how one should regard us, as servants of Christ and stewards of the mysteries of God" (1 Corinthians 4:1). By stewarding the divine mysteries, hierarchical authority unites the Church in the Trinitarian and Christological pattern of gifting and receptivity.[122] It is in this pattern of gifting/receptivity that the Church possesses her identity as

---

Character of Episcopal Orders," *The Thomist* 66 (2002): 369–94; idem, "Sacerdotal Character at the Second Vatican Council," *The Thomist* 67 (2003): 539–77. Citing among others Edward Schillebeeckx, OP's *Ministry* (London: SCM Press, 1981) and *Christ the Sacrament of the Encounter with God* (New York: Sheed and Ward, 1963), Mansini points out however that "the whole theology of sacramental character has been attacked and the notion sidelined as much as possible" ("Episcopal *Munera* and the Character of Episcopal Orders," 370).

121. ST III, q. 63, a. 6. For further discussion see Avery Dulles, SJ, *The Priestly Office: A Theological Reflection* (Mahwah, NJ: Paulist Press, 1997), 12–15.

122. For further discussion see Yves Congar, "The Hierarchy as Service," in idem, *Power and Poverty in the Church*, trans. Jennifer Nicholson (Baltimore: Helicon, 1964), 34–35. See also Congar's helpful discussion of the Church's apostolicity according to Thomas Aquinas: Congar, "L'apostolicité de l'Eglise chez S. Thomas d'Aquin," *Revue des sciences philosophiques et théologiques* 44 (1960): 209–24; as well as the insights developed in Bonino, "The Role of the Apostles in the Communication of Revelation According to the *Lectura super Ioannem* of St. Thomas Aquinas."

the Bride who shares in and manifests the unity and Trinity of the divine Bridegroom (cf. Revelation 19:7, 21:9).[123]

I began this chapter with Miroslav Volf's evaluation of Ratzinger's and Zizioulas's ecclesiologies in light of the principle that the Church should be an image of the Trinity. In Volf's view, as we have seen, Ratzinger falls into an essentialist monism by failing to distinguish adequately individual persons (divine or human). The collective absorbs the individuals, who do not have real agency of their own. The result is to leave the bishop's power unchecked. Zizioulas, Volf holds, falls into a monarchical monism whereby the bishop takes on the role of the divine Father in the giving of personhood, leaving the community utterly dependent on the bishop. In response, I first sought to ensure that the divine unity and Trinity not be opposed to each other as in a numerical schema. In this way I aimed at re-affirming, against suspicions of monism, the place of unity within the Church's imaging of the triune God. I then proposed that in the Father's begetting of the Son and the Father and Son's spirating of the Spirit, one can identify the gifting and (in a certain sense) receiving that constitute the communion of divine Persons without threatening their absolute unity. On this basis I asked what it would mean to speak of the Church as an image of the Trinity. I argued that the answer is found in the act of faith and in the sacraments, above all, the Eucharist.

In a hierarchical Church, the modes by which faith and the sacraments are mediated make present a Trinitarian pattern of gifting and receptivity that informs the Church's unity in faith and grace—a unity-in-communion that cannot be understood in terms of a power

---

123. As Congar remarks regarding the structure of gifting/receptivity that unifies the Church with Christ: "The whole body [the Church] thinks and actively uses its mind with regard to religious truth, but the structure of belief is hierarchic, because it does not originate in ideas in the minds of the faithful, but is a treasure of truth apostolically communicated from above, originating in Jesus Christ. The whole body receives the grace of the sacraments, but the structure of sacramental action is hierarchic because sacramental grace is a reality very different from the collective seal of believers or from its result; it is the treasure of grace communicated from above and originating in Jesus Christ." See his "The Eucharist and the Church of the New Alliance," in his *The Revelation of God*, trans. A. Manson and L. C. Sheppard (French 1962; New York: Herder and Herder, 1968), 168–88, at 187. On the Church as the Bride of Christ (with discussion of Mary's particular role by way of showing the significance of the particular members of the Church), see Hans Urs von Balthasar, "Who Is the Church?," trans. A. V. Littledale with Alexander Dru, in his *Explorations in Theology*, vol. 2, *Spouse of the Word* (German 1961; San Francisco: Ignatius Press, 1991), 143–91.

struggle between the one and the many, because it is a unity-in-communion that is radically gift and that can be truly experienced only as such. This pattern is not only Trinitarian, but also Christological: from within the divine pedagogy, one sees that the slain Lamb, by his cruciform gifting, opens the scroll of history and reveals (through the Love that is the Holy Spirit) history's true meaning, invisible to those who see reality in terms of worldly power (Revelation 5:5). By entering into the unity-in-communion that arises from the mediation of God's gifting in Christ and the Spirit, one receives the charity that enables one to serve others rather than to be trapped within the cycle of domination and victimization.

At this point, however, further questions arise regarding Jesus Christ and the earliest Church. Even if one grants this chapter's arguments regarding the hierarchical Church's imaging of Trinitarian gifting/receptivity, did Jesus in fact understand his cross as an exercise of cruciform gifting, a priestly or "cultic" action? Or did later interpreters, preeminently the author of the letter to the Hebrews, impose this understanding upon Jesus' life as a way of explaining how Jesus' cross fits into his proclamation of the kingdom? Likewise, did the early Church possess a cultic priesthood or liturgy? Or, as time passed, did a priestly hierarchy (in the case of the pope, a "hierarchy within the hierarchy") distort what was originally a community of equals sharing a meal that celebrated the Resurrection?[124] Even the briefest glance at the literature reveals that these questions are highly unsettled

---

124. See Thomas Hobbes's description in his *Leviathan*: "But as the inventions of men are woven, so also are they raveled out; the way is the same, but the order is inverted. The web begins at the first elements of power, which are wisdom, humility, sincerity, and other virtues of the Apostles, whom the people, converted, obeyed out of reverence, not by obligation. Their consciences were free, and their words and actions subject to none but the civil power. Afterwards, the presbyters (as the flocks of Christ increased), assembling to consider what they should teach, and thereby obliging themselves to teach nothing against the decrees of their assemblies, made it to be thought the people were thereby obliged to follow their doctrine, and when they refused, refused to keep them company (that was then called excommunication), not as being infidels, but as being disobedient. And this was the first knot upon their liberty. And the number of presbyters increasing, the presbyters of the chief city or province got themselves an authority over the parochial presbyters, and appropriated to themselves the names of bishops. And this was a second knot on Christian liberty. Lastly, the bishop of Rome, in regard of the imperial city, took upon him an authority (partly by the wills of the emperors themselves and by the title of Pontifex Maximus, and at last, when the emperors were grown weak, by the privileges of St. Peter) over all other bishops of the empire. Which was the third and last knot, and the whole synthesis and construction of the pontifical power" (Hobbes, *Leviathan*, ed. Edwin Curley [Indianapolis, IN: Hackett, 1994], ch. 47, par. 19, p. 481).

in contemporary academic Catholic theology.[125] The chapters that follow thus take up in more detail, even if still inevitably in a preliminary manner, the nature of Christ's priesthood, Christian hierarchical priesthood, and sacramental mediation.

---

125. Behind these questions is a broader one, well stated by John Behr: "With regard to the establishment by the end of the second century of catholic, orthodox or normative Christianity, the most important question must be: on what basis was this done? Was it a valid development, intrinsic to the proclamation of the Gospel itself, or an arbitrary imposition, dictated by a male, monarchical, power-driven episcopate suppressing all alternative voices by processes of exclusion and demonization, or however else the history might be written?" (Behr, *The Formation of Christian Theology*, vol. 1: *The Way to Nicaea* [Crestwood, NY: St. Vladimir's Seminary Press, 2001], 13). Behr's approach to answering this question calls into question the historicizing and fragmentizing assumptions that one finds in, e.g., Euan Cameron, *Interpreting Christian History: The Challenge of the Churches' Past* (Oxford: Blackwell, 2005). Cameron begins by explaining the earliest Christians as "a dissenting tendency within the Jewish communities of the Eastern Mediterranean" (11), as if "dissent" provided an adequate category for the proclamation of Jesus as Messiah.

Chapter 2

The Priesthood of Christ

The Second Vatican Council's Constitution on the Sacred Liturgy, *Sacrosanctum Concilium*, teaches that "it is quite right to think of the liturgy as the enacting of the priestly role of Jesus Christ."[1] As the Council Fathers remark earlier in the same document, "the liturgy, through which, especially in the divine sacrifice of the Eucharist, 'the act of our redemption is being carried out,' becomes thereby the chief means through which believers are expressing in their lives and demonstrating to others the mystery of Christ and the genuine nature of the true Church."[2] These affirmations, uncontroversial among Catholic theologians when *Sacrosanctum Concilium* was published, have since become the subject of much theological and exegetical disputation. Did Jesus really enact a "priestly role" in which the Christian priesthood shares by means of "the divine sacrifice of the Eucharist"? As Avery Dulles observes, "It is often said that the priesthood of Christ should be the starting point for any Christian concept of priesthood. But the priestly status of Jesus Christ is not self-evident. Some theologians insist that Christ was a layman, and deny that he was a priest except in a metaphorical sense."[3]

At first glance, the New Testament seems to settle this question. The letter to the Hebrews calls Jesus "the apostle and high priest of our confession" (Hebrews 3:1). Whereas the high priests of

---

1. *Sacrosanctum Concilium*, 7, in *Decrees of the Ecumenical Councils*, vol. 2: *Trent to Vatican II*, ed. Norman P. Tanner, SJ (Washington, DC: Georgetown University Press, 1990), p. 822.

2. Ibid., 2, p. 820 (translation slightly modified), citing the Roman Missal, prayer over the gifts for the ninth Sunday after Pentecost. Cf. John Paul II, *Ecclesia de Eucharistia* (2003), nos. 3, 5, and elsewhere.

3. Avery Dulles, SJ, *The Priestly Office: A Theological Reflection* (Mahwah, NJ: Paulist Press, 1997), 5. For discussion of these issues see also Benedict Ashley, OP, "The Priesthood of Christ, of the Baptized, and of the Ordained," in idem, *The Ashley Reader: Redeeming Reason* (Naples, FL: Sapientia Press, 2006), 125–43.

Israel were of Levitical descent, Jesus is "designated by God a high priest after the order of Melchizedek" (Hebrews 5:11).[4] The task of every "high priest chosen from among men" is "to act on behalf of men in relation to God, to offer gifts and sacrifices for sins" (Hebrews 5:1). Jesus performs this task perfectly, in contrast to the limited power of merely human priests. Unlike a merely human high priest, Jesus is "holy, blameless, unstained, separated from sinners, exalted above the heavens" (Hebrews 7:26). He is the "great high priest who has passed through the heavens, Jesus, the Son of God" (Hebrews 4:14); he is the one whom God "appointed the heir of all things, through whom also he created the world" (Hebrews 1:2). When he "made purification for sins" (Hebrews 1:3), Jesus did so as a man who "reflects the glory of God and bears the very stamp of his nature, upholding the universe by his word of power" (Hebrews 1:3). He is both a human high priest and the eternal Son of God.

Jesus' priestly sacrificial offering consists in his own suffering: "In the days of his flesh, Jesus offered up prayers and supplications, with loud cries and tears, to him who was able to save him from death, and he was heard for his godly fear. Although he was a Son, he learned obedience through what he suffered; and being made perfect he became the source of eternal salvation to all who obey him" (Hebrews 5:7–9). By his suffering on the cross, Christ accomplishes "once for all" (Hebrews 9:12, 26) the atoning work of the high priest as described in Exodus 30 and especially Leviticus 16. Christ "entered once for all into the Holy Place, taking not the blood of goats and calves but his own blood, thus securing an eternal redemption" (Hebrews 9:12). His blood possesses eternal expiatory power because of his perfect love on the cross: as the author of Hebrews puts it, "the blood of Christ, who through the eternal Spirit offered himself without blemish to God" (Hebrews 9:14). His "sacrifice of himself" (Hebrews 9:26) also possesses eternal expiatory power because, as the Son of God, he conquers death and thereby "holds his priesthood permanently, because he continues for ever. Consequently he is able for all time to save those

---

4. For historical-critical background, see Deborah W. Rooke, *Zadok's Heirs: The Role and Development of the High Priesthood in Ancient Israel* (Oxford: Oxford University Press, 2000). She shows that the high priesthood remained a cultic office through the Roman conquest, rather than primarily serving as the basis of political power.

who draw near to God through him, since he only lives to make intercession for them" (Hebrews 7:24–25).

By contrast to Hebrews, however, Jesus in the four Gospels
never names himself a "priest," and his actions are never described as
"priestly."[5] Albert Vanhoye points out, "In the Gospels the word
'priest' (*hiereus*) is never applied either to Jesus or to his disciples, but
always designates the Jewish priests."[6] Jesus could only have been a
Jewish priest if he had been from the tribe of Levi: as Vanhoye says,
"according to the Law, he was not a priest. No one thought of attrib-
uting this office to him and he himself never laid the least claim to it."[7]
Instead, the Gospels show that many of his contemporaries thought of
Jesus as a prophet (cf. Matthew 16:14, Luke 13:33, John 4:44, Mark

---

5. In favor of a biblical theology of Christ's priesthood (with prophetic and royal
dimensions), however, Avery Dulles observes:

> the inspired and canonical status of the Letter to the Hebrews, the Christian theologian
> is justified in forming a concept of priesthood that applies at least to Jesus himself.
> Such a concept would involve being designated and empowered by God to offer prayers
> and sacrifice of praise, thanksgiving, and atonement on behalf of the whole people,
> thereby pleasing God and bringing divine benefits upon those for whom intercession is
> made. . . . If the concept of priesthood in Hebrews is taken as a starting point, it
> becomes apparent that other New Testament authors such as Paul understand Jesus as a
> priestly figure, even though they do not use the term. They consider the death of Jesus
> on the cross to be a religious sacrifice. Indeed it becomes apparent that the idea of
> priesthood is pervasive in the New Testament descriptions of Jesus as the one who bore
> the sins of many and allowed his body to be broken and his blood poured forth on
> behalf of others. Many New Testament authors describe Jesus as shepherd or pastor.
> The First Letter of Peter, for example, calls him the chief shepherd and also the lamb
> without spot or blemish, offered up for the sins of the world. These themes are extensively
> developed in the gospel of John, in which Jesus says of himself, "I am the good
> shepherd" (Jn 10:11). The sacrificial role is brought out in the statement immediately
> following: "The good shepherd lays down his life for the sheep" (ibid.). He does so in
> obedience to the Father's command, in order to win eternal life for the sheep committed
> to his care. In his priestly sacrifice the shepherd becomes the victim whose body and
> blood are true food and drink (Jn 6:53). He has a prophetic task as leader and teacher
> of the community, for the sheep hear his voice and follow him to the pastures of eternal
> life (Jn 10:27–28). Even the concept of kingship is not absent from the Johannine vision,
> for Jesus dies with the inscription on the cross, "King of the Jews" (Jn 19:19). He has
> told Pontius Pilate, "my kingship is not of this world" (Jn 18:36). The category of
> priesthood, therefore, is biblically appropriate. (Dulles, *The Priestly Office*, 5–6; cf. 31–32)

6. Albert Vanhoye, sj, *Old Testament Priests and the New Priest According to the New
Testament*, trans. J. Bernard Orchard, osb (French 1980; Petersham, MA: St. Bede's
Publications, 1986), 3. Observing that "the priesthood constituted one of the fundamental
institutions of the Old Testament," Vanhoye rightly asks, "How could the Christian Church
claim to be faithful to the totality of biblical revelation and to possess in Christ its definitive
fulfillment, if it found itself in a negative relationship with regard to this fundamental
institution of the people of God?" (17).

7. Ibid., 48.

6:15). For his part, Jesus often describes himself and his mission in terms of kingship.

When he first begins to preach in the Gospel of Matthew, Jesus says, "Repent, for the kingdom of heaven is at hand" (Matthew 4:17).[8] The kingdom has come in the person of Jesus, as he makes clear when challenged by the Pharisees about his power of casting out demons: "But if it is by the Spirit of God that I cast out demons, then the kingdom of God has come upon you" (Matthew 12:28). He tells Peter that "I will give you the keys to the kingdom of heaven" (Matthew 16:19), and later promises his disciples that "there are some standing here who will not taste death before they see the Son of man coming in his kingdom" (Matthew 16:28). Enacting the prophecy of Zechariah 9:9—"Rejoice greatly, O daughter of Zion! / Shout aloud, O daughter of Jerusalem! / Lo, your king comes to you; / triumphant and victorious is he, / humble and riding on an ass, / on a colt the foal of an ass"—he enters Jerusalem and is hailed by the crowds as the royal "Son of David" (Matthew 21:9). At his birth, according to the Gospel of Matthew, "wise men from the East came to Jerusalem, saying, 'Where is he who has been born king of the Jews?'" (Matthew 2:1–2). At his death, he answers the high priest's question about whether he is the Christ by saying, "You have said so. But I tell you, hereafter you will see the Son of man seated at the right hand of Power, and coming on the clouds of heaven" (Matthew 26:64). He likewise responds to Pilate's question about whether he is "King of the Jews" by saying, "You have said so" (Matthew 27:11). He is mocked by the Roman soldiers and by his fellow Israelites as "King of the Jews" (Matthew 27:29, 42), and the soldiers nail to his cross the inscription, "This is Jesus the King of the Jews" (Matthew 27:37).

In the Gospel of Mark, too, he preaches the kingdom (cf. Mark 1:15, 9:1) and is crucified as "The King of the Jews" (Mark 15:26).[9]

---

8. Cf. the insights of Jacques Jomier, OP, "The Kingdom of God in Islam and Its Comparison with Christianity," trans. Stephen Wentworth Arndt, *Communio* 13 (1986): 267–71.

9. The biblical scholar Daniel J. Harrington, SJ, distinguishes strongly, but mistakenly I think, between the "kingdom of God" and the "Church." See Harrington, *The Church According to the New Testament: What the Wisdom and Witness of Early Christianity Teaches Us Today* (Franklin, WI: Sheed & Ward, 2001), 19. Cf. for the same view, Thomas P. Rausch, SJ, *Towards a Truly Catholic Church: An Ecclesiology for the Third Millennium* [Collegeville, MN: Liturgical Press, 2005], 52–54); Hans Küng, *The Church*, trans. Ray and Rosaleen Ockenden (German 1967; London: Burns & Oates, 1968), 96f.; Richard McBrien, *Do We Need the Church?* (New York: Harper & Row, 1969), 14–15. Compare *Lumen Gentium*'s account of "the church, as the

Likewise, in the Gospel of Luke, Jesus' enemies bring him to Pilate with the accusation, "We found this man perverting our nation, and forbidding us to give tribute to Caesar, and saying that he himself is Christ a king" (Luke 23:2). In the Gospel of John, his enemies warn Pilate, who is inclined to release Jesus, that, "If you release this man, you are not Caesar's friend; every one who makes himself a king sets himself against Caesar" (John 19:12).

Even if with Hebrews one identifies Jesus as in some sense a "priest" as well as a king, consider also the difficulties that arise in supposing, as *Sacrosanctum Concilium* does, that Jesus' followers participate in his priesthood, especially "in the divine sacrifice of the Eucharist."[10] Namely, what kind of "priesthood" do Jesus' followers receive?

The first letter of Peter announces the fulfillment in Christ of God's promise that if Israel obeys the commandments given at Sinai, "you [Israel] shall be to me a kingdom of priests and a holy nation" (Exodus 19:6).[11] Peter proclaims to all human beings, "Come to him, to that living stone, rejected by men but in God's sight chosen and precious; and like living stones be yourselves built into a spiritual house, to be a holy priesthood, to offer spiritual sacrifices acceptable to God through Jesus Christ. . . . You are a chosen race, a royal priesthood, a holy nation, God's own people" (1 Peter 2:4–5, 9). The

---

kingdom of Christ already present in mystery," which "grows visibly in the world through the power of God" (§3, in *Decrees of the Ecumenical Councils, vol. 2, Trent to Vatican II.* James Fredericks describes theologians who, to varying degrees, separate "kingdom" and "Church" as "regnocentric theologians," among whom he takes as a model Jacques Dupuis, sj. See Fredericks, "The Catholic Church and the Other Religious Paths: Rejecting Nothing That Is True and Holy," *Theological Studies* 64 (2003): 225–54. Alfred Loisy famously differentiated between the kingdom (announced by Jesus) and the Church in his L'Évangile et l'Église (Paris: Picard, 1902), 255; for the context and sources of this work see Harvey Hill, "Loisy's *L'Évangile et l'Église* in Light of the 'Essais,'" *Theological Studies* 67 (2006): 73–98.

10. Cf. Yves Congar, "The Different Priesthoods: Christian, Jewish and Pagan," in his *A Gospel Priesthood,* trans. P. J. Hepburne-Scott (New York: Herder and Herder, 1967), 74–89; idem, "Notes on Our Priesthood," in *A Gospel Priesthood,* 90–102; idem, *Lay People in the Church,* rev. ed., trans. Donald Attwater (London: Geoffrey Chapman, 1965), 145–52. In "Notes on Our Priesthood" Congar remarks of himself and his fellow ordained priests: "We are, then, ministerial, hierarchical and sacramental priests of the one sacrifice of Jesus Christ, sacramentally celebrated throughout time and space, in order to consummate, in union with this sacrifice, the sacrifice of his mystical body: that is, of the faithful who have been turned to God by our ministry" (97).

11. For further discussion see Jo Bailey Wells, *God's Holy People: A Theme in Biblical Theology* (London: Sheffield Academic Press, 2000).

task of the "holy" and "royal" priesthood that is the Church is "to offer spiritual sacrifices acceptable to God through Jesus Christ" (1 Peter 2:5) and to "declare the wonderful deeds of him who called you out of darkness into his marvelous light" (1 Peter 2:9), the light of divine mercy. Likewise envisioning the universal priesthood, the letter to the Hebrews suggests that Jesus' followers should offer spiritual sacrifices by suffering with him, by doing good works, and by proclaiming his name in worship; in this way, Jesus' followers partake in his "altar." Encouraging believers to depend solely upon Jesus for salvation, Hebrews states,

> We have an altar from which those who serve the tent have no right to eat. For the bodies of those animals whose blood is brought into the sanctuary by the high priest as a sacrifice for sin are burned outside the camp. So Jesus also suffered outside the gate in order to sanctify the people through his own blood. Therefore let us go forth to him outside the camp, bearing abuse for him. For here we have no lasting city, but we seek the city which is to come. Through him then let us continually offer up a sacrifice of praise to God, that is, the fruit of lips that acknowledge his name. Do not neglect to do good and to share what you have, for such sacrifices are pleasing to God. (Hebrews 13:10–16)

The book of Revelation similarly presents all Christians as priests who are enabled, in Christ and his Spirit, to worship God the Father in holiness. Thus in its opening invocation of praise, the book of Revelation states, "To him who loves us and has freed us from our sins by his blood and made us a kingdom, priests to his God and Father, to him be glory and dominion for ever and ever" (Revelation 1:5–6). In the vision recounted by the seer of Revelation, the 24 elders similarly emphasize the fulfillment of Exodus 19:6 in their "new song" of worship to the slain but living Lamb: "Worthy art thou to take the scroll and to open its seals, for thou wast slain and by thy blood didst ransom men for God from every tribe and tongue and people and nation, and hast made them a kingdom and priests to our God, and they shall reign on earth" (Revelation 5:9–10). This priesthood recurs in the description of the millennial kingdom before the final end of the world. The seer describes the martyrs, already enjoying the risen life, as "priests of God and of Christ, and they shall reign with him a thousand years" (Revelation 20:6).

If all of Jesus' followers are "priests to his God and Father" (Revelation 1:6) who are fit "to offer spiritual sacrifices acceptable to God through Jesus Christ" (1 Peter 2:5), how does this offering occur? Are "spiritual sacrifices," as both 1 Peter and Hebrews suggest, constituted simply by praise for God's name, suffering with Christ, and good works? Or is there also a hierarchical priesthood whose ministry unites our spiritual sacrifices cultically to the sacrifice of Christ?[12]

This chapter focuses on Christ as a "priest," leaving for the next chapter the question of the priesthood that emerges from his actions. I first examine some recent historical-critical scholarship on Jesus' Pasch, specifically the approaches of N. T. Wright, Steven Bryan, Scot McKnight, and Brant Pitre. Despite the differences among the four authors, together they bear historical-critical witness to an understanding of Jesus' death as a priestly action that is eschatological, sacrificial/eucharistic, sanctifying, and unitive. I then turn to Aquinas's theological investigation, in his question in the *Summa Theologiae* devoted to Christ as a priest, of these dimensions of Christ's priestly action.[13] I hope to offer a nuanced and ecumenically persuasive case in favor of *Sacrosanctum Concilium*'s affirmation that ecclesial hierarchy mediates the Church's participation in Jesus' priestly action.[14]

---

12. Cf. on this topic Gilles Emery, OP, "Le sacerdoce spiritual des fidèles chez saint Thomas d'Aquin," *Revue Thomiste* 99 (1999): 211–43. As Guy Mansini, OSB, pointed out to me, the visible sacrifice is the sacrament of the invisible sacrifice, and the former has no value apart from the charity and humility and obedience of the interior sacrifice of devotion. Believers, however, need the exterior, visible priesthood and its exercise, both to provoke their interior sacrifice and to express it; they need it to communicate to them the very grace in virtue of which their charity directs them to offer all things in the Spirit through Christ to the Father.

13. In uniting contemporary biblical scholarship with the theological tradition represented by Aquinas, my approach is somewhat similar to that of the evangelical theologian Hans Boersma, who remarks that his "understanding of the atonement has been shaped particularly by two theologians, one from the early Church (Irenaeus) and one who takes his place among contemporary students of New Testament theology (N. T. Wright)" (Boersma, *Violence, Hospitality, and the Cross: Reappropriating the Atonement Tradition* [Grand Rapids, MI: Baker Academic, 2004], 112). Boersma continues, "Irenaeus's understanding of the atonement is often described as 'recapitulation': Christ taking the place of Adam and of all humanity and as such giving shape to the genesis of a new humanity. N. T. Wright's understanding of the atonement, centering on the term 'reconstitution,' is quite similar. He regards Christ as the messianic representative of Israel and, as such, of all humanity. In his person he reconstitutes Israel and all humanity, so that his life and death overcome the failure of Israel and Adam and restore Jews as well as Gentiles to covenant fellowship with God" (112). Boersma's development of "recapitulation" fits with the various dimensions of Christ's priesthood envisioned by Aquinas.

14. A common view among theologians today is that the cultic understanding of Jesus' priesthood emerged in the East in the fourth century. See for example David N. Power, OMI, *The Eucharistic Mystery: Revitalizing the Tradition* (New York: Crossroad, 1992), building upon

CONTEMPORARY BIBLICAL SCHOLARSHIP AND JESUS' PRIESTHOOD

While granting that historical reconstructions of Jesus cannot be normative for the Gospels—not only because the Gospels are divine revelation received in faith, but also because historical reconstructions conflict with each other and change rapidly—the biblical scholar Scot McKnight observes that simple appeal to the canonical witness does not suffice to put entirely to the side historical questions about Jesus. As he says,

> Regardless of the many attempts to appreciate the *canonical witness*— whether through the lenses of aesthetic criticism or New Testament theology or Orthodox theology or kerygmatic theology or the "witness of the church"—and there is something important to each approach, one has difficulty in believing the atoning death of Jesus and then being told that we are not sure that Jesus thought of his death in this way.[15]

While it would not be possible to prove that Jesus thought of his death in this way, one might ask whether he plausibly did so. How might Jesus Christ have understood his actions to be "priestly"?[16] Does

---

his re-reading of Trent's definition of the Eucharist as a propitiatory sacrifice in his *The Sacrifice We Offer: The Tridentine Dogma and Its Reinterpretation* (New York: Crossroad, 1987). Power in *The Eucharistic Mystery* sees sacrifice as a negative holdover from religions of fear and finds in Jesus' cross a radical "reversal of values." In *The Sacrifice We Offer,* Power concludes that "propitiatory turns out to be one of those words that is more attached to a given practice than to a doctrinal understanding of what is involved in the practice, as well as to a particularly historically bound institutional way of mediating Christ's grace to the church. The particular meaning of the priestly act could be retained only in a church that could find given sacerdotal structures its most appropriate faith expression, and that was party to a cultural perspective that made this vision of church possible" (159–60). Thus evaporates the doctrinal definition. In *Lay People in the Church,* rev. ed., trans. Donald Attwater (London: Geoffrey Chapman, 1965), 145–52, Yves Congar interprets in the direction of continuity the same texts and problems that Power and others interpret in the direction of discontinuity. For discussion of Power's theology, see my "A Note on Joseph Ratzinger and Contemporary Theology of the Priesthood," *Nova et Vetera* 5 (2007): 271–83; idem, "John Paul II and Aquinas on the Eucharist," in *John Paul II and St. Thomas Aquinas,* ed. Michael Dauphinais and Matthew Levering (Naples, FL: Sapientia Press, 2006), 209–31.

15. Scot McKnight, *Jesus and His Death: Historiography, the Historical Jesus, and Atonement Theory* (Waco, TX: Baylor University Press, 2006), 52–53. For reflections on the understanding of "history" appropriate to Christian biblical exegesis, see my *Participatory Biblical Exegesis: A Theology of Biblical Interpretation* (Notre Dame, IN: University of Notre Dame Press, 2008).

16. Numerous other scholars could be canvassed: see for example Bruce Chilton, *The Temple of Jesus: His Sacrificial Program within a Cultural History of Sacrifice* (Philadelphia:

contemporary historical-critical reconstruction of the Jesus of the Gospels support the portrait of Christ the priest that the letter to the Hebrews offers? When Christians affirm, on the ground of the unity of the scriptures as divine revelation, that Hebrews makes theologically explicit what is implicit in the Gospels, does historical-critical research support this position?

N. T. Wright

Given the magnitude of N. T. Wright's achievement, examination of recent biblical scholarship on Jesus' understanding of his Paschal actions should begin with Wright's work.[17] In his *Jesus and the Victory of God*, Wright agrees with Jacob Neusner, Ben Meyer, and others in connecting Jesus' words and deeds about the Temple to Jesus' Last Supper. Wright argues in this regard that "Jesus intended his death to accomplish that which would normally be accomplished in and through the Temple itself. In other words, Jesus intended that his death should

University of Pennsylvania Press, 1992). Chilton notes that "sacrifice, the heart of cultic praxis, is more assumed than it is explained within the sources of early Judaism. Early Christianity and early Judaism both need to be viewed from a sacrificial perspective, if any speaker within their systems is to be understood in his use of cultic vocabulary" (ix). Chilton seeks to expose the "network of meanings" that reveals "the priestly aspect of Jesus' teaching, largely ignored by 'critical' scholarship and its Protestant bent, offensive to that Christianity which wishes Jesus to be done with Jewish forms, and invisible to the Judaism which relies on the Rabbis for its vocabulary" (x). For a position that more sharply differs from mine, see David Catchpole, *Jesus People: The Historical Jesus and the Beginnings of Community* (London: Darton, Longman and Todd, 2006), 279–84, which distinguishes between Jesus' intention, which was solely "to call Israel to prepare for the inauguration of God's kingdom" (284), and the unintended result, his death. See also Gerhard Lohfink, *Does God Need the Church? Toward a Theology of the People of God*, trans. Linda M. Mahoney (German 1998; Collegeville, MN: Liturgical Press, 1999), which argues that "if there are always exegetes who simply deny that Jesus could have interpreted his death as an existential representation on behalf of the many and as an atoning sacrifice for Israel, this is not ultimately a matter of historical-critical issues. The decision was already made beforehand" (196).

17. For the importance of Wright's work, see the eminent contributors to Carey C. Newman, ed., *Jesus and the Restoration of Israel: A Critical Assessment of N. T. Wright's Jesus and the Victory of God* (Downers Grove, IL: InterVarsity Press, 1999). For an ecclesiological application of Wright's biblical scholarship, see Rodney Clapp, "Practicing the Politics of Jesus," in *The Church as Counterculture*, ed. Michael L. Budde and Robert W. Brimlow (New York: State University of New York Press, 2000), 15–37. Clapp is concerned about how the norms of the state, rather than the Paschal Mystery of Jesus Christ, seem to dominate much of modern Christianity (which Clapp traces to "Constantinianism" without discussing the role of bishops pre– and post–Constantine).

in some sense function sacrificially."[18] Yet, Jesus did not envision his death as occupying a place within a continuum of sacrifice, in which his sacrificial death would be merely one of many. Instead, Jesus purposefully went to Jerusalem during Passover with the intention of dying a sacrificial death that would fulfill the original Passover and thereby "would establish a reality which would supersede the Temple."[19]

This account of Jesus' intention needs filling out, and Wright performs this task admirably. According to Wright, Jesus understood himself as the Messiah who was "Israel-in-person, Israel's representative, the one in whom Israel's destiny was reaching its climax."[20] As the Messiah, Jesus "embodied what he had announced. He was the true interpreter of Torah; the true builder of the Temple; the true spokesperson for Wisdom."[21] His goal was to renew the covenant by finally accomplishing the end of the Babylonian Exile, the restoration of the people and land in holiness. Due to the people's sins, YHWH had abandoned the Temple before the Babylonian Exile (cf. Ezekiel 10); now in and through Jesus' actions, YHWH would return to Zion as king. Yet first the divine judgment of Israel, Jerusalem, and the Temple had to be endured, the "day of YHWH" foretold by the prophets. Jesus found "himself called, like Ezekiel, symbolically to undergo the fate he had announced, in symbol and word, for Jerusalem as a whole."[22] Jesus would endure the judgment of sin by his sacrificial

---

18. N. T. Wright, *Jesus and the Victory of God* (Minneapolis, MN: Fortress Press, 1996), 604. See also Bruce Chilton's praise of William Robertson Smith, in contrast to G. B. Gray, regarding sacrifice in the Old Testament. Chilton observes that "Gray's model of a progressive movement in the religion of Israel away from the alleged materialism of sacrifice" continues to influence contemporary accounts of sacrifice (Chilton, *The Temple of Jesus*, 46).

19. Wright, *Jesus and the Victory of God*, 605, cf. 609: "Jesus, then, went to Jerusalem not just to preach, but to die. Schweitzer was right: Jesus believed that the messianic woes were about to burst upon Israel, and that he had to take them upon himself, solo." Cf. Chilton's critical engagement with Schweitzer in evaluating "the sacrifice of Jesus" (Chilton, *The Temple of Jesus*, 137–54). For Chilton, the Gospels' presentation of Jesus as predicting the Temple's destruction and claiming to be the Messiah refer to "the issues of a later day" (154). Rather, Jesus was engaged in a debate with the Temple authorities over whether or not "God preferred a pure meal to impure sacrifice in the Temple. Any such claim struck at the conception of the unique efficacy of the cult on Mount Zion" (ibid.). To my mind, Chilton's exegesis here seems strained.

20. Wright, *Jesus and the Victory of God*, 538.

21. Ibid.

22. Ibid., 594. In Wright's view, Israel's desire to rebel militarily against Roman rule indicated that Israel was still trying to imitate the pagan nations. Wright states, "Jesus therefore not only took upon himself the 'wrath' (which, as usual in Jewish thought, refers to hostile military action) which was coming upon Israel because she had compromised with

death. His death during Passover, as the death of the Messiah, would
be the sacrificial suffering that would trigger the eschatological
accomplishment of the kingdom of YHWH in holiness. His sacrificial
death "would be the new exodus, the renewal of the covenant, the
forgiveness of sins, the end of exile. It would do for Israel what Israel
could not do for herself. It would thereby fulfill Israel's vocation, that
she should be the servant people, the light of the world."[23] In dying,
moreover, Jesus would not merely be a passive victim awaiting divine
vindication. Rather, as already suggested, Jesus' entrance into Jerusalem
would "enact, symbolize and personify" the return of YHWH to
Zion, to Jerusalem, and the Temple mount.[24] After enacting YHWH's
judgment upon Israel by his suffering and death, Jesus would be
vindicated: as Jesus informs the high priest Caiaphas, "They would
witness something far more telling [than a mere vision]: the this-
worldly events which would indicate beyond any doubt that Israel's

paganism and was suffering exile. He also took upon himself the 'wrath' which was coming
upon Israel because she had refused his way of peace" (596). On the role of Jerusalem and the
Temple in Jesus' vision of restoration as set forth by the Gospels, as well as in Paul, Hebrews,
and the book of Revelation, see also P. W. L. Walker, *Jesus and the Holy City: New Testament
Perspectives on Jerusalem* (Grand Rapids, MI: Eerdmans, 1996). Walker draws heavily upon
Wright's work, especially upon Wright's "Jerusalem in the New Testament," in *Jerusalem Past
and Present in the Purposes of God*, ed. P. W. L. Walker, rev. ed. (Grand Rapids, MI: Baker,
1994), 53–78, and upon Wright's brilliant overview of his approach, *The New Testament and
the People of God: Christian Origins and the Question of God* (Minneapolis, MN: Fortress, 1992).

23. Wright, *Jesus and the Victory of God*, 597. Regarding the forgiveness of sins, Wright
notes, "This 'forgiveness' should not be thought of as a detached, ahistorical blessing, such as
might be offered by anyone at any time. Jesus' offer is not to be construed, as it has been so
often, as an attempt to play at 'being god'; nor is it to be rejected as unhistorical on the grounds
that such an attempt is unthinkable. Forgiveness was an eschatological blessing; if Israel went
into exile because of her sins, then forgiveness consists in her returning: returning to YHWH,
returning from exile. Jesus' action and claim indicated that this symbol of return was now
becoming a reality" (434; cf. 268f.). I would add, however, that without denying that "forgiveness
was an eschatological blessing," one can still affirm that Jesus acts with the power of the Son
of God. I agree with C. Stephen Evans's view that Wright operates somewhat within the
"methodological naturalism" of contemporary historiography: see Evans, "Methodological
Naturalism in Historical Biblical Scholarship," in Newman, *Jesus and the Restoration of Israel*,
180–205.

24. Wright, *Jesus and the Victory of God*, 615. As Wright later puts it, "he acted upon a
vocation to do and be for Israel and the world what, according to scripture, only Israel's god
can do and be" (649). He goes on to summarize his case: "I have argued that Jesus' underlying
aim was based on his faith-awareness of vocation. He believed himself called, by Israel's god,
to evoke the traditions which promised YHWH's return to Zion, and the somewhat more
nebulous but still important traditions which spoke of a human figure sharing the divine throne;
to enact those traditions in his own journey to Jerusalem, his messianic act in the Temple, and
his death at the hands of the pagans (in the hope of subsequent vindication); and thereby to
embody YHWH's return" (651).

god had exalted Jesus, had vindicated him after his suffering, and had raised him to share his own throne."[25]

Jesus' vindication would not, of course, leave Israel or the world just as it was before. Rather, the day of YHWH would fulfill the prophecies. As Wright argues, in Jesus' view "the moment had arrived for the great renewal, in which Torah would be written on people's hearts."[26] A new world-order would come about. Just as Jesus claimed authority over the Temple, so also, then, he claimed authority over the Torah. Since Jesus willed to go to his death in order to endure on behalf of Israel the judgment upon sin, and thus to bring Israel's exile to its end, his vindication would mean a new Israel ordered around himself as the victorious embodiment of Israel now indwelt by YHWH in holiness. Wright states, "If YHWH's return to Zion was to happen in and through him, he had the right and authority to reconstitute Israel around himself, as the forgiven, i.e. the returned-from-exile, people of the one true god."[27] By his suffering, death, and vindication, Jesus as the returned king "would build the true Temple."[28] He would do so as a priest-king "after the order of Melchizedek" (Psalm 110:4). As Wright points out, when teaching in the Temple,

---

25. Ibid., 643. Wright comments with regard to the sharing of the divine throne: "Here at last, I suggest, we have uncovered the reason why Caiaphas tore his robe and shouted 'Blasphemy!'" (643). He distances himself, however, from the view that Jesus knew himself to be the Son of God in the Nicene sense:

> I suggest, in short, that the return of YHWH to Zion, and the Temple-theology which it brings into focus, are the deepest keys and clues to gospel christology. Forget the "titles" of Jesus, at least for a moment; forget the pseudo-orthodox attempts to make Jesus of Nazareth conscious of being the second person of the Trinity; forget the arid reductionism that is the mirror-image of that unthinking would-be orthodoxy. Focus, instead, on a young Jewish prophet telling a story about YHWH returning to Zion as judge and redeemer, and then embodying it by riding into the city in tears, symbolizing the Temple's destruction and celebrating the final exodus. I propose, as a matter of history, that Jesus of Nazareth was conscious of a vocation: a vocation, given him by the one he knew as "father," to enact in himself what, in Israel's scriptures, God had promised to accomplish all by himself. He would be the pillar of cloud and fire for the people of the new exodus. He would embody in himself the returning and redeeming action of the covenant God. (653)

I think that this consciousness of vocation need not, and should not, be separated from his recognition of his divine Sonship vis-a-vis "the one he knew as 'father'."

26. Ibid., 646.

27. Ibid., 647. Joseph Ratzinger canvasses various perspectives on eschatology in his "Eschatology and Utopia," in his *Church, Ecumenism and Politics: New Essays in Ecclesiology*, trans. Robert Nowell (German 1987; New York: Crossroad, 1988), 237–54.

28. Wright, *Jesus and the Victory of God*, 494.

Jesus quotes Psalm 110:1 in order to suggest that the Messiah will
have authority over the Temple "not merely as David's son, but, more
particularly, as David's lord."[29] Thus, for Wright, Jesus' claims entail
his re-ordering the Temple, which in its physical form would be
destroyed, around his victorious sacrificial death.[30] Indeed, the entire
people of God would be re-ordered around him. Wright observes in
this regard that "Jesus' vision of an alternative Israel as, in the first
instance, a network of cells loyal to him and his kingdom-vision, was
bound to come into conflict with other first-century visions of the
kingdom."[31] The time of fulfillment meant that the new Israel would
be a "light to the world" by relativizing the "god-given markers of
Israel's distinctiveness."[32] As Wright says in concluding his analysis of
Jesus' prophetic critique of Israel's central symbols:

> Healing, forgiveness, renewal, the twelve, the new family and its new
> defining characteristics, open commensality, the promise of blessing for
> the Gentiles, feasts replacing fasts, the destruction and rebuilding of the
> Temple: all declared, in the powerful language of symbol, that Israel's
> exile was over, that Jesus was himself in some way responsible for this
> new state of affairs, and that all that the Temple had stood for was now
> available through Jesus and his movement.[33]

In my view, Wright's narrative provides good reason for
supposing that Jesus understood his death as "sacrificial," that is, as a
death on behalf of all Israel so as to bring about the eschatological
kingdom of YHWH. Likewise, Wright's narrative provides good
reason for supposing that Jesus intended that the worship offered by
his followers would replace the Temple sacrifices, and would accomplish
for his followers what the Temple sacrifices sought to accomplish. In

---

29. Ibid., 509.

30. Wright affirms the authenticity of Jesus' prophecies regarding the destruction of the
Temple. As Wright says, "the destruction of the Temple—predicted already in symbolic
action, and here in prophetic oracle—is bound up with Jesus' own vindication, as prophet and
as Messiah. In the eschatological law court scene, he has pitted himself against the Temple.
When his prophecy of its destruction comes true, that event will demonstrate that he was
indeed the Messiah who had the authority over it. Mark 13:2 and its parallels thus makes
explicit the meaning of Mark 11:15–17. 'There will not be one stone upon another that will
not be cast down' " (511; cf. 353, 362, and elsewhere).

31. Ibid., 317.

32. Ibid., 389.

33. Ibid., 436.

order to make a historically persuasive case, Wright presents Jesus as a prophet whose vocation gradually unveils itself and who makes a "Pascalian wager" in going to Jerusalem to die. By setting limits to Jesus' knowledge, Wright puts to the side New Testament passages that suggest that Jesus possesses not only miraculous powers, but also knowledge and love—of God the Father, the Holy Spirit, and his fellow human beings—far exceeding that of the prophets. Wright does not ask the question of what kind of knowledge and love would enable Jesus to be the sinless one who can accomplish for all Israel, and for all humankind, eschatological communion with God. In this regard it is instructive that John's Gospel, which does ask such theological questions, has little place in Wright's project.

Even with this caveat, Wright's exposition assists us greatly in understanding what Christ's priestly action meant—namely, an eschatological sacrifice in which, as the new Temple, his followers would participate.[34] Indebted to Wright, numerous biblical scholars have followed Wright's basic interpretation while seeking to deepen and solidify certain aspects of it. I will discuss three such contributions in order to ascertain what they add to our theme of the priesthood of Christ.

---

34. See in this regard N. T. Wright, "The Lord's Prayer as a Paradigm for Christian Prayer," in *Into God's Presence: Prayer in the New Testament,* ed. Richard N. Longenecker (Grand Rapids, MI: Eerdmans, 2001), 132–54. He interprets "Give us this day our daily bread" (Matthew 6:11) as the food of the eschatological New Exodus: "Manna was not needed in Egypt. Nor would it be needed in the promised land. It is the food of inaugurated eschatology, the food that is needed because the kingdom has already broken in and because it is not yet consummated. The daily provision of manna signals that the Exodus has begun, but also that we are not yet living in the land" (143). Brant Pitre comments on Wright's remark: "It should go without saying that if this was the meaning Jesus intended for this petition, then he saw himself as the Jewish Messiah who would once again rain down the new manna from heaven, the 'food of inaugurated eschatology'" (Pitre, "The Lord's Prayer and the New Exodus," *Letter and Spirit* 2 [2006]: 69–96, at 87). Frances Young offers a contrasting position. She holds that the New Testament discussions of the Eucharist do not in fact reflect Jesus' own views. As she remarks of Jesus, "It is possible that he intended the symbols [bread and wine] to be interpreted as a prophecy of his vicarious death, as the [New Testament] traditions imply, but, in the light of the eschatological setting, I incline to the view that they were rather a symbolic guarantee of his presence with them at the Messianic feast when God would have triumphed and vindicated him in spite of death. This would naturally lead to the kind of eschatological fellowship-meal with the Risen Christ which seems to have been the character of the primitive Eucharist" (Young, *The Use of Sacrificial Ideas in Greek Christian Writers from the New Testament to John Chrysostom* [1979; Eugene, OR: Wipf and Stock, 2004], 245, fn. 12).

Steven M. Bryan

In his *Jesus and Israel's Traditions of Judgement and Restoration*, Steven Bryan observes, "The scholar whose overall hypothesis about Jesus is perhaps most similar to that proposed here is N. T. Wright."[35] As one would expect, he nonetheless advances some critiques of Wright's interpretation. Above all, he casts into doubt Wright's use of the term *exile*: in Second-Temple Jewish texts, according to Bryan, exile meant literal exile from the land of Israel, and even this literal exile was minimized in some texts, which postulated an "extended age of wrath" that subsumed the literal exile "within a much longer period of divine punishment on Israel."[36] By contrast, Wright applies *exile* also to Israel's bondage to Roman rule and downplays the partial restoration, or return from Babylonian Exile, achieved under Ezra and Nehemiah.[37] Bryan also mentions a possible difficulty in Wright's account of Jesus' proclamation of judgment upon the nation of Israel, namely that Wright's account does not sufficiently address Jesus' view of the *final* judgment and the relationship of national judgment to the restoration of Israel: "Wright seems to invest this national judgement with climactic significance—he does not portray it as a return to exile—but it is decidedly not final judgement to which Jesus refers."[38] Leaving aside the issue of final judgment, Bryan argues through the course of the

---

35. Steven M. Bryan, *Jesus and Israel's Traditions of Judgement and Restoration* (Cambridge: Cambridge University Press, 2002), 12.

36. Ibid., 18, 19. In such texts, Bryan notes, one finds "not an expansion of exile to allow its use in an extended sense, but a reduction of the exile's significance in order to ameliorate the difficulty created by the prophets' close association of exile and redemption" (19). Bryan also points out that some Second-Temple Jews believed that Israel had indeed repented, and yet God had delayed the restoration nonetheless. Whereas in Wright "a continued sense of exile is inferred from a continued hope of restoration," Bryan states that "at least some Jews did not believe that the delay in the fulfillment of restoration promises was an indication of God's continued disapprobation, whether under the rubric of exile or otherwise. One of the primary ways in which Jewish writers dealt with the problem of delay was to attribute the time of the End to the sovereign mystery of the divine counsel: the End will come at the appointed time. Such a view was not fully compatible with the belief that the End was contingent on Israel's repentance, though repentance could itself be regarded as a divinely ordained precursor to restoration. But at various times, some came to believe that Israel had repented. For these, suffering was no longer simply God's chastisement of the rebellious nation but rather the unjust affliction of the righteous, and the delay of restoration was ascribed to God's inscrutable decree" (19).

37. Bryan seeks to distinguish "ongoing exile" from "incomplete restoration," favoring the latter (16).

38. Ibid., 4.

book that Jesus' understanding of national judgment corresponded to a radical reconfiguration of Second-Temple Jewish understanding of the restoration of Israel.[39] In Bryan's view, Jesus announces that a new Israel has been formed, the rejection of which brings about (simultaneously) national judgment.[40]

This thesis merits our attention. According to Bryan, Jesus held that "even constitutional features of the eschaton—the shape of eschatological Israel, the purity of God's people, and even the Temple of the eschaton—were already coming into existence."[41] Those who rejected "Israel's eschatological reconstitution" were undergoing the national judgment. Bryan states, "In Jesus' view, the eschatological reconstitution of Israel had already taken place through the creation by John of a penitent remnant. And on this remnant, and those individuals who join it, Jesus bestows the blessings which make it the eschatological remnant."[42] From this perspective, not the reconstitution of the 12 tribes, but rather John the Baptist's establishment of a purified remnant accomplished the restoration; Jesus' task, then, was to make the eschatological blessings available to this purified remnant,

---

39. Bryan remarks, "Previous prophets of national judgement had anticipated that Israel's restoration would follow judgement. It might, therefore, be expected that the announcement of national judgement would carry with it a message that restoration had been postponed by the necessity of further purgation. However, this does not appear to be the case with Jesus; his announcement of national judgement in no way meant that Israel's restoration had been pushed into the future" (243). For Jesus, national restoration, the formation of the eschatological Israel, was already occurring (cf. 129).

40. In Bryan's words,

> If, for the prophets, national judgement meant a disruption in the nation's experience of the blessings of election, it was nevertheless possible for them to affirm the continuity of Israel's election through judgement. This continuity of election would be experienced in the restoration of Israel after judgement. For Jesus, however, the climactic nature of Israel's judgement changed the nature of Israel's restoration and the sense in which Israel's election could be regarded as one of unbroken continuity. No longer was restoration to be experienced after judgement; such a scenario could not be possible, for in Jesus' view the announcement of Israel's judgement meant the end of Israel's election. But, paradoxically, even as the proclamation of climactic judgement brought Israel's election to an end, it allowed Jesus to reassert the continuity of Israel's election: the pronouncement of Israel's judgement carried with it the announcement of a new act of election. And who could question the absolute freedom of divine grace in determining the shape of the Israel constituted by this eschatological action of God? In Jesus' view, the restoration of the apostate nation could include even apostate individuals and could occur even while the pronouncement of unavoidable national judgement still stood. (87; cf. 130 and elsewhere)

41. Ibid., 243.

42. Ibid., 239; cf. the detailed argument of ch. 4, 88–129.

the new Israel.[43] With respect to national judgment, Bryan connects Jesus' weeping over Jerusalem's failure to recognize the eschatological fulfillment (Luke 19:41–44) with the fact that Jesus promises no "sign" other than the "sign of Jonah," which Bryan interprets as national judgment.[44] Similarly, Bryan holds, Jesus' parables about the vineyard warn of national judgment because Israel has failed to recognize the eschatological fulfillment, and Jesus associates with "sinners" because some of those thought to be "sinners" have in fact recognized the fulfillment brought by John.[45]

How does Jesus make the eschatological blessings available to those who have recognized the time of fulfillment? Bryan notes, "Central to the eschatological hopes of Second-Temple Judaism were the beliefs that Israel would be reassembled in a pure Land and reconstituted as a pure people. A crucial question, then, is how Jesus' message of national restoration *and* judgement affected his intentions concerning the purity and Land of Israel."[46] In answering this question, Bryan first discusses how the Pharisees and priests understood the degrees of ritual purity required of Israelites, and critiques E. P. Sanders's failure to apprehend the relationship between purity/holiness and election.[47] He then explores texts in 2 Maccabees and Jubilees that emphasize the importance of Exodus 19:6 for Second-Temple theologies of restoration. In this regard he concludes that restorationist programs assumed that all (eschatological) Israel would take on some, though not all, of the purity requirements for consecrated priests. He comments as well upon Zechariah 14 and Isaiah 66, which suggest that in eschatological Israel "the domain of the holy has become universal."[48]

Turning to Jesus' own views of purity/holiness, Bryan argues that Jesus denies that extra bodily purity requirements are needed for the restoration, as the Pharisees thought. Bryan also argues that Jesus

---

43. For a summary of the argument, see ibid., 128.

44. For Bryan's argument in this regard, see ibid., 41f.

45. Bryan states, "Opposition to Jesus' consorting with 'the wicked' was not prompted by pugnacious self-righteousness. Rather, Jesus' declaration that 'sinners' were among those already enjoying the blessings of the kingdom would have been seen as a hindrance to Israel's preparation for eschatological restoration, not least for its inclusion of those who on some understandings of Torah were definitely out" (ibid., 68).

46. Ibid., 130.

47. Ibid., 145.

48. Ibid., 154.

does not intend to reconstitute the 12 tribes in the land. Instead, Bryan thinks, Jesus held that "God's people would only be constituted as a pure society through the sanctification of the whole earth by an eschatological action of God."[49] After reviewing numerous texts, both biblical and extra-biblical, that identify the Messiah as the builder of the eschatological Temple, Bryan suggests that the best way to interpret Jesus' cleansing of the Temple is as a condemnation of the entirety of the Second Temple. For Jesus, God's eschatological action has arrived, and yet the Temple (like the fig tree that incurs Jesus' curse) continues to function as of old.[50] What kind of Temple, then, does Jesus require? Bryan proposes that Jesus, as Messiah, intends to build the eschatological Temple himself, a temple not made by human hands.[51] This eschatological Temple will bestow the blessings of the eschaton.[52]

What, for our purposes, does Bryan add to Wright's narrative? Recall that Wright argues that Jesus understood his death as

---

49. Ibid., 188.

50. See ibid., 222, and elsewhere. Cf. Bruce Chilton's view of Jesus and the Temple: Chilton, *The Temple of Jesus*, 91–136. Writing before Wright's work, Chilton argues that "Jesus' sacrificial program is an enactment of Zechariah's, insofar as the notions of immediate cleansing (resulting in purity), forgiveness, and the worship of all Israel in Jerusalem without trade are actualized. Jesus' distinctiveness seems to lie in the way he connected that eschatological program with inclusive definitions of purity and forgiveness, with the issue of how sacrifices were to be offered, and with his own ministry. In terms of the typology of sacrifice that has been developed, his program joins the normative pattern of the ideological connection of sacrifice and the covenant, where the covenant is understood to include the definitive and eschatological fulfillment of the promises to Israel" (136).

51. In this regard Bryan pays close attention to Mark 14:55–59. Bryan observes that for E. P. Sanders, Mark 14:58 "indicates an expectation that God himself would shortly construct a physical, eschatological Temple in Jerusalem" (Bryan, *Jesus and Israel's Traditions of Judgement and Restoration*, 232). In response to Sanders, Bryan argues that "Sanders has simply assumed that if Jesus spoke of an eschatological Temple he necessarily meant a new, physical Temple in Jerusalem, an assumption which would appear to be unwarranted in view of the foregoing survey of Jewish expectations concerning the eschatological Temple" (ibid.). Bryan points to Jewish texts that suggest that "the eschatological Temple would not be a Temple made with hands precisely because it was the sort of structure which could not be made with hands" (233).

52. Bryan points out that "to argue that Jesus probably did not expect a physical Temple is not to specify the sort of non-physical Temple that Jesus did expect. And here the sources permit us to say nothing more" (ibid., 235). Bryan also takes up the question of the early Christians' continued participation in the Temple cult. He states, "In view of the fact that only a relatively small portion of the cult was devoted to the expiation of sin, it is entirely conceivable that a Jewish Christian could have believed that Jesus' death obviated other forms of expiatory sacrifice and yet see no contradiction between this belief and continued participation in the rest of the cultic system" (234, emphasis his). As he remarks, Paul's action in Acts 21:23–26 "reveals the most stalwart defender of the exclusivity and finality of Christ's expiatory death within early Christianity freely offering non-expiatory sacrifices" (234, fn. 136).

"sacrificial"—a death on behalf of all Israel so as to establish the eschatological kingdom—and that Jesus envisioned a new liturgical worship that would accomplish for his followers what the Temple sacrifices sought to accomplish. To this schema, Bryan adds a focus on John the Baptist's preparation of a righteous remnant, a preparation that Jesus then fulfills by bestowing the eschatological blessings, namely the sanctification of the entire world. Jesus' understanding of "restoration," as Bryan sees it, involves a radical change for Israel.[53] The change results from the pouring out of holiness upon the whole world through Jesus' eschatological building of a new "Temple." Without diverging markedly from Wright's narrative, then, Bryan presses us to inquire more deeply into the mediation of holiness in eschatological Israel. What is the connection between Jesus' eschatological action, the new "Temple" that he builds, and his followers? If the "restoration" of Israel means a pouring out of holiness upon the whole world, and thus a radically new "Israel" and "Temple," how do the followers of Jesus receive and mediate the eschatological holiness brought about by his actions? Bryan thus places emphasis on the sanctifying dimension of Jesus' priestly action.

Scot McKnight

Scot McKnight offers a painstaking, cautious historical-critical exploration of how Jesus—the Jesus about whom the New Testament authors wrote, as distinguished at least conceptually from Jesus as depicted by the New Testament authors—might have understood his approaching death.[54] McKnight's conclusion to *Jesus and His Death*

---

53. For another view, rooted in Acts (in light of Isaiah), of the nature of Jesus' "restoration" of Israel, see David W. Pao, *Acts and the Isaianic New Exodus* (Grand Rapids, MI: Baker Academic, 2002), ch. 4. Pao relies upon N. T. Wright's thesis of Israel's ongoing exile (143–46).

54. In this section I focus on McKnight's *Jesus and His Death*. For a more popular treatment of the topic by the same author, see Scot McKnight, *A Community Called Atonement* (Nashville, TN: Abingdon Press, 2007). Indebted to Boersma's *Violence, Hospitality, and the Cross*, especially 99–114, McKnight argues in *A Community Called Atonement* that appreciating the various theologies of Christ's cross requires recognizing "the metaphorical nature of atonement language" (39). Although I would suggest that this language is at its best also metaphysical, I agree with McKnight's key proposal that "atonement is *crux et*—the cross and . . . the resurrection and Pentecost, each set into the incarnation and the manifestation of God in the ecclesial community" (53). Boersma rightly emphasizes "God's hospitality—his absolutely unconditional desire to draw us into eternal fellowship with him" (Boersma, *Violence, Hospitality, and the Cross*, 114).

exhibits this caution: only claims that seem incontrovertible even from a skeptical perspective survive. Consistently grounding himself in Mark's Gospel, McKnight proposes that historical study can verify five claims about how Jesus himself understood his approaching death. First, Jesus desired, at least in some sense, to avoid death. Second, Jesus nonetheless expected a premature death. Third, Jesus thought that this premature death belonged to God's plan for Israel. Fourth, Jesus' understanding of "the *fate of a prophet*" in Israel informed his expectation of a premature death.[55] Fifth, Jesus expected eventual vindication by "his Father" and urged his followers therefore not to fear risking their own lives.

McKnight admits that these conclusions are quite minimal. If this is all that we can say about how Jesus might have understood his own death, we have said no more than might be said about any human being who accepts martyrdom. Yet, he argues that on the basis of these five conclusions, we can move to more substantial historical-critical claims about how Jesus would have envisioned his approaching death. McKnight provides three such claims, which fit into the framework that we have seen in Wright and Bryan. The first claim links Jesus and John the Baptist, and argues that Jesus' understanding of his approaching death would have been shaped by his relationship to John the Baptist and by John the Baptist's beheading. The second claim holds that Jesus could not have seen his death as an "individualistic" event, an event involving only himself, as it were. If Jesus thought that the fate of others was bound up in his death, then in some sense his death was "a *representative* death."[56] McKnight expands upon this claim: "It is indeed possible, as I judge the evidence, that Jesus saw his death as vicarious; if not, however, the evidence is clear that he believed he was the representative Israelite: his death paved the way for others."[57] As evidence for this second claim, McKnight twice cites Jesus' action at the Last Supper. If Jesus "goes to meet his death having asked his followers to share in his body and his blood,"[58] then this request must mean that Jesus envisioned others as participating, in some sense, in

---

55. McKnight, *Jesus and His Death*, 336 (emphasis his).

56. Ibid., 337 (emphasis his).

57. Ibid.

58. Ibid.

his death—and thus also envisioned his death as a representative death, in which participation would be meaningful.

The third and final claim put forward by McKnight is that "Jesus saw his death as the *beginning of the eschatological ordeal*."[59] According to McKnight's reading of Jesus' place within Second-Temple Judaism, Jesus anticipated an "eschatological tribulation" and "knew (as a Jew) that the tribulation was to lead into the kingdom."[60] Jesus, in other words, expected that his death would be the trigger that inaugurated the kingdom of God, by bringing about the tribulation that was to occur before the final consummation. This separates Jesus, in McKnight's view, from other prophets, including John the Baptist, who did not envision their deaths as triggering the eschaton. Thus Jesus' self-understanding in approaching his death was that of someone who saw himself as more than a prophet and thereby as the one who could represent Israel in the day of tribulation.

Can more be said? McKnight thinks that Mark 10:45 and 14:24 provide sufficient evidence for two further conclusions. Mark 10:45 describes Jesus as saying to his disciples, "For the Son of man came not to be served but to serve, and to give his life as a ransom for many." In McKnight's view, the self-understanding implied by this text has its roots not in the servant songs of Isaiah, but in Daniel 7's presentation of the figure of the Son of Man. Seen in this light, Jesus' death has a "corporate" dimension, since his task is to lead "his followers through death and into vindication before the Ancient of Days."[61]

How might Jesus have understood this "corporate" dimension, in which others participate in Jesus' representative death so as to be vindicated in the eschatological tribulation? McKnight argues that the evidence of Mark 14:24 suggests that "Jesus *anticipated Pesah* in the last supper."[62] In anticipating the Passover, Jesus presented himself to his followers as the true Passover lamb. His followers could participate in the sacrificial death of the true Passover lamb by partaking of the bread and cup, which Jesus interprets "as his body and his blood."[63] Not only would Jesus' blood, as the blood of the true Passover lamb,

---

59. Ibid.
60. Ibid.
61. Ibid., 338.
62. Ibid.
63. Ibid.

"protect his followers from the imminent judgment of God" (a judgment against Israel), but more particularly it would do so through their partaking of the body and blood of the Lamb. As McKnight puts it, "Jesus' theory of atonement then is that his own death, and his followers' participation in that death by ingestion, protects his followers from the Day of YHWH. . . . As the avenging angel of the Passover in Egypt 'passed over' the first-born children whose fathers had smeared blood on the door, so the Father of Jesus would 'pass over' those followers who ingested Jesus' body and blood."[64]

McKnight's historical-critical analysis, then, attains not only to the conclusion that Jesus understood his death as "representative" and "corporate," but also to a theology of the Eucharist united to Jesus' own understanding of his approaching death. The Eucharist, on this view, is Jesus' way of enabling his followers to participate in the true Passover—his death, his sacrificial body and blood—and thereby be spared the eschatological tribulation so as to attain the eschatological kingdom. McKnight is somewhat unclear regarding whether Jesus expected this Passover meal involving "his own death, and his followers' participation in that death by ingestion," to continue after Jesus' vindication. For McKnight, Jesus anticipated that "when that kingdom arrived Jesus would once again resume table fellowship (bread and wine) with his followers."[65] While McKnight does not specify how this resumed eschatological table fellowship comports with the ingestion of Jesus' sacrificial body and blood, nonetheless McKnight's contribution to our inquiry into Jesus' priesthood will be evident. Beginning from the methodological principles of historical criticism, he adds a eucharistic dimension to Wright's emphasis on Jesus' enactment of the eschatological promises of YHWH and Bryan's emphasis on the outpouring of sanctification by means of Jesus' messianic and eschatological Temple-building.

---

64. Ibid., 339. For theological reflections on the eschatological dimension of the Eucharist see, e.g., William J. Hill, "The Eucharist as Eschatological Presence," *Communio* 4 (1977): 306–20; M. Francis Mannion, "Rejoice, Heavenly Powers! The Renewal of Liturgical Doxology," *Pro Ecclesia* 12 (2003): 37–60, especially 38–43.

65. McKnight, *Jesus and His Death*, 339.

Brant Pitre

Brant Pitre's *Jesus, the Tribulation, and the End of the Exile: Restoration Eschatology and the Origin of the Atonement* also augments the schema that Wright provides. Pitre investigates the emergence in the late Second-Temple period of conceptions of an eschatological tribulation, and asks how such conceptions might help us understand Jesus' words and deeds.[66] While noting that Wright's work constitutes "one of the most important dialogue partners in this study,"[67] Pitre attaches to his Introduction an "excursus" that differentiates his understanding of the "end of the exile" from Wright's (one recalls Bryan's similar clarifications, although Bryan moves in a somewhat different direction from Pitre). In a nutshell, Pitre emphasizes that the *literal* exile of the people of Israel had not come to an end in 539 BC, as Wright supposes. Rather, the exile continued for the ten northern tribes who had been carried off by the Assyrians in 722 BC. Pitre argues, "Wright has the *right insight* but the *wrong exile.* The Jews of the first century were certainly waiting for 'the End of the Exile'—but not the Babylonian Exile. Rather, they were waiting for the end of the Assyrian Exile, as we saw with the quote from Josephus."[68] In Pitre's view, Jesus, following the prophets, announced (among other things) the eschatological ingathering of all 12 tribes.

Interpreting Mark 10:45, Pitre holds that it does indeed bear reference to Isaiah 53's "suffering servant," but he explores the passage primarily in light of Daniel 7 and 9. He suggests that three points from Daniel and other prophets are paramount: "1. The Son of Man, as Messiah, will suffer and die in the tribulation. 2. The purpose of the sufferings of the tribulation is to atone for Israel's sins. 3. The forgiveness of Israel's sins will bring about the End of the Exile."[69] The third point, he notes, should be understood in terms of the ingathering of the ten northern tribes, scattered among the nations:

---

66. See Pitre, *Jesus, the Tribulation, and the End of the Exile: Restoration Eschatology and the Origin of the Atonement* (Grand Rapids, MI: Baker Academic, 2005). In addition to the work of Albert Schweitzer and more recently N. T. Wright, Pitre draws significantly upon the work of Dale Allison, especially his *The End of the Ages Has Come: An Early Interpretation of the Passion and Resurrection of Jesus* (Philadelphia: Fortress Press, 1985).

67. Pitre, *Jesus, the Tribulation, and the End of the Exile,* 19.

68. Ibid., 35.

69. Ibid., 398. Cf. Pitre, "The 'Ransom for Many,' the New Exodus, and the End of the Exile: Redemption as the Restoration of All Israel (Mark 10:35–45)," *Letter and Spirit* 1 (2005): 41–68.

Jesus understands his death as a "ransom" for these "many."[70] Was Jesus' sacrificial death, then, solely for the lost ten tribes or for the territorial reunification of Israel? Since the Jews remained scattered, was Jesus' death a failure?

Without directly raising such questions, Pitre seeks to show that what Jesus intended to bring about was "the *restoration of Israel in a final Passover*."[71] The Last Supper, viewed through this lens, thus functions as a "prophetic sign" of eschatological consummation in and through Jesus.[72] Pitre states in this regard that "Jesus reconfigured the Passover sacrifice around the offering of his own body and blood" and "did so in the presence of the Twelve disciples, representing the twelve tribes of Israel."[73] The first Passover had liberated Israel from

---

70. Pitre, *Jesus, the Tribulation, and the End of the Exile*, 398. Pitre states further on: "when Jesus gathered around him twelve disciples, he would have been making a striking, even startling prophetic statement: the time of the regathering of all Israel, including the lost ten tribes, was at hand" (434).

71. Ibid., 448 (emphasis his).

72. Ibid. Earlier Pitre remarks, "By means of the Last Supper, Jesus is engaging in a sacrificial act and prophetic sign intended to begin the re-gathering of the twelve tribes around himself and thereby bring about the restoration of Israel" (447). The eschatological importance of the Twelve is underestimated by Daniel Harrington, SJ, in his *The Church According to the New Testament*, 20f., 159f. For Harrington, "Jesus came to proclaim the kingdom of God, not to plan out an ecclesiastical organization or institution" (20), and "Jesus showed little concern for establishing the privileges and structural prerogatives of his first followers. What counted most was their willingness to be with Jesus and to share in his ministry and his cross. They were to adopt his simple lifestyle as they went from place to place and proclaimed the coming of God's kingdom. They were not appointed to preside over local communities. Instead, they were sent forth as 'apostles.' Jesus imparted his Spirit to those whom he chose to be his disciples" (21). Harrington grants that the Church that emerged was marked by "a continuity between Jesus' disciples who followed him before his death and Resurrection, and those who bore witness to him after his Resurrection. Also, the followers of Jesus carried on his practice of sharing meals with others as a sign pointing toward the coming kingdom of God" (22). This portrait of a group of men and women who, without "privileges and structural prerogatives," lived simply and shared meals together to signify their hope for the future, seems to miss much of what Jesus was doing. Harrington thinks of Jesus as launching "a small Jewish religious reform movement" (23).

73. Pitre, *Jesus, the Tribulation, and the End of the Exile*, 448. See also Pitre, "The Lord's Prayer and the New Exodus," where he provides numerous texts from Second-Temple Jewish sources to show that they expected that "when the Messiah finally came, he would cause the manna to come down from heaven again" (85). Pitre draws the Second-Temple texts from a variety of sources, including James Charlesworth, *The Old Testament Pseudepigrapha*, 2 vols. (Garden City: Doubleday, 1983); Raymond E. Brown, *The Gospel According to John* (New York: Doubleday, 1966); C. H. Dodd, *The Interpretation of the Fourth Gospel* (Cambridge: Cambridge University Press, 1953); Craig S. Keener, *The Gospel of John*, 2 vols. (Peabody, MA: Hendrickson, 2003); Bruce J. Malina, *The Palestinian Manna Tradition: The Manna Tradition in the Palestinian Targums and Its Relationship to the New Testament* (Leiden: Brill, 1968); B. Gärtner, *John 6 and the Jewish Passover* (Lund: Gleerup, 1959).

Egyptian slavery, but had not succeeded in establishing the people in the holiness necessary for God's continued indwelling and their continued unity. By contrast, the new Passover, accomplished by the sacrificial offering of Jesus' body and blood, would establish the people in such holiness: as an *"eschatological Passover,"* it "would do everything the first Passover had done, but which all those since the Exile had failed to do: atone for the sins of Israel, set in motion a New Exodus, and bring about the End of the Exile."[74] The participation of the Twelve disciples in the new Passover constituted by Jesus' sacrificial body and blood indicates, Pitre thinks, that Jesus anticipated his Passover would result in the ingathering of the ten lost tribes. Pitre suggests that Jesus expected this ingathering to be the literal return of the members of all 12 tribes of Israel to Zion, the eschatological uniting of the people of God. For our purposes, the crucial element emphasized by Pitre is the eschatological unity of the people of God brought about by Jesus' new Passover, a unity that Jesus reconstitutes around himself through his Twelve disciples (whether or not Jesus required the literal return of the ten lost tribes).

Pitre inquires, however, as to whether it is accurate to call the Last Supper a Passover meal. As he points out, even if one accepts John's chronology and holds that Jesus celebrated the Last Supper "before the feast of Passover" (John 13:1) and 24 hours before other Jews consumed the Passover meal, "the meal was nonetheless paschal in character, since *it still took place on the 'day' of Passover* (14 Nisan), which began, of course, the evening before the feast, not in the morning."[75] As descriptions of what is "proleptically" a Passover meal, then, the Last Supper accounts make clear that Jesus replaces the Passover lamb's flesh and blood, along with their liberative significance, with his own body and blood. Pitre therefore concludes, as we have

---

74. Pitre, *Jesus, the Tribulation, and the End of the Exile,* 448 (emphasis his). See also 443–44 on the notion of an "eschatological Passover," as well as Pitre, "The Lord's Prayer and the New Exodus," 94: "The *peirasmos* that is spoken of by Jesus in Mark 14:38 is not merely the coming period of eschatological tribulation, it is also an eschatological Passover, which is intrinsically linked to the prophetic sign Jesus has just enacted in the Last Supper. Hence, the 'cup' of which he speaks in Gethsemane and the Upper Room are one and the same: the cup of peirasmos and the cup of the paschal tribulation which will bring about the redemption of Israel and, therefore, a new Exodus." The eucharistic "cup" is the "cup" of his sacrificial Passover that accomplishes the New Exodus.

75. Pitre, *Jesus, the Tribulation, and the End of the Exile,* 442 (emphasis his).

seen, that "Jesus is *prophetically reconstituting the Passover sacrifice around his own suffering and death*, with himself as the new Passover lamb."[76]

Clearly, there are many similarities between Pitre's account and the positions of Wright, Bryan, and McKnight summarized above. For our purposes, however, Pitre gives added weight to two aspects of Jesus' priestly (Paschal) action: its sacrificial character, and its unitive character. Precisely as the "eschatological" Passover sacrifice, Jesus' self-offering intends to *unite* the previously fragmented people of God. This emphasis on the actual *unity* of the people of God recalls to mind a key task of cultic priesthood; namely, to bring about communion in unity. Although Pitre hypothesizes that Jesus saw this unity as the restoration of the literal unity of the 12 tribes of Israel, Pitre's emphasis on Jesus' priestly effort to establish the unity of the people of God expresses a crucial aspect of New Testament priesthood.

What therefore have we learned from Wright as followed in diverse ways by Bryan, McKnight, and Pitre? For these exegetes, with their differing emphases, Jesus' death constitutes a priestly action that is eschatological, sacrificial/eucharistic, sanctifying, and unitive. The next question, it will be clear, is how Christian theology of Christ's priesthood should integrate these four dimensions. As Pitre states,

> . . . at the level of theology, the link between the ransom saying and the restoration of Israel has the potential to open new doors in contemporary discussion of soteriology in general and the doctrine of the atonement in particular. It is widely known that the towering figure of St. Anselm and

---

76. Ibid., 443 (emphasis his). Following René Girard and Gil Bailie, Mark Heim argues that "the anthropological role of the church is to undermine the structure of sacred violence by keeping before our eyes the reality of the scapegoating process by which Jesus died, and then to illustrate a way to live without sacrifice, based on the way that Jesus lived" (Heim, *Saved from Sacrifice: A Theology of the Cross* [Grand Rapids, MI: Erdmans, 2006], 235). But Jesus' active way of living included his self-sacrificial cross; he was no mere passive victim of violence. Sacramental participation in Christ's sacrifice forms an active community of charity in which persons cleave not to their own lives but to God, and therefore can actively offer their lives in loving service (not victimization) to others. As Paul puts it, "We know that our old self was crucified with him so that the sinful body might be destroyed, and we might no longer be enslaved to sin" (Romans 6:6) and "we are children of God, and if children, then heirs, heirs of God and fellow heirs of Christ, provided we suffer with him in order that we may also be glorified with him" (Romans 8:17). See also L. Ann Jervis, "Becoming like God through Christ: Discipleship in Romans," in *Patterns of Discipleship in the New Testament*, ed. Richard N. Longenecker (Grand Rapids, MI: Eerdmans, 1996), 143–62; as well as in the same volume Gerald F. Hawthorne, "The Imitation of Christ: Discipleship in Philippians," 163–79. Hawthorne remarks, "In the divine economy of things one receives by giving, one is served by serving, one finds life by losing one's life, one is exalted by taking the lowly place" (178).

his influential formulation of the theory of substitutionary atonement in *Cur Deus Homo* has been strongly criticized for some time; yet many questions remain regarding how to understand this most central of Christian doctrines. In light of this situation, what may be needed now is a fresh reformulation of the discussion, one which draws directly on biblical language and imagery, so that the "sacred page" might truly be "the soul of sacred theology." . . . My hope is that theologians interested in this fundamental soteriological issue might also find these biblical categories helpful and illuminating for future discussion and reflection.[77]

How might one open these "new doors in contemporary discussion of soteriology in general and the doctrine of the atonement in particular," and offer "a fresh reformulation of the discussion, one which draws directly on biblical language and imagery"? It may seem that I am shirking the task when I propose that the "fresh reformulation" may best come about through an engagement with Aquinas's theology of Christ the priest. Yet, the "fresh reformulation" that is needed is one that unites Aquinas's insights into the biblical witness (insights drawn from a wide range of patristic and medieval exegete-theologians) with contemporary historical-critical contextualizations.

AQUINAS ON THE PRIESTHOOD OF JESUS CHRIST

Does Aquinas recognize and develop the four dimensions in his treatment in *Summa Theologiae* III, q. 22 of the priesthood of Christ?[78] Before taking up this question, I first ask why Aquinas considers Jesus to fulfill the role of "priest." After this introductory reflection, I examine Aquinas's theology of Christ's priesthood from the perspective of the four dimensions identified in the contemporary exegesis that we have surveyed.

Jesus the Priest

Wright locates his understanding of Jesus firmly within the context of ancient Israel, and Aquinas does the same. In asking whether the Messiah should be a "priest," Aquinas gives three reasons why one might

---

77. Pitre, "The Lord's Prayer and the New Exodus," 67–68.

78. A version of this section appears as "Christ the Priest: An Exploration of Sth III, q. 22," *The Thomist* 71 (2007).

answer in the negative. Each of these reasons expresses a spiritualization of Christ by which Christ is set in opposition to Israel.

The first reason is that Christ is far greater than the angels
(Hebrews 1:4). Aquinas quotes Zechariah 3:1, "Then he showed me
Joshua the high priest standing before the angel of the Lord."[79] The
angel is greater than the high priest of Israel, and the angel, by
contrast to a high priest of Israel, offers no sin-offering or cultic worship. If the Messiah is far greater than the angels, then surely the
Messiah, too, would stand above the kinds of cultic offerings for
which the high priest of Israel was consecrated to offer. On this logic,
the Messiah should not descend, as it were, to the level of the high
priests of Israel, who offered bloody sacrifices.[80] Rather, the Messiah
should raise the level of worship to that of the angels, an intelligible
worship of praise, as befits a Messiah who is greater than the angels.
From the premise that "a priest is less than an angel," the objection
draws the conclusion that "it is unfitting that Christ should be a priest."[81]

---

79. ST III, q. 22, a. 1, obj. 1.

80. Although some of her exegesis seems a stretch, Margaret Barker has shown that some
late Second-Temple non-canonical texts envision a high priesthood that attains to the rank of
the angels. She comments, for example, regarding a text from 2 Enoch, "The process of
passing from earthly to heavenly life was indicated by the change of garments, from earthly
clothing to garments of glory, and the oil conferred the Spirit, Wisdom, Divinity. In other
words, Enoch the high priest was resurrected and transformed into an angel by his consecration
as a high priest. It is one of the complications of the Hebrew Scriptures that to consecrate, as
in the English, is literally 'to make holy', but Hebrew has the added complication that angels
can be known as holy ones. When a high priest was consecrated, he was literally made into a
holy one. Moses' radiant face as he came down from Sinai (Exod. 34.29–35) is an early
example of this belief in apotheosis, and also an early example of Moses absorbing the traditions
of the temple" (Barker, "The Angel Priesthood," in her *The Great High Priest: The Temple Roots
of Christian Liturgy* [New York: T. & T. Clark, 2003], 103–45, at 129).

81. ST III, q. 22, a. 1, obj. 1. For discussion of Aquinas's treatment of Hebrews 1:4 in
his *Commentary on the Epistle to the Hebrews*, see Antoine Guggenheim, *Jésus Christ, Grand
Prêtre de l'ancienne et de la nouvelle Alliance. Étude du* Commentaire *de saint Thomas d'Aquin sur
l'Épitre aux Hébreux* (Paris: Parole et Silence, 2004), 415f. Thomas G. Weinandy, OFM CAP,
writes of Aquinas's Commentary: "what Aquinas does do is take seriously the inbuilt logical
structure of the Letter to the Hebrews and in so commenting on the first part of the Letter
(chapters 1–10) he clearly articulates two interrelated aspects that are essential to the Letter's
argument: first, the fulfilment of Old Testament revelation as found in the supremacy of the
Incarnation and, secondly, the ensuing fulfillment and supremacy of Christ's priestly sacrifice"
(Weinandy, "The Supremacy of Christ: Aquinas' *Commentary on Hebrews*," in *Aquinas on
Scripture: An Introduction to His Biblical Commentaries*, ed. Thomas G. Weinandy, OFM CAP,
Daniel A. Keating, and John P. Yocum [New York: T. & T. Clark, 2005], 223–44, at 225).
On Hebrews 1:4 see Weinandy, "The Supremacy of Christ," 230.

The second reason is that the Old Testament prefigures the New, and thus the realities of the New Testament—preeminently Christ—surpass the realities in the Old Testament that prefigured Christ, among them the Old Testament priesthood. Here Aquinas quotes Colossians 2:17 (to which we can add 2:16 by way of context): "Therefore let no one pass judgment on you in questions of food and drink or with regard to a festival or a new moon or a sabbath. These are only a shadow of what is to come; but the substance belongs to Christ."[82] Aquinas points out in this regard that it is significant that Christ did not descend from the tribe of Levi, to which the hereditary Old Testament priesthood belonged.[83] Christ is in no way a Jewish priest. The implication is that Christ's deeds cannot rightly be described as "priestly," since this would be to draw Christ once more into the ambit of the Old Testament priesthood, and to confuse the "figure" for the reality.

The third reason is that under the old covenant, God in his wisdom distinguished between lawgivers and priests. As Aquinas remarks, quoting Exodus 28, Moses was lawgiver, whereas his brother Aaron was priest. Why did God set up this distinction in his people Israel, if not to reveal something about the Messiah who was to fulfill and transform the law of Israel? In this respect Aquinas quotes the well-known prophecy from Jeremiah 31:33 (to which I add verses 31–32 and 34):

> Behold, the days are coming, says the Lord, when I will make a new covenant with the house of Israel and the house of Judah, not like the covenant which I made with their fathers when I took them by the hand to bring them out of the land of Egypt, my covenant which they broke, though I was their husband, says the Lord. But this is the covenant which I will make with the house of Israel after those days, says the Lord: I will put my law within them, and I will write it upon their hearts; and I will be their God, and they shall be my people. And no longer shall each man teach his neighbor and each his brother, saying, "Know the Lord," for they shall all know me, from the least of them to the greatest, says the Lord; for I will forgive their iniquity, and I will remember their sin no more.

---

82. Cf. Saint Thomas Aquinas, *Commentary on Colossians,* trans. Fabian Larcher, OP, ed. Daniel A. Keating (Naples, FL: Sapientia Press, 2006), nos. 118–21, pp. 65–67.

83. ST III, q. 22, a. 1, obj. 2.

The prophecy states that God will act again as lawgiver, but this time God will inscribe his law in the very heart of each member of Israel, so that all will know and follow the Lord. The actions of the lawgiver will suffice to accomplish the forgiveness of sins and the restoration of a holy people with whom God dwells intimately. If a lawgiver (a new and greater Moses) can accomplish so much, who needs a new and great Aaron, a new cultic priest? The inscription of divine wisdom in the heart, and the action of bloody cultic sacrifice, are obviously two quite different things. Since "Christ is the giver of the New Law," Aquinas concludes that "it is unfitting that Christ should be a priest."[84] Why would cultic worship, on the part of Christ or on the part of his followers, be necessary if God's wise law of love could be inscribed directly on the heart? A spiritual worship here seems entirely to replace cultic worship—as some modern readers of Jeremiah have also supposed. Although Aquinas does not quote it at this stage, one might also think of Jesus' words to the Samaritan woman in John 4:23–24, "But the hour is coming, and now is, when the true worshipers will worship the Father in spirit and truth, for such the Father seeks to worship him. God is spirit, and those who worship him must worship in spirit and truth."

Thus in all three objections raised by Aquinas to the description of Jesus as a "priest," the guiding theme is the surpassing of the carnal mode of the Old Testament, by the spiritual mode of the New— reflected already in the Old Testament through the ministry of the angels, the prophecies of a messiah, and the distinction between priest and lawgiver.[85]

---

84. Ibid., obj. 3.

85. For contemporary argumentation that cultic sacrifice, rooted in violence, has been abolished by Christ, see for instance the work of René Girard and those influenced by him. For Girard's approach, see especially his *Violence and the Sacred* (Baltimore: Johns Hopkins University Press, 1977); and idem, *The Scapegoat* (Baltimore: Johns Hopkins University Press, 1986). For work on sacrifice by theologians influenced by Girard, see, e.g., Raymond Schwager, *Brauchen wir einen Sündenbock? Gewalt und Erlösung in den biblishen Schriften* (Munich: Kösel, 1978); Gil Bailie, *Violence Unveiled: Humanity at the Crossroads* (New York: Crossroad, 1995); S. Mark Heim, *Saved from Sacrifice*. Hans Urs von Balthasar discusses Girard's approach in *Theo-Drama*, Vol. 4, *The Action*, trans. Graham Harrison (German 1980; San Francisco: Ignatius Press, 1994), 297–313. Von Balthasar points out the central weakness of Girard's approach: "God's forgiveness and the Cross (that is, the bearing of sin) cannot be left in mutual isolation: they are related. In this case, it will not be enough to follow Girard and Schwager in demythologizing the Old Testament picture of God so that he changes from a violent, wrathful God and becomes a powerless God who does not engage in retribution. What we

The High Priest of the Letter to the Hebrews

Aquinas's fundamental answer to these objections comes from the letter to the Hebrews, which freely uses the language of "high priest" to depict Christ's work: "Since then we have a great high priest who has passed through the heavens, Jesus, the Son of God, let us hold fast our confession" (Hebrews 4:14).[86] This verse from Hebrews, however, does not yet set forth what is meant by ascribing "priesthood" to Jesus. Aquinas defines priestly ministry as follows: "The office proper to a priest is to be a mediator between God and the people: to wit, inasmuch as He bestows Divine things on the people, wherefore *sacerdos* (priest) means a giver of sacred things (*sacra dans*)."[87] The priestly mediation of divine gifting occurs, Aquinas goes on to say, in two ways.

First, priestly mediation occurs through faithful communication of divine teaching: "according to Mal. ii. 7: *They shall seek the law at his*, i.e. the priest's, *mouth.*" This section of Malachi, which takes the

---

have, in fact, is a new form of the problem latent in both Old and New Covenants: What is the relationship between God's love and his justice, particularly in the case of the Cross? God's justice, which Girard never acknowledges as something primal, is evidently quite different from power. If we recognize this, Anselm's presentation of the problem acquires a new significance" (312). Yet von Balthasar agrees with Girard, mistakenly I think, that the incarnate Son is a "scapegoat." See also the biblical scholar Bruce Chilton's extended survey and critique of Girard's view of sacrifice, in Chilton, *The Temple of Jesus*, 15–42, and Appendix 1. In Chilton's view, the effort to understand sacrifice in any exhaustive fashion is misguided: "Now that vigorous efforts have been made for better than a century to 'explain' sacrifice in that manner, that is, by locating a primal or original explanation, and now that no such effort has won support, there is some practical warrant to consider the possibility that no such explanation exists" (39). Chilton grants that "violence, its concealment, its justification, and its propagation are involved within institutions of sacrifice," but he denies that "violence may be identified with sacrifice, in both its ritual and mythic components" (27).

86. Quoted by Aquinas in ST I, q. 22, a. 1, *sed contra.* On Jesus' priesthood according to Aquinas's reading of Hebrews 9, see Antoine Guggenheim, *Jésus Christ, Grand Prêtre*, Part II, ch. 7. Aquinas focuses on Christ's priestly action in discussing Hebrews 9:11–14: see Guggenheim, *Jésus Christ, Grand Prêtre*, 286–307. See also Gilles Berceville, OP, "Le sacerdoce du Christ dans le Commentaire de l'épître aux Hébreux de saint Thomas d'Aquin," *Revue Thomiste* 99 (1999): 143–58; Mario Caprioli, OCD, "Il sacerdozio di Cristo nella Somma Theologica e nel *Commento Super Epistolam ad Hebraeos*," in *Storia del tomismo* (Vatican City: Libreria Editrice Vaticana, 1992), 96–105; Thomas Weinandy, "The Supremacy of Christ," 236–40.

87. ST III, q. 22, a. 1. See also Serge-Thomas Bonino, OP, "Le sacerdoce comme institution naturelle selon saint Thomas d'Aquin," *Revue Thomiste* 99 (1999): 33–57; Gérard Remy, "Sacerdoce et médiation chez saint Thomas," *Revue Thomiste* 99 (1999): 101–18; and Roger Nutt's "From Within the Mediation of Christ: The Place of Christ in the Christian Moral and Sacramental Life According to St. Thomas Aquinas," *Nova et Vetera* 5 (2007):817–41.

form of a warning from the Lord, has to do with the mission of priests to teach the truth about God and about the covenant of life.

One form of the priestly mediation of divine gifting, therefore, consists in the communication of divine instruction or teaching. The second form involves the mediation of human offerings to God, both thanksgiving/praise/petition offerings and sin offerings. Following Hebrews, Aquinas states that a priest "offers up the people's prayers to God, and, in a manner, makes satisfaction to God for their sins; wherefore the Apostle says (Hebrews v. 1): *Every high-priest taken from among men is ordained for men in the things that appertain to God, that he may offer up gifts and sacrifices for sins*."[88] These "gifts and sacrifices," even when offered by human beings, come from God in the sense that God creates and sustains everything in being. The very offering of these "gifts and sacrifices," furthermore, is an exercise in divine gifting because the offering does not change God, but rather changes the offerers vis-à-vis God. God gifts human beings by enabling us to offer our gifts to him. In turn, our sacrifices to God aim to restore us to justice and holiness, so that we can dwell with God.

If this is what Hebrews means by the fullness of the priestly office—namely, mediating God's gifting and the people's (healing and deifying) participation in this gifting—Christ, says Aquinas, fulfills this office most perfectly.[89] Just as the Levitical priests taught the Torah and offered sacrifices on behalf of the people, Christ mediates the divine gifts to us both by his teaching and by his offering of the perfect sacrifice on the cross. To describe this twofold work, Aquinas turns to two biblical texts:

---

88. ST III, q. 22, a. 1. For discussion of Aquinas's treatment of this verse in his *Commentary on the Epistle to the Hebrews*, comparing Christ's priesthood to the Aaronic priesthood, see Guggenheim, *Jésus Christ, Grand Prêtre*, 159–67. See also Albert Vanhoye, sj, *Old Testament Priests and the New Priest According to the New Testament*, trans. J. Bernard Orchard, osb (French 1980; Petersham, MA: St. Bede's Publications, 1986), 116–20. Vanhoye argues that the text describes the high priesthood, not the Jewish priesthood in general.

89. For further discussion see Jean-Pierre Torrell, op, "Le sacerdoce du Christ dans la Somme de théologie," *Revue Thomiste* 99 (1999): 75–100; Guggenheim, *Jésus Christ, Grand Prêtre*, especially Part III; Vanhoye, *Old Testament Priests and the New Priest According to the New Testament*, 133–36, and elsewhere. As perfect, Christ's priesthood transcends the priesthood of the Old Testament, which could only prefigure it: his priesthood is not a continuation of the Levitical priesthood. Yet neither does his priesthood negate the Levitical priesthood, since the latter participates in its fulfillment in Christ.

> For through Him are gifts bestowed on men, according to 2 Pet. i. 4: *By Whom* (i.e. Christ) *He hath given us most great and precious promises, that by these you may be made partakers of the divine nature.* Moreover, He reconciled the human race to God, according to Col. i. 19,20: *In Him* (i.e. Christ) *it hath well pleased (the Father) that all fullness should dwell, and through Him to reconcile all things unto Himself.*[90]

Through Christ's priesthood, human beings become "partakers of the divine nature" and are reconciled to God. Thus Christ is the perfect priest, and indeed the only priest who can truly accomplish the mediation of divine gifting—the healing and deification[91] that God wills to bestow. Because of who Christ is, he is able to mediate these divine gifts through his human actions. As the letter to the Hebrews emphasizes, Christ mediates divine gifts with an efficacy that far exceeds what a merely human, and thus sinful and weak, priest could achieve.

The power that enables Christ to be such a priest requires explanation. Aquinas offers such an explanation in his replies to the three objections, which, as we recall, focused upon the view that the Messiah should entirely transcend the carnal and cultic office suggested by the term *priest.*

With respect to the first objection, Aquinas notes, following Pseudo-Dionysius, that the angels, too, possess "hierarchical

---

90. ST III, q. 22, a. 1. For Aquinas's account of deification, see Daniel A. Keating, "Justification, Sanctification and Divinization in Thomas Aquinas," in *Aquinas on Doctrine: A Critical Introduction*, ed. Thomas G. Weinandy, OFM CAP, Daniel A. Keating, and John P. Yocum (New York: T. & T. Clark, 2004), 139–58. Keating remarks, "It is noteworthy that among the several citations of 2 Pet. 1:4 in the *Summa*, the densest concentration appears in his *Treatise on Grace.* . . . Here we see quite clearly that Thomas' doctrine of grace is, in fact, a doctrine of divinization whereby God deifies the soul by granting to it (through Christ) a participation in his very nature. The biblical account of our new nature—of the new creation in Christ—is in fact at the centre of Aquinas' concern. By the power of the Holy Spirit, we are regenerated and given a new nature in Christ, enabling us to live a new way of life characterized principally by charity. For Thomas, this new, graced nature is our participation in the divine life" (154). See also A. N. Williams, *The Ground of Union: Deification in Aquinas and Palamas* (Oxford: Oxford University Press, 1999).

91. The themes of "image-restoration" (healing) and "image-perfection" (deification) recur throughout Romanus Cessario, OP's, *The Godly Image: Christ and Satisfaction in Catholic Thought from Anselm to Aquinas* (Petersham, MA: St. Bede's Publications, 1990). See also his "Aquinas on Christian Salvation," in Weinandy, Keating, and Yocum, *Aquinas on Doctrine,* 117–37. As Cessario notes in "Aquinas on Christian Salvation," "the essentially cruciform pattern of Christian life harmonizes the themes of image-perfection and satisfactory suffering" (127).

power."[92] Hierarchical power in Dionysius's sense is not the power to dominate, but the power to teach, heal, and uplift. This is the true meaning of "power." But how could Jesus, as a human "priest," possess more "hierarchical power" than the angels, as Hebrews claims? Aquinas responds that "Christ was greater than the angels, not only in His Godhead, but also in His humanity, as having the fullness of grace and glory."[93] That is to say, by the indwelling of the Holy Spirit transforming his human nature, Christ received "hierarchical power." The Holy Spirit, whom in the *prima pars* Aquinas names as "Love" and "Gift,"[94] bestows "hierarchical power" upon Christ. This power is the power to mediate divine gifting, divine love. Because the degree of transformation of his human nature by the indwelling Holy Spirit makes his human nature greater than any graced angelic nature, Christ, according to Aquinas, "had the hierarchical or priestly power in a higher degree than the angels, so that even the angels were ministers of His priesthood."[95] It is evident that we are dealing with an understanding of priestly "power" far different from what the understanding of power would be if the Holy Spirit were not the source of Christ's power. Following Hebrews 2:9, which teaches that Jesus "for a little while was made lower than the angels," Aquinas observes that Jesus' passibility makes him like "those wayfarers who are ordained to the priesthood."[96]

While Jesus' hierarchical power is strong in weakness, however, does power-as-domination inevitably overcome "hierarchical power" understood as the mediation of kenotic divine gifting? On the cross, Christ gives the divine answer: true hierarchical power will accomplish its work of mediation despite the most devastating abuses

---

92. ST III, q. 22, a. 1, ad 1.

93. Ibid.

94. See ST I, q. 36, a. 1; I, qq. 37–38; as well as Augustine, *De Trinitate*, Books 5 and 15. See also the extraordinarily rich biblical reflection on these Augustinian names for the Spirit by Joseph Ratzinger, "The Holy Spirit as Communion: On the Relationship between Pneumatology and Spirituality in the Writings of Augustine," in Ratzinger, *Pilgrim Fellowship of Faith: The Church as Communion*, ed. Stephan Otto Horn and Vinzenz Pfnür, trans. Henry Taylor (German 2002; San Francisco: Ignatius Press, 2005), 38–59. This article originally appeared in German in 1974.

95. Ibid. See also Albert Vanhoye, sj's, section on "The Expectation of a Great High Priest in Messianic Times," in his *Old Testament Priests and the New Priest According to the New Testament*, 43–47.

96. ST III, q. 22, a. 1, ad 1. See Guggenheim, *Jésus Christ, Grand Prêtre*, 131–39.

that worldly power, the distortion of love and gift, can devise. If this were not so, then the forgiveness of sins would lose its warrant. This point explains Aquinas's replies to the second and third objections. In answering these objections, Aquinas differentiates Jesus' priesthood from that of others because "Christ, as being the Head of all, has the perfection of all graces"—thereby holding that Jesus stands above the Old Testament priesthood and unifies in himself the offices of priest, prophet/lawgiver, and king.[97] Aquinas supposes not that Jesus dominates over the worldly, but only that his mediation of divine gifting cannot be rendered "powerless" but instead will be shown to be powerful despite operating in the very midst of sin. As Saint Paul puts it, "where sin increased, grace abounded all the more, so that, as sin reigned in death, grace also might reign through righteousness to eternal life through Jesus Christ our Lord" (Romans 5:20–21).

In short, for Aquinas as for contemporary historical scholarship, Jesus' priestly action locates him within the context of Israel, even as he also transcends this context. Recall now the four aspects of Jesus' priestly action, his "hierarchical power," that we found in Wright, Bryan, McKnight, and Pitre: eschatological, sacrificial, sanctifying, and unitive. In what ways does *Summa Theologiae* III, q. 22 enrich our understanding of these dimensions of Jesus' priestly action?

---

97. See ST III, q. 22, a. 1, ad 2 and 3. See also Benoît-Dominique de La Soujeole, OP, "Les tria munera Christi: Contribution de saint Thomas à la recherche contemporaine," *Revue Thomiste* 99 (1999): 59–74; Yves Congar, "Sur la trilogie: Prophète-roi-prêtre," *Revue des sciences philosophiques et théologiques* 67 (1983): 97–115. For Christ as prophet, priest, and king in Hebrews according to Aquinas's Commentary, see Guggenheim, *Jésus Christ, Grand Prêtre*, 535. Regarding Christ's tria munera and believers' participation in them, see also Herwi Rikhof, "Thomas on the Church: Reflections on a Sermon," in Weinandy, Keating, and Yocum, *Aquinas on Doctrine*, 204–5. Rikhof observes, "Thomas refers to the triplet priest-king-prophet. He uses it to explain the name 'Christ'. He also uses it to indicate the dignity or excellence of Christ, with an emphasis on his sanctifying work. Moreover, he uses the triplet with regard to the Christian and indicates a relationship between the two anointings. Again, one can perceive here a connection with *Lumen Gentium*, or rather with the Codex which translates Vatican II's insights within its definition of the *christifideles:* by baptism the faithful participate in the threefold task of Christ" (205). In a footnote, Rikhof notes that, given the absence of any reference to Christ's anointing in the *Summa Theologiae's* question on Christ's priesthood, "It seems therefore stretching the evidence too far if one argues that Thomas presents a more or less complete *munus triplex* doctrine" (222 note 26). The reality of the *munus triplex* is present in Aquinas's account of Christ's Person and work, but a complete doctrine, if by that one means a systematic elucidation, is lacking.

An Eschatological Action

Contemporary biblical scholars use the word *eschatological* with
reference to the Second-Temple Jewish context, where it meant ushering
in, through the Day of YHWH, the messianic age of the restoration
of Israel as a holy people who dwell with God. Does any comparable
notion play a role in Aquinas's theology of Christ's priesthood? For
Aquinas, Christ's priestly action inserts time (created and fallen, and
in Christ redeemed and elevated) into divine eternity, into the life of the
triune God.[98] Christ's priestly action thus marks the everlasting presence of God among his people, YHWH's permanent "return to Zion."[99]

One of the key problems for an "eschatological" understanding of Jesus' words and deeds in Israel is that little seems to have
changed after his death and Resurrection.[100] It comes as no surprise,

---

98. See Matthew L. Lamb, "The Eschatology of St. Thomas Aquinas," in Weinandy,
Keating, and Yocum, *Aquinas on Doctrine*, 225–40. Lamb writes, "The sapiential eschatology
of Aquinas, building upon patristic eschatologies, understands the eschatological and
apocalyptic passages in Scripture as revealing the transformation of the whole of creation so
that it fully manifests the divine wisdom, beauty and goodness. This contrasts with those who
view these passages as involving or portending widespread devastation or ultimate doom. A
wisdom approach indicates clearly how what is catastrophic from the viewpoint of this world is
only the purification needed for transition to the kingdom of God" (236).

99. For a historical-critical defense of Wright's claims about the ongoing exile and the
eschatological restoration inaugurated by Jesus, see Craig A. Evans, "Jesus and the Continuing
Exile of Israel," in Newman, *Jesus and the Restoration of Israel*, 77–100. Evans comments,

It is interesting to reflect on Jesus' use of traditions from Daniel, Zechariah and Isaiah.
All three of these books play a major role in Jesus' theology; and all three reflect periods
of exile in the life and history of Israel. Daniel reflected an exilic perspective, ostensibly
the Babylonian exile but in reality the Seleucid period of oppression and terror. Zechariah
stems from the exilic period and entertains hopes that Israel's kingdom will be restored
under the leadership of the "two sons of oil" (Zech 4:14)—Zerubbabel of Davidic
descent and Joshua the High Priest. Second Isaiah calls for a new exodus and a new
Israel, which he dubs the "servant" of the Lord. Jesus' use of these books, indeed his
being informed and shaped by them, is very revealing. It strongly suggests that Jesus
identified himself and his mission with an oppressed Israel in need of redemption and
that he himself was the agent of redemption. He was the Danielic "Son of Man" to whom
kingdom and authority were entrusted. He was the humble Davidic king of Zechariah's
vision who entered the temple precincts and offered himself to the High Priest and
took umbrage at temple polity. And, of course, he was the eschatological herald of
Second Isaiah who proclaimed the "gospel" of God's reign and the new exodus. (99–100)

100. This is the point that Dale C. Allison Jr. presses in his response to Wright's *Jesus and
the Victory of God:* Allison, "Jesus and the Victory of the Apocalyptic," in Newman, *Jesus and
the Restoration of Israel*, 126–41. Allison sees no reason to assume that the eschatological
descriptions of cosmic change employed by Jesus and his followers were intended metaphorically.
For Allison, Jewish apocalyptic prophecies (including those of Jesus) remain radically
unfulfilled by Jesus: "The last have not become first, nor have the meek inherited the earth.

for instance, that Albert Schweitzer's view that Jesus died expecting the end of the world—which in fact did not end in any evident sense—tended for some time to dampen enthusiasm for Schweitzer's insights into Jesus' eschatological worldview.[101] For Wright and Aquinas, Jesus' priestly action is better understood as the beginning of the eschatological "day" rather than the "end of the world." Recall Zechariah 14's announcement that the "day of the Lord" (14:1), a day of profound tribulation and restoration, will inaugurate "continuous day (it is known to the Lord), not day and not night, for at evening time there shall be light" (14:7).

Does Christ's priestly action constitute a "continuous day," a mediation of the divine gifting that draws time into divine eternity? Aquinas prepares his affirmative response by noting three reasons why the answer might be "no." The first objection states that Christ's priestly action cannot be eschatological because it has no part in the eschaton. Christ's action does not pour out eschatological blessings, but rather at best prepares for the eschaton. In this respect Aquinas quotes Isaiah 60:21, "Your people shall all be righteous." While this may come about through Christ's priestly action, Christ's priestly action has no place in it, because "those alone need the effect of the priesthood who have the weakness of sin."[102] The saints in heaven do not have the weakness of sin, whereas those in hell can no longer benefit from priestly expiation. On this view, a radical divide exists between historical redemption, to which Jesus' work belongs, and the eschaton. The messianic age is here separated radically from the work of the Messiah. The Messiah might have "eschatological" intentions, but no continuity exists between the Messiah's work to usher in the eschaton, and the eschaton itself.

Maybe, in the person of Jesus, we can speak of the initial or proleptic victory of God. But that victory remains agonizingly incomplete, and we cannot, if I may so put it, yet speak of the victory of the apocalyptic" (141). Wright responds to this concern in the same volume: "An eschatological reading of Jesus demands, I believe, that we get used to thinking in terms of the dialectic between achievement and implementation" ("In Grateful Dialogue: A Response," 244–77, at 272; cf. 261–72 for Wright's full discussion), although Wright seems to have primarily this-worldly ethical implementation in mind.

101. On Schweitzer's views see the different readings of Allison and Wright in Newman, *Jesus and the Restoration of Israel*, 129–30, 262.

102. ST III, q. 22, a. 5, obj. 1. This article takes up the question, "Whether the Priesthood of Christ Endures for Ever?"

The second and third objections likewise limit Jesus' priestly action in accord with the limitations of its historical plane. Granted that Jesus' priesthood "was made manifest most of all in His passion and death, when *by His own blood He entered into the Holies* (Heb. ix. 12)," one can observe that Jesus died once and rose from the dead.[103] Therefore Jesus was once a priest and is such no longer, since he dies no longer but instead enjoys everlasting life. Likewise, since a priest mediates the divine gifting, Jesus is priest as a man, not as God. In his human nature, Jesus can *mediate* to other human beings; in his divine nature, Jesus could act directly in the bestowal of divine gifts, in an unmediated fashion. Priestly mediation belongs to Jesus as man. Aquinas points out, however, that for three days, Jesus' body and soul were separated in death. One cannot call a separated soul a "man," nor can one call a corpse a "man." During this period of death, then, Jesus could not have acted as a priest; and thus his priestly act does not instantiate a "continuous day," but instead marks a historical rupture, whatever its other effects. His priestly action could not itself be fully "eschatological," because his priestly action and the eschaton are disjoined.

To some degree, the position of the objectors sounds like that of the biblical scholars. If Jesus envisioned his death as the trigger for the eschatological age, the "eschaton" itself—the restoration of Israel— would involve not his death but his triumphant vindication, when he will eat and drink once more with his followers. As he says to his disciples after giving them the wine as his "blood of the covenant" at the Last Supper, "Truly, I say to you, I shall not drink again of the fruit of the vine until that day when I drink it new in the kingdom of God" (Mark 14:25).

Aquinas certainly affirms that the fullness of the eschaton is not marred by death: "The Saints who will be in heaven will not need any further expiation by the priesthood of Christ" and "Christ's passion and death are not to be repeated."[104] He holds, rather, that Christ's priestly action inaugurates the eschatological day, both in this world by reconstituting Israel in holiness as "Christ's mystic body,"[105] and in the world to come (as Aquinas interprets it) by opening "the Holy Way" prophesied in Isaiah 35:8 by which "the ransomed of the Lord

---

103. Ibid., obj. 2.
104. Ibid., ad 1 and 2.
105. ST III, q. 49, a. 1.

shall return, and come to Zion with singing; everlasting joy shall be upon their heads; they shall obtain joy and gladness, and sorrow and sighing shall flee away" (Isaiah 35:10).[106] The actual eschaton involves neither Christ's ongoing suffering nor anything analogous to suffering.[107]

Because of what it achieves, however, Christ's priesthood endures in eternity, and is not simply a passing event. Aquinas explains, "In the priestly office, we may consider two things: first, the offering of the sacrifice; secondly, the consummation of the sacrifice, consisting in this, that those for whom the sacrifice is offered, obtain the end of the sacrifice."[108] It endures in its "end" or goal. Given Aquinas's understanding of causality, the goal of the action inheres in the action itself; likewise, when the goal is achieved, the action that brought about the goal is not lost, but instead shares in its completion or consummation. The consummation of Christ's priestly action is eternal life. Therefore, eternal life belongs to Christ's priestly action as its goal, and in this sense Christ's priesthood endures everlastingly. Eternally, the consummation enjoyed by the saints in heaven depends upon Jesus Christ. In this respect Aquinas quotes Revelation 21:23, "And the city [the heavenly Jerusalem] has no need of sun or moon to shine upon it, for the glory of God is its light, and its lamp is the Lamb."[109] The "Lamb standing, as though it had been slain"

---

106. Aquinas writes in ST III, q. 49, a. 5, "it is on account of sin that men were prevented from entering into the heavenly kingdom, since, according to Isa. xxxv. 8: 'It shall be called the holy way, and the unclean shall not pass over it.' Now there is a twofold sin which prevents men from entering into the kingdom of heaven. The first is common to the whole race, for it is our first parents' sin, and by that sin heaven's entrance is closed to man. Hence we read in Gen. iii. 24 that after our first parents' sin God 'placed . . . cherubim and a flaming sword, turning every way, to keep the way of the tree of life.' The other is the personal sin of each one of us, committed by our personal act. Now by Christ's Passion we have been delivered not only from the common sin of the whole human race, both as to its guilt and as to the debt of punishment, for which He paid the penalty on our behalf; but, furthermore, from the personal sins of individuals, who share in His Passion by faith and charity and the sacraments of faith. Consequently, then, the gate of heaven's kingdom is thrown open to us through Christ's Passion."

107. By contrast, Hans Urs von Balthasar argues that Christ's suffering and death—as an experience of hellish infinite "distance" from the Father that encompasses every possible created alienation from God—belongs analogously to the life of the Trinity, and thus to the kingdom of God as a participation in the Trinitarian life. For a critical evaluation of von Balthasar's position, see my *Scripture and Metaphysics: Aquinas and the Renewal of Trinitarian Theology* (Oxford: Blackwell, 2004), ch. 4.

108. ST III, q. 22, a. 5. Cf. Denis Chardonnens, OCD, "Éternité du sacerdoce du Christ et effet eschatologique de l'eucharistie. La contribution de saint Thomas d'Aquin à un theme de théologie sacramentaire," *Revue Thomiste* 99 (1999): 159–80.

109. ST III, q. 22, a. 5, ad 1.

(Revelation 5:6), is Christ the priest. Even though in heavenly glory he no longer performs his priestly action of expiatory sacrifice, nonetheless the heavenly glory enjoyed by the saints is enjoyed through him as the priestly mediator. His sacrificial action is consummated in the heavenly communion of the saints. Quoting Hebrews 10:14, "For by a single offering he has perfected for all time those who are sanctified," Aquinas observes that "the virtue [power] of that Victim endures forever."[110]

Even so, does the Old Testament, whose promises Jesus fulfills, envision an "eternity" that is not an extension of historical time? Is Aquinas's understanding of the "eschaton" fundamentally and unavoidably at odds with the resources available in Second-Temple Judaism for envisioning an "eschatological" restoration? Following the letter to the Hebrews, Aquinas suggests—and I would agree—that his understanding of the eschatological significance of Christ's priestly action accords with the liturgical pattern described by Leviticus 16, which gives instructions for Israel's observance of the Day of Atonement. Aquinas states, "Now this [eternal] consummation of Christ's sacrifice was foreshadowed in this, that the high-priest of the Old Law, once a year, entered into the Holy of Holies with the blood of a he-goat and a calf."[111] In Leviticus 16, God commands that the people of Israel, through the work of the high priest, make atonement "once in the year because of all their sins" (16:34). On this day alone, the high priest may enter into "the holy place" (16:2) in the Temple and sprinkle the sacrificial blood "upon the mercy seat and before the mercy seat" (16:15), the mercy seat on the Ark of the Covenant being where "I [YHWH] will appear in the cloud" (16:2). In order to make expiation for the people, the high priest enters into the very place where the Lord dwells with Israel. The divine presence there is so powerful that normally anyone who dares enter this holy place would die (16:2).

This historically concrete holy place, Aquinas suggests, evokes the trans-historical holy place where God dwells in the glory and majesty of the divine eternity. Christ enters as priest into that transcendent holy place. As Hebrews states, "But when Christ appeared as a high

---

110. Ibid., ad 2. See Guggenheim, *Jésus Christ, Grand Prêtre*, 520–33.
111. ST III, q. 22, a. 5. See Guggenheim, *Jésus Christ, Grand Prêtre*, 70–71, 467–68, and elsewhere.

priest of the good things that have come,[112] then through the greater and more perfect tent (not made with hands, that is, not of this creation), he entered once for all into the Holy Place, taking not the blood of goats and calves but his own blood, thus securing an eternal redemption" (Hebrews 9:11–12). The eschatological restoration of Israel hardly need exclude such a trans-historical dwelling with God, since Israel knew that, in the words ascribed to Solomon at the dedication of the Temple, "heaven and the highest heaven cannot contain thee [God]; how much less this house that I have built!" (1 Kings 8:27).[113]

Thus, although he does not have Wright's knowledge of the historical context of Second-Temple understandings of Israel's "restoration," Aquinas develops a nuanced view of the "eschaton" and places

---

112. The RSV includes a footnote here: "Other manuscripts read good things to come." Aquinas had this latter version of the verse.

113. For the trans-historical dimension of the Temple, see Jon D. Levenson, *Sinai and Zion: An Entry into the Jewish Bible* (San Francisco: Harper & Row, 1985), Part II. Levenson states, "Whereas Sinai, as we saw in Part I, represents the possibility of meaningful history, of history that leads toward an affirmation, Zion represents the possibility of meaning above history, out of history, through an opening into the realm of the ideal. Mount Zion, the Temple on it, and the city around it are a symbol of transcendence, a symbol in Paul Tillich's sense of the word, something 'which participates in that to which it points.' For the two tiers, the earthly and the heavenly, are not closed to each other, but open, and interpenetrating on Zion" (41–42). This sense of "interpenetration" of the trans-historical and the historical explains, Levenson argues, why

> Jewish tradition did not accept the finality of the destruction of the Temple and the absence of the redemption of which it was taken to be the symbol. On the contrary, the Jewish liturgy gives eloquent testimony to the longing for the reconstruction of the shrine and its city. The longing for the Temple was, as we have seen, a prominent theme in biblical times. It was only rendered more intense by the absence of the physical object of this passionate desire. . . . Throughout history, there have always been some Jews who wish to see not only God's presence, but also that of his people Israel restored to Zion even before the end of time. And thus it is appropriate that the movement for the restoration of Jewish sovereignty should have acquired the name *Zionism*, after the mountain tied so closely to the fortunes of the people Israel. However much Zionism may resemble a typical modern nationalism with the unfortunate consequences for outsiders that such movements entail, we should still not overlook Martin Buber's point that "this national concept was named after a place and not, like the others, after a people, which indicates that it is not so much a question of a particular people as such but of its association with a particular land, its native land." For the modern Zionist the ancient association of the people of Israel and the land of Israel has been rejoined. This return to the land was possible because for the most part, the Jewish tradition did not spiritualize the concept of Zion/Jerusalem/the land of Israel to the extent that it ceased to have any reference to real history. (179–80)

For further reflection, from a Christian perspective, upon the significance of the land of Israel and the Temple see Gregory Vall, " 'Man Is the Land': The Sacramentality of the Land of Israel," in *John Paul II and the Jewish People*, ed. David G. Dalin and Matthew Levering (Lanham, MD: Rowman and Littlefield, 2008).

Christ's priestly action at the center of this eschatological consummation. Christ's priesthood stands as the eschatological turning point,
both on earth (the new Israel) and in the new creation.[114]

A Sacrificial Action

What does Aquinas say about the sacrificial character of Christ's
"hierarchical power"? Aquinas raises the question of whether Jesus
intended to die a sacrificial death and thus saw himself as a sacrificial
"victim."[115] There are two obvious problems with this view, in addition
to a third problem, less obvious but equally troubling. First, Jesus did
not kill himself, nor was he slain by priests: could he really, then, have
envisioned his cross as a sacrificial offering? Those who crucified him
certainly did not intend to offer cultic sacrifice (thus making Jesus an
unlikely sacrificial "victim"), and whatever Jesus' "intentions," he had
no choice in the matter as he hung dying from the cross (thus making
Jesus an unlikely sacrificial "priest").[116]

Second, if Jesus was in fact acting as a "priest" in his Passion,
then he himself was the victim, and he thus was a human sacrifice.
Not only is the idea that God would desire human sacrifice appalling,
but furthermore in the Old Testament God frequently condemns
human sacrifice, which is a mark instead of pagan idolatry and moral
corruption. Aquinas quotes in this vein Psalm 106:38 (to which I will
add verses 36 and 37), "They served their idols, / which became a
snare to them. / They sacrificed their sons / and their daughters to the
demons; / they poured out innocent blood, / the blood of their sons
and daughters, / whom they sacrificed to the idols of Canaan; / and

---

114. As Walter Kasper states, "Thomas argues (against the progressive conception of
salvation history in Joachim of Fiore) that the time of the church is the 'last days.' Jesus Christ
has instituted the church to last until the end of time; the heavenly Jerusalem is already
descending upon the earth in the church, and the kingdom of God is already present in the
church. This eschatological dimension belongs to the sacramental structure of the church, for
Thomas sees the sacraments as *signa prognostica* of the world to come. In particular, the
Eucharist is an anticipatory image and foretaste of heaven and of the bliss that awaits us in the
heavenly Jerusalem. The apostolic office too shares in this eschatological dimension and is to
last until the end of the world (Matt. 28:20). The *pax ecclesiae* that the bishop's spiritual
authority is meant to serve is a fruit of the Holy Spirit and a proleptic image of the eschatological
peace that it makes present" (Kasper, *Leadership in the Church: How Traditional Roles Can Serve
the Christian Community Today*, trans. Brian McNeil [New York: Crossroad, 2003], 112–13).

115. ST III, q. 22, a. 2.

116. See ibid., obj. 1.

the land was polluted with blood." The "they" described here, of course, is the people of Israel—the psalmist and Aquinas, like modern archeologists, were well aware that some Israelites worshipped gods other than YHWH. The fact that some Israelites offered up human sacrifice does not legitimate human sacrifice in God's eyes; it also makes it even more appalling to suppose that Christ himself intended to offer a human sacrifice.[117]

The third problem is less evident, perhaps, but appears equally difficult to resolve. Namely, priests consecrated sacrifices to the Lord; the consecration was an integral part of the offering. But the human nature of Christ, by the indwelling Holy Spirit, "was from the beginning consecrated and united to God."[118] Therefore, why should Christ's human life be offered in sacrifice to God, if the very purpose of ritual "sacrifice"—namely, consecration and union of the offering with God—has already been achieved in the case of Christ?[119]

Without at first directly resolving these problems, Aquinas explores Christ's Passion in light of the Old Testament sacrifices. He takes this approach because Saint Paul interprets Christ's Passion through this Old Testament lens: "And walk in love, as Christ loved

---

117. Ibid., obj. 2. In this vein, Mark Heim, having presented the range of contemporary criticisms of sacrificial accounts of Christ's cross, rightly observes that they "assert no minor flaw in Christianity, but a consistent fault line in the whole foundation that runs from distorted views of God to spiritual guilt fixation to sacrificial bloodshed to anti-Semitic persecution to arrogant ignorance of world mythology. All this adds up to a fatally skewed faith, revolving around a central narrative based on sacred violence and the glorification of innocent suffering" (Heim, *Saved from Sacrifice*, 27). Following René Girard's argument that "sacrifice" is to be understood as human beings' effort to undo "bad" violence by means of supposedly "good" (sacred) violence, Heim seeks to preserve the place of the cross within Christianity by arguing that the cross is the ultimate repudiation of sacrifice: "The way of life that follows on the cross depends on recognition that the death of Jesus ought not to happen. It is not God's recipe that innocent suffering is the way to restore peace: God's purpose (to end such a pattern) is superimposed on that event of humanly sanctified violence. Sacrificial scapegoating is not something invented by those under the spell of the passion narratives, but something revealed and opposed there. Just as it is an error to think that it is somehow a Christian requirement to be a victim of redemptive violence, so it is an error to think there is a Christian responsibility to administer it" (252). Heim summarizes his position: "Scapegoating sacrifice is the stumbling block we placed between God and us. It is a root sin buried in our life together. The passion is a divine act revealing, reversing, and replacing our redemptive violence, which we so long and tenaciously hid from ourselves in the very name of the sacred. When our sin had so separated us from God and built our peace on blood, God was willing to come and die for us, to bear our sin and suffer the condemnation that we visit upon our victims and so deserve ourselves. God saved us from our form of reconciliation, healed us of our dependence on that sad medicine" (329).

118. ST III, q. 22, a. 2, obj. 3.

119. Ibid., obj. 3.

us and gave himself up for us, a fragrant offering and sacrifice to God" (Ephesians 5:2).[120] Like Paul, the Old Testament recognizes the spiritual core of "sacrifice." In this respect Aquinas quotes Psalm 51:17 (to which I add verses 14–16): Deliver me from bloodguiltiness, O God, / thou God of my salvation, / and my tongue will sing aloud thy deliverance. / O Lord, open thou my lips, / and my mouth shall show forth thy praise. / For thou hast no delight in sacrifice; / were I to give a burnt offering, thou wouldst not be pleased. / The sacrifice acceptable to God is a broken spirit; / a broken and contrite heart, / O God, thou wilt not despise.[121] If the words of this psalm are true, however, why does God command Israel to perform animal sacrifice? Aquinas turns to Augustine for insight into this question. In *City of God* Augustine, also with Psalm 50 in view, comments,

> If in times gone by our ancestors offered other sacrifices to God, in the shape of animal victims (sacrifices which the people of God now read about, but do not perform) we are to understand that the significance of those acts was precisely the same as that of those now performed amongst us—the intention of which is that we may cleave to God and seek the good of our neighbour for the same end. Thus the visible sacrifice is the sacrament, the sacred sign, of the invisible sacrifice.[122]

Augustine recognizes the importance of "signs" for human beings. Since human beings do not gaze directly upon intelligible realities, but rather acquire knowledge through sensible realities, human beings

---

120. Quoted in ST III, q. 22, a. 2, *sed contra*.

121. Cf. on the sacrifice of praise, Thomas P. Ryan, *Thomas Aquinas as Reader of the Psalms* (Notre Dame, IN: University of Notre Dame Press, 2000), 130–31, 133. For Aquinas, as Ryan says earlier, "the Psalms are not simply about Christ or prayer but about Christ praying" (108).

122. Augustine, *City of God*, trans. Henry Bettenson (New York: Penguin, 1972), Book X, ch. 5 (p. 377); Aquinas quotes the last sentence of this text in ST III, q. 22, a. 2. Both Augustine and Aquinas agree with Mark Heim that bloody sacrifice is by no means an end in itself. For Heim, following Girard, Christ's sacrifice makes possible charitable union with God and neighbor precisely by ending bloody sacrifice, now replaced by a communal meal: "The Last Supper can be seen in continuity with Jesus' practice of table fellowship, giving it an explicitly liturgical tone that casts it in explicit contrast with sacrificial practice. Instead of the rite of scapegoating sacrifice that lies at the base of historical human community, and instead of the cultic rite of animal sacrifice that reproduces its logic of exclusion and violence, this new community is founded on the communion meal. The early church was continually amazed and thankful that this table brought into one circle those who otherwise would be irrevocably separated by purity boundaries, who otherwise would be scapegoating each other and shedding each other's blood" (*Saved from Sacrifice*, 233–34 [cf. 232]).

require sensible signs to unite us in true worship of spiritual realities.[123] Following Augustine, then, Aquinas interprets the animal sacrifices of the Old Testament as important sensible "signs" that assisted the people of Israel in offering the spiritual sacrifice which God requires.

Granted that the animal sacrifices of the Old Testament are not to be despised, Aquinas pays attention to the fact that God ordains such a complex sacrificial system for Israel. Aquinas connects this sacrificial system with the diverse purposes of sacrificial offering, and he names three purposes, on an ascending scale: the "remission of sin," the preservation of the state of grace, and perfect union with God.[124] The first purpose belongs, he notes, to the very rationale of the divinely ordained priesthood, both that of the Old Testament and that of Christ. Here he quotes Hebrews 5:1, "For every high priest chosen among men is appointed to act on behalf of men in relation to God, to offer gifts and sacrifices for sins."[125] If the first purpose pertains to the sacrificial system in general, the second purpose has to do in particular, Aquinas suggests, with "the sacrifice of peace-offerings," as described in Leviticus 3. The state of grace is a state of "peace." Finally, the third purpose particularly involves the burnt offerings described in Leviticus 1, because such offerings signify the perfect union of human beings with God in the state of glory.[126]

---

123. Aquinas argues that before original sin, because of the right ordering of the higher and lower powers of the soul, "the first man was not impeded by exterior things from a clear and steady contemplation of the intelligible effects which he perceived by the radiation of the first truth, whether by a natural or by a gratuitous knowledge" (ST I, q. 94, a. 1). Nonetheless, sacrifice belongs to the natural law: "it is a dictate of natural reason in accordance with man's natural inclination that he should tender submission and honor, according to his mode, to that which is above man. Now the mode befitting to man is that he should employ sensible signs in order to signify anything, because he derives his knowledge from sensibles. Hence it is a dictate of natural reason that man should use certain sensibles, by offering them to God in sign of the subjection and honor due to Him" (ST II-II, q. 85, a. 1). See also ST I-II, q. 101, a. 2; I-II, q. 102, a. 3.

124. ST III, q. 22, a. 2.

125. Ibid.; cf. Guggenheim, *Jésus Christ, Grand Prêtre*, 160–61. Following Serge-Thomas Bonino, Guggenheim argues that neither Aquinas nor Hebrews has in view "priesthood" in a general sense common to Israel and other nations. Rather, Aquinas recognizes that what is at issue is the role of the Aaronic priesthood. As Guggenheim states in this regard, "Saint Thomas reflects on priestly mediation, and still more the mediation of the high priest, from within the Old and New Covenants" (161). See also Bonino, "Le sacerdoce comme institution naturelle selon saint Thomas d'Aquin," 34–35.

126. ST III, q. 22, a. 2.

Recalling, then, that the center of any "sacrifice" is the invisible sacrifice of charity signified by the visible sign, how might the Old Testament sacrifices assist in our comprehension of Christ's Passion as a priestly action of "sacrifice"?[127] First, regarding the three purposes of sacrifice: does Christ's Passion remove our sins, draw us into God's "peace," and unite us to God in glory? Aquinas answers with three biblical passages, corresponding respectively to the three purposes: Christ "was put to death for our trespasses" (Romans 4:25); Christ "became the source of eternal salvation to all who obey him" (Hebrews 5:9); and Christ unites us to God in glory "since we have confidence to enter the sanctuary by the blood of Jesus" (Hebrews 10:19).[128] By his Passion and death, then, Christ fulfills the three purposes of the "priest" offering "sacrifice." His sacrifice is also "once for all" (Hebrews 9:26): "For by a single offering he has perfected for all time those who are sanctified" (Hebrews 10:14).[129] Aquinas states with regard to the eucharistic sacrifice instituted by Christ, "The Sacrifice which is offered every day in the Church is not distinct from that which Christ Himself offered, but is a commemoration thereof. Wherefore Augustine says (*De Civ. Dei* x. 20): *Christ Himself both is the priest who offers it and the victim: the sacred token of which He wished to be the daily Sacrifice of the Church*."[130] The commemoration, as sacramental, truly unites the Church to Christ's historical sacrifice.[131]

---

127. Anscar Vonier, osb, cautions in his classic *A Key to the Doctrine of the Eucharist* (1925; Bethesda, MD: Zaccheus Press, 2003) that "no theory of sacrifice could ever adequately meet the case of Christ's sacrifice on the Cross. It is a sacrifice so entirely *sui generis* that it has to be defined by itself" (105) and that "the whole ancient sacrificial rite was figurative of Christ's sacrifice on the Cross. This means that we are to explain the ancient sacrifices through the sacrifice of the Cross and not vice versa" (106).

128. ST III, q. 22, a. 2.

129. For Aquinas on Hebrews 10:14 see Guggenheim, *Jésus Christ, Grand Prêtre*, 474.

130. ST III, q. 22, a. 3, ad 2.

131. For discussion of eucharistic sacrifice see my *Sacrifice and Community: Jewish Offering and Christian Eucharist* (Oxford: Blackwell, 2005). See also Vonier, *A Key to the Doctrine of the Eucharist;* Yves Congar, *Lay People in the Church,* rev. ed., trans. Donald Attwater (London: Geoffrey Chapman, 1965), 165f.; Avery Dulles, sj, "The Eucharist as Sacrifice," in *Rediscovering the Eucharist: Ecumenical Conversations,* ed. Roch Kereszty, o cist (New York: Paulist Press, 2003), 175–87; idem, "The Death of Jesus as Sacrifice," *Josephinum Journal of Theology* 3 (1996): 4–17; William T. Cavanaugh, "Eucharistic Sacrifice and Social Imagination in Early Modern Europe," *Journal of Medieval and Early Modern Studies* 31 (2001): 585–605. For an example of contemporary mainstream Catholic rejection of eucharistic sacrifice as taught by the Council of Trent, see Robert J. Daly, sj, "Sacrifice Unveiled or Sacrifice Revisited: Trinitarian and Liturgical Perspectives," *Theological Studies* 64 (2003): 24–42; idem, "Eucharistic Origins:

Thus, although we will explore how his shedding of blood takes away sins in more detail when discussing the "sanctifying" dimension of Christ's priesthood, we can already say that Christ accomplishes, in a unique and transcendent way, a sacrificial mission. Even so, what is offered in Christ's sacrifice is Christ's human life. Can his human life appropriately be conceived as a sacrificial "victim"? What kind of "priest" would offer his own life in "sacrifice"? This is the difficulty pressed, against the weight of the New Testament language, by the objections that we reviewed above. Is there a sense in which Christ's human life could be appropriately conceived as a sacrificial "victim"?

In addressing this question, Aquinas begins by emphasizing that the passive sense of "victim," which we associate with animal sacrifice, does not apply to Christ's Passion. If Christ is a sacrificial "victim," he is such only as an active agent, the Person of the Son of God, moved throughout by the charity with which the Holy Spirit graces Christ's human nature.[132] The fundamental "offering" of his human life, then, is the active offering that he makes spiritually out of love, not the more "passive" submission of his flesh to the nails of the Roman soldiers (although Aquinas also holds that Christ, as the incarnate Son, actively permits even this apparently wholly passive submission of the flesh).[133]

From the New Testament to the Liturgies of the Golden Age," *Theological Studies* 66 (2005): 3–22.

132. Miroslav Volf thus emphasizes that the significance of the Incarnation for understanding the crucifixion: "If we view Christ on the cross as a third party being punished for the sins of transgressors, we have widely missed the mark. . . . Christ is not a third party. On account of his divinity, Christ is one with God, to whom the 'debt' is owed. It is therefore God who through Christ's death shoulders the burden of our transgression against God and frees us from just retribution. But since on account of Christ's humanity he is also one with us, the debtors, it is we who die in Christ and are thus freed from guilt" (Volf, *The End of Memory: Remembering Rightly in a Violent World* [Grand Rapids, MI: Eerdmans, 2006], 117). Volf goes on to observe, "We also miss the mark if we believe that Christ's suffering somehow encourages the abused passively to accept their abuse. The message of the cross is not that it is legitimate to 'force people to serve in functions that ordinarily would have been fulfilled by someone else,' as Dolores Williams has stated. Since no third party is involved, in Christ's Passion no one is forced to do anything for anyone else. Substitution is a gift initiated and willingly given to wrongdoers by the One who was wronged, not a burden of service placed on an outsider. And it is a gift that, far from signaling the passive acceptance of abuse, most radically calls into question such abuse. For it condemns the wrongdoing while at the same time freeing the wrong-doers, who receive forgiveness in repentance, not just from punishment and guilt but also from the hold of the evil deed on their lives" (117). While "satisfaction" seems to me a more fruitful term than "substitution," Volf's reflections on Christ's Passion are theologically rich.

133. As Vonier says, however, "To entirely spiritualize the oblation and make of it exclusively an act of the created mind and will would be the abolition of the sacrifice; all

This point places at the forefront a crucial distinction between Christ's priesthood and the actions of Old Testament priests vis-à-vis their sacrificial victims: Christ the priest did not slay himself in sacrifice. Rather, through his active spiritual agency, he allowed himself to fall into the hands of those who sought to kill him: as Aquinas puts it, "of His own free-will He exposed Himself to death" and "freely offered Himself to suffering."[134] In allowing them to kill him, he did not kill himself, but rather permitted his enemies' wickedness to take its course. Aquinas relies here upon the suffering servant of Isaiah 53, who, in dying for "our iniquities" (Isaiah 53:5), does not kill himself but allows his persecutors to do their will: "He was oppressed, and he was afflicted, yet he opened not his mouth; like a lamb that is led to the slaughter, and like a sheep that before its shearers is dumb, so he opened not his mouth" (Isaiah 53:7).[135] Christ, like the suffering servant, is a sacrificial "victim" in the sense that he freely wills to undergo suffering and death, but he is only a sacrificial victim in this sense. He is not a "human sacrifice," because the only sense in which he is a sacrificial victim is the sense in which he allows his enemies to do their worst. In this sense, however, it is indeed his human life that, in freely and lovingly bearing our sins, he offers to the Father in a perfect priestly action.[136]

---

sacrifices are of the things that are bodily. . . . To give to Christ's crucifixion and death only moral worth, even if it be to an infinite degree, is not the whole of Christianity; there is something besides the moral worth of the suffering and dying Christ, there is the sacrifice" (*A Key to the Doctrine of the Eucharist*, 107–8). Not Christ's love alone, but Christ's love in union with his spilling of his blood changes the world. It remains the case that, as Romanus Cessario states, "it is not the sacrifice of his body on the altar of the cross in which this perfect worship formally consists, but his personal offering of obedience and love" ("Aquinas on Christian Salvation," 125). Thus when speaking about the crucifixion and death of Christ it is necessary to interpret "the efficacy of Christ's sufferings and death in relation to his human soul" (ibid.) without thereby leaving out the bodily dimension of his action.

134. ST III, q. 22, a. 2, ad 1 and 2.

135. Quoted in ibid., ad 1. Drawing largely upon 1 Enoch, Margaret Barker proposes that "the Servant figure was modeled on the one who performed the atonement rites in the first temple": see Barker, "Atonement: The Rite of Healing," in her *The Great High Priest*, 42–55, at 54.

136. For further discussion see Cessario, "Aquinas on Christian Salvation," 123–25. Cessario comments, "Three features of Aquinas' theology of satisfaction merit careful attention. First, Aquinas locates the essence of Christ's sacrifice in the perfect meshing of his human will with what the Father from all eternity wills for the salvation of the world. Aquinas offers no support for those who would advance a theory of penal substitution as the mechanism by which the benefits of Christ reach the human race. Love, not punishment, dominates Aquinas' account of the efficacy of the Passion. Thus and second, the love and obedience of the Incarnate Son inaugurates the new dispensation. Christ reveals the perfection of the beatitude that he himself teaches as constitutive of the new law: 'Blessed are those who are persecuted for righteousness' sake, for theirs is the kingdom of heaven' (Matt. 5:10). Third, Christ fulfils the

A Sanctifying Action

Even if God certainly does not require a "passive" human sacrifice—
and thus does not require a human sacrifice at all—does God nonetheless require a human "victim," however true it may be that Christ's
priestly action does not consist in slaying himself, but solely in allowing (through an action of spiritual sacrifice in perfect charity) his
enemies to do their worst? This question turns our attention to the
"sanctifying" dimension of Christ's priestly action. Why should
Christ's suffering and bloody death serve to make us holy? Why does
the eschatological and sacrificial expiation of sins come about through
the suffering and death of Christ?

First and foremost, God requires neither a human sacrifice
nor a human victim. God needs nothing from creatures. One cannot
emphasize enough that God did not institute the sacrificial worship of
Israel because he desired blood. In the chapter of *City of God* quoted by
Aquinas, Augustine observes, "When he [the author of Psalm 51] says
that God does not want sacrifices he means that he does not want them
in the way supposed by the fools, namely for his own gratification."[137]
Yet God does wish the salvation of human beings. As 1 Timothy says,
God "desires all men to be saved and to come to the knowledge of the
truth"—the truth that "there is one God and there is one mediator
between God and men, the man Christ Jesus, who gave himself as a
ransom for all" (1 Timothy 2:4–5). Why would Christ the mediator give
"himself as a ransom for all"? How could Christ's suffering and death be
the efficacious expression of God's desire for "all men to be saved"?[138]

---

role of Suffering Servant as described in Isaiah and in the Pauline writings. Although the
biblical theme of the Suffering Servant has occasioned an unbalanced theological presentation
of Christ's suffering, Aquinas presents Christ's obedience to God's plan of salvation without
suggesting a vengeful God who exacts a terrible punishment from an innocent victim. Instead,
he points to the example of virtue which Christ exhibits for our edification. In sum, the heart
of Aquinas' salvation theology lies in the loving service of a priest-Son to God" (124–25).
Compare Hans Urs von Balthasar's approach, for example in *Theo-Drama: Theological Dramatic
Theory*, vol. 5, *The Last Act*, trans. Graham Harrison (German 1983; San Francisco: Ignatius
Press, 1998), 256–69.

137. Augustine, *City of God*, Book X, ch. 5 (p. 378).

138. It is here that, in Mark Heim's view, Anselm's doctrine of satisfaction goes astray: "The
classic penal substitutionary theology of atonement (we will take Anselm as its representative)
constructs the terms of just such a hidden transaction. It posits a cosmic bargain that takes
place on a plane quite distinct from the historical reality of the crucifixion" (Heim, *Saved from
Sacrifice*, 297). For Heim "the Anselmian view of the cross is defined by two major additional
steps. The first is the decision to privilege legal images to represent the basic dynamic of 'death

In order to accomplish the salvation of human beings, Aquinas points out, God does not need human action. No mere human being can forgive sins. If God wills to forgive sins, he needs no human cooperation to do so, since the forgiveness of sins is entirely God's prerogative. In this regard, Aquinas quotes Isaiah 43:25, where God says, "I, I am He who blots out your transgressions for my own sake, and I will not remember your sins."[139] It would seem, then, that regarding the forgiveness of sins, Christ's priestly action—which, as the action of the mediator, is Christ's action as man, not as God—is of no account. Another difficulty arises from the fact that, even if Christ's suffering and death were supposed to be a sufficient "ransom," Christians continue to pray for the forgiveness of their sins and "the [eucharistic] Sacrifice is offered continuously in the Church."[140] Again

---

for us.' . . . The second step is to conflate this legal framework with a vision of divine justice that dictates God's purpose in suffering death. If Christ steps in to intercept a blow meant for us, where does that blow itself come from? It is occasioned by our sin (so far, a view fully in accord with the general tradition). Anselm's departure is to insist with new systematic rigor that it is actually coming from God. What we need to be rescued from is the deserved wrath and punishment of God. God wishes to be merciful, and so God becomes the one to be punished on behalf of us all. God strikes the same blow that God protects us from" (299). Heim goes on to note, "The key error is to refer both the meaning and need of Jesus' death to its character as an offering to God. What Anselm rejects at the level of human community, he re-creates at the level of community between God and humanity, a community whose reconciliation depends on the offering of an innocent victim. Most important, Anselm presents God as the one who requires this sacrifice and also as the one to whom it is offered. Scapegoating is a human practice, and Anselm is clear that such a practice cannot solve our estrangement from God. But in his view God has taken over a human scapegoating sacrifice (the execution of Jesus) and turned it into a unique scapegoating sacrifice of unimaginable magnitude. God is doing what human sacrifice does, but on a much larger scale, and one time only. God has not stepped into the process to oppose it, but to perfect it. Sacrifice to end sacrifice is an accurate and biblical way to describe Jesus' death, but it is an ambiguous and delicately poised idea. Anselm has taken it to mean that God does the same thing that human scapegoaters do, taking it to an ultimate extreme. Instead of God throwing a wrench into the gears of human sacrifice, Anselm's God has endorsed that machinery, borrowing it to perform the biggest and most effective sacrifice of all. Jesus has become our all-purpose scapegoat, whose suffering generates an infinite reservoir of merit that, like his shed blood, can be dispensed through the sacraments" (300). As Heim concludes, "These are fatal steps" (300), because "rather than a strategic act of resistance to overthrow sacred violence, the cross becomes a divine endorsement of it" (302). In response to Heim's critique, two questions should be posed: Is there a relational, personal "order" of justice (an "order" of offering what is due) inscribed in the very being of rational creatures (against the view of an extrinsic "divine wrath") that our sins against God and against other human beings wound? Does Jesus' active self-sacrifice, in which the defining element is love, make him a passive "scapegoat"?

139. ST III, q. 22, a. 3, obj. 1.

140. Ibid., obj. 2.

it would seem that Christ's human (priestly) action has hardly been sufficient, even if one were to suppose that it could be sufficient.

In light of these difficulties regarding the sanctifying effect of Christ's priestly action, Aquinas takes his bearings from three New Testament verses in particular: Romans 3:24–25, "they are justified by his grace as a gift, through the redemption which is in Christ Jesus, whom God put forward as an expiation by his blood"; Hebrews 9:14 (to which I will add verse 13), "For if the sprinkling of defiled persons with the blood of goats and bulls and with the ashes of a heifer sanctifies for the purification of the flesh, how much more shall the blood of Christ, who through the eternal Spirit offered himself without blemish to God, purify your conscience from dead works to serve the living God"; and John 1:29 (the words of John the Baptist), "Behold, the Lamb of God, who takes away the sin of the world!"[141] In each case, Jesus' sacrificial "blood" clearly causes, according to the New Testament, our sanctification. How could this be so?

Aquinas proposes two ways, both having to do not with a change in God, but with a change in human beings. Christ's priestly action does not cause God to forgive us by an outpouring of love, but rather removes the impediments in us to God's merciful outpouring of love. The change in us sanctifies us. But how, specifically, does Christ's priestly action accomplish a change in us? Aquinas first observes that we possess two impediments to our reception of God's mercy. Namely, our hearts are "stained" by sin, in that we willfully turn away from God's mercy, and in addition we owe a "debt of punishment" due in justice to those who willfully turn away from God. The twofold problem, then, is that our hearts are evil and that our evil merits punishment. We require, therefore, a twofold interior change: first, our hearts must be turned back to God (removing the "stain"), and second, our "debt of punishment" must be paid.[142]

---

141. The quotation from Romans comes from the corpus of ST III, q. 22, a. 3; that from Hebrews from the *sed contra;* and that from John from ad 3.

142. By contrast, Marilyn McCord Adams argues that God bears responsibility for the human predicament, and that therefore Christ's sacrifice is offered to us as payment for the debt that God, in Adams's view, incurs by creating us vulnerable to physical and moral evils. She writes, "God also sacrifices Godself—the Word made flesh, a material offering made holy by virtue of hypostatic union—to us. Certainly Emmanuel, God-with-us, counts as a communion sacrifice; so also as a gift sacrifice, a sweet smelling savor to honor us by His visitation. Strictly speaking God cannot make sin offerings, because—without obligations to others—God cannot sin no matter what God does. Nevertheless, because radical vulnerability to, inevitable

In human relationships, we can understand that a man who murders out of hatred not only needs healing in his heart, but also owes a debt of punishment to those he has offended. Or, to give another example, if one steals money, one cannot solely have a change of heart and experience true repentance; one must also make recompense for the injury of the theft. These juridical cases, however, seem ill-suited to the human relationship with God. We already owe everything to God, and God's mercy is infinite. Why would God demand "punishment" or "recompense" from us? Why would not simply healing our hearts be sufficient?

Aquinas certainly holds that Christ's priestly action heals our hearts. Inquiring into whether Christ's Passion was the most fitting way of liberating human beings from sin, for example, Aquinas notes, "In the first place, man knows thereby how much God loves him, and is thereby stirred to love Him in return, and therein lies the perfection of human salvation; since the Apostle says (Rom. v. 8): *God commendeth His charity towards us; for when as yet we were sinners . . . Christ died for us.*"[143] Similarly, Aquinas remarks upon the relationship that the members of Christ's mystical body have to their head and observes that Christ's merit in suffering for the sake of justice redounds to all his members.[144]

(at least collective) participation in horrors, is a harm to human beings for which God is responsible, God's offering of the Word made flesh to us bears analogies to sin offerings" (Adams, *Christ and Horrors: The Coherence of Christology* [Cambridge: Cambridge University Press, 2006], 275). In addition to lacking biblical warrant and to instantiating "original sin" in creation, Christ's sacrifice as offered "to us" requires that Christ's sacrifice, as an integral whole, be separated from worship (including Christ's human charity) so as not to become idolatrous.

143. ST III, q. 46, a. 3. In this section I employ some texts from outside q. 22.

144. ST III, q. 48, a. 1. On Aquinas's use of the phrase "*corpus mysticum*," see Martin Morard, "Les expressions 'corpus mysticum' et 'persona mystica' dans l'oeuvre de saint Thomas d'Aquin," *Revue Thomiste* 95 (1995): 653–64. In this regard Henri de Lubac, sj's, *Corpus Mysticum: The Eucharist and the Church in the Middle Ages*, trans. Gemma Simmonds, Christopher Stephens, and Richard Price (French 1949; Notre Dame, IN: University of Notre Dame Press, 2007) caused some misunderstanding. De Lubac argues that in the early Middle Ages the Eucharist's intrinsic ecclesial referent was lost due to a shift in theological terminology: the phrase "*corpus mysticum*" came to mean the Church rather than the Eucharist, with the result that ecclesiology became overly juridical. De Lubac holds that Aquinas's theology reflects a late stage of this deleterious shift due to the use of "*corpus Ecclesiae mysticum*" rather than "*corpus Christi mysticum.*" Morard, however, shows that Aquinas's theology does not in fact evidence such a shift. De Lubac's thesis informs Michel de Certeau, *The Mystic Fable*, trans. Michael B. Smith (Chicago: University of Chicago Press, 1992). In popularized form, one finds the thesis in the criticisms made by Paul McPartlan against medieval ecclesiology in his *Sacrament of Salvation: An Introduction to Eucharistic Ecclesiology* (Edinburgh: T. & T. Clark, 1995), 37–38.

Why then should Christ's priestly action also operate as an expiatory sin-offering, as "satisfaction" of the "debt of punishment"?[145] In addition to the New Testament texts noted above, Aquinas approaches this question through Isaiah 53:4, "he has borne our griefs and carried our sorrows," and Jeremiah 11:19, "I was like a gentle lamb led to the slaughter."[146] Such texts might be seen as implying an extrinsic juridical relationship between creature and creator. Aquinas, however, recognizes an order of justice inscribed in the very heart of human beings' relationship with God and each other. Justice is not extrinsic to any personal relationship. Aquinas, then, does not recoil from the New Testament's juridical language, which he understands to express the intimate, yet wounded, relationship between the creature and the creator. Even so, does God in fact demand "recompense"? If sinful human beings suffer from their self-inflicted wounds, why should a sinless human being suffer on their behalf, thus perpetuating, in some sense, the history of human suffering (even so as ultimately to end it)? Could not God sanctify human beings without any further suffering, let alone the agonizing suffering of the incarnate Son of God?

Indeed, Aquinas observes that God could have sanctified human beings in another way: "speaking simply and absolutely, it was

Regarding the ninth- and eleventh-century debates, Ephraim Radner has challenged de Lubac's thesis as well (while otherwise accepting it): see Radner, *The End of the Church: A Pneumatology of Christian Division in the West* (Grand Rapids, MI: Eerdmans, 1998), 208–10, 228–39. John Milbank takes up the thesis in his *Being Reconciled: Ontology and Pardon* (London: Routledge, 2003), 122–37, although he makes an exception for Aquinas and Bonaventure. Typical of the popularization, which cannot be blamed on de Lubac, is Joseph M. Powers, sj's, claim that the cultic priesthood gradually displaced the eucharistic community between the eighth and thirteenth centuries: see Powers, *Eucharistic Theology* (New York: Herder and Herder, 1967), 26–31.

145. On Christ's cross as "satisfaction" for sins, see the following studies, which are both historically and speculatively rich: Emmanuel Perrier, op, "L'enjeu christologique de la satisfaction" (I) and (II), *Revue Thomiste* 103 (2003): 105–36 and 203–47; Rik Van Nieuwenhove, "St Anselm and St Thomas Aquinas on 'Satisfaction': or How Catholic and Protestant Understandings of the Cross Differ," *Angelicum* 80 (2003): 159–76; Romanus Cessario, op, *The Godly Image: Christ and Satisfaction in Catholic Thought from Anselm to Aquinas;* idem, "Aquinas on Christian Salvation," especially 121–34.

146. ST III, q. 22, a. 3. The quotation from Jeremiah appears in obj. 3. For contemporary debates regarding the meaning of Isaiah 53 and its interpretation in the New Testament and later Christian writings, see, e.g., *The Suffering Servant: Isaiah 53 in Jewish and Christian Sources,* ed. Bernd Janowski and Peter Stuhlmacher, trans. Donald P. Bailey Grand Rapids, MI: Eerdmans, 2004); *Jesus and the Suffering Servant: Isaiah 53 and Christian Origins,* ed. William H. Bellinger Jr. and William R. Farmer (Harrisburg, PA: Trinity Press International, 1998). See also Christopher R. North, *The Suffering Servant in Deutero-Isaiah: An Historical and Critical Study,* 2nd ed. (New York: Oxford University Press, 1963).

possible for God to deliver mankind otherwise than by the Passion of Christ, because *no word shall be impossible with God* (Luke i. 37)."[147] In willing the Passion of Christ, God was not constrained by the order of justice, as if God, like a human judge, had to exact the proper penalty for the crime. On the contrary, God was entirely free. Aquinas points out that unlike a human judge, "God has no one higher than Himself, for He is the sovereign and common good of the whole universe."[148] When human beings sin against God (and all sin is ultimately against God), we wound our relationship with him—a relationship that, like any relationship, is constituted by an order of justice. God can mercifully forgive sins against himself without exacting just punishment, "just as anyone else, overlooking a personal trespass, without satisfaction, acts mercifully and not unjustly."[149] Why then did not God simply forgive all sins in this way, rather than through the bloody death of his incarnate Son?

Aquinas answers that God freely chose the most merciful way. Aquinas gives a number of reasons why salvation through Christ's Passion is more merciful than God simply forgiving our sins by fiat. The central reason has to do with the dignity that God gives human beings by allowing our injustice to be healed from within human nature. The dignity of human cooperation and achievement would be entirely lost if God had simply forgiven our sins by fiat. The seriousness of history, of human free actions, would have been greatly undermined. If God simply forgave sin by fiat, furthermore, he would not have conquered sin by uniting to himself a human nature in the Person of the Son, a union that affirms and augments human dignity in an unfathomably rich manner. As Aquinas states with regard to Christ's achievement as the new Adam, "it redounded to man's greater dignity, that as man was overcome and deceived by the devil [in Eden], so also it should be a man that should overthrow the devil; and as man deserved death, so a man by dying should vanquish death."[150] Jesus Christ, a

---

147. ST III, q. 46, a. 2.

148. ST III, q. 46, a. 2, ad 3.

149. Ibid.

150. ST III, q. 46, a. 3. N. T. Wright's approval of the "Christus Victor" theory of atonement is not foreign to Aquinas's theology, although Aquinas's doctrine is more complex. Wright states, "I find myself compelled toward one of the well-known theories of atonement, of how God deals with evil through the death of evil through the death of Jesus, not as a replacement for the events or the stories nor as a single theory to trump all others, but as a

man, establishes justice between humankind and God by his Passion, and this human achievement is possible because this man, while fully human, is the Son of God: "Although Christ was a priest, not as God, but as man, yet one and the same was both priest and God."[151]

But why does the new Adam die to restore our life? The proper penalty for sin against God is death: as Saint Paul puts it, "the wages of sin is death" (Romans 6:23). This is so because sin, in wounding the relationship of human beings to God, disorders the human person interiorly and leads ultimately to the rupture of the soul and body in death, and also because what Adam and Eve strove for was immortality on their own terms rather than as dependent creatures, and in so doing separated themselves willfully from the Source of life. The penalty of death is not an extrinsic requirement of a wrathful god, but rather belongs intrinsically to the relational wound or rupture that sin brings about. It pertains to human "dignity" that the relational wound be healed from within, from the side of human beings. Jesus Christ makes "satisfaction," heals the wound, by paying our penalty of death without, as a sinless man, owing it. Jesus' overflowing justice—the

---

theme which carries me further than the others toward the heart of it all. I refer to the Christus Victor theme, the belief that on the cross Jesus has won the victory over the powers of evil. Once that is in place, the other theories come in to play their respective parts. For Paul, Jesus' death clearly involves (for example in Romans 8:3) a judicial or penal element, being God's proper No to sin expressed on Jesus as Messiah, as Israel's and therefore the world's representative" (Wright, *Evil and the Justice of God* [Downers Grove, IL: InterVarsity Press, 2006], 95).

151. ST III, q. 22, a. 3, ad 1. Citing the Christology of the Council of Ephesus, Aquinas goes on to observe here, "Hence in so far as His human nature operated by virtue of the Divine, that sacrifice was most efficacious for the blotting out of sins." See also the discussion of the purpose of the Incarnation in ST III, q. 1, a. 2. Christ's priestly action is his human action of his Passion, but his human action, one must recall, is the action of the Son of God (since Christ is one Person). Aquinas observes, "Satisfaction may be said to be sufficient in two ways—first, perfectly, inasmuch as it is condign, being adequate to make good the fault committed, and in this way the satisfaction of a mere man cannot be sufficient for sin, both because the whole of human nature has been corrupted by sin, whereas the goodness of any person or persons could not make up adequately for the harm done to the whole of the nature; and also because a sin committed against God has a kind of infinity from the infinity of the Divine majesty, because the greater the person we offend, the more grievous the offense. Hence for condign satisfaction it was necessary that the act of the one satisfying should have an infinite efficiency, as being of God and man. Secondly, man's satisfaction may be termed sufficient, imperfectly—i.e., in the acceptation of him who is content with it, even though it is not condign, and in this way the satisfaction of a mere man is sufficient. And forasmuch as everything imperfect presupposes some perfect thing, by which it is sustained, hence it is that the satisfaction of every mere man has its efficiency from the satisfaction of Christ" (ST III, q. 1, a. 2, ad 3).

glorious goodness of his created charity, obedience, and humility as the incarnate Son of God—heals the woundedness of human beings' relationship with God by restoring superabundantly the lack of goodness that characterizes humankind due to the history of sin's destruction of human goods. Baptism unites us, his members, with his glorious goodness (holiness) in his salvific death: "Do you not know that all of us who have been baptized into Christ Jesus were baptized into his death? We were buried therefore with him by baptism into death, so that as Christ was raised from the dead by the glory of the Father, we too might walk in newness of life. For if we have been united with him in a death like his, we shall certainly be unity with him in a resurrection like his" (Romans 6:3–5). Reconciliation with God is accomplished by Christ's Pasch, rather than being merely a "word" spoken to us.

Similarly, commenting in the *Summa Theologiae* on Romans 3:24–25, Aquinas affirms that God's will that Christ's Passion make satisfaction for all sins "was in keeping with both His mercy and His justice."[152] He goes on to explain:

> With His justice, because by His Passion Christ made satisfaction for the sin of the human race; and so man was set free by Christ's justice: and with His mercy, for since man of himself could not satisfy for the sin of all human nature, as was said above (Q. 1, A. 2), God gave him His Son to satisfy for him. . . . And this came of more copious mercy than if He had forgiven sins without satisfaction. Hence it is said (Ephes. ii. 4): *God, who is rich in mercy, for His exceeding charity wherewith He loved us, even when we were dead in sins, hath quickened us together in Christ.*[153]

---

152. ST III, q. 46, a. 1, ad 3.

153. Ibid. In his recent *Saving Power: Theories of Atonement and Forms of the Church* (Grand Rapids, MI: Eerdmans, 2005), Peter Schmiechen seeks to uncover, among other things, "the relations between theories of atonement and the formation of the church—its basic structure, faith, life, and work" (353). In the context of his inquiry, he observes that Anselm's "theory of the restoration of creation . . . concludes with a direct connection with the sacrament of the Lord's Supper. The benefits of Christ, received from God the Father, are shared with believers who follow the mandates of Scripture and participate in the sacramental life of the church" (357–58). Could this theory of atonement, Schmiechen asks, exist outside the bounds of a sacramentally organized Church, for which Anselm's theory provides "a theological rationale" (ibid., 358)? He thinks that it could, but he remarks nonetheless that "if Jesus participates in our life to restore the creation, then our sacramental participation in his life is a natural and reasonable mode of transmission" (359–60), and he adds that "the interpretations of sacrifice, renewal (Athanasius), and restoration (Anselm) are tightly linked to sacramental transmission. These associations are so strong that it is difficult to decide whether it is the historical association or a truly natural link between interpretation and mode of transmission" (361).

As the son of Abraham and David through whom all nations are to be blessed (cf. Genesis 12:3; 22; 2 Samuel 7:13), Christ pours out the eschatological blessings not only through the justice that his priestly action achieves, but also, as we have seen, through the divine mercy and love that it reveals. Christ's incomparable manifestation of divine love stimulates human beings to love God in return, and Christ in his Passion displays the virtues—among them "obedience, humility, constancy, justice"—that "are requisite for man's salvation."[154] If God loves us so much as to become one of us, and suffer and die for us, then "man is all the more bound to refrain from sin, according to 1 Cor. vi. 20: *You are bought with a great price: glorify and bear God in your body.*"[155]

A Unitive Action

What about the unitive dimension of Christ's priestly action? In seeking the reason for the revealed truth that God designated Jesus "a high priest after the order of Melchizedek" (Hebrews 5:10), Aquinas holds that "the excellence of Christ's [priesthood] over the Levitical priesthood was foreshadowed in the priesthood of Melchisedech," in part because Abraham, from whom the Levitical priesthood descended, tithed to Melchizedek.[156] But the deeper reason, in Aquinas's view, has to do with how Melchizedek's priesthood foreshadows the unity accomplished by Christ's priestly action, a unity that could not be accomplished by the Levitical priesthood. The Levitical priesthood continually offered new sacrifices, and these sacrifices did not succeed in establishing a holy people. Had this not been the case, then the people of Israel would never have looked for a Messiah. As Aquinas

---

154. ST III, q. 46, a. 3. Here Aquinas quotes 1 Peter 2:21 (to which I will add verses 22–25), "For to this [the patient suffering of injustice] you have been called, because Christ also suffered for you, leaving you an example, that you should follow in his steps. He committed no sin; no guile was found on his lips. When he was reviled, he did not revile in return; when he suffered, he did not threaten; but he trusted to him who judges justly. He himself bore our sins in his body on the tree, that we might die to sin and live to righteousness. By his wounds you have been healed. For you were straying like sheep, but have now returned to the Shepherd and Guardian of your souls."

155. ST III, q. 46, a. 3. Cf. the valuable study of Karl Olav Sandnes, *Belly and Body in the Pauline Epistles* (Cambridge: Cambridge University Press, 2002).

156. ST III, q. 22, a. 6. On Christ and Melchizedek in Aquinas's *Commentary on the Epistle to the Hebrews*, see especially Antoine Guggenheim, *Jésus Christ, Grand Prêtre*, Part II, ch. 5. On Christ and Melchizedek, see also Vonier, *A Key to the Doctrine of the Eucharist*, 148–49.

puts it, the Levitical priesthood "did not wash away sins" and "was not eternal."[157]

By contrast, Jesus' priestly action is "once for all" (Hebrews 9:26); his sacrifice never needs to be repeated, because it permanently establishes holiness. His priesthood is "eternal": no high priest ever takes his place. Following Augustine's view that the many grains united in the bread and the many grapes united in the wine symbolize the unity of the Church, Aquinas argues that the Levitical priesthood symbolizes sacrifice (through the shedding of blood), while Melchizedek's priesthood symbolizes Communion (through the bread and wine).[158] Since human beings receive the effect of Jesus' saving sacrifice through Communion in faith in the eucharistic sacrifice, Melchizedek's priestly offering of bread and wine best symbolizes the unitive dimension of Jesus' priestly action. The unitive dimension of Christ's priesthood explains for Aquinas why Jesus' priesthood receives its primary definition through the letter to the Hebrews' application of Psalm 110:4, "Thou art a priest for ever, after the order of Melchizedek" (Hebrews 5:6, 7:17).

The fruit of Jesus' sacrifice, and of the eucharistic sacrament-sacrifice that represents Jesus' sacrifice, is the unity of the people of God, the mystical body of Christ, in the holiness attained in and through Jesus' sacrifice.[159] Jesus dies not for himself or his own needs, but to unify all others in himself.[160] Saint Paul speaks of the Father's "purpose which he set forth in Christ as a plan for the fullness of time, to unite all things in him, things in heaven and things on earth" (Ephesians 1:9–10): the Father "has put all things under his feet and has made him the head over all things for the church, which is his body, the fullness of him who fills all in all" (Ephesians 1:22–23). Aquinas explains, therefore, that "it is not fitting for Christ to be the recipient of the effect of His priesthood, but rather to communicate it to others."[161] His priestly action is the source of all unity in holiness,

---

157. ST III, q. 22, a. 6.

158. ST III, q. 22, a. 6, ad 2; see also ST III, q. 75, a. 2, obj. 3, and elsewhere for the citation from Augustine's *Tractate* 26 on the Gospel of John.

159. See most recently Gilles Emery, OP, "The Ecclesial Fruit of the Eucharist in St. Thomas Aquinas," trans. Therese C. Scarpelli, in his *Trinity, Church, and the Human Person: Thomistic Essays* (Naples, FL: Sapientia Press, 2007), 155–72.

160. ST III, q. 22, a. 4.

161. Ibid.

both Israel's (as the fulfillment of Torah and Temple) and the Church's: "Christ is the fountain-head of the entire priesthood: for the priest of the Old Law was a figure of Him; while the priest of the New Law works in His person."[162]

Emphasizing the unitive aspect of Christ's Pasch, Aquinas concludes his discussion of Christ's priesthood by attending to the symbolism of Melchizedek's offering of bread and wine. Aquinas refers to Hebrews 7:2's statement that Melchizedek "is first, by translation of his name, king of righteousness, and then he is also king of Salem, that is, king of peace."[163] As the true "king of righteousness" and "king of peace," Jesus Christ, through his priestly action, has the power to unite the human race in the holiness of God. By washing away sins, Jesus' eternal priesthood establishes the unity of the "church of God" (Galatians 1:13). The restoration that Jesus accomplishes thereby blesses all nations.[164]

CONCLUSION

In the context of questions about whether Christ is a "priest," we began by examining how contemporary New Testament scholarship, following the lead of N. T. Wright, identifies eschatological, sacrificial, sanctifying, and unitive dimensions of Jesus' Paschal action. Understanding his mission as a cultic one, Jesus seeks to unify Israel (and through Israel all the nations) in holiness, and thereby to accomplish the promised eschatological restoration. In his Pasch, he inaugurates the eschaton through his sacrificial undergoing of the final tribulation for the sins of the people of God, and through Baptism (Matthew 28:19) and the Eucharist (Luke 22:19) he enables his followers to share in his tribulation so as to share in his vindication.

Had Jesus understood his mission solely in terms of teaching and service, he could not be rightly described as a "priest"; but in fact the eschatological, sacrificial, sanctifying, and unitive dimensions of

---

162. Ibid.

163. See ST III, q. 22, a. 6, obj. 3.

164. For further discussion of the themes treated in this section of the chapter, see my *Sacrifice and Community*, especially chapters 2 and 3, and my *Christ's Fulfillment of Torah and Temple: Salvation according to Thomas Aquinas* (Notre Dame, IN: University of Notre Dame Press, 2002), as well as the further secondary sources cited in both works.

his Paschal action require theological reflection on his priesthood. The second section of this chapter contributed to such reflection by exploring Aquinas's theology of Christ's priesthood in q. 22 of the *Summa Theologiae*, where Aquinas draws upon the rich heritage of patristic and earlier medieval exegetical and theological work. It is well known that some contemporary theologians find Aquinas's account of Jesus' priestly action to be overly cultic and juridical, while others hold that Aquinas does not go far enough, largely because he somewhat limits the scope of Christ's human suffering and does not locate it within an intra–Trinitarian event. It seems to me, however, that Aquinas's theology of Jesus' priesthood illumines the witness of scripture by means of a careful investigation of the various dimensions of priestly action. Exegesis and theology—contemporary and patristic-medieval—here go together.

Because Jesus' mission culminates in a priestly action that he shares with his disciples at the Last Supper and in which the eschatological community constitutively partakes,[165] the mediation of the power of his Pasch requires a cultic priesthood, so that all believers may fully be "a chosen race, a royal priesthood, a holy nation, God's own people" (1 Peter 2:9). The Christian hierarchical priesthood sacramentally mediates to all believers the power of Jesus' Pasch. Yet, did a hierarchical priesthood of this nature exist in the earliest Christian communities? To this question we now turn.

---

165. Cf. Frances Young's view in *The Use of Sacrificial Ideas in Greek Christian Writers from the New Testament to John Chrysostom*. While considering the New Testament to be justified in interpreting Christ's cross by means of the Old Testament sacrificial cult, she interprets the Eucharist of the early Church to be a fellowship meal of thanksgiving, and at most a "gift-sacrifice of praise and thanksgiving" that shares in the eschatological liturgy (see 266). Much rests upon her claim that up through the fourth century, "the Eucharist was never regarded as an expiatory sacrifice in its own right" (267). But why should the Eucharist be understood strictly "in its own right," rather than understood always in relation to Christ's cross? Its association with the death of Christ is, as Jesus himself makes clear to his disciples at the Last Supper, at the very heart of the Eucharist. This association hardly need be merely nominal, a matter of words linking two thoroughly independent realities. For Young, the Eucharist, insofar as it has sacrificial dimensions, at most serves as a propitiatory "memorial of his saving death or actualising of the benefits of it" (275). If the Eucharist actualizes the benefits of Christ's expiatory sacrifice, however, would not expiation be among these benefits, and would not the Eucharist thus be in some (participatory) sense expiatory?

Chapter 3

The Priesthood of the First Christians

In his encyclical *Ecclesia de Eucharistia*, John Paul II states that "the apostles 'were both the seeds of the new Israel and the beginning of the sacred hierarchy.' By analogy with the Covenant of Mount Sinai, sealed by sacrifice and the sprinkling of blood, the actions and words of Jesus at the Last Supper laid the foundations of the new messianic community, the People of the New Covenant."[1] The sacramental mandate given to the disciples/apostles at the Last Supper requires that the eschatological "messianic community" be hierarchically structured. As *Lumen Gentium* remarks, "For the fulfillment of such great duties [*munera*], the apostles were enriched by Christ with a special outpouring of the Holy Spirit who came down upon them (see Acts 1:8; 2:4; John 20:22–23), and they, by the imposition of hands, handed on the spiritual gift to their helpers (see 1 Timothy 4:14; 2 Timothy 1:6–7); and this has been handed down to us in episcopal consecration."[2]

---

1. John Paul II, *Ecclesia de Eucharistia* (2003), 21, citing the Second Vatican Council's Decree on the Missionary Activity of the Church, *Ad Gentes*, 5.

2. *Lumen Gentium*, 21, in *Decrees of the Ecumenical Councils*, vol. 2, *Trent to Vatican II*, ed. Norman P. Tanner, sj (Washington, DC: Georgetown University Press, 1990), p. 865. See also *Dei Verbum*, 8. For the creedal understanding of the Church's "apostolicity," see Jared Wicks, sj, "Ecclesial Apostolicity Confessed in the Creed," *Pro Ecclesia* 9 (2000): 150–64. Commenting on *Lumen Gentium*, Alfonso Carrasco Rouco notes that in the document "the *potestas* of ministry thus appears as an objective reality whose nature, dynamism, and fruit are independent of the will of the minister. . . . In this way, the 'instrumental' nature of this service, whereby the real subject of action is Jesus Christ, keeps the minister from putting his own person at the center. After all, the minister cannot claim to be the principle of the believer's new life, thus putting himself in the place of the Spirit of Christ, nor does he have the right to decide the nature of the service to which he is called or of the communion that he serves. On the contrary, the mission of the minister entails a radical subordination on his part. His significance, his authority in the Church is, paradoxically, rooted in his obedience: it comes from working as the representative of Another, *in persona Christi*, and concretely, by his

Did the first Christians in fact understand ecclesial hierarchy to be intrinsically constitutive of the Church? In examining this question, I proceed in three steps. First, I summarize briefly two recent historical accounts of hierarchy in the early Church, by James Burtchaell and Francis Sullivan, respectively. While affirming that the first Christian communities were marked by hierarchy, Burtchaell and Sullivan present ecclesial hierarchy not as a sacramental reality arising from Christ's mediation of his priestly action, but as a functional form of leadership that Christ did not directly will.[3] Second, limiting myself to 1 Corinthians and the Gospel of Matthew, I propose that in the New Testament ecclesial hierarchy is intrinsic to, rather than merely conducive to, Christian communion.[4] I argue that the apostles received from Christ a unique (sacramental) participation in the

---

keeping and handing on the 'deposit of the faith,' by his being submitted to the Word of God and to the forms of its transmission in history" (Rouco, "Vatican II's Reception of the Dogmatic Teaching on the Roman Primacy," *Communio* 25 [1998]: 576–603, at 593–94).

3. Hans Urs von Balthasar refers to an "(uncrossable) limit: from a Protestant point of view, office, even the office of unity, can be quite useful, perhaps even indispensable, but is (*jure humano*) still merely a function which is designated by the Church. From a Catholic point of view, office will remain an aspect within the organism which takes its mission from Christ (*jure divino*)" (von Balthasar, "Catholicism and the Communion of Saints," trans. Albert K. Wimmer, *Communio* 15 [1988]: 163–68, at 167). Thus he points out, "In the Catholic Church, the office (with Peter as the symbol and guarantor of unity) belongs to the organism: the Church is, as proclaimed by the Second Vatican Council, the *communio hierarchica*" (167). For a theological argument in favor of a largely functional understanding, see Walter Kasper, "A New Dogmatic Outlook on the Priestly Ministry," *Concilium* 43, *The Identity of the Priest*, ed. Karl Rahner, sj (New York: Paulist Press, 1969), 20–33. Avery Dulles, sj, summarizes this essay in his *The Priestly Office: A Theological Reflection* (Mahwah, NJ: Paulist Press, 1997), 47–48. For Kasper, Dulles notes, Christ "breaks through all cultic barriers," with the result that in the New Testament "Christian leaders are designated not by sacral terms (such as *hiereus*, *sacerdos*, and *pontifex*) but rather by secular terms such as *episcopos* (supervisor), *presbyteros* (elder), and *diakonos* (servant)" (47). Dulles observes that while Kasper thinks that the priesthood "needs to be desacralized and demythologized," nonetheless Kasper considers Holy Orders to bestow an ontological configuration to Christ's self-giving service to others (47–48).

4. I focus in this chapter upon the distinctive authority given the disciples/apostles, but from another angle one could also show that the disciples/apostles are models for all Christians, and that their authority is unintelligible apart from the priesthood of all believers. Were this not the case, then the Christian laity would be an anomaly, as Hans Urs von Balthasar points out in his "Office in the Church," trans. A. V. Littledale with Alexander Dru, in *Explorations in Theology*, vol. 2, *Spouse of the Word* (German 1961; San Francisco: Ignatius Press, 1991), 81–141, at 83–87; cf. 139. Von Balthasar rightly warns against supposing that "the life of God among men, as described in the Gospel, would at its profoundest level be directed to the establishment of the clerical body—would, in fact, be a *grand séminaire* for the clergy on whom, after the ascension of the Founder, would devolve the task of handing on to the people the instruction imparted to them in virtue of the powers committed to them alone" (84).

communication of his sanctifying power, and not merely in the communication of his wisdom and example. Insofar as leadership in the earliest Church included this element of sanctifying power, ecclesial hierarchy has an intrinsic place in Christ's mediation of the power of his Pasch and cannot be viewed as a merely functional development. Third, engaging the theology of John Zizioulas and Thomas Aquinas, I inquire further into the "episcopal consecration" of which *Lumen Gentium* speaks. Zizioulas reflects on the bishop (and the presbyterate) in light of the context of the Eucharist, which defines episcopal presidency. Aquinas enriches Zizioulas's approach by grounding ontologically the eucharistic role of bishops and priests in a theology of sacramental "character."

Recent Historical Viewpoints: A Brief Overview

James Burtchaell, csc

James Burtchaell's *From Synagogue to Church: Public Services and Offices in the Earliest Christian Communities* attempts to set forth and evaluate the traditional debate between Catholics and Protestants over the structure of the earliest Church. He summarizes the traditional "Catholic" position, which we noted in *Lumen Gentium*, as holding that "certain offices were established by apostolic authority, and that the apostles in doing this were acting as plenipotentiaries of the Lord."[5] Contemporary scholarly opinion, he observes, generally supports the traditional "Protestant" position, namely that the "appearance of ordered authoritarian offices has its warrant, not from Jesus or the apostles, but from men like Clement and Ignatius, in defiance of the authentic egalitarianism they squelched."[6] Burtchaell calls for a third

---

5. James Tunstead Burtchaell, csc, *From Synagogue to Church: Public Services and Offices in the Earliest Christian Communities* (Cambridge: Cambridge University Press, 1992), 348. An earlier version of the first two sections of this chapter appears in my "Hierarchy and Holiness," in *Wisdom and Holiness, Science and Scholarship: Essays in Honor of Matthew L. Lamb*, ed. Michael Dauphinais and Matthew Levering (Naples, FL: Sapientia Press, 2007), 143–72.

6. Ibid., 349. For this position see, e.g., Daniel Harrington, sj's account of leadership in the early Christian communities: Harrington, *The Church According to the New Testament: What the Wisdom and Witness of Early Christianity Teach Us Today* (Franklin, WI: Sheed & Ward, 2001), 159f. He holds, "At the time of the Pastorals in the late first century or even early

position, a *via media*. He criticizes both the Catholic and the Protestant traditional positions for ignoring portions of the historical evidence:

> The "Catholic" theory projects backward a scenario of dominating clergy who are simply not to be found in the first documents. The "Protestant" theory has had to shrug off the exhibits in evidence—few but unequivocal— that they are unhappy to accept as precedents. For instance, they discount the *episkopoi* and *diakonoi* greeted by Paul in the address of his letter to the Philippians; Paul's call for deference to those put in charge of the Church when they give admonitions; the primacy of the Jerusalem church presided over by James, a non-apostle, with a bench of elders; and the assertion by Clement to the Corinthians who still remembered their earliest days as Church, that in their memory apostles had provided their churches with governing officers whose successors were to be chosen by due process (giving credibility to similar texts in Acts).[7]

---

second century AD, however, it appears that two distinct church orders had been in operation and were in the process of fusion. The *presbyteral* model found in Acts and 1 Timothy 5:17–20 (see also James 5:14; 1 Peter 5:5; 2 John 1; 3 John 1) was based on the organizational model of the Jewish synagogue. The 'bishop and deacon' pattern as it is mentioned in Philippians 1:1 and 1 Timothy 3:1–13 was founded more on the structures of voluntary associations in the Greco-Roman world" (162). According to Harrington, Ignatius of Antioch witnesses to, and bears significant responsibility for, the second century shift: "In fact, so strenuous is Ignatius's insistence on one bishop and the harmonious working together of bishop, presbytery, and deacons that one gets the idea that he 'protests too much' and that his ideas were not universally obvious or acceptable to everyone. Nevertheless, Ignatius and his fellow bishops apparently viewed the monoepiscopate and the threefold structure of church offices as the sure means of defense against Docetists, Judaizers, and other 'heretics.' Whatever the concrete historical circumstances may have contributed, the ecclesiastical structures that Ignatius promoted in his letters have been extraordinarily influential in church history" (164). Harrington goes on to say, "Where, then, did the 'ministerial priesthood' come from? It represents the combination of biblical elements that came together by the late second century AD" (167). A quite different position, grounded in an analysis of apostleship in the earliest Church, is set forth by Aidan Nichols, OP, in his *Holy Order: Apostolic Priesthood from the New Testament to the Second Vatican Council* (Dublin: Veritas Publications, 1990), 5–66. The opposition that Harrington finds between "presbyteral" and "episcopal" models relies upon a functional, rather than sacramental, account of apostolic ministry.

7. Burtchaell, *From Synagogue to Church*, 349. Regarding Clement, Raymond Brown states in a footnote, "The picture is simplified even further by Clement of Rome who asserts that the apostles who received the Gospel and their commands from Jesus Christ went forth to preach and appointed their first converts to be bishops and deacons, with the condition that if these should die, other approved men should succeed to their ministry (42:1–4; 44:1–2). Clement has combined the Twelve with Paul. The contention that this must be historical because it was written in 96, relatively few years after the events, is naive in its evaluation of historical memory" (Raymond E. Brown, ss, *Priest and Bishop: Biblical Reflections* [New York: Paulist Press, 1970], 72, fn. 52). By contrast, Nichols points out that it makes little sense to suppose that the apostolic preaching of the Gospel did not include the deliberate formation of apostolic communal structures (Nichols, *Holy Order*, 26).

Burtchaell argues, then, that there were authoritative offices, including presiding bishops, in the earliest Church, but not "dominating clergy" or carefully organized apostolic succession. He proposes that scholars seek to understand the role of authoritative positions in the earliest Church by attending to how authority functioned in the synagogue. As he says, "It was a Jewish view, not a Christian view, which Jesus tore away from the people and traditions of Abraham, Isaac, and Jacob. And if this be so in so many other usages, might it not be worthwhile to investigate whether and to what extent community organization among the earliest Christians might display and even be illuminated by continuities with its past?"[8]

Turning therefore to the structure of the synagogue, Burtchaell finds a variety of offices as well as a line of authority among the various synagogues. With regard to the latter point, he notes, "The mother of mothers, of course, was Jerusalem, and all synagogues looked to the great council there as to an ultimate authority."[9] This parallels the position of the earliest Christian community in Jerusalem, and later the position of the church of Rome. Among the officers of the synagogue, Burtchaell first treats elders, "presbyteroi": "Their precise function was to give wise counsel and to legitimate community policy, whether they actually formulated it or only ratified it. Elders were collegial."[10] How people became elders, Burtchaell notes, remains

---

8. Burtchaell, *From Synagogue to Church*, 192. Rudolph Schnackenburg emphasizes, on the contrary, that the earliest Church's leadership strongly differs from Jewish priestly hierarchy, primarily because the earliest Church accords all power to Jesus and recognizes no human qualifications such as bloodlines: see Schnackenburg, *The Church in the New Testament*, trans. W. J. O'Hara (New York: Seabury Press, 1965), 126–27. Schnackenburg writes, "Consequently if much in the external constitution of the original church of Jerusalem may suggest Qumran, the underlying conception is fundamentally different. . . . So even in ecclesiastical discipline, which in any case seems to be restricted to exceptional instances, the law of guidance by the Holy Spirit holds good (cf. also 1 Cor 5), and the apostles only act as God's delegates. If later a hierarchy of offices developed, that does not represent a relapse into Jewish modes of thought or abandonment of the fundamental New Testament idea of church order, as long as rule by the heavenly Lord, the origin of authority in God, and the obligation to service of the church were not forgotten" (128). Schnackenburg cites, e.g., S. Johnson, "The Dead Sea Manual of Discipline and the Jerusalem Church of Acts," in *The Scrolls and the New Testament*, ed. K. Stendahl (New York: Harper & Brothers, 1957), 129–42; B. Reicke, "The Constitution of the Primitive Church in the Light of Jewish Documents," in Stendahl, *The Scrolls and the New Testament*, 143–56; J. Schmitt, "L'organisation de l'Église primitive et Qumran," *Recherches bibliques* 4 (1959): 217–31.

9. Burtchaell, *From Synagogue to Church*, 217.

10. Ibid., 228.

unclear, but he suggests that the elders "expected to enjoy that dignity throughout their lifetimes."[11] Secondly, Burtchaell discusses "the notables" of the synagogue, "archontes," an elite group emerging out of the council of elders. Thirdly, the council of elders ("gerousia") possessed a "senior elder" or "president," the "gerousiarches."[12] Among the various synagogues in a large city such as Rome, there could also be an "archigerousiarches" distinguished above the other senior elders.[13] In addition, an "archisynagogos," or "community chief," had charge of the liturgical worship and, under the guidance of the elders and the notables, "he presided over the community, he convened it for its activities, he superintended its staff."[14] Burtchaell compares this position to the presiders, *episkopoi*, of the earliest Christian communities. Other offices include assistant, commissioner, scribe, and reader.

 Lastly, there were the priests, although they presided only at the Temple in Jerusalem, not in the synagogues. Burtchaell comments, "It is striking how decisively the priesthood vanished from the scene of power after the fall of Jerusalem in 70"[15] and the destruction of the Temple. Justifying his downplaying of the priesthood in his list of offices, he explains that well before 70 AD "the local synagogues had already chosen to deny priests any special privileges or position." Despite respect for the priesthood evident in the time of the Maccabean revolt and the elevated position of the priests in Jewish sects such as the one at Qumran, Burtchaell says, the laity had almost entirely decided that the priesthood no longer mattered outside Jerusalem: "in the villages and towns and cities, where priests in plenty dwelt and were available, a totally lay synagogue organization had long since decided it needed no legitimacy which the priests could give."[16] He sees this viewpoint as persisting in the earliest Christian communities, where "it is not that there are no longer any priests: there are no longer any who are not priests."[17] The earliest Christian churches, according to

---

11. Ibid., 231.

12. Ibid., 237.

13. Ibid., 239.

14. Ibid., 244.

15. Ibid., 253.

16. Ibid., 254.

17. Ibid., 323. Likewise, the Mennonite theologian John Howard Yoder remarks, "When Paul wrote, 'everyone has a gift,' he did not mean 'rich man, poor man, beggarman, thief' nor 'butcher, baker, candlestick-maker.' He meant apostles, teachers, healers, discerners of gifts,

Burtchaell, did not have ordained "priests" in the later sense of the word, associated with the celebration of the sacraments.

Comparing Christianity to "contemporaneous sectarian movements" within Judaism, Burtchaell observes that even radical critique of mainstream Judaism often went together with profound indebtedness to the synagogue's institutional structure.[18] With bishops, presbyters, and deacons in mind, he states, "The presiding officer, the college of elders, and the assistant appear to carry over from synagogue to church."[19] He points out, however, that as in the Jewish synagogue, the most important role in the earliest Church did not belong to the "presiding officer" or *episkopos*. Rather, the "apostles and prophets," and the charismatics, stood at the center of the earliest Church, although they did not preside. Burtchaell remarks, "The people who bore most powerfully in their persons the force of divine conviction and transformative impetus were people who, without community screening or authorization, did God's work. They spoke with authority."[20] Thus while the standard "Protestant" position is mistaken that there were no stable offices in the earliest Church, this position is right to accord emphasis to the charismatic leaders.[21] Similarly, the "Protestant"

---

helpers, speakers in tongues, and interpreters. These were all, in contrast, to post-medieval notions of 'the laity,' roles exercised in the assembly when Christians gathered for worship and deliberation. When he wrote, 'everyone has a gift,' the apostle was not empowering the laity; he was abolishing it. No-one is not a minister; but then the way the word 'ministry' is handled in professional ecumenism, namely, as limited to 'clergy,' has been strangely restricted when seen from the Pauline perspective. The concept of 'clergy' is itself heresy" (Yoder, "On Christian Unity: The Way From Below," *Pro Ecclesia* 9 [2000]: 165–83, at 181). Yoder adds that he is not "arguing against episcopacy" but rather is clarifying "what episcopacy, as one of the many ministries, is for. I am arguing that the task of all oversight ministries under the gospel (including their synodical and patriarchal variants, if that is what you believe in) is to provide the means whereby all the believers in one place can celebrate a normal common life, sacramental and moral" (ibid.). These "oversight ministries" may offer "counsel and comment, alerting local communities to both resources and pitfalls" (182) but should recognize that the "primary locus is the gathering of believers in each place, in the power of the Spirit of Christ, in their own language, with their own complementary diversity of charismatic enablements, following their own agenda" (ibid.). Compare the approach of John D. Zizioulas, "The Pneumatological Dimension of the Church," trans. W. J. O'Hara, *Communio* 1 (1974): 142–58.

18. Burtchaell, *From Synagogue to Church*, 344.

19. Ibid., 339.

20. Ibid., 350.

21. Cf. ibid., 351. For the argument that in the early Church "the bishops were the men who possessed the principal *charismatic gifts* in the community," see Yves Congar, "The Hierarchy as Service," in his *Power and Poverty in the Church*, trans. Jennifer Nicholson (Baltimore: Helicon, 1964), 44.

position is wrong to suppose that Jesus led his disciples away from the structure of communal offices, but the "Catholic" position is wrong to suppose that Jesus instituted offices. According to Burtchaell, "Jesus instigated no characteristic new organization or anarchy among those who shared faith in him. They proceeded from where they found themselves. And they found themselves in the synagogue."[22] Jesus' apparent lack of interest in organizing his disciples made the synagogue context the inevitable starting point.

On the basis of his reconstruction, Burtchaell provides an evaluation that also aims to chart terrain between the "Catholic" and "Protestant" evaluative standpoints. In his view, it is indisputable that a large organizational shift, as the "Protestant" position holds, occurred in the Church in the late first and early second centuries The officers overtook the charismatic leaders, and the bishops overtook the presbyters.[23] Rome replaced Jerusalem as the center of Christianity. But whether these shifts were a development or a retrogression cannot be determined historically. On the historical evidence alone, one cannot say that had the shift never taken place, the Church would have survived and developed as well as she did. Just as the authority of bishops can and has been used both well and ill, so also can authority arising from a more egalitarian community be used both well and ill; and there are strengths and weaknesses associated with both approaches to authority.

Burtchaell's emphasis on the determinative role of the synagogue (freed from the priestly cult of Jerusalem) thus would seem, in part, to support doubts about the exercise of hierarchical authority within a community of mutual self-subordination. Those who immediately

---

22. Burtchaell, *From Synagogue to Church*, 352. Robert Sokolowski makes the same point more positively: Christ "did not first establish a Church and then appoint its leaders, nor did he simply allow the membership to elect their rulers; after living with his disciples and forming them, he sent the apostles as the ones responsible for shaping the Church from the beginning, under the guidance of the Holy Spirit. There was no Church until it was formed around the apostles; the Church is apostolic by definition. The apostles are not an afterthought to the Church but are constitutive of it" (Sokolowski, "The Identity of the Bishop: A Study in the Theology of Disclosure," in his *Christian Faith and Human Understanding: Studies on the Eucharist, Trinity, and the Human Person* [Washington, DC: The Catholic University of America Press, 2006], 113–30, at 116). Sokolowski goes on to add that "the way they [the apostles] exercise their decisive role in the Church is through teaching, sanctifying, and governing. The central role of the bishops in the Church reflects the extraordinary prominence of the apostles in the four gospels and in the Acts of the Apostles" (ibid.).

23. Burtchaell, *From Synagogue to Church*, 347, 353.

followed Jesus, at least, emphasized according to Burtchaell more
egalitarian and diverse modes of leadership in their pursuit of *caritas*.
Furthermore, they devoted themselves to teaching and service, rather
than to a cultic/priestly ministry that mediated the saving power of
Christ's Paschal Mystery.[24]

Francis Sullivan

The view of the Catholic ecclesiologist Francis Sullivan points generally
in the same direction. With "the consensus of scholars," Sullivan
conjectures, for example, that "the church of Rome was led by a college
of presbyters, rather than by a single bishop, for at least several decades
of the second century."[25] According to Sullivan's reading of the First

---

24. These conclusions fit with the post–Vatican II shift among Catholic theologians away
from a "cultic" understanding of the priesthood. For discussion see Dulles, *The Priestly Office*,
1–4, 43–44. Dulles alludes to Hans Küng's *Why Priests?* (Garden City, NY: Doubleday, 1972)
and Edward Schillebeeckx, op's *Ministry: Leadership in the Community of Jesus Christ* (New
York: Crossroad, 1981), both of which reject a "cultic" and hierarchical understanding of the
priesthood. Both Küng's and Schillebeeckx's books provoked a formal doctrinal rebuke from
the Congregation for the Doctrine of the Faith: see *Mysterium Ecclesiae* (June 24, 1973) and
Sacerdotium Ministeriale (August 6, 1983). Dulles holds the post–Vatican II shift to be "partly
responsible for the crisis of priestly identity and for the paucity of vocations in parts of the
world where secularization has gone furthest" (43–44). Cf. Georges Chantraine, sj, "Apostolicity
According to Schillebeeckx: The Notion and Its Import," trans. Mark D. Jordan, *Communio*
12 (1985): 192–222. For evidence of the post–Vatican II shift one might see the essays in
Concilium 43, *The Identity of the Priest* (1969), ed. Karl Rahner, sj. The shift has recently been
analyzed sociologically by Dean R. Hoge and Jacqueline E. Wenger, *Evolving Visions of the
Priesthood: Changes from Vatican II to the Turn of the New Century* (Collegeville, MN: Liturgical
Press, 2003); and by Donald B. Cozzens, *The Changing Face of the Priesthood* (Collegeville,
MN: Liturgical Press, 2000). While primarily focusing on the growing number of men with
homosexual tendencies in the priesthood (in which regard Cozzens finds a tension with, and
challenge to, Catholic teaching about priestly celibacy and the immorality of homosexuality
acts), Cozzens also affirms the shift: "Saving souls through pastoral care and the celebration of
the sacraments is the primary function of the priest from the perspective of the cultic model.
Recent decades have seen that perspective expand to the point where the communal dimension
to salvation has received appropriate consideration" (8). In Cozzens's view, once the "communal
dimension to salvation" is rightly understood, the "cultic" understanding of the priesthood
fades away. Hoge and Wenger provide a helpful diagram on p. 114 comparing the "cultic model"
and the "servant-leader model." In "Priestly Ministry at the Service of Ecclesial Communion,"
Communio 23 (1996): 677–87, Marc Ouellet, ss, accepts the inadequacy of the cultic or " 'sacerdotal'
model" (681) and proposes instead that Baptism configures all believers to Christ the Head,
whereas Holy Orders is "the sacrament of Christ the Shepherd" because the priest "represents
the authority of the Father who causes the growth of the sons and daughters of God" (685).

25. Francis A. Sullivan, sj, *From Apostles to Bishops: The Development of the Episcopacy in
the Early Church* (New York: Paulist Press, 2001), 221–22. Sullivan observes earlier, "The
question dividing the churches is not whether or how rapidly the development from the
leadership of a college of presbyters to that of a single bishop took place, but whether the result

Epistle of Clement, written from Rome to the church at Corinth in the 90s, the letter gives no indication either that the Corinthian church has a bishop, or that the church in Rome has one. Instead, Clement always uses plural terms to refer to the leaders of the Corinthian church.[26] Similarly, *The Shepherd of Hermas*, composed in the first half of the second century in Rome, always uses plural terms when speaking of leadership in the Church. Sullivan, however, does envision a certain kind of "apostolic succession," although he grants that the available documents cannot demonstrate such an occurrence. Sullivan affirms that there is "New Testament evidence that the apostles shared their mandate with both their missionary coworkers and with the leaders in the local churches, and that when the apostles died both of these groups carried on their ministry."[27] When in the second century the "monoepiscopate" developed, it would not have been illegitimate, Sullivan suggests, for the local churches in which these bishops emerged to "establish his link with the apostles either through earlier coworkers or through a succession of presbyters in their church."[28] Some link, it

---

of that development is rightly judged an element of the divinely ordered structure of the Church. This is a question of the theological significance of a post–New Testament development, and history alone cannot give the answer" (218).

26. Similarly, Neil Ormerod, drawing upon Burtchaell's work and that of others, concludes,

There is little evidence that the orders of ministry are the result of some prior revealed datum that then finds expression in the practical construction of office in the early Church. Instead what we find is a creative theologizing, in both Clement and Ignatius, which attempts to place the emerging orders of ministry into some suitable framework of meaning. . . . Does the conclusion that the impetus for the structure of ministry lies in practical intelligence mean that there is no intrinsic norm operating, and that another structure would be just as valid? Here some caution is needed. Elsewhere I have argued for what might be called a "transcendental" basis for the three-fold order of ministry, grounded in Lonergan's scale of values and the notions of healing and creating in history. On that basis one could argue both that the three-fold order of ministry is the product of the practical intelligence of the community, and that the community, enlightened by the Holy Spirit, basically "got it right." That is, it produced a simple structure that met the recurrent needs of the community to preserve and develop its identity as a Christian community. One might easily find in this the hand of divine providence, confirming that in fact the three-fold order of ministry is divinely ordained, if not directly instituted divinely. (Ormerod, "The Structure of Systematic Ecclesiology," *Theological Studies* 63 [2002]: 3–30, at 26–27, citing his earlier "System, History, and the Theology of Ministry," *Theological Studies* 61 [2000]: 432–46).

But is not "hierarchy" already a "structure of ministry"?

27. Sullivan, *From Apostles to Bishops*, 223.

28. Ibid.; cf. Francis Sullivan, sj, *The Church We Believe In: One, Holy, Catholic, and Apostolic* (New York: Paulist Press, 1988), 182–84. For other efforts to account for "apostolic succession," see Joseph Ratzinger, *Pilgrim Fellowship of Faith: The Church as Communion*, ed.

would seem, could inevitably be found, given this broad definition of "apostolic succession."

Sullivan goes somewhat beyond Burtchaell by adding, in order to justify the claims of *Lumen Gentium*, a brief section arguing that "the post–New Testament development is consistent with the development that took place during the New Testament period," and that this development is both functionally necessary for the post–New Testament Church's "unity and orthodoxy" and guided by the Holy Spirit.[29] Drawing upon Raymond Brown's work, Sullivan proposes that Jesus left the disciples with a mandate to teach, but without much instruction about organization.[30] Perhaps unaware of Burtchaell's

---

Stephan Otto Horn and Vinzenz Pfnür, trans. Henry Taylor (German 2002; San Francisco: Ignatius Press, 2005), 187–91, 201–202; Walter Kasper, "The Apostolic Succession: An Ecumenical Problem," in idem, *Leadership in the Church: How Traditional Roles Can Serve the Christian Community Today*, trans. Brian McNeil (New York: Crossroad, 2003), 114–43; Yves Congar, "The Spirit Keeps the Church 'Apostolic,' " in his *I Believe in the Holy Spirit*, vol. 2, *He Is Lord and Giver of Life*, trans. David Smith (New York: Crossroad, 1997), 39–49; John D. Zizioulas, "La continuité avec les origines apostoliques dans la conscience théologique des Eglises orthodoxes," *Istina* 19 (1974): 65–94 (ch. 5 of Zizioulas's collection *Being in Communion: Studies in Personhood and the Church* (Crestwood, NY: St. Vladimir's Seminary Press, 1985), summarized by Congar in *I Believe in the Holy Spirit*, vol. 2, 50–51. Ratzinger conceives of "apostolic succession" as rooted in the apostles' mission to oversee the whole Church (not merely local churches), and he argues that by the second half of the second century "the leaders of the local Churches, the bishops, had to recognize that they had now become the successors of the apostles and that the apostles' task was now entirely borne on their shoulders" (Ratzinger, *Pilgrim Fellowship of Faith*, 190). For his part, Walter Kasper observes that apostolic succession is "not a succession in the linear sense, where one office-bearer follows another; rather, new members are co-opted and integrated into the apostolic college with its mission that is carried on from age to age" (Kasper, "The Apostolic Succession," 121). It seems to me that the linear dimension should not be entirely done away with: see *Lumen Gentium*, 20, in Tanner, *Trent to Vatican II*, pp. 863–64; cf. *Catechism of the Catholic Church*, 861–62.

29. See Sullivan, *From Apostles to Bishops*, 218, 225. Elsewhere Sullivan has proposed a conciliar hermeneutics that he thinks would, in some cases at least, justify a Catholic theologian in dissenting from a doctrine formally taught by a Council: see Francis Sullivan, SJ, *Creative Fidelity: Weighing and Interpreting Documents of the Magisterium* (New York: Paulist Press, 1996), ch. 9; cf. Piet Fransen, *Hermeneutics of the Councils and Other Studies* (Leuven: Leuven University Press, 1985). For further discussion of legitimate dissent, responding to the Congregation for the Doctrine of the Faith's 1990 *Instruction on the Ecclesial Vocation of the Theologian*, but weighed down by his casuistical framework, see Sullivan, *Creative Fidelity*, 23–26, as well as his "The Theologian's Ecclesial Vocation and the 1990 CDF Instruction," *Theological Studies* 52 (1991): 51–68. Responding to the *Instruction on the Ecclesial Vocation of the Theologian*, John P. Boyle likewise warns that it does not safeguard legitimate dissent, despite its claims about "dialogue": see Boyle, "The 1990 Instruction *Donum Veritatis*: On the Ecclesial Role of the Theologian," in his *Church Teaching Authority: Historical and Theological Studies* (Notre Dame, IN: University of Notre Dame Press, 1995), 142–60.

30. Brown strictly separates the bishops' hierarchical authority, which developed some time after Christ, from Christ's own activity. Instead, Brown argues that various forms of authority

view that the disciples therefore took up the synagogue's structure, Sullivan suggests that the New Testament demonstrates the ad hoc character of development in Church structure during the New Testament period. Without denying the continuance of "charismatic ministry,"[31] he finds in "the parts of the New Testament written during the subapostolic period, especially 1 Peter, Acts, and the Pastorals," an increasing concern for such tasks as "selecting the right persons for ministry in the local churches and ordaining them by the laying on of hands."[32] While he notes that only James, "the 'brother

---

arose in the Christian communities after Christ's death and Resurrection. He states, "The presbyter-bishops described in the NT were not in any traceable way the successors of the Twelve apostles. . . . And so the affirmation that all the bishops of the early Christian Church could trace their appointments or ordinations to the apostles is simply without proof—it is impossible to trace with assurance any of the presbyter-bishops to the Twelve and it is possible to trace only some of them to apostles like Paul" (Brown, *Priest and Bishop: Biblical Reflections*, 72–73). He holds that the most that can be said about the bishops' hierarchical authority is that the Holy Spirit inspired the early Christian communities to move in this direction. As he remarks, "The affirmation that the episcopate was divinely established or established by Christ himself can be defended in the nuanced sense that the episcopate gradually emerged in a Church that stemmed from Christ and that this emergence was (in the eyes of faith) guided by the Holy Spirit" (73). For Brown, the denial of the bishops' "apostolic succession," their direct link with Christ's commissioning of the apostles, does not pose a problem for the Church's hierarchical structure. He assumes that the Holy Spirit has simply guided a development of doctrine—although admittedly one based for centuries upon a false claim. Thus he remarks, "The claims of various sees to descend from particular members of the Twelve are highly dubious. It is interesting that the most serious of these is the claim of the bishops of Rome to descend from Peter, the one member of the Twelve who was almost a missionary apostle in the Pauline sense—a confirmation of our contention that whatever succession there was from apostleship to episcopate, it was primarily in reference to the Pauline type of apostleship, not that of the Twelve" (72, note 53). For similar views see also Harrington, *The Church According to the New Testament*, 170–71; Raymond E. Brown, ss, Carolyn Osiek, RSCJ, and Pheme Perkins, "Church in the New Testament," *The New Jerome Biblical Commentary* (Englewood Cliffs, NJ: Prentice Hall, 1990), 1339–46; Frederick J. Cwiekowski, *The Beginnings of the Church* (New York: Paulist Press, 1988). As George Lindbeck observes, "Under the pressure of historical evidence, providentially guided development has now generally replaced dominical or apostolic institution," which makes it difficult to claim more than a functional place for episcopacy in the Church (Lindbeck, "The Church," in *Keeping the Faith: Essays to Mark the Centenary of Lux Mundi*, ed. Geoffrey Wainwright [Allison Park, PA: Pickwick Publications, 1998], 179–208, at 198). I am arguing in this chapter for dominical institution of ecclesial hierarchy through Christ's sharing of his *exousia*.

31. Sullivan, *From Apostles to Bishops*, 227.

32. Ibid., 226. See also for "episkopos" as "household manager" in the pastoral letters, Frances Young, *The Theology of the Pastoral Letters* (Cambridge: Cambridge University Press, 1994), 103–4; cf. John J. Burkhard, OFM CONV., *Apostolicity Then and Now: An Ecumenical Church in a Postmodern World* (Collegeville, MN: Liturgical Press, 2004), 213. Burkhard finds that the term *episkopos*, in its sense of "overseer," "appears only once [1 Tim 3:1] in the whole of the New Testament. Moreover, it isn't even certain that the office is clearly distinguished from that of the group of presbyters found in many local churches. The individual who enjoys

of the Lord,' " is described as "having been left in charge of a local church," he suggests that the development in this direction, toward more defined leadership for local churches, allows us to recognize the rise of the episcopate as a legitimate development of doctrine, present already *in nuce* in the concerns of the earliest Christian communities.[33]

He goes on to emphasize that this second-century rise of the episcopate can be recognized historically as preserving the unity of the Church against the Gnostics in the second century, and can be recognized as the work of the Holy Spirit due to the Church's "reception" of the episcopate, a reception that paralleled the Church's reception of the canonical books of the Bible rather than the Gnostic books: "We have just as good reason for believing that the Spirit guided the Church in recognizing its bishops as successors of the apostles and authoritative teachers of the faith as we have for believing that the Spirit guided it in discerning the books that comprise the New Testament."[34] Since

episkope is one among many and his *episkope* is shared with others" (ibid.). Following Sullivan's *From Apostles to Bishops*, 103–125, Burkhard notes that even in the letters of Ignatius of Antioch, "the *episkopos* mentioned does not resemble the later monarchical *episkopos*. Ignatius' bishop is a figure who exercises his episcopal ministry in close interrelationship with his presbyters and deacons. He is not above them, and there is no sense that the latter derive their ministry from him" (Burkhard, *Apostolicity Then and Now*, 214–15). Burkhard argues that for Ignatius of Antioch, the presbyters, not the bishop, exercise the "teaching and governing functions" (215). In Burkhard's view, citing also William Henn's *The Honor of My Brothers: A Short History of the Relation between the Pope and Bishops* (New York: Crossroad, 2000), the "monarchical bishop" emerges only in the fourth century. As in Afanasiev and Zizioulas, Cyprian of Carthage, along with Constantine, shoulders much of the blame, although Burkhard blames Cyprian for different problems than do Afanasiev and Zizioulas. It seems to me that Ignatius of Antioch, and even 1 Timothy, contain more of the "monarchical" element (without the negative connotations) than Burkhard supposes.

33. Sullivan, *From Apostles to Bishops*, 227.

34. Ibid., 230. It must be noted that Sullivan's use of "reception" here has ramifications for other aspects of his theology of Church structure. He discusses "reception" in his *Magisterium: Teaching Authority in the Catholic Church* (New York: Paulist Press, 1983), especially 103–15. For similar approaches to "reception" see Patrick Granfield, OSB, *The Limits of the Papacy* (New York: Crossroad, 1987), 134–68; Richard R. Gaillardetz, *Teaching with Authority: A Theology of the Magisterium of the Church* (Collegeville, MN: Liturgical Press, 1997), 227–73; idem, "The Reception of Doctrine: New Perspectives," in *Authority in the Roman Catholic Church: Theory and Practice*, ed. Bernard Hoose (Aldershot: Ashgate, 2002), 95–115; Thomas P. Rausch, SJ, *Towards a Truly Catholic Church: An Ecclesiology for the Third Millennium* (Collegeville, MN: Liturgical Press, 2005), 152–59. See also Sullivan's "The Sense of Faith: The Sense/ Consensus of the Faithful," in Hoose, *Authority in the Roman Catholic Church*, 85–93. These theologians generally have in view *Humanae Vitae* and the teaching that only men can receive the sacrament of orders, which they wish to argue have not been "received" by the faithful as a whole. As John P. Boyle puts it in his *Church Teaching Authority*, "The multiple actions and gifts of the Spirit in the church (and outside it) suggest rather that a dialogic model of

the Spirit is the Spirit of Jesus Christ, the Spirit enacts Christ's will for the Church. Sullivan's defense of the episcopate seems to be an ecclesiological functionalism (the need to preserve orthodoxy and unity) ratified by the Holy Spirit—a ratification made known, crucially, by the "reception" accorded to the episcopate's authority by the various communities of believers.[35]

What is gained by our survey of Burtchaell's and Sullivan's positions? By raising the issue of the apostles' "mandate" and "ministry," Sullivan helps us to ask what the apostles thought they were doing. Were they merely teaching the scriptures (enlightened by Christ) and serving the community, as both Burtchaell and Sullivan surmise?[36]

---

magisterium is needed. In such a model the bishops' proposition of Christian belief and practice guided and protected by the Spirit is received by a community which has also received the gifts of the Spirit. It is scarcely an accident that Vatican II could teach with such confidence that the consent of the church will never be lacking to infallible teaching because of the work of the Holy Spirit" (61).

35. See also Yves Congar, "La 'réception' comme réalité ecclésiologique," *Revue des sciences philosophiques et théologiques* 56 (1972): 369–403. What if the "reception" begins to erode when confronted with a new cultural situation? As Avery Dulles, sj, points out, "Once one admits that *ius divinum* may depend upon a development in time, it is difficult to insist upon absolute irreversibility. What is appropriate or even necessary for a later age is admitted to have been inappropriate or even impossible for an earlier time. If this is so, how can we say that at some future time or in some other culture the previous development might not again become inappropriate or impossible? If development is acknowledged, the institution which develops becomes tied to certain historical and cultural conditions whose permanence might itself be questionable. Thus the theory of development [as presented by Karl Rahner, sj] seems to call for something like de-development, at least as a possibility" (Dulles, "'Ius Divinum' as an Ecumenical Problem," in his *A Church to Believe In: Discipleship and the Dynamics of Freedom* [1982; New York: Crossroad, 1987], 80–102, at 91–92). Dulles at this stage of his career does not reject this possibility; for a similar perspective see his "The Church, the Churches, and the Catholic Church," *Theological Studies* 33 (1972): 199–234; as well as his *The Resilient Church* (Garden City, NY: Doubleday, 1977), 34.

36. This "merely" should not be misunderstood. From a phenomenological perspective, Robert Sokolowski observes that teaching "establishes the space in which sanctification and governance can take their place, and it makes clear what the sanctification and governance truly are" (Sokolowski, "The Identity of the Bishop," 117). Sokolowski also points out that the episcopal authority to govern flows from teaching and sanctifying: "Because he must hand on the truth and grace of Christ, he must also govern" (119). On the relationship of the *munus docendi* to the *munus sanctificandi*, according to Vatican II and Thomas Aquinas, see Damien Logue, "Le *premier* et le *principal* du sacrement de l'ordre. Lecture de *Presbyterorum ordinis*, 4 et, 13," *Revue Thomiste* 102 (2002): 431–53; Guy Mansini, osb, "Episcopal *Munera* and the Character of Episcopal Orders," *The Thomist* 66 (2002): 369–94; idem, "Sacerdotal Character at the Second Vatican Council," *The Thomist* 67 (2003): 539–77; idem, "A Contemporary Understanding of St. Thomas on Sacerdotal Character," *The Thomist* 71 (2007): 171–98. In "Episcopal *Munera* and the Character of Episcopal Orders," Mansini argues that "the bishop's capacity to sanctify—his priesthood, his possession of *potestas ordinis*, and especially as this

Not enduring hierarchical ecclesial structure would seem necessary if the leaders are solely charged with teaching and serving, since, as Burtchaell makes clear, the leaders were (and are) often not the best ones at teaching or serving. Or, as *Lumen Gentium* affirms, did the apostles also possess and share with others a sacramental power, a distinct participation in the power of Christ's priestly action?[37]

If *Lumen Gentium* is correct, then it would be a mistake to speak (as Burtchaell does) of a situation after Christ in which there were no "priests" because "there are no longer any who are not priests."[38] If the apostles received from Christ and transmitted to others a unique power, however, one would expect to find some New Testament evidence of this "sacramental" mandate. Do the New Testament texts point to anything more than teaching and service as comprising the apostolic mandate? In seeking an initial answer to this question, with its implications for the understanding of the nature of ecclesial hierarchy among the first Christians, I will examine Paul's first letter to the Corinthians and the Gospel of Matthew. These two texts, from circa 50–85 AD, suggest that the earliest Christians envisioned more than functional leadership to be necessary for their witness to the activity of Christ and the Holy Spirit.

---

includes the power to ordain—just is a sort of competence to rule, and this means that he ought to teach those whom he rules and sanctifies. Therefore, objectively, it calls for jurisdiction, for a canonical mission" (393), as well as for grace. He distinguishes between "order" and "jurisdiction" as follows: "*Potestas ordinis* is given by sacrament, is for sacramental action, makes a man an instrument of Christ in such sacramental action, is stable and cannot be lost. Jurisdiction involves simple assignment (assignment of one's subjects) as by the instrument of the *missio canonica*, it is for ruling, it makes a man a vicar of Christ in teaching and ruling, and it is not stable in the same way *potestas ordinis* is and can be lost" (376). He further defends this position, by means of a detailed analysis of the *Acta Synodalia* for *Lumen Gentium*, 21 and *Presbyterorum Ordinis*, 2, in "Sacerdotal Character at the Second Vatican Council."

37. On the inability of historical research alone, because of its limited view of what counts as historical, to apprehend Christ's institution of the sacraments, see J. A. Di Noia, OP, and Bernard Mulcahy, OP, "The Authority of Scripture in Sacramental Theology: Some Methodological Observations," *Pro Ecclesia* 10 (2001): 329–45. See also Roch Kereszty, O CIST, "Historical Research, Theological Inquiry, and the Reality of Jesus: Reflections on the Method of J. P. Meier," *Communio* 19 (1992): 576–600.

38. Burtchaell, *From Synagogue to Church*, 323.

THE APOSTOLIC MANDATE IN 1 CORINTHIANS AND THE GOSPEL OF MATTHEW

1 Corinthians

The distinctions that Paul makes as he writes to the Corinthians illumine his view of the apostolic mandate.[39] On the one hand, he distinguishes between Jesus Christ and all Christians. The "church of God which is at Corinth" is "sanctified in Christ Jesus, called to be saints together with all those who in every place call on the name of our Lord Jesus Christ" (1 Corinthians 1:2).[40] Christ, not Christians, is the source of this sanctifying power. The Corinthian believers receive "the grace of God . . . in Christ Jesus," a grace that enriches them "with all speech and all knowledge" (1 Corinthians 1:5) so that they receive every "spiritual gift" (1 Corinthians 1:7) and are enabled by Christ to remain "guiltless" (1 Corinthians 1:8) on the day of judgment. Christ's power of sanctifying those who believe in him comes from his cross. Paul warns the Corinthians against relying upon any other source than Christ crucified for "our wisdom, our righteousness, and our sanctification and redemption" (1 Corinthians 1:30), "lest the cross of Christ be emptied of its power" (1 Corinthians 1:17). The sanctifying power of the cross is the mystery that Paul calls "a secret and hidden wisdom of God, which God decreed before the ages for our glorification" (1 Corinthians 2:7).

When Paul instructs the Corinthians about how human beings receive the power of the cross, he distinguishes between (without separating) ordinary believers and the apostles, along with those who share the apostles' mandate.[41] At first glance, he appears to locate this

---

39. For theological discussion of 1 Corinthians on the Body of Christ, see Benoît-Dominique de La Soujeole, OP, *Introduction au mystère de l'Église* (Paris: Parole et Silence, 2006), 72–74.

40. Paul's theology of the Church retains the election of Israel, although he holds that in Christ, God has drawn the Gentiles into this election: see for instance Bruce D. Chilton's remarks on Paul's theology of the Eucharist and the Church, in Jacob Neusner and Bruce D. Chilton, *The Body of Faith: Israel and the Church* (Valley Forge, PA: Trinity Press International, 1996), 143–62. The primacy of divine election accords with hierarchical ecclesial structure, in which one can see the covenantal pattern of gifting/receptivity. On covenantal gifting/receptivity in the Old and New Testaments, see Michael Dauphinais and Matthew Levering, *Holy People, Holy Land: A Theological Introduction to the Bible* (Grand Rapids, MI: Brazos Press, 2005).

41. Hans Urs von Balthasar comments on Paul's understanding of his "fellow workers": "It is significant that though the difference in rank between the Apostle and his coworkers

distinction solely in the relationship between teacher and learner, which need not require any particular power in the teacher beyond the ability to communicate the Gospel. Paul makes clear that faith, the work of the Holy Spirit in us, establishes believers' contact with the power of the cross: "Now we have received not the spirit of the world, but the Spirit which is from God, that we might understand the gifts bestowed on us by God. And we impart this in words not taught by human wisdom but taught by the Spirit, interpreting spiritual truths to those who possess the Spirit" (1 Corinthians 2:12–13). Faith illumines believers' minds with "the mind of Christ" (1 Corinthians 2:16). The apostles and those who share their mandate—Paul here names himself, Apollos, and Peter (1 Corinthians 1:12)—are teachers of faith. Their authority comes from "the will of God" (1 Corinthians 1:1); they have been sent by Christ (1 Corinthians 1:17). While the apostles and those who share their mandate are not the primary agents causing faith in believers, they are instrumentally agents. The faith of the Corinthian believers is owed not to Paul but to "the power of God" (1 Corinthians 2:5). Paul is the teacher who has delivered the Good News to the Corinthians; thus for those whom God calls, Paul's words inspire faith: "we preach Christ crucified, a stumbling block to the Jews and folly to the Gentiles, but to those who are

---

persists even when he names them in addressing a letter ('Paul, called as an apostle of Jesus Christ and Sosthenes, our brother' [1 Cor 1:1]), Paul wants his 'fellow workers' (that phrase again! [2 Cor 8:23]), Titus and Timothy, to be just as highly esteemed by the congregation as he is himself. When Timothy comes to Corinth, he is to be treated like the Apostle, 'for he is doing the Lord's work, as I also am. Let no one therefore despise him' (1 Cor 16:10–11). If Paul is his congregation's bishop, then his fellow workers may be designated as auxiliary bishops. The pastoral letters make it clear that they have the necessary authority (in Crete, Titus is instructed to 'appoint elders in every city as I directed you' [Titus 1:5]). . . . Precisely because the (fellow) workers are promoters (*auctores*) of the building, they have the right to exercise the determining influence (*auctoritas*). Despite what is sometimes claimed nowadays, there is no trace of Church democracy in Paul's writing. Instead there is *koinonia*, 'fellowship' (1 Cor 1:9; 10:16 and 2 Cor 13:14) based on, and called for, by Christ's love. *Koinonia* requires us to live for one another, which means being open and transparent in mutual love. This will turn out to be exactly what Paul demands of the pastoral office, This *mutual openness*, which should banish all mistrust, is the reason why Paul has no difficulty in uniting love and obedience in the Church (2 Cor 7:15). The paradigm of this unity is Christ's obedience, even unto death; therefore the Corinthians, too, must be 'obedient in all things' to the Apostle" (Von Balthasar, *Paul Struggles with His Congregation: The Pastoral Message of the Letters to the Corinthians*, trans. Brigitte L. Bojarska [German 1988; San Francisco: Ignatius Press, 1992], 25–26). For von Balthasar's richly developed exegesis of the Corinthian correspondence, see also von Balthasar, "Office in the Church," 116–21.

called, both Jews and Greeks, Christ, the power of God and the wisdom of God" (1 Corinthians 1:23–24).

Paul cautions against valuing the teachers over what they are teaching; namely, "Jesus Christ and him crucified" (1 Corinthians 2:2).[42] As he puts it, "Is Christ divided? Was Paul crucified for you?

---

42. Emphasis on this point is the great contribution of the work of John Webster, following in the footsteps of Karl Barth. As Webster puts it, "The Word is not *in* the church but announced *to* the church through Holy Scripture. The church is therefore not first and foremost a speaking but a hearing community. John the seer says that he turned to the voice that was speaking to him (Rev. 1.12); and there are few more succinct statements of the primary dynamic of the Christian assembly. The church *is* that turning. And, further, in making that movement, in fear and trembling, falling at the feet of the son of man, the church receives its appointment to a specific task: it is summoned to speech" ("On Evangelical Ecclesiology," in his *Confessing God: Essays in Christian Dogmatics II* [New York: T. & T. Clark, 2005], 153–93, at 190). Understanding the Church theocentrically as a graced "turning" enables Webster to critique both "postliberal" ecclesiologies (as too caught up in enumerating the Church's practices and Catholicizing the Reformation) and "communion" ecclesiologies. Regarding the latter, Webster asks, "does an ecclesiology centred on communion of necessity compromise the imparticipable perfection of God's triune life, and so disturb the fundamental asymmetry of Christ and the church?" (163). As he explains in a theologically rich passage: "It would be entirely improper to interpret communion ecclesiology as a systematic attempt to subsume God and creatures under a single reality of 'communion'. Nevertheless, the confluence of two factors—a mistrust of the category of 'pure nature', and a potent doctrine of the church's relation to God as both participatory and mediatorial—makes communion ecclesiology rather uneasy with at least some ways of speaking of the 'originality' of God, that is, of God's utter difference from creatures even in his acts towards and in them. In a telling passage, de Lubac suggests that 'nowhere within our world is there any absolute beginning of any kind, and if, *per impossibile*, everything could be destroyed it would be impossible to create all afresh.' At the very least, it is not self-evident that such an account can be coordinated with an account of *creatio ex nihilo*, still less with a theology of incarnation and atonement, resurrection, Spirit, justification and sanctification. For what are such acts if not absolute beginnings, the introduction into creation of an absolute *novum*, unconditioned and unexpected?" (163) Granting Webster's objections, one does not have to follow de Lubac's account of nature and grace in order to set forth a eucharistic and Trinitarian ecclesiology. See Reinhard Hütter, "*Desiderium Naturale Visionis Dei—Est autem duplex hominis beatitude sive felicitas*: Some Observations about Lawrence Feingold's and John Milbank's Recent Interventions in the Debate over the Natural Desire to See God," *Nova et Vetera* 5 (2007): 81–131. Missing from Webster's ecclesiological reflections, as from Karl Barth's, is a fully developed account of the Eucharist, which stands alongside the ministry of the Word at the heart of the graced "turning" in faith (cf. "On Evangelical Ecclesiology," 187). See also Webster's *Holiness* (Grand Rapids, MI: Eerdmans, 2003) and his "The Self-organizing Power of the Gospel of Christ: Episcopacy and Community Formation," in his *Word and Church: Essays in Christian Dogmatics* (New York: T. & T. Clark, 2001), 191–210 (he briefly mentions the "Lord's supper" on 202); as well as Charles Journet's warning, in response to Barth, against a "univocal metaphysic" that rules out instrumental causality (Journet, *The Church of the Word Incarnate: An Essay in Speculative Theology*, vol. 1: *The Apostolic Hierarchy*, trans. A. H. C. Downes [London: Sheed and Ward, 1955], 11).

Or were you baptized in the name of Paul?" (1 Corinthians 1:13).[43]
Vis-à-vis Christ, Paul, and those Paul teaches are on an equal level
with each other. They all serve Christ: "What then is Apollos? What
is Paul? Servants through whom you believed, as the Lord assigned to
each. I planted, Apollos watered, but God gave the growth. So neither
he who plants nor he who waters is anything, but only God who gives
the growth" (1 Corinthians 3:5–7). Yet, Paul also participates in Christ's
power in a way that sets Paul apart from those whom he teaches.
Paul has received a position of authority within "the kingdom of God"
(1 Corinthians 4:20). He thus can warn the Corinthian believers,
"Some are arrogant, as though I were not coming to you. But I will
come to you soon, if the Lord wills, and I will find out not the talk of
these arrogant people but their power. For the kingdom of God does
not consist in talk but in power" (1 Corinthians 4:19–20). Paul's
distinctive participation in the "power" of the kingdom of God
enables him to speak with authority to people who are otherwise his
equals. He asks, "What do you wish? Shall I come to you with a rod,
or with love in a spirit of gentleness?" (1 Corinthians 4:21).[44]

---

43. Given the unity of Christ affirmed by Paul, Richard B. Hays comments, "There can be
no doubt that our denominational divisions perpetuate the sort of fragmentation of Christ that
Paul deplored. Each one of us says, 'I belong to Luther,' or 'I belong to Calvin,' or 'I belong to
Wesley,' or 'I belong to the Church of Christ.' The division of the Christian communions is a
scandal, and we should hear in Paul's letter to Corinth a reproach to ourselves for perpetuating
this tragic state of affairs" (Hays, *First Corinthians* [Louisville, KY: John Knox Press, 1997],
25). Hays focuses in particular on the need for local congregations to avoid factions (ibid.).
Regarding 1 Corinthians 1:12, where Paul criticizes not only those who say, "I belong to Paul"
but also those who say, "I belong to Christ," Hays observes, "Such a claim ['I belong to
Christ'] might be coupled with a boastful pretension to have direct spiritual access to Christ
apart from any humanly mediated tradition" (23). Hays, however, does not discuss how this
mediation might be structured, preferring simply to appeal directly to the Lord's authority.
Thus, according to Hays, for Paul "the Corinthians must see themselves as part of a much larger
movement, subject to the same Lord whose authority governs the church as a whole. They are
not spiritual free agents. The church of God that is in Corinth is just one branch of a larger
operation" (17).

44. Hays remarks on this passage, "Paul believes himself invested with God's authority in
such a way that he has 'divine power to destroy strongholds . . . and every proud obstacle
raised up against the knowledge of God' (2 Cor. 10:4–5). This at least means that he will expose
the superficiality and falsehood of the arrogant Corinthian arguments. It probably means more
than that, however, for 'the kingdom of God consists not in rhetoric but in power' (1 Cor.
4:20). Presumably Paul expects that if necessary God will unleash some manifestation of the
power of the Spirit that will humble the arrogant ones" (Hays, *First Corinthians*, 75). But it
seems to me that Paul grounds his authority on something more than expectation of a
charismatic display or victory in argument, since he suggests that he will bear the "rod," and
thus that he participates distinctly in the working of the Holy Spirit in building up the

Paul describes himself and those who share the apostolic mandate as the "stewards" of Christ's saving power: "This is how one should regard us, as servants of Christ and stewards of the mysteries of God" (1 Corinthians 4:1).[45] As a "steward," Paul possesses "a rod" to enforce his authority. Indeed, this "rod" can be active in the Corinthian church without Paul being physically present. Paul can speak in the Lord's name, with the Lord's power: "For though absent in body, I am present in spirit; and as if present, I have already pronounced judgment in the name of the Lord Jesus on the man who has done such a thing. When you are assembled, and my spirit is present, with the power of our Lord Jesus, you are to deliver this man to Satan for the destruction of the flesh, that his spirit may be saved in the day of the Lord Jesus" (1 Corinthians 5:3–5). Paul's power as "steward of the mysteries of God" thus extends over the community for the exercise of judgment, as part of his task of building up the community of believers.

To this point, we have shown that Paul, by his own description, participates uniquely in the cruciform power that he proclaims, the sanctifying power of Christ's cross and Resurrection. We have noted that Paul identifies faith as the portal through which believers participate in this power. Paul is a "steward" of this faith. Believers also participate in the sanctifying power of Christ by means of Baptism and the Eucharist. Although Paul says that "Christ did not send me to baptize but to preach the Gospel" (1 Corinthians 1:17), among the Corinthians Paul baptized Crispus, Gaius, and the household of Stephanas. With respect to the Eucharist he asks rhetorically, "The cup of blessing which we bless, is it not a participation in the blood of Christ? The bread which we break, is it not a participation in the body of Christ?"

Church. On the "rod" as the power of the Holy Spirit, see also the text from Severian of Gabala in *1 Corinthians Interpreted by Early Christian Commentators*, trans. and ed. Judith L. Kovacs (Grand Rapids, MI: Eerdmans, 2005), 81.

45. For context, see Hays's observation that "within the social world of Paul's time, his point was perfectly understandable: Servants or slaves of powerful masters often enjoyed positions of considerable delegated authority, being charged with major administrative responsibility for the affairs of the household. Paul's image of the steward (*oikonomos*, 4:1) evokes this picture of the slave-in-charge. (In a world where there are no longer slaves in charge of big households, we might think analogically of the foreman in charge of a construction crew or the chief of staff in the White House.)" (*First Corinthians*, 65). Even though it lacks the ontological dimension, Hays's description here otherwise accords with the account of the mediation of Christ's power that I propose in this chapter.

(1 Corinthians 10:16).[46] Together with the response of faith, Baptism and the Eucharist unite believers to the sanctifying power of Christ crucified. Regarding this union with Christ's power, Paul states, "Because there is one bread, we who are many are one body, for we all partake in the one bread" (1 Corinthians 10:17). Their common participation in "the one bread," which itself is "a participation in the body of Christ," makes them "one body."

As one of the "stewards of the mysteries of God," Paul possesses authority with respect to certain modes of participating in Christ's sanctifying power. Put another way, certain modes of sharing in Christ's sanctifying power flow through Paul (and through the other men who share the apostolic mandate). Not only does Paul assert his authority with respect to the faith and morals upheld by the Corinthian community, but he also asserts his authority with respect to the celebration of the Eucharist. Thus, he observes that in common understanding, "those who eat the sacrifices" are "partners of the altar" (1 Corinthians 10:18), and he concludes from this that those who partake of the Eucharist may not partake of other sacrificial meals: "You cannot drink the cup of the Lord and the cup of demons. You cannot partake of the table of the Lord and the table of demons" (1 Corinthians 10:21). Similarly, he warns that the Corinthian mode of celebrating the Eucharist has not built up the Church's unity in the way that proper celebration of the Eucharist does. Although the Corinthians should be eating "the Lord's supper" (1 Corinthians 11:20), in fact, when they gather together, each eats his own supper, so that

---

46. Hays comments on this verse, "The references to sharing in the blood and body of Christ in verse 16 have nothing to do with mysteriously ingesting Christ in the meal; rather, Paul means that the participants in the supper are brought into partnership or covenant (cf. 11:25) with Christ through sharing the meal" (167). He notes that in Jewish and pagan ritual meals, "Each meal creates a relation of *koinonia* ('fellowship') among the participants and the deity honored in the meal. Paul takes this as a commonplace interpretation of such cultic meals" (ibid.). The question perhaps is whether this *koinonia* in Christ attains ontological dimensions, and if so, what this would mean for the "power" mediated through the ritual meal. Does the Christian Eucharist surpass the Jewish ritual meal? Hays appears to think not: "Paul is not thinking of some sort of mystical union affected through the meal—an idea foreign to the Old Testament. The meal is, however, to be eaten 'in the presence of the Lord' as a sign of the covenant relationship between God and the people, a covenant that also binds the people together" (168). Michael J. Gorman, like Hays, a Methodist biblical scholar, moves closer to a sense of "mystical union" by emphasizing the context of worship: "As an act of worship, it is an experience of participation (Greek *koinonia*, 1 Cor. 10:16) in Christ and his death" (Gorman, *Cruciformity: Paul's Narrative Spirituality of the Cross* [Grand Rapids, MI: Eerdmans, 2001], 356).

some go hungry. In this regard, Paul solemnly recalls the words of the Lord about the Eucharist as a warning against the Corinthians:

> For I received from the Lord what I also delivered to you, that the Lord Jesus on the night when he was betrayed took bread, and when he had given thanks, he broke it, and said, "This is my body which is for you. Do this in remembrance of me." In the same way also the cup, after supper, saying, "This cup is the new covenant in my blood. Do this, as often as you drink it, in remembrance of me." For as often as you eat this bread and drink the cup, you proclaim the Lord's death until he comes. (1 Corinthians 11:23–26)

Paul's apostleship or stewardship includes both watching over the Corinthians' faith, and instructing them on how to "remember" and "proclaim" the Lord in the Eucharist, and thereby participate in the power of his Pasch.

In short, Paul mediates between Christ and the Corinthians. Christ and the Corinthians are connected through the mediation of Paul, and yet the Corinthians are directly united with Christ. How can a mediated connection be direct? In a relationship of participation, mediation need not impede direct participation. By faith, Baptism, and the Eucharist, the Corinthians participate directly in Christ's cross and Resurrection. Yet this direct participation does not occur without apostolic mediation.[47] Paul's (apostolic) participation in Christ's power nourishes and safeguards the Corinthians' (all Christians') participation in Christ's power. Christ's power flows in a distinctive

---

47. Based upon his understanding of Paul's delegation of the task of baptizing (1 Cor 1:14–16), Hays takes a different view from mine: "Apparently Paul, after baptizing a few such [prominent] converts, entrusted the subsequent performance of baptisms to these prominent persons. Two significant observations follow from these facts. First, Paul has no conception of baptism as a sacrament that must be administered only by specially ordained persons, nor does he have any proprietary interest in regulating its administration. Second, the church at Corinth preserved and reproduced—apparently with Paul's implicit blessing—many of the status distinctions and household authority structures that were already present in the Corinthian social setting before Paul's arrival. . . . In contrast to the ministry of baptizing, Paul insists that his commission from Christ is 'to proclaim the gospel' " (Hays, *First Corinthians*, 24). In Hays's view, therefore, "in Paul's apostolic work the ministry of the Word is all-important, whereas the ministry of 'sacrament' has only secondary significance; the community should not be divided by different sacramental practices, because its fundamental ground of unity lies in the proclaimed gospel" (ibid.). I do not think that Paul rules out a conception of sacramental mediation, through hierarchical authority, of Christ's power. While the "ministry of the Word" is central in Paul, he regards the practices of baptism and the Eucharist as central to the community's self-understanding, and he does not disjoin his authority from these practices.

way through Paul, as apostle, precisely so that it might flow through the Corinthians.

Hierarchical authority in this way is not opposed to mutual self-subordination. The apostolic power that Paul receives from Christ is entirely subordinated, given over, to the power that the Corinthian believers thereby gain in Christ. Paul says in this regard, "I try to please all men in everything I do, not seeking my own advantage, but that of the many, that they may be saved" (1 Corinthians 10:33). Paul must be transparent to Christ: "For no other foundation can any one lay than that which is laid, which is Jesus Christ" (1 Corinthians 3:11).[48] Paul passes on this apostolic authority to his collaborators: "Therefore I sent to you Timothy, my beloved and faithful child in the Lord, to remind you of my ways in Christ, as I teach them everywhere in every church" (1 Corinthians 4:17). In turn, the Corinthian believers subordinate themselves to Paul's apostolic power to mediate Christ's power, and thereby they kenotically receive Christ's kenotic power. As Paul remarks, he is their "father in Christ Jesus through the Gospel" (1 Corinthians 4:15). No more than Paul can they claim any power that originates in themselves. Paul asks them, "What have you that you did not receive? If then you received it, why do you boast as if it were not a gift?" (1 Corinthians 5:7).[49]

Paul employs the human body as an image of this mediated unity with Christ. He writes, "For just as the body is one and has many members, and all the members of the body, though many, are one body, so it is with Christ. For by one Spirit we were all baptized into one body—Jews or Greeks, slaves or free—and all were made to drink of one Spirit" (1 Corinthians 12:12–13). In the unity of the body there is a hierarchy of parts, but this hierarchy does not place the parts

---

48. Serge-Thomas Bonino, OP, observes that "St. Thomas carefully notes that the movement of conversion must not stop in the participated perfection that is found in the apostle as secondary cause, but rather it is achieved only in union with subsistent perfection itself. The practical consequence: the apostle must efface himself; he must in no way interpose himself or turn toward himself the movement that carries the believer toward God" (Bonino, "The Role of the Apostles in the Communication of Revelation according to the *Lectura super Ioannem* of St. Thomas Aquinas," trans. Teresa Bede and Matthew Levering, in *Reading John with St. Thomas Aquinas*, ed. Michael Dauphinais and Matthew Levering [Washington, DC: The Catholic University of America Press, 2005], 318–46, at 341).

49. This understanding of kenotic power is explored throughout Gorman's *Cruciformity*: see in particular the summaries on 92–94 and 394–97, although Gorman does not give an account of Paul's unique apostolic authority in the community.

in opposition. Each part of the body participates in the others, so as to constitute a hierarchical unity: "For the body does not consist of one member but of many" (1 Corinthians 12:14), and "there are many parts, yet one body" (1 Corinthians 12:20). As Paul points out, the relationship among the members of the body is not therefore one of competition: "If the foot should say, 'Because I am not a hand, I do not belong to the body,' that would not make it any less a part of the body" (1 Corinthians 12:15). Similarly, although in a rightly functioning body the "lower" parts of the body are subordinated to the "higher" parts, nonetheless this subordination does not constrict the lower parts, but rather enables them to share in fulfilling the purposes of the entire body. In this regard Paul observes that "the parts of the body which seem to be weaker are indispensable" (1 Corinthians 12:22), and that "God has so adjusted the body, giving the greater honor to the inferior part, that there may be no discord in the body, but that the members may have the same care for one another" (1 Corinthians 12:24–25). The unity of the body does not negate the hierarchical ordering of the parts, but rather the hierarchy of parts serves the flourishing of the one body. Paul concludes, "If one member suffers, all suffer together; if one member is honored, all rejoice together" (1 Corinthians 12:26).

For Paul, then, mediated union with Christ through the Holy Spirit is like the hierarchical mediation and participation that marks human bodiliness. Christ's power, the sanctifying power of the cross and Resurrection, flows through the entire body, and each part of the body participates in it directly by the Holy Spirit. As Paul puts it, "Now there are varieties of gifts, but the same Spirit; and there are varieties of service, but the same Lord; and there are varieties of working, but it is the same God who inspires them all in every one. To each is given the manifestation of the Spirit for the common good" (1 Corinthians 12:4–7). Yet, Christ's power, as the cruciform power of self-giving "weakness," is participated through self-subordinating love. Thus, Christians directly receive Christ's power as mediated by self-subordinating relationships with others, founded upon love. In addition, because of the kind of power that it is—the power of sanctification in the Crucified One—this power must always have its source in Christ. It is not the kind of power that one can appropriate for oneself; only Christ can give it through his Holy Spirit. Christ does so through a hierarchical structure of participation and mediation that Paul describes as constituting the unity of the Church: "Now you are the body of Christ and individually members of it. Now God has appointed in the Church first apostles, second prophets, third teachers, then workers of miracles, then healers, helpers, administrators, speakers in various kinds of tongues" (1 Corinthians 12:27–28).[50]

In this "body of Christ," the hierarchical organization of offices is one way in which Christ mediates to believers his self-subordinating love. Each member of the "body" must depend upon and serve the other members. Paul asks rhetorically, "Are all apostles? Are all prophets? Are all teachers? Do all work miracles? Do all possess gifts of healing? Do all speak with tongues? Do all interpret?" (1 Corinthians 12:29–30). The fact that the believers possess distinct vocations provides the opening for self-subordinating love, which Paul calls the "still more excellent way" (1 Corinthians 12:31) that belongs at the heart of every vocation. As Paul depicts the primacy of love,

> If I speak in the tongues of men and of angels, but have not love, I am a noisy gong or a clanging cymbal. And if I have prophetic powers, and understand all mysteries and all knowledge, and if I have all faith, so as

---

50. Concerned to avoid any conflation of Christ and the Church (Augustine's *totus Christus*), John Webster argues that "the Church's acts do not realize, complete, continue or in any way extend or embody God's work, which is perfect, and which alone is properly holy. The Church's acts of holiness, having their origin and their sustaining energy in God, bear testimony to God's work, accompanying it with their witness, and, in all their human fragility and sinfulness, echoing the holy work of the holy God" (Webster, *Holiness*, 72). Without disagreeing with Webster's depiction of the Church's "acts of holiness," I wonder whether his view that the Church's acts do not "embody" God's work can be squared with the Church as the "body of Christ." If it does not in a real sense "embody" (even if in another sense not embodying), can it fittingly be described as the "body"? It seems to me that Paul has in view a deeper unity—ultimately grounded eucharistically—than Webster would allow. For Webster, following Calvin, Paul's mystical meaning cannot go further than a "fellowship": "What is the relationship between the Holy One and the saints? Because the relation is most properly conceived as a relation-in-distinction, the 'communion' between the church and its Lord is best articulated as *fellowship* rather than *participation*" ("On Evangelical Ecclesiology," 170). Quoting Calvin, Webster describes the union of Head and members as " 'spiritual bond' rather than 'essential indwelling'. That is, the church's relation to Christ is a fellowship in which distance or difference is as essential as union, for it is a mutuality ordered as precedence and subsequence, giving and receiving, and so one from which any identification is excluded" (ibid.). Certainly "distance or difference is as essential as union," but why should this mean that "any identification is excluded"? A deeper exploration of the "giving and receiving" is necessary, so as to appreciate how Christians may be united (eucharistically) to Christ's giving and receiving. (Von Balthasar argues that "[o]rthodox Protestantism, in contradistinction to pietism, has always, as it does today, rejected the idea of an *imitatio* of Christ as ignoring the distance between him and us, and tantamount to sacrilege" ["Office in the Church," 121].)

to remove mountains, but have not love, I am nothing. If I give away all I have, and if I deliver my body to be burned, but have not love, I gain nothing. (1 Corinthians 13:1–3)

As he puts it elsewhere with specific regard to his own mandate, "I do not run aimlessly, I do not box as one beating the air; but I pommel my body and subdue it, lest after preaching to others I myself should be disqualified" (1 Corinthians 9:26–27).

The apostolic mandate gives a special power with respect to the communication of Christ's sanctifying power, but it does not guarantee that its possessor will abide in cruciform love. Yet, it does assist in configuring Paul to the self-subordination of Christ's cross. As Paul says,

> For I think that God has exhibited us apostles as last of all, like men sentenced to death; because we have become a spectacle to the world, to angels and to men. We are fools for Christ's sake, but you are wise in Christ. We are weak, but you are strong. You are held in honor, but we in disrepute. To the present hour we hunger and thirst, we are ill-clad and buffeted and homeless, and we labor, working with our own hands. When reviled, we bless; when persecuted, we endure; when slandered, we try to conciliate; we have become, and are now, as the refuse of the world, the offscouring of all things. (1 Corinthians 4:9–13)

Paul's hierarchical authority leads to opposition and "disrepute" because his authority opposes the pride of other believers. Paul finds himself having to warn the Corinthians, "What! Did the word of God originate with you, or are you the only ones it has reached?" (1 Corinthians 14:36). Such exercise of hierarchical authority inevitably involves offense, and yet it affirms the crucial principle of Christian receptivity in contrast to pride. Receptivity is the key to Christian wisdom. As Paul states, "If any one thinks that he is a prophet, or spiritual, he should acknowledge that what I am writing to you is a command of the Lord. If any does not recognize this, he is not recognized" (1 Corinthians 14:37–38).

Paul shares his apostolic mandate with certain members of the Corinthian community, as well as with others whom he instructs the Corinthians to hear with obedience. Timothy is an important example: "When Timothy comes, see that you put him at ease among you, for he is doing the work of the Lord, as I am. So let no one despise him"

(1 Corinthians 16:10–11). Apollos, too, "will come when he has opportunity" (1 Corinthians 16:12). From within the Corinthian community, Paul identifies Stephanas: "Now, brethren, you know that the household of Stephanas were the first converts in Achaia, and they have devoted themselves to the service of the saints; I urge you to be subject to such men and to every fellow worker and labor" (1 Corinthians 16:15–16). Mentioning Stephanas, Fortunatus, and Achaicus, Paul again emphasizes that they participate in his authority: "Give recognition to such men" (1 Corinthians 16:18).[51]

For Paul, then, hierarchical authority in the Church belongs to Christ's mode of communicating, in the Holy Spirit, the power of Christ's self-subordinating love. Hierarchical authority befits Christ's Church because it makes manifest the fruitfulness of subordinating oneself to others in love, rather than placing oneself first. Paul is well aware of how difficult it is for believers to obey other Christians, but he insists upon it. He does so because such obedience expresses love (against the temptation of pride, the temptation to cling to oneself) and because of the very nature of the union of believers with Christ's sanctifying power—through faith and the sacraments of faith, which Paul oversees—as a direct *and* mediated union. As Paul says to the Corinthians, "Be imitators of me, as I am of Christ" (1 Corinthians 11:1; cf. 4:16).[52] It will also be clear that for the mediation of Christ's

---

51. Thomas Aquinas reads 2 Corinthians as focused on the ministers of God, whereas he finds 1 Corinthians to be concerned more directly with their sacramental ministry: for the interweaving of these themes, see Daniel A. Keating, "Aquinas on 1 and 2 Corinthians: The Sacraments and Their Ministers," in *Aquinas on Scripture: An Introduction to His Biblical Commentaries*, ed. Thomas G. Weinandy, Daniel A. Keating, and John P. Yocum (New York: T. & T. Clark, 2005), 127–48.

52. Joseph Ratzinger likewise points to the Corinthian correspondence as indicating an apostolic power, given by Christ, to communicate the power of the cross in a manner that other believers cannot communicate it. Commenting on 2 Corinthians 5, Ratzinger observes, "This text displays quite plainly that representative and missionary character of the apostolic ministry that we have just come to understand as the essence of a 'sacrament'; the God-given authority originating precisely in self-dispossession, in not speaking in one's own name, emerges clearly in this passage" (Joseph Ratzinger, *Called to Communion: Understanding the Church Today*, trans. Adrian Walker [German 1991; San Francisco: Ignatius Press, 1996], 118). He goes on to say that the "God-given authority" is to communicate "reconciliation with God, which springs from the Cross of Christ. . . . Since as a historical happening it [the Cross] belongs to the past, it can be appropriated only 'sacramentally' " (ibid.). To understand this appropriation Ratzinger turns to 1 Corinthians, saying, "when we listen to 1 Corinthians, we perceive that baptism and the Eucharist, which are inseparable from the word of preaching that produces faith and thus brings us to new birth, are essential for this event. Accordingly, it also becomes quite clear in Paul that the 'sacramental' authority of the apostolate is a specific

saving power, teaching and service do not suffice. Christ does not solely instruct and provide an example to believers. Rather, he shares with them a power that changes them, deifies them.

Thus Paul's mandate to communicate Christ's saving power to others sets him apart from other believers whom he serves. Since Christ alone can give what Paul (mediating Christ's gift) gives, Paul and his generation stand at the beginning of the "apostolic succession" by which the unique apostolic participation in Christ's power is passed down through the generations. This hierarchical authority, hierarchical mediation, belongs to the Church's witness to mutual self-subordinating love not only because receiving from others is opposed to pride, but also because those who give in the name of Christ must themselves become cruciform. Paul must be configured to Christ's self-subordinating love so as to fulfill, in its fullest dimensions, the apostolic vocation of spending his life in giving Christ to other believers.[53]

---

ministry and in no way describes Christian life as a whole, though many have wanted to draw this conclusion from the fact that the Twelve represent at the same time the future office and the Church as a whole" (118–19). Cf. for contemporary application Jeremy Driscoll, OSB, "Preaching in the Context of the Eucharist: A Patristic Perspective," *Pro Ecclesia* 11 (2002): 24–40.

53. Pheme Perkins agrees that Paul's understanding of authority in the Church merits imitation, but she interprets his view in a different manner than I do. She begins by noting, "Accustomed to the authoritarianism of today's hierarchy, most Catholics presume that Paul exercised apostolic authority in the same way" (Perkins, " 'Being of One Mind': Apostolic Authority, Persuasion, and *Koinonia* in New Testament Christianity," in *Common Calling: The Laity and the Governance of the Catholic Church*, ed. Stephen J. Pope [Washington, DC: Georgetown University Press, 2004], 25). For Paul, she says, "The true apostle was not to be found in the royal entourage of a triumphal parade, but among the condemned captives at its end, mere garbage in the world's estimation" (31). She presents his understanding of apostolic authority as grounded in an authenticity recognized by the community: Paul's "principle remains fundamental to authority within the Christian churches: there must be a discernable 'fit' or coherence between the concrete words and deeds of leaders (apostles, preachers, teachers) and the Gospel they proclaim" (30). Due to this principle, Paul's exercise of authority passes muster even today. Perkins states, "In Paul's case, the imitation of Christ crucified engendered a pastoral practice that acknowledged the need for local flexibility in preaching the Gospel and building up the community of faith" (33). While criticizing Paul's practice and doctrine on some points, she finds that for Paul, "The cross negates every form of human self-assertion and domination (2 Cor 13:3–4)" (35). Her praise of Paul, however, depends upon the idea that Paul claims no authority other than the insight into the Gospel—and thus his ability to teach the Gospel—that his sufferings have given him: "The local leaders and teachers of Paul's time had no 'office' that gave them the right to determine belief or action. Rather, the authority of communal prophets and teachers was a consequence of their activities in the Church, encouraging, exhorting, and instructing others" (34; she cites here Troels Engberg-Pedersen, "1 Corinthians 11:16 and the Character of Pauline Exhortation," *Journal of Biblical Literature* 110 [1991]: 679–689). It is this limited view of apostolic authority as rooted in teaching ability that I am contesting in this chapter.

The Gospel of Matthew

Does the Gospel of Matthew add to this understanding of the relationship of hierarchical authority and self-subordinating Christian
love? We have already noted two passages in Matthew that seem to
militate against the fittingness of hierarchical authority in the Church:
"unless you turn and become like children, you will never enter the
kingdom of heaven. Whoever humbles himself like this child, he is
the greatest in the kingdom of heaven" (Matthew 18:3–4),[54] and

> You know that the rulers of the gentiles lord it over them, and their great
> men exercise authority over them. It shall not be so among you, but who-
> ever would be great among you must be your servant, and whoever would
> be first among you must be your slave; even as the Son of man came not
> to be served but to serve, and to give his life as a ransom for many.
> (Matthew 20:25–28)

Again one might ask: Can Paul's strong sense of his own apostolic
authority—recall his claim that "if anyone does not recognize this, he
is not recognized" (1 Corinthians 14:38)—be squared with Jesus'
teaching in the Gospel of Matthew that Jesus' followers must humble
themselves like children and must be the slaves of all? As the Methodist
biblical scholar Ben Witherington observes, "Jesus' vision of leadership
is not of a person who lords it over others or wields authority like the
rulers of the Gentiles, but rather one who is the servant and slave of
all."[55] Can such a vision of leadership be combined with apostolic
authority? Turning from Paul to the Gospels, I will briefly identify
and discuss seven characteristics that belong to the mandate of the
disciple/apostle in the Gospel of Matthew.

First, the disciples/apostles are those who share Jesus' last
Passover supper with him, and who thus bear responsibility for
sharing it with the world.[56] As Matthew describes it,

---

54. Cf. the ecclesiological reflections in Guy Bedouelle, OP, "Reflection on the Place of
the Child in the Church: 'Suffer the Little Children to Come unto Me,'" trans. Esther
Tillman, *Communio* 12 (1985): 349–67.

55. Ben Witherington III, *Matthew* (Macon, GA: Smyth & Helwys, 2006), 378.

56. W. D. Davies and Dale C. Allison Jr. state with regard to Matthew 26:26–29, "Matthew's
text recounts a past event, the last supper of Jesus with his disciples. But all commentators
presume that Matthew's first readers saw in the last supper the foundation of the Lord's
Supper: 26.26–29 is an aetiological cult narrative. While agreeing, we observe that the text
does not say this about itself. Jesus does not invite repetition of his actions; there is no 'Do this

Now as they were eating, Jesus took bread and blessed and broke it and gave it to the disciples and said, "Take, eat; this is my body." And he took a cup, and when he had given thanks he gave it to them, saying, "Drink of it, all of you; for this is my blood of the covenant, which is poured out for many for the forgiveness of sins." (Matthew 26:26–28)

Earlier, Jesus feeds the crowds with his miraculous food through the mediation of the disciples/apostles. Jesus "took the seven loaves and the fish, and having given thanks he broke them and gave them to the disciples, and the disciples gave them to the crowds" (Matthew 15:36).[57] The disciples mediate Jesus' eucharistic feeding of the world.

Second, the disciples/apostles receive the mission to communicate Jesus' sanctifying power to the entire world. The risen Lord appears on a mountain in Galilee only to the eleven disciples, Judas having committed suicide: "And Jesus came and said to them, 'All authority in heaven and on earth has been given to me. Go therefore and make disciples of all nations, baptizing them in the name of the Father and of the Son and of the Holy Spirit, teaching them to observe all that I have commanded you' " (Matthew 28:18–20).[58]

---

in remembrance of me.' The last supper is then an example of how the text gives its full meaning only to readers who bring to it extra-textual knowledge, in this case knowledge of the Christian celebration of the eucharist" (Davies and Allison, *The Gospel According to Saint Matthew*, vol. III, *Commentary on Matthew XIX-XXVIII* [Edinburgh: T. & T. Clark, 1997] 465). See also Hans Urs von Balthasar, "The Priest of the New Covenant," in his *Explorations in Theology*, vol. 4, *Spirit and Institution*, trans. Edward T. Oakes, sj (German 1974; San Francisco: Ignatius Press, 1995, 353–81, at 360–65, on the apparent "silence of the New Testament texts regarding the exclusive authority of the ones sent by Jesus to celebrate his eucharistic memorial meal in the midst of the community" (360). Von Balthasar argues that Paul "looks on his whole apostolic ministry as completely liturgical" (364), and that the apostles receive a "foundational authority" that includes "the authority to celebrate the sacrament of the 'one bread' that is the foundation of all the Church's sacraments. By means of the Eucharist, the community becomes 'one Body', the 'Body of Christ' (1 Cor 10:6). Indeed, this celebration is the high point of the Christian proclamation, namely, the announcement of the death of the Lord (1 Cor 11:26)—which is also the very mandate given to the one sent by the Lord" (365).

57. Donald Senior, CP, remarks with regard to the disciples, "As in the previous feeding story [Matthew 14:15–21], the disciples have an important role. Here they seem to readily grasp their responsibility to feed the crowds (contrast 14:15–16) but do not know how to do so. The use of the term *eucharistesas* ('giving thanks,' 15:36) and the suppression of the blessing and distribution of the fish (note the elimination of Mark 7:7), with the resulting focus on the loaves and the baskets of leftover fragments, underscore the connection of this story to the eucharistic practice of the community" (Senior, *Matthew* [Nashville, TN: Abingdon Press, 1998], 186).

58. Roch Kereszty, O CIST, connects this passage in Matthew with the mission of the Apostle Paul: "According to Matthew, the eleven disciples-apostles received a share in the *exousia*, the full power of the Son (28:18–20). Paul was aware that, as an apostle of Jesus Christ, he was

Their mission to teach and baptize depends upon their ongoing sharing in the presence of the risen Jesus, who tells them, "Lo, I am with you always, to the close of the age" (Matthew 28:20). During his earthly ministry, too, Jesus calls the Twelve and sends them on mission. In calling them to follow him, Jesus promises them, " 'Follow me, and I will make you fishers of men' " (Matthew 4:19). He gives them the mission to proclaim, by words and deeds, the coming of the kingdom of God in the towns of Israel (at first not entering any gentile or Samaritan town).[59] Foreseeing their later journeying throughout the world, Jesus promises them that in bearing witness to him they will suffer, but that the Holy Spirit will speak through them: "When they deliver you up, do not be anxious how you are to speak or what you are to say; for what you are to say will be given to you in that hour; for it is not you who speak, but the Spirit of your Father speaking through you" (Matthew 10:19–20).

---

given *exousia* that he could use both for 'building up' and 'tearing down' (2 Cor 10:8). Analogously to the *exousia* of Jesus Christ, which Jesus used only in absolute dependence on the Father, the apostle used the participated *exousia* in absolute dependence on the person and gospel of Jesus Christ for the sake of the faithful. He acted both as father and mother, pleading, entreating, and persuading his faithful with tender affection whenever he could. But he did not hesitate to make the full weight of his apostolic *exousia* felt in giving norms for the eucharistic life (1 Cor 10–11), for marriages (1 Cor 7), for lawsuits in the church in Corinth (1 Cor 6), and for excommunication of an incestuous man 'in the name of our Lord Jesus Christ' and with his 'power' (1 Cor 5:4)" (Kereszty, "A Catholic Response to W. Pannenberg Regarding the Petrine Ministry of the Bishop of Rome," *Communio* 25 [1998]: 619–29, at 624). Regarding Matthew 28:18–20, Donald Senior notes the link to Daniel 7:14, "And to him was given dominion and glory and kingdom, that all peoples, nations, and languages should serve him; his dominion is an everlasting dominion, which shall not pass away, and his kingdom one that shall not be destroyed" (Senior, *Matthew*, 346).

59. Hans Urs von Balthasar remarks in this regard, "Even before the Resurrection, the missioned disciples were endowed with authority not only to preach his word but also to do his deeds, both of which were essential parts of a whole, enabling them to proclaim the message of the Kingdom" (von Balthasar, "The Priest of the New Covenant," 358). See also the astute comment of Louis Bouyer regarding the Twelve: "For Jesus especially, even if people still debate whether he proclaimed himself—indeed, quite simply believed himself—to be the Messiah, there is no doubt, according to even the most radical critics, that his mission, as he understood it, was addressed to this people [the People of God, Israel] and, more precisely, concerned the final conditions of belonging to it. The choosing of the Twelve and their function appear to imply not a break with the old People of God but their radical renewal, an eschatological *qahal* or *ekklesia*. Let us point out that modern exegesis has thereby joined hands with the fathers, for whom the Church had been founded since Abraham (if not since Abel or Adam), renewed at each covenant, and radically renewed (without break with the past) in Christ" (Bouyer, *The Church of God: Body of Christ and Temple of the Spirit*, trans. Charles Underhill Quinn [French 1970; Chicago: Franciscan Herald Press, 1982], 551).

Third, Jesus gives his disciples/apostles special explanations of his teachings. For example, after teaching the crowds at length in parables, Jesus interprets for his disciples/apostles alone the key parable, that of sower. As Matthew tells us,

> Then he [Jesus] left the crowds and went into the house. And his disciples came to him, saying, "Explain to us the parable of the weeds of the field." He answered, "He who sows the good seed is the Son of man; the field is the world, and the good seed means the sons of the kingdom; the weeds are the sons of the evil one, and the enemy who sowed them is the devil; the harvest is the close of the age." (Matthew 13:36–39)

His disciples/apostles have a unique authority, therefore, to proclaim his teaching: "[teach] them to observe all that I have commanded you" (Matthew 28:20).

Fourth, while all the disciples/apostles have a special share in Jesus' authority, Simon Peter stands out.[60] He is the first one of the disciples to confess in faith that Jesus is "the Christ, the Son of the living God" (Matthew 16:16). This faith comes not from Peter's own strength, but has been given Peter by "my [Jesus'] Father who is in heaven" (Matthew 16:17). Jesus gives Peter a unique share in his authority:

> And I tell you, you are Peter, and on this rock I will build my Church, and the powers of death shall not prevail against it. I will give you the keys to the kingdom of heaven, and whatever you bind on earth shall be bound in heaven, and whatever you loose on earth shall be loosed in heaven. (Matthew 16:18–19)

---

60. For mainstream works of historical-critical biblical scholarship on Peter in the Gospel of Matthew, see Arlo Nau, *Peter in Matthew: Discipleship and Dispraise* (Collegeville, MN: Liturgical Press, 1992); Timothy Wiarda, *Peter in the Gospels* (Tübingen: Mohr Siebeck, 2000); Raymond E. Brown et al., eds., *Peter in the New Testament* (New York: Paulist Press, 1973). These works grant Peter's unique role without attaching to it the traditional Catholic interpretations. For a perspective that underscores Peter's (and the Church of Rome's) ongoing importance, see Roch Kereszty, "Peter and Paul and the Founding of the Church of Rome: Forgotten Perspectives," *Communio* 15 (1998): 215–33. For commentary by Orthodox biblical scholars on the Gospel of Matthew's depiction of Peter see Theodore Stylianopoulos, "Concerning the Biblical Foundation of Primacy," in *The Petrine Ministry: Catholics and Orthodox in Dialogue*, ed. Walter Cardinal Kasper, trans. the staff of the Pontifical Council for Promoting Christian Unity (New York: Paulist Press, 2006), 37–64, at 42–53; Veselin Kesich, "Peter's Primacy in the New Testament and the Early Tradition," in *The Primacy of Peter: Essays in Ecclesiology and the Early Church*, ed. John Meyendorff (1963; Crestwood, NY: St. Vladimir's Seminary Press, 1992), 35–66, at 45–53, 59, and elsewhere. Kesich particularly downplays Peter's significance, whereas Stylianopoulos is more open to it.

Yet Jesus' gift to Peter of "the keys to the kingdom," significant though it is, hardly means that he does not recognize Peter's profound weakness.[61] Peter cannot as yet imagine a Messiah who would suffer and die, and he even dares to rebuke Jesus for saying that this is what will happen. Jesus responds, "Get behind me, Satan! You are a hindrance to me; for you are not on the side of God, but of men" (Matthew 16:23). Peter's strength is not his own. Likewise, when Jesus commands him to walk on water, Peter does so but then begins to falter and begs Jesus to save him. Matthew relates, "Jesus immediately stretched out his hand and caught him, saying to him, 'O man of little faith, why did you doubt?'" (Matthew 14:31). Peter is one with the rest of the disciples/apostles in this weakness of faith, and yet he receives a mandate that goes beyond theirs.

Fifth, the disciples/apostles leave everything to follow Jesus. The Twelve, more than any others of those who followed Jesus during his earthly ministry, abandoned their earlier pursuits so as to serve the Lord. Because of this, they have a special share in Jesus' power, a share which Jesus describes in eschatological terms: "Truly, I say to you, in the new world, when the Son of man shall sit on his glorious throne, you who have followed me will also sit on twelve thrones, judging the twelve tribes of Israel" (Matthew 19:28).[62] Others, too,

---

61. Describing the presentation of Peter in Aquinas's *Commentary on John*, Frederick Christian Bauerschmidt notes that for Aquinas "the diversity of ecclesiastical offices 'is for the beauty and completion of the Church' (*Ioan.* 6, lect. 5, n. 938; cf. 1, 4, n. 119) because they are the occasion for the decorous ordering of the community. In discussing the characteristics requisite for the pastoral office in the context of Peter's encounter with the risen Christ by the sea of Tiberius, Thomas quotes Aristotle's *Politics* to the effect that 'it is the natural order of things that the one who cares for and governs others should be better' (*Ioan.* 21, lect. 3, n. 2619). This applies in the Church militant no less than in Aristotle's *polis*. But we must also bear in mind that the Church is not the *polis*" (Bauerschmidt, " 'That the Faithful Become the Temple of God': The Church Militant in Aquinas's *Commentary on John*," in Dauphinais and Levering, *Reading John with St. Thomas Aquinas*, 305). The difference between the Church and the *polis* becomes clear in Peter's humbled state after his betrayal of Jesus: "It is this humbled Peter to whom Jesus gives the task of leadership in the Church militant, precisely because in his humility he embodies what Christ taught by his example" (ibid.). See also my "Ecclesial Exegesis and Ecclesial Authority: Childs, Fowl, and Aquinas," *The Thomist* 69 (2005): 407–67.

62. David Catchpole observes that Jesus envisioned the Twelve as rulers over the eschatological Israel (in which God will pour out his holiness upon Israel): see Catchpole, *Jesus People: The Historical Jesus and the Beginnings of Community* (London: Darton, Longman and Todd, 2006), 106. Likewise, Bruce Chilton grants Jesus' "eschatological imagination" (Neusner and Chilton, *The Body of Faith*, 111) but emphasizes that Jesus never defined systematically what the new Israel would look like. For his part, Yves Congar holds that Jesus did not found the Church "after the fashion of Solon, Lycurgus or Lenin, giving it a charter or a constitution. He

will share in the reward given to the followers of Jesus. Thus Jesus continues, "And every one who has left houses or brothers or sisters or father for my name's sake will receive a hundredfold, and inherit eternal life" (Matthew 19:29).

Sixth, the disciples/apostles' power depends entirely upon Jesus. When they try to act on their own, they are repeatedly shown to be incompetent. For instance, when a man whose son suffers from epilepsy reports that the disciples could not cure the child, Jesus answers, "O faithless and perverse generation, how long am I to be with you? How long am I to bear with you?" (Matthew 17:17). After Jesus has healed the child, the disciples ask him why they could not do it. He answers, "Because of your little faith" (Matthew 17:20). This same lack of faith appears when they wake Jesus out of fear that their boat will capsize. Jesus responds, " 'Why are you afraid, O men of little faith?' Then he rose and rebuked the winds and the sea; and there was a great calm" (Matthew 8:26). Yet their devoted following of Jesus also suggests, at their best, a childlike faith in him. Indeed, Jesus rejoices that some people have understood him:

> I thank thee, Father, Lord of heaven and earth, that thou hast hidden these things from the wise and understanding and revealed them to babes; yea, Father, for such was thy gracious will. All things have been delivered to me by my Father; and no one knows the Son except the Father, and no one knows the Father except the Son and any one to whom the Son chooses to reveal him. (Matthew 11:25–27)

When Jesus calls them, they do not hesitate: "Immediately they left their nets and followed him" (Matthew 4:20), and "Immediately they left the boat and their father, and followed him" (Matthew 4:22).[63]

Seventh, having sworn not to abandon Jesus in his hour of trial, the disciples abandon him. Quoting Zechariah's messianic

---

founded it by giving its very being and life, promising his Spirit to animate and assist it. He announced that, in virtue of living within it, we would have in it truth and life, because he would live in it himself, who is the way and the truth by his Spirit" (Congar, "The Church and Its Unity," in his *The Mystery of the Church*, trans. A. V. Littledale [French 1956; Baltimore: Helicon Press, 1960], 91). Thus the mission to the Gentiles emerged from within the context of the proclamation to Israel: see Congar, "The Life of the Church and Awareness of Its Catholicity," in idem, *The Mystery of the Church*, 138–46.

63. See Senior, *Matthew*, 63–64.

prophecy, Jesus tells them that they will fall away and then be gathered again. Led by Peter, they all deny that they will ever fall away:

> Peter declared to him, "Though they all fall away because of you, I will never fall away." Jesus said to him, "Truly, I say to you, this very night, before the cock crows three times, you will deny me three times." Peter said to him, "Even if I must die with you, I will not deny you." And so said all the disciples. (Matthew 26:33–35)[64]

One of the disciples, Judas, betrays Jesus to the Roman authorities and in his guilt kills himself (Matthew 27:5). They abandon Jesus even though three of them, Peter, James, and John, earlier witness the transfigured Lord beside Moses and Elijah (Matthew 17:1–7).[65]

The Gospel of Matthew thus presents at least seven ways that Jesus sets apart the apostles from his other followers.[66] The disciples/

---

64. In this regard, Davies and Allison quote Calvin's interpretation: "Peter, quitting the doubt of v. 22 for 'the intoxication of human self-confidence' (Calvin), not only contradicts his Lord (cf. 16.21–3) and the Scripture, but makes himself out to be more loyal than his fellow disciples" (Davies and Allison, *Commentary on Matthew XIX–XXVIII*, 486). Matthew 26:32, Davies and Allison note, provides crucial context for the disciples' failure: after his Resurrection Jesus will "reconstitute the flock that has been and then inaugurate the world mission" (ibid.).

65. This pattern of failure continues, of course, in the hierarchical priesthood of the Church. Thus Thomas Aquinas decries the sin of simony—the practice of receiving "money for the spiritual grace of the sacraments"—and his manner of enumerating this sin indicates his knowledge of its prevalence (see ST II-II, q. 100, aa. 1–2). Far from imagining that all members of the hierarchical priesthood are holy, Aquinas observes that "our Lord has good and wicked ministers or servants" (ST III, q. 82, a. 5).

66. On the basis of speculation about the community within which Matthew composed his Gospel, Davies and Allison present Matthew as highly concerned about Christian unity: "Matthew, engaged with a Pharisaism which sought to re-establish the unity of the Jewish people in terms of the written and oral Torah, himself sought a unity—the unity of Christians. He found such unity implicit in the story and teachings of Jesus. So the presentation of those two things in his Gospel was in part an attempt to overcome the divisions and tensions that characterized his own community as well as early Christianity in general" (Davies and Allison, *Commentary on Matthew XIX–XXVIII*, 704). They propose however that the evidence of Matthew's Gospel suggests that "the community's organization also seems to evidence a group only reluctantly and not finally separated from Judaism. The Matthean ecclesia appears to have been partly inchoate and ambivalent. The structures glimpsed in 10.41 and 18.15–18 appear rudimentary. Although the egalitarianism of 18.15–18 seems to give way in 16.16–19 to authority and the priority of Peter, organizationally one senses behind the text a community groping its way in search of forms, a group not yet too fully formed or cohesive or sure of itself. Even in 16.16–19 the image is 'that of building on a rock, that is, of a community in process of being structured' " (ibid., 697, citing H. C. Kee, "The Transformation of the Synagogue after 70 CE," *New Testament Studies* 36 [1990]: 21, and W. Carter, *Households and Discipleship* [Sheffield: Sheffield Academic Press, 1994]). Given that during Jesus' lifetime the community was indeed in the process of being structured, I think that the content of Matthew's Gospel is compatible with a more fully formed community.

apostles have a unique share in the Passover meal and the distribution of Jesus' food to the world; they are called by Jesus to undertake the mission of communicating Jesus' sanctifying power to the world; they receive fuller explanations of Jesus' teachings and thereby have unique authority to teach in his name; Peter stands out among the disciples/ apostles as sharing above the others in Jesus' power; they leave everything to follow Jesus and receive power accordingly; their power depends entirely upon Jesus; they all abandon Jesus in his hour of trial, confirming once and for all that their mandate does not depend upon their perfection.

The Gospel of Matthew ends with the risen Lord's commissioning of the apostles; the Gospel does not tell us whether the apostles' unique power in the Church can be or is passed down to others so as to establish a permanent hierarchical/sacramental leadership in the Church. However, the Gospel does indicate that the apostolic mandate in the Church is more than that of teachers of faith, requiring simply zeal and divine call.[67] While the apostles possess unique authority to teach faith in Jesus, their unique mission is rooted in their distinctive sharing in the sanctifying power of the cross and Resurrection by which Christ establishes the kingdom of God. As Louis Bouyer puts it, "what the apostles must first transmit to us through the special gift of the Spirit, given to them for us, is the very presence of the Head and his mystery, passing into us, operating in us, reaching out to us."[68] Their participation in the "presence of the Head and his mystery" includes their particular mandate to baptize in the name of the Father, the Son, and the Holy Spirit and their unique participation in Jesus' own Paschal meal, the Eucharist. Peter's sharing in Jesus' authority is particularly striking, although it should also be noted that Peter's authority is never separated from that of the other apostles, which provides its context.[69]

---

67. Thus Rudolph Schnackenburg finds that for the Gospel of Matthew, "in the Church there is an authority conferred by God and concerning salvation which, according to the evangelist's conception, can hardly repose in the community as such, but is rather made over to certain persons" (Schnackenburg, *The Church in the New Testament* [New York: Seabury Press, 1965], 74). He adds that "Matthew knows and acknowledges presiding functions and offices in the Church but also subjects them all to the law of service and responsibility before the Lord (cf. 24:45–51; 25:14–30)" (76).

68. Bouyer, *The Church of God*, 317.

69. See also Senior, *Matthew*, 188–95.

John D. Zizioulas and Thomas Aquinas

The above examination of 1 Corinthians and the Gospel of Matthew requires a reexamination of the portrait of the hierarchical structure of the earliest Church that Burtchaell and Sullivan provided. In so doing, I will draw attention in particular to John Zizioulas's emphasis on the eucharistic role of the bishop. In his theologically guided historical account of the development of the episcopacy (and presbyterate), Zizioulas stresses that the unique "power" of the bishop has its roots in the celebration of the Eucharist, and that if theologians want to understand ecclesial structure, they must do so from within the theology of the eucharistic synaxis.[70] I then show that Thomas Aquinas likewise underscores the eucharistic vocation of the bishop (which he grants also to priests). On a theological rather than historical level, furthermore, Aquinas inquires carefully into what the ability to celebrate the Eucharist requires. Specifically, he argues that the eucharistic celebration requires the presider to be conformed to Christ by means of a spiritual power—a sacramental "character"—that enables him to

---

70. See John D. Zizioulas [Metropolitan John of Pergamon], *Eucharist, Bishop, Church: The Unity of the Church in the Divine Eucharist and the Bishop during the First Three Centuries*, 2nd ed., trans. Elizabeth Theokritoff (Brookline, MA: Holy Cross Orthodox Press, 2001 [1965]). Zizioulas remarks that the Church's unity and organizational structure "was not borrowed or copied from the world around her, as historians have often contended, but arose naturally out of the eucharistic assembly" (59). Here his research would be enriched by James Burtchaell's argument that the position of *episkopos* arose out of the synagogue structure and parallels the *archisynagogos* who, in Burtchaell's words, "presided at worship" as well as "at all community functions." Yet even given Burtchaell's research into the synagogue structure, nonetheless one can see in Zizioulas how Christ's sacramental presence gave a new direction to this structure, one that required a *sacramental* "order." Zizioulas states, "So thanks to the Eucharist and, therefore, chiefly in it, the various forms of ministry grew up in the primitive Church, and these in turn gave rise to the various 'orders' in the Church and produced her law as a strictly Christocentric reality. All the ministries of Christ were reflected as historical realities in a way that created order and, therefore, 'orders.' In other words, while Christ was identified with the whole Church which was His body, and, therefore, *all* the members of the Church were 'sharers in Christ,' the powers or ministries of Christ were not expressed through all these members, but through certain ones" (61). Zizioulas develops, without significantly changing, the ecclesiological points made in *Eucharist, Bishop, Church* in his later influential study, *Being in Communion*, chapters 2–7. For discussion of Zizioulas's ecclesiology, see especially the appreciative reading of Paul McPartlan, *The Eucharist Makes the Church: Henri de Lubac and John Zizioulas in Dialogue* (Edinburgh: T. & T. Clark, 1993); Christopher Ruddy, *The Local Church: Tillard and the Future of Catholic Ecclesiology* (New York: Crossroad, 2006), 22–30. See also the criticisms lodged by Miroslav Volf in *After Our Likeness: The Church as the Image of the Trinity*, trans. Doug Stott (Grand Rapids, MI: Eerdmans, 1998), which we surveyed in chapter 1.

share in Christ's gifting. The sacrament of orders bestows the spiritual power that enables bishops/priests to celebrate the Eucharist.

In sum, as we will see, Zizioulas focuses attention on the Eucharist, and Aquinas gives to this focus on the bishop's eucharistic vocation a metaphysical sophistication that illumines the scriptural witness found in 1 Corinthians and the Gospel of Matthew.

John D. Zizioulas: The Eucharist and the Bishop

Building upon passages such as 1 Corinthians 11:18 and 11:20, which connect "when you assemble as a church" and "when you meet together" with the celebration of the Eucharist, Zizioulas aims at showing first that New Testament references to the "Church" in particular cities have in view the community gathered to celebrate the Eucharist.[71] Second, he argues that the passages about the Eucharist, combined with the passages about Christ and the Church as the "body of Christ," signal an already rich development of the theology of ecclesial unity (the unity of the members with Christ and with each other) in the earliest Church.[72] As he says, "The principal images used to depict and describe the Church in the New Testament are based on the relationship of the 'many' with the 'One,' exactly as this is dictated by the eucharistic

---

71. See Zizioulas, *Eucharist, Bishop, Church*, 46f. In a remark that could also perhaps characterize the situation in the Roman Catholic Church, Zizioulas states that "many Orthodox have it firmly entrenched in their mind that the bishop is in essence an administrator, and that in his liturgical function, including indeed the Divine Eucharist, he is not a person *constitutive* of the Mystery but more or less [a] *decorative* someone who is invited to 'embellish' the whole service by his presence and his vestments" (6). As Zizioulas goes on to say, the work of the Holy Spirit in the Church is then set in opposition to this merely administrative work of the bishop, and one begins to wonder whether the bishop's authority is needed at all, even for administration. Cf. for a Catholic perspective similar to the one Zizioulas critiques, Hugh Lawrence, "Ordination and Governance," in *Authority in the Roman Catholic Church: Theory and Practice*, ed. Bernard Hoose (Aldershot: Ashgate, 2002), 73–82. Lawrence holds that in the fourth century, "The clergy acquired the position of imperial officers" (75) with the result that a "hierocratic doctrine" developed in the Middle Ages. Assuming that ecclesial structure is fundamentally a sociological reality, he concludes, "The responsibility to direct and govern the Christian community rests, as it always has, with those whom the community (by whatever procedure) has chosen for that office and who have been ordained to the apostolic ministry. But the reorientation of ecclesiology through the Council, recognizing that all members of the Church share a common and royal priesthood, clearly involves a rethinking of roles and of the ways in which all can collaborate in the mission of Christ. Images of governance drawn from the political and social experience of Christians in past ages are no longer useful. The ordering of a community of equals involves the principles of representation by the governed and the responsibility of rulers to their people" (81).

72. See Zizioulas, *Eucharist, Bishop, Church*, 55f.

experience of the Church. . . . All these images become meaningless outside the ontological unity of the 'many' in Christ."[73] Third, Zizioulas finds that the Eucharist in the earliest Church required the presence of the "president" of the eucharistic assembly, the *episkopos*, although the *episkopos* was not the only one who could offer the Eucharist (the apostles and, according to the *Didache*, certain "prophets" also did so). Each "Church" in each city had only one "president" or *episkopos*, whose primary task was to lead the eucharistic worship.[74] Fourth, Zizioulas argues that these churches, or eucharistic assemblies under the presiding role of the *episkopos*, did not function as parts in a universal whole. Rather, because in and through the eucharistic celebration the whole Christ was made present and Christ's members were incorporated into him, each eucharistic assembly contains the fullness of the Church.[75] When parish structures later developed, with the resulting new authority of the *presbyters* for the Eucharist, the risk was that the

---

73. Ibid., 56–57. For studies that confirm Zizioulas's point and provide much ecclesiological insight, see Paul S. Minear, *Images of the Church in the New Testament* (Philadelphia: Westminster Press, 1960); Geoffrey Preston, OP, *Faces of the Church: Meditations on a Mystery and Its Images*, ed. Aidan Nichols, OP (Grand Rapids, MI: Eerdmans, 1997), 3–102.

74. See Zizioulas, *Eucharist, Bishop, Church*, 87f. In order to evaluate his argument historically, one would need to survey his interpretation of key passages from the New Testament, Clement of Rome, Ignatius of Antioch, Justin Martyr, Hippolytus, Irenaeus, and Cyprian, among others.

75. Ibid., 107f.; cf. 159–62. Drawing upon *Being in Communion* and two more recent essays by Zizioulas, "The Church as Communion," *St. Vladimir's Theological Quarterly* 38 (1994): 3–16; and idem, "Primacy in the Church: An Orthodox Approach," in *Petrine Ministry and the Unity of the Church*, ed. James F. Puglisi (Collegeville, MN: Liturgical Press, 1999), 115–25, Christopher Ruddy notes that for Zizioulas, "Conciliarity is the '*"sine qua non conditio"* for the catholicity of the Church,' because through it every local church is recognized as fully ecclesial, that is, catholic. On the theological level, conciliarity is an expression of God's own communion, in which oneness and multiplicity reciprocally involve each other, and of human participation in such communion through the eucharist (which, again, is always the one eucharist celebrated in many churches). . . . On account of this simultaneity of the one and the many in divine communion, Zizioulas rejects any notion of ecclesial priority, be it of the local or the universal Church. On the one hand, he thinks it is clear that the conciliar and eucharistic nature of the Church prohibits any kind of universal priority in which the many would be collapsed into or subjugated by, and not integrated within, the one; this, he argues, has been the perennial temptation of Roman Catholicism. On the other, arguing primarily against Afanasiev, he rejects local priority, because it would place the many before the one—or assent that a local church could exist independently of ecclesial communion—and consequently compromise each local church's essential relation—through eucharist and ordination—to other churches; the relationship between local churches would then be one of confederation, not communion" (Ruddy, *The Local Church*, 26–27). On the episcopal college, see Henri de Lubac, SJ, "The Episcopal College," in his *The Motherhood of the Church*, trans. Sister Sergia Englund, OCD (French 1971; San Francisco: Ignatius Press, 1982), 233–55 (in the section titled *Particular Churches in the Universal Church*).

bishop's integral connection with the Eucharist, and thereby with the unity of the Church, would be forgotten.[76]

In making this argument about the role in the earliest Churches of the *episkopos*, Zizioulas criticizes three influential ways of viewing the history of the early Church. First, F. C. Baur, and with him the Tübingen School, proposed a Hegelian (idealist) model for the development of authority in the early Church: a Jewish movement (Peter, James) struggles with a Hellenist movement (Paul), with the ultimate synthesis emerging in Irenaeus in the late second century. Baur holds that Christian diversity preceded Christian unity by nearly two centuries, and so it becomes hard to talk about unity as an *intrinsic* mark of the Church of Christ.[77] In addition, Baur defines

---

76. This is the theme of Part III of Zizioulas, *Eucharist, Bishop, Church*, 197f. John Howard Yoder underscores this problem:

> As I noted in 1980 in *Ecumenical Trends*, the standard discussion about episcopacy has routinely neglected a major dimension of what would need attention if everyone were to be in the conversation. In the earliest church every local church had its resident bishop, elected by his own people, on the basis of a local discernment process like that indicated in (for example) 1 Tim. 3. There was no theological mandate for having a church without its own resident bishop. The post–Reformation debate, as a result of the political shape of the troubles of the sixteenth century, has been about the question of succession, not an unimportant issue, although in principle ultimately a manageable one. The radical reformation debate, on the other hand, which has never begun seriously in ecumenical venues, is about the size of the diocese. . . . There would be no theologically important clash between congregationalists and Catholics, if the size of the diocese could be what it used to be. When I review the Roman Catholic and Anglo-Catholic arguments for the "historic episcopacy," I find no theological arguments which could count against ordaining more bishops, enough that every functioning congregation would have one. (Yoder, "On Christian Unity: The Way From Below," *Pro Ecclesia* 9 [2000]: 165–83, at 173–74).

77. This view is likewise set forth by Walter Bauer, *Orthodoxy and Heresy in Earliest Christianity*, trans. Philadelphia Seminar on Christian Origins, ed. Robert A. Kraft and Gerhard Krodel (German 1934; Mifflintown, PA: Sigler Press, 1996). For discussion of the views of Baur and Bauer as inadequate "myths of origins," see Luke Timothy Johnson, "Koinonia: Diversity and Unity in Early Christianity," *Theological Digest* 46 (1999): 303–13, at 304–7. In addition to diversity, Johnson points out, "In the beginning is also *koinonia*. The word means fellowship, and it denotes a sharing between parties who are not identical in every respect. It is this side of things that the conflict theories of origins tend to overlook. Not all difference is contradiction; not all disagreement spells division" (309). For a recent study indebted to Walter Bauer's perspective, see Peter Iver Kaufman, *Church, Book, and Bishop: Conflict and Authority in the Early Church* (Boulder, CO: Westview Press, 1996). As Kaufman puts it, "Despite stated opinion that their God was not a God of confusion, Christians appear almost addicted to confusion and conflict. And that addiction helped them come to some self-definition, to define the authority of the church, book, and bishop" (14). For a different view, without denying the disagreements among early Christians, see Yves Congar, *Diversity and Communion*, trans. John Bowden (French 1982; Mystic, CT: Twenty-Third Publications, 1985), 9–22; Rudolph Schnackenburg, *The Church in the New Testament* (New York: Seabury

unity solely in terms of ideas, thereby ruling out a eucharistic unity. Second, Adolf von Harnack finds that the dialectic in the early Church was between "localism" and "universalism," a dialectic eventually resolved—hardly in a satisfactory fashion—by the Church of Rome's claims to power. On this view, again, unity emerges late in the history of the Church, which begins as a movement dependent upon charismatic individuals operating freely in various localities, and ends as the institutional Church governed by bishops.[78]

The third way of looking at the early Church that Zizioulas opposes is one that he attributes to "Western theology, since scholasticism," and specifically since the emergence of the clearly defined list of seven sacraments.[79] The first step in the corruption of Western theology occurred when the bishop's role lost its mystical-sacramental significance: "the Divine Eucharist and the bishop had long since ceased to be connected either with each other, or with the essence of the Church and her unity, in the consciousness of Western theology."[80] Instead, the bishop came to be seen as an essential aspect of the functional success of the Church in warding off heresy, consolidating orthodoxy, and so forth. When viewed functionally, as an administrator, the bishop's role, however, is not intrinsic to "the nature of the Church."[81] Thus it would seem that if in a later time period the role of bishop becomes functionally inadequate and antiquated, one would have sufficient reason to replace episcopal authority with another more functional structure. Second, as one of the seven sacraments, no matter how unique, the Eucharist came to be treated under sacramental theology rather than ecclesiology: "it is one thing to say that the Eucharist is indispensable as one of the 'seven sacraments' of the Church, and

---

Press, 1965), 130–31. For a critique of Walter Bauer's book, see Walther Völker's book review in *Zeitschrift für Kirchengeschichte* 54 (1935): 628–31, recently translated in *Journal of Early Christian Studies* 14 (2006): 399–405, by Thomas P. Scheck; cf. Lewis Ayres's introduction (also critical of Bauer's thesis) to this number of the *Journal of Early Christian Studies*.

78. In response to these two views, Zizioulas notes that more recent historians are agreed that the oppositions on which these views rely—Judaism versus Hellenism and local versus universal—do not sufficiently describe the early Christian movement in its own historical context: see Zizioulas, *Eucharist, Bishop, Church*, 11–13.

79. Ibid., 14.

80. Ibid., 13.

81. Ibid., 14. For a historical study that views bishops as administrators seeking to consolidate power, see Kaufman, *Church, Book, and Bishop: Conflict and Authority in Early Latin Christianity*.

quite another to regard it as the supreme revelation of the Church herself."[82] Both the bishop and the Eucharist become functionalist realities, aimed at assisting individuals in arriving at salvation, rather than being the Church's very mode of sharing in Christ's Pasch. The former view is extrinsic to Christ's saving work, the latter view intrinsic. Zizioulas eloquently summarizes his position: "Only if we regard the Eucharist as the revelation of the Church in her ideal and historical unity, and the bishop first and foremost as the leader and head of the eucharistic assembly which unites the Church of God in space and time, do we recognize in each of these their profound ecclesiological content."[83]

Turning to recent Eastern Orthodox theology, Zizioulas adds two more points. First, ecclesiology belongs within Christology. Here he takes up a comment of Georges Florovsky, made in Florovsky's *La sainte Église universelle* (1948): "The theology of the Church is nothing but a chapter, and one of the principal chapters, of Christology. Without this chapter, Christology itself would not be complete. It is within the framework of Christology that the mystery of the Church is proclaimed in the New Testament. It was presented in the same way by the Greek and the Latin Fathers."[84] This is why episcopal authority cannot be understood outside the incorporation into Christ effected by the celebration of the Eucharist. As Zizioulas points out, once the Church is not seen as an entity over against Christ, but as the dynamic incorporation of human beings into Christ, "the revelation in Christ ceases to be a system of ideas as the Tübingen School conceived it, and becomes a truth *ontological in character*."[85] The Church is not, and never was, a matter of "Jewish" versus "Hellenist" ideas, of "local" versus "universal" domains, or of an extrinsic application of divine gifts. Rather, the Church is *"the very person of Christ* and man's union

---

82. Zizioulas, *Eucharist, Bishop, Church*, 14.

83. Ibid.

84. Quoted in ibid., 35, fn 39. The quotation is from p. 12 of Florovsky's book.

85. Ibid., 15. Likewise, see Joseph Ratzinger's observation that "the one Church always exists concretely in the concrete local community. The local community realizes itself as the Church in the religious assembly, that is, above all in the celebration of the Eucharist. Consequently, Christian brotherhood demands concretely the brotherhood of the individual parish community. This brotherhood has its source and center in the celebration of the eucharistic mysteries. In fact, in the classical theology of the Church, the Eucharist has been seen not so much as the soul's meeting with Christ, but rather as the *concorporatio cum Christo*— as the Christians' becoming one in the one body of the Lord" (Ratzinger, *The Meaning of Christian Brotherhood* [German 1960; San Francisco: Ignatius Press, 1993], 68).

with Him," that is to say, *"the whole Christ* in Augustine's apt phrase."[86] The unity of the Church is simply our incorporation into Christ.

Second, without downplaying the importance of the Holy Spirit for the theology of the Church, Zizioulas cautions against "a pneumatocentric ecclesiology"—here he cites Johann Möhler's *Die Einheit der Kirche*—"in which there is a risk of ecclesiology being made into 'charismatic sociology' and the unity of the Church becoming nothing more than a *societas fidei et Spiritus Sancti in cordibus*."[87] At stake is the correct theocentric, rather than anthropocentric, understanding of the Church.[88] Ecclesiology that seeks to be "pneumatocentric" begins with the experience of the gathered community, and as a result the Church comes primarily to be seen "as 'the body of Christians' united in the Holy Spirit."[89] By contrast, when one begins with Christ, the Word who contains all human beings within himself, the Church "is seen as the 'body of Christ' in an ontological sense."[90] Here Christ, not Christians, is primary—as Christ must rightly be.

---

86. Zizioulas, *Eucharist, Bishop, Church*, 15.

87. Ibid., 16. For an appreciative exposition of Möhler's ecclesiology, see Louis Bouyer, *The Church of God: Body of Christ and Temple of the Spirit*, trans. Charles Underhill Quinn (French 1970; Chicago: Franciscan Herald Press, 1982), 91–105. Bouyer holds that "it can be wondered if the pneumatological element has yet acquired in customary teaching of Catholic theology, whether official or not, the full place that Moehler gave it from the start" (104). See also Bouyer's positive reflections on Möhler's debt to Friedrich Schleiermacher, whose lectures Möhler audited (91–93, 95), as well as more recently Michael J. Himes, *Ongoing Incarnation: Johann Adam Möhler and the Beginnings of Modern Ecclesiology* (New York: Crossroad, 1997); Donald J. Dietrich and Michael J. Himes, eds., *The Legacy of the Tübingen School: The Relevance of Nineteenth-Century Theology for the Twenty-First Century* (New York: Crossroad, 1997), especially the essays by Bradford E. Hinze, Michael J. Himes, Reinhold Rieger, Stephen Fields, sj, Thomas F. O'Meara, op, and Anton van Harskamp. In light of this work, I wonder whether recent appropriation of Möhler's work is sufficiently theocentric.

88. For an illustration of Zizioulas's concern, see the ecclesiology of Thomas Rausch, sj. Rausch remarks, "It can be argued that a 'desacralization' of worship took place among the early Christian communities as the locus of God's presence shifted from Temple and priesthood to the community itself. Remembering the death and resurrection of Jesus through symbolic expression became more important than the Temple cult. David Power speaks of this as an assimilation of images attached to ritual and its significance into a non-ritualistic context, 'thus changing the meaning of the holy.' What was holy was the community itself, the Church, which Paul speaks of as the Temple or household of God, the dwelling place of God in the Spirit (Eph 2:19–22; cf. 1 Cor 3:16). For the Spirit dwells in the community of the disciples of Jesus, empowering them, creating the Church, a theology evident in Luke/Acts and John as well as Paul" (Rausch, *Towards a Truly Catholic Church*, 60–61). Rausch cites Power's *Unsearchable Riches: The Symbolic Nature of Liturgy* (New York: Pueblo, 1984).

89. Zizioulas, *Eucharist, Bishop, Church*, 16.

90. Ibid.

These two theological points, Zizioulas notes, cannot help but affect one's historical research, at least with respect to framing the questions that one asks. Zizioulas recognizes that the incorporation of human beings into Christ includes elements other than the Eucharist, elements that indeed belong to any celebration of the Eucharist: "The Church has always felt herself to be united in *faith, love, baptism, holiness of life*, etc."[91] In this regard, indeed, he warns that "eucharistic ecclesiology," of the kind advocated by Nicholas Afanasiev and Alexander Schmemann, can itself become one-sided through its focus on the Eucharist.[92] Yet, any ecclesial "unity" that is an "incorporation" of human beings into Christ must, Zizioulas argues, be sacramental: if it is not both an "incorporation" and a sign (since Christ's human body cannot be added to other than through divine signification), then there cannot be full ecclesial unity. While necessary to any unity, faith and holiness cannot suffice by themselves, because human unity must ultimately be a fully *embodied* unity, an "incorporation." Only thereby is the unity "ontological" so that the Church *is* "the whole Christ." Put another way, it cannot merely be a unity located spiritually in "the body of Christians" (pneumatocentric ecclesiology) to which Christ's incarnate embodiedness remains ontologically extrinsic. Historical research that seeks to uncover an intrinsic "unity" of the Church, therefore, must follow the path of the sacrament of the Eucharist. Likewise, for the presence of the *episkopos* to belong to the constitution of ecclesial unity, his presence must be understood eucharistically. This is so most fundamentally because the Eucharist is an action, not a thing. Only if the Church is unified in and through this constitutive action can the *episkopos* be an ecclesial agent of unity. Given the

---

91. Ibid., 17.

92. For Schmemann's ecclesiology see his *The Eucharist: Sacrament of the Kingdom*, trans. Paul Kachur (Crestwood, NY: St. Vladimir's Seminary Press, 1988), especially chapter 2. See also Gregory C. Faulkner, *Return to the Eucharist: The Eucharistic Ecclesiology of Alexander Schmemann's Liturgical Theology and Its Methodological Implications for a Reformed Liturgical Theology* (Ph.D. diss., Princeton: Princeton Theological Seminary, 2001). Faulkner argues that Schmemann successfully avoids "eucharistiamonism." Regarding the concern to avoid reductionism, see also Jean Galot's *Theology of the Priesthood* (San Francisco: Ignatius Press, 1984), which warns against the reduction of the priesthood to the liturgical ministry and emphasizes the pastoral office; cf. the summary of Galot's views in Dulles, *The Priestly Office*, 48–50; cf. similarly the emphasis on evangelization (the prophetic office) in John Paul II's *Pastores Dabo Vobis* (1992) and *Redemptoris Missio* (1990), summarized by Dulles on 25–27.

presence of the bishop, furthermore, no unity that included the bishop only extrinsically could be a fully expressed "unity."[93]

Thomas Aquinas: Giving Christ's Gift

In 1 Corinthians and the Gospel of Matthew, as well as in Zizioulas's portrait of the earliest Church, we have found evidence for a non-functionalist hierarchical priesthood whose mandate encompasses not solely teaching, but also the bestowal of the sacraments. But what is required in the bishop and/or priest for there to be an ontological, rather than solely functional, hierarchical priesthood? In order to answer this question, this final section of this chapter explores Aquinas's theology of the hierarchical priesthood. Although Aquinas has little to offer the historical debate to which Zizioulas contributes, Aquinas's scriptural and metaphysical depth serves our inquiry at this stage.

Aquinas takes as his starting point the Gospel accounts of the Last Supper and Ephesians 5:25–26, "Christ loved the Church and gave himself up for her, that he might sanctify her, having cleansed her by the washing of water with the word," a reference to the sanctifying power of Baptism.[94] The New Testament makes clear that Christ's invitation to share in his sacrificial body and blood and his cleansing his Church "by the washing of water with the word" do not come to

---

93. Although Zizioulas argues historically, his fundamental insight is theological: the "Church" is the locus of incorporation into the power of Christ's Pasch, and thus the Church is made present in the Eucharistic offering with its presider (the bishop).

94. *Summa Contra Gentiles* (SCG), Book IV, ch. 74, p. 286. In the *Summa Contra Gentiles*, the first way that Aquinas accounts for the existence of the hierarchical priesthood in the Church comes from the fact that sacramental actions mediate divine power through visible, corporeal signs. Since this is true, Aquinas reasons, those who perform sacramental actions should also be corporeal agents, rather than having the sacraments come directly from God or from angels. As he says, "Therefore, the sacraments mentioned must be dispensed by visible men who have spiritual power" (Book IV, ch. 74, p. 285). This spiritual power, dispensed through the sacraments, is what characterizes the priesthood. Thus sacramental unity with Christ requires not only the corporeal sign (the "thing," as it were) but also corporeal agents—men endowed with the spiritual power to communicate the power of Christ's Pasch. As Walter Kasper comments in discussing Aquinas's treatment of the priesthood and the sacraments in the *Summa Contra Gentiles*: "Since the mediation of salvation has a sacramental structure, it follows for Thomas that this mediation also has a hierarchical structure. Under a sacramental structure, the administration of the sacraments can occur only through visible human persons; and since it is impossible for human persons to perform this ministry out of any personal competence of their own, the initiation into ecclesiastical office must itself be a sacrament that mediates grace. This sacrament bestows the spiritual power (*virtus*) necessary for the correct exercise of the ministry and empowers the minister to help build up the body of Christ without any risk to the salvation of his own soul" (Kasper, *Leadership in the Church*, 98–99).

an end after Christ ascends to heaven. On the contrary, Christ charges his apostles with the task of giving his gift, with a sacramental mission. In this respect Aquinas quotes four biblical texts: 1 Corinthians 4:1, "This is how one should regard us, as servants of Christ and stewards of the mysteries of God"; Luke 22:19, "Do this in remembrance of me"; John 20:23, "If you forgive the sins of any, they are forgiven"; and Matthew 28:19, "Go therefore and make disciples of all nations, baptizing them."[95]

Even if Christ's gift endures through the apostles, however, why should this mean that the bishop/priest possesses a distinctive spiritual power from that of the ordinary Christian? Why should not the spiritual power subsist in the sacramental action of the community as led by the bishop/priest, without requiring a distinctive spiritual power to subsist in the bishop/priest? Aquinas argues that the human agent cannot be so easily set to the side: to be (in Saint Paul's phrase) a "steward" of the "mysteries of God" is itself a distinctive participation in those "mysteries." At the Last Supper, Aquinas says, "since Christ was about to withdraw His bodily presence from the Church, it was necessary that Christ should establish other ministers in His place who would dispense the sacraments to the faithful."[96]

Do these ministers require any particular power? Or could the dispensing be extrinsic to what is dispensed? If the sacraments were mere things, such extrinsicism might be possible. But since the nature of the sacrament is inseparable from the particular action that effects the sacrament, Aquinas states that "the instrument must be proportionate to the agent. Hence, the ministers of Christ must be in conformity with Him."[97] Might such "conformity" simply involve the possession and manifestation of cruciform charity, so that a bishop/priest would be suited to give Christ's gift simply by manifestly sharing, by the power of the Holy Spirit, in the faith and charity that all believers are called to possess? In this case, the bishop's role would differ from that of other believers only in terms of administrative function. Aquinas, however, rejects this solution. The bishop/priest, in instrumentally giving Christ's gift, must be likened to the true Giver (Christ) in a more profound manner.

---

95. SCG, Book IV, ch. 74 (286).
96. Ibid.
97. Ibid.

The Giver at the Last Supper, however, is God and man. How can mere human beings dare to celebrate the Last Supper? Here we arrive at the center of Aquinas's theology of the priesthood. He points out that "Christ, as the Lord, by His very own authority and power wrought our salvation, in that He was God and man: so far as He was man, in order to suffer for our redemption; and, so far as He was God, to make His suffering salutary for us."[98] In giving us the gift of salvation, Christ, in the unity of his Person, acted through his humanity and through his divinity. One can see how the ministers can be configured to Christ's human nature: charity accomplishes this configuration. But charitable human actions do not suffice for the kind of actions that Christ's ministers, the bishops/priests, are called to make. These actions, above all the celebration of the Eucharist *in persona Christi*, are a participation in Christ's action not only with respect to Christ as a charitable man, but also with respect to Christ as God.[99] The Last Supper is a human act and also a divine act, united in the action of the incarnate Son of God. Thus, as Aquinas suggests, the Eucharist teaches us that "the ministers of Christ must not only be men, but must participate somehow in His divinity through some spiritual power, for an instrument shares in the power of its principal agent"[100]—especially a living "instrument" whose action the consecration of the Eucharist must also be. This "spiritual power," or

---

98. Ibid.

99. For study of "in persona Christi," see Bernard D. Marliangeas, *Clés pour une théologie du ministère: In persona Christi, in persona Ecclesiae* (Paris: Beauchesne, 1978), with a preface by Yves Congar. More recently, see the work of Sara Butler, MSBT, "*In Persona Christi*," *CTSA Proceedings* 50 (1995): 146–55; Guy Mansini, OSB, "Representation and Agency in the Eucharist," *The Thomist* 62 (1998): 499–517; idem, "A Contemporary Understanding of St. Thomas on Sacerdotal Character"; and Lawrence J. Welch, "For the Church and within the Church: Priestly Representation," *The Thomist* 65 (2001): 613–37. Drawing upon the documents and *Acta* of Vatican II that treat "*in persona Christi capitis*," Welch critiques the view, set forth by David Coffey in "The Common and the Ordained Priesthood," *Theological Studies* 58 (1997): 209–36, that "the priest is capable of acting in the person of Christ the Head because he first represents the Church" (Welch, "For the Church," 613). See also Pierre-Marie Gy, OP's observation regarding a medieval iconographical image of Christ the Priest as representing "a kind of fusion between the priest offering the Mass and Christ himself in his sacrifice," so that "the priest is Christ himself." Gy concludes, "Such an image does not seem to me to be unfaithful to the theology of St. Thomas on the sacrament of Order." See Gy, "Évolution de saint Thomas sur la théologie de l'ordre," *Revue Thomiste* 99 (1999): 188.

100. SCG, Book IV, ch. 74 (286).

sacramental "character,"[101] that distinguishes bishops/priests from ordinary believers is a certain participation in Christ's divine power, through the instrumental power of Christ's humanity, that enables bishops/priests to give Christ's gift through their sacramental action.[102] Their sacramental action participates uniquely in Christ's divine-human action through the spiritual power that they receive.

Aquinas identifies this spiritual power with the power (ἐξουσία) to which Saint Paul refers in warning the Corinthians to obey his teachings: "it is this power that the Apostle calls 'the power which the Lord hath given me unto edification and not unto destruction' (II Cor. 13:10)."[103] The sacraments of Baptism and the Eucharist are the foundation of a hierarchical priesthood possessed of a spiritual power that builds up the Church in ways that extend the Church's baptismal and eucharistic unity. Paul appeals to his apostolic power or authority, therefore, in teaching and governing, not solely in sanctifying, the Corinthians.

Aquinas appreciates, however, the difference between Christ giving the gift of this spiritual power to apostles such as Paul, and the apostles giving the gift of this spiritual power to others. It makes

---

101. See Aquinas's discussion of sacramental "character," found in *Summa Theologiae* III, q. 63 (cf. my brief discussion in chapter 1). Following Augustine and Dionysius, Aquinas states that "the sacraments of the New Law produce a character, in so far as by them we are deputed to the worship of God according to the rite of the Christian religion. Wherefore Dionysius (*Eccl. Hier.* ii), after saying that God *by a kind of sign grants a share of Himself to those that approach Him*, adds *by making them Godlike and communicators of Divine gifts.* Now the worship of God consists either in receiving Divine gifts, or in bestowing them on others. And for both these purpose some power is needed; for to bestow something on others, active power is necessary; and in order to receive, we need a passive power. . . . But it must be observed that this spiritual power is instrumental: as we have stated above (Q. 62, A. 4) of the virtue which is in the sacraments. For to have a sacramental character belongs to God's ministers: and a minister is a kind of instrument, as the Philosopher says (*Polit.* i)" (ST III, q. 63, a. 2). Aquinas goes on to observe that these active and passive sacramental characters "are nothing else than certain participations of Christ's Priesthood, flowing from Christ Himself" (ST III, q. 63, a. 3). Holy Orders imparts an active sacramental character enabling the recipient to "bestow on others, things pertaining to Divine worship" (ST III, q. 63, a. 4). This theology of sacramental "character" enables Aquinas to distinguish between the common priesthood, pertaining to all the baptized, and the hierarchical priesthood. Aquinas observes that "it is the sacrament of Order that pertains to the sacramental agents: for it is by this sacrament that men are deputed to confer sacraments on others: while the sacrament of Baptism pertains to the recipients, since it confers on man the power to receive the other sacraments of the Church; whence it is called the *door of the sacraments*" (ST III, q. 63, a. 6).

102. On this point I am indebted to Bernhard Blankenhorn, OP, who emphasizes the significance of the instrumental power of Christ's humanity.

103. SCG, Book IV, ch. 74, p. 286.

sense that Christ can provide the apostles with a unique sharing in his power, but how can mere men share with other men a power that is more than human? Aquinas's inquiry assumes that Christ has given this spiritual power to the apostles so as to be passed on through the generations; otherwise the Church could not continue to be built up. In this regard he cites Matthew 28:20, "lo, I am with you always, to the close of the age" and Mark 13:37, "And what I say to you I say to all." When Aquinas states, "This spiritual power from Christ, then, flows into the ministers of the Church,"[104] the question is how this could occur.

The answer is through the sacrament of Holy Orders. Just as the sacrament of the Eucharist communicates what only Christ can give, so also does the sacrament of orders. The "spiritual power" that the apostles receive includes the power to share this spiritual power sacramentally, so that other men, too, might be able to give Christ's gift. In the other sacraments, Aquinas points out, spiritual changes are wrought in us by means of sensible signs. Regarding the spiritual power given the apostles, it follows that "this spiritual power also had to be passed on to men under certain sensible signs."[105] The apostles used bodily signs to pass on their spiritual power, and thereby they bestowed a sacrament, the sacrament of Holy Orders.

One recalls, however, that Christ directly chose his own twelve disciples, and one of them betrayed him, while the others did little better. If the apostles pass on this unique spiritual power for building up the Church to other men, and these men pass it on to still other men (whose office receives the name *episkopos*), and so forth, can this method of transmission really conduce to the upbuilding of the Church? Would not, on the contrary, things go from bad (the disciples) to worse (the bishops) once Christ no longer *directly* chooses the men who receive this unique spiritual power in the Church?[106]

---

104. Ibid., 287.

105. Ibid. For discussion of the importance of sensible signs, see Charles Morerod, OP, "John Paul II's Ecclesiology and St. Thomas Aquinas," in *John Paul II and St. Thomas Aquinas*, ed. Michael Dauphinais and Matthew Levering (Naples, FL: Sapientia Press, 2006), 45–73, at 47–51.

106. In fact, Aquinas does think that the movement from the apostles down through the generations is to some degree a decline, since he holds that the apostles' and to a lesser extent the Fathers' temporal closeness to Christ gives them a spiritual preeminence. Cf. Serge-Thomas Bonino, OP, "The Role of the Apostles in the Communication of Revelation According to the *Lectura super Ioannem* of St. Thomas Aquinas," trans. Teresa Bede and Matthew Levering, in Dauphinais and Levering, *Reading John with St. Thomas Aquinas*, 318–46; as well as C.

Relying on the divine goodness in bountifully bestowing the grace of the Holy Spirit, Aquinas notes that with respect to God's gifting, "if the power for some operation is conferred on one, there [will] be conferred also those things without which this operation cannot suitably be exercised."[107] In the case of the priesthood, what is needed for its suitable exercise is the grace of the Holy Spirit so as to configure the priest to Christ's cruciform wisdom and self-giving service to others. As with the other sacraments, therefore, the sacrament of Holy Orders bestows a special grace of the Holy Spirit that enables the recipient to attain the "end" of the sacrament.[108]

What is the "end" of the sacrament of orders, the service to which the priest is particularly called? Aquinas identifies the "end" as the giving of the sacraments. Priests are not called to just any service, but to a sacramental service. More precisely, however, the "end" is defined not simply by all the sacraments in general, but by the greatest sacrament, the Eucharist. To give the Eucharist is the ultimate reason for the priesthood. He explains that "among the sacraments that which is most noble and tends most to complete the others is the sacrament of the Eucharist."[109] For Aquinas, then, the Eucharist is the only adequate lens for understanding the spiritual power of Holy Orders. As he puts it, characteristically citing Aristotle's *De anima*, "Therefore, the power of orders must be weighed chiefly by reference to this sacrament [the Eucharist], for 'everything is denominated from its end.' "[110]

Halligan, "The Teaching of St. Thomas in Regard to Apostles," *American Ecclesiastical Review* 144 (1961): 32–47.

107. SCG, Book IV, ch. 74, 287.

108. Cf. Dermot Power, "The Priesthood and the Evangelical Counsels," *Communio* 23 (1996): 688–700, which focuses on Hans Urs von Balthasar's theology of the priesthood as a vocation of radical configuration to Christ by the grace of the Holy Spirit which enables the priest to live out the evangelical counsels. See also for a theology of priestly celibacy, de Lubac, *The Motherhood of the Church*, 113–39; Dulles, *The Priestly Office*, 68–71.

109. SCG, Book IV, ch. 74, 287.

110. Ibid., 287–88. For further discussion and development of this point, see Henri de Lubac, SJ, *The Splendor of the Church*, trans. Michael Mason (French 1953; San Francisco: Ignatius Press, 1986), 143–51. Citing a wide variety of sources including the *Summa Contra Gentiles*, de Lubac remarks, "To hold in their own hands the Eucharist—that is the supreme prerogative of those who form the hierarchy in the Church and are 'the ministers of Christ and the dispensers of the mysteries of God.' The hierarchy's 'most priestly action,' and the supreme exercise of its power, lies in consecrating Christ's body and thus perpetuating the work of the Redemption—in offering the 'sacrifice of praise,' which is the only one pleasing to God. In a broad sense, the whole Christian people is associated with that power at that point, and that is the meaning of St. Leo's words that the anointing of the Sovereign Pontiff 'reaches to the very

It is through the Eucharist that Aquinas explains the relationship of the spiritual power bestowed by the sacrament of Holy Orders
to the sacraments that bestow the forgiveness of sins; namely, Baptism,
Penance, and Extreme Unction. Why should priests have the power
to forgive the sins of fellow believers, when priests are sinners too? In
this regard Aquinas first employs an analogy from the realm of
physical power. "Fire," he points out, "has the power both to pass its
form on to another, and to dispose that other for the reception of the
form."[111] In order to catch fire, something must become hot. As
Aquinas states in philosophical terms, one would expect that "the
same power which grants a perfection" is also that "which prepares
matter for the reception of that perfection."[112] The perfection granted
by the spiritual power of Holy Orders is ultimately that of bestowing
the Eucharist. Thus, one should expect the spiritual power of Holy
Orders, like a spiritual "fire," to extend also to preparing believers for
properly receiving the Eucharist.

    Proper reception of the Eucharist requires above all rightly
ordered love. Aquinas observes that "a believer is made ready for the
reception of this sacrament [the Eucharist] and in harmony with it by
his freedom from sin; otherwise, he cannot be united spiritually with
that Christ to whom he is sacramentally conjoined by the reception of
this sacrament."[113] The ecclesial unity in Christ established by the
Eucharist, and correspondingly by the sacrament of orders, requires
holiness; lacking holiness there is no full incorporation into Christ. It
follows that "the power of orders must extend itself to the remission of
sins by the dispensation of those sacraments which are ordered to the
remission of sins,"[114] namely Baptism and Penance. Aquinas suggests
that this connection illumines, and is illumined by, scripture: "This,
indeed, is the power we understand by the 'keys' about which our
Lord said to Peter: 'I will give to thee the keys of the kingdom of
heaven' (Matt. 16:19). For to every man heaven is closed or opened by

---

extremities of the whole body of the Church'. That exercise of the hierarchical power, in the
name of Christ, is one which constitutes the hierarchy's 'primary and most august function'.
So, if we are to understand the role of the hierarchy—which is to understand the Church—we
must consider the hierarchy via the action by which this function is carried out" (147–49).

111. SCG, Book IV, ch. 74, 288.
112. Ibid.
113. Ibid.
114. Ibid.

this: he is subject to sin, or he is cleansed from sin; hence, too, the use of these keys is called 'to bind and to loose,' namely, from sins."[115] What seems to some like an overbearing assumption of power by bishops/priests—the power of excommunication and the forgiveness of sins—thus appears in its true eucharistic light.

Yet, by not differentiating priests and bishops regarding the power to consecrate the Eucharist, has Aquinas thereby severed the bishop from the special role regarding the Eucharist that Zizioulas envisions, and thus perhaps fallen short of an adequate understanding of the eucharistic unity of the Church? Certainly Aquinas does not possess the historical insight into *episkopoi* and *presbyteroi* that Zizioulas draws from modern research, but he is aware of a certain fluidity in the use of these terms in the earliest Church. In the *Summa Theologiae*, modifying Jerome, he concludes that "bishop" and "priest" originally could be used interchangeably. As an example, he notes that Saint Paul "employs the term *priests* in reference to both, when he says (1 Timothy v. 17): *Let the priests that rule well be esteemed worthy of double honor*; and again he uses the term *bishops* in the same way, wherefore addressing the priests of the Church of Ephesus he says (Acts xx. 28): *Take heed to yourselves* and *to the whole flock, wherein the Holy Ghost hath placed you bishops, to rule the church of God*."[116] Aquinas denies, however, that this interchangeability of name corresponded to an interchangeability of office in the earliest Church.

In setting forth this position, Aquinas seeks to take into account Jerome's viewpoint that the bishop's authority over priests has its roots in ecclesial custom rather than in Christ's institution. Commenting on Titus 1:5, Jerome holds that "bishops should recognize that, by custom rather than by the very ordinance of our Lord, they are above the priests."[117] In order to make the point that the distinction of office

---

115. Ibid.

116. ST II-II, q. 184, a. 6, ad 1.

117. For Jerome's comment as quoted by Aquinas, see ST II-II, q. 184, a. 6, obj. 1. Guy Mansini comments on the difficulties regarding the relationship of priest and bishop raised in the period after Aquinas: "if there is no *potestas ordinis* that consecration gives since, after all, it imprints no character, and if there is no power of ruling not to be identified with the power of jurisdiction, then the difference between bishop and priest reduces to the jurisdiction granted to the former, and the very institution of the episcopacy, as distinct from a simple priesthood, becomes an ecclesiastical, human institution. Such, roughly, is the position of John of Torquemada in the 15th century, Thomas da Vio Cardinal Cajetan in the 16th, and Diego Laynez, the Minister General of the Jesuits, at the Council of Trent. This position seems to be

(between bishop and priest) belongs to the earliest Church, Aquinas falls back upon a quotation from Pseudo-Dionysius's *Ecclesiastical Hierarchy* and upon a quotation from the *Glossa ordinaria*. Theologically, he points out that "to assert that priests nowise differ from bishops is reckoned by Augustine among heretical doctrines (*De Haeres*. liii), where he says that the Arians maintained that *no distinction existed between a priest and a bishop*."[118]

Aquinas does seek, therefore, to maintain a significant distinction between bishops and priests, even though he holds that this distinction does not rest upon the power to consecrate the Eucharist. He connects the distinction with the power to ordain.[119]

---

reinforced by the papal concession to ordain granted to certain abbots in the 15th century" (Mansini, "Episcopal *Munera* and the Character of Episcopal Orders," 380–81). Mansini adds, "If at first these concessions of the faculty to ordain meant that bishops were seen as priests with the addition of jurisdiction over a diocese, they can just as easily mean that priests are diminished bishops. And this is how Yves Congar interpreted the data. The distinction between bishops and priests is not of divine, but only of ecclesiastical institution. What is divinely instituted, dominically instituted, is the episcopacy—an office of apostolic ministry succeeding the apostles. It is this ministry, therefore, this ministry in its fullness, that we should think to be contemplating when we read the New Testament and consider the mystery of the Church. We must first make sense of the bishop before we make sense of the priest. It was precisely this kind of thinking, already in the 1930s, that helped lead to the Council's assertion of the sacramentality of the episcopacy, and of the episcopacy as the fullness of orders, and so, by implication, the primary analogate, as it were, of ministerial priesthood" (381–82). See also Brunero Gherardini, "La Sacramentalità dell' Episcopato in San Tommaso," in *Indubitanter ad Veritatem: Studies Offered to Leo J. Elders SVD*, ed. Jörgen Vijgen (Budel: Damon, 2003), 189–201.

118. ST II-II, q. 184, a. 6, ad 1.

119. On this point see Mansini's helpful summary of Aquinas's position: "When in the *Commentary on the Sentences* St. Thomas discusses episcopal consecration, he denies that it imprints a character. He does this, however, not because it does not have a permanent effect, but because the effect it has does not, he says, mean a new relation to the Eucharist, and 'characters' are numbered and distinguished by just such a relation. What is the effect of episcopal consecration in addition to that of presbyteral ordination? It is, he says, a relation to, a power with respect to, the Church" (Mansini, "Episcopal *Munera* and the Character of Episcopal Orders," 378). This "power," Mansini notes, is not jurisdiction: "It is understandable in view of later terminology that some have identified this power with jurisdiction. The Roman Catechism of 1566 identifies jurisdiction with power relative to the mystical body of Christ, the Church. The power St. Thomas is speaking of, however, is or at least includes the power to ordain. Jurisdiction, furthermore, is given *simplice injunctione* and is revocable; the power over the Church St. Thomas is speaking of is given by the sacrament of orders and cannot be lost. Moreover, it is by possession of this power that the bishop rules *in persona Christi*" (378–79). Mansini draws especially upon Joseph Lécuyer, "Les étapes de l'enseignement thomiste sur l'épiscopat," *Revue Thomiste* 57 (1957): 29–52; and Eugenio Corecco, "L'origine del potere di giurisdizione episcopale: Aspetti storico-giuridici e metodologico-sistematici della questione," *La scuola cattolica* 96 (1968): 3–42, 107–41. For an investigation of the nature of the power of the sacramental character, see Mansini, "A Contemporary Understanding of

We can gain more insight into Aquinas's position by attending to his discussion of the appointment of bishops in the Church. Here Jerome's discussion of Titus 1:5 appears again. Jerome says that "some seek to erect as pillars of the Church, not those whom they know to be more useful to the Church, but those whom they love more, or those by whose obsequiousness they have been cajoled or undone, or for whom some person in authority has spoken, and, not to say worse than this, have succeeded by means of gifts in being made clerics."[120] Aquinas recognizes this as a true description of a persistent problem for the Church. What then should a bishop be, in Aquinas's view? In choosing a bishop, Aquinas holds, one must above all choose "such a one as will dispense the divine mysteries faithfully."[121] Faithfully to dispense the divine mysteries—sacraments and doctrine—means to dispense them not for one's own benefit, but "for the good of the Church, according to 1 Cor. xiv. 12, *Seek to abound unto the edifying of the Church*."[122]

Through the sacrament of orders, a future bishop receives his priestly identity in celebrating the Eucharist, an identity that as bishop he shares with others by bestowing the sacrament of orders. Just as the Eucharist builds the Church's unity, so too the bishop must become thoroughly eucharistic so as to be able to assist the eucharistic unity of the Church. The bishop must renounce his own good, which he will receive "in the life to come," and instead totally give himself to "the good of the Church," to the upbuilding of Christ's Body.[123] He must hand himself entirely, eucharistically, over to Christ's Body, which is

---

St. Thomas on Sacerdotal Character." For further discussion of Aquinas on episcopal ordination, see also Kasper, *Leadership in the Church*, 101–5. Kasper credits Aquinas's treatment of this topic with taking "at least the first step toward healing the breach that had arisen, as a result of the first and second eucharistic controversies, between the sacramental and mystical reality of the church on the one hand and its institutional, hierarchical form on the other. Thanks to this breach, the church in its external form came more and more to seem a purely sociological reality, a mere apparatus of power. Thomas's theological conception broke through the boundaries of his own age, laying the foundations for a renewal in ecclesiology and sacramental theology that unfortunately came only much later on" (105).

120. Quoted in ST II-II, q. 185, a. 3.

121. ST II-II, q. 185, a. 3.

122. Ibid. See Frederick Christian Bauerschmidt, " 'That the Faithful Become the Temple of God,' " 293–311, at 299: " 'Teaching' must always be placed within the martyriological context of bearing witness with their lives. Christian teaching is about the formation of disciples; it is about the 'edification' or 'building' of God's temple." The bishop must exemplify such teaching.

123. ST II-II, q. 185, a. 3. See for further discussion of the bishop (during the period between Constantine and Gregory VII) as "a spiritual man, a man of God," Yves Congar, "The Hierarchy as Service," 50.

built up by the Eucharist that he celebrates. Since the chief good of the Church is her unity in Christ, the bishop must also be particularly adept at fostering unity. Aquinas is aware in this regard that there are charitable men who would not be particularly adept at such work. The one chosen to be bishop must eucharistically hand himself over to the Body of Christ, while also being "able to instruct, defend, and govern the Church peacefully."[124] Eucharistic self-giving must be joined to prudential ability to preserve and build up eucharistic unity. As Aquinas says in commenting on the risen Lord's thrice-repeated questioning of Peter's love (in conjunction with the command "Feed my sheep"), "Our Lord knew that, by His own bestowal, Peter was in other respects fitted to govern the Church: wherefore He questioned him about his greater love, to show that when we find a man otherwise fitted for the government of the Church, we must look chiefly to his pre-eminence in the love of God."[125]

In serving the unity of the Church, the bishop has to renounce even some spiritual goods that otherwise he could have obtained for himself. Comparing the episcopate with the religious life, Aquinas observes that the latter aims primarily at working out one's own salvation, whereas the former aims primarily at working out the salvation of others.[126] In this respect he notes the spiritual sacrifice made by Saint Paul, who, "on account of the needs of his subjects, suffered patiently to be delayed even from the contemplation of the life to come, according to Philip. i. 22–25, *What I shall choose I know not, but I am straitened between two, having a desire to be dissolved, and to be with*

---

124. ST II-II, q. 185, a. 3. On the bishop's subordination to the Body of Christ, see Alfonso Carrasco Rouco, "Vatican II's Reception of the Dogmatic Teaching on the Roman Primacy," trans. Adrian Walker, *Communio* 25 (1998): 576–603. Rouco argues that papal primacy assists such concrete subordination (or receptivity): "the ministry of the bishop, by its sacramental nature, claims to exist in order to serve the presence in history of something different from, and bigger than, what man can build on his own, that is, it claims to serve the reality of communion that is the Body of Christ. It cannot do so, however, except insofar as the minister really does objectively depend on this reality that he affirms is present in history. The papal ministry, as an objective criterion of the presence of this *Communio*, concretely enables the existence of this relation of objective dependence on the Church" (598). He adds, "For his part, the successor of Peter, like every Christian believer, must first live a dynamic of reception that above all acknowledges being bound by the fundamental features of the Tradition that comes from Christ" (602).

125. ST II-II, q. 185, a. 3, ad 1. See the commentary on John 21:15–19 in Timothy S. Laniak, *Shepherds after My Own Heart: Pastoral Traditions and Leadership in the Bible* (Downers Grove, IL: InterVarsity Press, 2006), 220–22.

126. ST II-II, q. 185, a. 4, ad 1.

Christ, a thing by far better. But to abide still in the flesh is needful for you. And having this confidence, I know that I shall abide."[127] Similarly, the bishop must sacrifice his own bodily and material goods for the sake of the upbuilding of the Church: here Aquinas quotes John 10:11, "The good shepherd lays down his life for the sheep."[128] For this reason, despite the sins of particular bishops, Aquinas sees the episcopate as a "state of perfection," that is, a state of life marked supremely, in its obligations, by charity.[129] Religious bind themselves to poverty, chastity, and obedience, and thereby more freely progress in the perfection of charity. Likewise, bishops bind themselves to the pastoral duty (John 10:11,15), in which they hand themselves over to God so as to devote their lives to shepherding his Body toward full union with God.[130]

Does the bishop then have to abandon completely his own spiritual and bodily good? Articulating a balanced position, Aquinas holds that the bishop cannot cease working out his own salvation by prayer and contemplation, and that there are some circumstances in which the bishop can protect his own life. He states that "if the salvation of his subjects can be sufficiently provided for by another person in the absence of the pastor, it is lawful for the pastor to

---

127. ST II-II, q. 185, a. 4.

128. Ibid. For further discussion of John 10 see my "Augustine and Aquinas on the Good Shepherd: The Value of an Exegetical Tradition," in *Aquinas the Augustinian*, ed. Michael Dauphinais, Barry David, and Matthew Levering (Washington, DC: The Catholic University of America Press, 2007), 205–42. See also Laniak, *Shepherds after My Own Heart*, 211–18.

129. Aquinas observes, "Some are in the state of perfection, who are wholly lacking in charity and grace, for instance wicked bishops or religious" (ST II-II, q. 184, a. 4, *sed contra*). He explains that "state properly regards a condition of freedom or servitude. Now spiritual freedom or servitude may be considered in man in two ways: first, with respect to his internal actions; secondly, with respect to his external actions. And since according to 1 Kings xvi.7, *man seeth those things that appear, but the Lord beholdeth the heart*, it follows that with regard to man's internal disposition we consider his spiritual state in relation to the Divine judgment, while with regard to his external actions we consider man's spiritual state in relation to the Church. It is in this latter sense that we are now speaking of states, namely insofar as the Church derives a certain beauty from the variety of states. . . . Accordingly, properly speaking, one is said to be in the state of perfection, not through having the act of perfect love, but through binding himself in perpetuity and with a certain solemnity to those things that pertain to perfection" (ST II-II, q. 184, a. 4). Yet "some persons bind themselves to that which they do not keep, and some fulfill that to which they have not bound themselves" (ibid.).

130. ST II-II, q. 184, a. 5. The episcopate is a state of perfection, whereas priesthood is not, because bishops "cannot abandon the episcopal cure, save by the authority of the Sovereign Pontiff (to whom alone it belongs also to dispense from perpetual vows), and this for certain causes" (ST II-II, q. 184, a. 6) and because "bishops have the chief cure of the sheep of their diocese, while parish priests and archdeacons exercise an inferior ministry under the bishops" (ibid., ad 2).

withdraw his bodily presence from his flock, either for the sake of some advantage to the Church, or on account of some danger to his person."[131] Similarly, the bishop may legitimately possess property of his own, as Paul did (Aquinas cites 2 Corinthians 11:8), but bishops must take care to avoid a situation where "while busy with their own they neglect those that concern the worship of God."[132]

In distributing the funds of the Church, the bishop cannot give all the money to the poor, as Christ commanded the rich young ruler, but must also consider the divine worship and its service. While some may see such prudence as detracting from the radicalism of Christian love, Aquinas sees this prudence as belonging to a true concern for the Church's good. This prudence is similar to the special privileges that go along with the office of bishop. Bishops are "placed above others" and receive "reverence, honor, and a sufficiency of temporalities."[133] Aquinas is adamant that "no man should seek to be raised thus."[134] Yet, the privileges of authority, honor, and sufficiency give the bishop the ability to serve on a wider scope the "principal and final" goal of the episcopal office, namely "the good of our neighbor."[135] Just as a temporal ruler has privileges that belong to his ability to serve the common good of the state, so also a spiritual ruler has privileges that belong to his ability to serve the common good of the Church. So long as the bishop loves not the privileges but the good of all his neighbors—namely, unity with Christ in the Church—the eminence

---

131. ST II-II, q. 185, a. 5; cf. II-II, q. 184, a. 7, ad 1, where Aquinas states that "bishops especially are bound to despise all things for the honor of God and the spiritual welfare of their flock, when it is necessary for them to do so, either by giving to the poor of their flock, or by suffering *with joy the being stripped of* their *own goods* [cf. Heb 10:34]."

132. ST II-II, q. 185, a. 6, ad 3; cf. II-II, q. 184, a. 7, ad 3. See the discussion of Aquinas's position on this point in Kasper, *Leadership in the Church*, 92–96. Kasper observes, "The test of Thomas's spiritual and pastoral vision was whether it could offer an answer to the question of poverty—the main problem of the church in his day. When his contemporaries asked about the wealth of the bishops and of the church, they were in fact putting a question mark against the entire institutional structure of the church. This wealth provoked an abundant criticism in the thirteenth century, not only among movements that were suspected of heresy or among the 'Spirituals,' but also among the simple people, who saw the church's wealth and therefore lent an open ear to the radical voices" (92). Kasper finds that Aquinas "opts for a spiritual form of the church and of the episcopal ministry in the midst of the world—and in the midst of the world's distress. In other words, he opts for a church that administers justly, generously, and compassionately the goods that it rightly possesses" (96).

133. ST II-II, q. 185, a. 1.

134. Ibid., ad 2.

135. ST II-II, q. 185, a. 1.

of the bishop is employed not to "lord it over" others (Matthew 20:25), but to serve the increasing unity of others in Christ. The "object of his desire" must be "the good work and not the precedence in dignity."[136]

CONCLUSION

Beginning with the view that "the church itself is primary, and ministry serves the church and does not found it first of all," the Catholic ecclesiologist John Burkhard observes that "[f]rom ancient times the church has known various forms of organized ministry and forms of transmitting that ministry," and he asks rehetorically, "If true ecclesiality is found in a church, is it possible to accept a variety of ministries [including Protestant ministries] as not incompatible with that fundamental ecclesiality?"[137] Assuming "ecclesiality" to be rooted by the Holy Spirit in the power of Christ's Pasch, one might respond to Burkhard's question by asking whether the "ministries" are Christologically and ontologically rooted, or merely functional results of the Church's development. If the "ministries" are intrinsically connected to what they mediate, then leadership in the Church will be more than a functional leadership. As Hans Urs von Balthasar puts it with respect to sacramental forgiveness of sins, "the dispensation of judgment from the eschatological grace presupposes an *office*, that is to say, a participation in the authority of Jesus."[138] Only Jesus can bestow this unique participation in his authority.

But did Jesus do this? Or did the ministries that arose in the early Christian communities only later claim sacramental rather than merely functional authority? In this regard, J. Augustine Di Noia points out that historical research alone cannot determine whether Jesus in fact willed "to constitute his brethren in the communion of

---

136. Ibid. For further discussion of Aquinas's theology of the episcopal state, see especially the articles by Lécuyer, Mansini, and Bonino.

137. Burkhard, *Apostolicity Then and Now*, 244–45.

138. Hans Urs von Balthasar, *The Glory of the Lord: A Theological Aesthetics*, vol. 7, *The New Covenant*, trans. Brian McNeil, CRV (German 1969; San Francisco: Ignatius Press, 1989), 182. Von Balthasar adds that this authority "is not separable from poverty and self-abandonment" (ibid.), although he is well aware that ecclesial authority has not always been exercised in a holy fashion. See also von Balthasar, *The Office of Peter and the Structure of the Church*, trans. Andrée Emery (German 1974; San Francisco: Ignatius Press, 1986), 9–26.

everlasting love of the Father, Son, and Holy Spirit."[139] Historical research alone cannot give proof of the divine action that in faith we recognize as constitutive of history. What then can we say about the evidence we have found in 1 Corinthians and the Gospel of Matthew, whose import we explored theologically through the insights of Zizioulas and Aquinas? On the basis of New Testament texts, von Balthasar argues in a passage worth quoting at length that Jesus bestowed a unique participation in his power:

> The question whether Jesus "founded" the Church can be a misleading formulation. One must distinguish two basic points here. The first refers to Jesus' mission, given him by the Father. It consists primarily in the "Word becoming flesh," who in human form—by his words, his deeds, by his work and rest, his fatigue and weariness, by his glory and his condemnation, his extreme exertion on the Mount of Olives, by his cross, his death, his descent to the netherworld—interprets to humanity the intentions of God the Father (John 1:18). . . . The second point [is] that Jesus definitely had an institution in mind that would preserve his fundamental pronouncements and his decisive deeds, and carry on after his death. He merely had to establish the fundamentals. He would leave the completion according to the triune will to the Holy Spirit. What he essentially intended was twofold. First, the continually renewed infusion of understanding his spirit of love . . . . The second thing that Jesus communicates are the powers of authority that are specifically his own. As a man he is human, and he will not accomplish his enterprise by himself alone. Very soon he chooses the Twelve (Mark 3), whom he gives authority (*exousiai*): first, to

---

139. J. Augustine Di Noia, OP, "The Church in the Gospel: Catholics and Evangelicals in Conversation," *Pro Ecclesia* 13 (2004): 58–69, at 68. On the historical question, Di Noia points out that "it is only in the light of faith that the events of Christ's life can be understood in their historical reality as such. For, a complete account of the events narrated in the Gospels must include a reference to the divine agency and intentions at work in them. There is a church because the triune God willed to share his divine life with human persons and to establish this communion through the incarnation, passion, death and resurrection of the only begotten Son" (69; see for a similar perspective on historical reality and biblical exegesis my *Participatory Biblical Exegesis: A Theology of Biblical Interpretation* [Notre Dame, IN: University of Notre Dame Press, 2008]). With regard to ecclesial hierarchy, Di Noia notes that the eminent evangelical theologian J. I. Packer holds that "the Catholic Church 'misconceives the nature of the church as the New Testament writers explain it' by giving institutional form to a 'sacramental and juridical organization sustained by priests channeling divine life through a set of rituals' " (Di Noia, "The Church in the Gospel," 59, citing Packer, "Crosscurrents among Evangelicals," in *Evangelicals and Catholics Together: Toward a Common Mission*, ed. Charles Colson and Richard John Neuhaus [Dallas: Word Publishing, 1995], 151). For the opposite view Di Noia cites Avery Dulles, SJ's contribution to *Evangelicals and Catholics Together*, "The Unity for Which We Hope," 125–34 (Di Noia, "The Church in the Gospel," 60).

"be with him," then "to proclaim," and finally, "to expel demons," that is, to bring the Holy Spirit so effectively that the spirit of contradiction has to give way. The actual ordination to the priesthood, however, takes place for the first time in closest connection with the "Passion and Resurrection": the Lord's Supper ("Do this in remembrance of me"; Luke 22:19) was understood by the disciples as meaning that it should be repeated. And the power to absolve ("Receive the Holy Spirit. If you forgive the sins of any . . . ."; John 20:22–23) is certainly more than a general prayer to forgive each other's faults. . . . These two main sacraments instituted before and after the Passion are sufficient to prove Jesus' will that official authority should continue in the Church and that the Lord's Supper offered after the Resurrection by the young community in the Acts of the Apostles suffices—irrespective of Paul's unprecedented consciousness of his office—to trace the origins of the powers of the office to Jesus.[140]

As we have seen, 1 Corinthians and the Gospel of Matthew likewise suggest that "the powers of the office" come from Jesus. Although the particular structure (bishop, presbyter) develops in the course of the first century, the New Testament indicates that Jesus wills a hierarchical mediation of his followers' communion in his gifts, and that this hierarchical mediation (not merely functional but "sacramental" regarding its claim to communicate the power of Christ's Pasch) is already embodied by the leaders of the earliest Christian communities.[141]

Yet, why should the very men who abandoned Jesus, let alone those who came later such as Paul, receive unique power to communicate the saving power of Christ's Pasch? Why not entrust this power to the community's response of faith, or to discrete individual encounters with Christ? As von Balthasar asks elsewhere, "can we trust an authority that has failed so often, failed so humanly?"[142]

---

140. Hans Urs von Balthasar, "Life and Institution in the Church," trans. Andrée Emery, *Communio* 12 (1985): 25–32, at 30–31. See also Miguel Ponce Cuéllar's emphasis on the participation of the apostles in Christ's eschatological and priestly *exousia*, in his valuable *Llamados a Servir: Teología del Sacerdocio Ministerial* (Barcelona: Herder, 2001).

141. For similar discussion of biblical (and early Christian) texts, see Yves Congar, "The Church and Its Unity," 58–96, at 80ff. On the Church of Acts see especially 85–86.

142. Von Balthasar, *The Office of Peter and the Structure of the Church*, 19. Von Balthasar later points out that many contemporary ecclesiologies "are incurably *romantic*. They lose sight of the real experience of two thousand years of Church history and hold on to the two extremes: on the one hand, a gospel—seen in the rosy light of Renan—of 'powerlessness' and the 'blessedness of the poor and oppressed'; on the other hand, a Marxist critique of society which, by 'changing the structures' (a new mythical-magical spell), hopes to establish that evangelical paradise" (35).

Providing an antidote to pride and the autonomy it seeks, Christ wills that his followers *receive* him from others; just as "being found in human form, he humbled himself and become obedient unto death, even death on the cross" (Philippians 2:8). Only such self-subordinating receptivity configures the Church to Christ's own humility, which is revealed to be true power: "Therefore God has highly exalted him and bestowed on him the name which is above every name" (Philippians 2:9). In this regard Avery Dulles observes, "Just as the career of Jesus reached its climax in the paschal mystery, so the activity of the ministerial priest culminates in the life of worship by which the church is brought into the mystery of Christ."[143] This "mystery," served by priestly mediation, involves cruciform receptivity.[144]

The Gospel of Matthew makes clear that hierarchical mediation can be abused: Peter himself abuses his role, placing himself in

---

143. Dulles, *The Priestly Office*, 44. Dulles notes earlier that the Council of Trent anathematized the position that the priesthood of the New Testament consisted in the mere power to preach the gospel. It defined priesthood primarily in terms of the powers to forgive sins and to offer the holy sacrifice of the mass (Session 23, ch. 1; DS 1764). The same Council stated that the sacrament of priestly orders was instituted at the Last Supper when Jesus uttered the words, "Do this in commemoration of me" (Session 22, can. 2; DS 1752; quoting Lk 22:19 and 1 Cor 11:24). . . . Vatican II did not clearly reject the view of Trent that the priesthood of bishops and presbyters is to be defined above all in terms of its sacred functions. For example, PO [*Presbyterorum Ordinis*] 2 begins its treatment of the presbyterate by asserting that Christ the Lord appointed some of the faithful as ministers "who would have the sacred power of order within the company of the faithful, to offer sacrifice and forgive sins, and who would publicly discharge their sacerdotal function for the people in the name of Christ." LG [*Lumen Gentium*] 28 describes presbyters as "true priests of the New Testament" and states that "it is above all in the eucharistic worship or synaxis that they exercise their sacred function." (Dulles, *The Priestly Office*, 33)

144. In an essay that focuses on 2 Corinthians, John M. McDermott, sj, observes that the mediator is Himself mediated. As already noted, Paul's service of the new covenant ([2 Cor] 3:6) is a mediation. Though there is only one Lord and one mediator (I Cor. 8:6; cp. 1 Tim. 2:3–7), He does not disdain further mediation since the Spirit mediates Him (cf. Rom. 8:1–17), and He wishes by the Spirit to make human beings participators in and communicators of His glory. This multiple mediation contributes to the movement in II Cor. 3: Paul is the mediating minister (διάκονος) of the new covenant (3:6); this introduces a comparison with Moses' mediating ministry (διακονία) of the old covenant (3:7–11), and Moses' veiled mediation gives way to Christ whose transforming glory is seen with unveiled face (3:12–18). The transition from Paul to Christ over Moses can occur because in Paul's hierarchical thinking—he is Christ's slave (Rom. 1:1)—the servant does not act in opposition to his Lord: "Be imitators of me as I am of Christ" (I Cor. 11:1f.; 4:15f.; I Thes. 1:6) is easily compatible with "Serve Christ the Lord" (Col. 3:24; Rom. 14:18) and "Serve the living and true God" (I Thes. 1:9). (McDermott, "II Cor. 3: the Old and New Covenants," *Gregorianum* 87 [2006]: 25–62, at 55)

front of Jesus rather than remaining transparent to Jesus. Yet Jesus wills to give Peter this role—and the rest of the apostles their role—even while knowing that all the apostles, even Peter, will abandon him in his time of trial, and even despite the fact that he has to rebuke Peter immediately after giving Peter his role. The mandate Jesus gives the apostles is not based on expectations that those who share this mandate will be particularly holy in how they exercise hierarchical mediation. The Church thus becomes a school for humility. In order to receive the divine gifting, we must learn to receive from other imperfect human beings.

What about, however, the persons at the "top" in terms of hierarchical authority?[145] Do not their exalted positions teach them the very opposite lesson; namely, that their power is their own, that their word is sufficient? In reply, one observes that bishops have not moved beyond the Church's structures of mediation. As Aquinas emphasizes, their lives are not their own, but are devoted to giving to the Church these very things that they themselves receive. Those who receive the mandate of the apostles are, as Paul and Barnabas say, merely "men, of like nature with you" (Acts 14:15). Recall Peter's words after hauling up "a great shoal of fish" (Luke 5:6) by following Christ's instructions, after spending the night catching nothing: "Depart from me, for I am a sinful man, O Lord" (Luke 5:8). Jesus responds, "Do not be afraid; henceforth you will be catching men" (Luke 5:10).[146] Jesus Christ sustains the ecclesial hierarchy so as to

---

145. Unlike the canonists of his time, Aquinas (in this regard like Bonaventure) does not raise the question of papal heresy, except perhaps indirectly in *Quaestiones quodlibetales* IX.16 (1257). On this point see Ulrich Horst, OP, *The Dominicans and the Pope: Papal Teaching Authority in the Medieval and Early Modern Thomist Tradition*, trans. James D. Mixson (Notre Dame, IN: University of Notre Dame Press, 2006), 14–21. This question becomes the central ecclesiological question in the late medieval period, along with the question of the papacy's temporal jurisdiction. See for example William of Ockham, *A Letter to the Friars Minor and Other Writings*, ed. Arthur Stephen McGrade and John Kilcullen, trans. John Kilcullen (Cambridge: Cambridge University Press, 1995). Cf. my "Ockham and the Papacy," forthcoming in a Festschrift for Stephen F. Brown.

146. Cf. Joseph Ratzinger, "The Papal Primacy and the Unity of the People of God," in idem, *Church, Ecumenism and Politics: New Essays in Ecclesiology*, trans. Robert Nowell (German 1987; New York: Crossroad, 1988), 29–45. Drawing upon Cardinal Reginald Pole's work *De Summo Pontifice* (written during the struggle with Henry VIII), Ratzinger emphasizes how the pope's task is to imitate Christ's humility and obedience: "Isaiah's next phrase 'And the government will be upon his shoulder' refers for Pole to the arduous burden Christ bears for our sake: it is not the word government but the bearing of a more than human burden on human shoulders that for him is the dominant element in this image. The honorific 'strong

fulfill his promises that "the powers of death shall not prevail" against the Church (Matthew 16:18), and that the Holy Spirit "will teach you all things" (John 14:26).[147] Ultimately the efficacy of hierarchical mediation in the Church cannot be proven but instead rests on the Trinity's wisdom and love in accomplishing the salvation won by Christ, in and through the lives of sinful, and repentant, human beings.

Could not the structure of gifting and receptivity be so radically deformed by sinful human beings as no longer to mediate Christ's saving truth and power? It would be absurd to deny this possibility from a merely human perspective.[148] But as the risen Lord promised his apostles at the great commission, "Lo, I am with you always, to the close of the age" (Matthew 28:20).

---

hero' is interpreted by the English cardinal on the basis of what 'strength' ultimately means in the Bible. This he finds in the Song of Songs: 'For love is strong as death' (8:6). The strength in which the vicar of Christ must become like his Lord is the strength of the love that is ready for martyrdom" (41).

147. Yves Congar distinguishes between the apostles' mission and that of the Holy Spirit in his "The Holy Spirit and the Apostolic Body, Continuators of the Work of Christ," in his *The Mystery of the Church*, 147–86. The Holy Spirit is "conjoined with the institutional Church and the apostolic body—these latter doing externally and visibly what he himself does interiorly" (172). As Congar makes clear, "The foundation of the union between the Holy Spirit and the institutional Church is the union of operation present, from the beginning, between the Holy Spirit and Christ. This union, deriving from the mystery of the divine being, of the eternal relations in God, of the consubstantiality and circuminsession of the divine Persons, was proclaimed, as regards Christ, at his baptism and, as regards the Church and the apostolate, at Pentecost, their baptism by the Holy Spirit" (169).

148. Klaus Schatz, SJ, argues that the Church must become clearer about what would happen "in the case of the most severe types of failure or defection on the part of the personal occupant of the Petrine office," as for instance if the pope were to go insane: see Schatz, *Papal Primacy: From Its Origins to the Present*, trans. John A. Otto and Linda M. Maloney (German 1990; Collegeville, MN: Liturgical Press, 1996), 181. Behind such concerns, I think, lies the more fundamental problem of obedience to an authoritative office within a religious communion. Writing after his own silencing, Henri de Lubac, SJ, comments in this respect that "it is scarcely surprising that many men consider the exercise of authority in the Church an intolerable tyranny. Moreover, whether the unbeliever condemns it or admires it, he cannot help but form a very misleading idea of it, for 'if the Church were only a human society, even though the most venerable and experienced ever known,' her demands would not be justified" (de Lubac, *The Splendor of the Church*, trans. Michael Mason [French 1953; San Francisco: Ignatius Press, 1986], 258–59; the citation is from Yves de Montcheuil, *Mélanges théologiques* [Paris: Aubier-Montaigne, 1946], 121–22). De Lubac argues that the authority of the Church, including that of the pope, in fact belongs to true "evangelical poverty; it is within the bosom of the Church that we learn to die to ourselves in order to live in dependence. An apprenticeship of this sort never comes to an end; it is hard on nature, and those very men who think themselves most enlightened are the ones who have most need of it (which is why it is particularly healthy for them), so that they may be stripped of their false wealth, 'to humble their spirits under a visible authority' " (de Lubac, *The Splendor of the Church*, 258).

Chapter 4

Priority or Primacy in the Church

Without claiming that the distinct forms of hierarchical priesthood that we know today were present in the same way among the first Christians, the previous chapter argued that the apostolic mandate was marked sacramentally by a hierarchical authority to mediate the salvific power of Christ's priestly action. As Avery Dulles comments, "What is essential to episcopacy . . . is not the particular features borrowed from secular organizations but the existence of a body of pastors having apostolic authority. The true source of this authority is neither the episcopal office nor the apostolic but, more fundamentally, Christ the Lord."[1] It is this sacramental power to mediate Christ's words and deeds, a power constitutive of ecclesial hierarchy, that enables the Church to participate receptively in the fullness of Christ's gifting.

At this stage, however, one might ask a further question, already at least implicitly raised by the Corinthians: Are not claims to "power" in the Church distorted when they become claims to "jurisdiction," trading the context of the particular eucharistic assembly for larger-scale contexts? For instance, even granting the power of bishops, how can one justify a pope with jurisdiction over the whole

---

1. Avery Dulles, SJ, *The Catholicity of the Church* (Oxford: Oxford University Press, 1985), 119. Dulles notes that there was "a gradual development in the emergence of the ecclesiastical hierarchy. The Church did borrow certain elements from the Hellenistic world and from the political organization of the Roman Empire" (ibid.). Drawing upon Joseph Ratzinger's work, Dulles goes on to point out, "Since the Church is a visible continuation of Christ's presence, ordination in the apostolic succession is the appropriate means of entering her official ministry. The office gives authority to the spoken word so that hearers can allow it to judge them, rather than make themselves its judges. The doctrine of the apostolic succession therefore upholds the function of the Church not only as sacrament but also as herald of the word" (120–21). Cf. Ratzinger, "Primacy, Episcopate, and Apostolic Succession," in Karl Rahner and Joseph Ratzinger, *The Episcopate and the Primacy* (New York: Herder and Herder, 1962), 37–63. More recently, see the remarks on apostolic succession by Benoît-Dominique de La Soujeole, OP, *Introduction au mystère de l'Église* (Paris: Parole et Silence, 2006), 597–99.

Church? In this respect, without neglecting episcopal dignity and collegiality, *Lumen Gentium* teaches that "the Roman Pontiff, by reason of his office as Vicar of Christ, and as pastor of the entire Church, has full, supreme, and universal power over the whole Church, a power which he can always exercise unhindered."[2] Does this affirmation go too far? Does it not undermine the authority of the bishop in the diocese and make the bishop of Rome a "bishop" only in a highly analogous sense?[3]

In contemporary academic theology, the answers to such questions are generally yes. David McLoughlin, for example, affirms, "The Council failed to clearly envision the bishop within the communion of his own local church," resulting in "a continuing seepage from the Church of those who hear the words but do not see the reality" of true *communio*.[4] For McLoughlin, "The use of Rome as a focus over and above the local church frustrates the development of true *communio* whose focus . . . is around the Eucharist."[5] While much more apprecia-

---

2. *Lumen Gentium*, 23, in *Decrees of the Ecumenical Councils*, vol. 2, *Trent to Vatican II*, ed. Norman P. Tanner, sj (Washington, DC: Georgetown University Press, 1990).

3. For a survey of the various positions taken by Lutheran, Anglican, and Catholic theologians on the topic of "Roman primacy," with a focus on the past two centuries, see Dulles, *The Catholicity of the Church*, 127–46. Regarding primacy in the early Church, Dulles observes that "it seems evident that the Church only gradually came to see the necessity of having within its episcopate someone who could speak and act for the whole Church. This insight, though gradually achieved, has lasting validity" (139). Dulles is encouraged by recent developments: "Never since the Reformation has there been such readiness on the part of Protestants, Anglicans, and Orthodox to acknowledge the value of the papacy as a bond of unity" (142). As he says, "Now that Christianity is becoming for the first time truly planetary and culturally pluralistic, it is more important than ever to have a central authority that will keep the regional groupings in communion. The centrifugal forces of social and cultural diversity must be counterbalanced by the centripetal attraction of a symbolic focus of unity" (142). He warns against envisioning the papacy primarily in terms of juridical power (135–36). Following Jean-Marie Tillard, op, he affirms "that the pope is responsible for the catholic unity of the whole Church, and that by assuring this unity he performs a service for all the particular churches" (137). Cf. Tillard's *The Bishop of Rome* (Wilmington, DE: Michael Glazier, 1983). One might also see Francis A. Sullivan, sj's response to Pope John Paul II's motu proprio *Apostolos Suos* (1998): Sullivan, "The Teaching Authority of Episcopal Conferences," *Theological Studies* 63 (2002): 472–93. Sullivan is concerned that "the conditions which the pope has laid down for the binding effect of a teaching statement made by an episcopal conference do imply the theory that properly speaking, teaching authority belongs only to the individual bishops or to the college of bishops with the pope" (491).

4. David McLoughlin, "*Communio* Models of Church: Rhetoric or Reality?" in *Authority in the Roman Catholic Church: Theory and Practice*, ed. Bernard Hoose (Aldershot: Ashgate, 2002), 187, 189.

5. Ibid., 187. McLoughlin seeks to make common cause with the Orthodox, and he concludes that "still in Eastern Byzantine theology holiness tends to win out over the juridical

tive of the Second Vatican Council, Paul McPartlan similarly remarks that "Catholics and Orthodox should have tremendous compassion for one another as fellow victims, in their different ways, of Constantine," who conflated Church and state in the fourth century and thereby produced a juridical ecclesiology whose consequences have victimized Christians ever since.[6] McPartlan concludes that "following the twentieth century's great revival of Trinitarian awareness, the present task of the Catholic Church is to find, in common with the other Churches and especially with the Orthodox, what sort of structure, what sort of collegiality and indeed what sort of primacy best reflects the Trinitarian mystery and serves the Eucharist."[7] In other words, after 17 Constantinian centuries of juridical ecclesiology, we can now hope to move forward again.

---

mentality eventually" (189). But his interpretation of holiness in action focuses largely on changing Church doctrine, rooted in Christ's teaching and practice, on divorce and on women in the priesthood: "The *communio* model of the Church is a rich one. In reflecting the shared life of God where identity does not destroy difference, it offers great promise for ecumenism. It has the capacity to encompass both Church as 'where two or three are gathered in my name then am I there in the midst' and Church as the communion of saints across the ages. But, if there are unreconciled members in the Church—for example, the divorced and remarried—if there are those self-evidently called to ministry but ignored—for example, clergy now married and gifted women—then what status has our rhetoric of *communio*?" (ibid.) The answer to this question, in order to be a theological answer, would have to push beyond allegedly self-evident sociological norms. For McLoughlin, "There has to be unity which respects the sheer plurality of the Spirit-given gifts over and against any fearful tendency to centralize and control according to a uniform mould. Somehow we are challenged to develop ways of working and speaking together which serve the Spirit's capacity, as at Pentecost, to communicate without demanding that we all speak the same language or share the same customs or even gender" (188). Given this opposition between "Spirit-given gifts" and the "fearful tendency to centralize and control," one wonders whether McLoughlin's account of the Spirit's work is sufficiently rich.

6. Paul McPartlan, "Trinity, Church and State," in Hoose, *Authority in the Roman Catholic Church*, 117–28, at 126. Highlighting the ecclesiological and Trinitarian work of Karl Barth, Jürgen Moltmann, Leonardo Boff, Jon Sobrino, John D. Zizioulas, McPartlan argues that Christians are poised to rediscover Trinitarian modes of ecclesial communion. In his view—which strikes me as hasty in its dismissal of centuries of Christian reflection—"The great era of Trinitarian awareness, we might say, lasted until the fourth century when the councils of Nicaea and Constantinople determined what should be said of the consubstantial Son and the co-worshipped Spirit in the Creed. This was, of course, also the great era of a communionally understood Church. I say this not in a fervour of nostalgia but as a prelude to suggesting that we are now entering a great *new* era of Trinitarian awareness. Every problem—and, in this case, the problem of Trinitarian amnesia—is also an opportunity, and the fact that Christians generally became so acutely aware of the problem during the twentieth century indicates that a rich new Trinitarian awareness has been forming" (123).

7. Ibid.

In light of this widespread view, this chapter first attends to the contributions of Orthodox theology, in particular Nicholas Afanasiev's influential contrast between "universal ecclesiology" and "eucharistic ecclesiology" and Olivier Clément's response to John Paul II's request in his encyclical *Ut Unum Sint* (1995) for ecumenical reflection on the role of the pope. Afanasiev's and Clément's works illumine the profoundly eucharistic character of all hierarchical priesthood in the Church, and call into question whether *Lumen Gentium's* affirmation (following Vatican I) of the pope's "full, supreme, and universal power over the whole Church" accords with a truly eucharistic understanding of the Church.[8] Second, I set forth aspects of Aquinas's theology of papacy as developed in the *Summa Contra Gentiles* and the *Summa Theologiae*. I propose that Aquinas's theology of the papacy flows from a eucharistic understanding of the Church. His insights into the reality of the papacy both enrich the contemporary Catholic dialogue with Orthodox theologians—as Walter Kasper has pointed out—and make clear that the standard narrative of ecclesiological decline lacks sufficient historical and theological nuance and contextualization.[9]

---

8. It is worth noting that the Orthodox theologian John Erickson calls for more attention to Baptism in Orthodox ecclesiology: see Erickson, "The Formation of Orthodox Ecclesial Identity," *St. Vladimir's Theological Quarterly* 42 (1998): 301–14; idem, "Baptism and the Church's Faith," in *Marks of the Body of Christ*, ed. Carl E. Braaten and Robert W. Jenson (Grand Rapids, MI: Eerdmans, 1999), 44–58; cf. the similar concerns of Stanley Samuel Harakas, "Doing Theology Today: An Orthodox and Evangelical Dialogue on Theological Method," *Pro Ecclesia* 11 (2002): 435–62, at 452. For efforts to develop an Orthodox Trinitarian ecclesiology, in response to Miroslav Volf, see Peter Anthony Baktis, "Orthodox Ecclesiology for the New Millennium," *Pro Ecclesia* 10 (2001): 321–28. See also the ecclesiological contributions of Emmanuel Clapsis, *Orthodoxy in Conversation: Orthodox Ecumenical Engagements* (Brookline, MA: Holy Cross Orthodox Seminary Press, 2000).

9. For appreciative remarks on Aquinas's theology of papal primacy, see Walter Kasper, *Leadership in the Church: How Traditional Roles Can Serve the Christian Community Today*, trans. Brian McNeil (New York: Crossroad, 2003), 106–8. On Catholic–Orthodox dialogue one might see, from a Catholic perspective, Paul McPartlan, "Towards Catholic–Orthodox Unity," *Communio* 19 (1992): 305–20; Adriano Garuti, OFM, *Primacy of the Bishop of Rome and the Ecumenical Dialogue*, trans. Michael Miller (San Francisco: Ignatius Press, 2004), ch. 2: "The Primacy and Catholic–Orthodox Dialogue," 12–86. For an effort to understand and heal the division between East and West, see also Yves Congar, "Ecclesiological Awareness in the East and in the West from the Sixth to the Eleventh Century," in *The Unity of the Churches of God*, ed. Polycarp Sherwood, OSB (Baltimore, MD: Helicon Press, 1963), 127–84. Congar remarks, "With regard to her reality as a great society—though surely not with regard to the mystery of the Church: her profound reality as Body of Christ—the first datum of Christian awareness seems to us to be the universal Church in the West, and in the East, the local church" (139). Congar holds that "Rome thinks juridically and views the Church as the reality

AFANASIEV AND CLÉMENT: BEYOND JURIDICIST "UNIVERSAL ECCLESIOLOGY"

Nicholas Afanasiev

In his influential essay "The Church Which Presides in Love," originally published in 1963, Nicholas Afanasiev draws the distinction between "universal ecclesiology" and "eucharistic ecclesiology" that, as we have seen, informs Zizioulas's thought, even though Zizioulas notes some reservations.[10] Afanasiev's eucharistic ecclesiology presents a distinctive

---

correlative to her universal authority" (ibid.), whereas the East "stayed with the idea of a communion between local churches—and so much the more so as the Church has been thought sacramentally, not juridically. Now, in the sacramental view, the local community is complete; and any one community is the equal of any other. Perhaps it is for this reason, too, that the East seems to us to be only slightly scandalized and disturbed by the breaking off of communion" (139–40). See also Congar, *After Nine Hundred Years: The Background of the Schism between the Eastern and Western Churches* (New York: Fordham University Press, 1959). Andrew Louth reports that as great an Orthodox theologian as Dumitru Stăniloae, despite his ecumenical engagements, held that "outside the Orthodox Church there is no proper apostolic succession" (Louth, "Review Essay: The Orthodox Dogmatic Theology of Dumitru Stăniloae," *Modern Theology* 13 [1997]: 253–67, at 260, summarizing Stăniloae's view as contained in his *Orthodoxe Dogmatik*, 3 vols. [Düsseldorf: Benziger Verlag, 1984–95], vol. 3: pp. 141–43). Stăniloae's contributions to ecumenism are chronicled by Ronald G. Robertson, "Dumitru Stăniloae on Christian Unity," *Dumitru Stăniloae: Tradition and Modernity in Theology*, ed. Lucian Turcescu (Oxford: Center for Romanian Studies, 2002), 104–25, especially 113, for the shift in Stăniloae's views after his participation in the 1982 Catholic–Orthodox dialogue at Munich.

10. Nicholas Afanassieff [Afanasiev], "The Church Which Presides in Love," in *The Primacy of Peter: Essays in Ecclesiology and the Early Church*, ed. John Meyendorff (1963; Crestwood, NY: St. Vladimir's Seminary Press, 1992), 91–143. For Orthodox responses to Afanasiev's position, in particular the criticisms offered by John Zizioulas and Dumitru Stăniloae, see Lucian Turcescu, "Eucharistic Ecclesiology or Open Sobornicity?" in Turcescu, *Dumitru Stăniloae*, 83–103. Turcescu rightly observes that "eucharistic ecclesiology" has serious difficulty accounting for the parish, which is headed by the priest rather than the bishop. For a Catholic discussion of Afanasiev's position, see Aidan Nichols, OP, *Theology in the Russian Diaspora: Church, Fathers, Eucharist in Nikolai Afanas'ev* (Cambridge: Cambridge University Press, 1989); Leo Cardinal Scheffczyk, "Das Problem der 'eucharistischen Ekklesiologie' im Lichte der Kichen und Eucharistielehre des heiligen Thomas von Aquin," in *Indubitanter ad Veritatem: Studies Offered to Leo J. Elders SVD*, ed. Jörgen Vijgen (Budel: Damon, 2003), 388–405; Louis Bouyer, *The Church of God*, Part I, ch. 10, which briefly places Afanasiev within the context of the vibrant renewal of Orthodox theology through Khomiakov, Soloviev, Florensky, Bulgakov, Lossky, and Florovsky. Bouyer finds that Afanasiev's reflections "furnish perhaps the only solid basis for an ecclesiology whose broadest and deepest visions would find support not on some *a priori* idea but on the most traditional experience of the Church" (141). Bouyer holds that Afanasiev "has put his finger on an essential point, which is, as it were, the key to the ecclesiology of the New Testament and the earliest fathers" (142). Yet Bouyer adds a criticism of Afanasiev's "absolute rejection of any juridical aspect in the life and the concept of the Church, which (for him) seems to be connected with this eucharistic ecclesiology" (ibid.). See

conception of the relationship of bishops to each other. Seeking to replace the "primacy" of one bishop over others with the "priority"— understood as a hierarchical ordering with respect to the "gift of witnessing"—of one local church, Afanasiev challenges us to think through Christian hierarchy in terms of concrete eucharistic love rather than domineering power.

He begins by noting that discussions between Catholic and Orthodox theologians regarding the Catholic doctrine of the primacy of the bishop of Rome often adopt the wrong starting point; namely, historical-critical exegetical questions about the role of Peter and similar historical questions about the status of the Church of Rome.[11] The real question, Afanasiev argues, is theological. As he puts it,

also Alvin F. Kimel's "Who Are the Bishops? Episkopé and the Church," *Anglican Theological Review* 77 (1995): 58–75, indebted to Afanasiev as corrected by Zizioulas.

11. For a study that proceeds along these lines, see Klaus Schatz, sj, *Papal Primacy: From Its Origins to the Present*, trans. John A. Otto and Linda M. Maloney (German 1990; Collegeville, MN: Liturgical Press, 1996). To the question of whether during the first millennium the East ever recognized a Roman primacy, Schatz answers "no" if one means "primacy of jurisdiction," but "yes" if one means "the ultimate norm of ecclesial communion": "It would not be difficult to find a continuing series of witnesses in the Eastern Church throughout the centuries who give a clear acknowledgment of that principle, and who speak in one way or another of the Roman church, or even the Roman bishop, as the head or presider over all churches" (60). He adds that "especially when the imperial throne was incapable of fully managing affairs the market value and theological status of the Roman See could rise remarkably, even among eastern authors" (61). As an example, he gives Theodore Abu Qurra (ca. 800 AD), who wrote in Syria around 800 against the Monophysites: "Only in the papacy did he find the ultimate criterion for the legitimacy of councils" (ibid.). Granting that Abu Qurra cannot be taken as representative, Schatz holds nonetheless that the orthodox Eastern Fathers generally held that doctrinal questions could not be solved without union with Rome, and thus " 'witnesses to primacy' are indeed significant as testimony to the *common* faith of East and West" (ibid.). For further insight, see also Brian E. Daley, sj, "Position and Patronage in the Early Church: The Original Meaning of 'Primacy of Honour,' " *Journal of Theological Studies* 44 (1993): 529–53. For an erudite study of the first millennium from an Orthodox perspective, see V. Nicolae Dură, "The 'Petrine Primacy': The Role of the Bishop of Rome according to the Canonical Legislation of the Ecumenical Councils of the First Millennium, an Ecclesiological-Canonical Evaluation," in *The Petrine Ministry: Catholics and Orthodox in Dialogue*, ed. Walter Cardinal Kasper, trans. the staff of the Pontifical Council for Promoting Christian Unity (New York: Paulist Press, 2006), 159–87. See also in the same volume Vlassios Phidas, "Papal Primacy and Patriarchal Pentarchy in the Orthodox Tradition," 65–82. Phidas notes that the Bishop of Rome possesses for Orthodoxy "the canonical prerogatives of the *prima sedes* in the system of the patriarchal pentarchy" (77), but Catholics since 1054 have developed the theology of papal primacy in a different direction; namely, with "*direct reference to the whole body of bishops of the Church*" (ibid.) rather than within the context of the pentarchy. See also for Orthodox perspectives the essays by John Zizioulas ("Primacy in the Church: An Orthodox Approach," 115–26), Dumitru Popescu ("Papal Primacy in Eastern and Western Patristic Theology: Its Interpretation in the Light of Contemporary Culture," 99–114), and Nicolas Lossky ("Conciliarity-Primacy in a Russian Orthodox Perspective," 127–36) in *Petrine*

"Can primacy—whether of Rome or of any other church—really exist in the Church? . . . If we are to solve the problem of primacy within the Church, our starting point must be ecclesiology; i.e., we must ask, does the doctrine of the Church contain the idea of primacy (in its present or any other form), or exclude it altogether?"[12] In order to answer this question, Afanasiev sets forth his argument that over the centuries two kinds of ecclesiology have emerged: universal and eucharistic.

Universal ecclesiology, Afanasiev says, holds that "the Church is a single organic whole, including in itself all church units of any kind, especially those headed by bishops. This organic whole is the Body of Christ or, to return to Catholic theological terms, the Mystical Body of Christ."[13] Universal ecclesiology is by no means exclusively Roman Catholic: Afanasiev finds examples of it in modern Byzantine and Russian Orthodox theology and conciliar definitions. It also has a long pedigree, with its roots in the third-century theologian Cyprian of Carthage.[14] Influenced by the structure of the Roman Empire

---

Ministry and the Unity of the Church, ed. James F. Puglisi (Collegeville, MN: Liturgical Press, 1999).

12. Afanasiev, "The Church Which Presides in Love," 91. Afanasiev's posthumously published major work, *The Church of the Holy Spirit*, has recently appeared in English: See Afanasiev, *The Church of the Holy Spirit*, translated by Vitaly Permikov, ed. Michael Plekon. (Notre Dame, IN: University of Notre Dame Press, 2007). For details on Afanasiev's life and work, including the influence of his teacher and colleague Sergius Bulgakov (as well as his colleague Alexander Schmemann), see Plekon's introduction to "*The Church of the Holy Spirit*: Nicolas Afanasiev's Vision of the Eucharist and the Church," ix–xx, as well as Plekon, *Living Icons: Persons of Faith in the Eastern Church* (Notre Dame, IN: University of Notre Dame Press, 2002), 149–77.

13. Afanasiev, "The Church Which Presides in Love," 92.

14. For the view that Cyprian initiates the blending of the bishop's role into that of the presbyters, see John D. Zizioulas, "*Episkope* and *Episkopos* in the Early Church: A Brief Survey of the Evidence," in *Episkope and Episcopate in Ecumenical Perspective*, Faith and Order Paper 102 (Geneva: World Council of Churches, 1980), 30–42. For a more positive reading of Cyprian's view of the local church, see Yves Congar, "The Hierarchy as Service," in idem, *Power and Poverty in the Church*, trans. Jennifer Nicholson (Baltimore: Helicon, 1964), 43f. Francis A. Sullivan, SJ, makes use of Cyprian in favor of democratic Church structures: see Sullivan, "St. Cyprian on the Role of the Laity in Decision Making in the Early Church," in *Common Calling: The Laity and Governance of the Catholic Church*, ed. Stephen J. Pope (Washington, DC: Georgetown University Press, 2004), 39–49. See also the texts and commentary in Sullivan, *From Apostles to Bishops: The Development of the Episcopacy in the Early Church* (New York: Paulist Press, 2001), 192–216. Similarly, Sullivan suggests that behind Ignatius of Antioch's insistence that he "obtained his ministry (*diakonian*) from God rather than from men or through his own efforts" (115), one might find the community's recognition that Ignatius possessed "the charism of leadership" (cf. 1 Cor 12:28; Rom 12:8)" (ibid.).

(with the emperor as the "soul" of the imperial body),[15] as well as by earlier theological accounts of the Church's unity as rooted in Christ's unity (Ignatius of Antioch and Tertullian), Cyprian argued that the many local churches within the one Church were comparable to the many members with Christ's Body. Thus, no local church is the "Catholic" Church; rather, the Catholic Church is the universal Church, composed of all the local churches as members of the Body.[16] Just as the many member churches are one in Christ's Body, so also the many member bishops are one in Peter. Quoting Cyprian, Afanasiev notes that for Cyprian *"Episopatus unus est*, because 'the throne of Peter is one,' 'in which God has established and shown the source of all unity.' 'There is one God alone, one Christ, one Church, one Throne of Peter, whom the word of the Lord had made his foundation-stone.' "[17] Yet all the bishops receive a share in the "Throne of Peter," which Cyprian conceives as belonging, in one sense, to the whole episcopate. In another sense, however, the Throne of Peter belongs specially to the Church of Rome, so that "the Bishop of Rome is the direct heir of Peter, whereas the others are heirs only indirectly, and sometimes only by the mediation of Rome."[18] While Cyprian does not, in Afanasiev's view, draw the logical conclusion regarding primacy, later bishops of Rome extend Cyprian's logic to this conclusion.

This "universal ecclesiology" inspired by Cyprian, Afanasiev notes, poses a difficult challenge to the rejection of papal primacy by Orthodox theologians. Namely, "If there is no primacy in the Universal Church, why do we allow a partial primacy within the boundaries of an autocephalous church? The head of an autocephalous church

---

15. For the role of the emperor in the early Church, see also Joseph Ratzinger, "Anglican–Catholic Dialogue: Its Problems and Hopes," trans. Dame Fridesweide Sandemann, osb, in his *Church, Ecumenism and Politics: New Essays in Ecclesiology* (German 1987; New York: Crossroad, 1988), 76–77; cf. his "Postscript" to this piece, 94. Ratzinger calls attention here to Vincent Twomey's *Apostolikos Thronos. The Primacy of Rome as Reflected in the Church History of Eusebius and the Historico-Apologetic Writings of St Athanasius the Great* (Münster: Aschendorff, 1982): "Vincent Twomey has already shown in a very well documented piece of research, that already in the contest at Nicaea two opposed options stand out clearly: the Eusebian and the Athanasian, i.e., the idea of an imperial universal Church as against a really theological conception in which it is not the emperor but Rome which plays the decisive role" (Ratzinger, "Postscript," 76).

16. Afanasiev, "The Church Which Presides in Love," 95.

17. Ibid., 96.

18. Ibid., 98.

makes manifest its unity: but how can the unity of the whole Orthodox Church be given empirical expression in the absence of a universal primacy?"[19] Given the perspective of universal ecclesiology, Afanasiev argues, it is futile to deny the necessity of primacy—although Orthodox theologians can still deny that, as Roman Catholic theology has held, primacy is necessarily connected to the Church of Rome and her Bishop.[20] But Afanasiev, as we observed above, does not assume the perspective of "universal ecclesiology" as normative. Before universal ecclesiology became the regnant model, he argues, the earliest Church held to a "eucharistic ecclesiology."[21] In his view, the earliest Church

---

19. Ibid., 100.

20. In this regard, Afanasiev quotes the Protestant theologian Oscar Cullman and the Orthodox theologian A. Kartashev, both of whom, in publications from the 1950s, rejected Roman primacy but allowed for the possibility of primacy in other forms (106).

21. Afanasiev's conception of "eucharistic ecclesiology" has had a major influence on contemporary Catholic ecclesiology. See for emphasis on the local church, Jean-Marie R. Tillard, OP, *L'Église locale: Ecclésiologie de communion et catholicité* (Paris: Cerf, 1995); idem, *Flesh of the Church, Flesh of Christ: At the Source of the Ecclesiology of Communion*, trans. Madeleine Beaumont (French 1992; Collegeville, MN: Liturgical Press, 2001); idem, *Church of Churches: The Ecclesiology of Communion*, trans. R. C. De Peaux, O. Praem. (French 1987; Collegeville, MN: Liturgical Press, 1992); cf. Joseph G. Aryankalayil, *Local Church and Church Universal: Towards a Convergence Between East and West: A Study of the Theology of the Local Church according to N. Afanasiev and J.-M. R. Tillard with Special Reference to Some of the Contemporary Catholic and Orthodox Theologians* (Ph.D. diss.; Fribourg: Université de Fribourg Suisse, 2004). For Tillard's negative reading of Aquinas's theology of the Church, see *L'Église locale*, 489–98. On the variety of "communion ecclesiologies" see Dennis M. Doyle, *Communion Ecclesiologies: Vision and Versions* (Maryknoll, NY: Orbis Books, 2000), which discusses Tillard at 152–56. See also Christopher Ruddy's *The Local Church*, which, while focusing on Tillard, accords with the concerns raised by Joseph Komonchak, "The Theology of the Local Church: The State of the Question," in *The Multicultural Church*, ed. William Cenkner (New York: Paulist, 1996), 35–53; cf. Komonchak, "The Local Realization of the Church," in *The Reception of Vatican II*, ed. Giuseppe Alberigo, Jean-Pierre Jossua, and Joseph A. Komonchak, trans. Matthew J. O'Connell (Washington, DC: The Catholic University of America Press, 1987), 77–90. Tillard seeks to avoid positing a tension between the "local" and "universal" Church by identifying the original Church of Jerusalem as simultaneously "local" and "universal," but both Doyle and Ruddy, while agreeing with Tillard's position, think that Tillard's views come under the censure of the Congregation for the Doctrine of the Faith's (CDF) "Some Aspects of the Church Understood as Communion," *Origins* 22 (June 25, 1992): 108–12, later clarified in "La Chiesa come Comunione," *L'Osservatore Romano*, June 23, 1993. At stake is whether the Body of Christ, the heavenly Jerusalem, exists "prior" ontologically to local realizations: does receptivity to divine gifting have primacy in ecclesiology, as suggested by the Holy Spirit's action at Pentecost? Avery Dulles, SJ, affirms the ontological priority of the "universal" Church: see Dulles, "The Trinity and Christian Unity," in *God the Holy Trinity: Reflections on Christian Faith and Practice*, ed. Timothy George (Grand Rapids, MI: Baker Academic, 2006), 69–82, at 79–80. See also Henri de Lubac, SJ, *The Motherhood of the Church*, trans. Sister Sergia Englund, OCD (French 1971; San Francisco: Ignatius Press, 1982), 171–335 (a section titled "Particular Churches in the Universal Church"). Cf. regarding the CDF's document, Joseph Ratzinger, "The Ecclesiology of the Constitution *Lumen Gentium*," in his *Pilgrim Fellowship of*

knew nothing of the "Universal Church." He observes in this regard, "We would never have found the idea of the Universal Church in the New Testament, and least of all in St Paul's writings, if it had not already been present in our minds."[22]

Afanasiev singles out in particular Paul's first letter to the Corinthians as the hermeneutical key to the earliest Church's "eucharistic ecclesiology." In chapter 12 Paul tells the Corinthians "you are the body of Christ and individually members of it" (1 Corinthians 12:27), while shortly earlier Paul asks rhetorically, "The bread which we break, is it not a participation in the body of Christ? Because there is one bread, we who are many are one body" (1 Corinthians 10:16–17). According to Afanasiev, the phrase "the body of Christ" means the same thing in both passages. It does so because of the kind of action that the Eucharist is: "When the Eucharist is celebrated, the bread becomes the Body of Christ, and by the bread the partakers become the Body of Christ."[23] Celebrating the Eucharist turns both the bread and its partakers into the Body of Christ. This Body of Christ is thus not only Christ, but also the local church that celebrates the Eucharist. It follows that each local church is fully the Church, since each local church is fully the Body of Christ. Just as the consecrated bread is not merely a part of Christ's Body, but rather is in fact Christ's true Body, so also the local church in the Eucharist is not merely a part of Christ's Body the Church. Where Christ's Body truly is, there Christ's whole Body is, because Christ's Body is indivisible. As Afanasiev states, " 'One plus one is still one' in ecclesiology. Every local church manifests all the fullness of the Church of God, because it *is* the Church of God and not just one part of it."[24]

Faith: The Church as Communion, ed. Stephan Otto Horn and Vinzenz Pfnür, trans. Henry Taylor (German 2002; San Francisco: Ignatius Press, 2005), 123–52. Ratzinger states, "Just as in the case of the term 'People of God,' one could not help but notice here an increasing emphasis on the horizontal dimension, the omission of the idea of God. 'Communion' ecclesiology began to be reduced to the theme of the relationship between the local Church and the Church as a whole, and that in turn, more and more, declined into the question of the assignment of competent authority as between the one and the other" (132). He defends the CDF's document explicitly at 133–39.

22. Afanasiev, "The Church Which Presides in Love," 108.

23. Ibid.

24. Ibid., 109. For the criticisms posed against this position by Lucian Turcescu, John Zizioulas, and Dumitru Stăniloae, see Turcescu, "Eucharistic Ecclesiology or Open Sobornicity?" 83–103.

Let me pose a question at this stage. Should one make a distinction between on the one hand the unity and multiplicity of the Eucharist as Christ's body and blood in sacramental mode, and on the other hand the unity and multiplicity of the Church that is constituted by partaking in the Eucharist? The many "Eucharists" are always none other than the one body and blood of the living Christ, because of the sacramental mode. Thus, while one can speak of many Eucharists, one cannot speak of more than one body and blood of Christ. Does this make a strict parallel with what one means in speaking of the local churches as the "Body of Christ"? I think not. While there is in fact only one body and blood of Christ, there are many local churches. Thus, the unity of the many Eucharists is a unity in the strict sense, and the diversity of the many Eucharists is a formal diversity; whereas the unity of the many churches is a formal unity, and the diversity of the many churches is a diversity in the strict sense (namely, many distinct human beings). In both cases, there is a real unity that enables one to call the Eucharist, and the church constituted in the celebration of the Eucharist, the "Body of Christ." What is in one case a formal diversity under which lies a material unity (the Eucharist as a sacrament), however, is in the other case a material diversity under which lies a formal unity (the Church as composed of many members and churches).

It would seem that this difference would affect the way in which one could speak of the "Body of Christ" as "indivisible." In both cases—Eucharist and Church—the "Body of Christ" would be indivisible, but the "materiality" of the Eucharist as Jesus' living body and blood is indivisible, while the "materiality" of the Church as various human beings is in fact divisible. In a certain sense, then, it is clearly true that where the Body of Christ is, there is the Church in its fullness. Yet, the different meanings at play will not allow us to defend this point solely on the basis of the fact that the Body of Christ is "indivisible," because the Church as Christ's members is not "indivisible" in the same way as the Eucharist as Christ's body and blood. The Church is divisible in its members in a way that the Eucharist is not divisible. In defending the Church's unity, the early Church would have had to possess some concept of the Church's formal universality/ unity, whereas this would not have had to be the case—presuming an understanding of the Eucharist as Christ's body and blood—with respect to the unity of the Eucharist as the "Body of Christ."

Thus, it may be that Afanasiev makes an overly sharp disjunction when he observes, "Eucharistic ecclesiology teaches that the unity and fullness of the Church attach to the notion of a local church, and not to the fluid and indefinite notion of the Universal Church."[25] Granted that the unity and fullness of the Church belong to the local church, whose members are eucharistically the "Body of Christ," still why not also hold that the unity and fullness also belong to, and indeed require, a "notion of the Universal Church"? Just as the unity of the many Eucharists requires an understanding of the one living body and blood of Christ, so also the unity of the many members and churches requires an understanding of the one Church encompassing all members and churches, which are divisible in a sense that the body and blood of Christ are not. Similarly, when Afanasiev states that "the Eucharist could never have been offered in a local church if it had been no more than one part of the Church of God,"[26] one can both agree and disagree. Certainly the local church is more than a "part" of the universal Church of God, but nonetheless, as is evident to the eyes, the local church does not encompass all the members of Christ's Body in the *same way* that the universal Church does. The local church cannot be understood without a corresponding "notion of the Universal Church." Afanasiev affirms, "By denying the idea of 'parts,' eucharistic ecclesiology also excludes any concept of the Universal Church, for the Universal Church consists of parts, if it exists at all."[27] As I have tried to show, this is not the case. The conceptual self-sufficiency of the local church, as containing in itself all the local churches,[28] no more follows than does the conceptual self-sufficiency of the local Eucharist. In both cases, the "Body of Christ" includes both the one and the many in a nuanced fashion.

---

25. Afanasiev, "The Church Which Presides in Love," 110. Cf. Turcescu, "Eucharistic Ecclesiology or Open Sobornicity?" 93–94, 97.

26. Afanasiev, "The Church Which Presides in Love," 110.

27. Ibid.

28. Afanasiev does not seek to isolate one local church from others. He writes, "Though a local church did contain everything it needed within itself, it could not live apart from the other churches. It could not shut itself in or refuse to be acquainted with happenings in other churches: for anything that happened in other churches, as well as in its own, happened in the Church of God, the one and only Church" (ibid., 112). On the issue of the relationship of the local and universal Church, Christopher Ruddy summarizes and critically engages Afanasiev's ecclesiology in *The Local Church*, 15–21.

Having sketched "universal ecclesiology" and "eucharistic ecclesiology," Afanasiev returns to the question of primacy in ecclesial hierarchy. If a "universal ecclesiology" requires sociologically one bishop as head of all the bishops, a "eucharistic ecclesiology" takes the quite different starting point than we saw in Zizioulas. Afanasiev connects the Eucharist closely with Jewish ritual meals. He states, "The Eucharist is a prolongation of the Supper in one special regard: it is an ecclesiological Last Supper, the 'feast of the Lord' celebrated in the Church, by whose celebration the Church has being. As in Jewish meals which served as the models for the Last Supper, so in the Eucharist one person must preside."[29] The presider at the eucharistic assembly is thereby also the head of the local church, and since the local church is the Body of Christ in its fullness, there is no need to contemplate one bishop as the head of the other bishops. Instead, each full instantiation of the Body of Christ is called to receive, in love, the witness of other full instantiations of the Body of Christ, "the Spirit bearing witness of the Spirit."[30] When other local churches reject

---

29. Afanasiev, "The Church Which Presides in Love," 111.

30. Ibid. A number of contemporary theologians have modified this understanding of the eucharistic presider in the direction of a functionalist, rather than sacramental and cultic, view of the priesthood. Compare for example Thomas Rausch, SJ's observation, "Eucharistic presidency belongs to the function of presiding over the community. . . . In the light of the original nexus between leading the community and eucharistic presidency, Leonardo Boff's suggestion that lay community coordinators be authorized to preside at the Eucharist for communities lacking ordained ministers may not be so untraditional" (Rausch, *Towards a Truly Catholic Church: An Ecclesiology for the Third Millennium* [Collegeville, MN: Liturgical Press, 2005], 106). Rausch is drawing upon Richard R. Gaillardetz's "The Ecclesiological Foundations of Ministry within an Ordered Communion," in *Ordering the Baptismal Priesthood: Theologies of Lay and Ordained Ministry*, ed. Susan K. Wood (Collegeville, MN: Liturgical Press, 2003), 26–51; and Leonardo Boff's *Ecclesiogenesis: The Base Communities Reinvent the Church* (Maryknoll, NY: Orbis, 1986). Avery Dulles, SJ, evaluates Boff's position negatively: "Following Küng and Schillebeeckx, . . . Leonardo Boff has urged that in the absence of an ordained minister, a basic community can truly celebrate the Lord's Supper in which Christ is truly, and in some degree sacramentally, present. This view, like those of Küng and Schillebeeckx, has been rejected by the CDF. The point at issue is that the sacraments are public acts of the church as such, and cannot be celebrated by an individual or a particular congregation except in union with the bishop and the body of bishops. Only through ordinations conferred by the apostolic body can individuals enter into the public ministry. The deviant views would make sense only in terms of a congregational ecclesiology that is far from Catholic. The ordained are not mere delegates of the assembly to which they minister. They receive their gifts through apostolic succession in office, which confers upon them the sacred character of order, empowering them to act in the name of the church and in the name of Christ as head of the church" (Avery Dulles, SJ, *The Priestly Office: A Theological Reflection* [Mahwah, NJ: Paulist Press, 1997], 35, referring to the Congregation for the Doctrine of the Faith's

what is being taught and done in another local church, such rejection shows that the rejected local church has failed to be what it should be.

Thus, far from supposing that one bishop/presider stands above others, Afanasiev holds that all bishops and all local churches stand on the same level of equality, even if "the witness of local churches might vary in weight."[31] He goes on to explain that the hierarchical ordering of the (fully equal) local churches' witness is dependent upon each local church's degree of "realization of the presence of the Church of God."[32] The local church that possesses priority does not possess power over the other local churches, but does possess an eminently authoritative witness and greater love. Since "primacy" involves one bishop's (legalistic) power rather than one local church's (love-based) "priority," Afanasiev concludes that "eucharistic ecclesiology excludes the idea of primacy by its very nature."[33]

From the historical evidence, too, he judges that the earliest Church did not envision any one local church or particular bishop

---

notification on Boff's *Church: Charism and Power* [Maryknoll, NY: Orbis, 1986] published in *Origins* 14 [April 4, 1985]: 683–87).

31. Afanasiev, "The Church Which Presides in Love," 111.

32. Ibid. As he explains further, "When a local church invokes the church-in-priority, it is not invoking judgment from a tribunal against which there is no appeal, but coming to the church-in-priority so as to find itself, by hearing the voice of the Church which dwells there" (114). Responding to this aspect of Afanasiev's essay, Henri de Lubac, SJ, argues that "in the essential act of his magisterium, the authority of Peter's successor is indeed one of testimony. He decides nothing at his own pleasure, rather he refers to the faith of the entire Church, that is, to the tradition coming from the Apostles, of which he is the guardian par excellence" (de Lubac, *The Motherhood of the Church*, 323, fn 28).

33. Afanasiev, "The Church Which Presides in Love," 115. For the view that "a distinction between 'primacy' and 'priority' is not possible," see Turcescu, "Eucharistic Ecclesiology or Open Sobornicity?," 89. Yves Congar remarks with regard to the charge of legalism: "It has often been observed that a theology which denies the eternal procession of the Holy Spirit from the Word tends to minimize the part played by definite forms or authority in actual life, and leaves the way more open to a kind of independent inspiration. The ecclesiology of the Orthodox Churches has a distinctly 'pneumatic' tendency and declines to accept Catholic ideas of authority which seem to savour of legalism. This legalism, however, is closely bound up with values of profound mystical importance, as may be seen in the following passage from St. Thomas Aquinas which brings out strikingly the ecclesiological counterparts of the theology of the Holy Ghost: 'To say that the Vicar of Christ, the Roman Pontiff, does not hold the Primacy in the universal Church is an error analogous to that which denies that the Holy Ghost proceeds from the Son. For Christ, the Son of God, consecrates his Church and consecrates it by the Holy Ghost as by his seal or stamp. Likewise, the Vicar of Christ by his primacy and governance, like a good servant, preserves the universal Church that is subject to Christ' " (Congar, "The Holy Spirit and the Apostolic Body, Continuators of the Work of Christ," in idem, *The Mystery of the Church*, trans. A. V. Littledale [French 1956; Baltimore: Helicon Press, 1960], 153).

having power over other local churches and bishops: such an idea only occurs after the shift from eucharistic ecclesiology to universal ecclesiology. Instead, in the earliest Church, the church of Jerusalem, possessed "priority," and at first Peter, then James, presided at that church.[34] Later in the first century, as suggested by the letters of Ignatius and Clement, as well as by Irenaeus, this "priority" shifted to the Church of Rome; after Constantine, "primacy" displaced "priority" due to the loss of eucharistic ecclesiology.[35] The key result is the introduction of Roman legalism, power rather than love, into Christian ecclesiology. As Afanasiev says, "universal ecclesiology and eucharistic ecclesiology have different conceptions on the question of Church government: the first conceives this government as a matter of law and rights, and the second regards it as founded on grace."[36] More pungently, he observes that "the concept of primacy is really the same as that of priority, only looked at from a lawyer's point of view."[37] This point of view distorts the entire reality of what "priority" sought to serve, namely, unity in love, a unity founded entirely upon the "gift of witnessing" rather than power over other Christians.[38] Afanasiev leaves us with a choice: "we

---

34. With regard to Peter, Paul, and the other apostles, Afanasiev is careful to note that the role of apostle differs significantly from that of bishop, since after the dispersion of the apostles from Jerusalem, they were (as founders) heads of many local churches, rather than members or presiders at any local church. As for Peter's role, Afanasiev notes that "for me, the problem of Peter's primacy seems to be a false problem; but the problem of Peter himself is real. . . . It is enough simply to say that Peter stood in a place apart among the apostles, and that his ministry was unique in kind and had no later parallels" (Afanasiev, "The Church Which Presides in Love," 122). With respect to Paul, Afanasiev remarks that in Galatians 2 "Paul applied to the church which possessed the greatest authority, and the Church of Jerusalem behaved as the church-with-priority" (120).

35. Afanasiev summarizes his position as follows: "The foundations of universal ecclesiology were formulated for the first time by Cyprian of Carthage. With Constantine, a new factor comes into the Church's life, namely the Roman Empire and the Roman Caesar. This new factor led to the predominance of universal ecclesiology in the mind of the Church. In spite of all the difference there is between these two types of ecclesiology, they agree in both accepting the idea that the whole Church must follow a single directive. For the pattern of universal ecclesiology, a unique, personal power founded on rights is a necessity. It is impossible to construct a universal ecclesiology without admitting the idea of primacy. . . . In the pattern of eucharistic theology, power of one single bishop simply does not exist in any case, because power based on right does not exist. But this is not to say that eucharistic ecclesiology rejects the idea that the whole church should follow a single directive; this idea springs from the basic doctrine of eucharistic ecclesiology" (ibid., 141)—namely, the doctrine of "priority."

36. Ibid., 141.

37. Ibid.

38. Ibid., 142. See also Yves Congar, "The Hierarchy as Service," 53: "we should note at this point that if Rome succeeded in obtaining, over and above her power, the *authority* of her

have simply to accept either priority and eucharistic ecclesiology or primacy and universal ecclesiology. By denying both we reject the idea that the Church has a single directive—and that is an essential proposition in the doctrine of the Church."[39]

Olivier Clément

Olivier Clément's *You Are Peter: An Orthodox Theologian's Reflection on the Exercise of Papal Primacy* was written explicitly in response to Pope John Paul II's encyclical *Ut Unum Sint*. For our purposes, Clément's last chapter—a postscript titled "For a Common Future"—has particular value. The modern world, he observes, is marked both by increasing unity and increasing fragmentation. Capitalism and technology are unifying the world, while religious belief and cultural identity are fragmenting it. Paradoxically, the long-sought unity

---

primacy, it was in large part due to the value and the wisdom of her answers to all the questions which were put to her from every region of Christendom. Genuine authority is moral authority." Congar, however, sees this "moral authority" as devolving into overly juridical forms beginning with Pope Gregory VII and exacerbated by late-medieval nominalist theology: see Congar, "Titles and Honours in the Church," in idem, *Power and Poverty in the Church*, 106–7. See also Congar, "Aspects ecclésiologiques de la querelle entre mendiants et séculiers dans la seconde moitié du XIIIe siècle et le début du XIVe," *Archives d'histoire doctrinale et littéraire du Moyen Age* 28 (1961): 35–151; idem, "The Idea of the Church in St. Thomas Aquinas," in idem, *The Mystery of the Church*, 97–117, where Congar encourages an ecclesiological "return to the infinitely wider and deeper viewpoints of the great theological traditions of the Fathers and the great scholastics" (98); Walter Ullmann, *Medieval Papalism: The Political Theories of the Medieval Canonists* (London: Methuen, 1949).

   39. Afanasiev, "The Church Which Presides in Love," 142. Critiquing both Roman Catholic and (at least modern) Orthodox ecclesiologies, Afanasiev argues that "eucharistic ecclesiology is still alive, deep down, in the Orthodox soul; but Orthodoxy on the surface is under the shadow of universal ecclesiology, and also of contemporary ecclesiastical organization. The attribute of 'catholicity,' which (in eucharistic ecclesiology) belongs to the episcopal church, has now been transferred to the autocephalous church—a unit, in fact, half political and half ecclesiastical. Naturally, the episcopal church loses its catholicity and becomes a part of the autocephalous church" (ibid.). He concludes, "In the long course of the struggle against the Roman Catholic position about the primacy of Rome, Orthodox doctrine has lost the very notion of priority. And the Catholic Church lost sight of the idea even earlier, during its struggle for a single directive in the Church, which it has now transformed into primacy" (143). On "catholicity" see also Benoît-Dominique de La Soujeole, OP, *Introduction au mystère de l'Église* (Paris: Parole et Silence, 2006), 567–78; Ratzinger, *Called to Communion: Understanding the Church Today*, trans. Adrian Walker (German 1991; San Francisco: Ignatius Press, 1996), 85–88; Henri de Lubac, SJ, *The Motherhood of the Church*, 171–79; Avery Dulles, SJ, *The Catholicity of the Church* (Oxford: Oxford University Press, 1985). For a recent Anglican perspectives on "catholicity" see Daniel H. Williams, "The Disintegration of Catholicism into Diffuse Inclusivism," *Pro Ecclesia* 12 (2003): 389–93 (responding to Episcopal Bishop William Griswold's "Experiencing Catholicity," *America* [September 27, 1997]).

contains despair within it, since it has no answer to death and evil, and in fact serves death and evil through a "human prometheanism";[40] while the feared fragmentation still retains internally some hope, both because the various religious beliefs offer a response to death and evil, and because fragmentation at least affirms the particularity and uniqueness of each human being, a particularity somewhat lost in economic and technological systematization.[41]

How should Christians respond to this situation? Should Christians give up on unity? No. Clément affirms that Christians must emphasize that faith in Christ serves a human unity that retains the particularity and uniqueness of each person, and that renounces all violence and evil-doing. On the level of God, the first point is that "God is innocent, that God has not wanted and *does not want death*, that God does not even have the idea of evil. We must be rid of the notion of a diabolical God made in the image of humanity, humanity at its worst."[42] Instead, the Christian God is a crucified God of *kenotic*

---

40. Olivier Clément, *You Are Peter: An Orthodox Theologian's Reflection on the Exercise of Papal Primacy*, trans. M. S. Laird (1997; New York: New City Press, 2003), 99. See the valuable review essay of Clément's book by Avery Dulles, SJ, "A New Orthodox View of the Papacy," *Pro Ecclesia* 12 (2003): 345–58. Dulles here also discusses Dumitru Popescu's, John Zizioulas's, and Nicolas Lossky's essays in Puglisi, *Petrine Ministry and the Unity of the Church*. Dulles notes with respect to Clément's survey of the Fathers: "With his mastery of the patristic tradition, Clément is able to marshal an extraordinary collection of testimonies from the early centuries regarding the transmission of Peter's primatial office to the bishops of Rome. . . . It is of great interest that the Council of Ephesus in 431 hailed Pope Celestine as 'the new Peter.' The Council of Chalcedon in 451 recognized Peter speaking through the mouth of Leo the Great. The Third Council of Constantinople in 681 heard Peter speaking through Pope Agatho. Before summoning the seventh ecumenical council, that of Nicaea II, the Empress Irene pleaded with Pope Hadrian as 'the most holy head,' who 'presides from the See of Peter,' to exercise his leadership in opposition to the iconoclasts. These and similar expressions, recalled by Clément, express the faith of the entire church in the first millennium. More remarkable still, Clément shows that the same regard for Roman and Petrine primacy extends well into the second millennium" (Dulles, "A New Orthodox View of the Papacy," 349–50).

41. For concerns about the modern world similar to Clément's, see also Paul Evdokimov, "To the Churches of Christ" (originally published in 1950), in *In the World, of the Church: A Paul Evdokimov Reader*, ed. and trans. Michael Plekon and Alexis Vinogradov (Crestwood, NY: St. Vladimir's Seminary Press, 2001), 49–60; Matthew L. Lamb, "Modern Liberalism, Authority and Authoritarianism: Political Theology against Deceptive Modern Categories," in *Missing God? Cultural Amnesia and Political Theology*, ed. John K. Downey, Jürgen Manemann, and Steven T. Ostovich (Berlin: LIT Verlag, 2006), 104–24. Drawing on the thought of Johann Baptist Metz, Lamb comments that in the modern period "the political way of living has become totally subordinated to the productive way of living. Praxis has been reduced to technique" (118).

42. Clément, *You Are Peter*, 102. The fault, Clément thinks, lies primarily with Israel and with Augustine, whose inheritors are the nominal Christians of today: The "notion of the

"infinite weakness," a God who, "in a certain sense, . . . has been excluded from his creation and only maintains it from without."[43] Thus, God is not responsible for fragmentation, nor does God seek to overcome fragmentation by power; instead, cruciform love, which cherishes the freedom/uniqueness of each human person, is God's sole means of unification.

As Clément puts it, then, "Self-emptying, emptiness expresses the entire mystery of love. God moves toward humanity in a reverse movement: it is not an over-full God, who would overwhelm humanity, but a God 'emptied' and awaiting our response in love."[44] In this regard Clément distinguishes between "*auctoritas*" and "*potestas*," noting that the latter constrains whereas the former means "to cause to grow in freedom."[45] Likewise, affirmation of the mystery of the Trinity should deepen our awareness that God enables a unification that respects the uniqueness of persons. In the triune God, oneness has an intensity that possesses interior room for the "other." Clément states, "The living God is so *one* that he bears within himself the reality, the pulsation of the *other* and, in the Spirit, in the holy Breath, overcomes all duality not by collapsing into an impersonal unity, but by a *coincidence of absolute unity and absolute diversity*."[46]

If a unity that upholds the particularity of persons character-izes the triune God, the same should also be true on the level of human beings, the *imago Dei*. Neither economic/technological unity nor religious/cultural fragmentation suffices for the true flourishing of the human person. Clément therefore seeks to evoke a religious belief that unifies without neglecting the uniqueness of persons. In this

---

diabolical God" is "born from the stories of the wars, in part legendary, fought by the people of Israel when they moved into the land of Canaan, first to conquer then to preserve the 'laboratory' of monotheism, a notion reinforced, in the theological history of the West, by the senile systematizations of an Augustine. It is a notion cultivated by the need of all those nominal Christians, so harshly criticized by Nietzsche, for vengeance or reparation" (ibid.).

43. Ibid., 102, 103. He adds that "the philosophical concept of a God who has foreknowledge of all things, a conception which turns us into puppets, is certainly not biblical" (102).

44. Ibid., 104. Thus "our God is not a God of 'holy wars' and crusades, but the God of the life-giving cross. Differences, even contradictions between religions should not be an occasion for war, but rather for friendship and prayer, if not shared at least together, as at Assisi. Moreover, these exchanges can immensely enrich Christianity, for in an eschatological perspective, it must be recognized that God's ways are many and various" (106).

45. Ibid., 111.

46. Ibid., 106.

regard, he speaks of "total unity in Christ, total diversity in the flames of the perpetual Pentecost."[47] The deepest interiority (unity), sought for example by Buddhism, becomes in Christianity also the deepest communion (divinization in the triune God). In contrast to the constrictions of the person imposed by economic/technological unity, Christians should offer a vision of "divinized humanity, which is the space of the Spirit and of creative freedom."[48]

Thus, far from conceiving of religious belief as a source of fragmentation, Christians should retrieve the value of *eros* and should emphasize a cosmic vision of renewal of the entire creation. The fulfillment of *eros* in *ascesis*, Clément states, "renders both man and woman 'separate from all and united to all,' as Evagrius Ponticus used to say."[49] Without appreciation for *eros*, religious belief becomes a sterile inwardness that serves fragmentation. With respect to Christianity's cosmic vision, Clément remarks, "There is no doubt that the future of Christianity lies in the rediscovery of a mystical and liturgical vision of the cosmos. The eucharist fulfills the sacramental potential of matter. It is the role of we humans, the priests of the world, to offer to God, in the great Christic sacrifice of reintegration, the spiritual essence of created things."[50] Renewed prayer, liturgical and personal, nourishes this union-in-communion.

---

47. Ibid. On the Holy Spirit's role in the unity of the Church, see Yves Congar, "The Church and Pentecost," in idem, *The Mystery of the Church.* Congar writes, "The Holy Spirit, through the love he instills, breaks our bondage to egoism, to our private inclinations, to the spirit of contradiction and distrust (Eph. ii. 2), to the spirit of the world of which St. Paul speaks (I Cor. ii. 12), which is a spirit of self-centeredness, exclusiveness, withdrawal from others. The spirit of Christ, on the other hand, is one of communion—see the magnificent programme of its practice in Rom. xii. 3–16—'no want of unity in the body, all the different parts of it to make each other's welfare their common care' (I Cor. xii. 25). The Spirit of love impels us from within to the service of others and harmony with them, in short, to communion" (27).

48. Clément, *You Are Peter,* 107.

49. Ibid., 108.

50. Ibid., 107–8. Clement argues that this Christian vision takes up and elevates contemporary concern for the environment: "It is up to us to give to this transforming vision the widest possible cultural and social scope and to use it to fertilize ecological concerns. The great Russian wisdom figures attempted this at the beginning of the century. Their ways of thinking were certainly awkward, but we will have to take up once again their meditation on Wisdom—this mysterious figure who appears above all in Proverbs 8 and in whom God and creation seem to mutually interpenetrate. Through wisdom, the ancient myths of the Sacred Earth can be integrated into Christianity in a poetic of communion. And most certainly there is a link between Wisdom and the Mother of God in whom the Earth at last discovers its face" (108).

It is this understanding of Christian "priesthood" (common and ordained) as a participation in "the great Christic sacrifice of reintegration" that, in my view, stands out in Clément's work.[51] Much could also be said of Clément's understanding of episcopacy and papacy. For Clément, who acknowledges his indebtedness to Afanasiev and Zizioulas,

> It is possible to conceive of a Church restructured around dynamic eucha-
> ristic communities, each gathered round its bishop, yet linked, through
> different groupings, to centers of unison and of communion: metropolitan
> sees, patriarchates (their composition based often on nationality, but more
> and more on common culture and destiny), with universal primacy ulti-
> mately pertaining to the bishop of Rome as the embodiment of both the
> presence of Peter and the charismatic inspiration of Paul.[52]

He allows the Bishop of Rome more authority than does Afanasiev, while like Afanasiev he underscores that the crucial step must be away from the juridical understanding of primacy: *"The one essential would be to pass from a situation where the hierarchical dovetailing of power structures has legal back-up, to one where tensions are held in balance without predetermined juridical solutions."*[53] Underlying his ecumenical reflection

---

51. Cf. for similar reflections Paul Evdokimov, *The Art of the Icon: A Theology of Beauty*, trans. Steven Bigham (French 1972; Redondo Beach, CA: Oakwood Publications, 1990), 114–15. Evdokimov writes, "Man assembles the disjointed cosmos in his love, introduces it into the Church, and opens it up to the therapeutic action of grace" (115). Likewise he says, "For the Fathers, the Church is the new Paradise in which the Spirit raises up 'trees of life,' that is, the sacraments and where the kingship of the saints over the cosmos is mystically restored. . . . The rhythms of nature, the flesh of this world, having been enrolled in the sacramental and liturgical action, integrate themselves into sacred history" (119).

52. Clément, *You Are Peter*, 92. Regarding the contributions of Zizioulas and Afanasiev, Clément writes, "In his magisterial book, *L'Eucharistie, l'évêque et l'unité de l'Église*, Zizioulas sees no other structure of grace in the Church than that of the episcopacy; the rest is the product of history. This is in contrast to this century's other great Orthodox ecclesiologist, Father Nicholas Afanassieff, who was a professor at the Institute Saint Serge of Paris: the latter descried that from the very earliest years of the Church, a greater 'priority of reception' was accorded to the church of Rome" (88). For discussion of Clément's relationship to Zizioulas's work, see Dulles, "A New Orthodox View of the Papacy," 351.

53. Ibid., 93–94 (emphasis his). He proposes "a link between the three forms of Peter's succession which we have indicated: the faith of the people of God, which can be expressed, on occasion, by a single prophet; the episcopacy in its collegiality, *in solidum*, as Cyprian of Carthage said; and finally the bishop of that church that was 'founded and constituted' by the apostles Peter and Paul. This does not mean that the pope must be merely a spokesman, like the sovereign in a constitutional monarchy who 'reigns without governing.' A certain right of appeal (to be clarified, as in the case of the canons of Serdica); the adoption of positions that, while not decisive, would carry great weight (like the celebrated 'Tomes' sent to ecumenical

on the "exercise of papal primacy" is Clément's commitment to a fundamental understanding of the priesthood as a *kenotic* service of unity to the world, in which the world, in and through Christ and his Spirit, is offered to the Father and thereby caught up into the pattern of divinization.[54] Priesthood (common and ordained), including the ministry of bishops and the particular ministry of the Bishop of Rome, finds its purpose in the participated work of divinization.

Summary

Afanasiev argues that "universal ecclesiology" originated in the third and fourth centuries due to the unfortunate influence of imperial notions of "primacy" over a universal jurisdiction. "Eucharistic ecclesiology" was grounded in the local eucharistic community as the fullness of the Body of Christ, but also recognized the "priority" of one local church, a priority in love to which belongs the "gift of witnessing" but not juridical power over other local churches. Afanasiev indicates that the entire post–Constantinian Church, and indeed the Church since Cyprian (even, to a certain degree, the Orthodox Church), has been under the spell of a radically false ecclesial vision.[55] For his part,

---

councils during the first millennium); the convocation of councils, which today the pope would be called upon to preside at and ratify—all these things would allow the pope to engage constructively both with moments of turbulence in public opinion and with hesitation and disagreements among the bishops" (93). See also Evdokimov's statement that "In the biblical view, salvation has nothing to do with legalism" (Evdokimov, *The Art of the Icon*, 116), but rather has to do with saving from death. Dulles judges that Clément's reading of Vatican I is too critical: see Dulles, "A New Orthodox View of the Papacy," 355–57.

54. See also Carl E. Braaten and Robert W. Jenson, eds., *In One Body through the Cross: The Princeton Proposal for Christian Unity* (Grand Rapids, MI: Eerdmans, 2003). The signatories of the Princeton Proposal exhibit concerns similar to Clément's: "In late modernity we fear unity, often with good reason. We cherish our particularity—our family and ethnic heritage, our established patterns of life and thought. We look with suspicion on the political and economic forces that impose homogeneity. We celebrate diversity and pluralism, sometimes as a good in its own right, because we fear the constraints of a single set of ideals. Christians, however, proclaim unity as a gift of God" (12). The Princeton Proposal goes on to add, "Unity is not merely a means to mission, but rather a constituent goal: God gathers his people precisely in order to bring unity to a divided humanity. If we accept division from other Christians as normal and inevitable, we turn away from the mission God has given us" (26). Cf. Pope John Paul II's encyclical *Ut Unum Sint* (1995); and Vatican II's *Unitatis Redintegratio*.

55. Cf. Vigen Guroian's warning, "Old forms of ethnocentrism, nationalism, and establishmentarianism prevail and divide Orthodox churches against one another and against other churches, viciously in some instances" (Guroian, "The Crisis of Orthodox Ecclesiology," in *The Ecumenical Future*, ed. Carl E. Braaten and Robert W. Jenson [Grand Rapids, MI: Eerdmans, 2004], 162–75, at 165).

Clément sets forth certain parameters within which an exercise of strictly non-juridical papal "primacy" would be acceptable. His focus is on the situation of the modern world, in which religious faith appears to be on the side of fragmentation, allowing economic and technological forces to place themselves at the vanguard of a disastrous "unity." Clément calls for a renewal of the sense of Christian priesthood (common and ordained) in which the entire cosmos is eucharistically re-integrated and lifted up to the Father in Christ and through the Holy Spirit. The key for Clément, as for Afanasiev, is that papacy (or the episcopate or priesthood) does not have to do with juridical power,[56] but rather has to do with the kenotic and eucharistic *auctoritas* in love that enables human beings to be truly free. While Clément is generally positive about the first millennium, he finds that

> Little by little, constrained alike by historical events and the logic of a juridical mindset deprived of the counter-balance of the East (the estrangement of the two halves of Christendom having deepened between the eleventh and the fourteenth centuries), Roman primacy showed signs of being contaminated by the problem of power: imperial power, to be precise, which, since the crowning of Charlemagne, had been seen as subordinate to pontifical power. . . . Already, in the works of Leo and its liturgical celebration of the apostles Peter and Paul, apostolic Rome appeared to have taken over from ancient imperial Rome. Was not the bishop of Rome now *pontifex maximus* just as the emperor had been?[57]

As a Western scholastic theologian, Thomas Aquinas might thus seem an unlikely source for constructive engagement with the insights

---

56. By contrast, see Joseph Ratzinger's insightful defense of "law" in his *Called to Communion*, 93–94. Ratzinger contrasts his position with that of Rudolph Sohm. For a summary of Rudolph Sohm's position within the context of liberal Protestantism, see Avery Dulles, sj, *A Church to Believe In: Discipleship and the Dynamics of Freedom* (New York: Crossroad, 1982), 23.

57. Clément, *You Are Peter*, 59. Clément also in certain respects bemoans "the senile systematizations of an Augustine" (102). Regarding the ecclesiology of the West in the second millennium, Clément's views are shared, to a large degree, by Yves Congar: see Congar, *Diversity and Communion*, trans. John Bowden (French 1982; Mystic, CT: Twenty-Third Publications, 1985), 29–33, although Congar praises the contributions of the twentieth-century popes.

into eucharistic ecclesial hierarchy set forth by these Orthodox thinkers.[58] As we will see, however, this is far from the case.[59]

AQUINAS ON THE PAPACY

The Papacy in the *Summa Contra Gentiles*

In his treatment of the papacy in the *Summa Contra Gentiles*, Aquinas places emphasis on the promises that Christ gave to Peter: "He said to Peter before His ascension: 'Feed My sheep' (John 21:17); and before His passion: 'Thou being once converted confirm thy brethren' (Luke 22:32); and to him alone did He promise: 'I will give to thee the keys of the kingdom of heaven' (Matt. 16:19)."[60] Yet why does not Christ

---

58. The relationship of Aquinas's theology to contemporary Orthodox theology has mainly been studied regarding the Trinity: see, e.g., Bruce Marshall, "*Ex Occidente Lux?* Aquinas and Eastern Orthodox Theology," *Modern Theology* 20 (2004): 23–50. Marshall notes that "Catholic as well as Protestant theology has for some time now made common cause with Orthodoxy against the common doctor. Finding a shared enemy in Aquinas has been a catalyst, and not just a result, of greater ecumenical agreement in theology" (23). In Marshall's view, by contrast, "Aquinas seems to offer considerable resources for coming to grips with problems Christian theologians—Orthodox, Catholic, and Protestant alike—now commonly regard as fundamental" (43).

59. Avery Dulles, sj's comments about the ecclesiology of Vatican II add a valuable perspective here. While noting that "the basic inspiration of Vatican II's ecclesiology is not scholastic or Thomistic" (Dulles, "The Church According to Thomas Aquinas," in his *A Church to Believe In*, 149–69, at 166)—because of Vatican II's use of "people of God" and its teaching on episcopal ordination and collegiality—Dulles notes that *Lumen Gentium* cites only Augustine more than Aquinas, and that Augustine provides the key source for Aquinas's ecclesiology. Thus "the theological authorities [including Cyprian] most used by Vatican II in its ecclesiology may be said to be Saint Thomas and the predecessors who inspired him. The post–Thomistic sources cited by Vatican II, including the official documents of popes and councils, were often dependent on Aquinas. Quite apart from the question of citations, one could list numerous Thomistic ecclesiological theses that were officially endorsed by Vatican II" (165). Dulles goes on to list twenty-four such theses, which he considers to "sufficiently demonstrate that Thomas' teaching on the Church remains very much alive in contemporary Catholicism" (166).

60. Thomas Aquinas, *Summa contra gentiles*, Book IV, ch. 76 (7). For a different approach to Aquinas's treatment of the papacy in the *Summa Contra Gentiles* see George Sabra, *Thomas Aquinas' Vision of the Church: Fundamentals of an Ecumenical Ecclesiology* (Mainz: Matthias-Grünewald-Verlag, 1987), 123–25, 129, which argues that "anti-Greek apologetics" (124) guides Aquinas's approach and emphasizes that Aquinas does not hold "that the pope is the source of sacramental power" (129). See also C. Ryan, "The Theology of Papal Primacy in Thomas Aquinas," in *The Religious Roles of the Papacy: Ideals and Realities, 1150–1300*, ed. Christopher Ryan (Toronto: Pontifical Institute of Mediaeval Studies, 1989), 193–225; Ulrich Hörst, op, "Das Wesen der *potestas clavium* nach Thomas von Aquin," *Münchener Theologische Zeitschrift* 11 (1960): 191–201; Serge-Thomas Bonino, op, "La place du pape dans l'Église selon saint Thomas

simply feed and strengthen the simple believer directly? The question, Aquinas suggests, does not take seriously enough the mediation that Christ requires of Peter. Christ feeds his sheep, and yet he also asks Peter to do so; Christ confirms and strengthens the members of the Church, and yet he asks Peter to do so; Christ alone unlocks salvation, and yet he gives to Peter the "keys." In other words, Christ feeds and strengthens the simple believer directly, but he does so through visible ministers. This visible, tangible action nourishes the invisible power of faith. Aquinas states,

> Christ Himself perfects all the sacraments of the Church: it is He who baptizes; it is He who forgives sins; it is He, the true priest, who offered Himself on the altar of the cross, and by whose power His body is daily consecrated on the altar—nevertheless, because He was not going to be with all the faithful in bodily presence, He chose ministers to dispense the things just mentioned to the faithful.[61]

Although Peter's office is unique, he participates in Christ's authority in accord with this pattern of visible sacramental mediation that Christ has willed for the strengthening of believers in the receptivity of love.[62]

Is it going too far to speak of Peter's mission as an "office"? Aquinas thinks that Christ's words to Peter have not solely Peter in mind, but rather the whole flock of believers, across the generations, that always needs feeding and strengthening. Here Aquinas quotes two additional biblical passages, "He [Christ] shall sit upon the throne of David and upon His kingdom to establish and strengthen it with

---

d'Aquin," *Revue Thomiste* 86 (1986): 392–422, which notes the importance of the "good shepherd" imagery for Aquinas.

61. *Summa Contra Gentiles*, IV, ch. 76 (7).

62. Drawing upon Henri de Lubac, Paul McPartlan comments that the pope's "worldwide responsibilities may themselves be understood in a eucharistic light, his task being that of holding together in harmony the witness given by the various local churches around the world to the one mystery of the Eucharist in which all participate" (McPartlan, "The Eucharist, the Church and Evangelization: The Influence of Henri de Lubac," *Communio* 23 [1996]: 776–85, at 781). McPartlan also finds that the *Catechism of the Catholic Church* (CCC) "gives a eucharistic view of the papacy: '*The whole Church is united with the offering and intercession of Christ.* Since he has the ministry of Peter in the Church, the *Pope* is united with every celebration of the Eucharist, wherein he is named as the sign and servant of the unity of the universal Church' (CCC 1369; italics in the original). At a time when Christians of many denominations are coming to a new appreciation of the importance of the Eucharist for the life of the Church, a eucharistic approach to the papacy has great ecumenical potential" (McPartlan, "The Eucharist, the Church and Evangelization," 781).

judgment and with justice from henceforth and forever" (Isaiah 9:7) and "Behold I am with you all days even to the consummation of the world" (Matthew 28:20). Since Christ will be with the apostles "all days even to the consummation of the world," his sharing of his authority with Peter belongs to how he envisions that his ongoing presence will take visible form. In other words, Christ's sharing his authority with Peter cannot be separated from the mode in which Christ wills to feed and strengthen his Church even after Peter's death. As Aquinas observes, therefore, "it cannot be said that, although He gave Peter this authority, it does not flow on to others."[63]

Yet, even if one accepts that Christ's words to Peter correspond intentionally to the needs of sacramental mediation (inclusive of the mediation of Christ's saving truth) in the Church through the generations, what happens if Peter, or any of those who follow him in the fulfillment of Peter's office, fails? If left to Peter, who abandoned Christ before Christ's Passion, are not believers ultimately left to the juridical wolf rather than to the Good Shepherd?[64]

---

63. *Summa contra gentiles*, IV, ch. 76 (8).

64. Focused on this fear, Francis Sullivan, sj, devotes a significant portion of his *Magisterium: Teaching Authority in the Catholic Church* (New York: Paulist Press, 1983) to exploration of when Catholics may legitimately dissent from authoritative teaching: see 109–73, 208–18. With *Humanae Vitae* in view, Sullivan notes that Catholic theologians have recently criticized the Church's ordinary magisterium because "on certain issues the official teaching of the Holy See (encyclicals, declarations of the CDF) seems to them to reflect, in too narrow a way, theological options which are not seen as representing the most widely respected theological opinion available in the Church today" (Sullivan, *Magisterium*, 210–11). He adds, "I do not see how one can deny to a theologian the right to express his criticism of what he perceives to be a strictly theological option, even when it is incorporated into a document of the ordinary magisterium. At the same time, of course, such criticism must be of the positive, not the destructive kind, and in choosing the manner and medium of its expression, the theologian has to observe the moral principle of personal and social responsibility," including "the religious respect which is due to the bearers of pastoral authority in the Church" (211). For Sullivan, much hinges upon the non-infallible character of the teaching of the "ordinary magisterium" (cf. 170–71). Sullivan returns to these themes in his *Creative Fidelity: Weighing and Interpreting the Documents of the Magisterium* (New York: Paulist Press, 1996), as well as his "Recent Theological Observations on Magisterial Documents and Public Dissent," *Theological Studies* 58 (1997): 509–15. On *Humanae Vitae* see Sullivan, *Creative Fidelity*, 105–6; on the ordinary magisterium, see especially chapters 7 and 10 of *Creative Fidelity*. Regarding John Paul II's appeal to the authority of the "ordinary and universal magisterium" in condemning abortion and euthanasia in his encyclical *Evangelium Vitae* (see Sullivan, *Creative Fidelity*, 154f.), Sullivan characteristically denies that these condemnations can be considered to have been infallibly taught. Regarding Pius IX's *Tuas Libenter* (December 21, 1863), which originates the term "ordinary magisterium," Sullivan refers to John P. Boyle, "The Ordinary Magisterium: Towards a History of the Concept," part 1, *Heythrop Journal* 20 (1979): 380–98; and part 2, 21 (1980): 14–29. See also Gaillardetz's "The Ordinary Universal Magisterium: Unresolved

In response, I would argue that Aquinas's insertion of Peter's mission of feeding and strengthening within the Church's sacramental mediation of Christ's nourishment has important implications. Christ wills for this sacramental mediation to be his mode of presence in the Church "all days even to the consummation of the world." This sacramental mediation will not fail; if it were to fail, then Christ's presence would fail. Belonging intrinsically to this sacramental mediation, Peter's office will not fail either. Aquinas does not treat Peter's office on its own, in terms of the exercise of power over the Church. Rather, Aquinas envisions Peter's office within the ecclesial structure of the mediation of Christ's nourishment to believers (inclusive of "all the truth" that the Holy Spirit will teach). Within this ecclesial structure of mediation, Peter's ministry is one of feeding and strengthening, a kenotic "power." In many ways Peter and his successors, as weak human beings, will fail; but the Petrine ministry of feeding and strengthening will not fail.

In other words, Aquinas addresses the papacy in a broader context—the whole structure of sacramental mediation—than is allowed for by the narratives of post–Constantinian decline. In this broader context, eucharistic unity with Christ the Mediator is the aim of all ecclesial mediation. Envisioning a unity-in-communion through faith and the sacraments of faith, Aquinas places his theology of the papacy within this theology of ecclesial unity.[65] Regarding unity of

---

Questions," *Theological Studies* 63 (2002): 447–71, which raises the concern that the (in his view misguided) effort to defend *Humanae Vitae* as "definitive" doctrine led to improper appeal to the "ordinary magisterium." In *Teaching with Authority* Gaillardetz concludes his section on the ordinary magisterium by observing that "appeal to this exercise of episcopal teaching is in fact ill-suited for resolving controversial points of doctrine" (187) and by limiting the definitive exercise of the ordinary magisterium to "central and noncontroversial teachings" (ibid.) such as the bodily resurrection of Jesus. See the helpful responses offered by Lawrence J. Welch, "Reply to Richard Gaillardetz on the Ordinary Universal Magisterium and to Francis Sullivan," *Theological Studies* 64 (2003): 598–609; idem, "On Recognizing Infallible Teachings of the Ordinary Magisterium: A Rejoinder to Francis Sullivan," *New Blackfriars* 86 (2005): 591–97; Avery Dulles, SJ, *Magisterium: Teacher and Guardian of the Faith* (Naples, FL: Sapientia Press, 2007). See also Richard Gaillardetz, *Witnesses to the Faith: Community, Infallibility, and the Ordinary Magisterium of Bishops* (New York: Paulist, 1992), along with Sullivan's review of this book in *Theological Studies* 54 (1993): 779.

65. For communion ecclesiology influenced by Aquinas, see Jerome Hamer, OP, *The Church Is a Communion* (French 1962; London: Geoffrey Chapman, 1964), as well as the reflections on wisdom, communion, and mystery—in light of a retrieval of the biblical and Christological roots of Aquinas's theology—in M.-J. Le Guillou, OP, *Le Christ et l'Église. Théologie du mystère* (Paris: Parole et Silence, 2005 [1963]). See more recently the work of Benoît-Dominique de La Soujeole, OP: *Introduction au mystère de l'Église* (Paris: Parole et Silence, 2006), especially

faith, Aquinas suggests that the centrifugal forces inherent in theological questioning are sufficiently strong that communities of Christians will not remain of one faith unless there is a mode of resolving questions regarding the content of faith. As Aquinas notes, "about matters of faith it happens that questions arise. A diversity of pronouncements, of course, would divide the Church, if it were not preserved in unity by the pronouncement of one."[66] Without this hierarchical structure of authority, eucharistic unity, which as we have seen requires unity of faith, would fragment.

Aquinas holds, then, that in his love for "the Church which He loved and for which He shed His blood," Christ ensures that unity of faith characterizes his Body.[67] The authority of the bishops flows from and serves the Church's sacramental unity.[68] The distinct role of the Bishop of Rome does the same: "Although people are set apart according to differing dioceses and states, yet, as the Church is one, so

---

chapter 4; *Le Sacrement de la communion. Essai d'ecclésiologie fondamentale* (Paris: Cerf, 1998); "Société et communion chez S. Thomas. Étude d'ecclésiologie," *Revue Thomiste* 90 (1990): 587–622; and "L'Église comme société et l'Église comme communion au deuxième concile du Vatican," *Revue Thomiste* 91 (1991): 219–58. Many theological streams contributed to the development of the diverse contemporary Catholic communion ecclesiologies whose fruit is Vatican II's Dogmatic Constitution *Lumen Gentium*. See Johann Adam Möhler, *Unity in the Church, or the Principle of Catholicism Presented in the Spirit of the Church Fathers of the First Three Centuries*, trans. Peter C. Erb (German 1825; Washington, DC: The Catholic University of America Press, 1996); idem, *Symbolism: Exposition of the Doctrinal Differences between Catholics and Protestants as Evidenced by Their Symbolical Writings*, trans. James Burton Robinson from the 4th ed. (German 1835; New York: Crossroad Herder, 1997; Henri de Lubac, *Catholicism*, trans. Lancelot C. Sheppard (French 1938; London: Burns and Oates, 1950); idem, *Corpus Mysticum: The Eucharist and the Church in the Middle Ages*, trans. Gemma Simmonds, Christopher Stephens, and Richard Price (French 1949; Notre Dame, IN: University of Notre Dame Press, 2007). See also Henri Donneaud, OP, "Note sur l'Église comme communion dans le Catéchisme de l'Église catholique," *Revue Thomiste* 95 (1995): 665–71.

66. *Summa contra gentiles* IV, ch. 76 (3), p. 291. On the centrifugal dynamisms within the Church, see also Roch Kereszty, O CIST, "A Catholic Response to W. Pannenberg Regarding the Petrine Ministry of the Bishop of Rome," *Communio* 25 (1998): 619–29, at 626–27; Klaus Schatz, SJ, *Papal Primacy*, 178, 182. Kereszty underscores the pope's role in preserving the Church's receptivity in "our encounter with the absolute authority of God's own Word" (628).

67. *Summa Contra Gentiles* IV, ch. 76 (3), p. 291.

68. Aquinas holds that the special authority of the bishops flows from the sacramental constitution of the Church, which requires that there be those competent to give the sacrament of orders. As the ones who oversee the sacrament of orders, the bishops oversee the Eucharist, even though the power of the bishops "does not exceed the power of the priest in the consecration of the body of Christ" (ibid., [1], p. 290). It follows that "the chief direction of the faithful belongs to the dignity of the bishops" (ibid.).

must the Christian people be one."[69] Again the question is not a solely juridical one, although Aquinas certainly grants the pope juridical authority for the common good of the Church.[70] Instead, as Yves Congar puts it, for Aquinas *"gubernatio* covers the whole activity by which a created or established reality is maintained in the truth that constitutes it and is directed to its goal."[71] In assenting to credal affirmations in faith, believers assent to the triune God, and do so by an intellectual power (faith) that is a sharing in the Trinitarian life. The pope's authority thus belongs to the broader *gubernatio* by which the triune God guides human beings to beatitude. Christ's love for his Mystical Body's interpersonal unity explains why there is "one who is at the head of the entire Church."[72]

Just as eucharistic unity participates in the heavenly liturgy of the saints, so also Aquinas draws a connection between the pilgrim

---

69. Ibid., (2), p. 290. On Aquinas's use of the phrase "populus Christianus" (with an eye to Vatican II's use of "people of God"), see Yves Congar, "'Ecclesia' et 'populus (fidelis)' dans l'ecclésiologie de S. Thomas," in *St. Thomas Aquinas, 1274–1974, Commemorative Studies*, vol. 1, ed. Armand Maurer (Toronto: Pontifical Institute of Medieval Studies, 1974), 159–73. See also Sabra, *Thomas Aquinas' Vision of the Church*, 43–49. Sabra argues that Aquinas's understanding of "populus" is overly shaped by its connection with "law and an ordered community" (ibid., 48), but I do not think that this connection is a problem.

70. Aquinas does so most strongly perhaps in his early work, *Contra impugnantes Dei cultum et religionem* (1256). As Ulrich Horst notes, in this work Aquinas affirms that since the pope can alter the positive law of the Church, the pope can give the mendicant orders license to teach in dioceses, since the pope has jurisdiction over the whole Church (Horst, "Thomas Aquinas on Papal Teaching Authority," in idem, *The Dominicans and the Pope: Papal Teaching Authority in the Medieval and Early Modern Thomist Tradition*, trans. James D. Mixson (Notre Dame, IN: University of Notre Dame Press, 2006, 9). On jurisdiction in Aquinas see also Joseph Lécuyer, "Aquinas' Conception of the Papal Primacy in Ecclesiastical Government," *Archives d'histoire doctrinale et littéraire du moyen âge* 40 (1973): 97–134; and Serge-Thomas Bonino, OP, "La place du pape dans l'Église selon saint Thomas d'Aquin," 398f.

71. Yves Congar, "Saint Thomas Aquinas and the Infallibility of the Papal Magisterium (*Summa Theol.*, II-II, q. 1, a. 10)," *The Thomist* 38 (1974): 81–105. Congar continues, "But the Church is founded by faith, it is the *'congregatio fidelium,'* according to a traditional definition to which St. Thomas gives a sense that is very precise and very rich in his synthesis. Thus the historical realization of this 'effectus gratiae' embraces, under the transcendent and infallible *gubernatio* of God, the First Truth who communicates himself in revealing himself, all the providentially disposed mediations of this communication, the prophets, sacred writers, Christ, the Apostles, and then, dependent on them, the Councils, Popes, doctors" (104). On "congregatio fidelium" in Aquinas see Congar, "Vision de l'Église chez S. Thomas d'Aquin," *Revue des sciences philosophiques et théologiques* 62 (1978): 523–41, at 525f.; Sabra, *Thomas Aquinas' Vision of the Church*, 50–58.

72. *Summa Contra Gentiles* IV, ch. 76 (4), p. 291. See also José Antonio Riestra, *Cristo y la plenitud del Cuerpo místico. Estudio sobre la cristología de santo Tomás de Aquino* (Pamplona: Universidad de Navarra, 1985).

Church as governed by the pope and the eschatological Church. Without supposing that the pilgrim Church is already the completed eschatological Church, nonetheless the unity of the former manifests the unity of the latter. For Aquinas, as for Clément, the pilgrim Church is a sign of the eschatological unity of humankind in Christ's love. Aquinas observes that the pilgrim Church or Church militant "derives from the triumphant Church by exemplarity; hence, John in the Apocalypse (21:2) saw 'Jerusalem coming down out of heaven'; and Moses was told to make everything 'according to the pattern that was shewn thee in the mount' (Exod. 25:40; 26:30)."[73]

The earthly "Jerusalem," the Church, should manifest an ordering to the heavenly pattern. In the heavenly Jerusalem's full and complete unity, the triune God is all in all: "in the triumphant Church one presides, the one who presides over the entire universe—namely, God—for we read in the Apocalypse (21:3): 'They shall be His people and God Himself with them shall be their God.' "[74] As the visible Head of the Church, Jesus Christ reveals this invisible reality: "And the people of Judah and the people of Israel shall be gathered together, and they shall appoint for themselves one head" (Hos 1:11). In this respect, Aquinas quotes Jesus' words in John 10:16, shortly after Jesus proclaims himself the Good Shepherd: "So there shall be one flock, one shepherd."[75] Yet Jesus prepares for his ascension by sharing his authority as the one Shepherd with Peter, so that the invisible divine pattern may still be represented by the visible: "Hence it is that He said to Peter before his ascension: 'Feed my sheep' (John 21:17)."[76] By giving visible unity to the pilgrim Church's ordering as

---

73. *Summa Contra Gentiles*, IV, 76 (5), p. 291.

74. Ibid.

75. Ibid., (6).

76. Ibid., (7). The Orthodox theologian Georges Florovsky does not do justice to Catholic theology in this regard. He writes, "In Roman consciousness, the feeling that through his Ascension into heaven, Christ truly and directly (albeit invisibly) abides and governs in the 'historical' and earthly Church, has not been completely fortified and expressed. It is as if, in the Ascension, he left and exited from history until the Second Coming (Parousia), until his return. It is as if history had been abandoned, as if little had changed in history. This can be called 'hyper-historicism.' Hence the need for and possibility of Christ's well-known replacement in history—the idea of a 'deputy' " (Florovsky, "Rome, the Reformation, and Orthodoxy," trans. Linda Morris, in *Ecumenism II: A Historical Approach*, Collected Works of Georges Florovsky, vol. 14, ed. Richard S. Haugh [Vaduz: Büchervertriebsanstalt, 1989], 52–58, at 57). The same view can be found in the work of Dumitru Stăniloae and elsewhere: see Dănuţ

the one shepherd "in [Christ's] place,"[77] the pope serves as a sign, willed by Christ and guided by his Spirit, of the eschatological unity of the Church in God.[78] In this way the pilgrim Church, even after Christ's Ascension, is a sacramental sign of the eschatological Church, in whose fullness the pilgrim Church already participates by unity with the triune God through faith, hope, and love.

The Papacy in the *Summa Theologiae*

The references to the papacy in the *Summa Theologiae* likewise revolve around the unity of faith and sacraments in the pilgrim Church. In discussing Christ's grace, Aquinas explores the nature of the Church as Christ's mystical body. Quoting Ephesians 1:22, "he [the Father] has put all things under his [Christ's] feet and has made him the head over all things for the church, which is his body," Aquinas suggests that Saint Paul's analogous use of the human "head" relies upon three aspects that belong to the role of the head in the human body; namely, "order, perfection, and power."[79] Christ's grace is first in the "order" of grace because "on account of His nearness to God His grace is the highest and first, though not in time, since all have received grace on account of His grace, according to Rom. viii. 29: *For whom He foreknew, He also predestinated to be made conformable to the image of His Son, that He might be the first-born amongst many brethren.*"[80] The order of grace is the Church, comprising the "head" and "members" of Christ's "body." Christ is the head because the grace of the Holy Spirit

---

Mănăstireanu, "Dumitru Stăniloae's Theology of Ministry," in *Dumitru Stăniloae: Tradition and Modernity in Theology*, 126–44, at 133, fn. 28.

77. *Summa Contra Gentiles*, IV, 76 (7), p. 291.

78. Ibid., (5). On the Petrine "ministry of unity," see also, in light of *Ut Unum Sint*, Wolfhart Pannenberg, "A Lutheran's Reflections on the Petrine Ministry of the Bishop of Rome," trans. Adrian Walker, *Communio* 25 (1998): 604–18; with a valuable response by Roch Kereszty, o cist, "A Catholic Response to W. Pannenberg Regarding the Petrine Ministry of the Bishop of Rome," *Communio* 25 (1998): 619–29; George Lindbeck, "The Church," in *Keeping the Faith: Essays to Mark the Centenary of Lux Mundi*, ed. Geoffrey Wainwright (Allison Park, PA: Pickwick Publications, 1998), 199–201; Geoffrey Wainwright, "A Primatial Ministry of Unity in a Synodical and Conciliar Context," *One in Christ* 38 (2003): 3–25; J. Robert Wright, "The Possible Contribution of Papal Authority to Church Unity: An Anglican/Episcopalian Perspective," in *The Ecumenical Future*, ed. Carl E. Braaten and Robert W. Jenson (Grand Rapids, MI: Eerdmans, 2004), 138–44.

79. *Summa Theologiae* (ST) III, q. 8, a. 1, *sed contra* and *corpus*.

80. Ibid., *corpus*.

flows from Christ to others and configures us to his image so that we become adopted sons in the Son. Second, as the incarnate Word, Christ receives in his human nature the absolute fullness of grace, which is the Holy Spirit's gift of created sharing in the Trinitarian life. In this way Christ is head because of the perfection of his grace. Third, the grace of the Holy Spirit in Christ gives Christ the power to bestow grace upon us; like the head of the human body, Christ moves and directs the members. Regarding these latter two aspects of Christ's grace of headship, Aquinas quotes John 1:14,16: "And the Word became flesh and dwelt among us, full of grace and truth; we have beheld his glory, glory as of the only Son from the Father. . . . And from his fullness have we all received, grace upon grace."[81]

If Christ's headship in the Church is so profound, eliciting our personal and relational response, what need is there for a pope? Surely one head suffices? Aquinas agrees that there is no head of the Church but Jesus Christ. It is Jesus alone, by his Spirit, who nourishes and unites the Church. Here he cites Colossians 2:19, where Paul exhorts believers to hold "fast to the Head [Christ], from whom the whole body, nourished and knit together through its joints and ligaments,

---

81. Ibid. Avery Dulles, sj, perceptively observes, "In no context does Aquinas discuss the Church more explicitly than when he treats of the grace of Christ" (Dulles, "The Church According to Thomas Aquinas," in *A Church to Believe In* [New York: Crossroad, 1985], 149–69, at 156). For the connection between Aquinas's theology of Christ's grace of headship and contemporary "communion ecclesiology," see, e.g., Pedro Rodríguez, "La Iglesia como 'communio' en la perspective de la gracia capital de Cristo," in *Problemi teologici alla luce dell' Aquinate*, ed. Pontificia Accademia di San Tommaso d'Aquino (Vatican City: Libreria Editrice Vaticana, 1991), 296–303; Janez Vodopivec, "La 'gratia capitis' in San Tommaso in relazione all'ecclesiologia di comunione," in *Prospettive teologiche moderne*, ed. Pontificia Accademia di S. Tommaso (Vatican City: Libreria Editrice Vaticana, 1981), 327–38. See also Colman E. O'Neill, op, "St. Thomas on the Membership of the Church," *The Thomist* 27 (1963): 88–140, which has in view Pius XII's encyclical *Mystici Corporis* (1943). On Aquinas's use of "corpus Christi mysticum," see also Herwi Rikhof, "*Corpus Christi Mysticum*. An Inquiry into Thomas Aquinas' Use of a Term," *Bijdragen* 37 (1976): 149–71; Sabra, *Thomas Aquinas' Vision of the Church*, 58–68. As these studies make clear, Hans Urs von Balthasar's assessment of Aquinas's theology, in his early work *The Theology of Karl Barth*, is mistaken: "We had earlier spoken of the treatises that interested Aquinas the most. Among these would *not* be the three central theological tractates: De Deo trino, which gave Thomas an excellent formal training but which had no further role to play in shaping the course of his *Summa*; De Christo, which Thomas wrote with extraordinary care but introduced only after he had treated the whole of natural-supernatural ontology, epistemology and ethics in the Tertia Pars; and De Ecclesia, which never did have much of an impact, either on Thomas himself or on any other theologian of his time" (von Balthasar, *The Theology of Karl Barth: Exposition and Interpretation*, trans. Edward T. Oakes, sj [German 1951; San Francisco: Ignatius Press, 1992], 263).

grows with a growth that is from God."[82] Yet Aquinas also makes an important distinction by observing that the head of the body works both interiorly ("inasmuch as motive and sensitive force flow from the head to the other members") and exteriorly ("inasmuch as by sight and the senses, which are rooted in the head, man is guided in his exterior acts").[83]

Applying this distinction to Christ's headship, certainly no one can share in Christ's interior nourishment and guidance of his members. As Aquinas says, only Christ's "manhood, through its union with the Godhead, has the power of justifying."[84] The interior nourishment of believers can be done by Christ alone, and in this sense Christ's headship cannot be shared in any way. With respect to the exterior guidance, on the other hand, Christ's headship can be shared: "the influence over the members of the Church, as regards their exterior guidance, can belong to others, and in this way others may be called heads of the Church."[85]

Even so, this exterior guidance can only be shared in a limited sense. Aquinas recounts two limits to episcopal and papal participation in Christ's exterior guidance of the Church. First, Christ guides the Church as head in every place and time, as well as in eternal life; while bishops and popes participate in the guiding of the Church only in particular places and times, and they do not retain their leadership role in eternal life. Second, Christ's headship (in its exterior dimension) is intrinsic to him "by His own power and authority."[86] By contrast,

---

82. ST III, q. 8, a. 6, *sed contra*.

83. ST III, q. 8, a. 6.

84. Ibid.

85. Ibid.; cf. Serge-Thomas Bonino, OP, "The Role of the Apostles in the Communication of Revelation according to the *Lectura super Ioannem* of St. Thomas Aquinas," 344–45. For further discussion see Rikhof, "Thomas on the Church," 217–18. Aquinas draws a parallel between this use of "head" and the use of "shepherd" explained in Augustine's *Tractates on John* (John 10): "As Augustine says (*Tract.* xlvi, *in Joan.*): *If the rulers of the Church are Shepherds, how is there one Shepherd, except that all these are members of one Shepherd?* So likewise others may be called foundations and heads, inasmuch as they are members of the one Head and Foundation. Nevertheless, as Augustine says (*Tract.* xlvii), *He gave to His members to be shepherds; yet none of us calleth himself the Door. He kept this for himself alone.* And this because by door is implied the principal authority, inasmuch as it is by the door that all enter the house; and it is Christ alone by *Whom also we have access . . . into this grace, wherein we stand* (Rom. v. 2); but by the other names above-mentioned [head, foundation, shepherd] there may be implied not merely the principal but also the secondary authority" (ST III, q. 8, a. 6, ad 3).

86. ST III, q. 8, a. 6.

each bishop or pope possesses the exterior dimension of headship extrinsically rather than intrinsically; Christ through the Holy Spirit enables him to act *in persona Christi*. Aquinas states in this regard that "others [bishops and popes] are called heads, as taking Christ's place, according to 2 Cor. ii. 10, *For what I have pardoned, if I have pardoned anything, for your sakes I have done it in the person of Christ,* and v. 20, *For Christ therefore we are ambassadors, God, as it were, exhorting by us.*"[87] In the person of Christ, Christ's ministers act as "heads" in the Church so as to build up the Church's unity in faith and sacraments. They do not thereby replace Christ as head of the Church, but they share in a limited fashion in his cruciform grace of headship.[88]

Thus, when Christ vivifies the Church by acting interiorly in his members through the grace of the Holy Spirit, this interior nourishment is not strictly invisible. Christ's interior nourishment of his members takes visible form through his exterior guidance, which he accomplishes partly by enabling his ministers to act sacramentally in his person, as sharers in his authority. The task of this exterior work is to make manifest and to strengthen the interior unity of the Church. In other words, the ministry of the bishops and the pope exists to serve and manifest visibly the interior nourishment of the graced community. This service occurs notably in the tasks of teaching the content of faith and of administering the Church's sacramental life. As Saint Paul says in Romans 10:14–15, "But how are men to call upon him in whom they have not believed? And how are they to believe in him of

---

87. ST III, q. 8, a. 6. On the pope as the "head" of the Church, see also Henri de Lubac, sj, *The Splendor of the Church*, 270–73. De Lubac responds to the criticism set forth by the Orthodox theologian A. S. Khomiakov in his *L'Église latine et le Protestantisme au point de vue de l'Église d'orient* (1872). On Khomiakov's theology, including his influential theory of "sobornost" (catholicity) and the relationship of his thought to that of Möhler, see the summary provided by Georges Florovsky, *Ways of Russian Theology, Part Two*, trans. Robert L. Nichols, vol. 6 in Florovsky's *Collected Works*, ed. Richard S. Haugh (Vaduz: Büchervertriebsanstalt, 1987), 42–53.

88. Aquinas's choice of 2 Corinthians here emphasizes the cruciform character of episcopal and papal "headship." For discussion of 2 Corinthians see Timothy B. Savage, *Power through Weakness: Paul's Understanding of the Christian Ministry in 2 Corinthians* (Cambridge: Cambridge University Press, 1996). In general, Aquinas's guiding biblical texts with regard to Christ's grace of headship are Colossians 2:19 ("holding fast to the Head [Christ], from whom the whole body, nourished and knit together through its joints and ligaments, grows with a growth that is from God"), John 1:14, 16 ("And the Word became flesh and dwelt among us, full of grace and truth; we have beheld his glory, glory as of the only Son from the Father"), and Romans 8:29 ("For those whom he foreknew he also predestined to be conformed to the image of his Son").

whom they have never heard? And how are they to hear without a preacher? And how can men preach unless they are sent?" Aquinas quotes this passage in the context of affirming that the grace of the Holy Spirit makes it possible for human beings to do what they could not do if left solely to their own resources.[89]

Certainly when exterior preachers are lacking, Christ as the divine Word can teach human beings solely interiorly.[90] Indeed, the New Law of Christ is primarily the interior operation of the grace of the Holy Spirit, and Aquinas points out that "the letter, even of the Gospel, would kill, unless there were the inward presence of the healing grace of faith."[91] Yet the exterior work, in which Christ gives his ministers a sacramental participation, is hardly useless or negligible, even if it is in a sense secondary. As Aquinas observes, "the New Law contains certain things that dispose us to receive the grace of the Holy Spirit, and pertaining to the use of that grace, . . . and the faithful need to be instructed concerning them, both by word and writing, both as to what they should believe and as to what they should do."[92] These things were preached by the apostles and written down in the New Testament, and they include the sacraments.

Although "the New Law consists chiefly in the grace of the Holy Spirit," we receive this grace through the incarnate Word. Given this principle of incarnation, Aquinas observes that "it was becoming that the grace which flows from the incarnate Word should be given to us by means of certain external sensible objects."[93] While the New Law sacraments in themselves cause grace and so pertain to Christ's interior work,[94] the administration of the sacraments, like the authoritative teaching of the truths of the Gospel, has to do with the "exterior

---

89. ST II-II, q. 2, a. 5, obj. 1; cf. ad 1.

90. Aquinas states, "If, however, some [Gentiles] were saved without receiving any revelation, they were not saved without faith in a Mediator, for, though they did not believe in Him explicitly, they did, nevertheless, have implicit faith through believing in Divine providence, since they believed that God would deliver mankind in whatever way was pleasing to Him, and according to the revelation of the Spirit to those who knew the truth, as stated in Job xxxv. 11: *Who teacheth us more than the beasts of the earth*" (ST II-II, q. 2, a. 7, ad 3).

91. ST I-II, q. 106, a.2; cf. aa. 1–3.

92. ST I-II, q. 106, a. 1.

93. ST I-II, q. 107, a. 1.

94. See ST III, q. 62, a. 1.

guidance" of believers by Christ.[95] It follows that Christ shares both the administration of the sacraments and the authoritative teaching of the Gospel with his ministers, even though, as we saw earlier, "Christ Himself perfects all the sacraments of the Church."[96] Again, Christ is the sole head, but through the Holy Spirit he enables the bishops and pope to participate in this headship regarding its exterior power.

As the successors of the apostles, then, the bishops and pope have authority in the Church, an authority that is comprehensible within the framework of Christ's grace of headship and of the nourishment that flows from Christ to believers. Aquinas points out that when Paul urges the Corinthians to imitate Paul (1 Corinthians 4:16), this is justified by Paul's participation in Christ's divine teaching: "it is not human knowledge, but the Divine truth that is the rule of faith."[97] Even if they get caught up in the erudite errors of theologians, Aquinas notes, simple believers will not go astray so long as they adhere to the Church above such theologians, because "the faith of the universal Church . . . cannot err, since Our Lord said (Luke xxii. 32): *I have*

---

95. Contrast this understanding with Thomas Rausch's remark, "The Second Vatican Council changed the way Roman Catholics understand their Church. Prior to Vatican II, most Catholics ascribed to the Church and its official ministers an authority that today they would give only to God. There was no distinction between God's will and Church pronouncement, particularly in the area of moral theology. To ignore a Church prohibition was to sin against God. Avery Dulles terms this understanding of the Church, stressing its structures of governance and its authority to impose doctrine and discipline with spiritual sanctions, an 'institutional' model of Church. While a Church will always have an institutional dimension, the almost exclusively institutional, or perhaps more accurately, juridical understanding of the Catholic Church was to change considerably with the council" (Rausch, *Towards a Truly Catholic Church*, 15). For Aquinas, God communicates through the ecclesial hierarchy's "exterior guidance," the doctrinal and moral truths of life in Christ, whereas Rausch seeks to bypass this ecclesial mediation and "give only to God" the authority to teach, "particularly in the area of moral theology." The result is that ecclesial mediation (gifting/receptivity) is cut off from Christian moral agency, which becomes a matter between God and the individual. Rausch refers to Dulles's *Models of the Church* (Garden City, NY: Doubleday, 1974), 35, but I do not think that Rausch's vision of post–Vatican II ecclesiology accords with that of Dulles. In a concluding chapter added to the 1987 Doubleday edition of *Models of the Church*, Dulles observes, "Some of the objections to the institutional model can be answered if the institution is understood not in the abstractions of modern sociology, but in terms of what God 'instituted' in Christ" (205). To illustrate what he means, he then proposes the model of "community of disciples" in which "the Church mediates the call of Christ and makes available the word of God and the sacraments, without which discipleship would scarcely be possible" (226).

96. *Summa Contra Gentiles*, IV, 76 (7), p. 292.

97. ST II-II, q. 2, a. 6, ad 3.

prayed for thee, Peter, *that thy faith fail not.*"[98] Furthermore, when Christ shares his grace of headship regarding its exterior power, he does so in prayer—that is, in accord with the divine (providential) wisdom and will. In this prayer one sees Christ's love for his "little ones" (Matthew 10:42; 18:14; cf. Matthew 11:25–27). Grace, not human erudition, is here the rule. Since the foundation of the papal ministry is Christ's grace of headship and Christ's prayer, Aquinas sees the papal ministry as the antidote to the inevitability of theological divisions.

Aquinas thus identifies as a loss of faith the refusal to "adhere, as to an infallible and Divine rule, to the teaching of the Church, which proceeds from the First Truth manifested in Holy Writ."[99] Since God's revelation to human beings is inseparable from the Church, individual believers, no matter how erudite theologically, cannot determine for themselves, according to their own wisdom, the content of faith. As we noted in chapter 1, Aquinas remarks of those members of the Church who reject the Church's mediation of Christ's saving truth: "if, of the things taught by the Church, he holds what he chooses to hold, and rejects what he chooses to reject, he no longer adheres to the teaching of the Church as to an infallible rule, but to his own will."[100]

The pope, however, is a member of the Church. Does not the pope, when called upon to pronounce authoritatively on disputed doctrine, fall precisely into the attitude described by Aquinas as heretical; namely, that of holding "what he chooses to hold" and determining doctrine by his own wisdom and will? As in the *Summa Contra Gentiles*, Aquinas appeals in the *Summa Theologiae* to Christ's

---

98. Ibid. Cf. the biblical perspectives in Kasper, *The Petrine Ministry*: Joachim Gnilka (Catholic), "The Ministry of Peter—New Testament Foundations," 24–36; and Theodore Stylianopoulos (Orthodox), "Concerning the Biblical Foundation of Primacy," 37–64. Gnilka affirms the uniqueness of Peter's role in the New Testament but notes that the texts "are far from thinking in the constitutional and juridical terms in which many people today are accustomed to think" ("The Ministry of Peter," 25). Stylianopoulos concludes that while "the New Testament bears witness to a rich ecclesiology of communion," the New Testament "gives evidence of no inkling whatever that the unity of the Church *requires* a single, universal leader other than Christ" ("Concerning the Biblical Foundation of Primacy," 62). He grants that the New Testament data allow for "a historically developed and universally acknowledged Petrine office as an option, but one fully based on the principles of shared authority, love, and service, rather than on exclusive status, rights, and jurisdiction," and he prefers Orthodoxy's option in favor of "the local bishop and the universal episcopate as signs and instruments of unity" (63).

99. ST II-II, q. 5, a. 3.

100. Ibid.

prayer for Peter in Luke 22:32. Peter's ministry depends not upon Peter, but radically upon the grace of the Holy Spirit given according to Christ's wisdom and will. Christ wills in the Holy Spirit that the pope be "that authority which is empowered to decide matters of faith finally, so that they may be held by all with unshaken faith."[101] Such "unshaken faith" in the pope's decision with respect to matters of faith does not rest on anticipation of the pope's holiness or erudition. Instead, this faith rests on Christ and the Holy Spirit, not on Peter, on the pope, or on any merely human theological expert. In light of Christ's prayer in the Holy Spirit, believers may safely bring to the pope "the more important and more difficult questions that arise in the Church."[102]

In turn, the pope, when faced with a decision on a difficult question, decides not as a private person but as one who possesses a limited participation, due to Christ and the Holy Spirit, in Christ's grace of headship.[103] This grace enables the pope to speak, despite his manifold and evident human limitations, on behalf of Christ's body, the Church. Within the framework of Christ's grace and prayer, the pope's confirmation of the true content of *sacra doctrina* serves the unity of the mystical body. It is for this unity in Christ the one Mediator, Aquinas says, that Jesus established the Petrine ministry: "there should be but one faith of the whole Church, according to 1 Cor. i. 10: *That you all speak the same thing, and that there be no schisms among you*: and this cannot be secured unless any question of faith that may arise be decided by him who presides over the whole Church, so that the whole Church may hold firmly to his decision."[104] Christ enables the pope to share in the exterior power of the head, but this sharing depends upon Christ's more profound interior direction of the

---

101. ST II-II, q. 1, a. 10.

102. Ibid., citing Gratian's *Decretum*, Dist. xvii, Canon 5. For further discussion see Bonino, "La place du pape dans l'Église selon saint Thomas d'Aquin," 409f. Cf. the debate over Maximus the Confessor's view of the pope's role: Adam G. Cooper, "St. Maximus the Confessor on Priesthood, Hierarchy, and Rome," *Pro Ecclesia* 10 (2001): 346–67; Jean-Claude Larchet, "The Question of the Roman Primacy in the Thought of Saint Maximus the Confessor," in Kasper, *The Petrine Ministry: Catholics and Orthodox in Dialogue*, 188–209. Larchet argues that Maximus's position offers Orthodoxy "a strong reminder of the church of Rome's essential role" (208), but Larchet rules out the idea that the pope embodies the "Petrine office" or serves as the "vicar of Christ."

103. Drawing upon and clarifying Congar, Bonino comments that "the pope represents first Christ, and it is solely in representing the Head of the Church that, in a certain way, he represents the Church" ("La place du pape dans l'Église selon saint Thomas d'Aquin," 413).

104. ST II-II, q. 1, a. 10.

Church. Thus the dual aspect of Christ's grace of headship grounds the efficacy of his prayer, that through Peter the Holy Spirit will sustain the Church's unity in truth. The "primacy" of the pope is indeed a "priority" in love (Afanasiev), but this love is Christ's in the Holy Spirit, not the achievement of any particular person or local church.[105]

Since faith is joined to the sacraments of faith, the references to the pope in the *Summa Theologiae* that do not have to do with faith cluster around the sacraments. For example, with regard to the question of whether priests should celebrate the sacrament-sacrifice of the Eucharist several times a day (on the supposition that the increased frequency would increase its spiritual fruits), Aquinas quotes the authority of Pope Alexander II and Pope Innocent III against this practice.[106] Similarly, regarding the sign character of the practice of breaking the sacramental body of Christ into three parts, he quotes Pope Sergius to the effect that the three parts indicate the three states of Christ's mystical Body: in heaven, on earth, and in the grave.[107] Regarding the issue of reserving the consecrated host, he quotes Pope Clement I, and with respect to the number of people who should be present at the celebration of the Eucharist, he quotes Pope Soter.[108] Treating what to do if some of Christ's sacramental blood falls to the ground, he quotes Pope Pius I.[109] Here, as always, Aquinas places the power of the pope in the context of Christ's nourishment of believers in the Holy Spirit. The pope's primacy serves the upbuilding of the whole community of believers in eucharistic faith and love.[110]

---

105. See also Reinhard Hütter's Lutheran response to *Ut Unum Sint*, "Ecumenism and Christian Unity—Abstract Reunification or Living Concord? A Lutheran Approach to the Encyclical '*Ut Unum Sint*—That They May Be One,'" trans. Beth A. Schlegel, *Pro Ecclesia* 7 (1998): 186–98. Hütter's ecumenical journey eventually brought him into the Catholic Church, as did that of another notable Lutheran ecclesiologist, Ola Tjørhom. See Tjørhom, *Visible Church—Visible Unity: Ecumenical Ecclesiology and "The Great Tradition of the Church"* (Collegeville, MN: Liturgical Press, 2004); idem, "Catholic Faith outside the Catholic Church: An Ecumenical Challenge," *Pro Ecclesia* 13 (2004): 261–74.

106. ST III, q. 83, a. 2, ad 5.

107. ST III, q. 83, a. 5, and 8. In passing, he affirms here the Assumption of the Virgin Mary into heaven. Lest this seem an odd place for Aquinas to discuss the Virgin Mary, see Yves Congar, *Christ, Our Lady and the Church: A Study in Eirenic Theology*, trans. Henry St. John, OP (London: Longmans, Green and Co., 1957).

108. ST III, q. 83, a. 5, ad 11 and ad 12.

109. ST III, q. 83, a. 6, ad 7.

110. Compare Thomas O'Meara, OP's recent strictures against Aquinas's ecclesiology. O'Meara cautions, "The thirteenth century was molded by the neo–Platonic theology of

CONCLUSION

Recall once more the positions of Afanasiev and Clément. Afanasiev argues that the local eucharistic community is the fullness of the Body of Christ, and therefore all bishops are strictly equals, although one local church may possess a unique, non-juridical "gift of witnessing" due to priority in love. Clément emphasizes that papal "primacy" can only be conceivable outside of juridical frameworks, and he focuses upon the need in the modern world to renew awareness of the hierarchical priesthood as assisting in the eucharistic unification of the cosmos in Christ.[111] We might add the similar view of Paul Evdokimov, for

ecclesial authority, namely, hierarchy. In that society the pattern of descending levels of beings or offices molded mysticism, aesthetics, and politics. Because the sources and antiquity of this theology (Plato, and a Dionysius understood to be both the convert of Areopagus and the bishop of Paris) were unassailable, hierarchy was a structural model for much of medieval public and ecclesiastical life. Church offices (mirroring those of the angels) were rungs on a ladder of descending illuminations; the lower was perfected and directed by actions moving downwards but not upwards. . . . Historicity was not prominent, as knowledge of and belief in the transcendent held sway. So ministerial and magisterial aspects of the church were constrained by a vertical hierarchy" (Thomas F. O'Meara, OP, *Thomas Aquinas, Theologian* [Notre Dame, IN: University of Notre Dame Press, 1997], 139–40). Likewise, O'Meara asks in a recent article: "What can we learn from Aquinas' ecclesiology? Little, if we are looking for a contemporary theology of diocesan offices, but quite a bit if we look beneath and find an ecclesial theology of intimations" (O'Meara, "Theology of the Church," in *The Theology of Thomas Aquinas*, ed. Rik Van Nieuwenhove and Joseph Wawrykow [Notre Dame, IN: University of Notre Dame Press, 2005], 303–25, at 320). Regarding these "intimations," he grants that "in Aquinas' theology the motifs of Spirit and individuality were never fully captured by a hierarchical and feudal clericalism" (319). O'Meara claims Congar in support of his views, but I do not think that this does justice to the context and content of Congar's work: see O'Meara, "Beyond Hierarchology: Johann Adam Möhler and Yves Congar," in *The Legacy of the Tübingen School*, ed. Michael D. Himes and Donald Dietrich (New York: Crossroad, 1997), 173–91; as well as O'Meara's "Yves Congar: Theologian of Grace in a Wide World," in *Yves Congar: Theologian of the Church*, ed. Gabriel Flynn (Louvain: Peeters, 2005), 371–99, which shows that O'Meara's principal source is Rahner. Paul McPartlan takes a similar view of medieval ecclesiology: "Scholasticism envisaged the Church as a pyramid. At the bottom were the lay-people for whom the priests said Mass. Governing priests and people were the bishops, who, in turn, received their jurisdiction from the pope at the top of the pyramid" (McPartlan, *Sacrament of Salvation: An Introduction to Eucharistic Ecclesiology* [Edinburgh: T. & T. Clark, 1995], 40). Such accounts do not do justice to the theological dimensions of ecclesial hierarchy.

111. Despite their rhetorical condemnation of "juridical" elements, one doubts that Afanasiev or Clément would go as far as proposing, in Susan K. Wood's words, that "it is precisely as sacrament, not as juridical institution, that the Church is the body of Christ" (Wood, *Spiritual Exegesis and the Church in the Theology of Henri de Lubac* [Grand Rapids, MI: Eerdmans, 1998], 152). Wood immediately clarifies her meaning: "The full revelation of the 'body of Christ,' that is, members united to the head, Christ, will occur in the eschaton" (ibid.). The problem is that if the "juridical institution" is not the "body of Christ" (even if not co-extensive with the Body of Christ), then the visibility of the Church is lost.

whom "the sacred space of the Church penetrates cosmic space and spreads out to the 'holy cities,' "[112] so long as this spiritualization is not reified: "Rome and Jerusalem are found in every eucharistic gathering place where the Church manifests itself. In the same way, Peter's chair is contained in the chair of every bishop."[113]

For his part, Aquinas emphasizes that it is in the Eucharist that the Holy Spirit achieves the Church's unity in faith and love, and that the pope serves this eucharistic unity. In this regard, Aquinas's approach connects with Clément's view of ecclesial hierarchy as assisting in the eucharistic unification of the cosmos. Does Aquinas's theology of the papacy, however, fall into what Afanasiev calls "universal ecclesiology" as well as the juridicism criticized by both Zizioulas and Clément? I think the answer is no. Rather, Aquinas approaches the Petrine role of the Bishop of Rome not through an analysis of the juridical needs of the universal Church, but through a meditation on Christ's grace of headship and the modes in which Christ (as the one Mediator) shares it. The source of the Church's unity is neither the Bishop of Rome nor any other bishop, but is Christ's grace of headship. Regarding the "office" of Peter with the Church, Aquinas appeals not to a juridical or functionalist framework, but specifically to Christ's prayer for Peter. Everything leads back to Christ the Head and to his prayer, by which he allows the Bishop of Rome (extrinsically, not intrinsically) to share in the exterior operation of his grace of headship. Aquinas thus begins not from the standpoint of a universal institution that must be run in a sane and functional manner, but from the standpoint of the Person and graced humanity of Jesus Christ who, in the Holy Spirit, lovingly shares himself with his Church.

---

112. Evdokimov, *The Art of the Icon*, 119.

113. Ibid., 120. Elsewhere Evdokimov states, "The authority conferred upon the twelve Apostles and their successors has been placed within the community of the Church and never above it. The identification of the Church with Christ, the Body with the Head, makes impossible all human authority over the People of God, for this would be to place a human authority over Christ himself. Since the time of St Irenaeus, the episcopate is not a power over the Church, but the expression of her very nature. The sacramental identity and charism of the truth of the bishops is not a personal infallibility but that of the local church, identified with the Church in her entirety" (Evdokimov, "Freedom and Authority," in *In the World, of the Church: A Paul Evdokimov Reader*, ed. and trans. Michael Plekon and Alexis Vinogradov [Crestwood, NY: St. Vladimir's Seminary Press, 2001], 217–30, at 229).

Yves Congar rightly observes with regard to Aquinas's theology of the Church that "the Eucharist is the final cause of all else," and that the hierarchy receives "powers over souls . . . solely from the power or ministry which she [the Church] has in the celebration of the Eucharist, the sacrament of Christ Crucified."[114] As the wise and loving head of the Church, nourishing and directing his members interiorly by the grace of his Holy Spirit, Christ provides for their interior nourishment and guidance through the exterior modes (including juridical ones) of the proclamation of faith and the administration of the sacraments of faith.[115] Because Aquinas does not divide this interior nourishment from concrete exterior modes that support it and make it visible in the world, his account of the Church's mediation of the divine love retains a place for a papal "office" that plays a role in upholding the unity of faith necessary for the Church's celebration of the Eucharist. In accord with Clément's goal of empha-

---

114. Yves Congar, "The Idea of the Church in St. Thomas Aquinas," 114–15. As Congar says, Aquinas holds that the hierarchy's "power over the Mystical Body involves principally the power to purify and enlighten souls by the preaching of the truth and that of preparing or disposing for the reception of the Eucharist by a juridical control: in the internal forum by the exercise of the power of the keys, in the external forum by the rule of the spiritual power" (115). Regarding contemporary theological efforts to clarify the scope of the hierarchical priesthood, see Avery Dulles, SJ's observation that Vatican II envisioned priesthood as "made up of three disparate elements—the prophetic, the priestly, and the royal. Since the Council, many theologians have wondered whether a convincing rationale can be given for assigning all three functions to the same individual and calling that individual a priest. Even if the confection of the eucharist and the absolution from sins are reserved to priests, could not the functions of preaching and pastoral governance be taken over by others? Is priesthood to be reduced to the few functions that cannot be performed by anyone except bishops and presbyters? If the prophetic and pastoral tasks are no less important than the ritual, does priestly ministry still have the high significance and centrality traditionally attributed to it? Since the Council there has been a considerable spread of opinion among theologians committed to defending the ministerial priesthood. Some, like Karl Rahner, take the ministry of the word as primary, and attempt to show that the fullness of this prophetic ministry involves the priestly and the pastoral as well. Others, like Otto Semmelroth and Joseph Lécuyer, begin with the ministry of worship and seek to integrate the prophetic and the pastoral ministries into it. Still a third school, represented by Walter Kasper, Hans Urs von Balthasar, and Jean Galot, takes the pastoral or shepherding function as primary, and derives the others from this" (Dulles, *The Priestly Office*, 4–5). Dulles himself gives preeminence to the priestly ministry of worship, without neglecting the prophetic and pastoral ministries (see 44).

115. See also Bonino, "La place du pape dans l'Église selon saint Thomas d'Aquin," 404: "If one wishes to enter further into the understanding of the juridical structure of the Church according to St. Thomas, it is necessary to define the structure of the Church as a society. The governmental structures of a society are relative to the nature of the society for which they provide governance. On this point, St. Thomas thoroughly exploits the fact that the mystery of the Church and the spiritual communion of believers in Jesus Christ are only concretely realized in a visible society."

sizing Christianity's witness to "divinized humanity, which is the space of the Spirit and of creative freedom,"[116] Aquinas affirms the New Testament witness to the emergence of "creative freedom" from within a love-filled "space of the Spirit" that, precisely as a unifying "space," is not antinomian. In this "space of the Spirit," human beings in every generation are configured eucharistically to the image of the eternal Son: "you will know the truth, and the truth will make you free" (John 8:32).

---

116. Clément, *You Are Peter,* 107.

Chapter 5

Sacramental Mediation

Let us pause to recall the ground we have covered thus far. The first chapter asked whether hierarchical structure makes ecclesiology monistic rather than properly Trinitarian. The second chapter then turned to Jesus Christ, and asked whether Christ's death constituted a priestly action capable of forming the basis for the development of a Christian hierarchical priesthood rooted in sacramental re-enactment of Christ's priestly action. The third chapter explored leadership in the first Christian communities, in order to see whether ecclesial hierarchy belongs intrinsically (as opposed to merely functionally) to the Church. Lastly, by reading contemporary Orthodox ecclesiology in light of Aquinas's thought, chapter four took up the theology of the papacy. These chapters both describe central challenges that contemporary theology of ecclesial hierarchy must address, and suggest that the theological rationale for hierarchy in the Church consists in the Trinitarian and Christological pattern of gifting and receptivity.

This final chapter addresses perhaps the most fundamental challenge of all. Namely, after the Reformation and the Enlightenment, is hierarchical sacramental mediation still viable? *Sacrosanctum Concilium* teaches, "Liturgical services . . . are celebrations of the Church which is the 'sacrament of unity,' namely, the holy people united and organized under the authority of the bishops."[1] But is it in fact reasonable to think that hierarchy—having been largely rejected in modern political, economic, and familial spheres—should retain its role, within "the holy people united and organized under the authority of the bishops," in mediating Christ's gifts?

---

1. *Sacrosanctum Concilium*, 26.

Miroslav Volf has advanced this challenge with particular cogency, and his arguments merit our attention once again.[2] Commenting in *After Our Likeness* on why many contemporary Catholic theologians advocate a more congregationalist Catholic Church, Volf suggests that behind the various theological rationales, ecclesiological congregationalism is simply among the inevitable signs of the times. Premodern unity of societies around one Church is, in the West at least, a thing of the past. He gives four reasons for this shift away from strongly defined unity: "the differentiation of societies, the privatization of decision, the generalization of values, and inclusion."[3] The differentiation of society means the division among

---

2. One might also see Hans Küng, *The Church*, trans. Ray and Rosaleen Ockenden (German 1967; London: Burns & Oates, 1968). Küng's first sentences exhibit his sociological perspective:

> The Church is rapidly approaching its third millennium. For the world in which the Church lives, the future has already begun. Science has begun to investigate both microcosm and macrocosm, both the atom and the universe; there are increasingly rapid and more efficient means of communication and transport; there is a wealth of new instruments, synthetic materials; methods of production are being rationalized; the expectation of human life has been increased by a decade or more; tremendous achievements have been made in physics, chemistry, biology, medicine, psychology, sociology, economics, historical research. All in all, despite those worldwide catastrophes and perils which have been the particular fate of our century, the story has been one of breathtaking progress. The highly industrialized nations of Europe and America have spread their knowledge throughout the world, the peoples of Asia and Africa have come to life; the world is becoming one and a single economic unit, a single civilization, perhaps even a single culture is emerging. And what of the Church? Has the future begun for it too? In some respect perhaps, but in many others it has not. At all events we have surely come to realize that the Church cannot, even if it wants to, stand aside from this world-wide reorientation which heralds a new era; for the Church lives in this, not in another world. (3)

For Küng, the "world-wide reorientation" will require the Church to separate itself from its medieval thought-patterns, including those of Pseudo-Dionysius and Aquinas. Küng adds that "there are two completely different ways in which the power of the bishops can be strengthened. One, the method of the sixth-century Neo-Platonist who assumed the mask of Dionysius the Areopagite, disciple of Paul, was based on verbose mystical interpretations of the Church's cult; the bishop was held up as the bearer of mystical powers and the community was seen as bound to him above all by the cultic mysteries; the earthly ecclesiastical organization was depicted as reflecting the heavenly hierarchy. A different method, as followed by the Frankish jurist at the beginning of the Middle Ages, who was believed to be Isidore of Seville, was based on ingenious forgeries of ecclesiastical laws; the bishop was seen as the bearer of all legal powers and the community as bound to him by the power of the keys" (9–10). Worldly power thus stands at the heart of Küng's summaries of the bishop's role.

3. Miroslav Volf, *After Our Likeness: The Church as the Image of the Trinity*, trans. Doug Stott (Grand Rapids, MI: Eerdmans, 1998), 13. By contrast, for approaches to ecclesiology that emphasize (within the context of contemporary evangelical Protestantism) the importance of the Church's sacramental constitution, see Gary D. Badcock, "The Church as 'Sacrament,' "

numerous entities of what had previously been solely the Church's role. Each entity marks an area of specialization, and churches now specialize in delivering diverse "religious offerings."[4] The privatization of decision means that "individuals now largely determine their own social roles," and so churches have become voluntary associations.[5] The generalization of values makes "freedom and equality" the controlling values and inclusion the key task. Thus any areas of structural inequality, such as the distinction between clergy and laity, are now recognizably anachronisms.

Volf does not argue against ecclesial hierarchy solely on the basis of historical developments. As he notes, "Although history does indeed teach that with regard to the development of its own order the church is to a large extent dependent on developments within society itself, the social form of the church must find its basis in its own faith rather than in its social environment."[6] Otherwise, the Church's foundation in Christ would not be possible, and witness to Christ would be displaced by complete assimilation to the culture. Volf contends, however, that "we are standing in the middle of a clear and irreversible 'process of congregationalization' of all Christianity."[7]

and Ellen T. Charry, "Sacramental Ecclesiology," in *The Community of the Word: Toward an Evangelical Ecclesiology*, ed. Mark Husbands and Daniel J. Treier (Downers Grove, IL: InterVarsity Press, 2005), 188–200 and 201–16. In the same volume William A. Dyrness comments appreciatively on Volf's "view of sociality": see Dyrness, "Spaces for an Evangelical Ecclesiology," 256–58.

4. Volf, *After Our Likeness*, 14.

5. Ibid., 15.

6. Ibid.

7. Ibid., 13. See also Nathan O. Hatch, *The Democratization of American Christianity* (New Haven, CT: Yale University Press, 1989). The opposite view is expressed by Klaus Schatz, SJ, who compares the contemporary situation to that of the fifteenth century: "At that time the alternative was that the council was superior to the pope, or the pope to the council. Mediation between the traditional papalist ecclesiology that saw the Church as a monarchy and a conciliarist ecclesiology that had rediscovered some forgotten aspects (including especially the Church as *communio*) but was also one-sided in its absolute perspective did not succeed. Then, as now, the *communio* ecclesiology was strongly influenced not only by tradition but also by secular models (at that time the corporative and guild models, today that of democracy). Does this not suggest that if we do not succeed in achieving an integration the results will be similar? Will it not again happen that a purely monarchical ecclesiology will triumph in theory and practice, and the newly discovered collegial and conciliar aspects will once again be repressed, just as in the fifteenth century?" (Schatz, *Papal Primacy: From Its Origins to the Present*, trans. John A. Otto and Linda M. Maloney [German 1990; Collegeville, MN: Liturgical Press, 1996], 170). While I do not share Schatz's fear about the rise of a "monarchical" ecclesiology, I have tried to suggest in this book that the appropriate link between "communion" and "jurisdiction" becomes clear when one focuses on the exigencies of the mediation of divine gifting, rather

This process is necessary and irreversible not solely for sociological reasons, but for more fundamental theological ones. The central theological reason, as we saw in chapter 1, is in his view the ability of congregationalist ecclesiology to nourish *communio*-structures that reflect and embody the communion and equality of the Trinitarian Persons.[8]

Theological reasons intertwine with sociological ones that display the providential current of history. Sociologically speaking, "People in modern societies . . . have little sympathy for top-down organizations, including for churches structured top-down."[9] This lack of sympathy for hierarchy has theological roots and implications, in addition to sociological causes. Most importantly, Volf thinks, top-down institutions do not value the talents and capacities of human persons to the same degree as do communities in which all share equally in leadership. Due in part to the beneficent influence of Christian principles over the centuries, modern human beings expect more appreciation for individual persons than was expected by premodern human beings. Volf states, "The search of contemporary human beings for community is a search for those particular forms of socialization in which they themselves are taken seriously with their various religious and social needs, in which their personal engagement is

---

than on the distribution of "power" per se. On the history of "collegiality," see Yves Congar, "Notes sur le destin de l'idée de collégialité épiscopale en occident au moyen âge (VIIe-XVI siècles)," in *La collégialité épiscopale. Histoire et théologie* (Paris: Cerf, 1969), 99–129.

8. Volf, *After Our Likeness*, 25.

9. Ibid., 17. Writing in 1980, before the fruits of John Paul II's new evangelization, Avery Dulles, SJ, comments similarly, "In an earlier day, when people were accustomed to being ruled by alien powers in every sphere of life, the institutionalism of the Church caused little difficulty. People took it for granted that they could have little control over their own lives and that someone would have to tell them what to believe and do. In a paternalistic society, a paternalistic Church was felt to be appropriate. In some respects it even offered relief from the tyranny of other institutions. But today, especially in North Atlantic nations, people take a critical view of all institutions" (Dulles, *A Church to Believe In: Discipleship and the Dynamics of Freedom* [1982; New York: Crossroad, 1987], 3–4). Whether this "earlier day" ever existed may be doubted, because it seems that in all times and places a number of people have rebelled against ecclesial authority. But Dulles rightly observes, "In combination with the general anti-institutionalism of the 1960s, the postconciliar developments resulted in acute polarization. Eager to follow the directives of the Council, popular expositors tended to oversimplify the Council's own statements, giving the impression that whatever support the Council has given to the hierarchical or institutional aspect of the Church was a grudging concession to a benighted minority, whereas the true thrust of Vatican II had been toward a Church that was charismatic, democratic, participatory, and pluralistic" (6). Following John Paul II's emphasis in *Redemptor Hominis* (1979) on following Christ, Dulles's solution is to conceive of the Church as a "community of disciples" (12).

valued, and in which they can participate formatively."[10] When leadership is not shared, the resulting lack of equality deprives persons of the chance to participate and engage fully in the Church, and these persons ultimately look elsewhere for an ecclesial home.

The sociological weaknesses of hierarchical ecclesial structures also *produce* notable theological weaknesses, according to Volf. He points especially to evangelization, the process of the transmission of the faith. Were hierarchical ecclesial structure the only ecclesial option, he notes, many people would choose instead to remain unchurched. In this sense, "The differentiation of various Christian traditions is not simply to be lamented as a scandal, but rather welcomed as a sign of the vitality of the Christian faith within multicultural, rapidly changing societies demanding diversification and flexibility."[11] Whereas the hierarchical Church (Roman Catholic and Eastern Orthodox) must in some sense claim to constitute the only ecclesial structure willed by Christ—any other claim would effectively dissolve the hierarchical structure—Volf argues that evangelization proceeds best, at least in the modern differentiated context, when there is no "one correct ecclesiology."[12] This ecclesiological pluralism, he holds, has its theological

---

10. Volf, *After Our Likeness*, 17. See also Duane A. Walker's letter-to-the-editor, "Strength in Disunity," published in the ecumenical monthly *First Things* 169 (January 2007): 10), in response to Richard John Neuhaus's "An Irrevocable Commitment" (The Public Square, *First Things* 167 [October 2006]). Behind the abstruse theological debates, Walker holds, stands the simple fact that different people prefer different kinds of ecclesial structure. Walker interprets John 17 as referring to "our Lord's desire that there be unity of purpose, intention, and mission" rather than one visible institution. One might ask whether there can truly be "unity of purpose, intention, and mission" without a unity of ecclesial structure, but Walker turns such functionalist arguments on their head, using them to make his own case. If visible ecclesial unity were so important, Walker asks, why, functionally speaking, has there been almost no progress in ecumenism? He observes, "In our pursuit of church unity maybe we have been chasing a fantasy, a theory, more than anything else; otherwise, why the dismal results and the moribund state of the discussion?"

11. Volf, *After Our Likeness*, 21. For reflections that likewise value "diversification and flexibility" but aim at sacramental and confessional unity, see Brian E. Daley, sj, "Rebuilding the Structure of Love: The Quest for Visible Unity among the Churches," in *The Ecumenical Future*, ed. Carl E. Braaten and Robert W. Jenson (Grand Rapids, MI: Eerdmans, 2004), 73–105.

12. Ibid. Volf notes, "One might reject the legitimacy of several ecclesial models with the following argument [which Volf finds in the writings of Joseph Ratzinger and, to a somewhat lesser degree, of John Zizioulas]: Anyone who does not wish to accept the one institutional church willed by Christ will necessarily create one's own church modeled according to one's own needs. Yet whoever argues in this way (contrary to the New Testament witness, I believe) will also have to face the question whether this appeal to the unchangeable will of God is not

justification in the New Testament itself: "exegetes speak of the several ecclesial models one can find in the New Testament. I proceed on the simple systematic assumption that what was legitimate during the New Testament period cannot be illegitimate today."[13]

Just as hierarchical ecclesial structure hampers evangelization by its requirement of uniformity, so also it hampers evangelization because it is so discordant with the modern mind's affirmation of pluralism.[14] While some might defend this discordance as a Christological "sign of contradiction," the logic of Volf's position is formidable: hierarchical ecclesial structures developed and succeeded during a time in which societal hierarchies were widely accepted, whereas the modern rejection of such hierarchies means that defending ecclesial hierarchy is equivalent to upholding monarchy, in politics, as the best form of government.[15] Hierarchical Christianity appears outmoded,

---

serving rather to veil ideologically one's own interest in maintaining certain ecclesial structures" (22).

13. Ibid., 21. Of course, Volf can have ecclesiological pluralism without needing to affirm hierarchical ecclesial structure, since the acceptance of pluralism collapses hierarchical structure theoretically if not necessarily practically (and thus the limits inscribed within Volf's pluralism are evident). See also Veli-Matti Kärkkäinen, "The Apostolicity of Free Churches," *Pro Ecclesia* 10 (2001): 475–86. Kärkkäinen is concerned to combat any exclusively "historical or juridical notion of apostolicity," which would rule out the apostolicity of what he calls "younger churches" (486).

14. Cf. Peter Henrici's "The Church and Pluralism," trans. Albert K. Wimmer, *Communio* 10 (1983): 128–32. See also Jacques Dupuis, sj, "Le Verbe de Dieu, Jésus-Christ et les religions du monde," *Nouvelle revue théologique* 123 (2001): 529–46; and the response by Henry Donneaud, op, "Chalcédoine contre l'unicité absolue du Médiateur Jésus-Christ? Autour d'un article recent," *Revue Thomiste* 102 (2002): 43–62. Benoît-Dominique de La Soujeole, op, takes up the broader problem in "Être ordonné à l'unique Église du Christ: L'ecclésialité des communautés non chrétiennes à partir des données oecuméniques," *Revue Thomiste* 102 (2002): 5–41; see also his "Et pourtant, . . . elle subsiste!" *Revue Thomiste* 99 (2000): 531–49, which treats the interpretation of *Lumen Gentium*'s phrase "subsistit in" (#8) up through *Dominus Iesus* (2000); cf. Francis A. Sullivan, "A Response to Karl Becker, sj, on the Meaning of *Subsistit In*," *Theological Studies* 67 (2006): 395–409. The editorial board of the *Revue Thomiste*, led by Serge-Thomas Bonino, op, published " 'Tout récapituler dans le Christ': À propos de l'ouvrage de Jacques Dupuis, *Vers une théologie chrétienne du pluralisme religieux*," *Revue Thomiste* 98 (1998): 591–630, which addresses the mediation of Christ and the relationship of the "Church" to the "Kingdom of God."

15. For instance, Robert Bellarmine, sj, in the largely monarchical political context of the seventeenth century sought to defend papal authority as the best form of government because of its approximation to monarchy: see Bellarmine, *Opera omnia*, ed. Justin Fèvre (Paris: Vives, 1870), vol. 1-2, *Tertia controversia generalis: De summo pontifice*. For discussion see, e.g., Richard F. Costigan, sj, *The Consensus of the Church and Papal Infallibility: A Study in the Background of Vatican I* (Washington, DC: The Catholic University of America Press, 2005), 23f. According to Costigan, Bellarmine grants nonetheless that "the Church is not like a temporal kingdom.

even fanatically so (if it is seriously defended), before the message of Christ's saving love is even heard. Volf remarks in this regard that "the mediation of faith can succeed only *if those standing outside that faith are able to identify with the church communities embodying and transmitting it.*"[16] Since modern human beings, by and large, cannot identify with hierarchical ecclesial structures, they will turn away from such communities' efforts to proclaim the Gospel. This impediment threatens the very survival of Christian faith, at least in societies where the Church is almost exclusively hierarchical. In such situations one can expect to find that " 'social dissonance' becomes too great between what one endorses in society at large and what one experiences in the church."[17] A Church that rejects hierarchy in marriage, economics, and politics, while affirming its own hierarchical institutional structure, cannot but alienate its members. That its teachings in one area are not reflected in its teachings in another area suggests theological as well as sociological incoherence.

To these criticisms of hierarchical ecclesiology as unfaithful in its imposition of uniformity to the New Testament witness and as antithetical to the evangelization of modern persons, Volf adds that hierarchy militates against the co-equality of the Persons of the Trinity and thereby conduces to authoritarian practices—arguments that we discussed in chapter 1.

In short, while Volf opposes individualism and the commodification of Christian faith, he argues that the bonds of community attained through hierarchical ecclesial structures are not adequate to Christian interpersonal communication of the Gospel, on at least three levels. First, top-down structures lack appreciation for the individual's decision-making role in modern societies, as well as for the values of freedom and equality. In modern societies, hierarchy

---

'For in the kingdom of Christ supreme power is in Christ and is not in any way derived from the people' " (26).

16. Volf, *After Our Likeness*, 17.

17. Ibid., 18. As Volf says earlier, "Americans quite clearly expect one thing from their churches, namely, more lay participation in church life. To the question, 'Who do you think should have greater influence in determining the future of religion in America: the clergy, or the people who attend the services?' sixty-one percent responded: 'Laity, the people who attend religious services, should have greater influence.' Among young adults (ages 18–29), seventy percent gave this answer, while only nine percent favored greater influence on the part of the clergy. As for any religion, so for Christianity the transmission of faith is a question of survival" (16).

thereby fosters exclusion, not inclusion.[18] Since a hierarchical understanding of ecclesial office does not allow for the free flourishing of
each person's gifts, hierarchy both prevents the Church from benefiting
from the contributions of each person, and excludes many persons
from exercising their full abilities in the Church. Second, a hierarchical
Church lacks the diversity and flexibility of ecclesial structure needed
to adjust to the rapidly shifting circumstances in which the Gospel is
proclaimed. Here again hierarchical office undermines the Christian
personalism that encourages the effective proclamation of the Gospel
in new cultural situations. In the current cultural situation, for
instance, the very presence of hierarchy makes the Gospel appear
outmoded. For modern persons, the connection of the Gospel with
hierarchical structures produces a social dissonance that has the effect
of distancing persons from the Gospel. Third, hierarchical ecclesial
structures instantiate inequality among Christians, thereby undercutting
the interpersonal communion of equals (as the image of the Trinity)
that true Christian personalism requires. The communication of the
Gospel is at odds with an instrument of communication that expresses
not equal filial adoption in Christ, but hierarchical inequality of persons.

Volf's concerns hinge upon the question of what constitutes
the core of Christian personalism. Specifically, how does Jesus Christ
encounter, heal, and elevate into Trinitarian communion the personhood of each of his members? At the heart of this question is whether
one understands the Church to be constituted by sacramental mediation
(and thus preeminently by the Eucharist).

If sacramental mediation is ultimately the issue that underlies
Volf's concerns, how should we understand sacramental mediation? I
begin by tracing an eighteenth-century Jewish–Christian debate that

---

18. Volf's account of "inclusion" is not uncritical. See his *Exclusion and Embrace: Theological
Exploration of Identity, Otherness, and Reconciliation* (Nashville, TN: Abingdon Press, 1996),
63: "A consistent drive toward inclusion seeks to level all the boundaries that divide and to
neutralize all outside powers that form and shape the self. . . . Does not such radical indeterminacy
undermine from within the idea of inclusion, however? I believe it does. Without boundaries
we will be able to know only what we are fighting against but not what we are fighting for.
Intelligent struggle against exclusion demands categories and normative criteria that enable us
to distinguish between repressive identities and practices that should be subverted and nonrepres-
sive ones that should be affirmed." His critique of exclusion attempts, therefore, to "satisfy two
conditions: (1) it must help us to name exclusion as evil with confidence because it enables us
to imagine nonexclusionary boundaries that map nonexclusionary identities; at the same time
(2) it must not dull our ability to detect the exclusionary tendencies in our own judgments and
practices" (64).

hinged upon the question of whether Judaism and Christianity mediate a sacred power, beyond educative and affective insights: the debate between Moses Mendelssohn and Johann Georg Hamann. Mendelssohn's *Jerusalem* sought to conceive of Judaism, including its ceremonial laws, fundamentally as a non-hierarchical mediation of truths;[19] whereas Hamann in response argued that Mendelssohn's perspective does not account for the full scope of God's gifting. On this basis, I take up another pair of Jewish and Christian thinkers, Franz Rosenzweig and Pseudo-Dionysius, who understand the people of God in terms of liturgical mediation. Their insights lead us some distance from Volf. As a third step, I turn to Thomas Aquinas's theology of the priesthood, which draws heavily upon Dionysius's understanding of mediation while also responding to concerns that resonate with those of Volf.

---

19. The place of the Old Testament in ecclesiology—and so far as I know Volf's *After Our Likeness* does not discuss the Old Testament—deserves more attention. Consider the Enlightenment philosopher John Stuart Mill's reasons for the alleged superiority of the prophets to the Israelite priesthood:

> The Egyptian hierarchy, the paternal despotism of China, were very fit instruments for carrying those nations up to the point of civilization which they attained. But having reached that point, they were brought to a permanent halt, for want of mental liberty and individuality; requisites of improvement which the institutions that had carried them thus far, entirely incapacitated them from acquiring; and as the institutions did not break down and give place to others, further improvement stopped. In contrast with these nations, let us consider the example of an opposite character afforded by another and a comparatively insignificant Oriental people—the Jews. They, too, had an absolute monarchy and a hierarchy, and their organized institutions were as obviously of sacerdotal origin as those of the Hindoos. These did for them what was done for other Oriental races by their institutions—subdued them to industry and order, and gave them a national life. But neither their kings nor their priests ever obtained, as in those countries, the exclusive moulding of their character. Their religion, which enabled persons of genius and a high religious tone to be regarded and to regard themselves as inspired from heaven, gave existence to an inestimably precious unorganized institution—the Order (if it may be so termed) of Prophets. . . . Accordingly, whoever can divest himself of the habit of reading the Bible as if it was one book, which until lately was equally inveterate in Christians and in unbelievers, sees with admiration the vast interval between the morality and religion of the Pentateuch, or even of the historical books (the unmistakable work of Hebrew Conservatives of the sacerdotal order), and the morality and religion of the Prophecies: a distance as wide as between these last and the Gospels. Conditions more favorable to Progress could not easily exist: accordingly, the Jews, instead of being stationary like other Asiatics, were, next to the Greeks, the most progressive people of antiquity, and, jointly with them, have been the starting-point and main propelling agency of modern cultivation. (Mill, *Considerations on Representative Government*, in Mill, *On Liberty and Other Essays*, ed. John Gray [Oxford: Oxford University Press, 1991], 235–36) Cf. Jean Stern, "Marcionisme, néo-marcionisme et tradition de l'Église," *Revue Thomiste* 105 (2005): 473–506.

Mendelssohn and Hamann: Posing the Problem

Mendelssohn: Teaching Authority in the "Church"

Moses Mendelssohn begins his masterwork, *Jerusalem*, with the observation: "State and religion—civil and ecclesiastical constitution—secular and churchly authority—how to oppose these pillars of social life to one another so that they are in balance and do not, instead, become burdens on social life, or weigh down its foundations more than they help to uphold it—this is one of the most difficult tasks of politics."[20] For Mendelssohn, "eternal life" for human beings is in fact an endless extension of temporality,[21] and so pursuit of true temporal welfare is pursuit of true eternal welfare. The goal of the "state," seeking the temporal and eternal common good of citizens, should be educating its citizens to perform good actions on the basis of the right convictions.[22] Since citizens should perform good actions—should

---

20. Moses Mendelssohn, *Jerusalem, or On Religious Power and Judaism*, trans. Allan Arkush (Hanover, NH: Brandeis University Press, 1983), 33. He reviews critically the solutions offered by Thomas Hobbes and John Locke, on the one hand, and Robert Bellarmine on the other. Hobbes's solution, he notes, ends by sanctioning the despotism of the state; Locke's solution constricts the meaning of temporal welfare; Bellarmine upholds an ecclesial despotism. For a more appreciative view of Mendelssohn, and of Rosenzweig's appropriation of Mendelssohn than I offer here, see Leora Batnitzky, *Idolatry and Representation: The Philosophy of Franz Rosenzweig Reconsidered* (Princeton: Princeton University Press, 2000), 33–43. Batnitzky's viewpoint is criticized by Randi Rashkover, *Revelation and Theopolitics: Barth, Rosenzweig and the Politics of Praise* (New York: T. & T. Clark, 2005), 176–77. See also Michael Mack, "Moses Mendelssohn's Other Enlightenment and German Jewish Counterhistories in the Work of Heinrich Heine and Abraham Geiger," in Mack, *German Idealism and the Jew: The Inner Anti-Semitism of Philosophy and German Jewish Responses* (Chicago: University of Chicago Press, 2003), 79–97.

21. Mendelssohn, *Jerusalem*, 39. For a better understanding see Matthew L. Lamb, *Eternity, Time, and the Life of Wisdom* (Naples, FL: Sapientia Press, 2007).

22. Mendelssohn, *Jerusalem*, 40. Against this conflation of Church and temporal society, see the texts and commentary in Hugo Rahner, SJ, *Church and State in Early Christianity*, trans. Leo Donald Davis, SJ (German 1961; San Francisco: Ignatius Press, 1992). Regarding the patristic Church, Rahner observes that "from her beginning the Church regarded the state as a form of social life established by God, and she confided herself to the state's protection with a confidence that was never abandoned. The cordial collaboration with the state, expressed in the word *Concordate*, is essential, because both Church and state derive their existence from God. But the Church was always wary of the state's smothering embrace, which was a danger to her members" (298). See also Joseph Ratzinger, "Biblical Aspects of the Question of Faith and Politics," in his *Church, Ecumenism and Politics: New Essays in Ecclesiology*, trans. Robert Nowell (German 1987; New York: Crossroad, 1988), 147–51; Henri de Lubac, SJ, *The Splendor of the Church*, trans. Michael Mason (French 1953; San Francisco: Ignatius Press, 1986),

sacrifice for the common good—not by despotic coercion but of their own free will, the best state will be that which "achieves its purposes by morals and convictions," and thus governs "by education itself."[23]

Much depends here upon Mendelssohn's analysis of the benevolent individual. As he says, "Man is conscious of his own worth when he performs charitable acts, when he vividly (*anschauend*) perceives how he alleviates the distress of his fellow man by his gift; when he gives because he *wants* to give. But if he gives because he *must*, he feels only his fetters."[24] The task of the "church" is complementary to that of the "state": the Church/synagogue/mosque should educate citizens so that their good actions toward their fellow human beings are also good actions in relation to God.

If citizens will not perform good actions from benevolence, however, the state must compel them. This power of coercion belongs only to the state, not to the "church": "Religious society lays no claim to the *right of coercion*, and cannot obtain it by any possible contract."[25] Mendelssohn explains that religious society "is founded on the relationship between God and man. God is not a being who needs our benevolence, requires our assistance, or claims any of our rights for his own use, or whose rights can ever clash or be confused with ours."[26] Insofar as human beings sacrifice for the common good, they serve the state, their fellow human beings, and God. No further "sacrifice" is necessary, because whereas our fellow human beings need our sacrifices (the "state"), God is not needy. God "desires no *service* from us, no sacrifice of our rights for his benefit, no renunciation of our independence for his advantage. His rights can never come into conflict and confusion with ours. He wants only what is best for us, what is best for every single individual."[27] The "church" or religious societies cannot be justified in restricting the "natural liberty" of

---

172–75, 196–99; François Daguet, "Saint Thomas et les deux pouvoirs. Élements de théologie politique," *Revue Thomiste* 102 (2002): 531–68; Paul Evdokimov, "The Church and Society: The Social Dimension of Orthodox Ecclesiology," in *In the World, of the Church: A Paul Evdokimov Reader*, ed. and trans. Michael Plekon and Alexis Vinogradov (Crestwood, NY: St. Vladimir's Seminary Press, 2001), 61–94, which responds to Paul VI's *Populorum progressio*.

23. Mendelssohn, *Jerusalem*, 42.

24. Ibid., 43.

25. Ibid., 45.

26. Ibid., 57.

27. Ibid., 58–59.

human beings so as to compel a sacrifice to God in addition to the sacrifice for fellow human beings that the state requires/coerces. As Mendelssohn concludes, "The only rights possessed by the church are to admonish, to instruct, to fortify, and to comfort; and the duties of the citizens toward the church are an *attentive ear* and a *willing heart.* Nor has the church any right to reward or to punish actions."[28]

Religious societies that reward or punish individuals on the basis of agreement or disagreement in convictions thereby become forces of oppression. Since convictions belong to the realm of individual liberty, the only instrument for changing them should be persuasion. This means—and here is the key conclusion—that religious societies have no need of a "government" of their own, with the ability to reward or punish individuals for their convictions. Mendelssohn states, "What form of government is therefore advisable for the church? None! Who is to be the arbiter if disputes arise over religious matters? He to whom God has given the ability to convince others."[29] In his view, rabbis, priests, and pastors must not be required by their respective religious societies to affirm particular doctrines, since such a requirement would sanction coercion within the "church."[30] As he sums up his position:

> . . . if principles are to make man happy, he must not be scared or whee-
> dled into adopting them. Only the judgment reached by his powers of

---

28. Ibid., 59–60.

29. Ibid., 62.

30. Cf. Joseph Ratzinger's reflections on "Freedom and Constraint in the Church," in *Church, Ecumenism and Politics*, 183–203. Ratzinger writes,

> In the Church it is a matter of freedom in the profoundest sense of that word, of opening up the possibility of sharing in the divine being. The fundamental organization of the Church's freedom must therefore be to ensure that faith and sacrament, in which this sharing in the divine being is mediated, are accessible without diminution or adulteration. The fundamental right of the Christian is the right to the whole faith. The fundamental obligation that flows from this is the obligation of everyone, but especially the Church's ministers, to the totality of the unadulterated faith. . . . With regard to the world the Church must defend the right to freedom of belief in a double sense: in the first place as the right freely to be able to choose one's faith in the sense of what the Second Vatican Council said about religious freedom; in the second place positively as the right to believe and to live as a believing Christian. Belonging to this context is also the classical subject of *libertas ecclesiae,* the right of the Church to be the Church and to live in its own way. The right to believe is the real core of human freedom; when this right is lacking the loss of all further rights of freedom follows after with inner logic. At the same time this right is the real gift of freedom that Christian faith has brought into the world. It was the first to break the identification of state and religion and thus to remove from the state its claim to totality. (202–3)

intellect can be accepted as valid. . . . Hence, neither church nor state has a right to subject men's principles and convictions to any coercion whatsoever. Neither church nor state is authorized to connect privileges and rights, claims on persons and title to things, with principles and convictions, and to weaken through outside interference the influence of the power of truth upon the cognitive faculty.[31]

He has mainly in view teaching appointments in state universities, governmental service, and so forth, but the principle covers religious offices and membership as well. In this regard he particularly speaks out against "excommunication and the right to banish," which he allows to the "state" but not to the "church."[32]

Section I of *Jerusalem* ends on this note. Thus far Mendelssohn's account of the "church" conceives of religious communities as the locus of affective meditation on the higher things, but as little more. The purpose of religious communities "is *mutual edification*. By the magic power of sympathy one wishes to transfer truth from the mind to the heart; to vivify, by participation with others, the concepts of reason, which at times are lifeless, into soaring sensations."[33] This view of religious communities raised questions among Mendelssohn's contemporaries, to whom he responds in section II of *Jerusalem*. In particular, one critic argued that Judaism itself is an example of what Mendelssohn condemns: "What are the laws of Moses but a system of religious government, of the power and right of religion?"[34]

In response, Mendelssohn offers a re-interpretation of the Jewish religion. He grants that many Jews would agree with his critic's account of the laws of Moses, but he denies that he ever intended to throw off his own Judaism, let alone imply a preference for Christianity (with its annulling of the ceremonial law). On the contrary, he observes that "a characteristic difference" between Judaism and Christianity is that Judaism holds only what human reason can verify. He argues that the difference lies in the Jewish and Christian understandings of revelation. From the Jewish perspective, revelation consists in laws regarding how God wills the Jewish people to act. Such revelation,

---

31. Mendelssohn, *Jerusalem*, 70.
32. Ibid., 73.
33. Ibid., 74.
34. Ibid., 84.

while divine, includes "no doctrinal opinions, no saving truths, no universal propositions of reason."[35] These latter are revealed not in sacred writings, but through nature to all human beings alike. In contrast, Christianity supposes that universal truths about God, Christ, and humankind have been revealed.

Mendelssohn goes on to differentiate eternal truths, "founded upon *reason*," from historical truths, which "can only be conceived as true in respect to that point in time and space."[36] Both kinds of truths require empirical observation, but historical truths are non-repeatable and therefore rest far more upon the authority of the witness. Jewish Scripture deals with historical truths, which must be supernaturally revealed to be authoritatively known, whereas God teaches eternal truths "through creation itself, and its internal relations, which are legible and comprehensible to all men."[37] Had it been otherwise, then all human beings prior to the spread of the Torah would have lacked access to the eternal truths necessary for temporal and eternal happiness, which would have been unbefitting God's goodness. Thus "Judaism boasts of no *exclusive* revelation of eternal truths that are indispensable to salvation, of no revealed religion in the sense in which that term is usually understood."[38] Instead, Judaism consists of revealed laws for the Jewish people.

Mendelssohn denies that eternal truths are central to the Torah, but he certainly does not deny that the Jewish Scriptures contain eternal truths. He argues, indeed, that these eternal truths form "one entity" with the laws in the Torah. The laws are connected to eternal truths, however, in a variety of ways: "All laws refer to, or are based upon, eternal truths of reason, or remind us of them, or rouse us to ponder them."[39] The laws themselves, however, pertain to the act of the will rather than to the act of the intellect. Even words in the Torah that are sometimes translated as "faith" are better translated as "trust." Passages in the Torah that express an eternal truth appear in the Torah as knowledge pertaining to reason, not as requiring the response of faith. For this reason ancient Judaism, unlike Christianity,

---

35. Ibid., 90.

36. Ibid., 91.

37. Ibid., 93.

38. Ibid., 97. Here Mendelssohn's debt to Spinoza is particularly apparent.

39. Ibid., 99.

did not develop a creed, although in later times, Mendelssohn notes, Maimonides's rational expression of Judaism eventually led to a Jewish catechism of 13 articles, which fortunately "have not yet been forged into shackles of faith."[40] No Jew has to swear assent to articles of Jewish faith. The laws must be believed and obeyed (and, following Rabbi Hillel, their essence can be reduced to "love thy neighbor as thyself"), but no Jew is required to believe by faith the Torah's eternal truths, since they are known by natural reason.[41]

In Mendelssohn's view, the written word (especially hieroglyphs) fostered the development of the worship of animals and human beings, because the sign was mistaken for the reality. Originally the patriarchs possessed a philosophically rich religion: "Abraham, Isaac, and Jacob remained faithful to the Eternal, and sought to preserve among their families and descendants pure concepts of religion, far removed from all idolatry."[42] God chose their descendants, therefore, to be a "*priestly* nation; that is, a nation which, through its establishment and constitution, through its laws, actions, vicissitudes, and changes was continually to call attention to sound and unadulterated ideas of God and his attributes."[43] In contrast to the signs that had fostered idolatry, the ceremonial laws serve as signs that foster a true understanding of God and morality. This did not make the laws a belief system, however: "The law, to be sure, did not impel them to engage in reflection; it prescribed only actions, only doing and not doing."[44] The actions were related to eternal truths, but the danger of becoming a religion of beliefs was averted. When, however, the oral tradition about God's commandments was written down, idolatry infiltrated even God's chosen people.

While scholars often focus on Mendelssohn's contributions to religious freedom, for our purposes the question is what, for Mendelssohn, is mediated through the Jewish people. The answer is twofold: first, eternal truths that sound philosophy attained among the Jews but that superstition corrupts; second, ceremonial laws that mandated actions to signify the sound philosophy. Judaism thus does

---

40. Ibid., 101.
41. Ibid., 102.
42. Ibid., 118.
43. Ibid.
44. Ibid.

not consist in divinely revealed beliefs, but in divinely revealed laws/
actions that support what sound philosophy knows.

Hamann: The Overcoming of Sin

In a letter to Mendelssohn, Immanuel Kant not surprisingly gave
Jerusalem high praise. The Romantic thinker Johann Gottfried Herder
disagreed with its key theses, but did so in a friendly manner.[45] The
most important negative response came from Johann Georg Hamann,
whose brief *Golgotha and Scheblimini* (1784)—which Hegel considered
to be Hamann's most significant work—is a critique of *Jerusalem*.[46]

Hamann suggests that *pace* Mendelssohn's effort to portray
Israel's religion as a witness to monotheism and to tolerance—a proto-
Enlightenment, as it were[47]—in fact God elected Israel for Golgotha
(the redemption of the world from sin) and for "sitting at God's right
hand" (perfect communion with God).[48] Mendelssohn's definition of

---

45. See Alexander Altmann's introduction to the translation of Mendelssohn's *Jerusalem*
that I have used, 26–27.

46. See James C. O'Flaherty's discussion of "Hamann's Life and Work" in his edition of
Hamann's *Socratic Memorabilia: A Translation and Commentary* (Baltimore, MD: Johns Hopkins
University Press, 1967), 40. Hegel's appreciation for Hamann was shared by Goethe, due to
Herder's influence upon Goethe (17). For Hegel on Hamann, see G. W. F. Hegel, "Hamann's
Schriften," in *Sämtliche Werke*, vol. XI, ed. Johannes Hoffmeister (Hamburg: Felix Meiner,
1956), 221–94. For theological appreciation of Hamann, see John Betz, "Hamann before
Kierkegaard: A Systematic Theological Oversight," *Pro Ecclesia* 16 (2007): 299–333; Oswald
Bayer, *Autorität und Kritik: Hermeneutik und Wissenschaftstheorie* (Tübingen: Mohr-Siebeck,
1991); Hans Urs von Balthasar, *The Glory of the Lord: A Theological Aesthetics*, vol. 3, *Studies in
Theological Style: Lay Styles*, trans. Andrew Louth, John Saward, Martin Simon, and Rowan
Williams (German 1969; San Francisco: Ignatius Press, 1986), 239–78.

47. Compare Avery Dulles, sj's discussion of nineteenth- and early twentieth-century
liberal Protestant views of Catholicism in his *The Catholicity of the Church* (Oxford: Oxford
University Press, 1985), 107–9. Dulles surveys Friedrich Schleiermacher, Adolf von Harnack,
Rudolph Sohm, and Ernst Troeltsch. Typical is Troeltsch's view that Catholicism (especially
in the medieval West) "carried objectification and institutionalization to excess, so that the
originally free movement of the spirit became imprisoned in a hierarchical, episcopally ordered
organization of sacrament and tradition" (108). For all of these thinkers Catholicism "puts
obstacles between the individual Christian and God, destroying the direct relationship required
by the gospel in its original and authentic form" (109). See also Dulles's *A Church to Believe In*,
23, where Dulles discusses Sohm as well as Auguste Sabatier, Emil Brunner, Hans Küng, and
Gotthold Hasenhüttl.

48. As von Balthasar says, commenting on Hamann's theology of the Word: "in the guise
of utmost humility God really does show his utmost love and glory. . . . 'Golgatha', God's
final *kenosis*, already contains within itself '*scheblimini*': 'Sit thou at my right hand'" (von Balthasar,
Studies in Theological Style: Lay Styles, 251). Von Balthasar goes on to observe that Hamann
requires that "present reality be experienced in its historical, ontological dimensions, pointing
to creation (protology) and transfiguration (eschatology); these dimensions alone can give a

the "church" simply as a society whose concern is the relations of human beings with God cannot suffice, in Hamann's view. The reason is that this definition takes no account of sin. In this regard Hamann observes with typical insight and rhetorical flourish,

> In the infinite mis-relation of man to God "public institutions concerned with the relation of man to God" are sheer unrhymed sentences in dry words which infect the inner sap the more a speculative creature sucks in of it. First of all, in order to abolish the infinite mis-relation, before one can speak of relations which are to serve as the basis of connection for public institutions, man must either participate in a divine nature, or the godhead must assume flesh and blood. The Jews with their divine law-giving, and the naturalists with their divine reason have seized a protective palladium for levelling down this mis-relation.[49]

First and foremost, therefore, Mendelssohn has watered down what "religion" truly seeks. Neither Judaism nor Christianity can be merely a matter of affective cognition of the truths of monotheism and divine forbearance. Rather, what is sought in "figure" by the ceremonial rites of Judaism, and fulfilled in Christ Jesus, is reconciliation with God, crossing over the abyss of sin and alienation.[50]

---

true account of experience in all its profundity. But these are dimensions of reality and as such *historical*, for that which is present is absolutely an historical instant. In this resides the whole force of Hamann's argument, developed in *Golgatha and Scheblimini* and *The Flying Letter*, against Moses Mendelssohn's construction of an enlightened Jerusalem, timeless and ideal. The *analogia* between God and man of which we have just spoken finds concrete interpretation in an *analogia temporum*, which, when known and understood, yields the key of truth" (267). See also David Novak's *The Election of Israel: The Idea of the Chosen People* (Cambridge: Cambridge University Press, 1995), which treats Spinoza and Rosenzweig at length. *Scheblimini* is the Hebrew for "Sit thou at my right hand" (see Psalm 110:1). For further discussion see W. M. Alexander, *Johann Georg Hamann: Philosophy and Faith* (The Hague: Martinus Nijhoff, 1966), 95.

49. Johann Georg Hamann, *Golgotha and Scheblimini*, from the partial English translation done by Ronald Gregor Smith and included in his *J. G. Hamann, 1730–1788: A Study in Christian Existence with Selections from His Writings* (New York: Harper & Brothers, 1960), 230. For the complete German text, see Johann Georg Hamann, *Sämtliche Werke*, critical edition by Josef Nadler (Vienna: Herder, 1949–57), vol. 3, 291–320.

50. Cf. Kierkegaard's labors to combat Hegel's historicizing of the realities of Christian faith. In cautioning against the modern idealist tendency "to universalize the incarnation" (Farrow, *Ascension and Ecclesia* [Grand Rapids, MI: Eerdmans, 1999], 255), Douglas Farrow points to Kierkegaard's effort to ground a "contemporaneity" or "genuine co-existence with Jesus of Nazareth" (224) and Kierkegaard's "early conviction (never consistently followed up but never abandoned) that the eucharist, dynamically understood as a relational act, provides the proper starting point for ecclesiology" (228). Farrow is indebted to Michael Plekon, "Kierkegaard and the Eucharist," *Studia Liturgica* 22 (1992): 214–36.

Second, and related to the first, God's action is missing from Mendelssohn's anthropocentric account of religion. Hamann attempts to restore a theocentric account of the "church": "The mystery of Christian devotion does not consist of services, sacrifices and vows, which God demands of men, but rather of promises, fulfillments and sacrifices which God has made and achieved for the benefit of men."[51] Whereas Mendelssohn would focus on what human beings do—a "religion" that through its ceremonies affirms Enlightenment understanding of God and morality—Hamann would focus on what God does. As Hamann describes "the mystery of Christian devotion," it is not about primarily "lawgiving and moral teaching which have to do merely with human dispositions and human actions, but of the performance of divine decrees by means of divine acts, works and measures for the salvation of the whole world."[52] Christians thus do not bog themselves down in a mere belief system when they affirm the Creed; rather, they participate in the power of redemption, they enter into the covenantal work that God has accomplished. By contrast, Mendelssohn, Hamann says (reflecting his own critique of visible churches and their officeholders), has "changed the idea of religion and the church into that of a public educational establishment."[53] Indeed, Hamann accuses Mendelssohn of having given himself over to a mere belief system of the kind that Mendelssohn seeks to reject. Mendelssohn has traded the true historical Judaism, with its historical experience of God's work to overcome sin, for philosophical platitudes. For its part, Hamann says, "Christianity . . . does not believe in philosophical tenets, which are nothing but alphabetical scribaceousness of human speculation, subject to the fickle changes of the moon and of fashion."[54] In short, Christianity is based not on philosophical tenets of any kind, but on Golgotha.

---

51. Hamann, *Golgotha and Scheblimini*, 229; *Sämtliche Werke*, ed. Nadler, 312–13.

52. Ibid., 230; ed. Nadler, *Sämtliche Werke*, 312. Cf. for a Catholic perspective, Joseph Ratzinger, *Many Religions—One Covenant: Israel, the Church and the World*, trans. Graham Harrison (German 1998; San Francisco: Ignatius Press, 1999).

53. Hamann, *Golgotha and Scheblimini*, 229; ed. Nadler, *Sämtliche Werke*, 312.

54. Hamann, *Golgotha and Scheblimini*, 228; ed. Nadler, *Sämtliche Werke*, 310. W. M. Alexander observes that Hamann also has Lessing in his sights here. Summarizing Hamann's critique, Alexander writes, "Whence this profound knowledge that history is not open to God, that somehow He is restricted to the world of eternal ideas, alienated from the historical world which He created, governs, and redeems? Lessing's program is in effect an abstraction of history from God, a removal of God from history. This is a Gnostic hate of the flesh. These

Third, Hamann takes up Mendelssohn's view that Judaism is a religion of divine laws that establish Jewish action in sound philosophical tenets of monotheism and forbearance, whereas Christianity is a belief system that turns the mind from orthopraxy to orthodoxy, with the resulting fanatical persecution of those who do not believe. For Hamann, this view turns Christianity into an idealism, whereas in fact Christianity is the concrete marriage of God and humankind. Hamann writes, "Hence the revealed religion of Christianity is rightly called faith, trust, confidence, and hopeful and childlike assurance of divine pledges and promises and of the glorious progress of its developing life in representations from glory to glory, till the full revelation and apocalypse of the mystery which was kept secret and believed since the world began, in the fullness of seeing face to face."[55] The revelation of human destiny in Christ reveals humankind's true "common good," and therefore Mendelssohn's effort to argue that the "church" adds nothing to our understanding of the "state" fails. When unguided by the true common good, temporal service of other human beings does not suffice to accomplish the "true fulfillment of our duties and of the perfection of man."[56] Rather, without the transcendent common good uniting "church" and "state," Hamann holds, "The state becomes a body without spirit and life—a carcass for eagles! The church becomes a ghost, without flesh and bone—a scarecrow for sparrows!"[57] The triumph of God over sin and God's union with humankind do not stop at the bounds of the "state," but even now bring hope to the actions of the "state" which otherwise would be hopelessly stuck in its own corruption.

Hamann, then, is led by Mendelssohn's work to insights about the Church. Recall Mendelssohn's utter rejection of structured religious authority: "What form of government is therefore advisable for the church? None! Who is to be the arbiter if disputes arise over religious matters? He to whom God has given the ability to convince others."[58]

---

philosophers are not human—i.e. historical beings, but super-historical; truth according to their canons cannot appear in flesh and blood, and be mediated to men through flesh and blood, i.e. historically through fallible sense-experience. On the other hand, their 'necessary truths' are dead bodies which do not manifest the living God" (Alexander, *Johann Georg Hamann*, 97).

55. Hamann, *Golgotha and Scheblimini*, 227; ed. Nadler, *Sämtliche Werke*, 306.

56. Hamann, *Golgotha and Scheblimini*, 225; ed. Nadler, *Sämtliche Werke*, 305.

57. Hamann, *Golgotha and Scheblimini*, 225; ed. Nadler, *Sämtliche Werke*, 303.

58. Mendelssohn, *Jerusalem*, 62.

For Mendelssohn, there is no need for structured authority in the "church," because the sole duty of the "church" is to educate her members in benevolent motives, and this duty carries with it no particular "power" in the community because it should depend only upon the persuasiveness of the teacher. By contrast, Hamann suggests that the "church" does indeed bear a particular power; namely, the power of Christ's victory over sin and his Resurrection-promise of marital intimacy with God. This Christological "power" fulfills God's work in Israel; the Church is called to be "Israel" to the entire world, by spreading the power of the Gospel. This power goes beyond teaching alone. It is the communication of the efficacious power of Christ's cross and Resurrection. It truly mediates divine power to the world, the divine power of the historical event of Christ's Pasch. No mere teaching could do this: the "church" is the bearer in history of a power that changes not merely ideas but the very being of the world.

To this point, Hamann and Mendelssohn represent well the dividing line in contemporary ecclesiology: does the "church" mediate, through faith, a unique causal power for salvation, or is the "church" better understood as a teacher whose power resides solely in its own persuasive authenticity as measured by the contemporary culture? Hamann's pietistic Christianity is rather close to Mendelssohn, however, in its estimation of visible ecclesial authority. Speaking of "dogmatics and Church law," Hamann remarks scornfully, "These visible, public and common institutions are neither religion nor wisdom from above, but are earthly, human and devilish, according to the influence of foreign cardinals or ciceroni, poetic confessors or prosaic pot-bellied priests, and the changing system of statistical equipoise and preponderance, or of armed tolerance and neutrality."[59] References in *Golgotha and Scheblimini* to the pope, Rome, and so forth are derogatory. When it comes to the actual human mediation of the power of Christ's Pasch, then, it might seem that Hamann would agree with Mendelssohn's critique. Thus, whether Hamann is able to provide a

---

59. Hamann, *Golgotha and Scheblimini*, 230; ed. Nadler, *Sämtliche Werke*, 312. Cf. early nineteenth-century Russian ecumenism, influenced by "German pietistic and mystical circles," especially the Russian Bible Society founded by Czar Alexander I, with its emphasis on the inner light and the religion of the heart: see Georges Florovsky, "Russian Orthodox Ecumenism in the Nineteenth Century," in *Ecumenism II: A Historical Approach*, vol. 14 of his *Collected Works*, ed. Richard S. Haugh (Vaduz: Büchervertriebsanstalt, 1989), 110–63, at 110–12.

sufficiently rich account of the human role in mediating God's work of salvation, other than through words/scripture, remains in question.[60]

ROSENZWEIG AND PSEUDO-DIONYSIUS: SACRAMENTAL MEDIATION

Rosenzweig and God's Action

Just as Hamann highlights the problem of sin, the early twentieth-century Jewish thinker Franz Rosenzweig's *The Star of Redemption*, whose lineage goes back to Mendelssohn through Rosenzweig's teacher Hermann Cohen, takes its starting point from the problem of death. Recognizing that philosophy cannot handle this problem except by a "compassionate lie," one whose fraudulence is immediately apparent, Rosenzweig seeks to uncover philosophically the particular contribution of the Jewish and Christian (and, in the first two parts of his book, also Muslim) worldviews to the problem of the universal and the particular. It would be impossible in this brief space to canvass all the paths that he traces.[61] Instead, I will focus upon briefly drawing out some of the insights of Part III, "The Configuration or The Eternal Hyper-Cosmos." These insights bear upon the question that

---

60. I turn to Rosenzweig and Pseudo-Dionysius at this point, but one could equally bring in John Henry Newman, profoundly involved in these post–Enlightenment discussions that we have been tracing. This work has been done by Geoffrey Wainwright, "Dispensations of Grace: Newman on the Sacramental Mediation of Salvation," *Pro Ecclesia* 12 (2003): 61–88; cf. John Tracy Ellis, "The Eucharist in the Life of Cardinal Newman," *Communio* 4 (1977): 321–40; Avery Dulles, sj, *John Henry Newman* (New York: Continuum, 2002), 23–24. See also the insights of Joseph Ratzinger, *The Spirit of the Liturgy*, trans. John Saward (German 1999; San Francisco: Ignatius Press, 2000); Roch Kereszty, "A Theological Meditation on the Liturgy of the Eucharist," *Communio* 23 (1996): 524–61.

61. For an introduction to *The Star of Redemption*, see Michael Wyschogrod's book review of the first English translation of Rosenzweig's book: Wyschogrod, "Franz Rosenzweig's *The Star of Redemption*," in Wyschogrod, *Abraham's Promise: Judaism and Jewish–Christian Relations*, ed. R. Kendall Soulen (Grand Rapids, MI: Eerdmans, 2004), 121–30. See also David Novak's valuable treatment of Rosenzweig's doctrine of election, in Novak, *The Election of Israel: The Idea of the Chosen People* (Cambridge: Cambridge University Press, 1995), ch. 3: "Franz Rosenzweig's Return to the Doctrine," 78–107. Novak suggests that Rosenzweig is better termed a "theologian" than a "philosopher," because "his thinking begins with God, unlike Hermann Cohen, Martin Buber, or Emmanuel Levinas, who begin their thinking with the human condition" (*The Election of Israel*, 96, fn 47). Cf. on Jewish theology, Novak, "Theology and Philosophy: An Exchange with Robert Jenson," in Novak, *Talking with Christians: Musings of a Jewish Theologian* (Grand Rapids, MI: Eerdmans, 2005), 229–46.

Mendelssohn's *Jerusalem* articulated for us—namely the question of whether "church" government or hierarchical ecclesial power is possible or desirable given the risk of power turning into oppression. Hamann's theocentric perspective makes clear that Christ's Paschal power, accomplishing the communion of human beings to God, must be historically *present* in the world. For his part, Rosenzweig shows why this historical presence must be one of human (liturgical) mediation of divine power rather than a merely extrinsic presence of God.

Rosenzweig introduces Part III with a section titled "On the Possibility of Entreating the Kingdom." This is a reflection on time, eternity, and prayer. The prayer of the believer, Rosenzweig says, "must really attain that which the prayer of the nonbeliever will not and the prayer of the fanatic cannot attain. It must hasten the future, must turn eternity into the nighest, the Today. Such anticipation of the future into the moment would have to be a true conversion of eternity into a Today."[62] Yet, the problem is that the moment continually passes: how can the moment embody and mediate eternity? Rosenzweig affirms, impossibly it would seem, that "the moment which we seek must begin again at the very moment that it vanishes; it must recommence in its own disappearance; its perishing must at the same time be a reissuing. For this purpose it is not enough that it come ever anew. It must not come anew, it must come back. It really must be the same moment."[63] To a degree, the cycle of seasons, weeks, and days anticipates the presence of eternity in time. Rosenzweig thus finds that "it is not for nothing that the words for cultivation and cult, for the service of earth and the service of God, for agriculture and the cultivation of the kingdom are one and the same in the sacred tongue."[64] The cult, the *leitourgia*, is prayer that enables eternity to enter time. Not only does the cult of the community of believers enable eternity to enter time, but for Rosenzweig it "compels the redemptive advent of the eternal into time" through its speaking from love to Love, begging for Love's advent in the world.[65]

---

62. Franz Rosenzweig, *The Star of Redemption*, trans. from the 2nd ed. by William W. Hallo (Notre Dame, IN: University of Notre Dame Press, 1985), 289.

63. Ibid.

64. Ibid., 292.

65. Ibid., 293.

By pointing out the significance of the liturgy, Rosenzweig already has added a crucial element to Hamann's response to Mendelssohn. The theocentric action that Hamann emphasizes— Christ's sacrificial atonement that establishes intimate communion between human beings and God—is mediated historically through the liturgy, itself primarily God's action. Mendelssohn, one recalls, limited the ceremonial practices of Israel to symbolizing truths about God known to Enlightenment philosophers. Thus understood, the ceremonial practices needed no "government" of a priestly hierarchy or authoritative structure of mediation—they simply needed good philosophers to interpret them. By contrast, Rosenzweig's communal cult, as primarily God's action, changes the world by bringing eternity into history.[66] For the Christian, this happens sacramentally through direct access, mediated through the cult, to the historical moment of Christ's Pasch, a moment that unites time with eternity. More than good philosophers are needed for such cultic rites. Equally, human mediation, necessary as it is, of the power of Christ's Pasch does not take center stage. Christ and his saving work are at the center of the rites; the theocentricity urged by Hamann cannot be urged too much.[67]

---

66. On Rosenzweig's relationship to Mendelssohn, Leora Batnitzky argues that "Rosenzweig shares with Mendelssohn two important points: first, that idolatry is a matter of worship that is alien, and second, that this alien worship is intimately linked to a mistaken understanding of the nature of religious authority and its relation to the past. Though Mendelssohn's and Rosenzweig's approaches to reason and enlightenment differ, they are linked by a common problematic. This problematic can be formulated in the question: What is Judaism's contribution to the modern world? For both Mendelssohn and Rosenzweig, the answer to this question is intimately linked to their views of Judaism's ability to avoid idolatry through its unique understanding of how human meaning is constituted" (Batnitzky, *Idolatry and Representation*, 33). Batnitzky finds that Mendelssohn, like Rosenzweig, is a liturgical thinker because "Mendelssohn argues that Jewish law recognizes the priority of religious performance, or worship, over ways of thinking" (34). While Batnitzky's reading of Mendelssohn seems a stretch, her posing of the problematic is insightful.

67. David Novak contrasts Rosenzweig on revelation and election with the anthropocentrism of Spinoza and of Hermann Cohen (1842–1918), the Kantian Jewish philosopher who was Rosenzweig's teacher. Novak observes, "For Rosenzweig, the trajectory of election is clearly from God to man. God elects man as the object of his self-revelation; then, and only then, is man able to respond to being so elected. Being an act founded in election from above, revelation is not just a metaphor for discovery of what is ever above by him or her who is now below. For if that were the case, election would be an essentially human act: the choice of concentration on a universal object by a rationally universalizing subject" (*The Election of Israel*, 85). A bit later Novak adds in the same theocentric vein, "For Rosenzweig, the love of the neighbor is not the primary act of love for which the love of God functions. The love of God has priority. And it has priority because the human love for God is in response to God's love for man, which is revealed in God's election of Israel" (97).

The "government" of the community that mediates divine time is thus not an end in itself, whose success or failure can be analyzed strictly sociologically. For example, Rosenzweig sees profound significance in the fact that the Jews are physically descended from Abraham. They are therefore able to be a sign of eternity's presence in time. As Rosenzweig puts it,

> There is only one community in which such a linked sequence of ever-lasting life goes from grandfather to grandson, only one which cannot utter the "we" of its unity without hearing deep within a voice that adds: "are eternal." . . . All eternity not based on blood must be based on the will and on hope. Only a community based on common blood feels the warrant of eternity warm in its veins even now.[68]

He argues that it is primarily this blood-relationship, detached from the other earthly bonds enjoyed by other peoples and nations, that signals the community's "claim to eternity."[69] This does not mean that he evacuates the land of its importance, but rather that he considers it the sign of an eschatological yearning for perfect communion with God: "In the most profound sense possible, this people has a land of its own only in that it has a land it yearns for—a holy land. . . . The holiness of the land removed it from the people's spontaneous reach while it could still reach out for it. This holiness increases the longing for what is lost, to infinity."[70] After discussing the Jewish understanding of God and man, he turns to the liturgical feasts of the Jewish year and to the Jewish communal meal. His purpose is to show that "only the eternal people, which is not encompassed by world

---

68. Rosenzweig, *The Star of Redemption*, 298–99. Novak emphasizes that, in contrast to Martin Buber, Rosenzweig sees the community rather than the individual as the recipient of God's revelation: "Buber speaks of the validity of the commandment being 'personal' rather than 'universal.' Rosenzweig, conversely, speaks of 'all great Jewish periods.' Thus Rosenzweig speaks of the Jewish *people* as the subject or addressee of the commandments (understanding *Gebot* generically), whereas Buber speaks of *himself* (or any other individual self) as that subject or addressee (understanding *Gebot* particularly). There is a fundamental difference whether one sees the commandment as being addressed to a communal self or an individual self. This difference, in this issue, lies in the continuity and extension of the commandments in time and space" (Novak, "Karl Barth on Divine Command: A Jewish Response," in *Talking with Christians*, 127–45, at 135). For further discussion of this point and its significance, see *The Election of Israel*, 86–87.

69. Rosenzweig, *The Star of Redemption*, 299. Cf. Michael Mack, "The Politics of Blood: Rosenzweig and Hegel," in Mack, *German Idealism and the Jew*, 125–35.

70. Rosenzweig, *The Star of Redemption*, 300. Rosenzweig is writing before the establishment of the state of Israel and the reclamation of the Hebrew language.

history, can—at every moment—bind creation as a whole to redemption while redemption is still to come."[71] As Rosenzweig presents it, the meaning of Judaism escapes those who would envision the Jewish people in strictly sociological terms: their very existence is a sign that divine power has laid claim to history.

How does Rosenzweig understand (philosophically) the relationship between Judaism and Christianity? Judaism finds eternity in history through "rootedness in the profoundest self"; Christianity through "diffusion throughout all that is outside."[72] In this diffusion, the Church inevitably comes "into conflict with the state."[73] No more than Mendelssohn or Hamann does Rosenzweig credit the structures of the visible Church:

> The Church is in the world, visible and with a universal law of its own, and thus not a whit more than Caesar's empire itself the kingdom of God. It grows toward the latter in its history which is secular both in the sense of worldly and of centuries-long; it remains a segment of the world and of life, and it becomes eternal only through its animation by the human act of love. Ecclesiastical history is no more the history of the kingdom of God than is imperial history.[74]

In the "human act of love" and especially in the word, Rosenzweig finds the center of Christianity. In this regard he contrasts Christianity with Judaism. In the latter, the word does not establish the community. Although the reading of scripture might seem to mark the center of the Jewish liturgy, in fact the scriptural reading "is rather a symbol only of that community which has already been established, that 'eternal life' which has arguably been planted."[75]

By contrast in Christianity "the word truly takes the individual by the hand and guides him on the way which leads to the community."[76] Here, perhaps, Rosenzweig's lack of familiarity with Catholic Christianity shapes his account. According to Rosenzweig, historical mediation of divine power occurs, in Christianity, through

---

71. Ibid., 335.
72. Ibid., 348.
73. Ibid., 353.
74. Ibid.
75. Ibid., 358.
76. Ibid.

beliefs. His understanding of Christianity in this regard is similar to
Mendelssohn's, both indebted to the Lutheranism that they knew.[77]
Rosenzweig, however, recounts how the mediation of divine power in
history occurs through the liturgical feasts that make divine eternity
present in time. The liturgy is for him the place where the mediated
immediacy of God's power occurs; in their worship, Jewish flesh and
blood, and Christian faith in the word of revelation, become what God
has made them, a locus of divine inbreaking, manifesting God's
governance of history through creation, revelation, and eschatological
redemption.[78]

---

77. By contrast, for a sacramental view of Lutheranism, see *The Catholicity of the
Reformation*, ed. Carl E. Braaten and Robert W. Jenson (Grand Rapids, MI: Eerdmans,
1996). See also Avery Dulles, sj, and George A. Lindbeck, "Bishops and the Ministry of the
Gospel," in *Confessing One Faith: A Joint Commentary on the Augsburg Confession by Lutheran
and Catholic Theologians*, ed. George Wolfgang Forell and James F. McCue (Minneapolis, MN:
Augsburg, 1982), 147–72; David S. Yeago, "The Office of the Keys: On the Disappearance of
Discipline in Protestant Modernity," and Carl E. Braaten, "The Special Ministry of the
Ordained," in *Marks of the Body of Christ*, ed. Carl E. Braaten and Robert W. Jenson (Grand
Rapids, MI: Eerdmans, 1999), 95–122 and 123–36; cf. Braaten's *Mother Church: Ecclesiology
and Ecumenism* (Minneapolis, MN: Fortress Press, 1998), 91–92, 96–97. Dulles and Lindbeck
base their interpretation upon the Augsburg Confession and argue for a "Catholic" reading of
Luther on ecclesial hierarchy (however see also Dulles, *The Catholicity of the Church*, 109). For
a contrasting view, see the congregationalist interpretation of Luther by Brian A. Gerrish,
"Priesthood and Ministry in the Theology of Luther," *Church History* 34 (1965): 404–22;
Walter Sundberg, "Ministry in Nineteenth Century European Lutheranism," in *Called and
Ordained*, ed. Todd Nichol and Marc Kolden (Minneapolis: Fortress Press, 1990). See also
especially the Lutheran essays in the volume devoted to this topic in the Lutheran–Catholic
dialogue, *Papal Primacy and the Universal Church*, ed. Paul C. Empie and T. Austin Murphy
(Minneapolis, MN: Augsburg Press, 1974); the historical essays in *Episcopacy in the Lutheran
Church? Studies in the Development and Definition of the Office of Church Leadership*, ed. Ivar
Asheim and Victor R. Gold (Philadelphia: Fortress Press, 1970); and most recently Karlheinz
Diez, *"Ecclesia—Non Est Civitas Platonica": Antworten katholischer Kontroverstheologen des 16.
Jahrhunderts auf Martin Luthers Anfrage an die "Sichtbarkeit" der Kirche* (Frankfurt: Josef
Knecht, 1997).

78. David Novak finds inadequate, as I do, Rosenzweig's attempt to account for the
complementarity and eschatological unification of Judaism and Christianity. For Rosenzweig,
"Judaism's task is to preserve the historical reality of revelation in all its purity and all its
concentration; Christianity's task is to gather the whole world into that reality. Without Judaism
Christianity is in danger of being diluted into the paganism of the unredeemed world; without
Christianity Judaism is in danger of being marginalized as the religion of an exotic tribe. Only
at the time of the final-redemption-yet-to-be will there be an *Aufhebung*, but it will be the
elevation-and-transformation of *both* Judaism *and* Christianity into the wholly unprecedented
kingdom of God. Rosenzweig is convinced that the task of both Jews and Christians is to
await that culmination of all history—but to wait for it separately. . . . Although there is a
beautiful symmetry in Rosenzweig's unique constitution of the relation of Judaism and
Christianity to each other, it does not correspond to the data of Jewish tradition" (*The Election
of Israel*, 100–1). Novak explains that, on the contrary,

Pseudo-Dionysius: The Trinitarian Communication of Unity

Our effort to respond to Volf's case against ecclesial hierarchy—
rooted in how one understands the constitutive elements of Christian
personalism—has to this point traversed the Enlightenment arguments
of Moses Mendelssohn, who rejected ecclesial structure on the ground
that the Church's task is solely educative, and the responses of Hamann
and Rosenzweig, who suggest on the contrary that Christianity and
Judaism communicate a sacred power (Hamann) by means of liturgical
mediation (Rosenzweig). By engaging these three thinkers, I have
sought to suggest that Volf's emphasis on equality, flexibility, and
persuasiveness does not sufficiently appreciate the theocentric and
sacramental depths of true Christian personalism, inseparable from
the mediation of the grace of the Holy Spirit to fallen human beings
in need of healing and transformation.

Let us next turn to the classic source of much Christian
theology of hierarchy, Pseudo-Dionysius. Does he add anything to
Rosenzweig's account of liturgical mediation? For Dionysius, a key
question is why the Trinity created our intelligence to be so dependent
upon sensible things.[79] Would it not be better if, like the angels, we

---

the tendency in rabbinic teaching was to emphasize that the redemption of the world
would in essence be God's redemption of the Jewish people, which would then include
all the rest of humankind. Thus a major effect of redemption would be the judaization of
humanity. However, this redemption would not be the result of the extension of
revelation by the Jews or by anyone else. Instead, it would be the mysterious act of
God. . . . My argument with Rosenzweig is that he has compromised the transcendence
of redemption by making it the culmination of a process, albeit a process unlike that
proposed by Idealism. In other words, he did not fully exorcise the tendencies of the
Idealism on which he cut his philosophical teeth. For this reason, Rosenzweig has
ultimately seen the election of Israel as the means to a higher end, which is the election
of humanity itself. However, there is a fundamental difference between the more
classical view, which sees the redemption of the world as its apocalyptic judaization, and
Rosenzweig's still liberally influenced view, which sees redemption as the *Aufhebung* of
Judaism (and Christianity) into a new humanity. In Rosenzweig's view, election is
teleologically derivative, whereas in the classical view it is non-derivative. (102–3)

79. See Pseudo-Dionysius, *The Celestial Hierarchy*, ch. 1, §1, in Pseudo-Dionysius, *The
Complete Works*, trans. Colm Luibheid with Paul Rorem (New York: Paulist Press, 1987), 145.
For Aquinas's reliance upon Dionysius's understanding of divine mediation of supernatural
knowledge, see Serge-Thomas Bonino, OP, "The Role of the Apostles in the Communication
of Revelation according to the *Lectura super Ioannem* of St. Thomas Aquinas," trans. Teresa
Bede and Matthew Levering, in *Reading John with St. Thomas Aquinas*, ed. Michael Dauphinais
and Matthew Levering (Washington, DC: The Catholic University of America Press, 2005),
318–46, at 318–20. As Bonino says, "The law of mediation, as a general structure of Thomas's
thought, profoundly illumines his theological reflection on the role of the apostles in the

simply understood the Light? He answers that "the gifts transcendently received by the beings of heaven," in other words the angels, "are granted to us in a symbolic mode."[80] God created us "lower" than the angels so that we might ascend to what they know by coming to recognize, through liturgical symbolism, the pattern of divine gifting.

In *The Celestial Hierarchy* Dionysius defines *hierarchy* as "a sacred order, a state of understanding and an activity approximating as closely as possible to the divine."[81] He offers a similar (Trinitarian) definition of the Church's hierarchy in *The Ecclesiastical Hierarchy*: "Our hierarchy consists of an inspired, divine, and divinely worked understanding, activity, and perfection."[82] Imaging God requires being configured to God's order, understanding, and activity. This

communication of *sacra doctrina*, of supernatural and salvific knowledge" (ibid., 320). For the similar indebtedness of Maximus the Confessor to Dionysius's theology of hierarchy, see Adam G. Cooper, "St. Maximus the Confessor on Priesthood, Hierarchy, and Rome," *Pro Ecclesia* 10 (2001): 346–67. Cooper takes issue with Lars Thunberg's handling of the Church in Thunberg's *Man and the Cosmos: The Vision of St. Maximus the Confessor* (New York: St. Vladimir's Seminary Press, 1985).

    80. Pseudo-Dionysius, *The Celestial Hierarchy*, ch. 1, §3, 146. The importance of the "symbolic mode" finds contemporary expression in David Fagerberg, *Theologia Prima: What Is Liturgical Theology?* (Chicago: Hillenbrand Books, 2004); see also Alexander Golitzin, *Et introibo ad altare dei: The Mystagogy of Dionysius Areopagita* (Thessalonica: Patriarchikon Idruma Paterikon Meleton, 1994); idem, "Dionysius Areopagita: A Christian Mysticism?" *Pro Ecclesia* 12 (2003): 161–212, which defends Dionysius against Reformation concerns.

    81. Pseudo-Dionysius, *The Celestial Hierarchy*, ch. 3, §1, 153. On Dionysius's understanding of hierarchy see also Alexander Golitzin, "Hierarchy versus Anarchy? Dionysius Areopagita, Symeon the New Theologian, Nicetas Stethatos, and Their Common Roots in the Ascetical Tradition," *St. Vladimir's Theological Quarterly* 39 (1994): 131–79; R. Roques, *L'Univers Dionysien. Structure hiérarchique du monde selon le Pseudo-Denys* (Paris: Cerf, 1983). For a standard critique of Dionysius's influence on Catholic ecclesiology see Ghislain Lafont, OSB, *Imagining the Catholic Church: Structured Communion in the Spirit*, trans. John J. Burkhard, OFM CONV (French 1995; Collegeville, MN: Liturgical Press, 2000). Lafont writes, "In an attempt to enlist the thought of late Platonism in the last great school of Athens, this thinker undertook the audacious enterprise of interpreting the structures and the sacraments of the Church in light of Neoplatonism. The author of the work *Ecclesiastical Hierarchy* saw in the person of the bishop the mediator between the angelic hierarchies, which had their source in God the Principle-beyond-principle, and the faithful of the Church. In a way, we can say that Pseudo-Dionysius applied to the Christian order what had already been accomplished in the religious dimension of politics in Hellenistic thought. In addition to the other elements of political theology mentioned above, our recourse to the thought of Pseudo-Dionysius helps us understand the ecclesiological theory for the primacy of the pope, an interpretation that is inspired by late Platonism" (52; cf. 58). See Avery Dulles, SJ's review of Lafont's book in *Theological Studies* 57 (1996): 768–69.

    82. Pseudo-Dionysius, *The Ecclesiastical Hierarchy*, ch. 1, §1, in idem, *The Complete Works*, 195. As Dionysius says later, "in our sacred tradition every hierarchy is divided in three" (ch. 5, I, §1, 233).

means different things for different beings, depending upon the roles to which God calls them, but in all cases it requires lifting up one's mind (hierarchically) toward the higher realities. If created beings lose this self-subordinating desire to know higher realities, and instead focus their intelligence upon lesser things—as is so often the case— then they have fallen away from "hierarchy." To be hierarchically ordered is to look "upward" in search of the gifting God, and in this way to be configured to the Light who is Jesus, the Light who receives all from his Father.[83] Dionysius explains, "The goal of a hierarchy . . . is to enable beings to be as like as possible to God and to be at one with him. A hierarchy has God as its leader of all understanding and action. . . . A hierarchy bears in itself the mark of God. Hierarchy causes its members to be images of God in all respects."[84]

The ecclesial hierarchy mediates to us the divine Light in forms befitting our mode of knowing. Dionysius observes, "We see our human hierarchy . . . pluralized in a great variety of perceptible symbols lifting us upward hierarchically until we are brought as far as we can be into the unity of divinization."[85] These perceptible symbols, by which our minds ascend to divine realities, are the sacred writings and sacraments set forth by the hierarchs.[86] A true hierarch, says

---

83. See *The Ecclesiastical Hierarchy*, ch. 1, §1: "Jesus who is transcendent mind, utterly divine mind, who is the source and the being underlying all hierarchy, all sanctification, all the workings of God, who is the ultimate in divine power. He assimilates them, as much as they are able, to his own light" (196). Looking upward means, for the human being, attending to the example of the angels, whose (biblically revealed) hierarchical ordering of intelligences shows us how the Church is to be ordered so as to practice looking upward in receptivity to the divine Light. The earthly ecclesial hierarchy thus imitates the angelic hierarchy. As Dionysius says, "our own hierarchy is blessedly and harmoniously divided into orders in accordance with divine revelation and therefore deploys the same sequence as the hierarchies of heaven" (ch. 6, III, §5, 248).

84. Pseudo-Dionysius, *The Celestial Hierarchy*, ch. 3, §2, 154. Discussing Dionysius's *The Celestial Hierarchy*, Aquinas observes that the unity of the (hierarchical) kingdom of God reflects the divine unity. As Aquinas is careful to add, however, "those err and speak against the opinion of Dionysius who place a hierarchy in the divine Persons, and call it the *supercelestial* hierarchy. For in the divine Persons there exists, indeed, a natural order, but no hierarchical order, for as Dionysius says (*Cael. Hier.* iii): 'The hierarchical order is so directed that some be cleansed, enlightened, and perfected; and that others cleanse, enlighten, and perfect'; which far be it from us to apply to the divine Persons" (ST I, q. 108, a. 1).

85. Pseudo-Dionysius, *The Ecclesiastical Hierarchy*, ch. 1, §2, 197.

86. Dionysius states, "The first leaders of our hierarchy received their fill of the sacred gift from the transcendent Deity. Then divine goodness sent them to lead others to this same gift. . . . In their written and unwritten initiations, they brought the transcendent down to our level. As they had been commanded to do they did this for us, not simply because of the

Dionysius, is "a holy and inspired man, someone who understands all sacred knowledge, someone in whom an entire hierarchy is completely perfected and known."[87] A hierarch embodies the goal of every hierarchy, namely "divinization," which consists in becoming like God (and thus united to God) through "the continuous love of God and of things divine."[88]

How is such divinization possible? Dionysius holds that the starting point is receptivity. Human beings must "dispose our souls to hear the sacred words as receptively as possible, to be open to the divine workings of God, to clear an uplifting path toward that inheritance which awaits us in heaven, and to accept our most divine and sacred regeneration."[89] Receptivity is first: we must be born of God. Because this receptivity itself occurs at the human level of perceptible symbols, it involves receiving from human hierarchs who mediate "an encounter with God and with things divine."[90] This is done through the performance of the rite of Baptism, as Dionysius describes in some detail. Prior to Baptism, the catechumenate prepares the person through "the mediation of people more advanced than he."[91] As the catechumen purifies his or her life and learns about the divine realities, he or she becomes more and more prepared for union with the triune God, in "the company of those who have earned divinization and who form a sacred assembly,"[92] through the sacramental mediation of the hierarch. Dionysius remarks that "whoever enters into communion with the One cannot proceed to live a divided life, especially if he hopes for a real participation in the One."[93]

profane from whom the symbols were to be kept out of reach, but because, as I have stated, our own hierarchy is itself symbolical and adapted to what we are" (ibid., ch. 1, §5, 199). Regarding "symbols" see also the observation of Paul Evdokimov: "In the Bible . . . the more nature is firm, living, and full of vigor within the realm of its own value, the greater is its symbolic meaning. The more man is man, the more he is an image, an icon of God" (Evdokimov, *The Art of the Icon: A Theology of Beauty*, trans. Steven Bigham [French 1972; Redondo Beach, CA: Oakwood Publications, 1990], 106). This point accords with Dionysius's insight that "our own hierarchy is itself symbolical."

87. Pseudo-Dionysius, *The Ecclesiastical Hierarchy*, ch. 1, §3, 197.

88. Ibid., 198.

89. Ibid., ch. 2, I, 200.

90. Ibid., ch. 2, II, §5, 202.

91. Ibid., ch. 2, III, §4, 206. Dionysius explains and defends infant Baptism at the conclusion of *The Ecclesiastical Hierarchy*: see ch. 7, III, §11–12, 258–59.

92. Ibid., ch. 2, III, §4, 206.

93. Ibid., ch. 2, III, §5, 206.

The interpersonal communication between the triune God and human beings in divinization, and between the members of the "sacred assembly," can be seen in the liturgical rite of the Eucharist to which Baptism leads. What are the "perceptible symbols" present in the Eucharist? There are "the mystical reading of the sacred volumes" and "the things praised through the sacredly displayed symbols";[94] both of these mediate the Light of the Father in the Holy Spirit, and thereby unite the recipients in the unity of divine communion. Dionysius observes in this regard, "Every sacredly initiating operation draws our fragmented lives together into a one-like divinization. It forges a divine unity out of the divisions within us. It grants us communion and union with the One."[95] Every "hierarchic sacrament" achieves this, and the Eucharist does so most perfectly.[96] To receive such divine gifts we cannot be stuck on the level of the symbols. We must look upward so as to receive the higher realities; namely, the divine realities communicated through the symbols.

This looking upward, which is none other than the hierarchical ordering of our soul (so as to value higher and lower realities in a proper, hierarchical order), corresponds to the liturgical actions of the hierarch. By looking upward toward the source, he leads the whole congregation in the pattern of "hierarchical" receptivity, receiving the divine realities from above. His work of active mediation—what Dionysius calls "the performance of the most divine acts"—comes about through solemn liturgical prayer "at the divine altar."[97] While others see the symbols but not the realities, the hierarch leads the way in lifting up his eyes to the divine gifting: he "is continuously uplifted by the divine Spirit toward the most holy source of the sacramental rite and he does so in blessed and conceptual contemplations, in that purity which marks his life as it conforms to God."[98]

Why such an emphasis on the superiority of the hierarch? As Volf reminds us, are not other members equally Christians, equally

---

94. Ibid., ch. 3, II, 211.

95. Ibid., ch. 3, I, 209.

96. Ibid.

97. Ibid., ch. 3, II, 210–11.

98. Ibid., ch. 3, II, 211. For Dionysius, the eucharistic gifts communicate Christ's will to unite us to his hierarchical (well-ordered, holy) life, so as to unite us to the unity of the divine communion (ibid., ch. 3, III, §§12–13, 221–23).

persons in Christ? And what if the hierarch fails to be a holy person? These concerns, I would suggest, have not yet grasped the point of Dionysius's exposition. Dionysius understands that sin weighs down human beings so that they do not seek the higher things. Human beings, after sin, do not come naturally to looking upward. The hierarch, within the community, belongs to the "perceptible symbols" by which the triune God leads human beings upward to communion in divine unity and Trinity. By his presiding at the eucharistic synaxis, the hierarch symbolizes the need for each member to receive from above, from Christ, and the hierarch symbolizes the reality that the gifts are not merely exchanged among the members but rather come down from the Father through Christ by his Spirit. The community becomes fully itself in worship—a richly symbolic worship in which the pattern of upward-looking receptivity is symbolized throughout.

Hierarchy thus fits the particular kind of interpersonal relationship that is the relationship of fallen/redeemed human beings with God. So as to share in the Trinitarian communion of equal Persons, human persons need to be formed by an embodied hierarchical symbolism to learn how once again to receive gifts from on high. Even an imperfect hierarch can take his place within the symbolic framework, although it is much better that the hierarch be what he should be.

As Dionysius explains, "From the very beginning human nature has stupidly glided away from those good things bestowed on it by God. It turned to the life of the most varied desires and came at the end to the catastrophe of death. There followed the destructive rejection of what was really good, a trampling over the sacred Law laid down in paradise for man."[99] Turning away from the creative Source, human beings clung to creatures as though creatures were God and could bring happiness. The result of cleaving to creatures was a radical disordering of human nature's proper interior hierarchy—since the soul, forgetting God, irrationally served the body's disordered passions—and the resulting fatal dissolution of the body. Dionysius summarizes this loss of interior hierarchical ordering: "He [man] freely turned away from the divine and uplifting life and was dragged

---

99. Ibid., ch. 3, III, §11, 220. Cf. Athanasius, *On the Incarnation*, trans. and ed. by a Religious of C.S.M.V. (Crestwood, NY: St. Vladimir's Orthodox Theological Seminary, 1993).

instead as far as possible in the opposite direction and was plunged into the utter mess of passion."[100]

In response, God poured out his "providential gifts" even more.[101] In Christ and through his Spirit,[102] the Father offered us again the hierarchical pattern, and did so not through power but through righteous love: Divinity

> took upon itself in a most authentic way all the characteristics of our nature, except sin. It became one with us in our lowliness, losing nothing of its own real condition, suffering no change or loss. It allowed us, as those of equal birth, to enter into communion with it and to acquire a share of its own true beauty. Thus, as our hidden tradition teaches, it made it possible for us to escape from the domain of the rebellious, and it did this not through overwhelming force, but, as scripture mysteriously tells us, by an act of judgment and also in all righteousness.[103]

The triune God's gifting "showed us a supramundane uplifting and an inspiring way of life in shaping our self to it as fully as lay in our power."[104] To be conformed to the triune God is, for the human being, to receive a hierarchical ordering of "uplifting," in which the lower strives to share in the wise pattern of the higher. Thus the body receives its form from the soul, the body-soul composite has Christ as its pattern, and Christ is the Image of the Father. "Hierarchical" ordering, as understood here, is the very opposite of domination.

---

100. Pseudo-Dionysius, *The Ecclesiastical Hierarchy*, ch. 3, III, §11, 220.

101. Ibid.

102. On the role of the Spirit see also ibid., ch. 4, III, §11, where Dionysius speaks of the effect of the sacrament of "ointment" (i.e., the sacrament of confirmation): "Furthermore, in being initiated in that sacred sacrament of divine birth [baptism], the perfect anointing of the ointment gives us a visitation of the divine Spirit. What this symbolic imagery signifies, I think, is that he who in human form received the sanctification of the divine Spirit for us, while at the same time remaining unchanged in respect of his own divinity, arranges now for the gift to us of the divine Spirit" (231).

103. Ibid., ch. 3, III, §11, 220–21.

104. Ibid., 221. Reinhard Hütter remarks with similar insight, "The church itself is nothing else than the thankful creature of God's saving work, not a proud executor but a glad recipient. Yet this receiving embodied in practices is precisely the way in and through which the Holy Spirit works the saving knowledge of God" (Hütter, "The Church: The Knowledge of the Triune God: Practices, Doctrine, Theology," in *Knowing the Triune God: The Work of the Spirit in the Practices of the Church*, ed. James J. Buckley and David S. Yeago [Grand Rapids, MI: Eerdmans, 2001], 23). For a contrary view, interpreting the Church anthropocentrically (as self-constituting) rather than theocentrically, see Roger Haight, sj, *Christian Community in History*, vol. 1: *Historical Ecclesiology* (New York: Continuum, 2004).

Rather, it pedagogically leads fallen human beings toward renewing in ourselves the pattern of openness and receptivity to gifting that comes "from above," not by power but by love.

Dionysius observes, therefore, that ecclesial hierarchy—the interpersonal structure through which the triune God communicates his gifts, at whose head is the divine "hierarch" Jesus Christ—serves fallen human beings by providing practice in hierarchical "uplifting." He asks, "This imitation of God, how else are we to achieve it if not by endlessly reminding ourselves of God's sacred works and doing so by way of the sacred hymns and the sacred acts established by the hierarchy?"[105] The eucharistic synaxis is the primary example of such a hierarchical practice. Dionysius says, "We do this, as the scriptures say, in remembrance of him. This is why the hierarch, the man of God, stands before the divine altar."[106] Before the altar, the hierarch first praises, in words that lift up the mind to the divine realities, the glorious saving works that Jesus performs "for the good pleasure of the most holy Father and the holy Spirit."[107] The hierarch then "proceeds to the task of the symbolic sacred act," the consecration of the Eucharist.[108] Dionysius is well aware that no human hierarch, no matter how holy, is worthy of this office. The hierarch consecrates the Eucharist "in accordance with the rules laid down by God himself, which is the reason why, at the same time, having sung the sacred praises of the divine works, he apologizes, as befits a hierarch, for being the one to undertake a sacred task so far beyond him. Reverently he cries out: 'It is you who said "Do this in remembrance of me." ' "[109] The hierarch's unworthiness, it should be clear, places the hierarch himself in the same position as all members of Christ: namely, in a position of neediness or receptivity, so as to be "hierarchically" uplifted by Christ and his Spirit to the Father.

Indeed, Dionysius finds in the Eucharist the pattern for the life of the hierarch. Just as "reception of the mysteries always comes before their mystical distribution," so also in the Eucharist it is fitting that the hierarch, having consecrated the Eucharist, should partake in

---

105. Pseudo-Dionysius, *The Ecclesiastical Hierarchy*, ch. 3, III, §12, 221.
106. Ibid.
107. Ibid.
108. Ibid.
109. Ibid.

it first. Dionysius says, "The sacred leader first of all participates in the abundance of the holy gifts which God has commanded him to give to others and in this way he goes on to impart them to others."[110] The "holy gifts" of the Eucharist are in this regard no different from any other holy gifts. Thus Dionysius warns, "Whoever wrongfully dares to teach holiness to others before he has regularly practiced it himself is unholy and is a stranger to sacred norms."[111] Without personal holiness, the hierarch embodies arrogance. In Dionysius's words, "Just as the finest and most luminous of beings are the first to be filled with the sun's rays and then pass on the superabundant light to others, so if God's inspiration and choice have not summoned one to the task of leadership, if one has not yet received perfect and lasting divinization, one must avoid the arrogance of guiding others."[112] Dionysius knows, of course, that some hierarchs are not holy but retain their office. Such hierarchs must be warned that their arrogance, precisely in not repenting and striving for holiness, both undermines their mission and brings on the eternal punishment due to the lawless. But such hierarchs do not defeat the symbolism of God.

Dionysius does not limit the Church's hierarchy to the bishops. Rather, the hierarchical pattern of the Church begins with the angels, who possess "the native sacramental power of a most completely immaterial conception of God and of things divine."[113] Hierarchy rightly orders the lower to the higher. In the hierarchies of the angels, which Dionysius describes at various points on the basis of scriptural passages, this hierarchical ordering comes about through their "native sacramental power."[114] In the ecclesial hierarchy of the Church (and Israel), the triune God employs sacramental symbolism: "To avoid harm it [the divinity] granted only as much light as suited the weak eyes looking up to it."[115] In the hierarchy of Israel, led by Moses and the priests, God focused on lifting up the Israelites to true worship. Dionysius explains, "In this hierarchy of the Law the 'sacrament'

---

110. Ibid., ch. 3, III, §14, 223.

111. Ibid.

112. Ibid.

113. Ibid., ch. 5, I, §2, 233.

114. Dionysius argues that mediation takes place in the angelic hierarchy, in a manner similar to mediation in the earthly ecclesial hierarchy (ibid., ch. 6, III, §6, 248–49).

115. Ibid., ch. 5, I, §2, 234.

consisted of an uplifting to worship in spirit. The guides were those
whom Moses, himself the foremost initiator and leader among the
hierarchs of the Law, had initiated into the holy tabernacle."[116] The
hierarchy of the Church "is a fulfillment and completion" of the
hierarchy of Moses.[117] But, like the latter hierarchy, it requires "a
threefold division; namely, the most holy operation of the sacraments,
the godlike dispensers of the sacred things, and those guided by them,
according to capacity, toward the sacred."[118] Each aspect of this three-
fold division is itself divided into three. For our purposes, we do not
need to go into all the divisions. Rather, the key is that hierarchy's
purpose, at all levels, is deification in worship.

In his account of hierarchy, Dionysius always begins with
the principle of mediation. God communicates divine realities in a
mediated fashion, so that we receive from others and thereby learn to
practice receptivity. As Dionysius puts the principle, "It is the all-holy
ordinance of the divinity that secondary things should be lifted up to
the most divine ray through the mediation of the primary things."[119]
Hierarchical mediation seeks to lead others higher into God's Light,
not to impose or retain domineering power. Just as angelic hierarchy
mediates divine Light, so too does ecclesial hierarchy. Since ecclesial
hierarchy aims at lifting up human minds to Jesus Christ, the Church
symbolically/liturgically represents this hierarchical goal by means of
a hierarchical structure that moves upward to the hierarch (the bishop).
The "order of hierarchs," or bishops, thus possesses an authority that
can only be understood in the context of deifying worship. This order
"completes every hierarchic rite of consecration. It revealingly teaches
others to understand, explaining their sacred things, proportionate
characteristics, and their holy powers."[120]

God's work in human beings involves purification, illumination,
and perfection. The bishops receive the power to accomplish "perfection," through consecration in sacramental symbolism and through

---

116. Ibid.

117. Ibid.

118. Ibid., 235.

119. Ibid., ch. 5, I, §4, 236.

120. Ibid., ch. 5, I, §6, 237. For Dionysius, bishops govern the religious orders because
hierarchical mediation, as a performative interpretation of symbols (sacramental and
scriptural), includes the office of teaching divine realities (ibid., ch. 6, I, §3, 244–45).

the teaching of revealed divine wisdom in scriptural symbolism. The "symbols" lead upward to union with the triune God. Likewise, Dionysius explains, the work of purification belongs specially to the order of deacons. Their work "makes clean the imperfect and incubates them by means of the cleansing enlightenments and teachings of scripture."[121] The order of priests then possesses, in particular, the task of illumination: "The light-bearing order of priests guides the initiates to the divine visions of the sacraments. It does so by the authority of the inspired hierarchs in fellowship with whom it exercises the functions of its own ministry."[122]

Dionysius trusts that the hierarchs are "inspired," that is, filled with the Holy Spirit. As we have observed, he is aware of the unworthiness of the hierarchs and of the failure of some. Yet because the communication of the divine gifts is organized hierarchically (for the reasons we have noted), he trusts that the hierarchs will be sufficiently "inspired" by the Holy Spirit to accomplish their symbolic task. Dionysius observes that "at his consecration the hierarch kneels on both knees in front of the altar. On his head he carries God's revealed word, together with the hand of the hierarch who is consecrating him."[123] On his knees and with the scriptures on his head, the hierarch being consecrated symbolically enacts before the altar of divine worship his receptivity before the triune Source. This receptivity is accomplished from within his submission to those hierarchs who have faithfully (guided by the Holy Spirit) taught before him, symbolized sacramentally by "the hand of the hierarch who is consecrating him." The consecrations of the priest and deacon take place in a similar manner.[124]

Commenting on the rites of consecration to Holy Orders, Dionysius brings out the pedagogy of *receptivity* inscribed in the rites. The hierarch's imposition of hands "teaches them to do all their clerical works as if they were acting on the orders of God and have him as guide in all their activities."[125] The hierarch's action, in other

---

121. Ibid., ch. 5, I, §6, 238.

122. Ibid., 237.

123. Ibid., ch. 5, II, 239.

124. For the differences between the rites of consecration for the offices of bishop, priest, and deacon, as well as for commentary on the placement of the scriptures on the head of the new bishop being consecrated, see ibid., ch. 5, III, §§7–8, 242–43.

125. Ibid., ch. 5, III, §3, 240.

words, indicates the pattern of divine gifting and human receiving. The Sign of the Cross likewise implies the receptivity to divine wisdom that must characterize all members of the ecclesial hierarchy, as it does the angelic members. Dionysius states, "The sign of the cross indicates the renunciation of all the desires of the flesh. It points to a life given over to the imitation of God and unswervingly directed toward the divine life of the incarnate Jesus, who was divinely sinless and yet lowered himself to the cross and to death."[126] All who would imitate Jesus, especially those who receive hierarchical office, do so under the mark of the cross, representing radical receptivity and divine gifting. In the same way Dionysius notes that the hierarch's words during the act of consecration proclaim his unworthiness of the consecratory power that he has received from God. Even Jesus, "our own first and divine consecrator—for Jesus in his endless love for us took on this task—'did not exalt himself,' as scripture declares."[127] Rather, Jesus set the example for his ecclesial hierarchy: "in hierarchic fashion he referred this act of consecration to his most holy Father and to the Divine Spirit."[128] Thus again, hierarchy in the Church is not about dominating, but about gifting and receiving. Ecclesial hierarchy teaches human beings to lift up their minds to divine realities and be configured to the "hierarchic" pattern that divine Wisdom and Love require.

Dionysius repeatedly affirms that "the reception of the divine mysteries [the Eucharist] is the high point of all hierarchic participation."[129] The ecclesial hierarchy has its purpose in the divine worship, which builds up the Church in wisdom and love. It is in the Eucharist, too, that the hierarchy possesses its dignity: "all the sacred orders, as they are uplifted and are more or less made godlike, have a

---

126. Ibid., ch. 5, III, §4, 240.

127. Ibid., ch. 5, III, §5, 241.

128. Ibid. Dionysius adds that "it is not by his own personal activity that a divine hierarch should work sacerdotal consecration. Rather, it is under God's impulse that he should perform these sacred rites in a way that is hierarchic and heavenly" (ibid.). The meaning of *hierarchic* is well expressed by Yves Congar in "The Church and Its Unity," in his *The Mystery of the Church*, trans. A. V. Littledale (French 1956; Baltimore: Helicon Press, 1960), 58–96, at 78: "Christ does not confine himself to sensible means of an inanimate nature for the formation of his mystical Body but uses, also, and for the same reason, living ones, persons who are themselves sacramental. The Church, then, is not only sacramental, but also apostolic and hierarchic (in the original sense of having sacred powers)."

129. Pseudo-Dionysius, *The Ecclesiastical Hierarchy*, ch. 6, III, §5, 248.

proportionate share in the divine gift of this communion."[130] The closer the configuration to Christ's self-giving love in his Pasch, the greater the Christian dignity. The goal of the hierarch, therefore, is a holy life of receiving and communicating divine gifts, followed by a holy death and eternal life with Christ.

IMITATING GOD'S FRUITFULNESS: AQUINAS'S DIONYSIAN PERSPECTIVE

What have we learned thus far? Recall that in addition to arguing that inequality among Christians is opposed to the Church's vocation to image the Trinity, Volf warns that top-down structures cannot include each individual member of the Church in decision-making and do not enable each individual's particular gifts to flourish. He also finds that the lack of structural diversity and flexibility reduces the ability of hierarchical Churches to evangelize in rapidly changing cultures. In light of Volf's concerns, I traced the Enlightenment debate over ecclesial mediation between Moses Mendelssohn and Johann Georg Hamann, in order to show how Hamann's deeper awareness of the mysteries mediated by Christianity challenges Mendelssohn's model of freedom within a religious society whose goals are educative and affective. This understanding of mediation is deepened by Franz Rosenzweig, whose emphasis on the problem of death enables him to recognize that Judaism and Christianity mediate liturgically the inbreaking of divine eternity into time. By means of this deepening of our understanding of Jewish and Christian mediation, I sought to broaden the parameters within which Volf's concerns about evangelization and the relationship of the one and the many in Christian community should be addressed. Dionysius's classic account of liturgical mediation provided a capstone upon these efforts.

Like Volf, Dionysius is concerned above all with the Church's vocation to image the Trinity. Yet Dionysius asks first how God's gifts flourish in the community and in the individual, rather than asking first how the community's and individual's gifts can flourish. From this theocentric perspective, Dionysius sees the triune God's gifting— healing and transforming each individual so that he or she achieves

---

130. Ibid.

full "hierarchical" personhood in looking upward—as occurring preeminently through the liturgical symbolism. The human flourishing that Volf seeks, marked by the equality of the members of the community and by the spreading of the good news of forgiveness, takes place through the healing and transformation of the *imago dei* through the practice of cruciform receptivity to the divine gifting.[131] As Hamann emphasizes, the community of full human flourishing is defined by Golgatha. Such human flourishing is constituted already by the dynamisms of eternal life (Rosenzweig), which believers experience from within the gifting and receptivity that re-establishes the hierarchical "looking upward" proper to Christian personhood (Dionysius).

In order to develop this perspective more fully, as a last step I will add some reflections from Aquinas's discussion of Holy Orders in his *Commentary on the Sentences*, which provided the material for the *Supplement* to the *Summa Theologiae* prepared after Aquinas's death by Reginald of Piperno.[132] Well aware of the problem of weak and sinful bishops, Aquinas raises the issue of whether the Christian dispensation has outmoded hierarchy, other than perhaps a hierarchy of merit.[133]

---

131. I think that Volf would be sympathetic with much of this argument. See also Ellen T. Charry, "The Crisis of Modernity and the Christian Self," in Jurgen Moltmann, Nicholas Wolterstorff, and Ellen T. Charry, *A Passion for God's Reign: Theology, Christian Learning, and the Christian Self* (Grand Rapids, MI: Eerdmans, 1998), 88–112.

132. For discussion of Aquinas's debt to the thought of Dionysius, see Fran O'Rourke, *Pseudo-Dionysius and the Metaphysics of Aquinas* (Notre Dame, IN: University of Notre Dame Press, 2005), although O'Rourke's discussion at times lacks metaphysical clarity.

133. Cf. Walter Kasper, *Leadership in the Church: How Traditional Roles Can Serve the Christian Community Today*, trans. Brian McNeil (New York: Crossroad, 2003), 108–10. Kasper observes that Aquinas "affirms that authority deprives people of their freedom only when it seeks to promote its own interests; it sets people free when its aim is the good of the other person" (108). For Aquinas, Kasper continues insightfully: "authority is an essential dimension of the Christian order of salvation, since no one can redeem himself. We all depend on redemption 'from outside' and 'from above.' The church's ministry represents this salvation 'from outside' and 'from above,' reminding the human person that salvation is a gift he receives, not a task that would place an intolerable burden on him. Spiritual authority is a sign that makes it clear that the reality of Christian salvation is gift and grace; though, to be precise, this authority does not mediate salvation itself, but only the means of salvation, namely, the sacraments" (110). Kasper's approach here is quite similar to the one I have taken in this book. For discussion of Aquinas's treatment of the sacrament of orders in his *Commentary on the Sentences* and its transposition in the *Supplement*, see Pierre-Marie Gy, OP, "Évolution de saint Thomas sur la théologie du sacrament de l'Ordre," *Revue Thomiste* 99 (1999): 181–89. Gy draws upon M. Turrini, "Réginald de Piperno et le texte original de la *Tertia Pars* de la *Somme de théologie* de S. Thomas d'Aquin," *Revue des sciences philosophiques et théologiques* 73 (1989): 233–47.

Question 34 of the *Supplement* begins with three objections that connect with Volf's concerns.

The first objection is that "Order requires subjection and preeminence. But subjection seemingly is incompatible with the liberty whereunto we are called by Christ."[134] At stake is the flourishing of individual believers in their Christian vocation. What kind of "subjection" does "order" require? Aquinas's language—"subjection" versus Christian "liberty"—recalls Saint Paul's rejoicing in Christian freedom from the power of sin: "There is therefore now no condemnation for those who are in Christ Jesus. For the law of the Spirit of life in Christ Jesus has set me free from the law of sin and death" (Romans 8:1–2). Saint Paul of course does not reject "subjection"; in fact, for Paul subjection to God is the foundation of true freedom.[135] Paul writes, "But now that you have been set free from sin and have become slaves of God, the return you get is sanctification and its end, eternal life. For the wages of sin is death, but the free gift of God is eternal life in Christ Jesus our Lord" (Romans 6:22–23).

In his answer to the objection, Aquinas points out that political/economic subjection or slavery is incompatible with the fullness of Christian freedom. He states, "The subjection of slavery is incompatible with liberty; for slavery consists in lording over others and

---

134. *Summa Theologiae, Suppl.* q. 34, a. 1, obj. 1.

135. For further discussion of the freedom constituted by obedience to God's will, see Richard Bauckham, *God and the Crisis of Freedom: Biblical and Contemporary Perspectives* (Louisville, KY: Westminster John Knox, 2002), 46–49, and elsewhere. From his perspective as an Anglican biblical scholar and theologian, however, Bauckham argues strongly against hierarchy: "It is a mistake to read the Bible through the lens of hierarchical thinking, as much of the Western Christian tradition in the past has read it and as much feminist theological criticism today reads it. The overall direction of biblical thought . . . is egalitarian. Its tendency is not in support of but away from hierarchical structures in human society, and biblical images of God's rule function not to legitimate human hierarchy, but to relativize or delegitimize it" (118). He sees Jesus as appropriating and extending "the radical egalitarian tradition of Israel" (123). By "hierarchy," Bauckham means worldly "power and pretensions" (123), and he focuses on political, social, and familial hierarchy rather than on priestly hierarchy. He thereby misses the aspect of gifting/receptivity that priestly hierarchy, as a participation in Christ's saving work, serves. Instructively, Bauckham's account of the churches founded by Paul leaves out the kenotic, but no less real, authority that Paul claims for himself and those who share in his mandate: "In the churches of the Pauline mission, which are the churches about which we know the most in this respect, Jesus' radical egalitarianism made a strong impact. Christians were a family of faith, brothers and sisters to each other, relating to each other without the structures of privilege and status that subordinated one to another in society around them" (124).

employing them for one's own profit."[136] Is the hierarchical structure
of the Church, in which ordinary believers have to receive from and
obey bishops/priests, a kind of "slavery" that "consists in lording over
others"? Aquinas responds that it is not: "Such subjection is not
required in Order, whereby those who preside have to seek the salvation
of their subjects and not their own profit."[137] This answer, it will be
seen, leaves open the possibility of corrupt use of the sacrament of order,
which in the hands of those who abuse it becomes oppressive. It
becomes oppressive when it is understood as a lever of worldly power
and profiteering, rather as an authoritative mission of teaching and
sanctifying. Having to be taught and sanctified by bishops/priests is
not in itself an instance of anti-Christian subjection.

The first objection thus asks whether subjection, per se, can
belong to the Christian dispensation, and the answer is in the affirmative. The second objection against hierarchical order in the Church
also probes the question of subjection, this time asking how the
subjection of some Christians to other Christians can be compatible
with the requirement that *all* Christians subject themselves to all
others. Aquinas notes that "he who has received an Order becomes
another's superior. But in the Church everyone should deem himself
lower than another (Phil. ii. 3): *Let each esteem others better than
themselves*."[138] A bishop or pope, however, receives much attention,
admiration, and flattery. Can such a situation truly accord with, or
foster the fulfillment of, Paul's injunction in Philippians 2:3? When
certain human beings have more power than other human beings,
does this not generally lead them to esteem themselves above others,
and thereby provide a portal for pride and the oppression of others
that results from pride? Aquinas certainly does not deny that pride
can follow upon ecclesial office, but he notes that office and merit,
according to the Christian understanding, are quite different realities.
No matter how elevated the office, "Each one should esteem himself
lower in merit" than others.[139] There is no need for everyone to possess
an office of equal rank. Christian charity requires instead a recognition

---

136. ST, *Suppl.*, q. 34, a. 1, ad 1.
137. Ibid.
138. ST, *Suppl.*, q. 34, a. 1, obj. 2.
139. Ibid., ad 2.

that one's merit is distinct from one's office: charity, not ecclesial office, is the ground of merit, which is the true power in the Church.

If the merit accrued by love is the true power or hierarchy in the Church, however, why have a hierarchy of office? Why not simply a hierarchy constituted by the witness of love? To use a contemporary example, should Mother Teresa's bishop really be in a position of authority over Mother Teresa, and should Mother Teresa have to receive the sacraments from one who is far less meritorious? Indeed, the third objection observes that among the angels, hierarchy is ordered in precisely this fashion, that is, in strict accord with merit: "we find Order among the angels on account of their differing in natural and gratuitous gifts."[140] Aquinas grants, in the voice of the objector, that angels differ more clearly in nature—each being its own species—and that the gratuitous gifts of angels are clear to all, whereas "all men are one in nature, and it is not known who has the higher gifts of grace."[141] It would appear, then, that a hierarchy ordered by degrees of virtue is not possible in this life for human beings. The objection concludes that if no hierarchy like the angelic hierarchy is possible, then there should be no visible hierarchy at all in the Church, built as the Church is upon charity.

In answering this objection, Aquinas notes that the sacraments of the Church, which hierarchical order in the Church serves, are not about the holiness of human beings, as if they were anthropocentric rituals. Rather, the sacraments are about participating (theocentrically) in the holiness of God in Christ Jesus and his Spirit. This has an important consequence for hierarchical order in the Church: such order is based not upon degrees of human holiness, but upon efficacious dispensing of the divine sacraments by which human beings are made holy. It is different among the angels in heaven, where order "results directly from their difference in grace" so that "their orders regard their participation of divine things, and their communicating them in the state of glory."[142] Among human beings, the situation is the other way around: hierarchical order exists not as the manifestation of diverse creaturely participations in the grace of the Holy Spirit, but as a

---

140. ST, *Suppl.*, q. 34, a. 1, obj. 3.

141. Ibid.

142. ST, *Suppl.*, q. 34, a. 1, ad 3.

means by which to *enable* creatures to participate in the grace of the Holy Spirit.

For the Church on earth, in short, hierarchical order is not itself an "order of grace" but a mode of transmitting the grace of the Holy Spirit sacramentally; it seeks to bring about what the angels already enjoy in heaven. Aquinas states that "the Orders of the Church militant regard the participation in the sacraments and the communication thereof, which are the cause of grace and, in a way, precede grace; and consequently our Orders do not require sanctifying grace, but only the power to dispense the sacraments."[143] Those who imagine the Church's hierarchical order as corresponding "to the difference of sanctifying grace" have misunderstood the instrumental purpose of hierarchical order in the Church, an instrumental purpose manifest in the power to perform the sacraments.[144]

In short, these three objections probe whether hierarchical power in the Church corresponds to and fosters Christian flourishing. Aquinas recognizes that ecclesial order can be and sometimes is distorted into a "lording over others," when authority is exercised for temporal gain rather than out of love for God. But the purpose of ecclesial order is to serve the flourishing of love by means of dispensing the sacraments. Ecclesial order thus finds its (instrumental) purpose, and its limitations, in its eucharistic/sacramental mission. Hierarchical order in the Church is not an end in itself. Rather, its role must be understood within the liturgical "symbolism" that enables human beings, informed by the Holy Spirit, to practice receptivity to the divine gifting.[145]

Even so, given the distortions and abuses that can come with hierarchical order, why would God risk hierarchical mediation in the

---

143. Ibid.

144. See ibid.

145. Approvingly citing a lengthy passage from Aquinas's commentary on 2 Corinthians 3 regarding theonomous Christian freedom, Bauckham observes in the concluding chapter of his *God and the Crisis of Freedom*: "The mystery of the Spirit's activity is that this divine presence at the center of human personhood does not reduce personal freedom but enables the free spontaneity of those who embrace God's will as their own. . . . It is the activity of the Spirit that transcends the alternative of autonomy and heteronomy by actualizing in our personal existence the truth that God's law is not the will of another, in the ordinary sense in which this would be true of the will of another creature, but, as the law of the Creator and his creation, also the law of our own being, in conforming to which we become most truly ourselves" (Bauckham, *God and the Crisis of Freedom*, 208; cf. 68).

Church? The body of q. 34 takes up this question along lines that return us to the theme of chapter 1, the Church as the image of the Trinity. Observing that God "laid this natural law on all things, that last things should be reduced and perfected by middle things, and middle things by the first, as Dionysius says (*Eccl. Hier.* v)," Aquinas affirms that hierarchical order imitates God in the Trinitarian action *ad extra*.[146] How so? First, he notes, "we find order in nature, in that some things are above others, and likewise in glory, as in the angels."[147] While God could have created a set of creatures perfectly alike in nature and in grace, instead he willed to create an amazingly diverse creation, hierarchically ordered both in nature and in grace. In this way, God willed that creation express manifold degrees of participation in his being, wisdom, goodness, beauty, and so forth. Where human beings might have chosen an absolute uniformity among creatures, God delights in an extraordinary diversity. God gives this "beauty" of order not only to nature and to the blessed in heaven, but also the Church on earth.[148] To come to know God as he is in his gratuitous gifting, we must be formed in receptivity to hierarchical diversity—a formation that requires sacramental practice, because of the consequences of our rebellion against the root of all hierarchical ordering: the creature's relationship to the creator. With Adam and Eve, we want to be foremost in any hierarchical relationship—foremost not in the love that deifies, but in disordered power.

Second, God's fruitful gifting *ad extra* can be imitated by human beings. In creating and sustaining creatures, God acts both directly and in a mediated fashion; for instance, God directly sustains the being of the tree, but he also works through nature's processes of

---

146. ST, *Suppl.*, q. 34, a. 1.

147. ST, *Suppl.*, q. 34, a. 1, *sed contra*.

148. Ibid., *respondeo*. On diversity in the Church, see Herwi Rikhof, "Thomas on the Church: Reflections on a Sermon," in *Aquinas on Doctrine: A Critical Introduction*, ed. Thomas Weinandy, OFM CAP, Daniel Keating, and John Yocum (New York: T. & T. Clark, 2004), 211–12. Rikhof points out, "In his [Aquinas's] commentary on the Creed, he uses the term *diversa membra*. Within the one body this diversity does not disappear of become irrelevant. The diversity stays and has a purpose. Diversity would be meaningless if it were not ordered toward diverse acts. With regard to *singuli autem alter alteris membra* (Rom. 12:5), Thomas remarks that Paul touches here upon the connection between the diversity and the common advantage (*utilitas*). He explains this phrase by saying that a member is called 'member of another' in so far as one member serves the other by its own proper activity. So, this diversity of members and acts is related to a common good on the one hand, and to the other members on the other" (211).

generation and growth, involving the acorn, soil, sunlight, and so forth. Similarly, Christ himself bestows the sacramental grace of the Holy Spirit, and yet he does so through the mediation of human priests. As Aquinas says, in order "that He might be portrayed in His works, not only according to what He is in Himself, but also according as He acts on others. . . . He established Order in her [the Church] so that some should deliver the sacraments to others, being thus made like God in their own way, as co-operating with God."[149]

Is it only the bishops/priests, however, who are "being thus made like God" and "co-operating with God," since only the bishops/priests sacramentally possess hierarchical "order" in the Church? Certainly, in mediating God's action in believers, bishops/priests are "imitating" or participating in God's action in a unique way, as "the co-operators of God."[150] But the bishops/priests' imitation of God's action serves the whole Church in its vocation of imitating and co-operating with God's action *ad extra*, the creation and perfecting of creatures. The recipients of the sacraments, who take on a new life and are nourished toward Christian perfection, imitate and co-operate with God through their fruitfulness in charity. Thus the hierarchical priesthood imitates and co-operates with the divine fruitfulness by enabling all believers to imitate and co-operate with the divine fruitfulness.

Since this imitation flows from sacramental grace, Aquinas defines the sacrament of Holy Orders as that "whereby man is ordained to the dispensation of the other sacraments,"[151] above all to the Eucharist: "the principal act of a priest is to consecrate the body and blood of Christ."[152] By the sacrament of Holy Orders, men are "appointed to lead others in Divine things"[153] and to exercise "a twofold action: the one, which is principal, over the true body of Christ; the other, which is secondary, over the mystical body of Christ."[154] Aquinas

---

149. ST, *Suppl.* q. 34, a. 1, *respondeo.*

150. See also ST, *Suppl.*, q. 37, a. 1, which likewise cites Pseudo-Dionysius.

151. ST, *Suppl.*, q. 35, a. 1.

152. ST, *Suppl.*, q. 37, a. 5, as well as the *sed contra.*

153. ST, *Suppl.*, q. 36, a. 1.

154. ST, *Suppl.*, q. 36, a. 2, ad 1. The action of the bishop/priest vis-à-vis the Church ("the mystical body of Christ") flows from the principal action of the Eucharist: as Aquinas says, "the second act depends on the first" (ST, *Suppl.*, q. 36, a. 2, ad 1). The bishop's mission, while requiring more of the "secondary" action than is required of the priest, depends upon the

describes bishops/priests as "instruments" of Christ's sacramental outpouring of the grace of the Holy Spirit: "the ministers of the Church
are placed over others, not to confer anything on them by virtue of
their own holiness (for this belongs to God alone), but as ministers,
and as instruments, so to say, of the outpouring from the Head to the
members."[155] This outpouring attains its highest point in the Eucharist,
which builds up the Church in charity. As Aquinas says, following
Dionysius, "the sacrament of Order is directed to the sacrament of the
Eucharist, which is the sacrament of sacraments."[156]

Aquinas thus helps us to understand *Ecclesia de Eucharistia*,
where John Paul II writes: "The fact that the power of consecrating
the Eucharist has been entrusted only to bishops and priests does not
represent any kind of belittlement of the rest of the People of God, for
in the communion of the one body of Christ which is the Church this

---

bishop's principal action in the eucharistic celebration. Regarding the distinction between
bishop and priest, Aquinas argues, "Order considered as a sacrament which imprints a
character is specially directed to the sacrament of the Eucharist, in which Christ Himself is
contained, because by a character we are made like to Christ Himself. Hence, although at his
promotion a bishop receives a spiritual power in respect of certain sacraments [e.g., the power
to ordain others], this power nevertheless has not the nature of a character. For this reason the
episcopate is not an Order, in the sense in which an Order is a sacrament" (ST, *Suppl.*, q. 40, a.
5, ad 2). The Second Vatican Council resolves this question otherwise: "The synod teaches
that the fullness of the sacrament of order is conferred by episcopal consecration" and "The
bishop, marked with the fullness of the sacrament of order, is 'the steward of the grace of the
supreme priesthood,' especially in the eucharist which he offers or which he ensures is offered,
and by which the church continuously lives and grows" (*Lumen Gentium*, nos. 21 and 26, in
Decrees of the Ecumenical Councils, vol. 2, *Trent to Vatican II*, ed. Norman P. Tanner, SJ
[Washington, DC: Georgetown University Press, 1990], pp. 865, 870). For discussion of
Aquinas's position in light of the teaching of *Lumen Gentium*, see Guy Mansini, OSB,
"Episcopal *Munera* and the Character of Episcopal Orders," *The Thomist* 66 (2002): 369–94,
at 377f.; idem, "A Contemporary Understanding of St. Thomas on Sacerdotal Character," *The
Thomist* 71 (2007): 171–98, especially 192–97. Regarding Vatican II's teaching, see also
Joseph Ratzinger, *Principles of Catholic Theology: Building Stones for a Fundamental Theology*,
trans. Sr. Mary Frances McCarthy, SND (German 1982; San Francisco: Ignatius Press, 1987),
242–44 and 254–57. Influenced by Karl Rahner and others, Susan K. Wood argues that the
bishop's reception of the "fullness of the sacrament of order" (*Lumen Gentium*, 21) involves
above all "the connection between the relational *ordo* of a bishop in his particular church and
his *ordo* in the college of bishops" (Wood, "The Sacramentality of Episcopal Consecration,"
Theological Studies 51 [1990]: 479–96, at 489). In her view locating the distinction between
priest and bishop in the power to ordain is insufficient, since "dogmatically speaking, the
validation of a priest by another simple priest under certain conditions does not appear
impossible" (481). Thus she holds, "The ecclesial signification of episcopal consecration is
what ultimately distinguishes it from the presbyterate" (482).

155. ST, *Suppl.*, q. 36, a. 3, ad 2.

156. ST, *Suppl.*, q. 37, a. 2. He cites Dionysius's *Ecclesiastical Hierarchy*, ch. 3.

gift redounds to the benefit of all."[157] True diversity, which entails gifting and receptivity, fosters the configuration of believers to God's own creative gifting. Understood eucharistically, hierarchy in the Church enables believers to enter into the pattern of the triune God's outpouring of love. Ecclesial hierarchy thereby serves Christian freedom, equality, and evangelization far more profoundly than Volf contends.

CONCLUSION

Religion, in Mendelssohn's view, is the communication of truth so as to inspire good action, and all that is needed for this communicative practice is the persuasiveness of a good teacher. On this view, Christianity has clouded true religion by setting up a belief-system outside the bounds of philosophical knowledge, and this mistake in turn produced structures of authority (both inside and outside the Church) where there should be none. These structures of authority are inevitably oppressive, because the intervention (potential or actual) of authority in truth-seeking cannot but chill and oppress those who are sincerely engaged in the free exercise of seeking truth in accord with conscience. Mendelssohn does not want to do away altogether with religious traditions and their communal structures; instead he wants to rework them along Enlightenment lines. In this important respect he is more like Schleiermacher, who wrote a generation later, than like his own contemporary Immanuel Kant. Mendelssohn's reworking hardly sounds radical today: as Alexander Altmann notes, "Mendelssohn was leading the way to a nontheological, nonmystical version of Judaism such as came to dominate nineteenth- and early twentieth-century Jewish society."[158]

---

157. John Paul II, *Ecclesia de Eucharistia* (2003), 30.

158. Alexander Altmann, introduction to Mendelssohn, *Jerusalem*, 28. Altmann is right to add, as well, that "*Jerusalem*, for all its rationalist outlook, still retains firm roots in the Jewish tradition" (28). Altmann goes on to say that *Jerusalem* exhibits an "unshakable loyalty" to the "values" of the Jewish tradition; this seems to me to be true only if one limits those "values" in the way that Mendelssohn does. Altmann also emphasizes the role of *Jerusalem* in seeking full inclusion of the Jewish people in the modern world, an emergence from the ghettos to which they had been restricted, for reasons that bring shame upon Christians, in medieval and early modern Christian societies: "the plea for liberty of conscience and civic equality, which is at the heart of the work as a whole, was meant to secure for the Jewish people a fair share in the modern world which was about to dawn" (28).

Insofar as Mendelssohn views religious communities as inspiring good actions through teaching whose authenticity is manifested by the persuasiveness of the teacher, his position accords with much present-day Christian ecclesiology. For this reason, not only Mendelssohn's work, but also the responses of Hamann and, indirectly, of Rosenzweig (both of whom experienced profound conversions or "reversions," to Christianity and Judaism respectively)[159] assist contemporary ecclesiology in exploring what might be missing in perspectives that hold that authority in the Christian community flows above all from a recognized persuasiveness or authenticity in teaching the Gospel. Hamann and Rosenzweig offer a set of insights that suggest that the communal mediation consists in more than teaching. First, given the radical brokenness of all human "relations" by sin, Christianity cannot be merely educative: it must mediate the power of Christ's sacrificial atonement (Hamann), which embodies God's covenantal relationship with Jewish flesh and blood (Rosenzweig). Second, human community seeks a "common good" that has now been revealed as marital intimacy with God: the community must mediate this divine indwelling in truth and love. Third, no human leaders can mediate on their own Christ's sacrificial atonement and the divine indwelling: this mediation, if it occurs, cannot be thanks to the goodness and wisdom of the leaders, but can only be (theocentrically) God's action in the world through human mediation. Fourth, this mediation will be above all liturgical: put another way, the Eucharist makes the Church.[160]

These reflections led us to Dionysius. Worship, for Dionysius, involves the mediated reception and communication of divine gifts. Worship also leads the mind upward to the intelligible divine Light,

---

159. Rosenzweig nearly converted to Christianity before his profound reclamation of his Judaism.

160. See the discussion in Henri de Lubac, sj, *The Splendor of the Church*, 151–60, drawing upon his *Corpus Mysticum*. See also Anscar Vonier, osb, *A Key to the Doctrine of the Eucharist* (1925; Bethesda, MD: Zaccheus Press, 2003), 168: "Christ's sacramental Body makes Christ's mystical Body"; Gilles Emery, op, "The Ecclesial Fruit of the Eucharist in St. Thomas Aquinas," trans. Therese C. Scarpelli, in Emery, *Trinity, Church, and the Human Person* (Naples, FL: Sapientia Press, 2007), 155–72; Martin Morard, "L'eucharistie clé de voûte de l'organisme sacramental chez saint Thomas d'Aquin," *Revue Thomiste* 95 (1995): 217–50; Jean-Pierre Torrell, op, *St. Thomas Aquinas*, vol. 2, *Spiritual Master*, trans. Robert Royal (French 1996; Washington, DC: The Catholic University of America Press, 2003), 295–96; Matthew Levering, *Sacrifice and Community: Jewish Offering and Christian Eucharist* (Oxford: Blackwell, 2005), ch. 3.

as opposed to our tendency after the Fall to cling to the sensible things of this world. Worship purifies, illumines, and perfects our minds through the sacramental and scriptural "symbols" that the triune God gives in order to unite us in a communion with him. As a sacramental practice, worship requires practicing the art of receiving divine realities from another. Whereas after the Fall we tend to seek to rely solely upon our own resources, we are in fact in a condition of profound neediness. How can our pride be overcome? In order to learn how to receive from God, we must learn how to receive from human beings. The purpose of hierarchical ecclesial structures, which flow from the Eucharist, is to teach this humility precisely in the liturgical context of divine gifting.

Within this context, every element of the worship, including the hierarch/bishop, has a "symbolic" value: as the congregation looks upward to the hierarch who accomplishes the consecration of the divine gifts at the altar, the congregation is formed in the practice of looking upward to the one who the hierarch "symbolizes," Jesus Christ, who gives the Father's gift in the Spirit. As the rites of consecration for the hierarchical orders show, this formation in receptivity, an utter dependence upon the divine gift that one cannot give oneself, is not for the congregation alone. Rather, the members of the hierarchical orders are configured by the Holy Spirit, in the rite of consecration, to the "hierarchic" image of the crucified one, in whom human beings are rightly ordered (hierarchically) so that the soul governs the body and God governs the body-soul composite. By the practice of hierarchically ordered worship, all members of Christ come to share in the interpersonal communion of divine gifting, precisely by learning how to receive from above.[161] As Louis Bouyer observes, therefore, hierarchy cannot "be understood as a simple armature, juxtaposed to the Body,

---

161. For further reflection on the eucharistic formation of believers, see Joseph Ratzinger, "Eucharist and Mission," in his *Pilgrim Fellowship of Faith: The Church as Communion*, ed. Stephan Otto Horn and Vinzenz Pfnür, trans. Henry Taylor (German 2002; San Francisco: Ignatius Press, 2005), 90–122. On the encounter with Christ at the center of the sacraments, see also Colman O'Neill, OP, *Meeting Christ in the Sacraments*, revised by Romanus Cessario, OP (New York: Alba House, 1991); idem, *Sacramental Realism* (Chicago: Midwest Theological Forum, 1998); Yves Congar, "The Two Forms of the Bread of Life: In the Gospel and Tradition," in his *A Gospel Priesthood*, trans. P. J. Hepburne-Scott (New York: Herder and Herder, 1967), 103–38; idem, *Jesus Christ*, trans. Luke O'Neill (French 1965; New York: Herder and Herder, 1966), 148–53.

but as its vital organization, which assures each member not only his place but his function within the whole."[162]

This eucharistic understanding of hierarchy in the Church, as the configuration of believers to God's gifting, is taken up in Aquinas's theology of priestly mediation. As we have seen, Aquinas seeks to answer arguments about Christian freedom and a hierarchy of merit.[163] Aquinas engages such concerns, which reflect Volf's, from the perspective of the instrumentality of hierarchical priesthood in the Church, an instrumentality that flows not from our goodness but from God's goodness. For Aquinas, as for Dionysius, it is far better that the hierarch/bishop be holy and wise, but holiness and wisdom are not *strictly* necessary to his "symbolic" place in the eucharistic worship that builds the Church.[164] Viewed as just a man, even a holy

---

162. Louis Bouyer, *The Church of God: Body of Christ and Temple of the Spirit*, trans. Charles Underhill Quinn (French 1970; Chicago: Franciscan Herald Press, 1982), 162. Here Bouyer is commenting on Ephesians 4:11–13, 15, in light of *Lumen Gentium*, but for a similar perspective see Bouyer's observation specifically on Dionysius's understanding of hierarchy: for Dionysius " 'hierarchy' had an essentially dynamic meaning, extending on the level of creation the 'thearchy' of the Divine Persons. This had nothing to do with a division of the Church (or the universe, in the case of the 'heavenly hierarchy') between masters and subjects, in which the former were the only ones who were active and the latter were purely passive and dependent. Quite the contrary. As Dionysius understood the hierarchical principle, it meant that the most exalted beings in nature and grace could possess what they received (the divine *agape*) only by communicating it. And Dionysius specified that this communication's agent, whoever he might be, far from being removed from his most lowly participants, as a screen between them and the divine source, produced immediate contact between each person and the divine gift. Consequently, in accordance with their individual response to the gift received, the least in the hierarchy could be raised as high as the most exalted, and even higher" (40). See also Bouyer's masterful exposition of Dionysius's theology of hierarchy in *The Church of God*, 258–60.

163. See also John Stuart Mill's concern regarding to the nineteenth-century Catholic Church: "The Catholic Church . . . . makes a separation between those who can be permitted to receive its doctrines on conviction, and those who must accept them on trust. Neither, indeed, are allowed any choice as to what they will accept; but the clergy, such at least as can be fully confided in, may admissibly and meritoriously make themselves acquainted with the arguments of opponents, in order to answer them, and may, therefore, read heretical books; the laity, not unless by special permission, hard to be obtained" (Mill, "On Liberty," in idem, *On Liberty and Other Essays*, ed. John Gray, 44). Or as he says elsewhere, "At some period, however, of their history, almost every people, now civilized, have consisted, in majority, of slaves" ("Considerations on Representative Government," in *On Liberty and Other Essays*, 233).

164. Compare this position to Stanley Hauerwas's statement, "For the church to *be* rather than to *have* a social ethic moreover means that a certain kind of people are required to sustain it as an institution across time. They must, above all, be a people of virtue—not simply any virtue, but the virtues necessary for remembering and telling the story of a crucified savior" (Hauerwas, "The Servant Community: Christian Social Ethics," in his *The Peaceable Kingdom: A Primer in Christian Ethics* [Notre Dame, IN: University of Notre Dame Press, 1983], 102–3). Hauerwas recognizes that "the church is God's creation" (103), and so almost certainly he

and wise man, the hierarch/bishop cannot do what is necessary for
human beings: merely human "power" cannot heal and elevate our
personhood. Viewed in his "symbolic" reality, however, the bishop or
priest mediates Christ's kenotic power, through which our freedom is
redeemed in a love born of receptivity to God's gifting.

In other words, as Aquinas emphasizes, hierarchy in the Church
does not correspond to diverse creaturely participations in the grace of
the Holy Spirit, but rather mediates that redemptive and transformative
grace. Hierarchy recalls the whole congregation to the practice of
looking upward to Christ's gifting in the Holy Spirit. This practice, in
the rite of eucharistic worship, configures us to the receptivity and
gifting of the incarnate Lord, so that we may "be imitators of God, as
beloved children" (Ephesians 5:1). The key here is an understanding
of the divine "symbolism," the sign-character of earthly realities
(scriptural, sacramental, liturgical). This understanding of divine
"symbolism" extends to a delight in our participation in the wondrous
diversity of the gifting of the Father, Son, and Holy Spirit. Recall
Paul's teaching that after Jesus' Ascension, "his gifts were that some
should be apostles, some prophets, some evangelists, some pastors and
teachers, for the equipment of the saints, for the work of ministry, for
building up the body of Christ, until we all attain to the unity of the
faith and of the knowledge of the Son of God, to mature manhood,
to the measure of the stature of the fullness of Christ" (Ephesians
4:11–13).

In sum, hierarchical mediation of the divine gifting, preeminently in the Eucharist, recalls us to the truth that real human power,
as opposed to the worldly power, is a participated power to give and to
receive divine love. In the liturgy, the hierarchical "symbolism"

---

would agree that only God, and not "a certain kind of people" however virtuous, can sustain
the Church "as an institution across time." Yet the different formulation has ecclesiological
significance, as suggested by his intriguing comments on his "ecclesial stance" at that time: "do
I write as a Catholic or as a Protestant? The answer is that I simply do not know. I do not believe
that theology when rightly done is either Catholic or Protestant. The object of the theologian's
inquiry is quite simply God—not Catholicism or Protestantism. The proper object of the
qualifier 'catholic' is the church, not theology or theologians. No theologian should desire anything less than that his or her theology reflect the catholic character of the church. Thus I
hope my theology is catholic inasmuch as it is true to those Protestants and Roman Catholics
who constitute the church catholic" (xxvi). For discussion of Hauerwas on the Church see Arne
Rasmusson, *The Church as Polis: From Political Theology to Theological Politics as Exemplified by
Jürgen Moltmann and Stanley Hauerwas* (Notre Dame, IN: University of Notre Dame Press,
1995).

manifests the power of divine gifting, and thereby invites us into the Trinitarian and Christological heights of interpersonal communion. To express the vision of the Church that follows from this understanding of hierarchy, we may conclude with a passage from Walter Kasper:

> The church therefore is neither a democracy nor a monarchy, nor even a constitutional monarchy. She is hierarchical in the original sense of the word, meaning "holy origin"; that is, she has to be understood on the basis of what is holy, by the gifts of salvation, by Word and Sacrament as signs and means of the Holy Spirit's effectiveness. This brings us to the original and authentic theological understanding of communion as the Catholic vision of unity.[165]

---

165. Walter Kasper, "Present Situation and Future of the Ecumenical Movement," *Information Service*, 109 (2002): 11–20, at 16, cited in Jeffrey Gros, FSC, "Toward Full Communion: Faith and Order and Catholic Ecumenism," *Theological Studies* 65 (2004): 23–43, at 40.

Conclusion:
Hierarchy and Holiness

In accord with Yves Congar's admonition that the Church cannot be understood outside "the Christian-Trinitarian mystery, outside the anthropological, Christological, sacramental reality which is the subject of theology,"[1] I have explored theological questions regarding ecclesial hierarchy while generally leaving to the side sociological concerns about its actual exercise.[2] Has this omission produced a distorted vision? However appealing the theological depiction of the hierarchical mediation of divine gifting, has hierarchy in fact served well the community of Christ? Must we not rather begin by attempting to bridge, in Richard Gaillardetz's words, "the tangible gap many perceive between Catholicism's *vision* of ecclesial authority and its concrete structures and practice"?[3] One might also ask whether the effort to give theological

---

1. Yves Congar, "The Idea of the Church in St. Thomas Aquinas," in his *The Mystery of the Church*, trans. A. V. Littledale (French 1956; Baltimore, MD: Helicon Press, 1960), 97–117, at 117 (translation slightly revised). Congar grants, as do I, that for a full account of ecclesiology one must also make use of "canonical, juridical, or sociological" elements, so long as they are not given primacy (117).

2. For the variety of possible sociological models that could be applied in ecclesiology, see Neil Ormerod, "A Dialectic Engagement with the Social Sciences in an Ecclesiological Context," *Theological Studies* 66 (2005): 815–40. As examples of the use of sociological analysis, Ormerod notes Joseph A. Komonchak, *Foundations in Ecclesiology*, ed. Fred Lawrence, vol. 11, *Lonergan Workshop Journal, Supplementary Issue* (Boston: Boston College, 1995); Patrick Granfield, OSB, *Ecclesial Cybernetics: A Study of Democracy in the Church* (New York: Macmillan, 1973). See also the emphasis on the pluralism of cultures within the communion of the Church in Carl F. Starkloff, SJ, "The Church as Covenant, Culture, and Communion," *Theological Studies* 61 (2000): 409–31, a pluralism that leads Starkloff to call for the Church to "open itself further to facilitate this diversity in its theology, its structures, its laws, and its liturgy" (431). One wonders whether this call pays sufficient attention to the unity in truth and love that communion requires. Cf. Starkloff, "Church as Structure and Communitas: Victor Turner and Ecclesiology," *Theological Studies* 58 (1997): 643–68; Clare Watkins, "Organizing the People of God: Social-Science Theories of Organization in Ecclesiology," *Theological Studies* 52 (1991): 689–711.

3. Richard R. Gaillardetz, *Teaching with Authority: A Theology of the Magisterium in the Church* (Collegeville, MN: Liturgical Press, 1997), 276. With regard to this perceived "gap,"

reasons for ecclesial hierarchy, without first evaluating such hierarchy sociologically, already belongs to the struggle for ecclesial power. Commenting on the "history of the discussions of power, importance, and eminence, of being 'first,' of honor and jurisdiction," Michael Buckley states, "Driven by unfaced 'interest,' the protagonist, while seeming to do theology, can actually be framing ideologies—theoretical justifications for either the current allocations of power or for radical changes demanded in the possession and uses of power."[4]

Rather than leave such concerns unaddressed, I wish to take them up in this Conclusion by setting forth two sociological-theological critiques of ecclesial hierarchy offered by Pheme Perkins and Nicholas M. Healy, respectively. I then close with a final *apologia* for my theological understanding of ecclesial hierarchy.

Gaillardetz emphasizes the need for "the testimony of the *sensus fidelium* to influence the formal teaching of the Church" (278). Revision of Church teaching, one supposes, would then emerge from this increased influence of the *sensus fidelium*. Similarly, he calls for the election of the bishops, which would ensure that local popular opinion was more deeply reflected in the local bishop. In this regard he states, "The slogan 'the Church is not a democracy,' as with many slogans, does contain a half-truth; the Church cannot succumb to a strictly liberal democratic conception of its constitution, viewing all authority as residing first in the people and then, only in a delegated fashion, in the clergy. However, support for the election of bishops no more requires seeing the bishop as a 'delegate' of the people than does papal appointment of a bishop require a view of a bishop as vicar of the pope. Since it is the Holy Spirit who is the transcendent subject of the life of the Church, there is no reason why the same Spirit, which now works through direct appointment by the Holy See, may not work through some form of local election" (280). Gaillardetz goes on to argue that election of bishops would not necessarily encourage more partisan practices than already exist (280–81). The question, however, is whether such elections constitute a practice that deepens believers' cruciform receptivity. Gaillardetz does not do justice to the theocentric understanding of divine gifting that lies behind the phrase "the Church is not a democracy." For a better approach see Leo Scheffczyk, "*Sensus fidelium*—Witness on the Part of the Community," trans. Charlotte C. Prather, *Communio* 15 (1988): 182–98; Avery Cardinal Dulles, SJ, *Magisterium: Teacher and Guardian of the Faith* (Naples, FL: Sapientia Press, 2007).

4. Michael J. Buckley, SJ, *Papal Primacy and the Episcopate: Towards a Relational Understanding* (New York: Crossroad, 1998), 23. While Nietzsche lurks in the background of this discussion, Buckley has in view the insights of Jürgen Habermas, "Knowledge and Interest," in *Sociological Theory and Philosophical Analysis*, ed. Dorothy Emmet and Alasdair MacIntyre (New York: Macmillan, 1970), 36–54. See Buckley's reflections on purity of heart in theological inquiry, in chapter one of *Papal Primacy and the Episcopate*. Cf. from a different perspective Joseph Ratzinger's "A Company in Constant Renewal," emphasizing the Church's need to enter more and more deeply into receptivity to the divine gifting, in his *Called to Communion: Understanding the Church Today*, trans. Adrian Walker (German 1991; San Francisco: Ignatius Press, 1995), 133–56.

PHEME PERKINS AND NICHOLAS M. HEALY

The biblical scholar Pheme Perkins proposes that Christianity is about actions that overturn worldly social structures.[5] If this is the theological meaning of Christianity, then the sociological impact of ecclesial hierarchy is determinative for measuring its theological validity. In this vein, Perkins compares the understanding of leadership found in Saint Paul and Bishop Ignatius of Antioch (d. ca. 110). She finds in the latter an ominous movement away from Paul's affirmation that the "cross negates every form of human self-assertion and domination (2 Cor 13:3–4)," an affirmation that, in her view, saves Paul from the implications of his assumptions about women and slaves.[6] For Perkins, the key question is how one accounts for the presence of the Holy Spirit in the Church: Does the Holy Spirit primarily guide the Church through a "hierarchical structure" or through the members of the Body of Christ? Only the latter, she holds, corresponds to the liberative impulse of the cross.

If one envisions the Holy Spirit as guiding the Church primarily through the ecclesial hierarchy—through "individuals who hold office at the top of a hierarchical structure, who possess authority to impose faith and practice without regard for particular contexts of faith and communal discernment"[7]—then according to Perkins one is following

---

5. See Pheme Perkins, "'Being of One Mind': Apostolic Authority, Persuasion, and *Koinonia* in New Testament Christianity," in *Common Calling: The Laity and the Governance of the Catholic Church*, ed. Stephen J. Pope (Washington, DC: Georgetown University Press, 2004), 25–38. She governs her reading of the biblical texts by the normative question, "Did it [the biblical language] illuminate and transform? Or did it reinforce and reflect inherited religious or social patterns?" (26) See also her *Peter: Apostle for the Whole Church* (Columbia, SC: University of South Carolina Press, 1994), along with John Reumann's review of this book in *Theological Studies* 55 (1994): 540–42. For related concerns, see William J. Abraham's presentation of Rosemary Radford Ruether's theology in his *The Logic of Renewal* (Grand Rapids, MI: Eerdmans, 2003), 45–54, 68–69. Abraham observes that Ruether "would really like the Roman Catholic Church to transform itself into a modern mainline Protestant denomination. . . . She wants a version of Free Church Protestantism that can still benefit from the resources mediated through the long-standing institutions of the church across the ages" (69).

6. Perkins, "'Being of One Mind,'" 35.

7. Ibid., 36. Sharing this concern, Michael Buckley, SJ, proposes the following as a possible solution (agreeing with Archbishop John R. Quinn and others): "For centuries in the early Church, 'the relationship of a bishop to his church was seen as a spiritual marriage.' This theological understanding carried with it two implications: (a) 'like the assent of the partners in a marriage, the [local] church's "yes" must be freely given'; (b) the translation of a bishop to another see was prohibited except in very rare cases. There were canons that specified the first

Ignatius rather than Paul. From her reading of "Paul's pastoral practice," she affirms that Paul finds the Holy Spirit primarily at work "in the community as body of Christ—a community whose life may be guided by apostolic service, but one that must be empowered to discern the Spirit working in its midst."[8] The local community of Christians is served by its leaders ("apostolic service"), but remains free to "discern the Spirit" for itself. For Perkins the Holy Spirit works through the liberative experience of believers, and it is this liberative experience that is normative for the community. If hierarchical leadership attempts to hold local communities to doctrinal orthodoxy despite the variations in communal contexts, these top-down decisions must be evaluated and if necessary reversed by local communities' experiences of Christian action in the Spirit.[9]

Perkins argues, in short, that for Paul the experience of cruciform liberative praxis is the locus of the Spirit's work in the community, and such experiences connect human beings with the liberative moral

---

and prohibited the second. This doctrine of the almost mystical unity between the bishop and his diocese deserves additional study in the contemporary Church" (Buckley, *Papal Primacy and the Episcopate*, 94). The result would be to increase the autonomy of local churches, not only through the "yes" (or "no"), but also by ensuring as much as possible that bishops have local ties and thus represent local perspectives. The analogy of marriage provides a theological rationale for this approach, but it also raises questions. For one, who would be the "groom" to which the local church says yes or no? It could not be Christ, since the local Church could not say "no" to Christ. But if not Christ, then does the analogy of marriage (between the local Church and the bishop of Rome?) suffice for a theological account of the mediation of divine gifting/receptivity? What if the local Church will say "yes" only to a bishop who himself says "no" to the Bishop of Rome? Second, why should the clergy alone embody the local Church's "yes" (or "no")? In other words, the danger is that the "solution" becomes, paradoxically, far more "juridical" (in the negative sense) than the problem—which may be why a different practice developed in the Church with respect to communion and jurisdiction. See also for positions similar to Buckley's: Archbishop John R. Quinn, "The Claims of the Primacy and the Costly Call to Unity," with responses by R. Scott Appleby, Elizabeth A. Johnson, John F. Kane, Thomas P. Rausch, and Wendy M. Wright, as well as Quinn's "Response," in *The Exercise of the Primacy: Continuing the Dialogue*, ed. Phyllis Zagano and Terrence W. Tilley (New York: Crossroad, 1998).

8. Perkins, " 'Being of One Mind,' " 36.

9. In the context of contemporary debates within Anglicanism, Philip Turner notes, "Arguments over sexual ethics have in fact sparked a fierce debate over the nature of the church. Is it to be understood as a 'communion of churches' in which the 'autonomy' of each is properly exercised only within the constraints of a wider fellowship of common belief and practice; or is it best understood as a 'federation of churches' in which each member church is autonomous in a way that makes it uniquely responsible for its stewardship of God's self-revelation in Christ?" (Turner, "Introduction: Unity, Obedience, and the Shape of Communion," in Ephraim Radner and Philip Turner, *The Fate of Communion: The Agony of Anglicanism and the Future of a Global Church* [Grand Rapids, MI: Eerdmans, 2006], 4). Perkins's viewpoint raises a similar question.

teachings of Jesus. By contrast, the supposition that the Holy Spirit guides the Church through hierarchical leaders results in uncritical acceptance of restrictive teachings regarding matters of sexuality, marriage, and claims to authority.[10] Not only magisterial teaching should be subject to the measure of the community's liberative experience, but also scriptural passages must be evaluated by the same critical measure before being accepted.[11] Since the theological key is Christ's overturning of all structures of domination, sociological measurement of liberative experience becomes normative for theological discourse about ecclesial structure. Otherwise such theological discourse will itself become an instrument of oppression.

Nicholas M. Healy's *Church, World and the Christian Life: Practical-Prophetic Ecclesiology* makes a case for "theodramatic" ecclesiology as opposed to what he calls "epic" ecclesiology. He defines "epic" ecclesiology as one that, seeking to affirm the Church's holiness, depicts an idealized Church that does not exist in this world and ignores the sins and weaknesses of the concrete Church.[12] By contrast, "theodramatic" ecclesiology witnesses to "the Church's belief that all people and institutions, itself included, should humbly acknowledge their

---

10. Perkins writes, for example, "In today's church, women have good reason to suspect that when ecclesiastical authorities use lofty Christological metaphors, the images are a rhetorical covering for exclusion and subordination" (Perkins, " 'Being of One Mind,' " 25). See also Gaillardetz's suggestion that the Church is not yet structurally a "communion": "It is useless to speak of a real communion within the Church if there are no concrete manifestations of communion in which authentic conversation and consultation can take place" (Gaillardetz, *Teaching with Authority*, 282).

11. Perkins, " 'Being of One Mind,'" 26.

12. For explanation of this terminology, see Nicholas M. Healy, *Church, World and the Christian Life: Practical-Prophetic Ecclesiology* (Cambridge: Cambridge University Press, 2000), 150–51, and elsewhere. He refers to "epic" ecclesiologies also as "blueprint" ecclesiologies. After emphasizing the distinction between the concrete sinful Church and the eschatological perfect Church, he remarks, "Blueprint ecclesiologies thus foster a disjunction not only between normative theory and normative accounts of ecclesial practice, but between ideal ecclesiology and the realities of the concrete Church, too. They undervalue thereby the theological significance of the genuine struggles of the Church's membership to live as disciples within the less-than-perfect Church and within societies that are often unwilling to overlook the Church's flaws. As a consequence, blueprint ecclesiologies frequently display a curious inability to acknowledge the complexities of ecclesial life in its pilgrim state. To take just one instance, we noted how Tillard believes that the Eucharist is the most perfect expression of 'communion.' While that may well be true, eucharists are concretely and frequently divided by race, class, gender, and political ideology, to say nothing of denominational divisions" (37). An earlier version of this discussion of Healy's work appears in my "Hierarchy and Holiness," in *Wisdom and Holiness, Science and Scholarship: Essays in Honor of Matthew L. Lamb*, ed. Michael Dauphinais and Matthew Levering (Naples, FL: Sapientia Press, 2007), 143–72, at 143–47.

sinfulness, finitude, and dependence upon the grace and mercy of God."[13] For Healy, the holiness of the Church belongs not to the concrete or pilgrim Church, but strictly to the "eschatological Church of the saints who can no longer sin and whose lives together no longer need continual reformation."[14] He affirms that the pilgrim Church and the eschatological Church are related, but he thinks that ecclesiology must carefully distinguish what can be affirmed about the former from what can be affirmed about the latter:

> The eschatological Church should continue to be the subject of theological inquiry since the pilgrim Church proleptically participates in the eternal Church and so an account of the latter bears upon what we say about the former. But the two forms of the Church are not the same and cannot be treated in the same manner. An ecclesiological method that is appropriate for describing the ideal, eternal Church is not broad enough to deal adequately with the Church on earth. We must say far more about the Church *in via* than about the heavenly Church, and say it in a different and more complex way.[15]

Without further explaining the "proleptic" participation, Healy develops the implications of his strong distinction between the concrete and eschatological Church. For instance, he argues that the call of all humankind to be united to the one Church (the Church's

---

13. Healy, *Church, World and the Christian Life*, 151. Earlier Healy explains that in his book "the word 'church' refers to all those diverse Christian groups who accept what is sometimes cumbersomely called the Niceno-Constantinopolitan creed" (6), although he expects that sometimes his Roman Catholic perspective will show through, as for instance "when I discuss the issue of ecclesial arrogance, my primary reference is, as it must be, to the Roman church, although the problem clearly arises in different forms within other denominations" (ibid.).

14. Ibid., 150.

15. Healy, *Church, World and the Christian Life*, 150. He observes that "in general, ecclesiology in our period has become highly systematic and theoretical, focused more upon discerning the right things to think about the Church rather than orientated to the living, rather messy, confused, and confusing body that the Church actually is. It displays a preference for describing the Church's theoretical and essential identity rather than its concrete and historical identity" (3). On the relationship of the eschatological and pilgrim Church see also *Lumen Gentium*, 8: "Christ, the one mediator, set up his holy church here on earth as a visible structure, a community of faith, hope and love; and he sustains it unceasingly and through it he pours out grace and truth on everyone. This society, however, equipped with hierarchical structures, and the mystical body of Christ, a visible assembly and a spiritual community, an earthly church and a church enriched with heavenly gifts, must not be considered as two things, but as forming one complex reality comprising a human and a divine element. It is therefore by no mean analogy that it is likened to the mystery of the incarnate Word" (translation in *Decrees of the Ecumenical Councils*, vol. 2, *Trent to Vatican II*, ed. Norman P. Tanner, SJ [Washington, DC: Georgetown University Press, 1990], 854).

unity and catholicity) can be referred simply to the eschatological
Church. Thus he states, "We can follow Rahner and the tradition
generally in claiming that salvation requires at least an orientation to
the Church; but we are not thereby obliged to understand this as an
orientation to the Church on earth."[16] Similarly, he decries the fact
that "Charles Journet's formula, asserting that 'the Church is not
without sinners, but she herself is sinless,' has been accepted as if it
were doctrine."[17] Granted that the Church flows from the activity of
Christ's Holy Spirit, it still does not follow, Healy argues, that "when
the Church is truly itself, or when considered at its most profound
level, it is something that is fundamentally free of sin."[18] The distinction
(apparently ontological) between the concrete Church and the

---

16. Healy, *Church, World and the Christian Life*, 151. For a better account of the Church's
visible and "invisible" membership, see Hans Urs von Balthasar, *Theo-Drama*, vol. 4, *The
Action*, trans. Graham Harrison (German 1980; San Francisco: Ignatius Press, 1994), 453–69,
especially 453–54: "the boundaries of the visible Church do not correspond to those of the
living Mystical Body of Christ, for the latter can have true members outside the *Catholica* and
many dead members within her." For discussion of Aquinas's position, in agreement with von
Balthasar, see Herwi Rikhof, "Thomas on the Church: Reflections on a Sermon," in *Aquinas
on Doctrine: A Critical Introduction*, ed. Thomas Weinandy, OFM CAP, Daniel Keating, and John
Yocum (New York: T. & T. Clark, 2004), 199–223, at 216.

17. Healy, *Church, World and the Christian Life*, 9.

18. Ibid., 10. For a more nuanced perspective on the Church's holiness, equally aware of
the "carnal" aspect of the Church, see Yves Congar, "The Spirit Is the Principle of the
Church's Holiness," in his *I Believe in the Holy Spirit*, vol. 2, *He Is Lord and Giver of Life*, trans.
David Smith (New York: Crossroad, 1997), 52–64. After first discussing Aquinas's commentary
on the Apostles' Creed, in which Aquinas affirms that the "holy" Church is the temple of
God, Congar observes that "if it is on the basis of charity that God (the Spirit) dwells fully,
then only the Church, as the Body of Christ, is certain always to have a faith that is fashioned
by charity, since every individual person is able to fail in this. It was to the Church that the
promises were made, and by 'Church' what is meant is not simply the assembled believers or
what H. de Lubac called the *ecclesia congregata*, but also the *ecclesia congregans*, the essential
elements of the apostolic institution, that is, its function and its teaching ministry together
with its sacraments" (54). For similar reflections, also drawing upon Aquinas's commentary on
the Apostles' Creed, see Herwi Rikhof, "Thomas on the Church: Reflections on a Sermon," in
Weinandy, Keating, and Yocum, *Aquinas on Doctrine*, 199–223, especially 203–6 on the
Church's holiness. See also on the holiness of the Church the biblical, patristic, and medieval
texts and commentary in Hans Urs von Balthasar, "Casta Meretrix," in *Explorations in Theology*,
vol. 2, *Spouse of the Word*, trans. John Saward (German 1961; San Francisco: Ignatius Press,
1991), 193–288; Henri de Lubac, SJ, *The Splendor of the Church*, trans. Michael Mason (1953;
San Francisco: Ignatius Press, 1986), 43, 111–19. De Lubac also points to the eschatological
Church, but with a much stronger emphasis on the eschatological Church as the "marrow"
(117) of the concrete Church, "the twofold aspect of the one Church" (119). See also *Lumen
Gentium*, 8: "While Christ 'holy, blameless, unstained' (Heb 7, 26) knew no sin (see 2 Cor 5,
21), and came only to expiate the sins of the people (see Heb 2, 17), the church, containing
sinners in its own bosom, is at one and the same time holy and always in need of purification
and it pursues unceasingly penance and renewal" (translation in Tanner, *Trent to Vatican II*,

eschatological Church makes it possible to avoid claims about the holiness of the Church on earth. As he puts it without qualification, "Sin and error, in short, are part of the Church's theological and concrete identity prior to the eschaton."[19]

Healy identifies the Church's understanding of ecclesial power as a particular locus of the Church's sinfulness. As he remarks, "The power of sin is manifested not only in the actions of individuals but in the Christian communal body, when the latter fosters practices, valuations, and beliefs in its membership that are incompatible with the Gospel. One of the more obvious examples of this is the failure of the Church's leadership to avoid the corruptions of power."[20] Thus Boniface VIII's papal bulls *Clericis laicos* (1296) and *Unam sanctam* (1302) sinfully taught false doctrine, inflated accounts of papal authority, although the sin may well reside not in Boniface but in the common assumptions, built up over centuries, of the Church of his time which was "corrupted by the ideology and practices of worldly power."[21]

Healy's critique extends, of course, beyond the medieval Church. He repeatedly suggests that similar corruptive "practices of worldly power" are still sinfully marginalizing groups of people within the Catholic Church:

> Laypeople, women, majorities, and minorities of various kinds may be marginalized within some forms of the Christian Church. They may not only have a different perspective upon the Church and its interaction with other traditions, they may have clearer insights into its sinfulness and inadequacies, into the challenges it faces, and perhaps as to how it should be reformed.[22]

---

855). For a Lutheran perspective see David S. Yeago, "Ecclesia Sancta, Ecclesia Peccatrix: The Holiness of the Church in Martin Luther's Theology," *Pro Ecclesia* 9 (2000): 331–54.

19. Healy, *Church, World and the Christian Life*, 11; cf. 175. He adds, "God is the solution to the problems of the world, not the church. The church, although oriented to, and governed by, the solution, still remains part of the problem" (12). He is careful to say that he does not mean to condemn the Church in a hypocritical fashion: "I try to discern the speck in my church's eye so that it may pluck it forth and then more readily help me discern the beam in my own" (13).

20. Ibid., 7.

21. Ibid., 8. For criticism of Boniface VIII's claims see Avery Dulles, sj, *The Catholicity of the Church* (Oxford: Oxford University Press, 1985), 135–36, 145; idem, "A New Orthodox View of the Papacy," *Pro Ecclesia* 12 (2003): 345–58, at 352–53.

22. Healy, *Church, World and the Christian Life*, 178.

Similarly, "it may well be that the more a Christian grows into her unique role, the more she will find herself having to challenge certain ecclesial cultural patterns, even if she has no leadership role."[23] Contrasting his view on women in the Church with Jean-Marie Tillard's call for calm reflection on the topic, Healy notes that "the history of the Church indicates that serene reflection is the perquisite of those in power. Reforms, like doctrinal agreements, are usually the result, not of serenity, but of struggle and eventual compromise."[24] A key task of his "practical-prophetic" and theodramatic ecclesiology is therefore "actively seeking out and bringing to light anti–Christian practices and beliefs and . . . proposing suitable reforms,"[25] although Healy leaves this task to a future book.

To sum up: Perkins holds that Christianity is about a liberative praxis measured by the experience of local communities, which are the primary locus of the Holy Spirit's guidance of the Church. For Perkins, the comparison of Paul with Ignatius of Antioch indicates that leaders in the Church need to understand themselves as hierarchically subordinate to the sociological experience of local churches, whose authenticity is manifested by their participation in Christ's liberative praxis. Healy contrasts "theodramatic" or "practical-prophetic" ecclesiology with "epic" ecclesiology. The latter holds up an idealized vision of the Church's holiness, whereas the former recognizes that the pilgrim Church (which participates proleptically, though perhaps not ontologically, in the holy eschatological Church) is sinfully marked by corruptive "practices of worldly power." For Healy, discussion of ecclesial hierarchy must proceed,

23. Ibid., 179. Richard Gaillardetz affirms, "God's word has been given to the whole Christian community in Jesus Christ by the power of the Holy Spirit. Any understanding of the structures and exercise of doctrinal teaching authority will be distorted or defective to the extent that it does not fully account for this basic conviction. God's word is not in the possession of a privileged few within the Church, however much Catholics may insist on an apostolic ministry with the privileged responsibility of safeguarding the authentic proclamation of that word" (Gaillardetz, *Teaching with Authority*, 293). Without denying that "God's word has been given to the whole Christian community," the question is how it has been given. Is it sufficient to describe the "apostolic ministry" in terms of "safeguarding"? What about the mediated pattern of gifting? Recognition of gifting/receptivity challenges the adequacy of conceiving of the Church as made up of official leaders on the one hand and those with "no leadership role" on the other. Christian "leadership" is constituted by receptivity.

24. Healy, *Church, World and the Christian Life*, 38. Without disagreeing with Healy on the question of the ordination of women, Christopher Ruddy defends Tillard's ecclesiology against Healy's charge that it is an "epic" ecclesiology: see Ruddy, *The Local Church: Tillard and the Future of Catholic Ecclesiology* (New York: Crossroad, 2006), 127–29.

25. Healy, *Church, World and the Christian Life*, 185.

if it is not to fall into "epic" ecclesiology, with sociological and historical awareness of the oppressions and falsehoods that the hierarchy of the Church has perpetrated in the past and continues to perpetrate today. On these terms, it would appear that any hierarchy that could be imagined for the future Church would need to be a severely chastened hierarchy, whose "hierarchical" claims could only be understood as a limited mode (disciplined by other communal leadership modes) of awaiting the manifestation of the true eschatological hierarchy of love.[26]

HIERARCHY AND THE THEODRAMA

In light of these critiques, has my effort to explore the theological foundations of ecclesial hierarchy been in vain? By not examining the personal and structural sins of ecclesial hierarchy in history, I have arguably ventured into the terrain of "epic" ecclesiology. Furthermore, I have held that ecclesial hierarchy is the manner by which Christ mediates, in the Holy Spirit, our participation in the goods of salvation that flow from his Paschal Mystery: hierarchy belongs to what Avery Dulles, delineating "catholicity," calls "adherence to the fullness of

---

26. Implying that such a chastened hierarchy is needed, Gaillardetz observes, "The attitude of many that informing the faithful of the various distinctions in the authority of Church doctrine will only bring confusion and widespread dissent needs to be named for what it is: an inexcusable ecclesiastical paternalism" (Gaillardetz, *Teaching with Authority*, 290; cf. idem, *By What Authority? A Primer on Scripture, the Magisterium, and the Sense of the Faithful* [Collegeville, MN: Liturgical Press, 2003], 129). That there is "widespread dissent" from Catholics on almost every area of Church doctrine is true, and perhaps the question is whether "inexcusable ecclesiastical paternalism" is the most serious problem. Gaillardetz goes on to say, "If a particular teaching of the Church and the arguments adduced in support of it are not persuasive, simply 'ratcheting up' the authoritative status of the teaching, or arbitrarily closing off debate, will not substitute for persuasive argumentation and dialogue" (*Teaching with Authority*, 291). How to judge when the argumentation should be deemed "persuasive"? When the majority agree with it? Likewise, what are the grounds for the "dialogue"? Gaillardetz states, "A frequent consultation of theologians representing divergent views on a matter need not threaten the legitimate authority of those who hold Church office" (292). Again the question is whether this "legitimate authority" is not in fact under threat in the Church today. Are theologians' "divergent views" ever changed by the exercise of papal or episcopal "legitimate authority" in the contemporary Church? Gaillardetz is certainly aware of these concerns. As he remarks in *By What Authority?*, "Too often a minister will struggle with an official teaching of the Church because of inadequate theological formation. Teachings on Mary, eschatology, original sin, eucharistic real presence, sexual morality, etc. are often ignored because the minister finds popular/traditional treatments of the subject less than persuasive. Proper theological formation and ongoing education for ministry is absolutely essential. The minister must be able to present adequately the teaching of the Church in language and concepts intelligible to the modern Catholic" (*By What Authority?* 128–29).

God's gift in Christ."[27] My account of ecclesial hierarchy likewise denies that local communities' experiences of liberative praxis are the primary mode by which Christians should recognize the presence of Christ. Does my analysis therefore simply defend the oppressive imposition by distant hierarchs of restrictive anti–Christian legalism upon local communities?

In response to this concern, I would recall the common good that ecclesial hierarchy serves to mediate. By the Holy Spirit, ecclesial hierarchy mediates the power of Christ's kenotic love. This takes place above all in and through the unity of the Eucharistic sacrifice, inclusive of the communion meal.[28] As a participation in the gifting and receptivity of Christ, this hierarchically structured unity allows for true diversity, the many individual participations in Christ's love. As the communion of saints, the members of the one body commune together in the spiritual goods of the Church, not despite the hierarchical structure but because of it.[29]

---

27. Avery Dulles, SJ, *The Catholicity of the Church*, 9. Dulles's full point is worth quoting: "In intellectual circles today catholicity is commonly praised, whereas Catholicism is an object of suspicion. Whoever is catholic, in the sense of having *catholicity*, is esteemed as open-minded, tolerant, and undogmatic. But to be Catholic in the sense of professing *Catholicism* is regarded as signifying a closed, intolerant, and dogmatic spirit. According to the view I shall propose, catholicity and Catholicism are closely correlated. Catholicity always implies, in principle, adherence to the fullness of God's gift in Christ. Christianity is inclusive not by reason of latitudinarian permissiveness or syncretistic promiscuity, but because it has received from God a message and a gift for people of every time and place, so that all can find in it the fulfillment of their highest selves" (9). On our theme see especially Dulles's chapter 6, "Structures of Catholicity: Sacramental and Hierarchical," 106–26.

28. See Michael McGuckian, SJ, *The Holy Sacrifice of the Mass: A Search for an Acceptable Notion of Sacrifice* (Chicago: Hillenbrand Books, 2005).

29. Cf. Claude Dagens, "Hierarchy and Communion: The Bases of Authority in the Beginning of the Church," trans. Sister Isaac Jogues, SU, *Communio* 9 (1982): 67–78. For discussion of the "communion of saints," see, e.g., Jean-Pierre Torrell, OP, *St. Thomas Aquinas*, vol. 2, *Spiritual Master*, trans. Robert Royal (French 1996; Washington, DC: The Catholic University of America Press, 2003), 194–99; Geoffrey Preston, OP, *Faces of the Church: Meditations on a Mystery and Its Images*, ed. Aidan Nichols, OP (Grand Rapids, MI: Eerdmans, 1997), 261–71. Preston draws upon Stephen Benko, *The Meaning of 'Sanctorum Communio'* (London: SCM Press, 1964), which argues (along lines disputed by J. N. D. Kelly, *Early Christian Creeds* [London: Longmans, Green & Co., 1950]) that the credal phrase originally has the (theocentric) meaning of " 'participation in the holy things' " (Preston, *Faces of the Church*, 261) and later "came to be understood more and more as referring to the social character of the Church itself. It was taken to stand for the communion of the members of the Church with one another rather than simply the communion of each of them in holy things" (ibid.). For Aquinas in his commentary on the Apostles' Creed, Preston shows, it refers to both, although primarily to the sacramental communion in the holy things; whereas for Henri de Lubac, SJ, it refers solely to the communion in holy things. See de Lubac, *The Christian Faith:*

Yet, what about Perkins's and Healy's view that hierarchy, when distorted by the sinfulness of its members, becomes oppressive domination? I would first ask whether Perkins's ideal of the normative role of the liberative experience of the local community allows the Gospel to define Christian freedom, or whether in fact her proposal is rooted in a valorization of autonomy. Similarly, I would ask whether Healy's "practical-prophetic" criticisms of the Church's hierarchy are grounded in adequate theological understanding of the Church's doctrine. At stake is the theological framework within which one adjudicates the possibility that the sins of the members of the ecclesial hierarchy have derailed the Church's communion in the goods of Christ's Pasch through true faith and true sacraments (that is, the Church's "holiness"). Does Christ continue to uphold the whole Church, and not solely the eschatological Church, in holiness by means of his grace of headship in the Holy Spirit? Does a hierarchically ordered Church assist its members in attaining the "end" of Trinitarian communion in truth and love that Christ wills for believers through the Spirit?

A fully "theodramatic" approach answers yes to these questions by underscoring the Trinity's action in the Church, which ensures that the Church's faith and sacraments mediate Christ's salvific holiness.[30] In the theodrama thus understood, the Trinity is

---

An Essay on the Structure of the Apostles' Creed (San Francisco: Ignatius Press, 1986), 218. On the *communio sanctorum* in Aquinas's commentary on the Apostles' Creed, see also Herwi Rikhof, "Thomas on the Church," 211–12. See also Robert Louis Wilken, "*Sanctorum Communio*: For Evangelicals and Catholics Together," *Pro Ecclesia* 11 (2002): 159–66; Christoph Schönborn, "The 'Communion of Saints' as Three States of the Church: Pilgrimage, Purification, and Glory," trans. Walter Jüptner, OMI, *Communio* 15 (1988): 169–81.

30. For a better approach that attempts to integrate Healy's concerns, see Frederick Christian Bauerschmidt, " 'That the Faithful Become the Temple of God': The Church Militant in Aquinas's *Commentary on John*," in *Reading John with St. Thomas Aquinas*, eds. Michael Dauphinais and Matthew Levering (Washington, DC: The Catholic University of America Press, 2004): 293–311, although Bauerschmidt's treatment of the sinfulness of the Church according to Aquinas needs a more nuanced explication. Bauerschmidt writes, "Thomas believes, of course, in the holiness of the Church: that the Church lives by grace and the promise of Jesus that the gates of hell shall not prevail against her. But this is something different from the view, heard these days in certain ecclesiastical circles, that, while *Christians* may sin, the *Church* cannot, because she is objectively holy in her structures and sacraments" (309). What would it mean for the "Church" to "sin"? Would it require that the Church, in her actions *qua* Church, teach false doctrine or bestow objectively graceless sacraments? The issues involved are profoundly engaged by Joseph Ratzinger, "The Church's Guilt: Presentation of the Document *Remembrance and Reconciliation* from the International Theological Commission," in idem, *Pilgrim Fellowship of Faith: The Church as Communion*, ed. Stephan

present in the visible Church not merely extrinsically, but intrinsically and efficaciously, bringing forth believers' "liberative" and "prophetic" action recognizable through its conformity to the eucharistic pattern of receptivity and gifting.[31] Saint Paul's almost impossibly bold practice at the end of his letters, namely sending greetings from the "saints" (Romans 16:15, 2 Corinthians 13:13, and so forth), signals this efficacious mediation of divine gifting. Indeed, von Balthasar points out that from a "theodramatic" perspective, the form of Christ and the form of the Church cannot be separated: one cannot imagine Jesus without his apostles or vice versa.[32] As von Balthasar puts it, "In concrete terms, Christ only exists together with the community of saints united in the *Immaculata*, together with the communion of the ministerial office visibly united in Peter and his successors and

---

Otto Horn and Vinzenz Pfnür, trans. Henry Taylor (German 2002; San Francisco: Ignatius Press, 2005), 274–83.

31. See especially Servais Pinckaers, OP, "La morale et l'Église Corps du Christ," *Revue Thomiste* 100 (2000): 239–58, as well as the profound study of Jean-Marie Roger Tillard, OP, *Flesh of the Church, Flesh of Christ: At the Source of the Ecclesiology of Communion*, trans. Madeleine Beaumont (French 1992; Collegeville, MN: Liturgical Press, 2001); cf. Leo Scheffczyk, "Faith and Witness: *Confessio* and *Martyrium*," trans. Albert Wimmer, *Communio* 22 (1995): 406–17. From a Protestant perspective see Barry Harvey, "The Eucharistic Idiom of the Gospel," *Pro Ecclesia* 9 (2000): 297–318. It is such liberative and prophetic action that is sought, but without an adequate articulation of the Church as a sacramental organism (and without engaging the devastation wrought by abortion in the African American community), by Jamie T. Phelps, OP, "Communion Ecclesiology and Black Liberation Theology," *Theological Studies* 61 (2000): 672–99.

32. While the Church is thus truly the body of Christ, Christ's headship means that Christ, not the Church, is the one mediator of salvation, although the Church participates in this mediation. Cf. the concerns of Colin Gunton: "Much recent theology, particularly as the result of ecumenical discussion, has rediscovered the centrality of the church; it has also sometimes inflated its role, as if the church were itself the mediator of salvation. God uses the church as he uses Israel, but it is only by overmatching their all too obvious limits and weaknesses. Insofar as the church, in both worship and life, is *enabled* to set forth Christ, thus far does it mediate the work of the mediator. The other danger is to make the church merely instrumental, merely the means to something that is essentially external to it. Perhaps Calvin is near to that danger when he speaks of the church as among the external means used by God for the sanctification of the believer" (Gunton, "One Mediator . . . The Man Jesus Christ," *Pro Ecclesia* 11 [2002]: 146–58, at 157). One might also see Susan K. Wood's helpful effort, in light of Henri de Lubac's emphasis on the identity between Christ and the Church, to explain how "Christ transcends, is more than, his body and, as head of that body, cannot be considered a 'member' of the body in the same sense that the Christian is a member of the body" (145): Wood, *Spiritual Exegesis and the Church in the Theology of Henri de Lubac* (Grand Rapids, MI: Eerdmans, 1998), 144–48.

together with the living, ongoing tradition united in the great councils and declarations of the Church."[33]

In this light, Christ instructs his followers in self-disposses-sive receptivity by enabling us to receive him hierarchically from priests who are human and sinful as we are. In the Eucharist and through the practice of hierarchical receptivity to the divine gifting, we learn the power of Christ's obedience and grow in the ability to embody his kenotic power in lives of charity.[34] This "power" is truly "liberative" and "prophetic," but it is also a power that cannot be simply measured sociologically. The eyes of faith remain necessary in order to see this theodrama of holiness within the hierarchical Church. Von Balthasar observes,

> Even within the communities founded by Paul and stamped with his spirit, there are dissensions practically everywhere. The Letters to the Corinthians are full of accusations of strife in the community: there are *schismata* (1 Cor 1:10), there is *hairesis* (1 Cor 11:19), "for you bear it if a man makes slaves of you, or preys upon you, or takes advantage of you, or puts on airs, or strikes you in the face. . ." (2 Cor 11:20). In Philippi, two women have acquired opposing coteries; the Galatians should beware, lest in "biting and devouring one another" they are totally "consumed by one another" (Gal 5:15). And, as soon as Paul has turned his back, alien teachings insinuate themselves, Jewish teachings from Jerusalem, early Gnostic teachings in Colossae and no doubt in Corinth too. Hardly is the Church founded when she is deeply rent by strife.[35]

33. Von Balthasar, *Theo-Drama*, vol. 4, *The Action*, 456. See also Yves Congar, *The Meaning of Tradition*, trans. A. N. Woodrow (New York: Hawthorn Books, 1964). Von Balthasar affirms Christ's presence in other Christian communities, while denying that this presence ever loses its reference to the Catholic Church. He remarks that other Christian communities "bear flowers and fruits that are undeniably part of the Christian totality. So we have a paradoxical situation: the *Catholica* finds that things that are fundamentally hers, but which she has somehow forgotten or inadequately realized, are exhibited—to her shame—by other Christian communities" (von Balthasar, *The Action*, 456–57). See for further discussion Rodney A. Howsare, *Balthasar and Protestantism* (New York: T. & T. Clark, 2005), especially chapter 1.

34. I agree with Stanley Hauerwas's observation, in his foreword to Radner and Turner's *The Fate of Communion*, that "the politics of communion must also be a politics of holiness" (x). Hauerwas explains his observation by noting that "I do not believe it possible to be a good society without people being good" (xi). I would add that this is why Christian community, which cannot depend upon the goodness of people, must be built on baptism and the Eucharist, because *Christ* is good: "But God shows his love for us in that while we were yet sinners Christ died for us" (Romans 5:8). Cf. Michael J. McCarthy, sj, "An Ecclesiology of Groaning: Augustine, the Psalms, and the Making of Church," *Theological Studies* 66 (2005): 23–48.

35. Von Balthasar, *The Action*, 454.

What would outsiders have made of so many worldly power struggles among those called to be "saints"? Despite his role in the mediation of Christ's gifting, Paul tells the Corinthians, "I do not run aimlessly, I do not box as one beating the air; but I pommel my body and subdue it, lest after preaching to others I myself should be disqualified" (1 Cor 9:26–27). If even the apostle might be "disqualified," one can hardly expect to prove empirically the theodrama of divine love and forgiveness in the Church, notwithstanding the ongoing witness of the Church's saints. As Reinhard Hütter remarks, "Precisely the external, visible church *is* the hidden church, for only faith itself can perceive the externality of the Holy Spirit's activities at issue here; they are to be *believed* as *works* of the Holy Spirit. As activities of the *Holy Spirit*, precisely their straightforward, concrete externality makes them radically 'invisible' to unbelief."[36]

An "Answer that We Ourselves Have Not Devised"

Ecclesial hierarchy thus cannot be proven efficacious on either functionalist grounds (as assuring lack of strife) or on the grounds of the moral superiority of the hierarchs (who themselves may be "disqualified"). Rather, ecclesial hierarchy finds itself, and its power, inscribed within the Church's eucharistic participation in Christ's Pasch. Von

---

36. Hütter, *Suffering Divine Things: Theology as Church Practice*, trans. Doug Stott (German 1997; Grand Rapids, MI: Eerdmans, 2000), 131. Hütter is speaking about "works of the Holy Spirit" that "are tied to specific church practices which Luther calls the seven principal parts of Christian sanctification according to the first table of commandments" (129). See also Douglas Farrow, *Ascension and Ecclesia: On the Significance of the Doctrine of the Ascension for Ecclesiology and Christian Cosmology* (Grand Rapids, MI: Eerdmans, 1999), 3–4: "To grapple with the mystery of the *quodammodo praesens et quodammodo absens* is indeed ecclesiology's constant challenge. Where either side of that mystery is neglected, the mystery of the church itself is undone. Not long along ago a rather cheeky editorial in *Theology Today* encouraged us to learn to appreciate 'the presence of the absence,' something we propose to do; but to take such advice at face value, eschewing the eucharistic movement from absence to presence, would be to give up believing in the church altogether. On the other hand, those who are content to build lopsidedly on the wonderful promises of presence in Matthew 18:20 or 28:20, for example, will still find it difficult to press through to a serious view of the church. In neither case are presence and absence brought into their right relation, for they are not seen *together*, as the eucharist demands. Thus the intimate association between ecclesiology and eschatology is lost from view and the church is gradually assimilated to some more or less worldly agenda." One might also see Heinrich Schlier, "The Holy Spirit as Interpreter According to St. John's Gospel," trans. W. J. O'Hara, *Communio* 1 (1974): 128–41.

Balthasar comments in this vein that "the archetypal call of Peter at the end of the Gospel of John is followed by the promise of martyrdom that is inseparable from it."[37] The theology of ecclesial hierarchy comes into focus only in light of a wider theological accounting, inclusive of the triune God, Christ's Pasch, and sacramental mediation.[38] On this basis, this book has offered reasons for why the triune God's plan of salvation includes hierarchical priesthood in the Church.

These reasons cannot claim to "resolve" the mystery of hierarchy in the Church. They contribute instead to the task of faith seeking understanding. As Joseph Ratzinger has remarked, "If theology wishes and should be something other than religious studies, other than occupying ourselves with ever unsolved questions concerning what is greater than ourselves and nonetheless makes us what we are, then it can only be based on starting from an answer that we ourselves have not devised; yet in order for this to become a real answer for us, we

---

37. Von Balthasar, *The Action*, 468.

38. For a sampling of contemporary proposals to alter the hierarchical structure of the Church, generally by putting in place a democratic substratum with varying degrees of power, see Paul Lakeland, *The Liberation of the Laity: In Search of an Accountable Church* (New York: Continuum, 2003); Edward Schillebeeckx, OP, *Church: The Human Story of God*, trans. John Bowden (New York: Crossroad, 1990); Kenan B. Osborne, OFM, *Ministry: Lay Ministry in the Roman Catholic Church: Its History and Theology* (New York: Paulist, 1993); Eugene C. Bianchi and Rosemary Radford Ruether, eds., *A Democratic Catholic Church: The Reconstruction of Roman Catholicism* (New York: Crossroad, 1993); Leonard Swidler, *Toward a Catholic Constitution* (New York: Crossroad, 1996); Paul Collins, *Papal Power: A Proposal for Change in Catholicism's Third Millennium* (London: HarperCollins, 1997); Stephen J. Pope, ed., *Common Calling: The Laity and Governance of the Catholic Church* (Washington, DC: Georgetown University Press, 2004); Zagano and Tilley, *The Exercise of the Primacy: Continuing the Dialogue*; Francis Oakley and Bruce Russett, eds., *Governance, Accountability, and the Future of the Catholic Church* (New York: Continuum, 2004). Even Christopher Ruddy's *The Local Church: Tillard and the Future of Catholic Ecclesiology* (New York: Crossroad, 2006)—which concentrates in large part upon the ecclesiology of Jean-Marie Tillard, OP, whose approach Nicholas Healy criticizes as "epic" ecclesiology—decries "papal maximalization" under John Paul II (Ruddy, *The Local Church*, 154). For his part, Lakeland wishes to get away from the two-tiered hierarchical system and return to a "servant leadership" in which priests and bishops make decisions with the community. In so doing, he hopes to return the Church to its roots: "the picture of ministries outlined here approximates that which seems to have marked the early Church. A clergy/lay distinction was foreign to the consciousness of the early Christians" (Lakeland, *The Liberation of the Laity*, 285). He proposes therefore re-integrating the community into the Church's decision making: "When the time comes for the community to have new servant leaders, or when the community is so moved by the qualities of one of its members that it wishes to have that person called to servant leadership, the bishop becomes part of the mix" (284). See also Luke Timothy Johnson, *Scripture and Discernment: Decision-Making in the Church* (Nashville, TN: Abingdon Press, 1996), 132.

have to try to understand it, not to resolve it."[39] In this case, the "answer that we ourselves have not devised" is the Trinitarian and Christological pattern of gifting and receptivity that is the hierarchical Church.

Discussing John 21:15, Thomas Aquinas sums up his ecclesiology: "Prelates need grace because if they do not have grace they do not have anything: 'By the grace of God I am what I am' (1 Cor 5:10); 'And when they perceived the grace that was given to me, James and Cephas and John, who were reputed to be pillars, gave to me and Barnabas the right hand of fellowship' (Gal 2:9)."[40] The entire Church rests on this: "if they do not have grace they do not have anything." But can we trust the Holy Spirit to give the needed grace to prelates? Still discussing John 21:15, Aquinas continues, "So Peter, who before had denied Christ because he was afraid to die, now, after our Lord has arisen, feared nothing. Why should he be afraid, since he now realized that death has died?"[41] Death has died; Peter, in repentance and joy, need not fear.

---

39. Joseph Ratzinger, "What in Fact Is Theology?" in idem, *Pilgrim Fellowship of Faith*, 29–37, at 31. This article of Ratzinger's originally appeared in German in 2000. Ratzinger elsewhere makes similar points: "we must see to it that in this we do not silently make ourselves the absolute rulers of our faith and thus by pressing on thoughtlessly destroy the living thing that we cannot create but can only cherish" (Ratzinger, "Postscript" to "Anglican–Catholic Dialogue: Its Problems and Hopes," in his *Church, Ecumenism and Politics: New Essays in Ecclesiology*, trans. Robert Nowell [German 1987; New York: Crossroad, 1988], 98). For the difference between theology and religious studies see also Ratzinger's "The Truth of Christianity?" in his *Truth and Tolerance: Christian Belief and World Religions*, trans. Henry Taylor (German 2003; San Francisco: Ignatius Press, 2004), 138–209, especially 185.

40. Thomas Aquinas, *Commentary on the Gospel of John*, trans. Fabian Larcher, OP, Part II (Petersham, MA: St. Bede's Publications, 1999), 640 (#2616).

41. Ibid., 2617.

Bibliography

Abraham, William J. *Canon and Criterion in Christian Theology: From the Fathers to Feminism*. Oxford: Oxford University Press, 2002.

———. *The Logic of Renewal*. Grand Rapids, MI: Eerdmans, 2003.

Ackermann, Stephan. "The Church as Person in the Theology of Hans Urs von Balthasar," translated by Emily Rielley. *Communio* 29 (2002): 238–49.

Adams, Marilyn McCord. *Christ and Horrors: The Coherence of Christology*. Cambridge: Cambridge University Press, 2006.

Afanassieff (Afanasiev), Nicholas. "The Church Which Presides in Love." In *The Primacy of Peter: Essays in Ecclesiology and the Early Church*, edited by John Meyendorff, 91–143. 1963. Crestwood, NY: St. Vladimir's Seminary Press, 1992.

———. *The Church of the Holy Spirit*, translated by Vitaly Permiakov, edited by Michael Plekon. Notre Dame, IN: University of Notre Dame Press, 2007.

Alberigo, Giuseppe, Jean-Pierre Jossua, and Joseph A. Komonchak, eds. *The Reception of Vatican II*, translated by Matthew J. O'Connell. Washington, DC: The Catholic University of America Press, 1987.

Albertson, David. "On 'the Gift' in Tanner's Theology: A Patristic Parable." *Modern Theology* 21 (2005): 107–18.

Alexander, W. M. *Johann Georg Hamann: Philosophy and Faith*. The Hague: Martinus Nijhoff, 1966.

Allison Jr., Dale C. *The End of the Ages Has Come: An Early Interpretation of the Passion and Resurrection of Jesus*. Philadelphia: Fortress Press, 1985.

———. "Jesus and the Victory of the Apocalyptic." In *Jesus and the Restoration of Israel: A Critical Assessment of N. T. Wright's Jesus and the Victory of God*, edited by Carey C. Newman, 126–41. Downers Grove, IL: InterVarsity Press, 1999.

Altmann, Alexander. Introduction to *Jerusalem, or On Religious Power and Judaism* by Moses Mendelssohn, translated by Allan Arkush. Hanover, NH: Brandeis University Press, 1983.

Aquinas, Thomas. *Commentary on Colossians*, translated by Fabian Larcher, OP, edited by Daniel A. Keating. Naples, FL: Sapientia Press, 2006.

———. *Commentary on the Gospel of John*, trans. Fabian Larcher, OP, Part II. Petersham, MA: St. Bede's Publications, 1999.

———. *Summa Contra Gentiles*. Book Four: Salvation, translated by Charles J. O'Neil. Notre Dame, IN: University of Notre Dame Press, 1975.

———. *Summa Theologiae*, translated by the Fathers of the English Dominican Province. Westminster, MD: Christian Classics, 1981.

Aryankalayil, Joseph G. *Local Church and Church Universal: Towards a Convergence Between East and West*. PhD dissertation. Fribourg: Université de Fribourg Suisse, 2004.

Asheim, Ivar, and Victor R. Gold, eds. *Episcopacy in the Lutheran Church? Studies in the Development and Definition of the Office of Church Leadership*. Philadelphia: Fortress Press, 1970.

Ashley, Benedict, OP. "The Priesthood of Christ, of the Baptized, and of the Ordained." In idem, *The Ashley Reader: Redeeming Reason*, 125–43. Naples, FL: Sapientia Press, 2006.

———. "Hierarchy in Ecclesiology." In idem, *The Ashley Reader: Redeeming Reason*, 171–83. Naples, FL: Sapientia Press, 2006.

Athanasius. *On the Incarnation*, translated by a Religious of C.S.M.V. Crestwood, NY: St. Vladimir's Orthodox Theological Seminary, 1993.

Augustine. *City of God*, translated by Henry Bettenson. New York: Penguin, 1972.

Badcock, Gary D. "The Church as 'Sacrament.'" In *The Community of the Word: Toward an Evangelical Ecclesiology*, edited by Mark Husbands and Daniel J. Treier, 188–200. Downers Grove, IL: InterVarsity Press, 2005.

Bader-Saye, Scott. *Church and Israel after Christendom: The Politics of Election*. Boulder, Colorado: Westview Press, 1999.

Bailie, Gil. *Violence Unveiled: Humanity at the Crossroads*. New York: Crossroad, 1995.

Baktis, Peter Anthony. "Orthodox Ecclesiology for the New Millennium." *Pro Ecclesia* 10 (2001): 321–28.

Bandera, Armando, OP. *Configuración teologal-eucarística de la Iglesia según santo Tomás de Aquino*. Toledo: Servicio de Publicaciones del Instituto Teológico San Ildefonso, 1988.

Barker, Margaret. *The Great High Priest: The Temple Roots of Christian Liturgy*. New York: T&T Clark, 2003.

Barth, Karl. *The Church and the Churches*. German 1936. Grand Rapids, MI: Eerdmans, 2005.

Batnitzky, Leora. *Idolatry and Representation: The Philosophy of Franz Rosenzweig Reconsidered*. Princeton: Princeton University Press, 2000.

Bauckham, Richard. *God and the Crisis of Freedom: Biblical and Contemporary Perspectives*. Louisville, KY: Westminster John Knox, 2002.

Bauer, Walter, *Orthodoxy and Heresy in Earliest Christianity*, translated by Philadelphia Seminar on Christian Origins, edited by Robert A. Kraft and Gerhard Krodel. German 1934. Mifflintown, PA: Sigler Press, 1996.

Bauerschmidt, Frederick Christian. " 'That the Faithful Become the Temple of God': The Church Militant in Aquinas's *Commentary on John*." In *Reading John with St. Thomas Aquinas*, edited by Michael Dauphinais and Matthew Levering, 293–311. Washington, DC: The Catholic University of America Press, 2005.

Bayer, Oswald. *Autorität und Kritik: Hermeneutik und Wissenschaftstheorie*. Tübingen: Mohr-Siebeck, 1991.

Bedouelle, Guy, OP. "Reflection on the Place of the Child in the Church: 'Suffer the Little Children to Come unto Me,' " translated by Esther Tillman. *Communio* 12 (1985): 349–67.

Behr, John. *The Formation of Christian Theology*. Vol. 1, *The Way to Nicaea*. Crestwood, NY: St. Vladimir's Seminary Press, 2001.

Bellarmine, Robert. *Opera omnia*, edited by Justin Fèvre. Vol. 1–2, *Tertia controversia generalis: De summo pontifice*. Paris: Vives, 1870.

Bellinger Jr., William H., and William R. Farmer, eds. *Jesus and the Suffering Servant: Isaiah 53 and Christian Origins*. Harrisburg, PA: Trinity Press International, 1998.

Benko, Stephen. *The Meaning of 'Sanctorum Communio.'* London: SCM Press, 1964.

Berceville, Gilles, OP, "Le sacerdoce du Christ dans le *Commentaire de l'épître aux Hébreux* de saint Thomas d'Aquin." *Revue Thomiste* 99 (1999): 143–58.

Betz, John R. "Hamann before Kierkegaard: A Systematic Theological Oversight." *Pro Ecclesia* 16 (2007): 299–333.

Bianchi, Eugene C., and Rosemary Radford Ruether, eds. *A Democratic Catholic Church: The Reconstruction of Roman Catholicism.* New York: Crossroad, 1993.

Billings, J. Todd. "John Milbank's Theology of the 'Gift' and Calvin's Theology of Grace: A Critical Comparison." *Modern Theology* 21 (2005): 87–105.

Boersma, Hans. *Violence, Hospitality, and the Cross: Reappropriating the Atonement Tradition.* Grand Rapids, MI: Baker Academic, 2004.

Boff, Leonardo. *Ecclesiogenesis: The Base Communities Reinvent the Church.* Maryknoll, NY: Orbis, 1986.

Bonino, Serge-Thomas, OP. "La place du pape dans l'Église selon saint Thomas d'Aquin." *Revue Thomiste* 86 (1986) 392–422.

———. "The Role of the Apostles in the Communication of Revelation According to the *Lectura super Ioannem* of St. Thomas Aquinas," translated by Teresa Bede and Matthew Levering. In *Reading John with St. Thomas Aquinas*, edited by Michael Dauphinais and Matthew Levering, 318–46. Washington, DC: The Catholic University of America Press, 2005.

———. "Le sacerdoce comme institution naturelle selon saint Thomas d'Aquin." *Revue Thomiste* 99 (1999): 33–57.

Bourgeois, D. " 'Inchoatio vitae aeternae': La dimension eschatologique de la virtue théologique de foi chez S. Thomas d'Aquin." *Sapientia* 17 (1974): 276–86.

Bouyer, Louis. *The Church of God: Body of Christ and Temple of the Spirit.* Translated by Charles Underhill Quinn. French 1970. Chicago: Franciscan Herald Press, 1982.

———. *The Spirituality of the New Testament and the Fathers*, translated by Mary P. Ryan. French 1960. London: Burns & Oates, 1963.

Boyle, John P. *Church Teaching Authority: Historical and Theological Studies.* Notre Dame, IN: University of Notre Dame Press, 1995.

———. "The Ordinary Magisterium: Towards a History of the Concept (1)." *Heythrop Journal* 20 (1979): 380–98

———. "The Ordinary Magisterium: Towards a History of the Concept (2)." *Heythrop Journal* 21 (1980): 14–29.

Braaten, Carl E. *Mother Church: Ecclesiology and Ecumenism.* Minneapolis, MN: Fortress Press, 1998.

———. "The Special Ministry of the Ordained." In *Marks of the Body of Christ*, edited by Carl E. Braaten and Robert W. Jenson, , 123–36. Grand Rapids, MI: Eerdmans, 1999.

Braaten, Carl E. and Robert W. Jenson, eds. *The Catholicity of the Reformation.* Grand Rapids, MI: Eerdmans, 1996.

———. *The Ecumenical Future*, Grand Rapids, Michigan: Eerdmans, 2004.

———. *In One Body through the Cross: The Princeton Proposal for Christian Unity.* Grand Rapids, Michigan: Eerdmans, 2003.

———. *Marks of the Body of Christ.* Grand Rapids, MI: Eerdmans, 1999.

Brown, Raymond E., ss. *The Gospel According to John.* New York: Doubleday, 1966.

———. *Priest and Bishop: Biblical Reflections.* New York: Paulist Press, 1970.

Brown, Raymond E., ss, Carolyn Osiek, RSCJ, and Pheme Perkins. "Church in the New Testament." *The New Jerome Biblical Commentary*, 1339–46. Englewood Cliffs, NJ: Prentice Hall, 1990.

Brown, Raymond E., ss, et al., eds. *Peter in the New Testament*. New York: Paulist Press, 1973.

Bryan, Steven M. *Jesus and Israel's Traditions of Judgement and Restoration*. Cambridge: Cambridge University Press, 2002.

Buckley, James J. "The Wounded Body: The Spirit's Ecumenical Work on Divisions among Christians." In *Knowing the Triune God: The Work of the Spirit in the Practices of the Church*, edited by James J. Buckley and David S. Yeago, 205–230. Grand Rapids, MI: Eerdmans, 2001.

Buckley, James J., and David S. Yeago, eds. *Knowing the Triune God: The Work of the Spirit in the Practices of the Church*. Grand Rapids, MI: Eerdmans, 2001.

Buckley, Michael J., SJ. *Papal Primacy and the Episcopate: Towards a Relational Understanding*. New York: Crossroad, 1998.

Budde, Michael L., and Robert W. Brimlow, eds. *The Church as Counterculture*. New York: State University of New York Press, 2000.

Burkhard, John J., OFM CONV. *Apostolicity Then and Now: An Ecumenical Church in a Postmodern World*. Collegeville, MN: The Liturgical Press, 2004.

Burtchaell, James Tunstead, CSC. *From Synagogue to Church: Public Services and Offices in the Earliest Christian Communities*. Cambridge: Cambridge University Press, 1992.

Butler, Sara, MSBT. *The Catholic Priesthood and Women*. Chicago: Hillenbrand, 2007.

———. "*In Persona Christi*." *CTSA Proceedings* 50 (1995): 146–55.

Cameron, Euan. *Interpreting Christian History: The Challenge of the Churches' Past*. Oxford: Blackwell, 2005.

Caprioli, Mario, OCD. "Il sacerdozio di Cristo nella *Somma Theologica* e nel Commento *Super Epistolam ad Hebraeos*." In *Storia del tomismo*, 96–105. Vatican City: Libreria Editrice Vaticana, 1992.

Carter, W. *Households and Discipleship*. Sheffield: Sheffield Academic Press, 1994.

Catchpole, David. *Jesus People: The Historical Jesus and the Beginnings of Community*. London: Darton, Longman and Todd, 2006.

Catherine of Siena. *The Dialogue*, translated by Suzanne Noffke, OP. New York: Paulist Press, 1980.

Cavanaugh, William T. "Eucharistic Sacrifice and Social Imagination in Early Modern Europe." *Journal of Medieval and Early Modern Studies* 31 (2001): 585–605.

Cenkner, William, ed. *The Multicultural Church*. New York: Paulist, 1996.

Cessario, Romanus, OP. "Aquinas on Christian Salvation." In *Aquinas on Doctrine: A Critical Introduction*, edited by Thomas G. Weinandy, OFM CAP, Daniel A. Keating, and John P. Yocum, 117–37. New York: T&T Clark, 2004.

———. *Christian Faith and the Theological Life*. Washington, DC: The Catholic University of America Press, 1996.

———. *The Godly Image: Christ and Satisfaction in Catholic Thought from Anselm to Aquinas*. Petersham, MA: St. Bede's Publications, 1990.

Chantraine, Georges, SJ. "Apostolicity According to Schillebeeckx: The Notion and Its Import," translated by Mark D. Jordan. *Communio* 12 (1985): 192–222.

Chapp, Larry S. "Who Is the Church? The Personalistic Categories of Balthasar's Ecclesiology." *Communio* 23 (1996): 322–38.

Chardonnens, Denis, OCD. "Éternité du sacerdoce du Christ et effet eschatologique de l'eucharistie. La contribution de saint Thomas d'Aquin à un theme de théologie sacramentaire." *Revue Thomiste* 99 (1999): 159–80.

Charlesworth, James. *The Old Testament Pseudepigrapha*, 2 vols. Garden City: Doubleday, 1983.

Charry, Ellen T. "The Crisis of Modernity and the Christian Self." In Jurgen Moltmann, Nicholas Wolterstorff, and Ellen T. Charry, *A Passion for God's Reign: Theology, Christian Learning, and the Christian Self*, 88–112. Grand Rapids, MI: Eerdmans, 1998.

———. "Sacramental Ecclesiology." In *The Community of the Word: Toward an Evangelical Ecclesiology*, edited by Mark Husbands and Daniel J. Treier, 201–16. Downers Grove, IL: InterVarsity Press, 2005.

Chilton, Bruce. *The Temple of Jesus: His Sacrificial Program within a Cultural History of Sacrifice*. Philadelphia: University of Pennsylvania Press, 1992.

Cirillo, A. *Cristo Rivelatore del Padre nel Vangelo di S. Giovanni secondo il Commento di San Tommaso d'Aquino*. Rome: Angelicum, 1998.

Clapp, Rodney. "Practicing the Politics of Jesus." In *The Church as Counterculture*, edited by Michael L. Budde and Robert W. Brimlow, 15–37. New York: State University of New York Press, 2000.

Clapsis, Emmanuel. *Orthodoxy in Conversation: Orthodox Ecumenical Engagements*. Brookline, MA: Holy Cross Orthodox Seminary Press, 2000.

Clément, Olivier. *You Are Peter: An Orthodox Theologian's Reflection on the Exercise of Papal Primacy*, translated by M. S. Laird. New York: New City Press, 2003.

Coakley, Sarah, ed. *Re-Thinking Gregory of Nyssa*. Oxford: Blackwell, 2003.

Coffey, David. "The Common and the Ordained Priesthood." *Theological Studies* 58 (1997): 209–36.

Collins, Paul. *Papal Power: A Proposal for Change in Catholicism's Third Millennium*. London: HarperCollins, 1997.

Colson, Charles, and Richard John Neuhaus, ed. *Evangelicals and Catholics Together: Toward a Common Mission*. Dallas: Word Publishing, 1995.

Congar, Yves, OP. *A Gospel Priesthood*, translated by P. J. Hepburne-Scott. New York: Herder and Herder, 1967.

———. *After Nine Hundred Years: The Background of the Schism between the Eastern and Western Churches*. New York: Fordham University Press, 1959.

———. "L'apostolicité de l'Eglise chez S. Thomas d'Aquin." *Revue des sciences philosophiques et théologiques* 44 (1960): 209–24.

———. "Aspects ecclésiologiques de la querelle entre mendiants et séculiers dans la seconde moitié du XIIIe siècle et le début du XIVe." *Archives d'histoire doctrinale et littéraire du Moyen Age* 28 (1961): 35–151.

———. *Christ, Our Lady and the Church: A Study in Eirenic Theology*, translated by Henry St. John, OP. London: Longmans, Green and Co., 1957.

———. "De la communion des églises à une ecclésiologie de l'Église universelle." In *L'Épiscopat et l'Église universelle*, edited by Y. Congar and B. Dupuy, 227–60. Paris: Cerf, 1962.

———. *Diversity and Communion*, translated by John Bowden. French 1982. Mystic, CT: Twenty-Third Publications, 1985.

———. " 'Ecclesia' et 'populus (fidelis)' dans l'ecclésiologie de S. Thomas." In *St. Thomas Aquinas, 1274–1974, Commemorative Studies*. Vol. 1, edited by Armand Maurer, 159–73. Toronto: Pontifical Institute of Mediaeval Studies, 1974.

———. "Ecclesiological Awareness in the East and in the West from the Sixth to the Eleventh Century." In *The Unity of the Churches of God*, edited by Polycarp Sherwood, OSB. Baltimore, MD: Helicon Press, 1963.

———. "L'ecclésiologie de la Révolution française au Concile du Vatican, sous la signe de l'affirmation de l'autorité." In *L'ecclésiologie au XIXe siècle*, edited by Maurice Nédoncelle et al., 77–114. Paris: Cerf, 1960.

———. *L'Église de saint Augustin à l'époque moderne*. Paris: Cerf, 1970.

———. *I Believe in the Holy Spirit*, translated by David Smith. New York: Crossroad, 1997.

———. *Jesus Christ*, translated by Luke O'Neill. French 1965. New York: Herder and Herder, 1966.

———. *Lay People in the Church*, translated by Donald Attwater. Rev. ed. London: Geoffrey Chapman, 1965.

———. "*Lumen Gentium*, 7: L'Église, Corps mystique du Christ, vu au terme de huit siècles d'histoire de la théologie du Corps mystique." In *Au service de la Parole de Dieu. Mélanges offerts à Mgr. A.-M. Charue*, 179–202. Gembloux: Duculot, 1969.

———. *The Meaning of Tradition*, translated by A. N. Woodrow. New York: Hawthorn Books, 1964.

———. *The Mystery of the Church*, translated by A. V. Littledale. French 1956. Baltimore: Helicon Press, 1960.

———. "Notes sur le destin de l'idée de collégialité épiscopale en occident au moyen âge (VIIe–XVI siècles)." In *La collégialité épiscopale. Histoire et théologie*, 99–129. Paris: Cerf, 1969.

———. "La personne de l'Église." *Revue Thomiste* 71 (1971): 613–40.

———. *Power and Poverty in the Church*, translated by Jennifer Nicholson. Baltimore: Helicon, 1964.

———. "La 'réception' comme réalité ecclésiologique." *Revue des sciences philosophiques et théologiques* 56 (1972): 369–403.

———. *The Revelation of God*, translated by A. Manson and L. C. Sheppard. French 1962. New York: Herder and Herder, 1968.

———. "Saint Thomas Aquinas and the Infallibility of the Papal Magisterium (*Summa Theol.*, II-II, q. 1, a. 10)." *The Thomist* 38 (1974): 81–105.

———. "St. Thomas Aquinas and the Spirit of Ecumenism." *New Blackfriars* 55 (1974): 196–209.

———. "Sur la trilogie: Prophète-roi-prêtre." *Revue des sciences philosophiques et théologiques* 67 (1983): 97–115.

———. "Vision de l'Église chez S. Thomas d'Aquin." *Revue des sciences philosophiques et théologiques* 62 (1978): 523–41.

Congar, Yves, OP, and B. Dupuy. *L'Épiscopat et l'Église universelle*. Paris: Cerf, 1962.

Congregation for the Doctrine of the Faith. *Dominus Iesus*. 2000.

———. *Instruction on the Ecclesial Vocation of the Theologian*. 1990.

———. *Mysterium Ecclesiae*. June 24, 1973.

———. "Notification Regarding on L. Boff, *Church: Charism and Power.*" *Origins* 14 (1985): 683–87.

———. *Sacerdotium Ministeriale.* August 6, 1983.

———. "Some Aspects of the Church Understood as Communion." *Origins* 22 (1992): 108–12.

Cooper, Adam G. "St. Maximus the Confessor on Priesthood, Hierarchy, and Rome." *Pro Ecclesia* 10 (2001): 346–67.

Corecco, Eugenio. "L'origine del potere di giurisdizione episcopale: Aspetti storico-giuridici e metadologico-sistematici della questione." *La scuola cattolica* 96 (1968): 3–42, 107–41.

Costigan, Richard F., sj. *The Consensus of the Church and Papal Infallibility: A Study in the Background of Vatican I.* Washington, DC: The Catholic University of America Press, 2005.

Cozzens, Donald B. *The Changing Face of the Priesthood.* Collegeville, MN: The Liturgical Press, 2000.

Cuéllar, Miguel Ponce. *Llamados a Servir: Teología del Sacerdocio Ministerial.* Barcelona: Herder, 2001.

Cwiekowski, Frederick J. *The Beginnings of the Church.* New York: Paulist Press, 1988.

Dagens, Claude. "Hierarchy and Communion: The Bases of Authority in the Beginning of the Church," translated by Sister Isaac Jogues, su. *Communio* 9 (1982): 67–78.

Daguet, François. "Saint Thomas et les deux pouvoirs. Élements de théologie politique." *Revue Thomiste* 102 (2002): 531–68.

Dalin, David G., and Matthew Levering, eds. *John Paul II and the Jewish People.* Lanham, MD: Rowman and Littlefield, 2007.

Daley, Brian E., sj. "Position and Patronage in the Early Church: The Original Meaning of 'Primacy of Honour.'" *Journal of Theological Studies* 44 (1993): 529–53.

———. "Rebuilding the Structure of Love: The Quest for Visible Unity among the Churches." In *The Ecumenical Future,* edited by Carl E. Braaten and Robert W. Jenson, 73–105. Grand Rapids, MI: Eerdmans, 2004.

Daly, Robert J., sj. "Eucharistic Origins: From the New Testament to the Liturgies of the Golden Age." *Theological Studies* 66 (2005): 3–22.

———. "Sacrifice Unveiled or Sacrifice Revisited: Trinitarian and Liturgical Perspectives." *Theological Studies* 64 (2003): 24–42.

Dauphinais, Michael, and Matthew Levering. *Holy People, Holy Land: A Theological Introduction to the Bible.* Grand Rapids, MI: Brazos Press, 2005.

———, eds. *John Paul II and St. Thomas Aquinas.* Naples, FL: Sapientia Press, 2006.

———, eds. *Wisdom and Holiness, Science and Scholarship: Essays in Honor of Matthew L. Lamb.* Naples, FL: Sapientia Press, 2007.

———, eds. *Reading John with St. Thomas Aquinas.* Washington, DC: The Catholic University of America Press, 2005.

Dauphinais, Michael, Barry David, and Matthew Levering, eds. *Aquinas the Augustinian.* Washington, DC: The Catholic University of America Press, 2007.

Davies, W. D., and Dale C. Allison Jr. *The Gospel According to Saint Matthew.* Vol. III, *Commentary on Matthew XIX–XXVIII.* Edinburgh: T&T Clark, 1997.

de Certeau, Michel. *The Mystic Fable*, translated by Michael B. Smith. Chicago: The University of Chicago Press, 1992.

de La Soujeole, Benoît-Dominique, OP. "L'Église comme société et l'Église comme communion au deuxième concile du Vatican." *Revue Thomiste* 91 (1991): 219–58.

———. "Et pourtant. . . , elle subsiste!" *Revue Thomiste* 99 (2000): 531–49.

———. "Être ordonné à l'unique Église du Christ: L'ecclésialité des communautés non chrétiennes à partir des données oecuméniques." *Revue Thomiste* 102 (2002): 5–41.

———. *Introduction au mystère de l'Église*. Paris: Parole et Silence, 2006.

———. *Le Sacrement de la communion. Essai d'ecclésiologie fondamentale*. Paris: Cerf, 1998.

———. "Société et communion chez S. Thomas. Étude d'ecclésiologie." *Revue Thomiste* 90 (1990): 587–622.

———."Les *tria munera Christi*: Contribution de saint Thomas à la recherche contemporaine." *Revue Thomiste* 99 (1999): 59–74.

de Lubac, Henri, SJ. *Catholicism*, translated by Lancelot C. Sheppard. French 1938. London: Burns and Oates, 1950.

———. *Corpus Mysticum: The Eucharist and the Church in the Middle Ages*, translated by Gemma Simmonds, Christopher Stephens, and Richard Price. French 1949. Notre Dame, IN: University of Notre Dame Press, 2007.

———. *The Christian Faith: An Essay on the Structure of the Apostles' Creed*. San Francisco: Ignatius Press, 1986.

———. *The Motherhood of the Church*, translated by Sister Sergia Englund, OCD. French 1971. San Francisco: Ignatius Press, 1982.

———. *The Splendor of the Church*, translated by Michael Mason. French 1953. San Francisco: Ignatius Press, 1986.

de Montcheuil, Yves. *Mélanges théologiques*. Paris: Aubier-Montaigne, 1946.

Diez, Karlheinz. *"Ecclesia—Non Est Civitas Platonica": Antworten katholischer Kontroverstheologen des 16. Jahrhunderts auf Martin Luthers Anfrage an die "Sichtbarkeit" der Kirche*. Frankfurt: Josef Knecht, 1997.

Di Noia, J. Augustine, OP. "The Church in the Gospel: Catholics and Evangelicals in Conversation." *Pro Ecclesia* 13 (2004): 58–69.

Di Noia, J. A., OP, and Bernard Mulcahy, OP. "The Authority of Scripture in Sacramental Theology: Some Methodological Observations." *Pro Ecclesia* 10 (2001): 329–45.

Dietrich, Donald J., and Michael J. Himes, eds. *The Legacy of the Tübingen School: The Relevance of Nineteenth-Century Theology for the Twenty-First Century*. New York: Crossroad, 1997.

Dodd, C. H. *The Interpretation of the Fourth Gospel*. Cambridge: Cambridge University Press, 1953.

Donneaud, Henry, OP. "Chalcédoine contre l'unicité absolue du Médiateur Jésus-Christ? Autour d'un article recent." *Revue Thomiste* 102 (2002): 43–62.

———. "Note sur l'Église comme communion dans le Catéchisme de l'Église catholique." *Revue Thomiste* 95 (1995): 665–71.

———. "Objet formel et objet matériel de la foi: Genèse d'un instrument philosophique chez s. Thomas et quelques autres." *Revue Thomiste* 100 (2000): 5–44.

Downey, John K., Jürgen Manemann, and Steven T. Ostovich, eds. *Missing God? Cultural Amnesia and Political Theology.* Berlin: LIT Verlag, 2006.

Doyle, Dennis M. *Communion Ecclesiology: Vision and Versions.* Maryknoll, NY: Orbis Books, 2000.

Driscoll, Jeremy, OSB. "Preaching in the Context of the Eucharist: A Patristic Perspective." *Pro Ecclesia* 11 (2002): 24–40.

Dulles, Avery, SJ. *A Church to Believe In: Discipleship and the Dynamics of Freedom.* 1982. New York: Crossroad, 1987.

———. "A Half Century of Ecclesiology." *Theological Studies* 50 (1989): 419–42.

———. "A New Orthodox View of the Papacy." *Pro Ecclesia* 12 (2003): 345–58.

———. *The Catholicity of the Church.* Oxford: Oxford University Press, 1985.

———. "The Church as Communion." In *New Perspectives on Historical Theology: Essays in Memory of John Meyendorff,* edited by Bradley Nassif, 125–39. Grand Rapids, MI: Eerdmans, 1996.

———. "The Church, the Churches, and the Catholic Church." *Theological Studies* 33 (1972): 199–234.

———. "The Ecclesial Dimension of Faith." *Communio* 22 (1995): 418–32.

———. "The Eucharist as Sacrifice." In *Rediscovering the Eucharist: Ecumenical Conversations,* edited by Roch Kereszty, O CIST, 175–87. New York: Paulist Press, 2003.

———. *John Henry Newman.* New York: Continuum, 2002.

———. *Magisterium: Teacher and Guardian of the Faith.* Naples, FL: Sapientia Press, 2007.

———. *Models of the Church.* Garden City, NY: Doubleday, 1974.

———. *The Priestly Office: A Theological Reflection.* Mahwah, NJ: Paulist Press, 1997.

———. *The Resilient Church.* Garden City, NY: Doubleday, 1977.

———. Review of *Imagining the Catholic Church: Structured Communion in the Spirit* by Ghislain Lafont, OSB. *Theological Studies* 57 (1996): 768–69.

———. "The Trinity and Christian Unity." In *God the Holy Trinity: Reflections on Christian Faith and Practice,* edited by Timothy George, 69–82. Grand Rapids, MI: Baker Academic, 2006.

———. "The Unity for Which We Hope." In *Evangelicals and Catholics Together: Toward a Common Mission,* edited by Charles Colson and Richard John Neuhaus, 125–34. Dallas: Word Publishing, 1995.

Dulles, Avery, SJ, and George A. Lindbeck. "Bishops and the Ministry of the Gospel." In *Confessing One Faith: A Joint Commentary on the Augsburg Confession by Lutheran and Catholic Theologians,* edited by George Wolfgang Forell and James F. McCue, 147–72. Minneapolis, MN: Augsburg, 1982.

Dulles, Avery, SJ, Eugene L. Brand, Ephraim Radner, Geoffrey Wainwright, Gabriel Fackre, and Timothy George. "A Symposium on the Declaration *Dominus Iesus* (August 6, 2000)." *Pro Ecclesia* 10 (2001): 5–16.

Dupuis, Jacques, SJ. "Le Verbe de Dieu, Jésus-Christ et les religions du monde." *Nouvelle revue théologique* 123 (2001): 529–46.

Durã, V. Nicolae. "The 'Petrine Primacy': The Role of the Bishop of Rome According to the Canonical Legislation of the Ecumenical Councils of the First Millennium, an Ecclesiological-Canonical Evaluation." In *The Petrine Ministry: Catholics and Orthodox in Dialogue,* edited by Walter Cardinal

Kasper, translated by the staff of the Pontifical Council for Promoting
Christian Unity, 159–87. New York: Paulist Press, 2006.

Dyrness, William A. "Spaces for an Evangelical Ecclesiology." In *The Community of
the Word: Toward an Evangelical Ecclesiology*, edited by Mark Husbands and
Daniel J. Treier, 251–72. Downers Grove, IL: InterVarsity Press, 2005.

Ellis, John Tracy. "The Eucharist in the Life of Cardinal Newman." *Communio* 4
(1977): 321–40.

Emery, Gilles, OP. "Le sacerdoce spiritual des fidèles chez saint Thomas d'Aquin."
Revue Thomiste 99 (1999): 211–43.

———. "Trinitarian Theology as Spiritual Exercise in Augustine and Aquinas,"
translated by John Baptist Ku, OP. In *Aquinas the Augustinian*, edited by
Michael Dauphinais, Barry David, and Matthew Levering, 1–40.
Washington, DC: The Catholic University of America Press, 2007.

———. *Trinity, Church, and the Human Person: Thomistic Essays.* Naples, FL:
Sapientia Press, 2007.

———. *Trinity in Aquinas*, translated by Matthew Levering et al. Ypsilanti, MI:
Sapientia Press, 2003.

Emmet, Dorothy, and Alasdair MacIntyre, eds. *Sociological Theory and Philosophical
Analysis.* New York: Macmillan, 1970.

Empie, Paul C., and T. Austin Murphy, eds. *Papal Primacy and the Universal Church.*
Minneapolis, MN: Augsburg Press, 1974.

Engberg-Pedersen, Troels. "1 Corinthians 11:16 and the Character of Pauline
Exhortation." *Journal of Biblical Literature* 110 (1991): 679–689.

Erickson, John. "Baptism and the Church's Faith." In *Marks of the Body of Christ*,
edited by Carl E. Braaten and Robert W. Jenson, 44–58. Grand Rapids, MI:
Eerdmans, 1999.

———. "The Formation of Orthodox Ecclesial Identity." *St. Vladimir's Theological
Quarterly* 42 (1998): 301–14.

Evans, Craig A. "Jesus and the Continuing Exile of Israel." In *Jesus and the
Restoration of Israel: A Critical Assessment of N. T. Wright's* Jesus and the Victory
of God, edited by Carey C. Newman, 77–100. Downers Grove, IL:
InterVarsity Press, 1999.

Evans, C. Stephen. "Methodological Naturalism in Historical Biblical Scholarship."
In *Jesus and the Restoration of Israel: A Critical Assessment of N. T. Wright's* Jesus
and the Victory of God, edited by Carey C. Newman, 180–205. Downers
Grove, IL: InterVarsity Press, 1999.

Evans, G. R. *The Church and the Churches: Toward an Ecumenical Ecclesiology.*
Cambridge: Cambridge University Press, 1994.

Evdokimov, Paul. *The Art of the Icon: A Theology of Beauty*, translated by Steven
Bigham. French 1972. Redondo Beach, CA: Oakwood Publications, 1990.

———. *In the World, of the Church: A Paul Evdokimov Reader*, edited by and translated
by Michael Plekon and Alexis Vinogradov. Crestwood, NY: St. Vladimir's
Seminary Press, 2001.

Fagerberg, David. *Theologia Prima: What Is Liturgical Theology?* Chicago:
Hillenbrand Books, 2004.

Farrow, Douglas. *Ascension and Ecclesia: On the Significance of the Doctrine of the
Ascension for Ecclesiology and Christian Cosmology.* Grand Rapids, MI:
Eerdmans, 1999.

Faulkner, Gregory C. *Return to the Eucharist: The Eucharistic Ecclesiology of Alexander Schmemann's Liturgical Theology and Its Methodological Implications for a Reformed Liturgical Theology.* Ph.D. Dissertation. Princeton: Princeton Theological Seminary, 2001.

Florovsky, Georges. *Collected Works of Georges Florovsky*, vol. 6, *Ways of Russian Theology, Part Two*, translated by Robert L. Nicholsin, edited by Richard S. Haugh. Vaduz: Büchervertriebsanstalt, 1987.

———. "On the History of Ecclesiology." In *Collected Works of Georges Florovsky*, vol. 14, *Ecumenism II: A Historical Approach*, edited by Richard S. Haugh, 9–17. Vaduz: Büchervertriebsanstalt, 1989.

———. "Rome, the Reformation, and Orthodoxy," translated by Linda Morris. In *Collected Works of Georges Florovsky*, vol. 14, *Ecumenism II: A Historical Approach*, edited by Richard S. Haugh, 52–58. Vaduz: Büchervertriebsanstalt, 1989.

Flynn, Gabriel, ed. *Yves Congar: Theologian of the Church.* Louvain: Peeters, 2005.

Forell, George Wolfgang, and James F. McCue, eds. *Confessing One Faith: A Joint Commentary on the Augsburg Confession by Lutheran and Catholic Theologians.* Minneapolis, MN: Augsburg, 1982.

Forte, Bruno. "The Church Confronts the Faults of the Past." *Communio* 27 (2000): 676–87.

Fransen, Piet. *Hermeneutics of the Councils and Other Studies.* Leuven: Leuven University Press, 1985.

Fredericks, James. "The Catholic Church and the Other Religious Paths: Rejecting Nothing that Is True and Holy." *Theological Studies* 64 (2003): 225–54.

Fries, Heinrich, and Karl Rahner, *Einigung der Kirchen—reale Möglichkeit.* Freiburg: 1983.

Gaillardetz, Richard R. *By What Authority? A Primer on Scripture, the Magisterium, and the Sense of the Faithful.* Collegeville, MN: The Liturgical Press, 2003.

———. "The Ecclesiological Foundations of Ministry within an Ordered Communion." In *Ordering the Baptismal Priesthood: Theologies of Lay and Ordained Ministry*, edited by Susan K. Wood, 26–51. Collegeville, MN: The Liturgical Press, 2003.

———. "The Ordinary Universal Magisterium: Unresolved Questions." *Theological Studies* 63 (2002): 447–71.

———. "The Reception of Doctrine: New Perspectives." In *Authority in the Roman Catholic Church: Theory and Practice*, edited by Bernard Hoose, 95–115. Aldershot: Ashgate, 2002.

———. *Teaching with Authority: A Theology of the Magisterium of the Church.* Collegeville, MN: The Liturgical Press, 1997.

———. *Witnesses to the Faith: Community, Infallibility, and the Ordinary Magisterium of Bishops.* New York: Paulist, 1992.

Galot, Jean, SJ. *La nature du caractère sacramentel. Étude de théologie médiévale.* Paris: Desclée, 1956.

———. *Theology of the Priesthood.* San Francisco: Ignatius Press, 1984.

Galvin, John P. "Papal Primacy in Contemporary Roman Catholic Theology." *Theological Studies* 47 (1986): 653–67.

Gärtner, B. *John 6 and the Jewish Passover.* Lund: Gleerup, 1959.

Garuti, Adriano, OFM. *Primacy of the Bishop of Rome and the Ecumenical Dialogue*, translated by Michael Miller. San Francisco: Ignatius Press, 2004.

George, Timothy. "The Sacramentality of the Church: An Evangelical Baptist Perspective." *Pro Ecclesia* 12 (2003): 309–23.

———, ed. *God the Holy Trinity: Reflections on Christian Faith and Practice*. Grand Rapids, MI: Baker Academic, 2006.

German National Bishops' Conference Bilateral Working Group and the Church Leadership of the United Evangelical Lutheran Church of Germany. *Communio Sanctorum: The Church as the Communion of Saints*, translated by Mark W. Jeske, Michael Root, and Daniel R. Smith. Collegeville, MN: The Liturgical Press, 2004.

Gerrish, Brian A. "Priesthood and Ministry in the Theology of Luther." *Church History* 34 (1965): 404–22.

Gherardini, Brunero. "Sacramentalità dell'episcopato in San Tommaso." In *Indubitanter ad Veritatem: Studies Offered to Leo J. Elders SVD*, edited by Jörgen Vijgen, 189–201. Budel: Damon, 2003.

Girard, René. *The Scapegoat*. Baltimore: Johns Hopkins University Press, 1986.

———. *Violence and the Sacred*. Baltimore: Johns Hopkins University Press, 1977.

Glazov, Gregory. "Vladimir Solovyov and the Idea of the Papacy." *Communio* 24 (1997): 128–42.

Gnilka, Joachim. "The Ministry of Peter—New Testament Foundations." In *The Petrine Ministry: Catholics and Orthodox in Dialogue*, edited by Walter Cardinal Kasper, translated by the staff of the Pontifical Council for Promoting Christian Unity, 24–36. New York: Paulist Press, 2006.

Golitzin, Alexander. "Dionysius Areopagita: A Christian Mysticism?" *Pro Ecclesia* 12 (2003): 161–212.

———. *Et introibo ad altare dei: The Mystagogy of Dionysius Areopagita*. Thessalonica: Patriarchikon Idruma Paterikon Meleton, 1994.

———. "Hierarchy versus Anarchy? Dionysius Areopagita, Symeon the New Theologian, Nicetas Stethatos, and Their Common Roots in the Ascetical Tradition." *St. Vladimir's Theological Quarterly* 39 (1994): 131–79.

Goris, Harm. "Theology and Theory of the Word in Aquinas: Understanding Augustine by Innovating Aristotle." In *Aquinas the Augustinian*, edited by Michael Dauphinais, Barry David, and Matthew Levering, 62–78. Washington, DC: The Catholic University of America Press, 2007.

Gorman, Michael J. *Cruciformity: Paul's Narrative Spirituality of the Cross*. Grand Rapids, MI: Eerdmans, 2001.

Gouyard, Christian. *L'Église instrument du Salut*. Paris: Pierre Téqui, 2005.

Granfield, Patrick, OSB. *Ecclesial Cybernetics: A Study of Democracy in the Church*. New York: Macmillan, 1973.

———. *The Limits of the Papacy*. New York: Crossroad, 1987.

Gros, Jeffrey, FSC. "Toward Full Communion: Faith and Order and Catholic Ecumenism." *Theological Studies* 65 (2004): 23–43.

Guggenheim, Antoine. *Jésus Christ, Grand Prêtre de l'ancienne et de la nouvelle Alliance. Étude du* Commentaire *de saint Thomas d'Aquin sur l'*Épître aux Hébreux. Paris: Parole et Silence, 2004.

Gunton, Colin. "One Mediator . . . The Man Jesus Christ." *Pro Ecclesia* 11 (2002): 146–58.

———. *The Promise of Trinitarian Theology*. Edinburgh: T&T Clark, 1991.

Guroian, Vigen. "The Crisis of Orthodox Ecclesiology." In *The Ecumenical Future*, edited by Carl E. Braaten and Robert W. Jenson, 162–75. Grand Rapids, MI: Eerdmans, 2004.

Gy, Pierre-Marie, OP. "Évolution de saint Thomas sur la théologie de l'ordre." *Revue Thomiste* 99 (1999) : 181–89.

Habermas, Jürgen. "Knowledge and Interest." In *Sociological Theory and Philosophical Analysis*, edited by Dorothy Emmet and Alasdair MacIntyre, 36–54. New York: Macmillan, 1970.

Haight, Roger, SJ. *Christian Community in History*, vol. 1: *Historical Ecclesiology*. New York: Continuum, 2004.

Halligan, C. "The Teaching of St. Thomas in Regard to Apostles." *American Ecclesiastical Review* 144 (1961): 32–47.

Hamer, Jerome, OP. *The Church Is a Communion*. French 1962. London: Geoffrey Chapman, 1964.

Hamann, Johann Georg. *Exposure and Transfiguration: A Flying Letter to Nobody the Notorious*. 1786.

———. *Golgotha and Scheblimini*. Partial English translation in Ronald Gregor Smith, *J. G. Hamann, 1730–1788: A Study in Christian Existence with Selections from His Writings*. New York: Harper & Brothers, 1960.

———. *Hamann's* Socratic Memorabilia*: A Translation and Commentary*, edited and translated by James C. O'Flaherty. Baltimore, MD: Johns Hopkins University Press, 1967.

———. *Sämtliche Werke*, edited by Josef Nadler. Vol. 3. Vienna: Herder, 1949–1957.

Harakas, Stanley Samuel. "Doing Theology Today: An Orthodox and Evangelical Dialogue on Theological Method." *Pro Ecclesia* 11 (2002): 435–62.

Harrington, Daniel J., SJ. *The Church According to the New Testament: What the Wisdom and Witness of Early Christianity Teach Us Today*. Franklin, WI: Sheed & Ward, 2001.

Harvey, Barry. "The Eucharistic Idiom of the Gospel." *Pro Ecclesia* 9 (2000): 297–318.

Hatch, Nathan O. *The Democratization of American Christianity*. New Haven, CT: Yale University Press, 1989.

Hauerwas, Stanley. Foreword to *The Fate of Communion: The Agony of Anglicanism and the Future of the Global Church* by Ephraim Radner and Philip Turner. Grand Rapids, MI: Eerdmans, 2006.

———. *The Peaceable Kingdom: A Primer in Christian Ethics*. Notre Dame, IN: University of Notre Dame Press, 1983.

Hawthorne, Gerald F. "The Imitation of Christ: Discipleship in Philippians." In *Patterns of Discipleship in the New Testament*, edited by Richard N. Longenecker, 163–79. Grand Rapids, MI: Eerdmans, 1996.

Hays, Richard B. *First Corinthians*. Louisville, KY: John Knox Press, 1997.

Healy, Nicholas M. *Church, World and the Christian Life: Practical-Prophetic Ecclesiology*. Cambridge: Cambridge University Press, 2000.

Hegel, G. W. F. "Hamann's Schriften." In *Sämtliche Werke*. Vol. XI, edited by Johannes Hoffmeister, 221–94. Hamburg: Felix Meiner, 1956.

Heim, S. Mark. *Saved from Sacrifice: A Theology of the Cross*. Grand Rapids, MI: Eerdmans, 2006.

Henn, William. *The Honor of My Brothers: A Short History of the Relation between the Pope and Bishops.* New York: Crossroad, 2000.

Henrici, Peter. "The Church and Pluralism," translated by Albert K. Wimmer. *Communio* 10 (1983): 128–32.

Hill, Harvey. "Loisy's *L'Évangile et l'Église* in Light of the 'Essais.'" *Theological Studies* 67 (2006): 73–98.

Hill, William J. "The Eucharist as Eschatological Presence." *Communio* 4 (1977): 306–20.

Himes, Michael D., and Donald Dietrich, eds. *The Legacy of the Tübingen School.* New York: Crossroad, 1997.

Himes, Michael J. *Ongoing Incarnation: Johann Adam Möhler and the Beginnings of Modern Ecclesiology.* New York: Crossroad, 1997.

Hobbes, Thomas. *Leviathan*, edited by Edwin Curley. Indianapolis, IN: Hackett, 1994.

Hogan, Linda. *Confronting the Truth: Conscience in the Catholic Tradition.* New York: Paulist, 2000.

Hoge, Dean R., and Jacqueline E. Wenger. *Evolving Visions of the Priesthood: Changes from Vatican II to the Turn of the New Century.* Collegeville, MN: The Liturgical Press, 2003.

Hoose, Bernard. "Authority in the Church." *Theological Studies* 63 (2002): 107–22.

———. *Received Wisdom? Reviewing the Role of Tradition in Christian Ethics.* New York: Geoffrey Chapman, 1994.

———, ed. *Authority in the Roman Catholic Church: Theory and Practice.* Aldershot: Ashgate, 2002.

Hörst, Ulrich, OP. "Das Wesen der *potestas clavium* nach Thomas von Aquin." *Münchener Theologische Zeitschrift* 11 (1960): 191–201.

———. *The Dominicans and the Pope: Papal Teaching Authority in the Medieval and Early Modern Thomist Tradition*, translated by James D. Mixson. Notre Dame, IN: University of Notre Dame Press, 2006.

Howsare, Rodney A. *Balthasar and Protestantism.* New York: T&T Clark, 2005.

Hunt, Anne. "The Trinity and the Church: Explorations in Ecclesiology from a Trinitarian Perspective." *Irish Theological Quarterly* 70 (2005): 215–35.

Husbands, Mark, and Daniel J. Treier, eds. *The Community of the Word: Toward an Evangelical Ecclesiology.* Downers Grove, IL: InterVarsity Press, 2005.

Hütter, Reinhard. "The Church: The Knowledge of the Triune God: Practices, Doctrine, Theology." In *Knowing the Triune God: The Work of the Spirit in the Practices of the Church*, edited by James J. Buckley and David S. Yeago, 23–47. Grand Rapids, MI: Eerdmans, 2001.

———. "*Desiderium Naturale Visionis Dei—Est autem duplex hominis beatitude sive felicitas*: Some Observations about Lawrence Feingold's and John Milbank's Recent Interventions in the Debate over the Natural Desire to See God." *Nova et Vetera* 5 (2007): 81–131.

———. "Ecumenism and Christian Unity—Abstract Reunification or Living Concord? A Lutheran Approach to the Encyclical '*Ut Unum Sint*—That They May Be One,'" translated by Beth A. Schlegel. *Pro Ecclesia* 7 (1998): 186–98.

———. *Suffering Divine Things: Theology as Church Practice*, translated by Doug Stott. German 1997. Grand Rapids, MI: Eerdmans, 2000.

Janowski, Bernd, and Peter Stuhlmacher, eds. *The Suffering Servant: Isaiah 53 in Jewish and Christian Sources*, translated by Donald P. Bailey. Grand Rapids, MI: Eerdmans, 2004.

Jenson, Robert W. *Systematic Theology.* Vol. 1, *The Triune God.* Oxford: Oxford University Press, 1997.

Jervis, L. Ann. "Becoming like God through Christ: Discipleship in Romans." In *Patterns of Discipleship in the New Testament*, edited by Richard N. Longenecker, 143–62. Grand Rapids, MI: Eerdmans, 1996.

John Paul II, Pope. *Apostolos Suos.* 1998.

———. *Ecclesia de Eucharistia.* 2003

———. *Pastores Dabo Vobis.* 1992

———. *Redemptoris Missio.* 1990.

———. *Ut Unum Sint.* 1995.

Johnson, Luke Timothy. "Koinonia: Diversity and Unity in Early Christianity." *Theological Digest* 46 (1999): 303–13.

———.*Scripture and Discernment: Decision-Making in the Church.* Nashville, TN: Abingdon Press, 1996.

Johnson, S. "The Dead Sea Manual of Discipline and the Jerusalem Church of Acts." In *The Scrolls and the New Testament*, ed. K. Stendahl, 129–42. New York: Harper & Brothers, 1957.

Jomier, Jacques, OP. "The Kingdom of God in Islam and Its Comparison with Christianity," translated by Stephen Wentworth Arndt. *Communio* 13 (1986): 267–71.

Journet, Charles. *The Church of the Word Incarnate: An Essay in Speculative Theology.* Vol. 1, *The Apostolic Hierarchy*, translated by A. H. C. Downes. London: Sheed & Ward, 1955.

———. *L'Église du Verbe Incarné.* Vol. 2. Paris: Desclée de Brouwer, 1951.

———. *L'Église du Verbe Incarné.* 4 vols. Saint-Maurice: Saint-Augustin, 1999–2000.

———. "La sainteté de l'Église. Le livre de Jacques Maritain." *Nova et Vetera* (French) 46 (1971): 1–33.

Kärkkäinen, Veli-Matti. "The Apostolicity of Free Churches." *Pro Ecclesia* 10 (2001): 475–86.

Kasper, Walter. "A New Dogmatic Outlook on the Priestly Ministry." In *Concilium* 43, *The Identity of the Priest*, edited by Karl Rahner, SJ, 20–33. New York: Paulist Press, 1969.

———. "The Church as Sacrament of Unity," translated by Charles R. Hohenstein. *Communio* 14 (1987): 4–11.

———. *I Believe in the Holy Spirit.* Vol. 2, *"He Is Lord and Giver of Life,"* translated by David Smith. New York: Crossroad, 1997.

———. *Leadership in the Church: How Traditional Roles Can Serve the Christian Community Today*, translated by Brian McNeil. New York: Crossroad, 2003.

———. "Present Situation and Future of the Ecumenical Movement." *Information Service* 109 (2002): 11–20.

———, ed. *The Petrine Ministry: Catholics and Orthodox in Dialogue*, translated by the staff of the Pontifical Council for Promoting Christian Unity. New York: Paulist Press, 2006.

Kaufman, Peter Iver. *Church, Book, and Bishop: Conflict and Authority in the Early Church.* Boulder, CO: Westview Press, 1996.

Keating, Daniel. "Aquinas on 1 and 2 Corinthians: The Sacraments and Their Ministers." In *Aquinas on Scripture: An Introduction to His Biblical Commentaries*, edited by Thomas G. Weinandy, Daniel A. Keating, and John P. Yocum. New York: T&T Clark, 2005.

———. "Justification, Sanctification and Divinization in Thomas Aquinas." In *Aquinas on Doctrine: A Critical Introduction*, edited by Thomas G. Weinandy, OFM CAP, Daniel A. Keating, and John P. Yocum, 139–58. New York: T&T Clark, 2004.

Kee, H. C. "The Transformation of the Synagogue after 70 CE." *New Testament Studies* 36 (1990): 1–24.

Keefe, Donald J. "Authority in the Church: An Essay in the Theology of History." *Communio* 7 (1980): 343–63.

Keener, Craig S. *The Gospel of John*, 2 vols. Peabody, MA: Hendrickson, 2003.

Kelly, J. N. D. *Early Christian Creeds*. London: Longmans, Green & Co., 1950.

Kereszty, Roch, O CIST. "A Catholic Response to W. Pannenberg Regarding the Petrine Ministry of the Bishop of Rome." *Communio* 25 (1998): 619–29.

———. "A Theological Meditation on the Liturgy of the Eucharist." *Communio* 23 (1996): 524–61.

———. " 'Bride' and 'Mother' in the *Super Cantica* of St. Bernard: An Ecclesiology for Our Time?" *Communio* 20 (1993): 415–36.

———. "The Death of Jesus as Sacrifice." *Josephinum Journal of Theology* 3 (1996): 4–17.

———. "Historical Research, Theological Inquiry, and the Reality of Jesus: Reflections on the Method of J. P. Meier." *Communio* 19 (1992): 576–600.

———. "Peter and Paul and the Founding of the Church of Rome: Forgotten Perspectives." *Communio* 15 (1998): 215–33.

———, ed. *Rediscovering the Eucharist: Ecumenical Conversations*. New York: Paulist Press, 2003.

Kerr, Fergus, OP. "Yves Congar and Thomism." In *Yves Congar: Theologian of the Church*, edited by Gabriel Flynn, 67–97. Louvain: Peeters, 2005.

Kesich, Veselin. "Peter's Primacy in the New Testament and the Early Tradition." In *The Primacy of Peter: Essays in Ecclesiology and the Early Church*, edited by John Meyendorff, 35–66. 1963. Crestwood, NY: St. Vladimir's Seminary Press, 1992.

Khomiakov, A. S. *L'Église latine et le Protestantisme au point de vue de l'Église d'orient*. 1872.

Kimel, Alvin F. "Who Are the Bishops? Episkopé and the Church." *Anglican Theological Review* 77 (1995): 58–75.

Komonchak, Joseph. *Foundations in Ecclesiology*, edited by Fred Lawrence. Vol. 11, *Lonergan Workshop Journal, Supplementary Issue*. Boston: Boston College, 1995.

———. "The Local Realization of the Church." In *The Reception of Vatican II*, edited by Giuseppe Alberigo, Jean-Pierre Jossua, and Joseph A. Komonchak, translated by Matthew J. O'Connell, 77–90. Washington, DC: The Catholic University of America Press, 1987.

———. "The Theology of the Local Church: The State of the Question." In *The Multicultural Church*, edited by William Cenkner, 35–53. New York: Paulist, 1996.

Kovacs, Judith L., trans. and ed. *1 Corinthians Interpreted by Early Christian Commentators*. Grand Rapids, MI: Eerdmans, 2005.

Küng, Hans. *The Church*, translated by Ray and Rosaleen Ockenden. German 1967. London: Burns & Oates, 1968.

———. *Why Priests?* Garden City, NY: Doubleday, 1972.

Lafont, Ghislain, OSB. *Imagining the Catholic Church: Structured Communion in the Spirit*, translated by John J. Burkhard, OFM CONV. French 1995. Collegeville, MN: The Liturgical Press, 2000.

Lakeland, Paul. *The Liberation of the Laity: In Search of an Accountable Church*. New York: Continuum, 2003.

Lamb, Matthew L. "The Eschatology of St. Thomas Aquinas." In *Aquinas on Doctrine: A Critical Introduction*, edited by Thomas G. Weinandy, OFM CAP, Daniel A. Keating, and John P. Yocum, 225–40. New York: T&T Clark, 2004.

———. *Eternity, Time, and the Life of Wisdom*. Naples, FL: Sapientia Press, 2007.

———. "Modern Liberalism, Authority and Authoritarianism: Political Theology against Deceptive Modern Categories." In *Missing God? Cultural Amnesia and Political Theology*, edited by John K. Downey, Jürgen Manemann, and Steven T. Ostovich, 104–24. Berlin: LIT Verlag, 2006.

Laniak, Timothy. *Shepherds after My Own Heart: Pastoral Traditions and Leadership in the Bible*. Downers Grove, IL: InterVarsity Press, 2006.

Larchet, Jean-Claude. "The Question of the Roman Primacy in the Thought of Saint Maximus the Confessor." In *The Petrine Ministry: Catholics and Orthodox in Dialogue*, edited by Walter Cardinal Kasper, translated by the staff of the Pontifical Council for Promoting Christian Unity, 188–209. New York: Paulist Press, 2006.

Lash, Nicholas. "Authors, Authority and Authorization." In *Authority in the Roman Catholic Church: Theory and Practice*, edited by Bernard Hoose, 59–71. Aldershot: Ashgate, 2002.

Lawrence, Hugh. "Ordination and Governance." In *Authority in the Roman Catholic Church: Theory and Practice*, edited by Bernard Hoose, 73–82. Aldershot: Ashgate, 2002.

Le Guillou, M.-J., OP. *Le Christ et l'Église. Théologie du mystère*. 1963. Paris: Parole et Silence, 2005.

Lécuyer, Joseph. "Aquinas' Conception of the Papal Primacy in Ecclesiastical Government." *Archives d'histoire doctrinale et littéraire du moyen âge* 40 (1973): 97–134.

———. "Les étapes de l'enseignement thomiste sur l'épiscopat." *Revue Thomiste* 57 (1957): 29–52.

Levenson, Jon D. *Sinai and Zion: An Entry into the Jewish Bible*. San Francisco: Harper & Row, 1985.

Levering, Matthew. "A Note on Joseph Ratzinger and Contemporary Theology of the Priesthood." *Nova et Vetera* 5 (2007): 271–83.

———. "Augustine and Aquinas on the Good Shepherd: The Value of an Exegetical Tradition." In *Aquinas the Augustinian*, edited by Michael Dauphinais, Barry David, and Matthew Levering, 205–42. Washington, DC: The Catholic University of America Press, 2007.

———. *Christ's Fulfillment of Torah and Temple: Salvation According to Thomas Aquinas.* Notre Dame, IN: University of Notre Dame Press, 2002.

———. "Ecclesial Exegesis and Ecclesial Authority: Childs, Fowl, and Aquinas." *The Thomist* 69 (2005): 407–67.

———. "Friendship and Trinitarian Theology: Response to Karen Kilby." *International Journal of Systematic Theology* 9 (2007): 39–54.

———. "Hierarchy and Holiness." In *Wisdom and Holiness, Science and Scholarship: Essays in Honor of Matthew L. Lamb,* edited by Michael Dauphinais and Matthew Levering, 143–72. Naples, FL: Sapientia Press, 2007.

———. "John Paul II and Aquinas on the Eucharist." In *John Paul II and St. Thomas Aquinas,* edited by Michael Dauphinais and Matthew Levering, 209–31. Naples, FL: Sapientia Press, 2006.

———. "Ockham and the Papacy." In a Festschrift for Stephen F. Brown, forthcoming.

———. *Participatory Biblical Exegesis: A Theology of Biblical Interpretation.* Notre Dame, IN: University of Notre Dame Press, 2008.

———. *Sacrifice and Community: Jewish Offering and Christian Eucharist.* Oxford: Blackwell, 2005.

———. *Scripture and Metaphysics: Aquinas and the Renewal of Trinitarian Theology.* Oxford: Blackwell, 2004.

———. "St. Thomas and William Abraham." *New Blackfriars* 88 (2007): 46–55.

Lindbeck, George. "The Church." In *Keeping the Faith: Essays to Mark the Centenary of Lux Mundi,* edited by Geoffrey Wainwright, 179–208. Allison Park, PA: Pickwick Publications, 1998.

Logue, Damien. "Le *premier* et le *principal* du sacrement de l'ordre. Lecture de *Presbyterorum ordinis,* 4 et, 13." *Revue Thomiste* 102 (2002): 431–53.

Lohfink, Gerhard. *Does God Need the Church? Toward a Theology of the People of God,* translated by Linda M. Mahoney. German 1998. Collegeville, MN: The Liturgical Press, 1999.

Loisy, Alfred. *L'Évangile et l'Église.* Paris: Picard, 1902.

Longenecker, Richard N., ed. *Into God's Presence: Prayer in the New Testament.* Grand Rapids, MI: Eerdmans, 2001.

———. *Patterns of Discipleship in the New Testament.* Grand Rapids, MI: Eerdmans, 1996.

Lossky, Nicolas. "Conciliarity-Primacy in a Russian Orthodox Perspective." In *Petrine Ministry and the Unity of the Church,* edited by James F. Puglisi, 127–36. Collegeville, MN: The Liturgical Press, 1999.

Lossky, Vladimir. *In the Image and Likeness of God.* London: Mowbray, 1975.

Louth, Andrew. "Review Essay: The Orthodox Dogmatic Theology of Dumitru Stăniloae." *Modern Theology* 13 (1997): 253–67.

Mack, Michael. *German Idealism and the Jew: The Inner Anti-Semitism of Philosophy and German Jewish Responses.* Chicago: The University of Chicago Press, 2003.

Malina, Bruce J. *The Palestinian Manna Tradition: The Manna Tradition in the Palestinian Targums and Its Relationship to the New Testament.* Leiden: Brill, 1968.

Mănăstireanu, Dănuț. "Dumitru Stăniloae's Theology of Ministry." In *Dumitru Stăniloae: Tradition and Modernity in Theology*, edited by Lucian Turcescu, 126–44. Oxford: Center for Romanian Studies, 2002.

Mannion, M. Francis. "Rejoice, Heavenly Powers! The Renewal of Liturgical Doxology." *Pro Ecclesia* 12 (2003): 37–60.

Mansini, Guy, OSB. "A Contemporary Understanding of St. Thomas on Sacerdotal Character." *The Thomist* 71 (2007): 171–98.

———. "Episcopal *Munera* and the Character of Episcopal Orders." *The Thomist* 66 (2002): 369–94.

———. "On the Relation of Particular to Universal Church." *Irish Theological Quarterly* 69 (2004): 177–87.

———. "Representation and Agency in the Eucharist." *The Thomist* 62 (1998): 499–517.

———. "Sacerdotal Character at the Second Vatican Council." *The Thomist* 67 (2003): 539–77.

———. *The Word Has Dwelt Among Us: Explorations in Theology*. Ave Maria, FL: Sapientia Press, 2008.

Marion, Jean-Luc. *God Without Being: Hors-Texte*, translated by Thomas A. Carlson. Chicago: The University of Chicago Press, 1991.

———. " 'They Recognized Him; and He Became Invisible to Them.' " *Modern Theology* 18 (2002): 145–52.

Maritain, Jacques. *De l'Église du Christ*. Paris: Desclée de Brouwer, 1970.

Marliangeas, Bernard D. *Clés pour une théologie du ministère: In persona Christi, in persona Ecclesiae*. Paris: Beauchesne, 1978.

Marshall, Bruce D. "Aquinas the Augustinian? On the Uses of Augustine in Aquinas's Trinitarian Theology." In *Aquinas the Augustinian*, edited by Michael Dauphinais, Barry David, and Matthew Levering. Washington, DC: The Catholic University of America Press, 2007.

———. "*Ex Occidente Lux?* Aquinas and Eastern Orthodox Theology." *Modern Theology* 20 (2004): 23–50.

———. "Review Essay: The Divided Church and Its Theology," a review of *The End of the Church: A Pneumatology of Christian Division in the West* by Ephraim Radner. *Modern Theology* 16 (2000): 377–96.

———. "What Does the Spirit Have to Do?" In *Reading John with St. Thomas Aquinas*, edited by Michael Dauphinais and Matthew Levering, 62–77. Washington, DC: The Catholic University of America Press, 2005.

Martin, Francis. "The Integrity of Christian Moral Activity: The First Letter of John and *Veritatis Splendor*." *Communio* 21 (1994): 265–85.

Maurer, Armand, ed. *St. Thomas Aquinas, 1274–1974, Commemorative Studies*. Vol. 1. Toronto: Pontifical Institute of Mediaeval Studies, 1974.

McBrien, Richard. *Do We Need the Church?* New York: Harper & Row, 1969.

McCarthy, Michael J., SJ. "An Ecclesiology of Groaning: Augustine, the Psalms, and the Making of Church." *Theological Studies* 66 (2005): 23–48.

McDermott, John M., SJ. "II Cor. 3: the Old and New Covenants." *Gregorianum* 87 (2006): 25–62.

McDonnell, Kilian. "The Ratzinger/Kasper Debate: The Universal Church and Local Churches." *Theological Studies* 63 (2002): 227–50.

————. "Walter Kasper on the Theology and the Praxis of the Bishop's Office." *Theological Studies* 63 (2002): 711–29.

McGuckian, Michael, SJ, *The Holy Sacrifice of the Mass: A Search for an Acceptable Notion of Sacrifice*. Chicago: Hillenbrand Books, 2005.

McKnight, Scot. *Jesus and His Death: Historiography, the Historical Jesus, and Atonement Theory*. Waco, TX: Baylor University Press, 2006.

————. *A Community Called Atonement*. Nashville, TN: Abingdon Press, 2007.

McLoughlin, David. "*Communio* Models of Church: Rhetoric or Reality?" In *Authority in the Roman Catholic Church: Theory and Practice*, edited by Bernard Hoose, 181–92. Aldershot: Ashgate, 2002.

McPartlan, Paul. *The Eucharist Makes the Church: Henri de Lubac and John Zizioulas in Dialogue*. Edinburgh: T&T Clark, 1993.

————. "The Eucharist, the Church and Evangelization: The Influence of Henri de Lubac." *Communio* 23 (1996): 776–85.

————. *Sacrament of Salvation: An Introduction to Eucharistic Ecclesiology*. Edinburgh: T&T Clark, 1995.

————. "Towards Catholic-Orthodox Unity." *Communio* 19 (1992): 305–20.

————. "Trinity, Church and State." In *Authority in the Roman Catholic Church: Theory and Practice*, edited by Bernard Hoose, 117–28. Aldershot: Ashgate, 2002.

Mendelssohn, Moses. *Jerusalem, or On Religious Power and Judaism*, translated by Allan Arkush. Hanover, NH: Brandeis University Press, 1983.

Mersch, Emile, SJ. *The Theology of the Mystical Body*, translated by Cyril Vollert, SJ. St. Louis: Herder, 1951.

Meyendorff, John, ed. *The Primacy of Peter: Essays in Ecclesiology and the Early Church*. 1963. Crestwood, NY: St. Vladimir's Seminary Press, 1992.

Milbank, John. *Being Reconciled: Ontology and Pardon*. London: Routledge, 2003.

————. *The Suspended Middle: Henri de Lubac and the Debate Concerning the Supernatural*. Grand Rapids, MI: Eerdmans, 2005.

Mill, John Stuart. "Considerations on Representative Government." In idem, *On Liberty and Other Essays*, edited by John Gray. Oxford: Oxford University Press, 1991.

————. "On Liberty." In idem, *On Liberty and Other Essays*, edited by John Gray. Oxford: Oxford University Press, 1991.

Miller, Charles. *The Gift of the World: An Introduction to the Theology of Dumitru Stăniloae*. Edinburgh: T&T Clark, 2000.

Min, Anselm K. *Paths to the Triune God: An Encounter between Aquinas and Recent Theologies*. Notre Dame, IN: University of Notre Dame Press, 2005.

Minear, Paul S. *Images of the Church in the New Testament*. Philadelphia: Westminster Press, 1960.

Möhler, Johann Adam. *Symbolism: Exposition of the Doctrinal Differences between Catholics and Protestants as Evidenced by Their Symbolical Writings*, translated by James Burton Robinson. 4th ed. German 1835. New York: Crossroad Herder, 1997.

————. *Unity in the Church, or the Principle of Catholicism Presented in the Spirit of the Church Fathers of the First Three Centuries*, translated by Peter C. Erb. German 1825. Washington, DC: The Catholic University of America Press, 1996.

Moltmann, Jürgen, Nicholas Wolterstorff, and Ellen T. Charry. *A Passion for God's Reign: Theology, Christian Learning, and the Christian Self.* Grand Rapids, MI: Eerdmans, 1998.

Morard, Martin. "L'eucharistie clé de voûte de l'organisme sacramental chez saint Thomas d'Aquin." *Revue Thomiste* 95 (1995): 217–50.

———. "Les expressions 'corpus mysticum' et 'persona mystica' dans l'oeuvre de saint Thomas d'Aquin. Références et analyse." *Revue Thomiste* 95 (1995): 653–64.

Morerod, Charles, OP. "John Paul II's Ecclesiology and St. Thomas Aquinas." in *John Paul II and St. Thomas Aquinas*, edited by Michael Dauphinais and Matthew Levering, 45–73. Naples, FL: Sapientia Press, 2006.

Nassif, Bradley, ed. *New Perspectives on Historical Theology: Essays in Memory of John Meyendorff.* Grand Rapids, MI: Eerdmans, 1996.

Nau, Arlo. *Peter in Matthew: Discipleship and Dispraise.* Collegeville, MN: The Liturgical Press, 1992.

Nédoncelle, Maurice, et al., ed. *L'ecclésiologie au XIXe siècle.* Paris: Cerf, 1960.

Neuhaus, Richard John. "An Irrevocable Commitment." The Public Square. *First Things* 167 (October 2006).

Neusner, Jacob, and Bruce D. Chilton. *The Body of Faith: Israel and the Church.* Valley Forge, PA: Trinity Press International, 1996.

Newman, Carey C., ed., *Jesus and the Restoration of Israel: A Critical Assessment of N. T. Wright's* Jesus and the Victory of God. Downers Grove, IL: InterVarsity Press, 1999.

Nichol, Todd, and Marc Kolden, eds. *Called and Ordained.* Minneapolis: Fortress Press, 1990.

Nichols, Aidan, OP. *Holy Order: Apostolic Priesthood from the New Testament to the Second Vatican Council.* Dublin: Veritas Publications, 1990.

———. "Solovyov and the Papacy: A Catholic Evaluation." *Communio* 24 (1997): 143–59.

———. *Theology in the Russian Diaspora: Church, Fathers, Eucharist in Nikolai Afanas'ev.* Cambridge: Cambridge University Press, 1989.

———. *The Theology of Joseph Ratzinger.* Edinburgh: T&T Clark, 1988.

Nichols, Terence L. "Participatory Hierarchy." In *Common Calling: The Laity and the Governance of the Catholic Church*, edited by Stephen J. Pope, 111–26. Washington, DC: Georgetown University Press, 2004.

———. *That All Might Be One: Hierarchy and Participation in the Church.* Collegeville, Minnesota: The Liturgical Press, 1997.

North, Christopher R. *The Suffering Servant in Deutero-Isaiah: An Historical and Critical Study.* 2nd ed. New York: Oxford University Press, 1963.

Novak, David. *The Election of Israel: The Idea of the Chosen People.* Cambridge: Cambridge University Press, 1995.

———. *Talking with Christians: Musings of a Jewish Theologian.* Grand Rapids, MI: Eerdmans, 2005.

Nutt, Roger. "From within the Mediation of Christ: The Place of Christ in the Christian Moral Sacramental Life According to Thomas Aquinas," *Nova et Vetera* 5 (2007): 817–41.

O'Callaghan, John P. "St. Augustine's Mind and the Imago Dei in St. Thomas." In *Aquinas the Augustinian*, edited by Michael Dauphinais, Barry David, and

Matthew Levering, 100–44. Washington, DC: The Catholic University of America Press, 2007.

O'Flaherty, James C. *Hamann's* Socratic Memorabilia: *A Translation and Commentary.* Baltimore, MD: Johns Hopkins University Press, 1967.

O'Meara, Thomas F., OP. "Beyond Hierarchology: Johann Adam Möhler and Yves Congar." In *The Legacy of the Tübingen School,* edited by Michael D. Himes and Donald Dietrich, 173–91. New York: Crossroad, 1997.

———. "Theology of the Church." In *The Theology of Thomas Aquinas,* edited by Rik Van Nieuwenhove and Joseph Wawrykow, 303–25. Notre Dame, IN: University of Notre Dame Press, 2005.

———. *Thomas Aquinas, Theologian.* Notre Dame, IN: University of Notre Dame Press, 1997.

———. "Yves Congar: Theologian of Grace in a Wide World." In *Yves Congar: Theologian of the Church,* edited by Gabriel Flynn, 371–99. Louvain: Peeters, 2005.

O'Neill, Colman, OP. "The Instrumentality of the Sacramental Character." *Irish Theological Quarterly* 25 (1958): 262–68.

———. *Meeting Christ in the Sacraments,* revised by Romanus Cessario, OP. New York: Alba House, 1991.

———. *Sacramental Realism.* Chicago: Midwest Theological Forum, 1998.

———. "St. Thomas on the Membership of the Church." *The Thomist* 27 (1963): 88–140.

O'Rourke, Fran. *Pseudo-Dionysius and the Metaphysics of Aquinas.* Notre Dame, IN: University of Notre Dame Press, 2005.

Oakley, Francis, and Bruce Russett, eds. *Governance, Accountability, and the Future of the Catholic Church.* New York: Continuum, 2004.

Ormerod, Neil. "A Dialectic Engagement with the Social Sciences in an Ecclesiological Context." *Theological Studies* 66 (2005): 815–40.

———. "The Structure of Systematic Ecclesiology." *Theological Studies* 63 (2002): 3–30.

———. "System, History, and the Theology of Ministry." *Theological Studies* 61 (2000): 432–46.

Osborne, Kenan B., OFM. *Ministry: Lay Ministry in the Roman Catholic Church: Its History and Theology.* New York: Paulist, 1993.

Ouellet, Marc, SS. "Priestly Ministry at the Service of Ecclesial Communion." *Communio* 23 (1996): 677–87.

Packer, J. I. "Crosscurrents among Evangelicals." In *Evangelicals and Catholics Together: Toward a Common Mission,* edited by Charles Colson and Richard John Neuhaus. Dallas: Word Publishing, 1995.

Pannenberg, Wolfhart. "A Lutheran's Reflections on the Petrine Ministry of the Bishop of Rome," translated by Adrian Walker. *Communio* 25 (1998): 604–18.

Pao, David W. *Acts and the Isaianic New Exodus.* Grand Rapids, MI: Baker Academic, 2002.

Papanikolaou, Aristotle. *Being with God: Trinity, Apophaticism, and Divine-Human Communion.* Notre Dame, IN: University of Notre Dame Press, 2006.

Patterson, Sue. *Realist Christian Theology in a Postmodern Age.* Cambridge: Cambridge University Press, 1999.

Paul VI, Pope. *Humanae Vitae.* 1968.

———. *Populorum progressio.* 1967.

Perkins, Pheme. " 'Being of One Mind': Apostolic Authority, Persuasion, and *Koinonia* in New Testament Christianity." In *Common Calling: The Laity and the Governance of the Catholic Church*, edited by Stephen J. Pope, 25–38. Washington, DC: Georgetown University Press, 2004.

———. *Peter: Apostle for the Whole Church.* Columbia, SC: University of South Carolina Press, 1994.

Perrier, Emmanuel, OP. "L'enjeu christologique de la satisfaction" (I). *Revue Thomiste* 103 (2003): 105–36.

———. "L'enjeu christologique de la satisfaction" (II). *Revue Thomiste* 103 (2003): 203–47.

Phelps, Jamie T., OP, "Communion Ecclesiology and Black Liberation Theology." *Theological Studies* 61 (2000): 672–99.

Phidas, Vlassios. "Papal Primacy and Patriarchal Pentarchy in the Orthodox Tradition." In *The Petrine Ministry: Catholics and Orthodox in Dialogue*, edited by Walter Cardinal Kasper, translated by the staff of the Pontifical Council for Promoting Christian Unity, 65–82. New York: Paulist Press, 2006.

Pinckaers, Servais, OP. "La morale et l'Église Corps du Christ." *Revue Thomiste* 100 (2000): 239–58.

———. *The Sources of Christian Ethics.* 3rd ed. translated by Sister Mary Thomas Noble, OP. Washington, DC: The Catholic University of America Press, 1995.

Pitre, Brant. *Jesus, the Tribulation, and the End of the Exile: Restoration Eschatology and the Origin of the Atonement.* Grand Rapids, MI: Baker Academic, 2005.

———. "The Lord's Prayer and the New Exodus." *Letter and Spirit* 2 (2006): 69–96.

———. "The 'Ransom for Many,' the New Exodus, and the End of the Exile: Redemption as the Restoration of All Israel (Mark 10:35–45)." *Letter and Spirit* 1 (2005): 41–68.

Pius IX, Pope. *Tuas Libenter.* 1863.

Pius XII, Pope. *Mystici Corporis.* 1943.

Plekon, Michael. "The Church of the Holy Spirit: Nicolas Afanasiev's Vision of the Eucharist and the Church," Introduction to Nicholas Afanasiev, *The Church of the Holy Spirit*, translated by Vitaly Permiakov, edited by Michael Plekon, ix–xx. Notre Dame, IN: University of Notre Dame Press, 2007.

———. "Kierkegaard and the Eucharist." *Studia Liturgica* 22 (1992): 214–36.

———. *Living Icons: Persons of Faith in the Eastern Church.* Notre Dame, IN: University of Notre Dame Press, 2002.

Pope, Stephen J. "Accountability and Sexual Abuse in the United States: Lessons for the Universal Church." *Irish Theological Quarterly* 69 (2004): 73–88.

———, ed. *Common Calling: The Laity and the Governance of the Catholic Church.* Washington, DC: Georgetown University Press, 2004.

Popescu, Dumitru. "Papal Primacy in Eastern and Western Patristic Theology: Its Interpretation in the Light of Contemporary Culture." In *Petrine Ministry and the Unity of the Church*, edited by James F. Puglisi, 99–114. Collegeville, MN: The Liturgical Press, 1999.

Power, David N., OMI. *The Eucharistic Mystery: Revitalizing the Tradition.* New York: Crossroad, 1992.

————. *The Sacrifice We Offer: The Tridentine Dogma and Its Reinterpretation*. (New York: Crossroad, 1987.

————. *Unsearchable Riches: The Symbolic Nature of Liturgy*. (New York: Pueblo, 1984.

Power, Dermot. "The Priesthood and the Evangelical Counsels." *Communio* 23 (1996): 688–700.

Powers, Joseph M., SJ. *Eucharistic Theology*. New York: Herder and Herder, 1967.

Preston, Geoffrey, OP. *Faces of the Church: Meditations on a Mystery and Its Images*, edited by Aidan Nichols, OP. Grand Rapids, MI: Eerdmans, 1997.

Pseudo-Dionysius. *The Celestial Hierarchy*. In idem, *The Complete Works*, translated by Colm Luibheid with Paul Rorem, 143–92. New York: Paulist Press, 1987.

————. *The Ecclesiastical Hierarchy*. In idem, *The Complete Works*, translated by Colm Luibheid with Paul Rorem, 193–260. New York: Paulist Press, 1987.

Puglisi, James F. *Petrine Ministry and the Unity of the Church*. Collegeville, MN: The Liturgical Press, 1999.

Quinn, John R. "The Claims of the Primacy and the Costly Call to Unity." In *The Exercise of the Primacy: Continuing the Dialogue*, edited by Phyllis Zagano and Terrence W. Tilley, 1–28. New York: Crossroad, 1998.

————. "Response." In *The Exercise of the Primacy: Continuing the Dialogue*, edited by Phyllis Zagano and Terrence W. Tilley, 107–18. New York: Crossroad, 1998.

Radner, Ephraim. *The End of the Church: A Pneumatology of Christian Division in the West*. Grand Rapids, MI: Eerdmans, 1998.

Radner, Ephraim, and Philip Turner. *The Fate of Communion: The Agony of Anglicanism and the Future of the Global Church*. Grand Rapids, MI: Eerdmans, 2006.

Rahner, Hugo, SJ. *Church and State in Early Christianity*, translated by Leo Donald Davis, SJ. German 1961. San Francisco: Ignatius Press, 1992.

Rahner, Karl, and Joseph Ratzinger. *The Episcopate and the Primacy*. New York: Herder and Herder, 1962.

Rashkover, Randi. *Revelation and Theopolitics: Barth, Rosenzweig and the Politics of Praise*. New York: T&T Clark, 2005.

Rasmusson, Arne. *The Church as Polis: From Political Theology to Theological Politics as Exemplified by Jürgen Moltmann and Stanley Hauerwas*. Notre Dame, IN: University of Notre Dame Press, 1995.

Ratzinger, Joseph. *Called to Communion: Understanding the Church Today*, translated by Adrian Walker. German 1991. San Francisco: Ignatius Press, 1996.

————. *Church, Ecumenism and Politics: New Essays in Ecclesiology*, translated by Robert Nowell. German 1987. New York: Crossroad, 1988.

————. "The Church's Guilt: Presentation of the Document *Remembrance and Reconciliation* from the International Theological Commission." In *Pilgrim Fellowship of Faith: The Church as Communion*, edited by Stephan Otto Horn and Vinzenz Pfnür, translated by Henry Taylor, 274–83. German 2002. San Francisco: Ignatius Press, 2005.

————. *Dogma and Preaching*. Chicago: Franciscan Herald, 1984.

————. "Freedom and Liberation: The Anthropological Vision of the Instruction 'Libertatis Conscientia,'" translated Stephen Wentworth Arndt. *Communio* 14 (1987): 55–72.

————. *Introduction to Christianity*. London: Burns & Oates, 1969.

——. "The Local Church and the Universal Church: A Response to Walter Kasper." *America* 185 (November 19, 2001): 7–11.

——. *Many Religions—One Covenant: Israel, the Church and the World*, translated by Graham Harrison. German 1998. San Francisco: Ignatius Press, 1999.

——. *The Meaning of Christian Brotherhood*. German 1960. San Francisco: Ignatius Press, 1993.

——. "The New Covenant: A Theology of Covenant in the New Testament," translated by Maria Shrady. *Communio* 22 (1995): 635–51.

——. *Pilgrim Fellowship of Faith: The Church as Communion*, edited by Stephan Otto Horn and Vinzenz Pfnür, translated by Henry Taylor. German 2002. San Francisco: Ignatius Press, 2005.

——. "Primacy, Episcopate, and Apostolic Succession." In Karl Rahner and Joseph Ratzinger, *The Episcopate and the Primacy*, 37–63. New York: Herder and Herder, 1962.

——. *Principles of Catholic Theology: Building Stones for a Fundamental Theology*, translated by Sister Mary Frances McCarthy, SND. German 1982. San Francisco: Ignatius Press, 1987.

——. *The Spirit of the Liturgy*, translated by John Saward. German 1999. San Francisco: Ignatius Press, 2000.

——. *Theological Highlights of Vatican II*. New York: Paulist Press, 1966.

Rausch, Thomas P., SJ. *Towards a Truly Catholic Church: An Ecclesiology for the Third Millennium*. Collegeville, MN: The Liturgical Press, 2005.

Reicke, B. "The Constitution of the Primitive Church in the Light of Jewish Documents." In *The Scrolls and the New Testament*, edited by K. Stendahl, 143–56. New York: Harper & Brothers, 1957.

Remy, Gérard. "Sacerdoce et médiation chez saint Thomas." *Revue Thomiste* 99 (1999): 101–18.

Reumann, John. Review of *Peter: Apostle for the Whole Church* by Pheme Perkins. *Theological Studies* 55 (1994): 540–42.

Revue Thomiste, editorial board led by Serge-Thomas Bonino, OP. "'Tout récapituler dans le Christ': À propos de l'ouvrage de Jacques Dupuis, *Vers une théologie chrétienne du pluralisme religieux*." *Revue Thomiste* 98 (1998): 591–630.

Riestra, José Antonio. *Cristo y la plenitude del Cuerpo místico. Estudio sobre la cristología de santo Tomás de Aquino*. Pamplona: Universidad de Navarra, 1985.

Rikhof, Herwi. "*Corpus Christi Mysticum*. An Inquiry into Thomas Aquinas' Use of a Term." *Bijdragen* 37 (1976): 149–71.

——. "Thomas on the Church: Reflections on a Sermon." In *Aquinas on Doctrine: A Critical Introduction*, edited by Thomas G. Weinandy, OFM CAP, Daniel A. Keating, and John P. Yocum, 199–223. New York: T&T Clark, 2004.

Robertson, Ronald G. "Dumitru Stăniloae on Christian Unity." In *Dumitru Stăniloae: Tradition and Modernity in Theology*, edited by Lucian Turcescu, 104–25. Oxford: Center for Romanian Studies, 2002.

Rodríguez, Pedro. "La Iglesia como 'communio' en la perspective de la gracia capital de Cristo." In *Problemi teologici alla luce dell' Aquinate*, edited by Pontificia Accademia Romana di San Tommaso d'Aquino, 296–303. Vatican City: Libreria Editrice Vaticana, 1991.

Rooke, Deborah W. *Zadok's Heirs: The Role and Development of the High Priesthood in Ancient Israel*. Oxford: Oxford University Press, 2000.

Roques, R. *L'Univers Dionysien. Structure hiérarchique du monde selon le Pseudo-Denys.* Paris: Cerf, 1983.

Rosenzweig, Franz. *The Star of Redemption,* translated from the 2nd edition by William W. Hallo. Notre Dame, IN: University of Notre Dame Press, 1985.

Rouco, Alfonso Carrasco. "Vatican II's Reception of the Dogmatic Teaching on the Roman Primacy." *Communio* 25 (1998): 576–603.

Ruddy, Christopher. *The Local Church: Tillard and the Future of Catholic Ecclesiology.* New York: Crossroad, 2006.

Ryan, Christopher. "The Theology of Papal Primacy in Thomas Aquinas." In *The Religious Roles of the Papacy: Ideals and Realities, 1150–1300,* edited by Christopher Ryan, 193–225. Toronto: Pontifical Institute of Mediaeval Studies, 1989.

Ryan, Thomas P. *Thomas Aquinas as Reader of the Psalms.* Notre Dame, IN: University of Notre Dame Press, 2000.

Sabra, George. *Thomas Aquinas' Vision of the Church: Fundamentals of an Ecumenical Ecclesiology.* Mainz: Matthias-Grünewald-Verlag, 1987.

Sandnes, Karl Olav. *Belly and Body in the Pauline Epistles.* Cambridge: Cambridge University Press, 2002.

Savage, Timothy B. *Power through Weakness: Paul's Understanding of the Christian Ministry in 2 Corinthians.* Cambridge: Cambridge University Press, 1996.

Schatz, Klaus, SJ. *Papal Primacy: From Its Origins to the Present,* translated by John A. Otto and Linda M. Maloney. German 1990. Collegeville, MN: The Liturgical Press, 1996.

Scheffczyk, Leo. "Faith and Witness: *Confessio* and *Martyrium,*" translated by Albert Wimmer. *Communio* 22 (1995): 406–17.

———. "*Sensus fidelium*—Witness on the Part of the Community," translated by Charlotte C. Prather. *Communio* 15 (1988): 182–98.

———. "Das Problem der 'eucharistischen Ekklesiologie' im Lichte der Kichen- und Eucharistielehre des heiligen Thomas von Aquin." In *Indubitanter ad Veritatem: Studies Offered to Leo J. Elders SVD,* edited by Jörgen Vijgen, 388–405. Budel: Damon, 2003.

Schillebeeckx, Edward, OP. *Church: The Human Story of God,* translated by John Bowden. New York: Crossroad, 1990.

———. *Ministry: Leadership in the Community of Jesus Christ.* New York: Crossroad, 1981.

Schindler, David L. "Christology and the *Imago Dei*: Interpreting *Gaudium et Spes.*" *Communio* 23 (1996): 156–84.

———. "Towards a Eucharistic Evangelization." *Communio* 19 (1992): 549–75.

Schlier, Heinrich. "The Holy Spirit as Interpreter According to St. John's Gospel," translated by W. J. O'Hara. *Communio* 1 (1974): 128–41.

Schmemann, Alexander. *Church, World, Mission: Reflections on Orthodoxy in the West.* Crestwood, NY: St. Vladimir's Seminary Press, 1979.

———. *The Eucharist: Sacrament of the Kingdom,* translated by Paul Kachur. Crestwood, NY: St. Vladimir's Seminary Press, 1988.

Schmiechen, Peter. *Saving Power: Theories of Atonement and Forms of the Church.* Grand Rapids, MI: Eerdmans, 2005.

Schmitt, J. "L'organisation de l'Église primitive et Qumran." *Recherches bibliques* 4 (1959): 217–31.

Schmitz, Kenneth L. "The Authority of Institutions: Meddling or Middling?" *Communio* 12 (1985): 5–24.

———. *The Gift: Creation*. The Aquinas Lecture, 1982. Marquette: Marquette University Press, 1982.

Schnackenburg, Rudolf. *The Church in the New Testament*, translated by W. J. O'Hara. New York: Seabury Press, 1965.

Schönborn, Christoph. "The 'Communion of Saints' as Three States of the Church: Pilgrimage, Purification, and Glory," translated by Walter Jüptner, OMI. *Communio* 15 (1988): 169–81.

Schwager, Raymond. *Brauchen wir einen Sündenbock? Gewalt und Erlösung in den biblishen Schriften*. Munich: Kösel, 1978.

Senior, Donald, CP. *Matthew*. Nashville, TN: Abingdon Press, 1998.

Sesboüé, SJ, Bernard. *Le Magistère à l'épreuve. Autorité, vérité et liberté dans l'Église*. Paris: Desclée, 2001.

Sherwood, Polycarp, OSB, ed. *The Unity of the Churches of God*. Baltimore, MD: Helicon Press, 1963.

Shortt, Rupert. *God's Advocates: Christian Thinkers in Conversation*. Grand Rapids, MI: Eerdmans, 2005.

Sicari, Antonio. "Mary, Peter and John: Figures of the Church," translated by Michael Waldstein. *Communio* 19 (1992): 189–207.

Simon, Yves. *A General Theory of Authority*. Notre Dame, IN: University of Notre Dame Press, 1962.

Skublics, Ernest. "Communion Ecclesiology: A Vision of the Church Reshaping Theology and Seminary Formation." *Pro Ecclesia* 7 (1998): 288–306.

Smith, Ronald Gregor. *J. G. Hamann, 1730–1788: A Study in Christian Existence with Selections from His Writings*. New York: Harper & Brothers, 1960.

Sokolowski, Robert. *Christian Faith and Human Understanding: Studies on the Eucharist, Trinity, and the Human Person*. Washington, DC: The Catholic University of America Press, 2006.

Somme, Luc-Thomas, OP. *Fils adoptifs de Dieu par Jésus Christ: La filiation divine par adoption dans la théologie de saint Thomas d'Aquin*. Paris: Vrin, 1997.

Stagaman, David. *Authority in the Church*. Collegeville, MN: The Liturgical Press, 1999.

Stăniloae, Dumitru. *Orthodoxe Dogmatik*, 3 vols. Düsseldorf: Benziger Verlag, 1984–1995.

Starkloff, Carl F., SJ. "The Church as Covenant, Culture, and Communion." *Theological Studies* 61 (2000): 409–31.

———. "Church as Structure and Communitas: Victor Turner and Ecclesiology." *Theological Studies* 58 (1997): 643–68.

Stern, Jean. "Marcionisme, néo-marcionisme et tradition de l'Église." *Revue Thomiste* 105 (2005): 473–506.

Stylianopoulos, Theodore. "Concerning the Biblical Foundation of Primacy." In *The Petrine Ministry: Catholics and Orthodox in Dialogue*, edited by Walter Cardinal Kasper, translated by the staff of the Pontifical Council for Promoting Christian Unity, 37–64. New York: Paulist Press, 2006.

Sullivan, Francis A., SJ. "A Response to Karl Becker, S.J., on the Meaning of *Subsistit In*." *Theological Studies* 67 (2006): 395–409.

——. *The Church We Believe In: One, Holy, Catholic, and Apostolic.* New York: Paulist Press, 1988.

——. *Creative Fidelity: Weighing and Interpreting the Documents of the Magisterium.* New York: Paulist Press, 1996.

——. *From Apostles to Bishops: The Development of the Episcopacy in the Early Church.* New York: Paulist Press, 2001.

——. *Magisterium: Teaching Authority in the Catholic Church.* New York: Paulist Press, 1983.

——. "Recent Theological Observations on Magisterial Documents and Public Dissent." *Theological Studies* 58 (1997): 509–15.

——. Review of *Witnesses to the Faith: Community, Infallibility, and the Ordinary Magisterium of Bishops* by Richard Gaillardetz. *Theological Studies* 54 (1993): 779.

——. "St. Cyprian on the Role of the Laity in Decision Making in the Early Church." In *Common Calling: The Laity and Governance of the Catholic Church,* edited by Stephen J. Pope, 39–49. Washington, DC: Georgetown University Press, 2004.

——. "The Sense of Faith: The Sense/Consensus of the Faithful." In *Authority in the Roman Catholic Church: Theory and Practice,* edited by Bernard Hoose, 85–93. Aldershot: Ashgate, 2002.

——. "The Teaching Authority of Episcopal Conferences." *Theological Studies* 63 (2002): 472–93.

——. "The Theologian's Ecclesial Vocation and the 1990 CDF Instruction." *Theological Studies* 52 (1991): 51–68.

Sundberg, Walter. "Ministry in Nineteenth Century European Lutheranism." In *Called and Ordained,* edited by Todd Nichol and Marc Kolden. Minneapolis: Fortress Press, 1990.

Swidler, Leonard. *Toward a Catholic Constitution.* New York: Crossroad, 1996.

Tanner, Norman P., SJ. *Decrees of the Ecumenical Councils.* Vol. 2, *Trent to Vatican II.* Washington, DC: Georgetown University Press, 1990.

Thunberg, Lars. *Man and the Cosmos: The Vision of St. Maximus the Confessor.* New York: St. Vladimir's Seminary Press, 1985.

Tierney, Brian. *Origins of Papal Infallibility 1150–1350: A Study of the Concepts of Infallibility, Sovereignty and Tradition in the Middle Ages.* Leiden: E. J. Brill, 1972.

Tillard, Jean-Marie R., OP. *The Bishop of Rome.* Wilmington, DE: Michael Glazier, 1983.

——. *Church of Churches: The Ecclesiology of Communion,* translated by R. C. De Peaux, O PRAEM. French 1987. Collegeville, MN: The Liturgical Press, 1992.

——. *L'Église locale: Ecclésiologie de communion et catholicité.* Paris: Cerf, 1995.

——. *Flesh of the Church, Flesh of Christ: At the Source of the Ecclesiology of Communion,* translated by Madeleine Beaumont. French 1992. Collegeville, MN: The Liturgical Press, 2001.

Timms, Noel, and Kenneth Wilson, eds. *Governance and Authority in the Roman Catholic Church: Beginning a Conversation.* London: SPCK, 2000.

Tjørhom, Ola. "Catholic Faith outside the Catholic Church: An Ecumenical Challenge." *Pro Ecclesia* 13 (2004): 261–74.

———. *Visible Church—Visible Unity: Ecumenical Ecclesiology and "The Great Tradition of the Church."* Collegeville, MN: The Liturgical Press, 2004.

Torrell, Jean-Pierre, OP. "Le sacerdoce du Christ dans la *Somme de théologie.*" *Revue Thomiste* 99 (1999): 75–100.

———. *Saint Thomas Aquinas,* vol. 2, *Spiritual Master,* translated by Robert Royal. French 1996. Washington, DC: The Catholic University of America Press, 2003.

———. "Saint Thomas et l'histoire. État de la question et pistes de recherches." *Revue Thomiste* 105 (2005): 355–409.

———. "Yves Congar et l'ecclésiologie de saint Thomas d'Aquin." *Revue des sciences philosophiques et théologiques* 82 (1998): 201–242.

Turcescu, Lucien. "Eucharistic Ecclesiology or Open Sobornicity?" In *Dumitru Stăniloae: Tradition and Modernity in Theology,* edited by Lucian Turcescu, 83–103. Oxford: Center for Romanian Studies, 2002.

———. " 'Person' versus 'Individual', and Other Modern Misreadings of Gregory of Nyssa." In *Re-Thinking Gregory of Nyssa,* edited by Sarah Coakley, 97–110. Oxford: Blackwell, 2003.

———. ed. *Dumitru Stăniloae: Tradition and Modernity in Theology.* Oxford: Center for Romanian Studies, 2002.

Turner, Philip. "Episcopal Authority within a Communion of Churches." In *The Fate of Communion: The Agony of Anglicanism and the Future of the Global Church,* by Ephraim Radner and Philip Turner, 135–62. Grand Rapids, MI: Eerdmans, 2006.

———. "Introduction: Unity, Obedience, and the Shape of Communion." In *The Fate of Communion: The Agony of Anglicanism and the Future of a Global Church,* by Ephraim Radner and Philip Turner, 1–14. Grand Rapids, MI: Eerdmans, 2006.

Turrini, M. "Réginald de Piperno et le texte original de la *Tertia Pars* de la *Somme de théologie* de S. Thomas d'Aquin." *Revue des sciences philosophiques et théologiques* 73 (1989): 233–47.

Twomey, Vincent. *Apostolikos Thronos. The Primacy of Rome as Reflected in the Church History of Eusebius and the Historico-Apologetic Writings of St Athanasius the Great.* Münster: Aschendorff, 1982.

Ullmann, Walter. *Medieval Papalism: The Political Theories of the Medieval Canonists.* London: Methuen, 1949.

Vall, Gregory. "'Man Is the Land': The Sacramentality of the Land of Israel." In *John Paul II and the Jewish People,* edited by David G. Dalin and Matthew Levering. Lanham, MD: Rowman and Littlefield, 2008.

Van Nieuwenhove, Rik. "St Anselm and St Thomas Aquinas on 'Satisfaction': or How Catholic and Protestant Understandings of the Cross Differ." *Angelicum* 80 (2003): 159–76.

Van Nieuwenhove, Rik, and Joseph Wawrykow, eds. *The Theology of Thomas Aquinas.* Notre Dame, IN: University of Notre Dame Press, 2005.

Vanhoye, Albert, SJ. *Old Testament Priests and the New Priest According to the New Testament,* translated by J. Bernard Orchard, OSB. French 1980. Petersham, MA: St. Bede's Publications, 1986.

Vatican Council II. *Ad Gentes.* In *Decrees of the Ecumenical Councils.* Vol. 2, *Trent to Vatican II*, edited by Norman P. Tanner, sj, 1011–1042. Washington, DC: Georgetown University Press, 1990.

———. *Dei Verbum.* In *Decrees of the Ecumenical Councils.* Vol. 2, *Trent to Vatican II*, edited by Norman P. Tanner, sj, 971–81. Washington, DC: Georgetown University Press, 1990.

———. *Lumen Gentium.* In *Decrees of the Ecumenical Councils.* Vol. 2, *Trent to Vatican II*, edited by Norman P. Tanner, sj, 849–900. Washington, DC: Georgetown University Press, 1990.

———. *Sacrosanctum Concilium.* In *Decrees of the Ecumenical Councils.* Vol. 2, *Trent to Vatican II*, edited by Norman P. Tanner, sj, 820–43. Washington, DC: Georgetown University Press, 1990.

———. *Unitatis Redintegratio.* In *Decrees of the Ecumenical Councils.* Vol. 2, *Trent to Vatican II*, edited by Norman P. Tanner, sj, 908–20. Washington, DC: Georgetown University Press, 1990.

Vodopivec, Janez. "La 'gratia capitis' in San Tommaso in relazione all'ecclesiologia di comunione." In *Prospettive teologiche moderne*, edited by Pontificia Accademia di S. Tommaso e di Religione Cattolica, 327–38. Vatican City: Libreria Editrice Vaticana, 1981.

Volf, Miroslav. *After Our Likeness: The Church as the Image of the Trinity*, translated by Doug Stott. Grand Rapids, MI: Eerdmans, 1998.

———. *The End of Memory: Remembering Rightly in a Violent World.* Grand Rapids, MI: Eerdmans, 2006.

———. *Exclusion and Embrace: Theological Exploration of Identity, Otherness, and Reconciliation.* Nashville, TN: Abingdon Press, 1996.

———. " 'The Trinity Is Our Social Program': The Doctrine of the Trinity and the Shape of Social Engagement." *Modern Theology* 14 (1998): 403–23.

———. "Trinity, Unity, Primacy: On the Trinitarian Nature of Ecclesial Unity and Its Implications for the Question of Primacy." In *Petrine Ministry and the Unity of the Church*, edited by James F. Puglisi, 171–84. Collegeville, MN: The Liturgical Press, 1999.

Völker, Walther. Book review of *Rechtgläubigkeit und Ketzerei im ältesten Christentum* [*Orthodoxy and Heresy in Earliest Christianity*] by Walter Bauer. *Zeitschrift für Kirchengeschichte* 54 (1935): 628–31. English translation in *Journal of Early Christian Studies* 14 (2006): 399–405, translated by Thomas P. Scheck.

von Balthasar, Hans Urs. "Catholicism and the Communion of Saints," translated by Albert K. Wimmer. *Communio* 15 (1988): 163–68.

———. *Explorations in Theology*, vol. 2, *Spouse of the Word*, translated by A. V. Littledale with Alexander Dru. German 1961. San Francisco: Ignatius Press, 1991.

———. *Explorations in Theology.* Vol. 4, *Spirit and Institution*, translated by Edward T. Oakes, sj. German 1974. San Francisco: Ignatius Press, 1995.

———. *The Glory of the Lord: A Theological Aesthetics.* Vol. 3, *Studies in Theological Style: Lay Styles*, translated by Andrew Louth, John Saward, Martin Simon, and Rowan Williams. German 1969. San Francisco: Ignatius Press, 1986.

———. *The Glory of the Lord: A Theological Aesthetics.* Vol. 7, *The New Covenant*, translated by Brian McNeil, crv. German 1969. San Francisco: Ignatius Press, 1989.

———. "Life and Institution in the Church," translated by Andrée Emery. *Communio* 12 (1985): 25–32.

———. *The Office of Peter and the Structure of the Church*. Translated by Andrée Emery. German 1974. San Francisco: Ignatius Press, 1986.

———. *Paul Struggles with His Congregation: The Pastoral Message of the Letters to the Corinthians*. 1988. San Francisco: Ignatius Press, 1992.

———. *Theo-Drama: Theological Dramatic Theory*. Vol. 3, *Dramatis Personae: Persons in Christ*, translated by Graham Harrison. German 1978. San Francisco: Ignatius Press, 1992.

———. *Theo-Drama: Theological Dramatic Theory*. Vol. 4, *The Action*, translated by Graham Harrison. German 1980. San Francisco: Ignatius Press, 1994.

———. *Theo-Drama: Theological Dramatic Theory*. Vol. 5, *The Last Act*, translated by Graham Harrison. German 1983. San Francisco: Ignatius Press, 1998.

———. "Theology and Holiness," translated by Peter Verhalen, o CIST. *Communio* 14 (1987): 341–50.

———. *The Theology of Karl Barth*, translated by Edward T. Oakes, SJ. German 1951. San Francisco: Ignatius Press, 1992.

———. "Thoughts on the Priesthood of Women," translated by Adrian Walker. *Communio* 23 (1996): 701–9.

———. *Truth Is Symphonic: Aspects of Christian Pluralism*, translated by Graham Harrison. German 1972. San Francisco: Ignatius Press, 1987.

———. *Unless You Become Like This Child*, translated by Erasmo Leiva-Merikakis. German 1988. San Francisco: Ignatius Press, 1991.

Vonier, Anscar, OSB. *A Key to the Doctrine of the Eucharist*. 1925. Bethesda, MD: Zaccheus Press, 2003.

Wainwright, Geoffrey. "A Primatial Ministry of Unity in a Synodical and Conciliar Context." *One in Christ* 38 (2003): 3–25.

———. "Dispensations of Grace: Newman on the Sacramental Mediation of Salvation." *Pro Ecclesia* 12 (2003): 61–88.

Wainwright, Geoffrey, ed. *Keeping the Faith: Essays to Mark the Centenary of Lux Mundi*. Allison Park, PA: Pickwick Publications, 1998.

Waldstein, Michael. Introduction to *Man and Woman He Created Them: A Theology of the Body*, by John Paul II, translated by Michael Waldstein, 1–128. Boston: Pauline Books & Media, 2006.

Walker, Duane A. "Strength in Disunity," letter to the editor. *First Things* 169 (January 2007): 10.

Walker, P. W. L. *Jesus and the Holy City: New Testament Perspectives on Jerusalem*. Grand Rapids, MI: Eerdmans, 1996.

———, ed. *Jerusalem Past and Present in the Purposes of God*. Rev. ed. Grand Rapids, MI: Baker, 1994.

Watkins, Clare. "Organizing the People of God: Social-Science Theories of Organization in Ecclesiology." *Theological Studies* 52 (1991): 689–711.

Webster, John. *Confessing God: Essays in Christian Dogmatics II*. New York: T&T Clark, 2005.

———. *Holiness*. Grand Rapids, MI: Eerdmans, 2003.

———. *Word and Church: Essays in Christian Dogmatics*. New York: T&T Clark, 2001.

Weinandy, Thomas G., OFM CAP. *Does God Suffer?* Notre Dame, IN: University of Notre Dame Press, 2000.

———. "The Supremacy of Christ: Aquinas' *Commentary on Hebrews*." In *Aquinas on Scripture: An Introduction to His Biblical Commentaries*, edited by Thomas G. Weinandy, OFM CAP, Daniel A. Keating, and John P. Yocum, 223–44. New York: T&T Clark, 2005.

Weinandy, Thomas G., OFM Cap, Daniel A. Keating, and John P. Yocum, eds. *Aquinas on Doctrine: A Critical Introduction*. New York: T&T Clark, 2004.

———. *Aquinas on Scripture: An Introduction to His Biblical Commentaries*. New York: T&T Clark, 2005.

Welch, Lawrence J. "For the Church and within the Church: Priestly Representation." *The Thomist* 65 (2001): 613–37.

———. "On Recognizing Infallible Teachings of the Ordinary Magisterium: A Rejoinder to Francis Sullivan." *New Blackfriars* 86 (2005): 591–97.

———. "Reply to Richard Gaillardetz on the Ordinary Universal Magisterium and to Francis Sullivan." *Theological Studies* 64 (2003): 598–609.

Wells, Jo Bailey. *God's Holy People: A Theme in Biblical Theology*. Sheffield: Sheffield Academic Press, 2000.

Wiarda, Timothy. *Peter in the Gospels*. Tübingen: Mohr Siebeck, 2000.

Wicks, Jared, SJ. "Ecclesial Apostolicity Confessed in the Creed." *Pro Ecclesia* 9 (2000): 150–64.

Wilken, Robert Louis. "*Sanctorum Communio*: For Evangelicals and Catholics Together." *Pro Ecclesia* 11 (2002): 159–66.

William of Ockham. *A Letter to the Friars Minor and Other Writings*, edited by Arthur Stephen McGrade and John Kilcullen, translated by John Kilcullen. Cambridge: Cambridge University Press, 1995.

Williams, A. N. *The Ground of Union: Deification in Aquinas and Palamas*. Oxford: Oxford University Press, 1999.

Williams, Daniel H. "The Disintegration of Catholicism into Diffuse Inclusivism." *Pro Ecclesia* 12 (2003): 389–93.

Witherington III, Ben. *Matthew*. Macon, GA: Smyth & Helwys, 2006.

Wojtyła, Karol. *Sources of Renewal: The Implementation of the Second Vatican Council*, translated by P. S. Falla. San Francisco: Harper & Row, 1980.

Wood, Susan K. "The Sacramentality of Episcopal Consecration." *Theological Studies* 51 (1990): 479–96.

———. *Spiritual Exegesis and the Church in the Theology of Henri de Lubac*. Grand Rapids, MI: Eerdmans, 1998.

———. ed. *Ordering the Baptismal Priesthood: Theologies of Lay and Ordained Ministry*. Collegeville, MN: The Liturgical Press, 2003.

World Council of Churches. *Episkope and Episcopate in Ecumenical Perspective*, Faith and Order Paper 102. Geneva: World Council of Churches, 1980.

Wright, J. Robert "The Possible Contribution of Papal Authority to Church Unity: An Anglican/Episcopalian Perspective." In *The Ecumenical Future*, edited by Carl E. Braaten and Robert W. Jenson, 138–44. Grand Rapids, MI: Eerdmans, 2004.

Wright, N. T. *Evil and the Justice of God*. Downers Grove, IL: InterVarsity Press, 2006.

————."In Grateful Dialogue: A Response." *Jesus and the Restoration of Israel: A Critical Assessment of N. T. Wright's* Jesus and the Victory of God, edited by Carey C. Newman, 244–77. Downers Grove, IL: InterVarsity Press, 1999.

————. "Jerusalem in the New Testament." In *Jerusalem Past and Present in the Purposes of God*, ed. P. W. L. Walker, rev. ed. Grand Rapids, MI: Baker, 1994.

————. *Jesus and the Victory of God*. Minneapolis, MN: Fortress Press, 1996.

————. "The Lord's Prayer as a Paradigm for Christian Prayer." In *Into God's Presence: Prayer in the New Testament*, edited by Richard N. Longenecker, 132–54. Grand Rapids, MI: Eerdmans, 2001.

————. *The New Testament and the People of God: Christian Origins and the Question of God*. Minneapolis, MN: Fortress, 1992.

Wyschogrod, Michael. *Abraham's Promise: Judaism and Jewish–Christian Relations*, edited by R. Kendall Soulen. Grand Rapids, MI: Eerdmans, 2004.

Yeago, David S. " 'A Christian, Holy People': Martin Luther on Salvation and the Church." *Modern Theology* 13 (1997): 101–20.

————. "Ecclesia Sancta, Ecclesia Peccatrix: The Holiness of the Church in Martin Luther's Theology." *Pro Ecclesia* 9 (2000): 331–54.

————. "The Office of the Keys: On the Disappearance of Discipline in Protestant Modernity." In *Marks of the Body of Christ*, edited by Carl E. Braaten and Robert W. Jenson, 95–122. Grand Rapids, MI: Eerdmans, 1999.

Yocum, John P. "Sacraments in Aquinas." In *Aquinas on Doctrine: A Critical Introduction*, edited by Thomas G. Weinandy, OFM CAP, Daniel A. Keating, and John P. Yocum, 159–81. New York: T&T Clark, 2004.

Yoder, John Howard. "On Christian Unity: The Way From Below." *Pro Ecclesia* 9 (2000): 165–83.

Young, Frances. *The Theology of the Pastoral Letters*. Cambridge: Cambridge University Press, 1994.

————. *The Use of Sacrificial Ideas in Greek Christian Writers from the New Testament to John Chrysostom*. 1979: Eugene, OR: Wipf and Stock, 2004.

Zagano, Phyllis, and Terrence W. Tilley, eds. *The Exercise of the Primacy: Continuing the Dialogue*. New York: Crossroad, 1998.

Zizioulas, John D. *Being in Communion: Studies in Personhood and the Church*. Crestwood, NY: St. Vladimir's Seminary Press, 1985.

————. "The Church as Communion." *St. Vladimir's Theological Quarterly* 38 (1994): 3–16.

————. *Communion and Otherness*, edited by Paul McPartlan. New York: T&T Clark, 2006.

————. "La continuité avec les origines apostoliques dans la conscience théologique des Eglises orthodoxies." *Istina* 19 (1974): 65–94.

————. "*Episkope* and *Episkopos* in the Early Church: A Brief Survey of the Evidence." In *Episkope and Episcopate in Ecumenical Perspective*, Faith and Order Paper 102, 30–42. Geneva: World Council of Churches, 1980.

————. *Eucharist, Bishop, Church: The Unity of the Church in the Divine Eucharist and the Bishop during the First Three Centuries*, translated by Elizabeth Theokritoff. 2nd ed. 1965. Brookline, MA: Holy Cross Orthodox Press, 2001.

————. "The Pneumatological Dimension of the Church," translated by W. J. O'Hara. *Communio* 1 (1974): 142–58.

————. "Primacy in the Church: An Orthodox Approach." In *Petrine Ministry and the Unity of the Church*, edited by James F. Puglisi, 115–25. Collegeville, MN: The Liturgical Press, 1999.

Index